Dear Valued Customer,

We realize you're a busy professional with deadlines to hit. Whether your goal is to learn a new technology or solve a critical problem, we want to be there to lend you a hand. Our primary objective is to provide you with the insight and knowledge you need to stay atop the highly competitive and ever-changing technology industry.

Wiley Publishing, Inc., offers books on a wide variety of technical categories, including security, data warehousing, software development tools, and networking — everything you need to reach your peak. Regardless of your level of expertise, the Wiley family of books has you covered.

- For Dummies® – The ***fun*** and ***easy*** way™ to learn
- The Weekend Crash Course® –The ***fastest*** way to learn a new tool or technology
- Visual – For those who prefer to learn a new topic ***visually***
- The Bible – The ***100% comprehensive*** tutorial and reference
- The Wiley Professional list – ***Practical*** and ***reliable*** resources for IT professionals

The book you now hold, *SQL Bible*, is the most up-to-date and complete reference available on SQL. It covers the latest approved SQL specification, SQL99, in its standard format, and you can apply the code and techniques in this book to SQL databases from any major vendor, including Microsoft SQL Server, Oracle, and IBM DB2. With the authors' emphasis on standard SQL, you can implement heterogeneous database applications and be confident that the code will work across any major vendor offering. Whether you are a database administrator making your first foray into database programming or an experienced database programmer in need of a solid SQL99 reference, you'll find *SQL Bible* your complete solution.

Our commitment to you does not end at the last page of this book. We'd want to open a dialog with you to see what other solutions we can provide. Please be sure to visit us at www.wiley.com/compbooks to review our complete title list and explore the other resources we offer. If you have a comment, suggestion, or any other inquiry, please locate the "contact us" link at www.wiley.com.

Thank you for your support and we look forward to hearing from you and serving your needs again in the future.

Sincerely,

Richard K. Swadley

Richard K. Swadley
Vice President & Executive Group Publisher
Wiley Technology Publishing

15 HOUR WEEKEND CRASH COURSE

Bible

Wiley Publishing, Inc.

SQL Bible

Alex Kriegel and Boris M. Trukhnov

Wiley Publishing, Inc.

SQL Bible

Published by
Wiley Publishing, Inc.
10475 Crosspoint Boulevard
Indianapolis, IN 46256
www.wiley.com

Published simultaneously in Canada

Library of Congress Control Number: 2003101832

ISBN: 0-7645-2584-0

Manufactured in the United States of America

10 9 8 7 6 5 4 3 2 1

1B/QU/QU/QT/IN

For general information on our other products and services or to obtain technical support, please contact our Customer Care Department within the U.S. at (800) 762-2974, outside the U.S. at (317) 572-3993 or fax (317) 572-4002.

Wiley also publishes its books in a variety of electronic formats. Some content that appears in print may not be available in electronic books.

About the Authors

Alex Kriegel, MCP/MCSD, has worked for Pope & Talbot, Inc., in Portland, Oregon, since 2001 as Senior Programmer/Analyst; prior to that, he worked for Psion Teklogix International, Inc., in the same capacity. He received his B.S. in Physics of Metals from Polytechnic Institute of Belarus in 1988, discovered PC programming in 1992, and has never looked back since. He is also the author of *Microsoft SQL Server 2000 Weekend Crash Course* (Wiley, 2001).

Boris M. Trukhnov, OCP, has been working as Senior Technical Analyst/Oracle DBA for Pope & Talbot, Inc., in Portland, Oregon, since 1998. His previous job titles include Senior Programmer Analyst, Senior Software Developer, and Senior Operations Analyst. He has been working with SQL and relational databases since 1994. Boris holds a B.S. in Computer Science from the University of Minnesota.

Credits

Acquisitions Editor
Jim Minatel

Project Editor
Eric Newman

Technical Editors
Ken Slovak
Peter MacIntyre

Copy Editor
Maarten Reilingh

Editorial Manager
Mary Beth Wakefield

Vice President & Executive Group Publisher
Richard Swadley

Vice President and Executive Publisher
Bob Ipsen

Vice President and Publisher
Joseph B. Wikert

Executive Editorial Director
Mary Bednarek

Project Coordinator
Regina Snyder

Graphics and Production Specialists
Beth Brooks
Amanda Carter
Jennifer Click
Carrie Foster
Joyce Haughey
Kristin McMullan

Quality Control Technician
Charles Spencer

Media Development Specialist
Greg Stafford

Proofreading and Indexing
TECHBOOKS Production Services

I dedicate this book to the future of my sons, Phillip and Michael. —Alex

In loving memory of my mother. —Boris

Preface

This book is about Structured Query Language. Known familiarly as SQL, it is the standard language of relational databases and the lingua franca of the database world. It has been around for more than 20 years and shows no signs of aging. This is mostly because of numerous revisions: proprietary inventions frequently introduced by database vendors are either adopted into the standard, or become obsolete as the database community moves on. The latest SQL standard was introduced in 1999, and even though ANSI/ISO SQL standards do exist, many of these standards remain rather theoretical and differ significantly from implementation to implementation. That makes it difficult to find an SQL book "that has it all." One author might be biased toward a particular vendor so that you might get a decent Oracle or MS SQL Server book but not necessarily a good SQL one; a single explanation of all SQL ANSI/ISO standards alone would hardly be useful to anyone on a practical level. We believe that only a combination of these two approaches can produce a good result.

Note

The RDBMS world is divided between people who pronounce SQL as "ess-cue-ell" and those who pronounce it as "sequel." This book holds the former as the correct pronunciation, hence the usage "an SQL keyword" rather than "a SQL keyword."

A comparison of modern database vendors shows that Oracle, IBM DB2, and Microsoft SQL Server have and are likely to continue to have the lion's share of the market. This does not mean that other vendors are irrelevant. Some features they offer can meet or even exceed those of the "big three" (as we call them); they have their devoted customers, and they are going to be around for years to come. But because we cannot possibly cover each and every proprietary SQL extension, we decided to concentrate on the "big three" and explain SQL features with an emphasis on how they vary among Oracle, DB2, and MS SQL Server and how they differ from the SQL99 standard.

Sybase Adaptive Server SQL syntax is similar to the Microsoft SQL Server's syntax in many respects, and most of this book's MS SQL Server examples would also work with the Sybase RDBMS.

Whom This Book Is For

This book is for readers of all levels — from beginners to advanced users. Our goal was to provide a comprehensive reference that would help everyone who needs to communicate with relational databases, especially in a heterogeneous environment. Programmers and database administrators can find up-to-date information on the

SQL standard and the dialects employed by most popular database products. Database users can gain a deeper understanding of the behind-the-scenes processes and help with their daily tasks regardless of which of the three major RDBMS they are working with. Managers evaluating database products will gain an insight into internals of RDBMS technology. For managers who must plan for the RDBMS needs of their organizations, this book also explains the role SQL is playing in modern businesses and what is in store for SQL in the future.

How This Book Is Organized

The book contains seventeen chapters presented in six parts. There are also twelve appendixes.

Part I: SQL Basic Concepts and Principles

The three chapters in Part I introduce you to SQL — the standard language of relational databases. Chapter 1 describes the history of the language and relational database systems (RDBMS), and Chapters 2 and 3 provide a high-level overview of the major principles upon which SQL is built, as well as an in-depth discussion of SQL data types. We emphasize the differences between the SQL standard and that of the three major RDBMS implementations — Oracle 9*i*, IBM DB2 UDB 8.1, and Microsoft SQL Server 2000.

Part II: Creating and Modifying Database Objects

Part II's two chapters continue with a thorough explanation of database objects — tables, views, indices, sequences, and the like. They include SQL syntax for creating, modifying, and destroying database objects, again highlighting differences between the standard and its specific implementations.

Part III: Data Manipulation and Transaction Control

In Part III, Chapter 6 introduces you to Data Manipulation Language (DML), which handles inserting, updating, and deleting records in database tables. It also discusses in detail advanced `MERGE` and `TRUNCATE` statements. Once again, we give special consideration to differences among the Oracle, IBM, and Microsoft RDBMS implementations. Chapter 7 explains sessions, transactions, and locking mechanisms in a multiuser environment from the point of the view of the SQL standard and compares it with the actual implementations.

Part IV: Retrieving and Transforming Data

Part IV introduces one of the most important SQL statements — `SELECT` — in Chapters 8 and 9. We proceed from simple single-table queries to advanced multi-table `SELECT` statements, explaining the differences between vendor-specific implementations. Chapter 10 is dedicated to the SQL functions. It covers dozens of functions either mandated by the SQL standard or supplied by RDBMS vendors. We cross-reference the most common functions for all three major implementations. Chapter 11 discusses SQL operators, their implementation across the RDBMS vendors, and their uses in different contexts.

Part V: Implementing Security Using System Catalogs

One cannot underestimate the importance of information security in our increasingly interconnected world. Chapter 12 introduces the key concepts of database security, including basic security through SQL and advanced security incorporated by the vendors into their respective products. Chapter 13 looks at the issue of accessing metadata information in the RDBMS through SQL standard–mandated `INFORMATION_SCHEMA` and system catalogs.

Part VI: Beyond SQL: Procedural Programming and Database Access Mechanisms

The chapters in Part VI deal with the topics that are not the domain of SQL proper, such as procedural extensions (like Oracle's PL/SQL and Microsoft's Transact SQL) for creating stored procedures, functions, and triggers. Here you'll find a comprehensive overview of both Embedded and Dynamic SQL that delves into the complex topic of RDBMS access interfaces (like ODBC, OLEDB, ADO.NET, and JDBC) with programming examples in C, Visual Basic, Java, and C#. The last chapter is dedicated to new developments taking place today in the SQL world: XML integration, OLAP business intelligence, and object-oriented features of RDBMS.

Appendixes

The appendixes provide "How-to" guides and reference material too voluminous and dry for the main text.

- ✦ Appendix A describes the contents of the CD-ROMs.
- ✦ Appendix B describes the ACME sample database structure used in virtually every example in the book.

- Appendix C discusses the basics of relational database design.
- Appendixes D, E, and F explain in detail how to install RDBMS software, how to access the RDBMS of your choice, and how to install the ACME sample database (the full SQL scripts are included with the book's CD-ROM).
- Appendix G lists more than 500 SQL functions for Oracle, IBM DB2 UDB, and Microsoft SQL Server 2000, with a brief description of the functionality of each.
- Appendix H provides the syntax reference for SQL for quick lookup of needed statements.
- Appendix I is a list of all SQL reserved keywords that should not be used in your programming as identifiers.
- Appendix J provides a comparison between the SQL99 standard and its actual implementation by the "big three" vendors.
- Appendix K lists dozens of different RDBMS products that you could use besides those developed by Oracle, IBM, and Microsoft.
- Appendix L provides a brief introduction to the theory of sets and discrete math, which will be helpful to you in understanding the general principles that govern SQL.

CD-ROM

As noted previously, the book includes a CD-ROM. For detailed information on its content, see Appendix A.

Conventions Used in This Book

All the programming code in this book, including SQL statements, database object names, variable declarations, and so on, appears in this `fixed-width font`.

Hierarchical menu choices are shown in the following way: File⇨Save, which in this example means to select File on a menu bar, then choose Save from the submenu that appears.

Throughout the book you will also find the following icons, among others:

Notes provide additional information on the topic at hand.

Tips show you ways of getting your work done faster or more efficiently.

A Caution provides additional information that you should take into consideration.

Cross-References show where in another part of the book you can find related subject matter.

What Is a Sidebar?

Sidebars present relevant but sometimes off-the-main-topic information.

Acknowledgments

Alex: My deep gratitude goes to my wife, Liana, for helping me to organize material and make sure that examples in this book work as we say they should. I also thank Liana for putting up with my insane schedules.

Boris: I sincerely thank my wife, Kate, for her professional help, moral support, and unconditional understanding. Writing a book was a stressful process for both authors and their families. Kate not only helped me to go through these difficult times, but she also actively participated in the writing of this book by reviewing the chapters, helping with SQL examples, and making valuable suggestions and comments.

I am grateful to all my friends who were with me when I needed them.

My gratitude also goes to Professor Jaideep Srivastava, who introduced me to the relational database world.

Alex and Boris: Thanks to Jim Minatel, Senior Acquisitions Editor at Wiley Publishing, for his help with the project and his guidance through the maze of editorial procedures.

We thank the Wiley editorial team, especially Eric Newman and Maarten Reilingh, for helping to make this book better than it would otherwise have been, providing valuable suggestions on how to improve the book's content, and pointing out omissions, oversights, and outright bloopers.

Finally, we thank our technical editors for their help with preparing the publication.

Contents at a Glance

Contents

P A R T

I

SQL Basic Concepts and Principles

In This Part

SQL and Relational Database Management Systems (RDBMS)

✦ ✦ ✦ ✦

In This Chapter

Understanding databases

Characteristics of a good database

The database market

Real-life database examples

Brief database history

SQL standards and implementation differences

✦ ✦ ✦ ✦

Information may be the most valuable commodity in the modern world. It can take many different forms — accounting and payroll information, information about customers and orders, scientific and statistical data, graphics–to mention just a few. We are virtually swamped with data. And we cannot — or at least we'd like to think about it this way — afford to lose it, but these days we simply have too much data to keep storing it in file cabinets or cardboard boxes. The need to safely store large collections of persistent data, efficiently "slice and dice" it from different angles by multiple users and update it easily when necessary is critical for every enterprise. That need mandates the existence of databases, which accomplish all the tasks listed above, and then some. To put it simply, a *database* is just an organized collection of information — with emphasis on *organized*.

A more specific definition often used as a synonym for "database" is *database management system* (DBMS). That term is wider and, in addition to the stored information, includes some methods to work with data and tools to maintain it.

Note

DBMS can be defined as a collection of interrelated data plus a set of programs to access, modify, and maintain the data. More about DBMS later in this chapter.

Desirable database characteristics

There are many ideas about what a database is and what it should do. However, all modern databases should have at least the following characteristics.

Sufficient capacity

A database's primary function is to store large amounts of information. For example, an order management system for a medium-sized company can easily grow into gigabytes of data; the bigger the company, the more data it needs to store and rely upon. A company that wants to keep historical (archival) data will require even more storage space. The need for storage capacity is growing rapidly, and databases provide for *structured* storage.

Adequate security

As was noted previously, enterprise data is valuable and must be stored safely. That means protection of the stored data not only from malicious or careless human activities, such as unauthorized logins, accidental information deletions/modifications, and so on, but also from hardware failures and natural disasters.

Multiuser environment

It's also important to note that in order to be useful, the information stored in a database must be accessible to many users simultaneously at different levels of security, and, no matter what, the data must stay consistent. For example, if two users try to change the same piece of information at the same time, the result can be unpredictable (e.g., data corruption), so situations like that have to be handled appropriately by internal database mechanisms. Also, certain groups of users may be allowed to modify several pieces of information, browse other parts of it, and be prevented from even viewing yet another part. (Some company data can be strictly confidential with a very restricted access.)

Effectiveness

Users need *quick* access to the data they want. It is very important not only to be able to store data, but also to have efficient algorithms to work with it. For example, it would be unacceptable for users to have to scroll through each and every record to find just one order among millions stored in the database; the response to someone's querying the database must be fast, preferably instantaneous.

As an analogy, suppose you wanted to find all the occurrences of the word "object" in a book. You could physically browse through the entire book page by page until you reach the end. Or you could use the index and determine that the word is used on pages 245, 246, and 348. This situation is comparable to using bad or good programming algorithms.

Scalability

Databases must be flexible and easily adaptable to changing business needs. That primarily means that the internal structure of database objects should be easily modified with minimum impact on other objects and processes; for example, to add a field in a legacy database you would have to bring the whole dataset offline, that is, make it inaccessible to users, modify it, change and recompile related programs, and so on. We'll talk more about that in the "Database Legacy" section of this chapter.

Another scalability aspect is that data typically lives longer than the hardware and software used to access and manipulate it, so it would not be very convenient to have to redesign the entire database to accommodate the current "flavor-of-the-month" development environment; for example, in case of a takeover or when company management suddenly decides to switch production environment from Java to C#.

User-friendliness

Databases are not just for programmers and technical personnel (some would say not for programmers — period). Nontechnical users constitute the majority of all database users nowadays. Accountants, managers, salespeople, doctors and nurses, librarians, scientists, technicians, customer service representatives — for all these and many more people, interaction with databases is an integral part of their work. That means data must be easy to manipulate. Of course, most users will access it through a graphical user interface with a predefined set of screens and limited functionality, but ad-hoc database queries and reports become more and more popular, especially among sophisticated, computer-literate users.

Note

Consider this. An order management application has a screen to view all orders and another window to browse customers. It can also generate a number of reports, including one to analyze orders grouped by customer. But accountant Jerry is working on a report for his boss and needs to find the ten customers with the highest debt. He can request a new report from the IT department, but it will take days (or even weeks) because of bureaucratic routine, programmers' busyness, or something else. The knowledge of SQL can help Jerry to create his own ad-hoc query, get the data, and finish his report.

Selecting Your Database Software

Every single DBMS on the market follows essentially the same basic principles, there is a wide variety of database products on the market, and it is very difficult for a person without solid database background to make a decision on what would be the right product to learn or use. The database market is chockfull of different RDBMS: IBM DB2 UDB, Oracle, Microsoft SQL Server, Sybase, Informix, PostgreSQL, to name just a few.

No two DBMS are exactly alike: There are relatively simple-to-use systems, and there are some that require serious technical expertise to install and operate on; some products are free, and some others are fairly expensive — all in addition to a myriad of some other little things like licensing, availability of expertise, and so on. There is no single formula to help you in the DBMS selection process but rather several aspects to consider while making the choice. Here are the most common ones to start with.

Market share

According to a study by Gartner Dataquest, in 2001 the three major DBMS implementations shared about 80 percent of the database market. Oracle accounted for 32 percent, IBM DB2 about 31.6 percent, and Microsoft SQL Server 16.3 percent. Informix (now part of IBM) ranked fourth with 3 percent, followed by Sybase (2.6 percent); the rest of the market (14.4 percent) is shared among dozens (or maybe hundreds) of small vendors and nonrelational "dinosaurs." It's also worth noticing that the share of the "top three" is constantly growing (at the expense of their smaller competitors) — in 1997 the combined share of the "big three" was less than 70 percent.

Total cost of ownership

The prices for the three major implementations are comparable but could vary depending on included features, number of users, and computer processors from under a thousand dollars for a standard edition with a handful of licenses to hundreds of thousands or even millions for enterprise editions with unlimited user access. Many small database vendor implementations are free. Skills are a different story. Database expertise is a costly thing and usually is in short supply. On average, Oracle expertise is valued a little higher than comparable expertise for Microsoft SQL Server or DB2. The total cost of ownership (TOC) analysis released by vendors themselves tends to be biased, so use your best judgment and do your homework before committing your company to a particular vendor. Make no mistake about it: This is a long-term commitment, as switching the database vendors halfway into production is an extremely painful and costly procedure.

Support and persistency

One may ask, why spend thousands of dollars on something that can be substituted with a free product? The answer is quite simple: For a majority of businesses the most important thing is support. They pay money for company safety and shareholders' peace of mind, in addition to all the bells and whistles that come with an enterprise level product with a big name. (As the adage goes: "No one was ever fired for buying IBM"....) First, they can count on relatively prompt support by qualified specialists in case something goes wrong. Second, the company management can make a reasonable assumption that vendors like IBM, Microsoft, or Oracle would still be around ten years from now. (Nobody can guarantee that, of course, but their chances definitely look better against the odds of their smaller competitors.) So, the less expensive (and sometimes free) products by smaller database vendors might be acceptable for small businesses, nonprofit organizations, or noncritical projects, but very few serious companies would even consider using them for, say, their payroll or accounting systems.

Everything in Details: DBMS Implementations

One book cannot possibly cover all existing database implementations, and taking into consideration all these aspects, we've decided to concentrate on "the big three": Oracle Database, IBM DB2 UDB, and Microsoft SQL Server. These implementations have many common characteristics: They are all industrial-strength enterprise level relational databases (relational database model and SQL standards are covered later in this chapter), they use Structured Command Language (SQL) standardized by the American National Standards Institute (ANSI) and the International Organization for Standardization (ISO), and all three are able to run on Windows operating system. Oracle also is available on virtually any UNIX flavor, Linux, MVS, and OpenVMS; DB2 UDB is running on UNIX/Linux, NUMA-Q, MVS, OS/2, and AS/400.

Note

ANSI is a private, nonprofit organization that administers and coordinates the U.S. voluntary standardization and conformity assessment system. The Institute's mission is to enhance both the global competitiveness of U.S. business and the U.S. quality of life by promoting and facilitating voluntary consensus standards and conformity assessment systems, and safeguarding their integrity. ANSI was founded October 18, 1918 and is the official U.S. representative to the International Organization for Standardization (ISO) and some other international institutions.

The problem is, none of the databases mentioned earlier is 100 percent ANSI SQL compliant. (We'll talk about three levels of conformance on the following pages; the feature compliance list is given in Appendix J.) Each of these databases shares the basic SQL syntax (though some diversity exists even there), but the language operators, naming restrictions, internal functions, datatypes (especially date and time related), and procedural language extensions are implemented differently.

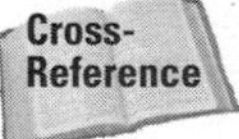

See Chapter 14 for more information on the SQL procedural extensions.

Table 1-1 compares some data on maximum name lengths supported by different database implementations.

Table 1-1
Maximum Name Length Restrictions for Some of Database Objects

	IBM DB2 8.1	*MS SQL Server 2000*	*Oracle 9i*
Table name length (characters)	128	128	30
Column name length (characters)	30	128	30
Constraint name length (characters)	18	128	30
Index name length (characters)	128	128	30
Number of table columns	255	1023	1000

In an ideal world the standards would rule supreme, and SQL would be freely shared among different implementations for the benefit of humanity. Unfortunately, the reality looks somewhat different. While it is possible to distill a standard SQL understood by all database vendors' products, anything above some very trivial tasks would be better, quicker accomplished with implementation-specific features.

Real-Life Database Examples

To say that the databases are everywhere would be an understatement. They virtually permeate our lives: Online stores, health care providers, clubs, libraries, video stores, beauty salons, travel agencies, phone companies, government agencies like FBI, INS, IRS, and NASA—they all use databases. These databases can be very different in their nature and usually have to be specifically designed to cater to some special customer needs. Here are some examples.

All relational databases can be divided into two main categories according to their primary function—*online transaction processing* (OLTP) and *data warehouse* systems. OLTP typically has many users simultaneously creating and updating individual records; in other words it's volatile and computation-intensive. Data warehouse is a database designed for information processing and analysis, with focus on planning for the future rather than on day-to-day operations. The information in these is not going to change very often, which ensures the information consistency (repeatable result) for the users. In the real world most systems are hybrids of these two, unless specifically designed as data warehouse.

Order management system database

A typical database for a company that sells building materials might be arranged as follows: The company must have at least one customer. Each customer in the database is assigned one or more addresses, one or more contact phones, and a default salesperson who is the liaison between the customer and the company. The company sells a variety of products. Each product has a price, a description, and some other characteristics. Orders can be placed for one or more product at a time. Each product logically forms an order line. When an order is complete it can be shipped and then invoiced. Invoice number and shipment number are populated automatically in the database and can not be changed by users. Each order has a status assigned to it: `COMPLETE`, `SHIPPED`, `INVOICED`, and so on. The database also contains specific shipment information (bill of lading number, number of boxes shipped, dates, and so on). Usually one shipment contains one order, but the database is designed in such a way that one order can be distributed between more than one shipment, as well as one shipment can contain more than one order. Some constraints also exist in the database. For example, some fields cannot be empty, and some other fields can contain only certain types of information.

You already know that a database is a multiuser environment by definition. It's a common practice to group users according to the functions they perform and security levels they are entitled to. The order management system described here could have three different user groups: Sales department clerks' function is to enter or modify order and customer information; shipping department employees create and update shipment data; warehouse supervisors handle products. In addition, all three user groups view diverse database information under different angles, using reports and ad-hoc queries.

We'll use this database, which we'll call ACME, throughout this book for examples and exercises. ACME database is a simplified version of a real production database. It has only 13 tables, and the real one would easily have over a hundred.

See Appendix B (The ACME Sample Database) and Appendix F (Installing ACME Database) for more detailed descriptions of the database and installation instructions.

Health care provider database

A health provider company has multiple offices in many different states. Many doctors work for the company, and each doctor takes care of multiple patients. Some doctors just work in one office, and others work in different offices on different days. The database keeps information about each doctor, such as name, address, contact phones, area of specialization, and so on. Each patient can be assigned to one or more doctors. Specific patient information is also kept in the database (name, address, phones, health record number, date of birth, history of appointments, prescriptions, blood tests, diagnoses, etc.). Customers can schedule and cancel appointments and order prescription drugs either over the phone or using the company Web site. Some restrictions apply — for example, to see a specialist, the patient needs an approval from his/her primary physician; to order a prescription the patient should have at least one valid refill left, and so on.

Now, what are the main database user groups? Patients should be able to access the database using a Web browser to order prescriptions and make appointments. This is all that patients may do in the database. Doctors and nurses can browse information about their patients, write and renew prescriptions, schedule blood tests and X-Rays, and so on. Administrative staff (receptionists, pharmacy assistants) can schedule appointments for patients, fill prescriptions, and run specific reports.

Again, in real life this database would be far more complicated and would have many more business rules, but our main goal now is just to give a general idea what kind of information a database could contain.

The health provider and order management system databases are both examples of a typical *hybrid* database (though the former is probably closer to an OLTP).

Scientific database

A database for genome research and related research areas in molecular and cellular biology can be a good example of a scientific database. It contains gene catalogs for completely sequenced genomes and some partial genomes, genome maps and organism information, and data about sequence similarities among all known genes in all organisms in the database. It also contains information on molecular interaction networks in the cell and chemical compounds and reactions.

This database has just one user group — all researchers have the same access to all the information. This is an example of a data warehouse.

Nonprofit organization database

A database of an antique automobile club can be pretty simple. Also, such an organization would not typically have too many members, so the database is not going to be very large. You need to store members' personal information such as address, phone number, area of interest, and so on. The database might also contain the information about the autos (brand, year, color, condition, etc.). Autos are tied to their owners (members of the club). Each member can have one or more vehicles, and a vehicle can be owned by just one member.

The database would only have a few users — possibly, the chairman of the club, an assistant, and a secretary.

The last two examples are not business-critical databases and don't have to be implemented on expensive enterprise software. The data still have to be kept safely and should not be lost, but in case of, let's say, hardware failure it probably can wait a day or two before the database is restored from a backup. So, the use of a free database, like mySQL, PostgreSQL, or even nonrelational Posgres is appropriate. Another good choice might be MS Access, which is a part of Microsoft Office Tools; if you bought MS Office just because you want to use Word and Excel, you should be aware that you've got a free relational database as well. (MS Access works well with up to 15 users.)

Database Legacy

Flat file, hierarchy, and network databases are usually referred as *legacy* databases. They represent the ways people used to organize information in prehistoric times — about 30 years ago.

Flat file databases

The flat file database was probably one of the earliest database management systems. The idea behind flat file is a very simple one: one single, mostly unstructured data file. It mirrors "ancient" precomputer data storage systems: notebooks, grocery lists, and so on. You could compare it to a desk drawer that holds virtually everything — bill stubs, letters, small change. While requiring very little effort to put information *in*, such a "design" becomes a nightmare to get the information *out*, as you would have to scroll through each and every record searching for the right one. Putting relevant data into separate files and even organizing them into tables (think of a file cabinet) alleviates the problem somewhat but does not remove the major obstacles: data redundancy (the same information might be stored more than once in different files), slow processing speed ("I know it was there somewhere..."), error-prone storage and retrieval. Moreover, it required intimate knowledge of the database structure to work at all — it would be utterly useless to search for, say, orders information in the expenses file.

Let's design a flat database system for an order entry system that gathers information about customers, orders they've placed and products the customers had ordered. If data is accumulated sequentially, your file will contain information about customers, then orders and products, then about some new customer, and so on — all in the order the data is entered (Table 1-2). Just imagine a task of extracting any meaningful information from this mess, not to mention that a lot of the cells will remain empty. (What would you fill Quantity column for the "Ace Hardware" or Address column for "Nails" with?)

Table 1-2
Flat File Records Keeping

Name	*Type*	*Address*	*Price*	*Quantity*
Nails	Product	n/a	100	2000
Ace Hardware	Customer	1234 Willow Ct Seattle, Washington	n/a	n/a
Cedar planks	Product	n/a	2000	5000

Dissatisfaction with these shortcomings stimulated development in the area of data storage-and-retrieval systems.

Excel is often used to create flat file databases.

Hierarchical databases

The concept of a hierarchical database was around since the 1960s and — believe it or not — it is still in use. The hierarchical model is fairly intuitive: As the name implies, it stores data in hierarchical structure, similar to that of a family tree, organization chart, or pyramid; some readers could visualize a computer file system as it is presented through some graphical interface.

The most popular hierarchical database product is IBM's Information Management System (IMS) that runs on mainframe computers. First introduced in 1968, it is still around (after a number of reincarnations), primarily because hierarchical databases provide impressive raw speed performance for certain types of queries.

It is based on "parent/child" paradigm in which each parent could have many children but each child has one and only one parent. You can visualize this structure as an upside down tree, starting at the root (trunk) and branching out at many levels (Figure 1-1).

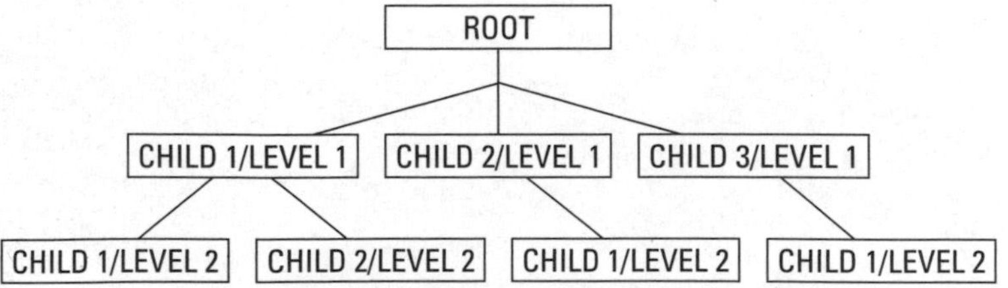

Figure 1-1: Hierarchical structure

Since the records in a child table are accessed through a hierarchy of levels there could not be a record in it without a corresponding pointer record in the parent table — all the way up to the root. You could compare it to a file management system (like a tree-view seen in the Microsoft Windows Explorer) — to get access to a file within a directory one must first open the folder that contains this file.

Let's improve upon the previously discussed flat file model. Instead of dumping all the information into a single file you are going to split it among three tables, each containing pertinent information: business name and address for the CUSTOMER table; product description, brand name, and price for the PRODUCT table; and an ORDER_HEADER table to store the details of the order.

In the hierarchical database model redundancy is greatly reduced (compared with flat file database model): You store information about customer, product, and so on once only. The table ORDER_HEADER (Figure 1-2) would contain pointers to the customer and to the product this customer had ordered; whenever you need to see what products any particular customer purchased, you start with ORDER_HEADER table, find list of id(s) for all the customers who placed orders and list of product id(s) for each customer; then, using CUSTOMER table you find the customer name you are after, and using products id(s) list you get the description of the products from the PRODUCT table.

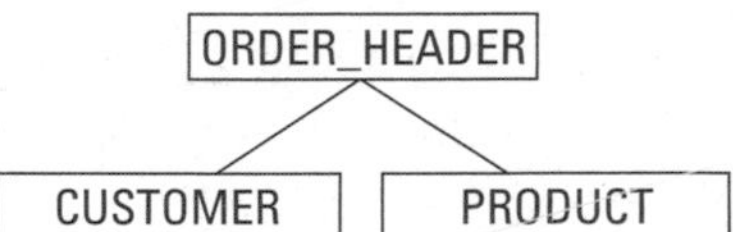

Figure 1-2: Hierarchical database example

Everything works great as long as one is willing to put up with a somewhat nonintuitive way of retrieving information. (No matter what information is requested one always has to start with the root, i.e., ORDER_HEADER table.) Should you need only customers' names the hierarchical database would be blazingly fast — going straight from a parent table to the child one. To get any information from the hierarchical database a user has to have an intimate knowledge of the database structure; and the structure itself was extremely inflexible — if, for instance, you'd decided that the customers must place an order through a third party, you'd need to rewire all relationships because CUSTOMER table would not be related to ORDER_HEADER table anymore, and all your queries will have to be rewritten to include one more step — finding the sales agent who sold this product, then finding customers who bought it. It also makes obvious the fact that you did not escape the redundancy problem — if you have a customer who places an order through more than one sales agent, you'll have to replicate all the information for each agent in a number of customer tables.

But what happens if you need to add a customer that does not have a placed order, or a product that no one yet ordered? You cannot — your hierarchical database is incapable of storing information in child tables without a parent table having a pointer to it: by the very definition of hierarchy there should be neither a product without an order, nor a customer without an order — which obviously cannot be the case in the real world.

The hierarchical databases handle one-to-many relationship (see Chapter 2 for definition) very well. However, in many cases you will want to have the child be related to more than one parent: Not only one product could be present in many orders, but one order could contain many products. There is no answer (at least not an easy one) within the domain of hierarchical databases.

Network databases

Attempts to solve the problems associated with hierarchical databases produced the *network* database model. This model has its origins in the Conference on Data Systems Languages (CODASYL), an organization founded in 1957 by the U.S. Department of Defense. CODASYL was responsible for developing COBOL — one of the first widely popular programming languages — and publishing the Network Database standard in 1971 The most popular commercial implementation of the network model was Adabas (long since converted to the *relational* model).

The network model is very similar to the hierarchical one; it is also based on the concept of parent/child relationship but removes the restriction of one child having one and only one parent. In the network database model a parent can have multiple children, and a child can have multiple parents. This structure could be visualized as several trees that share some branches. In network database jargon these relationships came to be known as *sets*.

In addition to the ability to handle a one-to-many relationship, the network database can handle many-to-many relationships.

One-to-one, one-to-many, and many-to-many relationships are explained in Chapter 2.

Also, data access did not have to begin with the root; instead one could traverse the database structure starting from any table and navigating a related table in any direction (Figure 1-3).

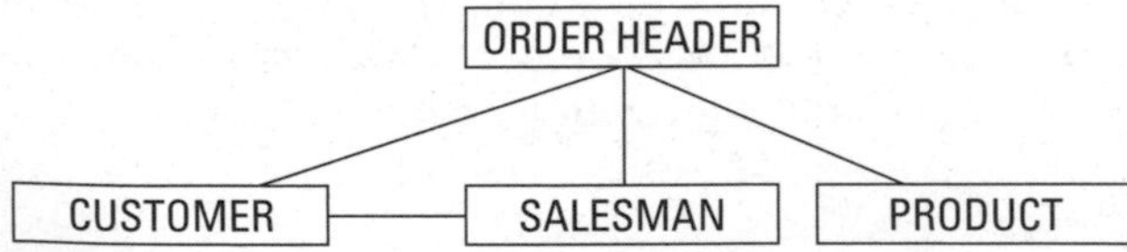

Figure 1-3: Network database example

In this example, to find out what products were sold to what customers we still would have to start with ORDER_HEADER and then proceed to CUSTOMER and PRODUCT — nothing new here. But things greatly improve for the scenario when customers place an order through more than one agent: no longer does one have to go through agents to list customers of the specific product, and no longer has one to start at the root in search of records.

While providing several advantages, network databases share several problems with hierarchical databases. Both are very inflexible, and changes in the structure (for example, a new table to reflect changed business logic) require that the entire database be rebuilt; also, set relationships and record structures must be predefined.

The major disadvantage of both network and hierarchical database was that they are programmers' domains. To answer the simplest query, one had to create a program that navigated database structure and produced an output; unlike SQL this program was written in procedural, often proprietary, language and required a great deal of knowledge — of both database structure and underlying operating system. As a result, such programs were not portable and took enormous (by today's standards) amount of time to write.

Relational Databases

The frustration with the inadequate capabilities of network and hierarchical databases resulted in the invention of the *relational data model*. The relational data model took the idea of the network database some several steps further. Relational models — just like hierarchical and network models — are based upon tables and use parent/child relationships. (Though this relationship was implemented through column values as opposed to a low-level physical pointer defining the relationship; more on that later in the chapter.)

Tables

A table is a basic building unit of the relational database. It is a fairly intuitive way of organizing data and has been around for centuries. A table consists of rows and columns (called *records* and *fields* in database jargon). Each table has a *unique* name in the database (i.e., unique *fully qualified name*, the one that includes schema or database name as a prefix).

Note The Dot (.) notation in a fully qualified name is commonly used in the programming world to describe hierarchy of the objects and their properties. This could refer not only to the database objects but also to the structures, user-defined types, and such. For example, a table field in an MS SQL Server database could be referred to as ACME.DBO.CUSTOMER. CUST_ID_N where ACME is a database name, DBO is the table owner (Microsoft standard), CUSTOMER is the name of the table, and CUST_ID_N is the column name in the CUSTOMER table.

Cross-Reference

See Chapter 4 for more on table and other database object names.

Each field has a unique name within the table, and any table must have at least one field. The number of fields per table is usually limited, the actual limitation being dependent on a particular implementation. Unlike legacy database structure, records in a table are not stored or retrieved in any particular order (although, records can be arranged in a particular order by means of using *clustered index*—discussed in Chapter 4); the task of sorting the record in relational databases systems (RDBMS) is relegated to SQL.

A record thus is composed of a number of cells, where each cell has a unique name and might contain some data. A table that has no records is called an empty table.

Data within the field must be of the same type, for example, the field `AMOUNT` contains only numbers, and field `DESCRIPTION`, only words. The set of the data within one field is said to be column's *domain*.

Note

Early databases—relational or otherwise—were designed to contain only text data; modern databases store anything that could be converted into binary format: pictures, movies, audio records, and so on.

The good relational design would make sure that such a record describes an *entity*—another relational database term to be discussed later in the book but worth mentioning here. To put it in other words, the record should not contain irrelevant information: `CUSTOMER` table deals with the customer information only, its records should not contain information about, say, products that this customer ordered.

Note

The process of grouping the relevant data together, eliminating redundancies along the way is called *normalization* and will be discussed in Chapter 2. It is not part of SQL per se, but it does impose limits on the SQL query efficiency.

There is no theoretical limit on the number of rows a table could have, though some implementations impose restrictions; also there are (or at least ought to be) practical considerations to the limits: data retrieval speed, amount of storage, and so on.

Relationships

Tables in RDBMS might or might not be related. As it was mentioned before, RDBMS is built upon parent/child relationship notion (hence the name—*relational*), but unlike in legacy databases (hierarchical, network) these relations are based solely on the values in the table columns; these relationships are meaningful in logical terms, not in low-level computer specific pointers. Let's take the example of our fictitious order entry database (the one that we will design, build, and use throughout the book). The ORDER_HEADER table is related to CUSTOMER table since both of these tables have a *common set of values*: The field ORDHDR_CUSTID_FN (customer ID) in ORDER_HEADER (and its values) corresponds to CUST_ID_N in CUSTOMER. The field CUST_ID_N is said to be a *primary key* for the CUSTOMER table and a *foreign key* for the ORDER_HEADER table (under different name).

Primary key

The *primary key* holds more than one job in RDBMS. We've said already that it is used to define a relationship; but its primary role is to uniquely identify each record in a table.

In the days of legacy databases, the records were always stored in some predefined order; if such an order had to be broken (because somebody had inserted records in a wrong order or business rule was changed), then the whole table (and, most likely, the whole database) had to be rebuilt. The RDBMS abolishes fixed order for the records, but it still needs some mechanism of identifying the records uniquely, and the primary key, based on the idea of a field (or fields) that contains set unique values, serves exactly this purpose.

By it is very nature, the primary key cannot be empty; this means that in a table with defined primary key, the primary key fields must contain data for each record.

Note

Though it is not a requirement to have a primary key on each and every table, it is considered to be a good practice to have one; in fact, many RDBMS implementations would warn you if you create a table without defining a primary key. Some purists go even further, specifying that the primary key should be *meaningless* in the sense that they would use some generated unique value (like EMPLOYEE_ID) instead of, say, Social Security numbers (despite that these are unique as well).

A primary key could consist of one or more columns, i.e., though some fields may contain duplicate values, their combination (set) is unique through the entire table. A key that consists of several columns is called a *composite key*.

Note

In the world of RDBMS, only tables that have primary keys can be related. Though the primary key is a cornerstone for defining relation in RDBMS, the actual implementations (especially early ones) have not always provided a built-in support for this logical concept. In practice, the task of enforcing uniqueness of a chosen primary key was the responsibility of programmers (requiring them to check for existing values before inserting new records, for example). Today all major relational database products have built-in support for primary keys; on a very basic level this means that the database does its own checking for unique constraint violations and will raise an error whenever an attempt to insert a duplicate record is made.

Foreign key

Let's go back to our CUSTOMER and ORDER_HEADER tables. By now you understand why the CUST_ID_N was designated as a primary key — it has unique value, no customer can possibly have more than one ID, and no ID could be assigned to more than one customer. To track what customers placed which orders, you need something that will provide a link between customers and their orders.

Table ORDER_HEADER has its own primary key — ORDHDR_ID_N which uniquely identifies orders; in addition to that it will have a foreign key ORDHDR_CUSTID_FN field. The values in that field correspond to the values in the CUST_ID_N primary key field for the CUSTOMER table. Note that, unlike the primary key, the foreign key is not required to be unique — one customer could place several orders.

Now, by looking into ORDER_HEADER table you can find which customers placed particular orders. The table ORDER_HEADER became related to table CUSTOMER. It became easy to find a customer based on orders, or find orders for a customer. You no longer need to know database layout, order of the records in the table, or master some low-level proprietary programming language to query data; it's now possible to run ad-hoc queries formulated in standard English-like language — the Structured Query Language.

Invasion of RDBMS

In spite of the clear advantages of the relational database model, it took some time for it to become workable. One of the main reasons was the hardware. The logically clear and clean model proved to be quite a task to implement, and even then it required much more in terms of memory and processing power than legacy databases.

The development of relational databases was driven by the need of the medium to big businesses to gather, preserve, and analyze data. In 1965, Gordon Moore, the cofounder of Intel, made his famous observation that the number of transistors per square inch on the integrated circuits (IC) doubles every year ever since the IC were invented. Surprisingly, this rule still holds true. More powerful machines made it feasible to implement and sell RDBMS; cheap memory and powerful processors made them fast; perpetually growing appetites for information made RDBMS products a commodity, drastically cutting their price down. Today, according to some estimates, less than 10 percent of the market is being held by the database legacy "dinosaurs" — mostly because of significant investment made by their owners more than 20 years ago. For better or for worse, relational database systems have come to rule on planet Earth.

Object Database and Object-Relational Database Models

The innovation did not stop here. At the end of the 1980s the buzzword was *object-oriented programming* (OOP). Because of very similar reasons (memory requirements, processing power) as those preventing widespread adoption of RDBMS, object-oriented programming did not take off until well into the 1990s. OOP languages are based on the notion that a programming (or business) problem could be modeled in terms of objects.

While the code of the program remained practically the same, the way the code was organized changed dramatically; it also changed the way programs were constructed, coded, and executed. For programming applications that communicate with the databases it would be only natural to store objects on an as-is basis instead of disassembling them into text and putting them back together when needed.

Modern RDBMS have the ability to store binary objects (e.g., pictures, sounds, etc.), in the case of OO databases, they need to store conceptual objects: customer, order, and so on. The emerging standard (SQL3) was designed to work with object-oriented databases. There are several products on the market for OODBS (object-oriented database systems) and OORDBMS (object-oriented relational database systems) that offer object-oriented features combined with reasonable performance, though none of these meet with a widespread adoption — as yet.

While SQL itself is not an object-oriented language now, it might as well be — in the future. Meanwhile, several vendors (Oracle, IBM) supplied their flagship database products with capability to use Java as procedural language that has some embedded SQL statements.

The other development worth noticing is a wide adoption of eXtensible Markup Language (XML). XML was developed as a logical evolution of the plain static HyperText Markup Language (HTML) used to generate Web pages. XML is discussed in the final chapters of this book as it has not become a part of the SQL standard yet, and is implemented through proprietary extensions to the RDBMS. An XML document contains self-describing data in a platform-independent industry-standard format that makes it easy to transform into different types of documents, to search, or to transfer across heterogeneous network.

Every major RDBMS release is either a new version of its product or an add-in to the existing one to handle XML. The logical step in this direction would be to create an XML native database, that is, a database that stores data in XML format, without parsing XML documents when storing the records nor reconstituting them from text-based data for retrieval. In theory, that would speed up XML-related database operation.

Brief History of SQL and SQL Standards

As we already know, prerelational databases did not have a set of commands to work with data. Every database either had its own proprietary language or used programs written in COBOL, C, and so on to manipulate records. Also, the databases were virtually inflexible and did not allow any internal structure changes without bringing them offline and rewriting tons of code. That worked more or less effectively until the end of the 1960s, when most computer applications were based strictly on batch processing (running from beginning to end without user interaction).

Humble beginnings: RDBMS and SQL evolution

In the early 1970s, the growth of online applications (programs that require user's interaction) triggered the demand for something more flexible. The situations when an extra field was required for a particular record or a number of subfields exceeded the maximum number in the file layout became more and more common.

For example, imagine that `CUSTOMER` record set has two fixed-length fields, `ADDRESS1` (for billing address) and `ADDRESS2` (for shipping address), and it works for all customers for some period of time. But what if a customer, who owns a hardware store, has bought another store, and now this record must have more than one shipping address? And what if you have a new customer, `WILE ELECTRONICS INC.`, who owns ten stores? Now, you have two choices. You can take the whole dataset offline, modify the layout, and change/recompile all programs that work with it. But then, all other customers that just have one store each will have nine unnecessary fields in their records (Figure 1-4). Also, nobody can guarantee that tomorrow some other customer is not going to buy, say, 25 stores, and then you'll have to start over again. Another choice would be to add ten identical records for Wile Electronics Inc., completely redundant except for the shipping address. The programs would still have to be changed, because otherwise they may return incorrect results (Figure 1-5).

NAME	BILLADDR	SHIPADDR_1	SHIPADDR_2	SHIPADDR_N	SHIPADDR_10
MAGNETICS USA INC.	123 LAVACA ST.	444 PINE ST.			
WILE ELECTRONICS INC.	411 LONDON AVE.	232 EEL ST.	454 OAK ST.	...	999 ELK AVE.

Figure 1-4: Multiple columns to resolve multiple addresses for CUSTOMER

So, as you can see, most problems are actually rooted in the structure of the database, which usually consisted of just one file with records of a fixed length. The solution is to spread data across several files and reassemble the required data when needed. We already mentioned hierarchical and network database models that definitely were attempts to move in this direction, but they still had had too many shortcomings, so the relational model became the most popular technique. The problem we just discussed would not be a problem at all in a relational database, where CUSTOMER and ADDRESS are separate entities (tables), tied by primary/foreign key relationship (Figure 1-6). All we have to do is to add as many ADDRESS records as we want with a foreign key that refers to its parent (Figure 1-7).

NAME	BILLADDR	SHIPADDR
MAGNETICS USA INC.	123 LAVACA ST.	444 PINE ST.
WILE ELECTRONICS INC.	411 LONDON AVE.	232 EEL ST.
WILE ELECTRONICS INC.	411 LONDON AVE.	454 OAK ST.
WILE ELECTRONICS INC.	411 LONDON AVE.	456 WILLOW ST.
WILE ELECTRONICS INC.	411 LONDON AVE.	678 MAPLE AVE.
WILE ELECTRONICS INC.	411 LONDON AVE.	332 WALNUT ST.
WILE ELECTRONICS INC.	411 LONDON AVE.	531 DEER ST.
WILE ELECTRONICS INC.	411 LONDON AVE.	865 CEDAR AVE.
WILE ELECTRONICS INC.	411 LONDON AVE.	911 MYRTLE ST.
WILE ELECTRONICS INC.	411 LONDON AVE.	777 SITKA AVE.
WILE ELECTRONICS INC.	411 LONDON AVE.	999 ELK AVE.

Figure 1-5: Multiple records to resolve multiple addresses for CUSTOMER

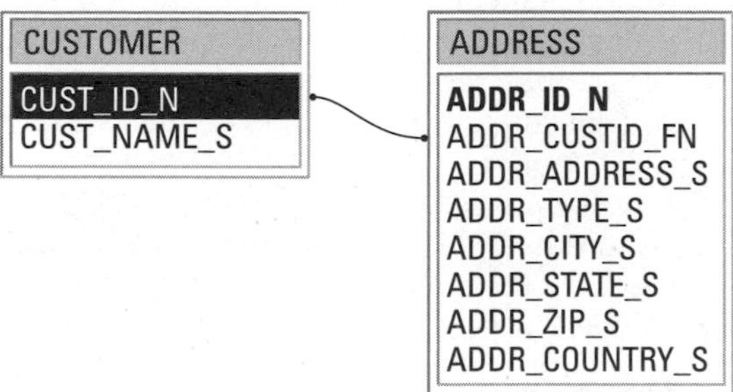

Figure 1-6: Primary/Foreign Key relationship between tables

Note

Our example might not look very convincing—it almost looks like that instead of adding new shipping addresses to CUSTOMER, we just added the same records to a separate ADDRESS table. In fact, the difference is huge. In a real-life legacy database, CUSTOMER file would not have just NAME and ADDRESS fields, but rather it would contain tons of other information: about orders, products, invoices, shipments, etc. All that would be repeated every time you accessed the database, even for something as simple as adding a new shipping address.

CUST_ID_N	CUST_NAME_S
7	WILE ELECTRONICS INC.

ADDR_CUSTID_FN	ADDR_ADDRESS_S	ADDR_TYPE_S
7	411 S LONDON AVE.	BILLING
7	454 OAK ST.	SHIPPING
7	678 MAPLE AVE.	SHIPPING
7	999 ELK AVE.	SHIPPING
7	777 SITKA AVE.	SHIPPING
7	911 MYRTLE ST.	SHIPPING
7	865 CEDAR AVE.	SHIPPING
7	531 DEER ST.	SHIPPING
7	332 WALNUT ST.	SHIPPING
7	456 WILLOW ST.	SHIPPING
7	232 EEL ST.	SHIPPING

Figure 1-7: Resolving the multiple customer addresses problem within relational model

Another advantage of the relational schema was a simplified logic for the applications that worked with data. For example, let's assume the nonrelational `CUSTOMER` dataset has fields for a maximum of five customer orders. (That easily could be a couple fields per order, by the way.) If you want to display all orders for a specific customer, a program will have to scroll through all these fields, determine which ones are not empty, and display their contents. In the relational case, all you need to do is to display all records in `ORDER_HEADER` table that have the required customer number. All that made ad-hoc query languages relatively easy to write and finally resulted in appearance of SQL.

The concept of a relational database and thus SQL was first introduced by Dr. Edward Frank Codd, who worked for IBM as a researcher, in his paper "A Relational Model of Data for Large Shared Data Banks" in 1970. In simple words, his idea of a relational database model was based on data independence from hardware and storage implementation and a nonprocedural high-level computer language to access the data. The problem was, IBM already had declared its own product, called IMS, as its sole strategic database product; the company management was not convinced at all that developing new commercial software based on relational schema was worth the money and the effort. A new database product could also potentially hurt the sales of IMS.

In spite of all that, a relational database prototype called System R was finally introduced by IBM in the late 1970s, but it never became a commercial product and was more of a scientific interest, unlike its language SQL (first known as SEQUEL) that finally became the standard for all relational databases (after years of evolution). Another relational product called Ingres was developed by scientists in a government-funded program at the University of California, Berkeley at about the same time, and also had its own nonprocedural language, QUEL, similar to IBM's SQL.

But the first commercial relational database was neither System R nor Ingres. Oracle Corporation released its first product in 1979, followed by IBM's SQL/DS (1980/81) and DB2 (1982/83). The commercial version of Ingres also became available in the early 1980s. Sybase Inc. released the first version of its product in 1986, and in 1988 Microsoft introduced SQL Server. Many other products by other companies were also released since then, but their share of today's market is minimal.

A brief history of SQL standards

The relational database model was slowly but surely becoming the industry standard in the late 1980s. The problem was, even though SQL became a commonly recognized database language, the differences in major vendors' implementations were growing, and some kind of standard became necessary.

Around 1978, the Committee on Data Systems and Language (CODASYL) commissioned the development of a network data model as a prototype for any future database implementations. This continued work started in the early 1970s with the Data Definition Language Committee (DDLC). By 1982, these efforts culminated in the data definition language (DDL) and data manipulation language (DML) standards proposal. They became standards four years later — endorsed by an organization with an improbably long name, the American National Standards Institute National Committee on Information Technology Standards H2 Technical Committee on Database (ANSI NCITS H2 TCD).

NCITS H2 was given a mandate to standardize relational data model in 1982. The project initially was based on IBM SQL/DS specifications, and for some time followed closely IBM DB2 developments. In 1984, the standard was redesigned to be more generic, to allow for more diversity among database products vendors. After passing through all the bureaucratic loops it was endorsed as an American National Standards Institute in 1986. The International Standard Organization (ISO) adopted the standard in 1987. The revised standard, commonly known as SQL89, was published two years later.

SQL89 (SQL1)

SQL89 (or SQL1) is a rather worthless standard that was established by encircling all RDBMS in existence in 1989. The major commercial vendors could not (and still to certain degree cannot) agree upon implementation details, so much of the SQL89 standard is intentionally left incomplete, and numerous features are marked as implementer-defined.

SQL92 (SQL2)

Because of the aforesaid, the previous standard had been revised, and in 1992 the first solid SQL standard, SQL92 or SQL2, was published. ANSI took SQL89 as a basis, but corrected several weaknesses in it, filled many gaps in the old standard, and presented conceptual SQL features, which at that time exceeded the capabilities of any existing RDBMS implementation. Also, the SQL92 standard is over five times longer than its predecessor (about 600 pages more), and has three levels of conformance.

Entry-level conformance is basically improved SQL89. The differences were insignificant — for example, circular views and correlated subqueries became prohibited in SQL92

Intermediate-level conformance was a set of major improvements, including, but not limited to, user naming of constraints; support for varying-length characters and national character sets, case and cast expressions, built-in join operators, and dynamic SQL; ability to alter tables, to set transactions, to use subqueries in updatable views, and use set operators (`UNION`, `EXCEPT`, `INTERSECT`) to combine multiple queries' results.

Full-level conformance included some truly advanced features, including deferrable constraints, assertions, temporary local tables, privileges on character sets and domains, and so on.

The conformance testing was performed by the U.S. Government Department of Commerce's National Institute of Standards and Technology (NIST). The vendors hurried to comply because a public law passed in the beginning of the 1990s required an RDBMS product to pass the tests in order to be considered by a federal agency.

As of this writing, all major database vendors (Oracle, DB2, MS SQL Server, and Sybase) meet only the first level of SQL92 conformance in full. Each of the vendors has individual features that venture into higher levels of conformance. The only vendor that claims its product meets all three levels, or 100 percent SQL92 compliant, is a small company called Ocelot Computer Services, Inc., and their RDBMS implementation of the same name does not seem to be very popular.

In 1996, NIST dismantled the conformance testing program (citing "high costs" as the reason behind the decision). Since then, the only verification of SQL standards compliance comes from the RDBMS vendors themselves; this understandably increased the number of vendor-specific features as well as nonstandard implementation of the standard ones. By 2001, the original number of RDBMS vendors belonging to the ANSI NCIT had shrunk from 18 (at the beginning of the 1990s) to just 7, though some new companies came aboard.

The current members of the ANSI NCIT H2 Technical Committee on Database are IBM, Oracle, Microsoft, NCR, Computer Associates, Compaq, Pervasive, FileTek, and InterSystems.

SQL99 (SQL3)

SQL3 represents the next step in SQL standards development. The efforts to define this standard began virtually at the same time when its predecessor — SQL92

(SQL2)—was adopted. The new standard was developed under guidance of both ANSI and ISO committees, and the change introduced into the database world by SQL3 was as dramatic a shift from nonrelational to relational database model; its sheer complexity is reflected in the number of pages describing the standard—over 1,500—comparing to 120 or so pages for SQL89 and about 600 pages for SQL92. Some of the defined standards (for example, stored procedures) existed as vendor-specific extensions, some of them (like OOP) are completely new to SQL proper. SQL3 was released as an ANSI/ISO draft standard in 1999; later the same year its status was changed to a *standard* level.

Note

We can draw a parallel between SQL ANSI/ISO standards and Latin. These standards are good to know; they may help one to learn the actual SQL implementations, but it is impossible (or almost impossible) to write a real 100 percent ANSI SQL compliant production script. The knowledge of Latin can help someone to learn Spanish, Italian, or Portuguese, but people would hardly understand you if you started speaking Latin on the streets of Madrid, Rome, or Lisbon. The main difference is the general direction—Latin is an ancestor of all the above (and many more) languages, and ANSI/ISO SQL standards are rather a goal for all proprietary SQL flavors.

SQL3 extends traditional relational data models to incorporate objects and complex data types *within* the relational tables, along with all supporting mechanisms. It brings into SQL all the major OOP principles, namely *inheritance*, *encapsulation,* and *polymorphism,* all of which are beyond the scope of this book, in addition to "standard" SQL features defined in SQL92. It provides seamless integration with the data consumer applications designed and implemented in OO languages (SmallTalk, Eiffel, etc.).

There are several commercial implementations of OODBMS on the market as well as OO extensions to existing commercial database products; not all of them adhere to the standards and a number of proprietary "features" makes them incompatible. For a time being OODBMS (OORDBMS) occupy an insignificant portion of the database market, and the judgment is still out there.

While it is impossible to predict what model will emerge as a winner in the future, it seems reasonable to assume that relational databases are here in for a long haul and have not yet reached their potential; SQL as *the* language of the RDBMS will keep its importance in the database world.

Summary

Databases penetrate virtually every branch of human activity, with relational databases (RDBMS) becoming the de-facto standard. Some legacy database models—hierarchical and network databases—are still in use, but relational database model (RDBM) holds the lion's share of the market.

The RDBM resolves some of the inherent problems of the legacy databases, and — with the advent of faster hardware and support from the industry heavyweights — became the staple of every business enterprise. The new object-oriented databases (OODMS) and object-oriented relational database systems (OORDBMS) are evolving, though none has reached the level of acceptance comparable with that of RDBMS.

Most of the existing applications on the market database use SQL as the standard language. There are three (four, by some counts, if SQL86 is included) standards: SQL89, SQL92, and SQL99, with virtually every RDBMS product being at least partially SQL92 compliant.

✦ ✦ ✦

Fundamental SQL Concepts and Principles

In This Chapter

SQL standards revisited

First look at SQL

Four basic SQL statements: introduction

Advanced SQL capabilities

Platform independence

Ever since SQL89 was adopted as the first SQL standard, SQL aimed to be just that — the standardized, generic, nonprocedural vendor independent language of relational databases. It did succeed — to a certain extent.

Promises and Deliverables

Unlike many popular programming languages (C++, Java, Visual Basic, C#, to mention just a few), SQL was designed to be nonprocedural. That means that the features one takes for granted in any other programming language — control flow statements (`IF. . .THEN`), looping constructs (`FOR. . . NEXT`), and the like — were completely excluded.

SQL was designed for data storage, retrieval, and manipulation, and as such it was tightly coupled with database management systems (DBMS); it neither exists outside DBMS nor could it be executed without. All one has to do is to submit a query to a DBMS and receive results in some client program — either actual data from the database or status results of a task (like inserting/deleting records).

In contrast to programming-style *variable manipulation*, inserting, updating, and retrieving data are *set-based procedures*. SQL statements operate on datasets, and though an operation itself might be lengthy, it does not really have any *flow*. From the programmer's point of view, a SQL program is just one statement, no matter how long, that executes as a whole, or not at all.

To overcome problems introduced with SQL procedural deficiency, database vendors came up with procedural extensions of their own: PL/SQL for Oracle Transact-SQL for Microsoft SQL Server, SQL PL for IBM DB2 UDB; the latest developments allow for using high-level language like Java or Visual Basic inside RDBMS. These are gradually making their way into the SQL99 standard (SQL/JRT).

Use of SQL is intertwined with the paradigm of client/server computing — long before this became a buzzword of the day. A *client* was supposed to know how to connect to a server, request data, and represent it for a user in some, usually graphical, format; a *server* is supposed to understand clients' request and return data — in addition to managing this data internally for best performance and providing safe storage and security services.

The complexity of low-level implementation — how the SQL statements are translated into machine language and executed — is hidden behind concise statements like `SELECT`, `INSERT`, or `UPDATE`, and the task of translating them into actual machine commands is left with the RDBMS.

This opened a whole can of worms; not only had RDBMS vendors chosen to implement different pieces of the SQL standard, but also in some cases those pieces were implemented differently. Vendor specific extensions — which often provided a base for the next iteration of SQL standard — complicated the matter even more.

As you learned in Chapter 1, the ANSI SQL standard (SQL89) instituted three levels of conformance for every database product aspiring to be ANSI compliant. SQL3 (SQL99) introduced two levels of conformance: Core SQL99 and Enhanced SQL99. Every major RDBMS is at least first (core) conformance-level compliant.

Nevertheless, SQL could hardly be considered portable; it is rather adaptable. There are quite a few points left up to the vendors to implement:

- **Semantic and syntactic differences.**
- **Opening database for processing.** The interfaces of ODBC, CLI, OLEDB, and others are not part of any SQL standard.
- **Dynamic and Embedded SQL implementations might differ from vendor to vendor.**
- **Collating order.** How results of a sorted query are presented; this depends on whether ASCII or EBCDIC characters are used. (Though the UNICODE standard alleviates this problem.)
- **Different data types extensions.**
- **Differences in database catalog tables.** Because this is mentioned at the full conformance level standard only; vendors working in the core level have no incentive to abandon their own proprietary structures.

ANSI/ISO Standard Documents

The following documents constitute the main body of ANSI/ISO standards:

- **ANSI/ISO/IEC 9075-1:1999.** Information technology — Database languages — SQL — Part 1: Framework (SQL/Framework)
- **ANSI/ISO/IEC 9075-1:1999/Amd 1:2001.** On-Line Analytical Processing (SQL/OLAP)
- **ANSI/ISO/IEC 9075-2:1999.** Information technology — Database languages — SQL — Part 2: Foundation (SQL/Foundation)
- **ANSI/ISO/IEC 9075-2:1999/Amd 1:2001.** On-Line Analytical Processing (SQL/OLAP)
- **ANSI/ISO/IEC 9075-3:1999.** Information technology — Database languages — SQL — Part 3: Call-Level Interface (SQL/CLI)
- **ANSI/ISO/IEC 9075-4:1999.** Information technology — Database languages — SQL — Part 4: Persistent Stored Modules (SQL/PSM)
- **ANSI/ISO/IEC 9075-5:1999.** Information technology — Database languages — SQL — Part 5: Host Language Bindings (SQL/Bindings)
- **ANSI/ISO/IEC 9075-5:1999/Amd 1:2001.** On-Line Analytical Processing (SQL/OLAP)
- **ANSI/ISO/IEC 9075-9:2001.** Information technology — Database languages — SQL — Part 9: Management of External Data (SQL/MED)
- **ANSI/ISO/IEC 9075-10:2000.** Information technology — Database languages — SQL — Part 10: Object Language Bindings (SQL/OLB)
- **ANSI/ISO/IEC 9075-13:2002.** Information technology — Database languages — SQL — Part 13: SQL Routines and Types Using the Java TM Programming Language (SQL/JRT)
- **ANSI/ISO/IEC 9579:2000.** Information technology — Remote database access for SQL with security enhancement
- **ANSI/ISO/IEC 13249-1:2000.** Information technology — Database languages — SQL multimedia and application packages — Part 1: Framework
- **ANSI/ISO/IEC 13249-2:2000.** Information technology — Database languages — SQL multimedia and application packages — Part 2: Full-Text
- **ANSI/ISO/IEC 13249-3:1999.** Information technology--Database languages — SQL Multimedia and Application Packages — Part 3: Spatial
- **ANSI/ISO/IEC 13249-5:2001.** Information technology — Database languages — SQL multimedia and application packages — Part 5: Still Image

These documents are available for a fee on the Web at `www.iso.org` and `www.ansi.org`.

Table 2-1 introduces the key SQL99 features areas that have been added to the previous SQL89, SQL92 standards. The more detailed and complete list of all major SQL99 features and compliance among major RDBMS vendors is given in Appendix J.

Table 2-1
Key SQL99 Areas

Features	*Description*
Call level interface (CLI)	The specification defining access to the database through a set of routines that could be called by a client application (ODBC, JDBC, etc.).
Information schema	A set of database views to access metadata for a particular database.
ROLES Security Enhancements	A security paradigm defining ability to fine-tune security privileges while grouping them into logically relevant groups.
Recursion	Refers to the nested relationship needed to model hierarchical structures.
Savepoint	An ability to add granularity to the transactional operation where a transaction could be rolled back not to the beginning but to a certain named step.
SQL Data types: `BLOB`, `CLOB`, `BOOLEAN`, `REF`, `ARRAY`, `ROW`, User Defined types	New data types to accommodate complexity of modern computing. (See Chapter 3 for in-depth discussion.)
SQL Multimedia data types: Full Text, Still Image, Spatial	New data formats developed for multimedia
SQL/MED	Defines extensions to Database Language SQL to support management of external data through the use of foreign tables and datalink data types.
SQL Programming Language	The domain ruled by proprietary procedural extensions like Oracle's PL/SQL or Microsoft Transact-SQL; defines standard programming Control-Of-Flow constructs (`IF...THEN...ELSE`), looping, etc.
Triggers	Defining action taken automatically in response to some predefined event; new standard fine-grained basic trigger functionality.
Management facilities for Connections, Sessions, Transactions, and Diagnostics	Infrastructure supporting for centralized or distributed processing.

SQL is a living language; it continues to grow and adapt to ever-changing demands. Despite the market pressures to standardize features and data exchange between the databases, vendors prefer to lock their customers into a specific RDBMS package by getting them hooked on some convenient nonstandard features that, while sometimes significantly improving performance, make it hard, expensive, or altogether impossible to port SQL routines to a different RDBMS.

Every vendor is encouraged to submit papers with new ideas and ANSI/ISO committees are reviewing these on an ongoing basis, which eventually would lead to yet another SQL standard in the future. The SQL of tomorrow might not turn out to be how we imagine it to ourselves today. Some of the emerging standards include XML (eXtensible Markup Language) and OLAP (On-Line Analytical Processing).

XML and OLAP are discussed in Chapter 17.

DB2 boasts being a major contributor to the current SQL99 standard, IBM being the number-one submitter of accepted papers for SQL99 for every single year from 1993 to 1999.

SQL: The First Look

Throughout this book we are going to use the ACME order management database of a fictitious hardware store. For full a description of this database as well as detailed instructions on how to install it on the RDBMS of your choice (as long as you choose Oracle 9*i*, Microsoft SQL Server 2000, or IBM DB2 UDB 8.1) please refer to Appendixes B and F, respectively. The whirlwind tour of SQL for this chapter will be using ACME tables exclusively. We've tried to create as generic as possible syntax that would be acceptable for every RDBMS discussed in the book.

Database example

As far as SQL is concerned the database starts with the `CREATE` statement. It is used to create all the objects that comprise a database: tables, indices, constraints, and so on. We look into creating, altering, and destroying database objects in Chapters 4 and 5.

You start with a `CREATE TABLE` statement. The syntax is virtually identical across all three databases: name of the column and its data type, which defines what kind of information it will hold in the future.

```
CREATE TABLE status
(
    status_id_n INT,
    status_code_s CHAR(2),
    status_desc_s VARCHAR(30)
)
```

This statement executed against an RDBMS will create a structure—an empty table, with columns of the specified *data types*: status id, status code, and description.

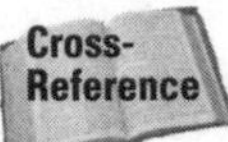

Data types are discussed in Chapter 3.

The procedure may be repeated as many times for as many tables you wish to add to your database. The relationships between these tables will be defined through *constraints*. To keep this introduction simple none of the constraints (or default values) are specified here.

Constraints are discussed in Chapter 4.

To dispose of a table (or many other objects in the RDBMS) one would issue a `DROP` statement:

```
DROP TABLE status
```

In real life, referential integrity constraints may prevent you from dropping the table outright; in the Chapter 1 we talked about what makes a database relational, in context of database integrity. You may need to disable constraints or cascade them. More about referential integrity and constraints is in Chapters 4 and 5.

A database is more than just a collection of the tables; there are many more objects as well as associated processes and structures that work together to keep and serve data; for now we can afford a more simplistic view.

Getting the data in and out

Once the tables are created, you probably would want to populate them with some data—after all, that's what databases are for. The SQL defines four basic statements, which are fairly self-explanatory, to query and manipulate data inside the database tables (Table 2-2). The exact uses of these statements will be discussed in depth in Chapters 6 through 9.

Table 2-2
Four Basic SQL Statements

SQL Statement	Purpose
INSERT	Adds new data to the table
UPDATE	Updates data — i.e., changes existing values — in the database table
SELECT	Retrieves data from database table
DELETE	Removes data from the table

Later in the book you will learn of data definition language (DDL) (Chapters 4 and 5), data manipulation language (DML) (Chapter 6), data query language (DQL) (Chapters 8 and 9), and data control language (DCL) (Chapter 12). These are parts of SQL proper.

To add new status for the table created in the previous example one would use the following statement:

```
INSERT INTO status
       (STATUS_ID_N, STATUS_CODE_S, STATUS_DESC_S)
VALUES (8,'70','INVOICED')
```

This statement could be entered directly through RDBMS access utility (Appendix E); in that case the database usually would acknowledge insertion with a message, or would generate an error message if the insertion failed for some reason.

The values for STATUS_CODE_S and STATUS_DESC_S are enclosed in single quotes because these columns are of character data type. STATUS_ID_N is of numeric data type and does not need quotes.

If you need to change some existing data (e.g., an acquisition status code might be changed while other related data elsewhere remains the same) you would use an UPDATE statement. Again, the syntax is completely portable across the three RDBMS products used in the book — Oracle 9*i* Database Server, IBM DB2 UDB 8.1, and Microsoft SQL Server 2000.

```
UPDATE status
SET    status_desc_s = 'APPROVED'
WHERE  status_id_n = 8
```

You update on a column basis, listing all the columns you want to update with the values you want to change; if every column in the record needs to be updated, they all must be listed with corresponding values.

```
UPDATE status
SET    status_desc_s = 'APPROVED',
       status_code_s = '90'
WHERE  status_id_n = 8
```

The UPDATE statement has a WHERE clause to limit the number of updated rows to exactly one customer whose ID is 8; if omitted from the query, the result would be that the existing value will be replaced with a new one for each and every customer.

The same applies to deleting data. If you need to completely remove a particular customer record from your database, then you might issue the following command:

```
DELETE status
WHERE  status_id_n = 8
```

Omitting the WHERE clause could be disastrous as all records in the table will be blown away; usually databases have some built-in mechanisms for recovering deleted data, which does not mean that you should not pay attention to what you're doing with the data.

The basic SELECT statement retrieves the data from a table or a view. You need to specify the columns you wish to be included in the resultset.

View is a virtual table that is being populated at the very moment it is queried. Views are discussed in detail in Chapter 4.

The following script selects CUSTOMER_NAME, ORDER_NUMBER and TOTAL_PRICE columns from the V_CUSTOMER_TOTALS view:

```
SELECT customer_name,
       order_number,
       total_price
FROM   v_customer_totals

customer_name              order_number     total_price
-------------------------  ---------------- -----------
WILE BESS COMPANY          523720               7511.00
WILE BESS COMPANY          523721               8390.00
WILE BESS COMPANY          523722               6608.00
```

```
WILE BESS COMPANY           523723                  11144.00
WILE ELECTROMUSICAL INC.    523726                   6608.00
WILE ELECTROMUSICAL INC.    523727                   6608.00
WILE ELECTROMUSICAL INC.    523728                   6608.00
```

Slice and dice: Same data, different angle

There is always more than one way to look at data. SQL provides you with the means to manipulate data while retrieving it. You can arrange the data in ascending or descending order by virtually any column in the table; you can perform calculations while retrieving the data; you can impose some restrictions on what data should be displayed. Here are just a few examples of these capabilities.

Basic SELECT query returns a resultset based on the selection criteria you've specified. What if one would like to see, for instance, net sales figures, with state and federal taxes subtracted? You could perform fairly complex calculations within the query itself. This example is based on the view V_CUSTOMER_TOTALS, which contains columns CUSTOMER_NAME, ORDER_NUMBER, and TOTAL_PRICE.

Assuming tax at 8.5%, the query might look like follows:

```
SELECT customer_name,
       order_number,
       (total_price-(total_price * 0.085)) net_sale
FROM   v_customer_totals

customer_name             order_number        net_sale
------------------------- ------------------- --------
WILE BESS COMPANY         523720               6872.56
WILE BESS COMPANY         523721               7676.85
WILE BESS COMPANY         523722               6046.32
WILE BESS COMPANY         523723              10196.76
WILE ELECTROMUSICAL INC.  523726               6046.32
WILE ELECTROMUSICAL INC.  523727               6046.32
WILE ELECTROMUSICAL INC.  523728               6046.32
```

By default, every column in the returned results has it is own name, in cases of calculated columns like the one in the example above, RDBMS will use the whole string (SALE_AMOUNT-(SALE_AMOUNT * 0.085) as the name. For readability, you may substitute this unwieldy string for something more descriptive using alias—in our case NET_SALE.

The results returned by the query include calculated values; in other words, the original data from the table has been transformed. SQL also provides several useful functions that could be used in the query to manipulate data as it is being extracted.

Chapter 10 gives an in-depth description of all popular functions and their uses across three RDBMS vendors (IBM, Microsoft, and Oracle); Appendix G lists virtually all SQL functions.

With SQL, you have full control over how data is displayed: you could order it by any column — alphabetically or numerically. Let's say that you want the list of your companies and sales arranged according to the amount of sales for each customer's order.

```
SELECT    customer_name,
          order_number,
          (total_price-(total_price * 0.085)) net_sale
FROM      v_customer_totals
ORDER BY  net_sale

customer_name              order_number     net_sale
------------------------   --------------   --------
WILE ELECTROMUSICAL INC.   523726            6046.32
WILE ELECTROMUSICAL INC.   523727            6046.32
WILE ELECTROMUSICAL INC.   523728            6046.32
WILE BESS COMPANY          523722            6046.32
WILE BESS COMPANY          523720            6872.56
WILE BESS COMPANY          523721            7676.85
WILE BESS COMPANY          523723           10196.76
```

Now you want to see the customers with the most sales at the top of the list; use DESC modifier (stands for *descending*); default order is *ascending*.

```
SELECT    customer_name,
          order_number,
          (total_price-(total_price * 0.085)) net_sale
FROM      v_customer_totals
ORDER BY  net_sale DESC

customer_name              order_number     net_sale
------------------------   --------------   --------
WILE BESS COMPANY          523723           10196.76
WILE BESS COMPANY          523721            7676.85
WILE BESS COMPANY          523720            6872.56
WILE BESS COMPANY          523722            6046.32
WILE ELECTROMUSICAL INC.   523726            6046.32
WILE ELECTROMUSICAL INC.   523727            6046.32
WILE ELECTROMUSICAL INC.   523728            6046.32
```

Aggregation

Using SQL, you could transform your data while retrieving it. For instance, you need to know the total sum of the sales. Let's assume your database contains the V_CUSTOMER_TOTALS view with the information for all the sales you've had up to date; now you need to sum it up.

To find out your total for all orders across all products, you would use the SQL built-in SUM function; it will simply add up all the amounts it finds in the TOTAL_PRICE column of the view.

```
SELECT SUM(total_price) net_sale_total
FROM   v_custome_totals

net_sale_total
--------------
     457000.40
```

To find out the average size of the orders, you would run this query, using AVG aggregate function on the TOTAL_PRICE column:

```
SELECT AVG(total_price) net_sale_average
FROM   v_custome_totals

net_sale_average
----------------
     8960.792156
```

In the real life you would want even further limit the query by requesting the average sales for a particular customer or date range.

Using other predicates like GROUP_BY and HAVING, one could sum NET_SALE by customer, or date, or product, and so on; grouping allows for aggregating within a group.

We used these samples just to give you a sense of what could be accomplished using SQL and RDBMS.

See Chapter 10 for more on SQL functions, including aggregate functions.

Data security

SQL provides a number of built-in mechanisms for data security. It is fine-grained, though granularity greatly depends on the particular implementation. Essentially, it comes down to granting access on the object level: ability to connect and view a particular table or set of tables, execute particular command (e.g., ability to view data—execute SELECT statement, while lacking privileges to INSERT new data).

Privileges

Assuming that there is a user JOHN_DOE defined in the database, to grant a permission to this user, the following SQL statement could be used:

```
GRANT  SELECT
ON     v_custome_totals
TO     john_doe
```

To grant SELECT and UPDATE simultaneously one could use this syntax:

```
GRANT  SELECT, UPDATE
ON     v_custome_totals
TO     john_doe
```

To revoke this privilege:

```
REVOKE  SELECT
ON      v_custome_totals
FROM    john_doe
```

Here is the syntax to quickly revoke all privilege from JOHN_DOE:

```
REVOKE  ALL
ON      v_custome_totals
FROM    john_doe
```

Views

One of the common mechanisms for implementing security is using views. A view is a way to limit the data accessible to a user. You may think of a view as a virtual table: It could join columns from several tables in the database, limit the number of columns available for viewing, and so on. It does not contain any data but fetches it on demand whenever a SELECT statement is executed against it. For most practical purposes, selecting from a view is identical to selecting from a table.

For example, the view V_CUSTOMER_TOTALS collects information from the CUSTOMER, ORDER_HEADER, ORDER_LINE, and PRODUCT tables, while summing and grouping some data along the way.

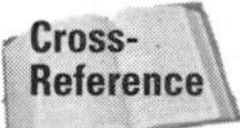

To see the full SQL syntax for creating view V_CUSTOMER_TOTALS, please refer to Appendix B.

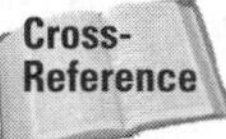

Some views limit access to underlying data (e.g., no UPDATE or INSERT statements could be executed). Views are discussed in Chapter 4.

There is much more to the security than discussed here; for example, all three RDBMS discussed in this book implement role-based security, where individual users are assigned to a particular role (e.g., accountants) and all the privileges are granted to the role.

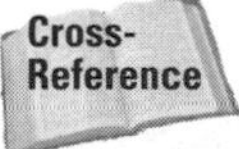

For a comprehensive discussion of the SQL security features, see Chapter 12.

Accessing data from a client application

A wide range of client applications is being used to access RDBMS data. They all use SQL to do that in two radically different ways.

Embedded SQL allows users to create programs that can access RDBMS through SQL statements *embedded* in an ANSI/ISO standard host programming language such as C or COBOL. That means that you program an application in the standard programming language and switch to SQL only where there is a need to use a database. Usually vendors provide special development tools to create such applications.

Dynamic SQL is all the embedded SQL is and then some more. The major difference is that dynamic SQL is not blended into some programming language, but is rather built on the fly *dynamically* and passed to RDBMS as a simple text. This allows for flexibility that embedded SQL cannot possibly have: there is no need in hard-coded tables names or column names, or even database name—it all could be changed.

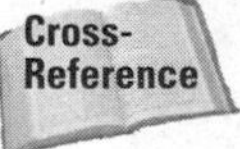

Embedded and dynamic SQL are discussed in Chapter 15.

New developments

The SQL99 standard also reflected a concept that had been evolving for quite some time—*online analytical processing* (OLAP). It was neither a new nor an obscure concept. The OLAP council was established in 1995, and most of the analysis was done manually since then. It soared in popularity with the advent of data warehousing — another database-related concept.

OLAP is about making sense out of data: analyzing complex trends, viewing the data under a variety of different angles; it transforms raw data into a multidimensional view, crafted to the user's perspective. OLAP queries could answer more intelligent questions than plain SQL, asking, for example, "what would be the effects of burger sales if prices of beef rise by 10 cents a pound?" These kinds of problems were usually solved with custom-made proprietary applications; SQL99 introduced built-in support for it. OLAP products complement the RDBMS, and all three major vendors (IBM, Oracle, and Microsoft) support it with some proprietary extensions. There are over 30 vendors on the market supplying RDBMS-based OLAP solutions.

Another relatively new feature supported by SQL is eXtensible Markup Language (XML). XML is all about data exchange. It is often called a *self-describing format* as it represents data in hierarchical structure, which, coupled with eXtensible Stylesheet Language (XSL), provides for visual representation via a browser or serves as a data format exchange between several parties.

Because it is an open standard that is not locked in by one particular vendor, it will be eventually supported by all vendors, enabling truly universal data interoperability. One of the major strengths of XML is that it could be transferred using HTTP protocol — the very protocol of the Internet — thus making any proprietary networks obsolete; it could be encrypted for better security or sent over the Secure Socket Layer (SSL). This versatility comes at a price — XML is inherently slower than compiled code, being a text that needs to be parsed and interpreted each time.

Any Platform, Any Time

SQL is different from standard programming languages such as C, Visual Basic, Java because it cannot be used to create stand-alone applications. It does not exist outside some database engine that is capable of translating its statements into machine language and execute. SQL does not have all the programming constructs that are the staples of other languages: for example, conditional logic, loops, and use of variables.

While these deficiencies are being alleviated, first with the introduction of procedural extensions, and then adding object-oriented features to SQL, it was never meant to be just another multipurpose programming language. This "weakness" is the key to SQL ubiquity — since it is dependent on RDBMS to execute, it is the first truly platform-independent language.

Every program is created by typing in some commands in plain ASCII. These commands are then compiled into binary machine code executable files for most of the programming languages. The problem with this approach is that for each and every platform the program has to be recompiled using the platform-specific compiler, e.g., a program compiled for Microsoft Windows would not work on UNIX, and vice versa. The solution proposed by Java still requires its platform-agnostic byte-code to be executed on platform-specific Java Virtual Machine (JVM).

An SQL query is created in very much the same way as the rest of the programs—by typing in SQL keywords; but here the similarity ends. The SQL program could be stored as a simple ASCII file that could be copied on UNIX, Windows, Mac OS, Linux, and so on—without any changes. Moreover, it could be opened, modified, and saved in any of these operating systems with some standard editing tools; there is no need to take into consideration any platform-specific features. As long as SQL remains a script, it is easily transferable between different platforms (but not between different RDBMS!); in a sense, the RDBMS works like a JVM. Even when SQL becomes part of a host language (e.g., embedded in a C program), it is still only text. It behaves in exactly the same way as HTML, which is just a collection of ASCII characters until it is fed into some Web browser to be executed. In case of SQL, its statements need to be sent to an RDBMS to be translated into executable machine codes; all it needs is a platform-specific database engine implementation.

One of the truly platform-independent features of SQL are basic data types: no matter whether you execute your SQL on UNIX or Windows (32-bit or 64-bit OS), the size and the structure of the reserved storage blocks will be exactly the same. `INTEGER` data type will always be 4 bytes and `DOUBLE` data type will occupy 8 bytes no matter what (proprietary data types might behave differently, depending on implementation). It may sound like an obvious thing, but this is not the case with all other programming languages. For C programming language `INTEGER` is 4 bytes on a 32-bit OS and 8 bytes on a 64-bit OS. (Of course, this also might depend on particular C compiler.) More about data types in Chapter 3.

In a sense, SQL shares the idea of platform independence with the Java programming language: just as Java Virtual Machine translates Java byte-code into platform-specific machine code, RDBMS executes platform-independent SQL code, translating it into OS machine-specific code. Because of this, an SQL program written using Notepad on Windows could be run by an Oracle RDBMS installed on UNIX or Linux.

Note

Oracle 9*i* database (different editions) is available for Sun SPARC Solaris, HP-UX, Compaq TRU64 UNIX, IBM OS/390 (MVS), Compaq Alpha Open VMS, Microsoft Windows (NT4.0/2000/XP and 95/98/Me), Linux(Intel), and IBM AIX.

IBM DB2 UDB 8.1 software (different editions) could be installed on IBM OS/2, Microsoft Windows (NT4.0/2000/XP and 95/98), Linux, IBM AIX, HP-UX, Sun Solaris, NUMA-Q, and SGI IRIX.

Microsoft SQL Server 2000 (different editions) is available for Microsoft Windows 2000 Server, Windows 2000 Advanced Server, Windows 2000 Datacenter Server, Windows XP (both Professional and Home Edition), Windows 2000 Professional, Windows NT (SP5 or later), Windows Millennium (Me), and Windows 98; Microsoft SQL Server CE also is available for Windows CE.

It was noted before, that there are numerous differences between dialects of SQL: a query written for SQL Server 2000, for example, might not execute on IBM DB2 UDB, and vise versa. But a query that runs on Oracle installed on Windows would require no changes to be executed on Oracle installed on Linux or UNIX. That, in turn, means that as long as one uses SQL features and keywords that are common across all three databases, exactly the same query could run — unchanged! — by any of these RDBMS.

There are virtually dozens of RDBMS products out there running on every imaginable platform (OS): Sybase, Ingres, Informix, Empress, MySQL, mSQL, PostgreSQL, LEAP RDBMS, FirstBase, Ocelot, Progress, Typhoon, SQL/DS, Daffodil DB, Compaq Non-Stop SQL/MX & SQL/MP, Linter RDBMS SQL, Interbase, UniVerse, GNU SQL Server — to name just a few, and new developments continue to sprout.

Note It is worth noticing that, although the overwhelming majority of RDBMS vendors choose to have their product ANSI-compliant, there are small segments of the market that run proprietary databases that use sometimes proprietary, non-SQL, language.

Of course, each of these RDBMS sports its own SQL dialect, but the good news is that majority of these are SQL standard-compliant. Basic SQL statements in every implementation require either no changes or very few changes to be executed on any of them; you could easily adapt your knowledge of SQL to any of these systems.

Summary

SQL is not just another programming language, it is a database language designed specifically to retrieve and manipulate data.

There is an SQL standard that is generally supported by all the major RDBMS vendors; though one must pay close attention to the dialect used by any particular RDBMS, SQL is nevertheless lingua franca of the database world.

Using SQL, you can create (and destroy) a number of database objects, insert, select, update or delete data.

There are two different types of SQL used in the client applications — embedded SQL and dynamic SQL — and each has its own use.

OLAP is relatively new to SQL. Part of the rapidly evolving field of business intelligence, OLAP facilitates analyzing data for business support information.

XML has emerged as a standard data exchange format, with pledged support by virtually every vendor in the field. Some of the RDBMS products (and all three major RDBMS vendors chosen for this book) are coming up with a native support for XML — an open standard for structuring and describing data. It is becoming the de-facto data exchange standard for the industry, especially over the Internet.

✦ ✦ ✦

SQL Data Types

Previously we defined database as an organized collection of information. Not only does that mean that data have to be organized according to a company's business rules, but also the database organization should reflect the nature of the information. Databases can store dollar amounts, quantities, names, date and time values, binary files, and more. These can be further classified by type, which reflects the "nature" of the data: numbers, characters, dates, etc.

Data type is a characteristic of a database table column that determines what kind of data it can hold.

One can ask: why do we need data types at all? Wouldn't it be easier simply have one uniform data type and store everything, let's say, in the form of character strings?

There are many reasons why we don't do that. Some of them are historical. For example, when relational databases were born in the late twentieth century, hard disk space and memory storage were at premium, so the idea was to store everything as efficiently as possible. Already existing programming languages had some built-in rules for how to store different types of data. For example, any English character (plus special characters and digits) could be represented using its ASCII equivalent and the necessary storage for it was one byte (more about ASCII later in this chapter). Numbers are traditionally stored in the form of binary strings (native to computer architecture). To represent a number from negative 32,768 to positive 32,767, two bytes (or sixteen bits) of storage are sufficient (2^{16}). But if we used ASCII characters to represent numbers, we would need six bytes to store any integer greater than 9,999 (five bytes for digits, and one for the plus or minus sign), five bytes for whole numbers greater than 999 (four bytes for digits, one byte for the sign), and so on. Now imagine — if we have a million of records, we could save four million bytes (about 4M). Sounds like almost nothing today, but back in the 1970s that was incredibly large storage space. The principle of effectiveness is still in place, of course, but now we are talking different scales.

✦ ✦ ✦ ✦

In This Chapter

Implementation differences

Character strings

Binary strings

Precise numbers

Approximate numbers

Dates and time

User-defined data types

Object data types

Literals (constants)

Null — substitute for any data type

✦ ✦ ✦ ✦

One byte consists of eight bits. Each bit is a binary number that can either be 0 or 1. All information is stored in memory or on the hard disk in form of ones and zeroes, representing the only two states computers understand: zero means no signal, and one indicates the presence of the signal.

Another reason is logical consistency. Every data type has its own rules, sort order, relations with other data types, implicit conversion rules, and so on. It is definitely easier to work with sets of like values, say dates, rather than with a mixture of dates, numbers, and character strings. Try comparing library shelves where all materials are sorted and classified (fiction is in one room, kids' literature in another, audio books in their special area, videotapes somewhere else) with a pile of chaotically mixed books, tapes, white papers, and CDs and think what would you prefer for finding information.

And the last thing to mention — some modern data types (particularly movie files) are too large and too complicated to store them in a traditional way. Now we are going to discuss existing SQL data types in more details.

No Strings Attached

Generally all strings could be divided into character strings (to store plain text) and binary strings which contain either machine code (computer programs) or special binary instructions for other programs.

Character strings

A character string can be defined simply as a sequence of bytes. The length of the string is the number of bytes in the sequence. A string of zero length is called an *empty string.* It can be an equivalent to `NULL` (special concept introduced at the end of this chapter) or not, depending on implementation. SQL99 specifically differentiates between empty strings and nulls.

All strings in SQL can be of fixed length or varying length. The difference is quite simple, but sometimes not very easy to understand for people with no technical background, so let us explain it in some greater detail.

Fixed-length character strings

If you define string to be of a fixed length, the system preallocates the desired number of bytes in memory and/or computer hard disk. It does not matter if the actual value to be stored in that string is exactly that many bytes, twice smaller, or just one character long — it is still going to occupy the whole allocated space (unused bytes will be padded with blank characters), so all strings will have exactly the same length. For example, imagine you defined a column `DATABASE` as having a character field of length 13, and now we want to store three strings in that column: ORACLE, UDB2, and MS SQL SERVER. Figure 3-1 illustrates the results of that operation. Note that all strings are exactly 13 bytes long.

O	R	A	C	L	E	blank	blank	blank	blank	blank	blank	blank
U	D	B	2	blank	blank	blank	blank	blank	blank	blank	blank	blank
M	S	blank	S	Q	L	blank	S	E	R	V	E	R

Figure 3-1: Fixed-length character string storage

Character strings of varying length

If you define DATABASE column as a varying-length string with maximum 13 characters to store, the picture will be different. The actual memory or disk space required to hold our values is allocated dynamically. As a result, all three strings will be of different length and will require different numbers of bytes to hold them. String ORACLE occupies 6 bytes, DB2 UDB—4 bytes and MS SQL SERVER takes maximum allowed 13 bytes. (See Figure 3-2.)

O	R	A	C	L	E							
U	D	B	2									
M	S	blank	S	Q	L	blank	S	E	R	V	E	R

Figure 3-2: Varying-length character string storage

Here is the general platform-independent recommendation: use a fixed-length data type when your values are expected to be of the same size, and a varying-length one for values when size is expected to vary considerably. In the example above it rather looks logical to use the varying-length strings, but if we need a column to store, say, gender in form M or F, a fixed-length string is more appropriate.

National character strings

Even though English is a very popular language, it is not the only language on Earth. And in spite of the fact that practically all major software companies reside in the United States, the market dictates its own rules. For example, Oracle is a very popular database vendor around the world with customers in China, India, Korea, Germany, France, Israel, Russia, Saudi Arabia, and many other countries.

Note

Oracle has customers in 145 countries. But would that be the case if the English language was the only option customers were able to use? Most likely, the answer is "no." Customers have to be able to store and use information in their native language—otherwise they would rather use some less-efficient and/or more expensive DBMS vendor who provides that option.

Now we have a little bit of a problem. So far we've used terms "character" and "byte" as synonyms. Byte is a computer term for a unit of information storage that consists of 8 bits. Each bit can either be 1 or 0 and the combination of 8 bits allows us to store 256 (2^8) distinct values (or 256 different characters represented by numbers from 0 to 255). That looks like a lot, but ... not actually. We need separate holders for uppercase and lowercase letters, punctuation marks, digits, math symbols, and so on. That barely leaves space for distinct characters used in other languages that employ the Latin alphabet. And what about the ones which don't? There are about 3,000 different languages in the world, dead and living, in addition to constructed languages like J.R.R. Tolkien's Quenya, Sindanin, or Entish, and most of them have their own distinct alphabets!

ASCII (American Standard Code for Information Interchange) was published in 1968 as a standard of ANSI. It uses the aforementioned 256 holders to store different characters, and it remains a useful standard to this day.

The solution seems to be rather intuitive — use two bytes per character instead of one. That allows 65,535 (2^{16}) distinct combinations, which is enough to store all existing characters from every major language on Earth.

SQL has two data types to store strings in national characters — national character string and national character string of varying length — that behave in exactly same way as previously described character string and character string of varying length correspondingly, but use the two-byte Unicode standard. So, if you declared your DATABASE column as a national character field of size 13, it would still hold 13 characters, but would reserve 2 bytes for each letter, for a total of 26 bytes. The difference is, now it can hold the names from previous examples spelled in practically any language, for example, in Russian. Figure 3-3 illustrates that.

O	P	A	K	π								
y	Λ	ß	2									
M	C		S	Q	L		C	E	P	B	E	P

Figure 3-3: Fixed-length Unicode character storage

Figure 3-4 shows same concept for national characters of varying length.

O	P	A	K	π								
y	Λ	ß	2									
M	C		S	Q	L		C	E	P	B	E	P

Figure 3-4: Varying-length Unicode character storage

Introducing Unicode

The ultimate successor to ASCII is *Unicode*. It is a standard double-byte character set that assigns a unique number to every single character, so all of them can be represented in one character set. To speak in database terminology, the Unicode character number serves as a primary key to index virtually all the world's characters. (Another good example of database use!) The Unicode standard has been adopted by such industry leaders as Apple, HP, IBM, Microsoft, Oracle, SAP, Sun, Sybase, Unisys, and many others. Unicode is required by modern standards such as XML, Java, JavaScript, CORBA, WML, HTML, and is the official way to implement ISO standard 10646. It is supported in many operating systems, all modern browsers, major RDBMS vendors, and many other products. The emergence of the Unicode standard and the availability of tools supporting it are among the most significant recent global software technology trends.

In Russian Oracle is spelled with only five characters rather than six in English, so only five memory (or hard disk) holders are occupied, but now each holder is two bytes long.

Let's talk about SQL99 standards and implementation specifics for all types of character strings. These are summarized in Table 3-1.

SQL99

SQL99 has two major character sets: `CHARACTER` and `CHARACTER VARYING`. In addition, there are also `NATIONAL CHARACTER` and `NATIONAL CHARACTER VARYING`.

`CHARACTER` can also be abbreviated with `CHAR`. The size can optionally be specified in the form `CHARACTER(n)`. For example, `CHARACTER(15)` can hold character strings up to 15 characters long. If size is omitted, the default is 1. An error occurs if one tries to store a string that is bigger than the size declared.

`CHARACTER VARYING` can be abbreviated with `CHAR VARYING` or `VARCHAR`. You have to specify the maximum size for strings to be stored, for example, `CHARACTER VARYING(15)` holds 15-character strings, or smaller.

`NATIONAL CHARACTER` (`NATIONAL CHAR`, `NCHAR`, `CHARACTER CHARACTER SET <char_set_name>`) specifies the default data type for the country of implementation. This is a fixed-length character string data type.

`NATIONAL CHARACTER VARYING` (`NATIONAL CHAR VARYING`, `NCHAR VARYING`, `CHARACTER VARYING CHARACTER SET < char_set_name>`, `CHAR VARYING CHARACTER SET < char_set_name>`) is a varying-length country-specific character string data type.

`CLOB` is a new SQL99 data type to store large nondatabase-structured text objects of varying size and complexity, such as employees' resumes, collections of papers, books, and other similar data.

Oracle 9*i*

Oracle is fully compliant with SQL99 standards for character strings.

✦ `CHAR` is used for fixed-length strings. The default length for a `CHAR` column is 1 byte with a maximum of 2,000 bytes.

✦ `VARCHAR2` is an Oracle data type to store varying-length character strings. It does not have the default length, so you have to specify a value from 1 to 4,000 (maximum number of bytes for `VARCHAR2`).

✦ `NCHAR` and `NVARCHAR2` are used to store fixed-length and varying-length national character strings. Beginning with Oracle9*i*, they were redefined to be Unicode-only data types and can hold up to 2,000 and 4,000 *characters* (not bytes!) correspondingly. That means if you declare a column to be `CHAR(100)` it will allocate 100 bytes per column, but `NCHAR(100)` Unicode-based column requires 200 bytes.

Note

The `VARCHAR` data type in Oracle is currently a synonym to `VARCHAR2`. If you declare a column as `VARCHAR(30)`, it will be converted it to `VARCHAR2(30)` automatically. Oracle does not recommend the use of `VARCHAR` as a data type, but rather recommends `VARCHAR2` instead because keyword `VARCHAR` may be later used in some different way.

✦ `CLOB` and `NCLOB` can store up to four gigabytes of data in Oracle. Both fixed-length and variable-length character sets are supported. `CLOB` uses the `CHAR` database character set, and `NCLOB` stores Unicode data using the national character set.

✦ `LONG` is an old Oracle data type to store variable-length character strings containing up to two gigabytes. It is similar to `VARCHAR2`, but has many limitations. For example, you cannot use `LONG` in the `WHERE` clause of a `SELECT` statement (discussed in Chapter 8), a table can't have more than one `LONG` column, it can't be indexed, and so on. Oracle strongly recommends to discontinue the use of the `LONG` data type and use `CLOB` instead.

Note

Oracle has synonyms for SQL99 compatibility. For example, you can use `CHARACTER(100)` rather than `CHAR(100)` or `CHARACTER VARYING` rather than `VARCHAR2` to attain the same results. See Table 3-1 for more details.

Table 3-1
Major Vendor Implementations Character String Data Types

SQL99	*Oracle 9i*	*DB2 UDB 8.1*	*MS SQL SERVER 2000*
CHAR[ACTER] [(n)]	CHAR[ACTER] [(n)]	CHAR[ACTER] [(n)]	CHAR[ACTER] [(n)]
CHAR[ACTER] VARYING**(n) OR** VARCHAR**(n)**	CHAR[ACTER] VARYING(n)	CHAR[ACTER] VARYING(n)	CHAR[ACTER] VARYING[(n)]
	VARCHAR(n)		
			VARCHAR[(n)]
	VARCHAR2(n)	VARCHAR(n)	
			TEXT
	LONG [VARCHAR]	LONG VARCHAR	
CLOB	CLOB		
NATIONAL CHAR[ACTER][(n)] **OR**	NATIONAL CHAR[ACTER] [(n)]	GRAPHIC[(n)]	NATIONAL CHAR[ACTER] [(n)]
NCHAR[(n)]			
	NCHAR[(n)]		NCHAR[(n)]
OR CHARACTER[(n)] CHARACTER SET <char_set_name>			
NATIONAL CHAR[ACTER] VARYING(n)	NATIONAL CHAR[ACTER] VARYING(n)	VARGRAPHIC(n)	NATIONAL CHAR[ACTER] VARYING[(n)]
OR		LONG VARGRAPHIC(n)	NCHAR VARYING[(n)]
NCHAR VARYING(n)	NCHAR VARYING(n)		
OR		DBCLOB(n)	NVARCHAR[(n)]
CHARACTER VARYING(n) CHARACTER SET <char_set_name>	NVARCHAR2(n)		
	NCLOB		

DB2 UDB 8.1

DB2 has following character string data types:

✦ CHARACTER is compliant with SQL99 standards. The maximum length is 254 characters. The default length is 1.

✦ VARCHAR is used for varying-length strings and has a maximum of 32,672 characters.

✦ LONG VARCHAR is virtually same as VARCHAR, but can hold larger values (up to 32,700) and can't be limited to a certain number of characters.

✦ CLOB types are SQL99 compliant varying-length strings of up to two gigabytes. An optional maximum length can be supplied in kilobytes (K|k), megabytes (M|m), or gigabytes (G|g). For example, CLOB (10M) would allow maximum of 10,048,576 characters.

✦ GRAPHIC is a rough DB2 equivalent to NATIONAL CHARACTER. It is a double-byte data type, which may range from 1 to 127 characters. If the length specification is omitted, a length of 1 is assumed.

✦ VARGRAPHIC is a varying-length double-byte character string data type, comparable to SQL99 NATIONAL CHARACTER VARYING. The range is from 1 to 16,336.

✦ LONG VARGRAPHIC is similar to VARGRAPHIC with a maximum length of 16,350. It does not have an optional length limit to be supplied by user.

✦ DBCLOB is a double-byte equivalent to CLOB. Maximum storage is one gigabyte of character data. DBCLOB accepts a maximum length in the same way as CLOB.

GRAPHIC, VARGRAPHIC, and DBCLOB data types are not supported in the Personal Edition of DB2 supplied with your book.

See Table 3-1 for more information.

MS SQL Server 2000

The following character string data types are supported by MS SQL Server:

✦ CHAR and VARCHAR are used for fixed-length and variable-length character data correspondingly. The maximum length is 8,000 characters. Unlike Oracle, you don't have to specify length for VARCHAR—it defaults to 1 like CHAR.

✦ TEXT is similar to VARCHAR, but can hold much larger values. Its maximum length is two gigabytes or $2^{31} - 1$ (2,147,483,647) characters.

✦ NCHAR and NVARCHAR, and NTEXT are Unicode equivalents to CHAR, VARCHAR, and TEXT. NCHAR and NVARCHAR can hold up to 4,000 characters; NTEXT is much larger—one gigabyte or $2^{30} - 1$ (1,073,741,823) characters.

For SQL99 compatibility synonyms see Table 3-1. If one data type has more than one name (or synonym) the most widely used name is given in italics.

Character string literals

The terms *literal* and *constant* refer to a fixed data value, for instance

```
'Frozen Margarita'
'ALEX'
'2003/08/07'
'10101101'
```

---

are all character literals. Character literals are enclosed in single quotes. To represent one single quotation mark within a literal, you can enter two single quotation marks:

```
'O''Neil'
```

Character literals are surprisingly consistent between all our three major vendors, with only slight variations. For example, MS SQL Server allows double quotes for character literals instead of single ones if the option QUOTED_IDENTIFIER is set off for a connection. To represent a national character set literal, it has to be preceded by capital letter N (DB2 understands G in addition to N):

```
N'Jack Smith'
N'Boris M. Trukhnov'
N'123 OAK ST.'
```

Text entered using this notation is translated into the national character set.

Binary strings

A binary string is a sequence of bytes in the same way that a character string is, but unlike character strings that usually contain information in the form of text, a binary string is used to hold nontraditional data such as images, audio and video files, program executables, and so on. Binary strings may be used for purposes similar to those of character strings (e.g., to store documents in MS Word format), but the two data types are not compatible; the difference being like text and a photo of the same text. Binary string data types are summarized in Table 3-2.

Character vs. Special Files

It might sound a little bit confusing—why plain text documents can be stored as character strings, and a Word document has to be treated as a binary string. The thing is, a Word file is a text document from user's point of view, but from computer storage perspective it is not. In addition to plain text characters it contains many special signs and instructions that only MS Word software can interpret. The same is true for any other special files—bitmaps, spreadsheets, audio and video files, and so forth. You can think of it in this way: a special file (e.g., of the DOC, XLS, BMP, or AVI type) is like a tape for VCR, whereas a program (MS Word, Excel, Paint, QuickTime Player) is like a VCR. You have to have a VCR to play a tape, and it has to be the right VCR—if you try to play a standard US VHS tape in NTSC format on a European video recorder (PAL format), it's not going to work. You might see some blinking on your screen, you will hear some noise, but you will definitely not be able to watch the movie. Just try to open a Word file with, say, Notepad and you will see what we are talking about.

SQL99

SQL99 has following data types to store binary strings: `BIT`, `BIT VARYING`, and `BLOB`.

- `BIT` is a fixed-length binary string somewhat similar to `CHAR`. If you declare a column to be `BIT(100)`, 100 bytes will be allocated in memory/disk, and if the object you store is just 60 bytes, it's still going to occupy all 100 bytes.
- `BIT VARYING` is similar to `VARCHAR`—even if you specify `BIT VARYING(100)` to be the data type lasting the previous example, it will only take 60 bytes to store the object.
- `BLOB` is a binary equivalent to CLOB.

Oracle 9*i*

Oracle doesn't have an equivalent to SQL99 BIT, but has two data types that correspond to `BIT VARYING`—`RAW` and `LONG RAW`. `BLOB` data type is also supported.

- `RAW` can hold a maximum of 2,000 bytes. The size has to be specified.
- `LONG RAW` can accumulate up to two gigabytes of data. This data type is obsolete, and Oracle strongly recommends converting it to `BLOB`.
- `BLOB` can store up to four gigabytes of binary data in Oracle.

DB2 UDB 8.1

The only data type for binary strings in DB2 is `BLOB`, which can be up to 2 gigabytes long.

MS SQL Server 2000

MS SQL Server has three different data types for binary strings: `BINARY`, `VARBINARY`, and `IMAGE`.

✦ BINARY is a fixed-length data type to store binary data. The size can be specified from 1 to 8,000; the actual storage volume is size + 4 bytes.

✦ VARBINARY can hold variable-length binary data. The size is from 1 through 8,000. Storage size is the actual length of the data entered + 4 bytes. The data entered can be 0 bytes in length.

✦ IMAGE is a variable-length binary data type that can hold from 0 through 2,147,483,647 bytes (two gigabytes) of data.

Table 3-2
Binary String Data Types

SQL99	*Oracle 9i*	*DB2 UDB 8.1*	*MS SQL SERVER 2000*
BIT			BINARY[(n)]
BIT VARYING	RAW(n)		VARBINARY[(n)]
	LONG RAW		
BLOB	BLOB	BLOB(n)	IMAGE

Binary string literals

MS SQL Server allows literals for binary string fields (BINARY, VARBINARY, IMAGE) either in the form of hexadecimal numbers prefixed with 0x or as binary strings. The value has to be unquoted:

```
0xAE
0101010010100110
```

MS SQL Server implicitly converts these literals into appropriate binary format. Oracle and DB2 don't have binary string literals; the values have to be converted into proper format using special functions (see Chapter 10).

Literals are barely needed for large objects that can store gigabytes of data. In most cases LOBs are not manipulated by traditional SQL statements, but rather accessed by special programs and interfaces that know how to handle such objects without reading them directly into memory.

In Numbers Strength

All numeric data could generally be divided into two categories: *exact numbers* and *approximate numbers.*

Exact numbers

Exact numbers can either be whole integers (numeric primary keys, quantities, such as number of items ordered, age) or have decimal points (prices, weights, percentages). Numbers can be positive and negative and have precision and scale. *Precision* determines the maximum total number of decimal digits that can be stored (both to the left and to the right of the decimal point). *Scale* specifies the maximum number of decimals allowed. Exact numeric data types are summarized in Table 3-3.

SQL99

SQL99 specifies the following data types for exact numbers: `INTEGER`, `SMALLINT`, `NUMERIC`, `DECIMAL` (as well as some synonyms found in Table 3-3).

- `INTEGER` represents countable numbers; its precision is implementation-specific.
- `SMALLINT` is virtually same as INTEGER, but maximum precision can be smaller than that for INTEGER.
- `NUMERIC` data type supports storage of numbers with specific decimal component as well as whole numbers. Optional scale specifies the number of decimal locations supported.
- `DECIMAL` is very similar to `NUMERIC`. The only difference is the precision (but not the scale) used by a vendor-specific implementation can be greater than that used in declaration.

Oracle 9*i*

Oracle has one data type, `NUMBER`, to represent all numeric data and numerous synonyms for it to comply with SQL99 (see Table 3-3). `INTEGER` and `SMALLINT` will translate into `NUMBER(38)`; `NUMERIC` and `DECIMAL` will be substituted with `NUMBER`. The `NUMBER` data type stores zero, positive, and negative fixed and floating-point numbers with magnitudes between $1.0 * 10^{-130}$ and $9.9...9 * 10^{125}$ with 38 digits of precision. The space is allocated dynamically, so Oracle claims having one numeric data type for all numeric data won't hurt performance.

DB2 UDB 8.1

DB2 has four data types for exact numbers: `INTEGER`, `SMALLINT`, `BIGINT`, and `DOUBLE`.

- `INTEGER` is a four-byte integer with a precision of 10 digits. It can store values from negative 2^{31} (2,147,483,648) to positive $2^{31} - 1$ (2,147,483,647).

Precision and Scale for NUMERIC and DECIMAL Datatypes

NUMERIC and DECIMAL values' scale and precision often cause confusion. Please remember, precision specifies the maximum number of ALL digits allowed for a value. For example, if a hypothetic table has these columns

```
column1  NUMERIC(10, 4)
column2  NUMERIC(10,2)
column3  NUMERIC(10,0)
```

then the maximum number you can store in column1 is 999,999.9999; column2 can hold values up to 99,999,999.99 inclusive; and column3 is good enough for 9,999,999,999. To determine the maximum number of figures before the decimal point, subtract scale from precision. If you try to insert a value with more figures before the decimal point than column allows, you will get an error, but values with more decimal points than specified will simply be rounded. For example, 999,999.9999 inserted into column2 (or column3) will be rounded to 1,000,000, but an attempt to set column1 to 99,999,999.99 would fail.

- SMALLINT is reserved for smaller size integers. The storage size is two bytes, and the range is from negative 2^{15} (32,768) to positive $2^{15} - 1$ (32,767).
- BIGINT is an eight-byte integer with precision of 19 digits. It ranges from negative $2^{63} - 1$ (9,223,372,036,854,775,808) to positive 2^{63} (9,223,372,036,854,775,807).
- DECIMAL data type (corresponds to NUMERIC) is designated for decimal numbers with an implicit decimal point. The maximum precision is 31 digits, and the range is from negative $2^{31} + 1$ to positive $2^{31} - 1$.

MS SQL Server 2000

MS SQL Server has more numeric data types for exact numeric data than Oracle and DB2. In addition to INT, BIGINT, SMALLINT, and TINYINT it also offers MONEY and SMALLMONEY.

- INT (or INTEGER) is to store whole numbers from negative 2^{31} to positive $2^{31} - 1$. It occupies four bytes.
- BIGINT is to store large integers from negative 2^{63} through positive $2^{63} - 1$. The storage size is eight bytes. BIGINT is intended for special cases where INTEGER range is not sufficient.
- SMALLINT is for smaller integers ranging from negative 2^{15} to positive $2^{15} - 1$
- TINYINT is convenient for small nonnegative integers from 0 through 255. It only takes one byte to store such number.

✦ DECIMAL is compliant with SQL99 standards. NUMERIC is a synonym to DECIMAL. (See Table 3.3 for other synonyms.) Valid values are in the range from negative 10^{38} +1 through positive 10^{38} – 1.

✦ MONEY is a special eight-byte MS SQL Server data type to represent monetary and currency values. The range is from negative 922,337,203,685,477.5808 to positive 922,337,203,685,477.5807 with accuracy to a ten-thousandth.

✦ SMALLMONEY is another monetary data type designated for smaller amounts. It is four bytes long and can store values from negative 214,748.3648 to positive 214,748.3647 with the same accuracy as MONEY.

Why have special data types for monetary values? One good reason is consistency. Probably all accountants know how much trouble so-called rounding errors can cause. For example, one column for dollar amounts is declared as NUMERIC(12,2) and another is NUMERIC(14,4). If we operate large sums, discrepancies can easily reach hundreds and even thousands of dollars. From another point of view, many different data types for virtually the same entities can cause confusion, so Oracle has its reasons for allowing only one data type for all numeric data. We'll let you decide which approach has more validity.

Table 3-3
Exact Numeric Data Types

SQL99	*Oracle 9i*	*DB2 UDB 8.1*	*MS SQLSERVER 2000*
INT[EGER]	NUMBER(38)	INT[EGER]	INT[EGER]
		BIGINT	BIGINT
SMALLINT	SMALLINT	SMALLINT	SMALLINT
	NUMBER(38)		TINYINT
NUMERIC[(p[,s])] **OR** DEC[IMAL] [(p[,s])]	NUMERIC[(p[,s])]	NUMERIC[(p[,s])]	NUMERIC[(p[,s])]
	DEC[IMAL] [(p[,s])]	DEC[IMAL] [(p[,s])]	DEC[IMAL] [(p[,s])]
	NUMBER[(p[,s])		MONEY
			SMALLMONEY

Literals for exact numbers

Literals for exact numbers are represented by string of numbers optionally preceded by plus or minus signs with an optional decimal part for NUMERIC and DECIMAL data types separated by a dot (.):

```
123
-33.45
+334.488
```

Oracle optionally allows enclosing literals in single quotes:

```
'123'
'-677.34'
```

MS SQL Server has literal formats for MONEY and SMALLMONEY data types represented as strings of numbers with an optional decimal point optionally prefixed with a currency symbol:

```
$12
$542023.14
```

Selecting Correct Data Types

The incorrect use of data types is quite typical for inexperienced database developers and can result in serious problems.

For example, defining a money-related field as a FLOAT or NUMERIC(12,1) causes rounding errors. (Accountants are just going to hate you!) Insufficient precision for a primary key column (say, ORDHDR_ID_N NUMBER(5) in an ORDER_HEADER table) will work for a while, but after inserting a certain number of records (99,999 in our case), you will not be able to insert new rows anymore—the next value for the primary key (100,000) won't fit NUMBER(5) precision.

The last example is easily fixable—the precision of a numeric column can easily be adjusted (more details in the next chapter). That is one of the benefits of a relational database over the old legacy systems. But still, it might take some time to figure out what causes the problem and fix it, and if your database is, for example, a large 24/7 order management system, your users are not going to be happy with the delay.

Approximate numbers

Approximate numbers are numbers that cannot be represented with absolute precision (or don't have a precise value). Approximate numeric data types are summarized in Table 3-4.

A classic example is number π, which is usually approximated to 3.14. The number was known in ancient Babylon and Egypt some 4,500 years ago and has been a matter of interest for mathematicians from Archimedes to modern scientists. As of today, 206,158,430,208 ($3 * 2^{36}$) decimal digits of π have been calculated. It would take approximately forty million pages, or fifty thousand volumes to store it in written form!

SQL99

SQL99 specifies the following data types for approximate numbers: `FLOAT`, `REAL`, and `DOUBLE PRECISION`.

- ✦ `FLOAT` is to store floating-point numbers with precision optionally specified by user.
- ✦ `REAL` is similar to `FLOAT`, but its precision is fixed.
- ✦ `DOUBLE PRECISION` is virtually the same as `REAL`, but with a greater precision.

Oracle 9*i*

As we already know, Oracle has one numeric data type, `NUMBER`, for both exact and approximate numbers. Another supported data type is `FLOAT`, which is mostly used to represent binary precision. The maximum decimal precision for `FLOAT` is 38; maximum binary precision is 126.

In addition to positive precision, Oracle allows negative precision as well. For example, if you have a column specified as `NUMBER(10, –2)`, all inserted values will be implicitly rounded to the second significant digit. For example, 6,345,454,454.673 will be stored as 6,345,454,500

DB2 UDB 8.1

DB2 has `REAL` single-precision data type as well as `DOUBLE` double-precision data type for approximate numbers. `FLOAT` is a synonym to `DOUBLE`.

- ✦ `REAL` is a four-byte long approximation of a real number. The range is from negative 3.402E + 38 to negative 1.175E – 37 or from positive 1.175E – 37 to 3.402E + 38. It also includes 0.
- ✦ `DOUBLE` requires eight bytes of storage and is much more precise than `REAL`. The number can be zero or can range from –1.79769E + 308 to –2.225E – 307, or from 2.225E - 307 to 1.79769E + 308.

MS SQL Server 2000

MS SQL Server has one data type for floating-point numbers — `FLOAT`. It also has a number of synonyms for SQL99 compliance (Table 3-4).

`FLOAT` data type can hold the same range of real numbers as `DOUBLE` in DB2. The actual storage size can be either four or eight bytes.

Table 3-4
Approximate Numeric Data Types

SQL99	*Oracle 9i*	*DB2 UDB 8.1*	*MS SQL SERVER 2000*
FLOAT[(p)]	FLOAT[(p)] NUMBER	FLOAT[(p)]	FLOAT[(p)]
REAL	REAL NUMBER	REAL	REAL
DOUBLE PRECISION	DOUBLE PRECISION NUMBER	DOUBLE [PRECISION]	DOUBLE PRECISION

Literals for approximate numbers

In addition to literals for exact numbers you can specify a real number as two numbers separated by upper- or lowercase character `E` (scientific notation). Both numbers may include plus or minus; the first number may also include a decimal point:

```
+1.23E2
-3.345e1
-3.44488E+002
```

The value of the constant is the product of the first number and the power of 10 specified by the second number.

Once Upon a Time: Date and Time Data Types

Handling dates and times is probably one of the most complicated and inconsistent topics in SQL. According to our personal experiences, operations with dates often cause confusion and even frustration not only among database users, but in the developers' community, too.

Introduction to complex data types

One of the problems is dates are not actually what they look like. So far we were talking only about simple data types that store one value per row. Date and time data types hold a number of elements (year, day, month, hour, etc.). In programming, such data types are called *complex* and are often represented as structures. When returned as a database query result, date and time fields appear like strings, but in fact they rather are parts of structures, similar to ones in the example below. (We don't use any specific programming language in this example, but rather some kind of pseudocode.)

```
STRUCTURE DATE
{
  YEAR          DECIMAL(4,0),
  MONTH         DECIMAL(2,0),
  DAY           DECIMAL(2,0)
}
```

```
STRUCTURE TIME
{
  HOUR          DECIMAL(2,0),
  MINUTE        DECIMAL(2,0),
  SECOND        DECIMAL(5,2)
}
```

```
STRUCTURE DATETIME
{
  YEAR          DECIMAL(4,0),
  MONTH         DECIMAL(2,0),
  DAY           DECIMAL(2,0),
  HOUR          DECIMAL(2,0),
  MINUTE        DECIMAL(2,0),
  SECOND        DECIMAL(5,2)
}
```

The displayed value just formats and concatenates the fields of this structure. For example, for the YYYY/DD/MM format, the pseudocode may look like this:

```
CONCAT(CAST(DATETIME.YEAR, STRING), '/',
       CAST(DATETIME.DAY, STRING), '/',
       CAST(DATETIME.MONTH, STRING))
```

The Dot (.) notation used in the above example is explained in Chapter 1.

These structures should also have some methods to handle situations when users want to display dates and times in different formats, for example to display time on the 12- or 24-hour scale, show day of week for a certain date, display century, convert it into a different time zone, and so on.

We'll talk more about complex data types later in this chapter.

Date and time implementations

As we've mentioned before, date and time data types are mandated by SQL99 and handled by different RDBMS implementations quite in a different way. Date and time data types are summarized in Table 3-5.

SQL99

SQL99 supports `DATE`, `TIME`, `TIMESTAMP`, `TIME WITH TIME ZONE`, and `TIMESTAMP WITH TIME ZONE` data types.

✦ `DATE` data type is a structure that consists of three elements: year, month, and day. The year is a four-digit number that allows values from 0000 through 9999; the month is a two-digit element with values from 01 through 12; and the day is another two-digit figure with range from 01 through 31. SQL99 does not have any strict rules on how to implement `DATE` internally, so vendors can make their own decisions. One vendor could choose something similar to the structures above; others could implement characters, numbers with different scale, and so on.

✦ `TIME` consists of hour, minute, and second components. The hour is a number from 00 to 23, the minute is a two-digit number from 00 to 59, and the second is either another integer from 00 to 61 or a decimal number with scale of 5 and precision of 3 that can hold values from 00.000 to 61.999.

The range of values for seconds greater than 59 is to handle the representation of leap seconds, occasionally added to Earth's time. None of our three major vendors has that feature implemented.

✦ `TIMESTAMP` is a combination of `DATE` and `TIME` data types and includes year, month, day, hour, minute, and second.

✦ `TIME WITH TIME ZONE` is basically an improvement to the `TIME` data type. It stores time zone information in addition to standard `TIME` elements.

✦ `TIMESTAMP WITH TIME ZONE` is an extension to the `TIMESTAMP` with information on time zone.

Oracle 9*i*

Oracle has DATE, TIMESTAMP, TIMESTAMP WITH TIME ZONE, and TIMESTAMP WITH LOCAL TIME ZONE data types.

- DATE is a slightly confusing data type, because in spite of its name it stores both date and time information and rather corresponds to SQL99 TIMESTAMP. In addition to standard SQL99 TIMESTAMP fields (year, month, date, hour, minute, and second), it also includes century.
- TIMESTAMP data type is practically same as DATE, but you can specify an optional precision for the number of digits in the fractional part of seconds. The valid values are numbers from 0 to 9 with the default of 6.
- TIMESTAMP WITH TIME ZONE data type speaks for itself. The only difference from TIMESTAMP is a time zone displacement included in its value, which is the difference in hours and minutes between local time and Coordinated Universal Time (UTC), also known as Greenwich Mean Time (GMT).
- TIMESTAMP WITH LOCAL TIME ZONE data type is another variation of TIMESTAMP (or TIMESTAMP WITH TIME ZONE). The difference is that it is normalized to the database time zone and the displacement value is not stored with it, but when users query the column, the result is returned in user's local session time zone.

Understanding TIMESTAMP WITH LOCAL TIME ZONE Data Type

This example will help you to understand the difference between TIMESTAMP and TIMESTAMP WITH LOCAL TIME ZONE data types.

Imagine ACME expanded, and it now has its offices all around the world. John is a head of Sales department located in Seattle, WA, and needs to see all new invoices created yesterday at each location. (We assume each location has its own database, and the databases can communicate to each other.) The problem is, one of the offices is in New York, another one is in Amsterdam, yet another is located in Bangkok, and so on; of course, each location is in its own time zone. But as far as John is concerned, he wants to see all new orders created whatever is considered to be yesterday in Seattle, in other words, according to the Pacific Standard Time (PST). Each of the mentioned offices belongs to a different time zone, without even mentioning the Daylight Savings. So, 08/31/2003 6:00 PM in Seattle is equivalent to 08/31/2003 9:00 PM in New York, 09/01/2003 3:00 AM in Amsterdam, and 09/01/2003 8:00 AM in Bangkok. That means not only different days, but even different months!

If the data type of ORDER_HEADER.ORDHDR_INVOICEDATE_D column is TIMESTAMP, John would need a report that programmatically translates all the different locations' invoice dates into PST.

Life would definitely be easier if we declared ORDHDR_INVOICEDATE_D as a TIMESTAMP WITH LOCAL TIME ZONE—then each time John queries a remote database from Seattle the result is returned in his session's time, that is, invoices created in Bangkok at 8 AM on September 1 (Thailand local time) will appear as belonging to August 31 Pacific Standard Time.

✦ INTERVAL YEAR TO MONTH data type stores a period of time using year and month fields.

✦ INTERVAL DAY TO SECOND data type can store a period of time in days, hours, minutes, and seconds.

The Oracle format value for minutes is MI, not MM like most other databases. So, be aware that if you want specify a time format it should look like HH:MI:SS, not HH:MM:SS. MM in Oracle stands for months.

DB2 UDB 8.1

DB2 has three standard SQL99 date and time data types — DATE, TIME, and TIMESTAMP.

✦ DATE consists of year, month, and day. The range of the year part is 0001 to 9999; month can be from 1 to 12; and the day part ranges from 1 to 28, 29, 30, or 31, depending on the month. DATE in DB2 is stored internally as a string of four bytes. Each byte represents two decimal digits. The first two bytes are for the year, the third is reserved for the month, and the fourth one holds day value. The length of a DATE column is 10 bytes to fit character string representation in literals.

✦ TIME data type is represented internally as a string of three bytes — one byte for hours, one for minutes, and one for seconds. Hour ranges from 0 to 24 (if value is 24, minutes and seconds will be all zeroes). Minute and second components have to be from 0 through 59. The length of a TIME column in DB2 is 8 bytes to allow the appropriate length for a character string representation.

✦ TIMESTAMP data type is a combination of DATE and TIME elements plus a microsecond component. The internal representation is a string of ten bytes (four DATE bytes, three TIME bytes, and additional three bytes for microseconds). The length of a TIMESTAMP column is 26 bytes.

MS SQL Server 2000

MS SQL Server has two date and time data types, DATETIME and SMALLDATETIME that both represent the combination of date and time values, but have different ranges.

✦ DATETIME can store values from 01/01/1753 to 12/31/9999 with accuracy of 0.00333 seconds. It is stored internally as an eight-byte string. The first four bytes represent the number of days before (or after) 01/01/1900, which is the system reference date. The second four bytes store time in milliseconds passed since midnight.

✦ SMALLDATETIME can hold dates from January 1, 1900 to June 6, 2079, with accuracy to the minute. The internal storage for that data type is four bytes. Again, the first portion (two bytes) stores the number of days after the system reference date (01/01/1900), and the second portion stores time (in minutes after midnight).

Table 3-5
Date and Time Data Types

SQL99	*Oracle 9i*	*DB2 UDB 8.1*	*MS SQL SERVER 2000*
DATE	DATE	DATE	DATETIME SMALLDATETIME
TIME [WITH TIME ZONE]	DATE	TIME	DATETIME SMALLDATETIME
TIMESTAMP[(p)] [WITH TIME ZONE]	DATE TIMESTAMP [WITH [LOCAL] TIME ZONE]	TIMESTAMP	DATETIME SMALLDATETIME
INTERVAL	INTERVAL DAY TO SECOND INTERVAL YEAR TO MONTH		

Date and time literals

Date and time literals are implementation-specific and vary significantly among different vendors.

Oracle 9*i*

Oracle lets you specify DATE values as literals if they match special database initialization parameter NLS_DATE_FORMAT, which defaults to DD-MON-YY. (Oracle initialization parameters are usually handled by DBA and are not covered in this book.) You can also use SQL99 literal standard (YYYY-MM-DD) with a DATE prefix, or convert literals into string using the Oracle function TO_DATE (covered in Chapter 10). The three following statements are valid date literals examples. (SHIPMENT_ARRIVDATE_D is a DATE field in Oracle ACME database.)

```
UPDATE shipment
SET shipment_arrivdate_d = '03-SEP-02'
WHERE shipment_id_n = 30661;
```

```
UPDATE shipment
SET shipment_arrivdate_d = DATE '2003-09-02'
WHERE shipment_id_n = 30661;
```

```
UPDATE shipment
SET shipment_arrivdate_d = TO_DATE('September, 02 2003',
'Month, DD YYYY')
WHERE shipment_id_n = 30661;
```

But these are illegal:

```
UPDATE shipment
SET shipment_arrivdate_d = 'YYYY-MM-DD'
WHERE shipment_id_n = 30661;
```

```
UPDATE shipment
SET shipment_arrivdate_d = '03-SEP-02 23:12:45'
WHERE shipment_id_n = 30661;
```

TIMESTAMP and TIMESTAMP WITH TIME ZONE data types also accept the DD-MON-YY format for literals (with optional TIME part); in addition, you can specify literals with a TIMESTAMP prefix:

```
TIMESTAMP '1997-01-31 09:26:50.124'
TIMESTAMP '1997-01-31 09:26:56.66 +02:00'
TIMESTAMP '1999-04-15 8:00:00 -8:00'
TIMESTAMP '1999-04-15 8:00:00 US/Pacific'
TIMESTAMP '1999-10-29 01:30:00 US/Pacific PDT'
```

The first of these lines is for TIMESTAMP data type, and the other four are for TIMESTAMP WITH TIME ZONE.

TIMESTAMP WITH LOCAL TIME ZONE data type does not have any literals associated with it.

Oracle gives you a great deal of flexibility when specifying interval values as literals. Reference Table 3-6 for examples.

Table 3-6
Interval Literals in Oracle

INTERVAL LITERAL	*INTERPRETATION*
`INTERVAL '23-5' YEAR TO MONTH`	Interval of 23 years and 5 months
`INTERVAL '67' YEAR(3)`	Interval of 67 years and 0 months
`INTERVAL '500' MONTH(3)`	Interval of 500 months
`INTERVAL '7' YEAR`	Interval of 4 years (maps to INTERVAL '7-0' YEAR TO MONTH)
`INTERVAL '74' MONTH`	Maps to INTERVAL '6-2' YEAR TO MONTH and indicates 6 years and 2 months
`INTERVAL '7 6:15' DAY TO MINUTE`	Interval of 7 days, 6 hours and 15 minutes
`INTERVAL '40' DAY`	Interval of 40 days
`INTERVAL '11:20' HOUR TO MINUTE`	Interval of 11 hours and 20 minutes
`INTERVAL '10:22' MINUTE TO SECOND`	Interval of 10 minutes 22 seconds
`INTERVAL '25' HOUR`	Interval of 25 hours
`INTERVAL '40' MINUTE`	Interval of 40 seconds

DB2 UDB 8.1

The following formats for `DATE` literals are recognized: `YYYY-MM-DD` (ANSI/ISO), `MM/DD/YYYY` (IBM US), and `DD.MM.YYYY` (IBM Europe).

So, these three statements are legal:

```
UPDATE shipment
SET shipment_arrivdate_d = '2003-09-02'
WHERE shipment_id_n = 30661
```

```
UPDATE shipment
SET shipment_arrivdate_d = '09/02/2003'
WHERE shipment_id_n = 30661
```

```
UPDATE shipment
SET shipment_arrivdate_d = '02.09.2003'
WHERE shipment_id_n = 30661
```

But this one is not:

```
UPDATE shipment
SET shipment_arrivdate_d = '02-SEP-2003'
WHERE shipment_id_n = 30661
```

The valid TIME literal formats are: HH.MM.SS (ANSI/ISO and IBM Europe), HH:MM AM|PM (IBM USA), and HH:MM:SS (Japanese Industrial Standard). Also, trailing blanks may be included, and a leading zero may be omitted from the hour part of the time; seconds may be omitted entirely:

```
'12.23.56'
'23:15 AM'
'8:45'
```

The valid string formats for TIMESTAMP literals are YYYY-MM-DD-HH.MM.SS.NNNNNN and YYYY-MM-DD HH:MM:SS.NNNNNN:

```
UPDATE shipment
SET shipment_createdate_d = '2003-10-12-23.34.29'
WHERE shipment_id_n = 30661
```

```
UPDATE shipment
SET shipment_createdate_d = '2003-10-12 23:34:29.345678'
WHERE shipment_id_n = 30661
```

MS SQL Server

MS SQL Server is probably the friendliest RDBMS in terms of handling date and time. It recognizes the date and time literals enclosed in single quotation marks in many different formats. For example:

```
'August 15, 2003'
'15 August, 2003'
'15-AUG-2003'
'15 Aug, 2003'
'030815'
'2003/08/15'
'08/15/03'
'14:30:24'
'04:24 PM'
'15 August, 2003 23:00'
'15-AUG-2003 22:45:34.345'
```

All these (and many other) formats are valid for both `DATETIME` and `SMALLDATETIME`.

Object and User-Defined Data Types

You are already familiar with the concept of complex data types (date and time), but their complexity is hidden from the users. Now, we are going to talk about some complex data types that do require more user involvement. Understanding these data types requires some background in object-oriented programming and design.

SQL99

In general, SQL99 defines two new groups of complex data types: Abstract types (ADT) and collections.

ADT

ADT provides means to explicitly define a structural type within the larger context of the database structure. It is a series of attribute names paired with system data types plus optional methods to manipulate those properties. ADT can virtually be anything one can imagine and describe by the means of the language—a car, a person, an invoice.

We already mentioned in Chapter 1 that object-oriented design and principles are very popular today. All modern computer languages (Java, C#, VB.NET) are strictly based on those principles. Nevertheless, we would like to remind you that object-oriented databases are hardly mainstream; their market share is marginal at best, and their future existence is still questionable. Major database vendors seem to prefer embedding some object-oriented features into their existing RDBMS engines (OORDBMS approach). We are not going to list all pros and contrast once again, but in our opinion the major advantage of traditional relational databases is they are based on strong mathematical and theoretical platforms and time-proven standards.

Collections

Collections can be of reference type, set type, and list type.

Reference type

Reference type is a special type through which an instance of another type can be referenced. The reference values are read-only and unique in database system catalog.

Set and list types

These types extend a field's capabilities by storing a collection of homogeneous data. For instance, we could make a good use of array data type for a phone number field.

Until recently, phone numbers didn't cause database programmers and designers any troubles. It was conventional for a person to have only one home number and a work number. The situation has dramatically changed in recent years. Cell phones are now as popular as TVs, VCRs, and watches. Many people even have more than one cell phone! That is not such a big deal for a correctly designed relational database—we simply can store phone numbers in a separate table with pointers to their parent. But using an array data type would be another elegant solution in this situation.

Sets and lists can consist of built-in data types (for example, array of strings), abstract data types, reference data types, or named row data types. The only difference between the two collection types is that the list has to be ordered.

Oracle 9*i*

Oracle supports ADT in the form of object types. Collections are supported as nested tables, varying arrays, and ref types.

Objects

Objects in Oracle can either simply describe an entity or have some methods (functions) to manipulate it in addition to that. We can create an object in Oracle using this syntax:

```
CREATE TYPE     addr_type AS OBJECT (
street          VARCHAR(30),
city            VARCHAR(30),
state           CHAR(2),
zip             VARCHAR(10),
country         VARCHAR(30)
type            CHAR(1));
```

We can now create table `CUST1` with address field of type `ADDR_TYPE`:

```
CREATE TABLE cust1 (
id           NUMBER,
name         VARCHAR(30),
address      addr_type);
```

Figure 3-5 is the illustration of what we've just created, assuming some records have been populated. Now we can access the attributes of address field using dot notation:

```
address.street
address.city
address.state
address.zip
address.country
address.type
```

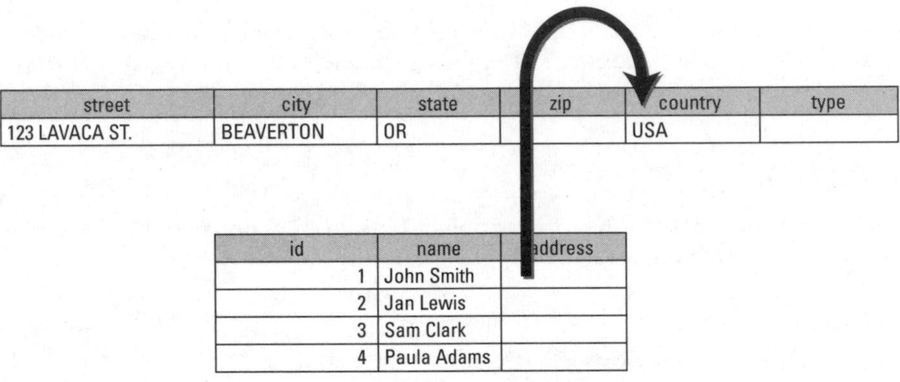

Figure 3-5: Table with column declared as an object type

Not much benefit so far — basically we just store multiple address fields in one column — but we'll take advantage of our new custom type in later examples.

Nested tables

A nested table in Oracle corresponds to SQL99 set type. It can be defined as a table that is a column of another table with unlimited number of rows. The actual data for a nested table is physically stored in another table, but from a user's viewpoint it looks like an integral part of the main table.

For example, we have a parent-child relationship between tables `CUST2` and `ADDRESS` and want to eliminate it using a nested column instead. Assuming we already have `ADDR_TYPE` created, what we do next is

```
CREATE TYPE addr_type_tab
AS TABLE OF addr_type
```

This creates a new user-defined type `ADDR_TYPE_TAB` of nested table type. Now, we can create the actual table `CUST2` so that each row may contain a table of addresses:

```
CREATE TABLE cust2 (
id       NUMBER,
name     VARCHAR(30),
address  addr_type_tab)
NESTED TABLE address STORE AS addr_storage;
```

The last line of code specifies the name of the storage table where the rows of all the values of the nested table reside. Figure 3-6 shows how addresses for CUST2 are stored in a nested table.

street	city	state	zip	country	type
454 OAK ST.	ALOHA	OR		USA	SHIPPING
411 LONDON AVE.	TIGARD	OR		USA	BILLING
232 EEL ST.	KING CITY	OR		USA	SHIPPING

id	name	address
1	John Smith	
2	Jan Lewis	
3	Sam Clark	
4	Paula Adams	

Figure 3-6: Nested tables in Oracle

Varying arrays

VARRAY data type is very similar to NESTED TABLE. The main difference is that VARRAY has to be ordered. Also, you have to specify the maximum number of elements for VARRAY and don't have to indicate the name for the storage:

```
CREATE TYPE addr_type_varray
AS VARRAY(50) OF addr_type;
```

```
create table cust3 (
id       NUMBER,
name     VARCHAR(30),
address  addr_type_varray);
```

DB2 UDB 8.1

DB2 supports user-defined structured types, reference types, and user-defined distinct types.

User-defined types

User-defined types are very similar to Oracle's object types. This example shows how to create an address structure:

```
CREATE TYPE       addr_type AS (
street            VARCHAR(30),
city              VARCHAR(30),
state             CHAR(2),
zip               VARCHAR(10),
country           VARCHAR(30)
type              CHAR(1))
MODE DB2SQL
```

Now we can create a table that uses the new user-defined data type ADDR_TYPE:

```
CREATE TABLE cust1 (
id        INTEGER,
name      VARCHAR(30),
address   addr_type)
```

Reference types

Reference types are used to define references to a row in another table (or user-structured type). The references are similar to referential integrity constraints but do not enforce relationships between the tables:

```
CREATE TABLE cust2 (
id        INTEGER,
name      VARCHAR(30),
address   REF(addr_type))
```

The address column of the CUST2 table references the user-defined ADDR_TYPE.

Distinct types

Distinct types are defined using existing data types and have the same features of the built-in type. For example, we can create a new data type usd for U.S. dollars:

```
CREATE DISTINCT TYPE usd AS DECIMAL(12,2) WITH COMPARISONS
```

Now we can use it throughout the whole database in a way similar to the way MS SQL Server uses its MONEY data type. For example, we can create tables with column of a type USD:

```
CREATE TABLE employee (
id        INTEGER,
same      VARCHAR(30),
salary    USD);
```

Other Data Types

We covered all the major SQL data types in detail. Now let's briefly describe a couple more that either are not implemented by any of the major vendors or are implemented in such a way that the data type name would not match SQL99 standards.

BOOLEAN

SQL99 has a special BOOLEAN data type with a range that includes only two values: TRUE and FALSE. Oracle, DB2, and Microsoft SQL Server don't have a BOOLEAN data type. (Or, to be more precise, DB2 has it, but for internal use only, i.e., you cannot declare a column of type BOOLEAN.) But the BOOLEAN data type can be easily simulated, for example by using a user-defined data type of type VARCHAR that only allows FALSE and TRUE for its values.

This example illustrates how to do it in MS SQL Server:

```
CREATE RULE bool_rule AS @list in ('TRUE', 'FALSE')
sp_addtype BOOLEAN, 'VARCHAR(5)', 'NULL'
sp_bindrule 'bool_rule', 'BOOLEAN'
```

Now you can use it just as another data type in your instance of MS SQL Server.

ROWID

ROWID is a special Oracle data type to store unique addresses for each row in the database. Tables can be created with ROWID columns, but that's not recommended.

UROWID

UROWID is similar to ROWID but used for index-organized tables.

BFILE

`BFILE` Oracle data type enables read-only access to binary files stored outside the Oracle database.

DATALINK

`DATALINK` is an DB2 data type to manage large objects in the form of external files. The files can reside in a file system on the same server or on a remote server. Internal database functions are used to manipulate `DATALINK` columns.

BIT

`BIT` data type in MS SQL Server stores a bit of data (0 or 1) and does not correspond to previously described SQL99 `BIT`. The literal value for bit is a single character from its range optionally enclosed into single quotes.

Tip

MS SQL Server BIT data type is yet another way to simulate SQL99 BOOLEAN data type. 1 corresponds to TRUE and 0 denotes FALSE.

TIMESTAMP

`TIMESTAMP` data type in MS SQL Server is not the same as `TIMESTAMP` SQL99 data type. You can only have one column per table of type `TIMESTAMP`. It exposes automatically generated binary numbers (unique within a database) and is basically used to uniquely identify a database row in a manner similar to (but not identical to) Oracle's `ROWID` and primarily serves version control purposes. The main difference between `TIMESTAMP` and `ROWID` is that the value of a `TIMESTAMP` column gets updated every time the row is changed, whereas Oracle's `ROWID` is assigned to a row for as long as the row exists.

Microsoft is planning to replace this data type with a `ROWVERSION` data type in future releases for SQL99 compliance. Currently `ROWVERSION` is a synonym to `TIMESTAMP`.

The storage size of `TIMESTAMP` data type is 8 bytes; it is semantically identical to binary(8).

Tip

Another related concept in MS SQL Server (and DB2 UDB) is an *identity column*. It is not a data type, but rather a special numeric column property that requires the column to contain system-generated sequential values that uniquely identify each row within table. More about identity columns is in Chapter 4.

NULL

NULL is a special database concept to represent the absence of value. It is neither a zero nor an empty string, but a special character that can be substituted for any data type. Nulls are usually used when the value is unknown or meaningless. NULL columns can later be updated with some real data.

For example, when a new employee is hired, he/she might neither yet have the phone number nor be assigned to a department. In such situation the NULL values are appropriate for PHONE and DEPARTMENT columns.

Another situation is when a value is nonapplicable; like STATE field in a European address. It can also be set to NULL.

The NULL value requires special handling and has to be dealt with carefully. In fact, any operator that involves NULL as an operand also returns NULL.

NULL can cause you serious troubles if not used properly. For example, imagine you have two columns in your table and you want to calculate the difference between them. If one of your columns has NULL values, the result of your calculation is undefined (NULL), i.e., 100 – 0 = 100, but 100 – NULL = NULL. That means you have to use special mechanisms (discussed in Chapters 10 and 11) to handle this and similar situations.

Summary

While it may not be apparent at the first look, the data types are there to safeguard us and make our life easier. This chapter describes and categorizes all existing data types (character and binary strings, precise and approximate numbers, dates and time, user-defined and object types, as well as few others that don't fit well any of the above) and analyzes variations between vendor implementations and SQL99 standards.

It is very important to know what data types are available in each implementation and to understand the correspondence between them and SQL99 standards.

You also need to consider ramifications of using a particular data type to store a particular kind of data.

Each of the three RDBMS vendors discussed in this book has its own proprietary extensions — in addition to SQL99 standard mandated data types.

The concept of NULL is introduced in this chapter. While not defining a data type, this concept is crucial for understanding how data is created, retrieved, and compared.

✦ ✦ ✦

PART II

Creating and Modifying Database Objects

✦ ✦ ✦ ✦

In This Part

✦ ✦ ✦ ✦

CHAPTER 4

Creating RDBMS Objects

✦ ✦ ✦ ✦

In This Chapter

Tables — the main RDBMS objects

Understanding constraints

Creating indexes to improve performance

Creating views

Creating synonyms

Creating schemas

Creating tablespaces, sequences, and other databases objects

✦ ✦ ✦ ✦

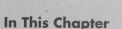

By definition, a database is a collection of objects and processes that manage these objects. Before you can start doing anything with a database, you (or somebody else) has to design it and then create its objects. The database design is a separate (though related to) SQL topic; we give a crash course in RDBMS design basics in Appendix C. This chapter is about creating objects in a relational database.

To be able to create database objects you must have sufficient (implementation specific) security privileges. See Chapter 12 for detailed discussion of SQL security.

Tables

Tables are the central and the most important objects in any relational database. The primary purpose of any database is to hold data that is logically stored in tables.

One of the relational database design principles is that each table holds information about one specific type of thing, or *entity*. For example, a CUSTOMER table would contain data about customers only, not about the products they ordered, invoices issued to them, or salesmen who placed orders for them. The ACME database doesn't even have customers' addresses and phone numbers because those are separate entities represented by ADDRESS and PHONE tables respectively.

Rows (sometimes also called records) are horizontal slices of data; each row contains data about one entity item. A row from the CUSTOMER table contains information about one single customer, a row from the ORDER_HEADER, about one single order, and so on.

The vertical cuts of table data are called columns. A column holds a particular type of information for all entity records. The CUST_NAME_S column in the CUSTOMER table encloses all customers' names; ORDHDR_INVOICENBR_N in ORDER_HEADER contains all invoice numbers.

While for the sake of simplicity it is possible to visualize tables as rows and columns sequentially stored somewhere on your hard disk, such a picture does not reflect the actual state of things. First, tables are not sequential, and second, they are not necessarily on your disk. (For example, Oracle keeps all new and modified rows, committed and uncommitted, in memory until a special database event occurs that synchronizes the memory contents with what's on the hard disk.) This is something to consider for a database administrator; as a user (and even as a programmer) it remains to your advantage to use this simple visualization and to concentrate on the table creation process.

CREATE TABLE statement

Even though we can make some generalizations about the database table creation process, internal table implementations and CREATE TABLE statement clauses differ from vendor to vendor significantly. For example, Oracle's CREATE TABLE syntax diagram is about fifteen pages long; DB2's takes roughly seven pages; MS SQL Server has the shortest definition — only one-and-a-half pages.

We are going to concentrate on the most common clauses as described in the SQL99 standards with emphasis on vendor implementation differences.

SQL99 syntax

SQL99 offers the following CREATE TABLE syntax:

```
CREATE [{GLOBAL | LOCAL} TEMPORARY] TABLE <table_name>
(
 <column_name> [<domain_name> |
                 <datatype> [<size1>[,<size2>]
                ]
                [<column_constraint>,...]
                [DEFAULT <default_value>]
                [COLLATE <collation_name>],...
 [<table_constraints>]
 [ON COMMIT {DELETE | PRESERVE} ROWS]
)
```

Oracle 9*i* syntax

In Oracle 9*i*, you can create three different types of tables: relational tables, object tables, and XML type tables. The latter two are out of scope of this book; the simplified CREATE TABLE syntax for relational tables is shown below:

```
CREATE [GLOBAL TEMPORARY] TABLE [<schema>.]<table_name>
(
```

```
  <column_name> <datatype> [<size1>[,<size2>]]
               [DEFAULT <default_value>]
               [<column_constraint>,...],...
 [<table_constraint>,...]
 [<physical_properties>]
)
[ON COMMIT {DELETE|PRESERVE} ROWS];
```

DB2 UDB 8.1 syntax

In DB2 UDB 8.1, you can create tables using this syntax (some complex clauses are omitted):

```
CREATE TABLE [<schema>.]<table_name>
(
  <column_name> <datatype> [<size1>[,<size2>]]
                [<column_constraint>,...]
                [[WITH] DEFAULT [<default_value>] |
                 GENERATED {ALWAYS |
                            BY DEFAULT
                           }
                 AS IDENTITY [<identity_clause>]
                ],...
  [<table_constraint>,...] |
  [[LIKE <table_name> [{INCLUDING | EXCLUDING}
                          {[COLUMN] DEFAULTS | IDENTITY}
                      ]
    ] |
   [AS   <select_statement>
         [{DEFINITION ONLY |
           DATA INITIALLY DEFERRED REFRESH DEFERRED |
           IMMEDIATE
          }
         ]
   ]
  ]
  [<tablespace_options>]
)
```

MS SQL 2000 syntax

Here is MS SQL Server 2000 syntax:

```
CREATE TABLE [[<database_name>.]<owner>.][#|##]<table_name>
(
 <column_name> <datatype> [<size1>[,<size2>]]
               [COLLATE <collation_name>]
               [[DEFAULT <default_value>] |
                [IDENTITY [ ([<seed>, <increment>])
```

```
                      [NOT FOR REPLICATION]
                  ]
                ]
   [<column_constraint>,...],...
   [<table_constraint>,...]
   [ON <filegroup>]
   [TEXTIMAGE_ON <filegroup>]
  )
```

Permanent and temporary tables

Database tables can be permanent or temporary, based upon the lifespan of table data.

Usually you want tables to be permanent, meaning that inserted data stays there until somebody explicitly deletes table rows. In some less common situations, you may want the table data to disappear as soon as one *commits* changes in other tables or logs off. Typically, that may be the case when you are issuing SQL statements from other programs (embedded SQL) or using procedural SQL extensions, such as PL/SQL (Oracle) or Transact SQL (MS SQL Server) to perform complex tasks. For example, you might want a program to select columns from dozens of different tables, apply formulas to perform calculations on them, store the intermediate results in a temporary table, and then update another group of tables based on those results.

Temporary tables in SQL99

SQL99 mandates two types of temporary tables: LOCAL and GLOBAL. The difference is in their data visibility. Even though the data in a temporary table is visible only within the *session* (or *transaction*) that populated it, GLOBAL tables can be accessed by any program or module within the session; thus, a stored procedure sp_1 can create the global temporary table TEMP_TABLE1; another stored procedure sp_2 can populate it with data, and then other stored procedures sp_3, sp_4, and sp_5 can use the data in their processing as long as all five stored procedures are started from the same session.

Unlike temporary table data, the temporary table's definition is permanent; so, if user A creates a temporary table B, populates it with data, and logs off, when s/he logs back the next day (or next year), the table is still there, but it is empty.

A session is one or more transactions during the interval from when a user logs into the database until s/he logs off. A transaction can be defined as a logical unit of work that consists of SQL statement(s) that usually change data (update, insert, or delete rows); at the end of a transaction *all* changes are either saved in the database using the COMMIT statement or discarded (rolled back). More about sessions, transactions, and COMMIT and ROLLBACK statements in Chapter 7

Temporary tables in Oracle 9*i*

You can create GLOBAL TEMPORARY tables in Oracle; LOCAL TEMPORARY tables are not yet implemented. The idea of a GLOBAL TEMPORARY table is slightly different from that described in the SQL99 concept. The table definition is visible to all sessions, but the data in a temporary table is only visible to the session that populated the data:

```
CREATE GLOBAL TEMPORARY TABLE tmp_customer_order_totals
(
 customer_name   VARCHAR2(30),
 customer_total  NUMBER
)
ON COMMIT DELETE ROWS;
```

In other words, user John might have created the TMP_CUSTOMER_ORDER_TOTALS table a year ago; users Mary, Susan, and Kyle are using the table concurrently (assuming they have appropriate privileges), but from their point of view it's like each of them was using his or her own temporary table; see Figures 4-1, 4-2, and 4-3.

CUSTOMER_NAME	CUSTOMER_TOTAL
WILE ELECTROMUSICAL INC.	19824
WILE ELECTRONICS INC.	28672.8

Figure 4-1: Mary's rows in the TMP_CUSTOMER_ORDER_TOTALS temporary table

CUSTOMER_NAME	CUSTOMER_TOTAL
WILE ELECTROMATIC INC.	30956.2
WILE SEAL CORP.	100771.8

Figure 4-2: Susan's rows in the TMP_CUSTOMER_ORDER_TOTALS temporary table

CUSTOMER_NAME	CUSTOMER_TOTAL
WILE BESS COMPANY	276775.6

Figure 4-3: Kyle's rows in the TMP_CUSTOMER_ORDER_TOTALS temporary table

Temporary tables in DB2 UDB 8.1

Temporary tables cannot be created in DB2 UDB 8.1 with CREATE TABLE; you can instead declare a temporary table for current session with the DECLARE GLOBAL TEMPORARY TABLE statement.

The declared temporary table cannot be shared with other sessions; when a session is terminated, rows and the table definition are both dropped.

The syntax of the DECLARE GLOBAL TEMPORARY TABLE statement is similar to DB2's CREATE TABLE statement; here is an example:

```
DECLARE GLOBAL TEMPORARY TABLE tmp_customer_order_totals
(
 customer_name    VARCHAR(30),
 customer_total   DECIMAL(12,2)
)
ON COMMIT PRESERVE ROWS NOT LOGGED
```

One important thing to mention here is that if you try this statement on your sample database, it will fail with an error saying that the user does not have a large enough temporary tablespace. We explain the concept of tablespace later in this chapter.

Temporary tables in MS SQL Server 2000

The MS SQL Server syntax used to create a temporary table is not consistent with SQL99 standards. To create a local temporary table, you prefix it with the pound sign (#); the double pound sign (##) indicates a global temporary table.

Local temporary tables are visible only to the current session; both the table data and table definition are deleted when the user logs off (comparable to DB2 temporary tables created with the DECLARE GLOBAL TEMPORARY TABLE statement):

```
CREATE TABLE #tmp_customer_order_totals
(
 customer_name    VARCHAR(30),
 customer_total   MONEY
)
```

Global temporary tables are visible to all users; they are destroyed after every user who was referencing the table disconnects from the SQL Server:

```
CREATE TABLE ##tmp_customer_order_totals
(
 customer_name    VARCHAR(30),
```

```
    customer_total  MONEY
  )
```

Column definitions

The table has to have one or more column definitions, which consist of the column name and the data type.

SQL99

According to SQL99, a *domain* can be used for a column instead of a data type. (Domains are covered later in this chapter.)

Oracle 9*i*, DB2 UDB 8.1, and MS SQL Server 2000 are reasonably consistent in their column definition clauses; the only difference is each implementation uses its own data types. For instance, this Oracle column definition:

```
customer_name    VARCHAR2(30)
customer_total   NUMBER
```

Would have to be replaced in MS SQL Server with:

```
customer_name    VARCHAR(30)
customer_total   MONEY
```

None of the above vendors allows domains in column definitions. (As a mattrer of fact, they don't have domains at all.)

Column constraints

Each column can have one or more column constraints. SQL99 specifies the following column constraints:

- ✦ NOT NULL means that the NULL values are not permitted in the column.
- ✦ UNIQUE means all values in the column must be distinct values; NULLs are permitted.
- ✦ PRIMARY KEY specifies that all column values must be unique and the column can't contain NULLs. In other words, it's a combination of the above two constraints.
- ✦ REFERENCES means the column is a foreign key to the referenced table.
- ✦ CHECK verifies that the column values obey certain rules; for example, only positive numbers are permitted, or only a certain set of strings is valid.

All three implementations have all the above constraints and handle them in similar ways. You can either name constraints accordingly with your database naming conventions, or don't specify constraint names at all. In the latter case, RDBMS will generate default names. The following examples illustrate the use of column constraints (Oracle or MS SQL Server):

```
CREATE TABLE salesman
(
  salesman_id_n       INT    CONSTRAINT pk_salesmanprim PRIMARY KEY,
  salesman_code_s     VARCHAR (2)  CONSTRAINT uk_salescode UNIQUE,
  salesman_name_s     VARCHAR (50)  NOT NULL,
  salesman_status_s   CHAR (1)    CONSTRAINT chk_salesstatus CHECK
                                  (salesman_status_s in ('N', 'Y'))
)

CREATE TABLE address
(
    addr_id_n          INT CONSTRAINT pk_addrprimary PRIMARY KEY,
    addr_custid_fn     INT,
    addr_salesmanid_fn INT CONSTRAINT fk_addr_salesman
                       REFERENCES salesman (salesman_id_n),
    addr_address_s     VARCHAR(60),
    addr_type_s        VARCHAR(8) CONSTRAINT chk_addr_type CHECK
                       (addr_type_s IN ('BILLING', 'SHIPPING')),
    addr_city_s        VARCHAR(18) CONSTRAINT nn_addr_city   NOT NULL,
    addr_state_s       CHAR(2),
    addr_zip_s         VARCHAR(10)    NOT NULL,
    addr_country_s     CHAR(3)
 )
```

You would need to make a couple of modifications for this statement to run in DB2:

```
salesman_id_n      INT    CONSTRAINT pk_salesmanprim PRIMARY KEY NOT NULL
salesman_code_s    VARCHAR (2)  CONSTRAINT uk_salescode UNIQUE NOT NULL

addr_id_n          INT CONSTRAINT pk_addrprimary PRIMARY KEY NOT NULL
```

Oracle and MS SQL Server implicitly create NOT NULL constraints on all primary keys and unique columns, but DB2 does not, so you have to specify both NOT NULL and PRIMARY KEY constraints on a primary key column of a DB2 table or an error will be generated.

Column default values

Each column can optionally be given a default value (in range of its data type). In this case, if an INSERT statement omits the column, the default value will automatically be populated:

```
CREATE TABLE product
(
    prod_id_n             INTEGER          NOT NULL,
    prod_price_n          DECIMAL(10,2),
    prod_num_s            VARCHAR(10),
    prod_description_s    VARCHAR(44)      NOT NULL,
```

```
    prod_status_s          CHAR(1)          DEFAULT 'Y',
    prod_brand_s           VARCHAR(20)      NOT NULL,
    prod_pltwid_n          DECIMAL(5,2)     NOT NULL,
    prod_pltlen_n          DECIMAL(5,2)     NOT NULL,
    prod_netwght_n         DECIMAL(10,3),
    prod_shipweight_n      DECIMAL(10,3)
)

INSERT INTO product
 ( prod_id_n,
   prod_price_n,
   prod_num_s,
   prod_description_s,
   prod_brand_s,
   prod_pltwid_n,
   prod_pltlen_n,
   prod_netwght_n,
   prod_shipweight_n
 )
VALUES
 (990,
  18.24,
  '990',
  'SPRUCE LUMBER 30X40X50',
  'SPRUCE LUMBER',
  4,
  6,
  21.22577,
  24.22577
 )

SELECT   prod_id_n,
         prod_price_n,
         prod_status_s
FROM     product

PROD_ID_N PROD_PRICE_N PROD_STATUS_S
--------- ------------ -------------
      990        18.24 Y
```

This example will work with all our "big three" databases.

Column collating sequence

Character string columns can optionally have a collating sequence; thus, you can specify nondefault character precedence order.

Out of our three database vendors only MS SQL Server allows collations as a part of the column definition. The collation name specifies the collation for the column of a character string data type; you can use both MS SQL Server and MS Windows predefined collations. For example, if you want all customer names in the ACME database to be handled according to French collation rules, you can modify the CUSTOMER table:

```
CREATE TABLE customer
(
    cust_id_n            INT           NOT NULL,
    cust_paytermsid_fn   INT,
    cust_salesmanid_fn   INT,
    cust_status_s        VARCHAR(1)    DEFAULT 'Y' NOT NULL,
    cust_name_s          VARCHAR(50)   COLLATE FRENCH_CI_AI NOT NULL,
    cust_alias_s         VARCHAR(15),
    cust_credhold_s      VARCHAR(1)    DEFAULT 'Y' NOT NULL
)
```

CI in the above collation definition stands for CASE INSENSITIVE, and AI means ACCENT INSENSITIVE; to use a case-sensitive, accent sensitive collation, use FRENCH_CS_AS instead. See MS SQL Server and MS Windows documentation for full lists and descriptions of the available collations.

Table constraints

Table constraints are similar to column constraints; the main difference is that table constraints can be used not only on individual columns, but also on column lists. The valid table constraints are listed here:

- ✦ UNIQUE. Similar to the column constraint, but can ensure uniqueness of the combination of two or more columns.
- ✦ PRIMARY KEY. The combination of values in constrained column(s) must be unique; NULL values are not allowed.
- ✦ FOREIGN KEY. Specifies a column or group of columns in the table that references a column (or group of columns) in the referenced table.
- ✦ CHECK. Defines a predicate that refers values in one or more tables; similar to the column CHECK constraint.

The following example illustrates the use of table constraints:

```
CREATE TABLE order_header
(
    ordhdr_id_n            INTEGER          NOT NULL,
    ordhdr_payterms_fn     INTEGER,
    ordhdr_statusid_fn     INTEGER,
    ordhdr_custid_fn       INTEGER,
    ordhdr_salesmanid_fn   INTEGER,
    ordhdr_nbr_s           VARCHAR(30)     NOT NULL,
    ordhdr_invoicenbr_n    INTEGER,
```

```
    ordhdr_orderdate_d          DATETIME,
    ordhdr_invoicedate_d        DATETIME,
    ordhdr_canceldate_d         DATETIME,
    ordhdr_credithold_s         CHAR(1),
    ordhdr_readytoinvoice_s     CHAR(1)         DEFAULT 'N',
    ordhdr_notes_s              VARCHAR(60),
    ordhdr_createdby_s          VARCHAR(10),
    ordhdr_createdate_d         DATETIME,
    CONSTRAINT chk_ordhdr_ready CHECK
            (ordhdr_readytoinvoice_s IN ('N', 'Y')),
    CONSTRAINT chk_ordhdr_credh CHECK
            (ordhdr_credithold_s IN ('N', 'Y')),
    CONSTRAINT pk_ordhdrprim PRIMARY KEY (ordhdr_id_n),
    CONSTRAINT idx_ordhdr_ordnbr  UNIQUE (ordhdr_nbr_s)
)
CREATE TABLE shipment
(
    shipment_id_n              INTEGER          NOT NULL,
    shipment_bolnum_s          VARCHAR(6),
    shipment_shipdate_d        DATETIME,
    shipment_arrivdate_d       DATETIME,
    shipment_totalcases_n      INTEGER,
    shipment_trailernbr_s      VARCHAR(12),
    shipment_shpmntfrght_n     DECIMAL(12,2),
    shipment_frtterms_s        VARCHAR(3),
    shipment_createdby_s       VARCHAR(10),
    shipment_createdate_d      DATETIME,
    CONSTRAINT chk_shipfrtterms CHECK
            (shipment_frtterms_s IN ('COL', 'PPD')),
    CONSTRAINT pk_shipmentrprim PRIMARY KEY (shipment_id_n)
)
CREATE TABLE order_shipment
(
    ordship_ordhdr_id_fn       INTEGER     NOT NULL,
    ordship_shipment_id_fn     INTEGER     NOT NULL,
    CONSTRAINT pk_ordhdrship PRIMARY KEY
                           (ordship_ordhdr_id_fn, ordship_shipment_id_fn),
    CONSTRAINT fk_ordsh_ord FOREIGN KEY (ordship_ordhdr_id_fn)
                           REFERENCES order_header(ordhdr_id_n)
)
```

This example is for MS SQL Server syntax; to make it work in Oracle 9*i* or DB2 UDB 8.1, modify the DATETIME data type for columns ORDHDR_ORDERDATE_D, ORDHDR_INVOICEDATE_D, ORDHDR_CANCELDATE_D, ORDHDR_CREATEDATE_D, SHIPMENT_SHIPDATE_D, SHIPMENT_ARRIVDATE_D, and SHIPMENT_CREATEDATE_D to be of a valid data type for the particular implementation (DATE or TIMESTAMP).

Referential integrity constraints optional clauses

SQL99 assumes an optional clause on the creation of FOREIGN KEY and REFERENCES constraints that specifies what happens to a row if that row has a referential relationship and the referenced row is deleted from the parent table or changes are made to the referenced table. The syntax is as follows:

```
[ON DELETE {NO ACTION | CASCADE | SET NULL}]
[ON UPDATE {NO ACTION | CASCADE | SET NULL | SET DEFAULT}]
```

`NO ACTION` is the default behavior and means an error will be generated if one tries to delete the row (or update the primary key value) referenced by other table(s).

`CASCADE` assumes that the same changes will automatically be done to the foreign key as were made to the parent; thus, if the parent row is deleted, all child rows that referenced it will also be deleted; if the parent's primary key is updated, all child rows' foreign keys that reference it will also be updated with the same value.

`SET NULL` means if the parent row was deleted or its primary key was changed, all child tables' referencing foreign key values will be set to `NULL`.

`SET DEFAULT` is very similar to `SET NULL`, but the child tables' columns are set to their default values rather than to `NULL`s. This assumes that column default values exist.

All our three vendors implemented the above SQL99 standard to certain degree.

Oracle 9*i* does not have the `ON UPDATE` clause; the `ON DELETE` clause syntax is:

```
[ON DELETE { NO ACTION | CASCADE | SET NULL }]
```

DB2 UDB 8.1 has an additional optional `RESTRICT` that in most cases behaves like `NO ACTION`:

```
[ON DELETE {NO ACTION | RESTRICT | CASCADE | SET NULL}]
[ON UPDATE {NO ACTION | RESTRICT}]
```

MS SQL Server 2000 has two options — `NO ACTION` and `CASCADE` for both `ON DELETE` and `ON UPDATE` clauses:

```
[ON DELETE {NO ACTION | CASCADE}]
[ON UPDATE {NO ACTION | CASCADE}]
```

The default is `NO ACTION` for all three implementations.

The following examples illustrate the difference between NO ACTION and CASCADE using Oracle 9*i* syntax.

Listing 4-1 uses previously created SALESMAN and ADDRESS tables with default (NO ACTION) option on the referential integrity constraint FK_ADDR_SALESMAN.

Listing 4-1: **Default (NO ACTION) option**

```
SQL> INSERT INTO salesman
     (
      salesman_id_n,
      salesman_code_s,
      salesman_name_s,
      salesman_status_s
     )
     VALUES
     (
      23,
      '02',
      'FAIRFIELD BUGS ASSOCIATION',
      'Y'
     );

1 row created.

SQL> INSERT INTO address
     (
      addr_id_n,
      addr_custid_fn,
      addr_salesmanid_fn,
      addr_address_s,
      addr_type_s,
      addr_city_s,
      addr_state_s,
      addr_zip_s,
      addr_country_s
     )
     VALUES
     (
      49,
      NULL,
      23,
      '223 E FLAGLER ST.',
      NULL,
      'MIAMI',
      'FL',
      '33131',
```

Continued

Listing 4-1 *(continued)*

```
    'USA'
  );

1 row created.

SQL> commit;

Commit complete.

SQL> DELETE FROM salesman;
DELETE FROM salesman
*
ERROR at line 1:
ORA-02292: integrity constraint (TEMP.FK_ADDR_SALESMAN)
violated - child record found
```

Listing 4-2—with `CASCADE` **option on the referential integrity constraint** `FK_ADDR_SALESMAN`:

Listing 4-2: **CASCADE option**

```
SQL> drop table ADDRESS;

Table dropped.

SQL> CREATE TABLE address
  (
      addr_id_n           INT CONSTRAINT pk_addrprimary PRIMARY KEY,
      addr_custid_fn      INT,
      addr_salesmanid_fn  INT CONSTRAINT fk_addr_salesman
                          REFERENCES salesman (salesman_id_n)
                          ON DELETE CASCADE,
      addr_address_s      VARCHAR(60),
      addr_type_s         VARCHAR(8) CONSTRAINT chk_addr_type CHECK
                          (addr_type_s IN ('BILLING', 'SHIPPING')),
      addr_city_s         VARCHAR(18) CONSTRAINT nn_addr_city   NOT NULL,
      addr_state_s        CHAR(2),
      addr_zip_s          VARCHAR(10)    NOT NULL,
      addr_country_s      CHAR(3)
  );

Table created.

SQL> INSERT INTO address
  (
   addr_id_n,
```

```
 addr_custid_fn,
 addr_salesmanid_fn,
 addr_address_s,
 addr_type_s,
 addr_city_s,
 addr_state_s,
 addr_zip_s,
 addr_country_s
)
VALUES
(
 49,
 NULL,
 23,
 '223 E FLAGLER ST.',
 NULL,
 'MIAMI',
 'FL',
 '33131',
 'USA'
);

1 row created.

SQL> COMMIT;

Commit complete.

SQL> SELECT * FROM ADDRESS;

 ADDR_ID_N   ADDR_CUSTID_FN  ADDR_SALESMANID_FN      ADDR_ADDRESS_S
----------   --------------  ------------------      -----------------
        49               23                 223      E FLAGLER ST.

SQL> DELETE FROM salesman;

1 row deleted.

SQL> SELECT * FROM address;

no rows selected
```

Deferrable constraints

SQL99 standards say that constraints can be either DEFERRABLE or NOT DEFERRABLE (default). A NOT DEFERRABLE constraint is checked after each DDL statement; DEFERRABLE constraints can either be checked immediately after every INSERT, DELETE, or UPDATE (INITIALLY IMMEDIATE) or at the end of the transaction (INITIALLY DEFERRED).

That feature can be especially helpful when data loads are performed with no particular order; that allows you to load data into child table(s) first, then into parent table(s). Another use would be loading data that does not comply with a `CHECK` constraint and then updating it appropriately.

The only vendor out of our "big three" who provides deferrable constraints is Oracle 9*i*. The syntax is

```
[[NOT] DEFERRABLE [INITIALLY {IMMEDIATE | DEFERRED}]]
```

or

```
[[INITIALLY {IMMEDIATE | DEFERRED}] [NOT] DEFERRABLE]
```

Like any other programming language, SQL allows you to add comments to your code. A line in SQL code is treated as a comment (i.e., RDBMS does not try to compile and execute it) if it is prefixed with a double dash (`--`). Yet another way to "comment out" text (which is usually used for multiline comments) is to enclose it into `/* */`.

Listing 4-3 illustrates the use of deferrable constraints.

Listing 4-3: **Using deferrable constraints**

```
-- Create SALESMAN table with NOT DEFERRABLE CHECK constraint
-- chk_salesstatus on salesman_status_s column

SQL> DROP TABLE salesman;

Table dropped.

SQL> CREATE TABLE salesman
  (
       salesman_id_n         NUMBER          NOT NULL,
       salesman_code_s       VARCHAR2(2)     NOT NULL,
       salesman_name_s       VARCHAR2(50)    NOT NULL,
       salesman_status_s     CHAR(1)         DEFAULT 'Y',
       CONSTRAINT chk_salesstatus CHECK
                  (salesman_status_s in ('N', 'Y')),
       CONSTRAINT pk_salesmanprim PRIMARY KEY (salesman_id_n)
  );

Table created.

-- Now, try to insert a row with salesman_status_s = 'A'
SQL> INSERT INTO salesman
  (
```

```
    salesman_id_n,
    salesman_code_s,
    salesman_name_s,
    salesman_status_s
  )
  VALUES
  (
    23,
    '02',
    'FAIRFIELD BUGS ASSOCIATION',
    'A'
  );

/*
  The result is a constraint violation error
  (constraint is checked immediately).
*/

INSERT INTO SALESMAN
*
ERROR at line 1:
ORA-02290: check constraint (TEST.CHK_SALESSTATUS) violated

-- Drop SALESMAN table and re-create it with DEFERRABLE CHECK constraint
SQL> DROP TABLE salesman;

Table dropped.

SQL> CREATE TABLE salesman
  (
      salesman_id_n         NUMBER           NOT NULL,
      salesman_code_s       VARCHAR2(2)      NOT NULL,
      salesman_name_s       VARCHAR2(50)     NOT NULL,
      salesman_status_s     CHAR(1)          DEFAULT 'Y',
      CONSTRAINT chk_salesstatus CHECK (salesman_status_s in ('N', 'Y'))
                                 DEFERRABLE INITIALLY DEFERRED,
      CONSTRAINT pk_salesmanprim PRIMARY KEY (salesman_id_n)
  );

Table created.

-- Try to insert the same row again - works this time
SQL> INSERT INTO salesman
  (
    salesman_id_n,
    salesman_code_s,
    salesman_name_s,
    salesman_status_s
  )
  VALUES
  (
```

Continued

Listing 4-3 *(continued)*

```
 10    23,
 11    '02',
 12    'FAIRFIELD BUGS ASSOCIATION',
 13    'A'
 14  );

1 row created.

-- Try to commit changes
SQL> COMMIT;

-- Error occurs - the constraint is checked at the end of the transaction.
COMMIT
*
ERROR at line 1:
ORA-02091: transaction rolled back
ORA-02290: check constraint (TEST.CHK_SALESSTATUS) violated

-- Trying to insert again
SQL> INSERT INTO salesman
  2  (
  3    salesman_id_n,
  4    salesman_code_s,
  5    salesman_name_s,
  6    salesman_status_s
  7  )
  8  VALUES
  9  (
 10    23,
 11    '02',
 12    'FAIRFIELD BUGS ASSOCIATION',
 13    'A'
 14  );

1 row created.

-- Now update it with an appropriate value ('Y')
SQL> UPDATE salesman
  2  SET salesman_status_s = 'Y'
  3  WHERE salesman_status_s = 'A';

1 row updated.

-- COMMIT works this time.
SQL> COMMIT;

Commit complete.
```

Using INITIALLY DEFERRED Constraints

The INITIALLY DEFERRED constraint status is usually used for special cases (data loads, conversions, etc.); when used in everyday database operations, the deferred constraints can be confusing and even harmful.

For example, imagine someone issued a couple dozen DML statements and then tries to commit their changes, but the commit fails because the very first INSERT statement violates an INITIALLY DEFERRED constraint. The transaction will be rolled back, so the user would have to retype all the statements. If the constraint were checked after each statement, the user would have known to correct data before going any further.

The solution is simple: only use INITIALLY DEFERRED constraint status for special needs and change it to INITIALLY IMMEDIATE whenever the deferred functionality is no longer desirable. (You can always change it back and forth if your constraint was created as DEFERRABLE.) We'll learn more about that in Chapter 5.

ON COMMIT clause

This clause can be used for temporary tables only. It specifies if the table rows are implicitly deleted at the end of a transaction or preserved until the session ends, so consequent transactions can use the temporary table data.

The clause can be used within Oracle's CREATE TABLE statement or DB2's DECLARE TABLE. See the previous examples in the section about temporary tables.

Physical properties clause

Now, it's a little bit of a simplification, but generally data is physically stored on a database server's hard disk(s). The precise definition is beyond the scope of a book about SQL, but we are going to cover the very basics to help you better understand the creation of the database objects.

The implementations use quite diverse approaches, but the idea is the same: to be able to separate different database objects by type and, ideally, to put them on separate physical disks to speed up database operations. For example, all table data would live on Disk1, all table indexes on Disk2, and all LOBs would be placed on Disk3. The importance of such an approach varies from vendor to vendor; many other factors, like database size, workload, server quality, and so on can also play their role.

This book assumes the ACME sample database will be used primarily for educational purposes. We don't expect you to use a real big server with multiple disks, so the physical storage has rather theoretical significance for now.

Oracle 9*i*

Oracle uses *tablespaces* (logical database structure explained later in this chapter). You can specify separate tablespaces for table data, table indexes, and table LOBs:

```
CREATE TABLE phone
(
    phone_id_n           NUMBER      CONSTRAINT pk_phonerimary
                                     PRIMARY KEY USING INDEX
                                     TABLESPACE INDEX01,
    phone_custid_fn      NUMBER,
    phone_salesmanid_fn  NUMBER,
    phone_phonenum_s     VARCHAR2(20),
    phone_type_s         VARCHAR2(20),
    CONSTRAINT chk_phone_type CHECK
              (phone_type_s IN ('PHONE', 'FAX'))
)
TABLESPACE DATA01
```

This example assumes the existence of tablespaces DATA01, where the table data will reside, and INDEX01, to store the index for the primary key.

DB2 UDB 8.1

DB2 also uses tablespaces much as Oracle does. You can specify separate tablespaces for table data, indexes, and large objects:

```
CREATE TABLE phone
(
    phone_id_n           INTEGER           NOT NULL,
    phone_custid_fn      INTEGER,
    phone_salesmanid_fn  INTEGER,
    phone_phonenum_s     VARCHAR(20),
    phone_type_s         VARCHAR(20),
    CONSTRAINT chk_phone_type CHECK
              (phone_type_s IN ('PHONE', 'FAX')),
    CONSTRAINT pk_phonerimary PRIMARY KEY (phone_id_n)
)
IN USERDATA01
```

The system-managed tablespace USERDATA01 presumably exists. We'll show how to create it at the end of the chapter in the section about tablespaces.

Index Organized Tables and Other Physical Properties

The ability to specify where data is physically stored on the server is just one of many options you can specify when creating a database table. For example, you can specify how much space will be left for updates when a row is inserted, regulate the physical table growth, slice the table based on certain conditions (either horizontally or vertically), place the different partitions on separate physical devices, and so on.

Oracle also allows you to create index-organized tables. An index-organized table is a special type of table in which the table rows are maintained in an index built on the primary key. In other words, unlike regular tables in which rows are stored in no particular order, the rows of an index-organized table are always sorted by the primary key field. The access to such tables based on primary key is therefore much faster, but the DML statements can be considerably slower. For example, to insert a row into an index-organized table, an RDBMS has to re-sort and rebuild the whole physical table structure.

This syntax creates an index-organized table named ORDER_LINE:

```
CREATE TABLE ORDER_LINE
(
    ORDLINE_ID_N            NUMBER          NOT NULL,
    ORDLINE_ORDHDRID_FN     NUMBER          NOT NULL,
    ORDLINE_PRODID_FN       NUMBER,
    ORDLINE_ORDQTY_N        NUMBER,
    ORDLINE_SHIPQTY_N       NUMBER,
    ORDLINE_CREATEDATE_D    DATE,
    ORDLINE_CREATEDBY_S     VARCHAR2(10),
    CONSTRAINT PK_ORDLINEPRIM PRIMARY KEY (ORDLINE_ID_N)
)
ORGANIZATION INDEX
;
```

MS SQL Server implements a similar concept in *clustered indexes,* which are explained later in this chapter.

MS SQL Server 2000

Instead of tablespaces, MS SQL Server employs *filegroups*. Again, the idea is very similar; the difference is mostly in the syntax:

```
CREATE TABLE phone
(
    phone_id_n            INTEGER         NOT NULL,
    phone_custid_fn       INTEGER,
    phone_salesmanid_fn   INTEGER,
    phone_phonenum_s      VARCHAR(20),
    phone_type_s          VARCHAR(20),
```

```
    CONSTRAINT chk_phone_type CHECK
              (phone_type_s IN ('PHONE', 'FAX')),
    CONSTRAINT pk_phonerimary
               PRIMARY KEY (phone_id_n) ON INDEX01
)
ON DATA01
```

In this example, we have presumed the existence of previously created filegroups DATA01 and INDEX01. MS SQL filegroups are covered in more detail later in this chapter.

Identity clause

Sometimes in your database, you want to generate unique sequential values, for example for a primary key column, for order or invoice numbers, customer IDs, and so on. We already mentioned the concept of identity columns in Chapter 3; now we are going to cover it in greater detail.

Oracle 9*i*

Oracle does not have identity columns; it uses special database objects called *sequences* instead. You can simply create a table with a numeric field to be populated; at the moment of table creation the RDBMS does not need to know that, for example, you intend to populate the PAYTERMS_ID_N field of the PAYMENT_TERMS table using a sequence:

```
CREATE TABLE payment_terms
(
    payterms_id_n           NUMBER   NOT NULL,
    payterms_code_s         VARCHAR(6),
    payterms_desc_s         VARCHAR(60),
    payterms_discpct_n      NUMBER,
    payterms_daystopay_N    NUMBER,
    CONSTRAINT pk_payterms PRIMARY KEY (payterms_id_n)
)
```

More about sequences can be found in the CREATE SEQUENCE section that follows in this chapter as well as in the ALTER SEQUENCE, and DROP SEQUENCE sections of Chapter 5.

DB2 UDB 8.1

Identity properties for a column can be specified *instead* of the default clause. You can specify the starting value, the increment, the minimum and maximum values, whether the sequence should cycle around when it reaches the maximum value or whether it should stop, and the number of values cached in memory:

```
CREATE TABLE payment_terms
(
    payterms_id_n          INTEGER   NOT NULL
                           GENERATED ALWAYS AS IDENTITY
                           (START WITH 1, INCREMENT BY 1, CACHE 5),
    payterms_code_s        VARCHAR(6),
    payterms_desc_s        VARCHAR(60),
    payterms_discpct_n     DECIMAL(5,2),
    payterms_daystopay_N   INTEGER,
    CONSTRAINT pk_payterms PRIMARY KEY (payterms_id_n)
)
```

The default number of values to cache is 20; you can specify `NO CACHE` if you don't want to cache values.

MS SQL Server 2000

An identity column is created in a very similar way with slightly different syntax:

```
CREATE TABLE payment_terms
(
    -- The first 1 means "start with"; the second stands for "increment by"
    payterms_id_n          INT   NOT NULL IDENTITY (1,1),
    payterms_code_s        VARCHAR(6),
    payterms_desc_s        VARCHAR(60),
    payterms_discpct_n     DECIMAL(5,2),
    payterms_daystopay_n   INT,
    CONSTRAINT pk_payterms PRIMARY KEY (payterms_id_n)
)
```

The caching option is not available in MS SQL Server.

Creating new table as a copy of another table

Sometimes it's very useful to be able to create a table as a copy of another table. You can "clone" an existing table by creating its exact copy (with or without data) in all "big three" databases with slightly different syntax.

Oracle 9*i*

The statement below creates a temporary table that is a copy of the `PAYMENT_TERMS` table (including all rows):

```
CREATE GLOBAL TEMPORARY TABLE payment_terms2
AS
(SELECT * FROM payment_terms);
```

The proper use of the SELECT statement enables you to create a table that only contains certain columns and/or rows from the target table:

```
CREATE TABLE customer
(
    cust_id_n              NUMBER          NOT NULL,
    cust_paytermsid_fn     NUMBER,
    cust_salesmanid_fn     NUMBER,
    cust_status_s          VARCHAR2(1)     DEFAULT 'Y' NOT NULL,
    cust_name_s            VARCHAR2(50)    NOT NULL,
    cust_alias_s           VARCHAR2(15),
    cust_credhold_s        VARCHAR2(1)     DEFAULT 'Y' NOT NULL,
    CONSTRAINT chk_cust_status CHECK (cust_status_s IN ('N', 'Y')),
    CONSTRAINT chk_cust_credhold CHECK (cust_credhold_s IN ('N', 'Y')),
    CONSTRAINT pk_custprimary PRIMARY KEY (cust_id_n)
);

CREATE TABLE phone
(
    phone_id_n           NUMBER          NOT NULL,
    phone_custid_fn      NUMBER,
    phone_salesmanid_fn  NUMBER,
    phone_phonenum_s     VARCHAR2(20),
    phone_type_s         VARCHAR2(20),
    CONSTRAINT chk_phone_type CHECK (phone_type_s IN ('PHONE', 'FAX')),
    CONSTRAINT pk_phonerimary PRIMARY KEY (phone_id_n)
);

CREATE TABLE customer_phone AS
(
 SELECT      cust_name_s,
phone_phonenum_s
 FROM        customer,
phone
 WHERE       cust_id_n = phone_custid_fn
);
```

To create an empty table in Oracle, deliberately use a FALSE condition in the WHERE clause:

```
/*
We know that all primary keys in ACME database are positive
integers so we know that PAYTERMS_ID_N < 0 condition always
evaluates to "FALSE"
*/
CREATE GLOBAL TEMPORARY TABLE payment_terms3
AS
(SELECT * FROM payment_terms WHERE PAYTERMS_ID_N < 0);
```

See more about TRUE and FALSE conditions in Appendix L.

DB2 UDB 8.1

Either one of two statements below will create a copy of the PAYMENT_TERMS table in DB2 UDB:

```
CREATE TABLE payment_terms2
AS (SELECT * FROM payment_terms)
DEFINITION ONLY
```

```
CREATE TABLE payment_terms2
LIKE payment_terms
```

The first syntax (DB2 considers it a special case of a *summary table* — see the sidebar "Creating Summary Tables") is more flexible because it allows you to create tables based on a subset of the original table columns or even on a multitable query:

```
CREATE TABLE customer
(
    cust_id_n            NUMBER           NOT NULL,
    cust_paytermsid_fn   NUMBER,
    cust_salesmanid_fn   NUMBER,
    cust_status_s        VARCHAR2(1)      DEFAULT 'Y' NOT NULL,
    cust_name_s          VARCHAR2(50)     NOT NULL,
    cust_alias_s         VARCHAR2(15),
    cust_credhold_s      VARCHAR2(1)      DEFAULT 'Y' NOT NULL,
    CONSTRAINT chk_cust_status CHECK (cust_status_s IN ('N', 'Y')),
    CONSTRAINT chk_cust_credhold CHECK (cust_credhold_s IN ('N', 'Y')),
    CONSTRAINT pk_custprimary PRIMARY KEY (cust_id_n)
)

CREATE TABLE phone
(
    phone_id_n          NUMBER          NOT NULL,
    phone_custid_fn     NUMBER,
    phone_salesmanid_fn  NUMBER,
    phone_phonenum_s    VARCHAR2(20),
    phone_type_s        VARCHAR2(20),
    CONSTRAINT chk_phone_type CHECK (phone_type_s IN ('PHONE', 'FAX')),
    CONSTRAINT pk_phonerimary PRIMARY KEY (phone_id_n)
)

CREATE TABLE customer_phone AS
```

```
(
 SELECT      cust_name_s,
phone_phonenum_s
 FROM        customer,
phone
 WHERE       cust_id_n = phone_custid_fn
)
DEFINITION ONLY -- required clause
```

The foregoing statement creates an empty CUSTOMER_PHONE table with two columns, CUST_NAME_S and PHONE_PHONENUM_S, with the same data types as the corresponding columns in the underlying tables; you could have achieved the same result using this syntax:

```
CREATE TABLE customer_phone AS
(
 cust_name_s        VARCHAR(50)    NOT NULL,
 phone_phonenum_s   VARCHAR(20)
)
```

The advantage of CREATE TABLE ... LIKE syntax is that it can optionally create a copy of table with all column defaults and/or identity columns.

The CREATE TABLE ... AS and CREATE TABLE ... LIKE syntaxes both create empty tables in DB2. The data can be populated by using the INSERT INTO ... SELECT FROM statement discussed in later chapters.

MS SQL Server 2000

In MS SQL Server, you can create a copy of the PAYMENT_TERMS table using this syntax:

```
SELECT *
INTO #PAYMENT_TERMS2
FROM PAYMENT_TERMS
```

This syntax creates a MS SQL local temporary table; if the pound sign were omitted, PAYMENT_TERMS2 would be created as a permanent table.

You can use the same trick (a deliberately "FALSE" condition) as in Oracle to create an empty table in MS SQL Server.

Creating Summary Tables

Some RDBMS tables can be very large, so querying them can take a long time. Even when all appropriate indexes are in place and the database is properly tuned, some queries still have to perform full table scans, in which each and every record is searched for specific values, to return the desired results. That is especially true when you want a query to retrieve records summarized with a GROUP BY clause using aggregate functions.

The concept of summary tables introduced in DB2 allows you to maintain a summary of table (or multiple tables) data in another table, refreshing it every time when the underlying table(s) data changes. The most interesting fact about DB2 summary tables is that not only users can query them to obtain results faster, but the RDBMS *optimizer* can also use them to execute users' queries that indirectly request information already summarized in the summary tables.

Keep in mind that this only works well on tables that are more or less static; if the source tables change frequently (i.e., many DDL statements run against them), the overhead may become too big and the overall performance may actually degrade.

You can have two types of summary tables in DB2. Tables created with the REFRESH DEFERRED clause can be refreshed on demand with the REFRESH TABLE table_name statement; if the REFRESH IMMEDIATE clause was used, the summary table will delete and reinsert rows automatically every time the table(s) used in its WHERE clause change. In both cases, you have to use the REFRESH TABLE ... statement at least once on a summary table before you (or the optimizer) can start using it.

Summary tables are subject to many limitations. For example, you cannot use ORDER BY, outer joins, or nondeterministic functions in the select_statement; you must have GROUP BY clause and COUNT (*) column; all columns must be named, and so on. See DB2 UDB documentation for all rules and restrictions.

Here is an example of the table ORDERLINE_SUMMARY that summarizes ordered and shipped product quantities by order on demand:

```
CREATE TABLE   orderline_summary
AS
(
 SELECT         ordline_ordhdrid_fn,
SUM(ordline_ordqty_n) AS ord_qty_summary,
SUM(ordline_shipqty_n) AS ship_qty_summary,
COUNT (*) AS rowcount
 FROM            order_line
 GROUP BY        ordline_ordhdrid_fn
)
DATA INITIALLY DEFERRED REFRESH DEFERRED
```

Oracle provides similar capabilities by using MATERIALIZED VIEWS discussed latter in this chapter.

Indexes

Index is another database physical structure that occupies disk space in a way similar to that of a table. The main difference is that indexes are hidden from users and are not mentioned in any DML statements, even though they are often used behind the scene.

Assume our PHONE table created previously in this chapter has been populated with records. Assume you issue the following query:

```
SELECT *
FROM phone
WHERE PHONE_CUSTID_FN = 152
```

The RDBMS first checks if the index exists on the condition column (PHONE_CUSTID_FN). If the answer is yes, the index is used to determine the physical location of the corresponding rows (i.e., the two rows with PHONE_CUSTID_FN = 152). If no index is found on the column, the whole table is scanned to find rows with appropriate values.

A database index is similar to an index at the end of a book—it stores pointers to the physical row locations on the disk in the same way a book's index points to the page numbers for the appropriate topics. From another viewpoint, it is similar to a database table with two or more columns: one for the row's physical address, and the rest for the indexed table columns. In other words, index tells the RDBMS where to look for a specific table row (or a group of rows) on the disk as illustrated on Figure 4-4.

As you can see, the table column and the index have the same set of values; the main difference is that in the index, these values are sorted, so it takes much less time to find what you need.

In most databases indexes are implemented as B-Tree indexes, that is, they use the so called B-Tree algorithm that minimizes the number of times the hard disk must be accessed to locate a desired record, thereby speeding up the process. Because a disk drive has mechanical parts, which read and write data far more slowly than purely electronic media, it takes thousands of times longer to access a data element from a hard disk as compared with accessing it from RAM.

B-Trees save time by using nodes with many branches (called children). The simplest version of a B-Tree is called a binary tree because each node has only two children. Figure 4-5 illustrates a search for the value 100 using a binary tree. The algorithm is very simple. Starting at the top, if the top node value is less than what you are looking for, move to the left; if it's greater than 100, go to the right, until the value is found.

PHONE TABLE

PHONE_ID_N	PHONE_PHONENUM_S	PHONE_CUSTID_FN
16	(555) 394-9957	1
53	(555) 394-9956	1
		...
		...
		...
		...
37	(555) 957-8979	152
		...
		...
		...
		...
		...
17	(555) 674-0002	144
		...

NON-UNIQUE INDEX ON PHONE_CUSTID_FN

PHONE_CUSTID_FN	PHYSICAL ADDRESS
1	AAAA8kAABAAAC9WAAP
1	AAAA8kAABAAAC9WAA0
...	
...	
...	
...	
...	
...	
...	
...	
144	AAAA8kAABAAAC9WAA1
152	AAAA8kAABAAAC9WAAk
...	

SERVER HARD DISK

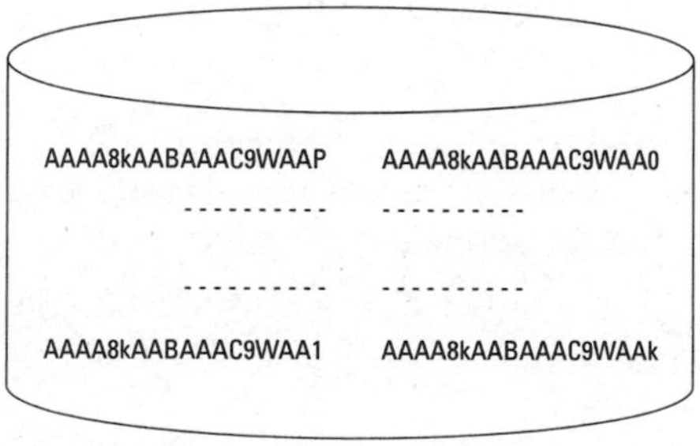

AAAA8kAABAAAC9WAAP AAAA8kAABAAAC9WAA0

---------- ----------

---------- ----------

AAAA8kAABAAAC9WAA1 AAAA8kAABAAAC9WAAk

Figure 4-4: Index use

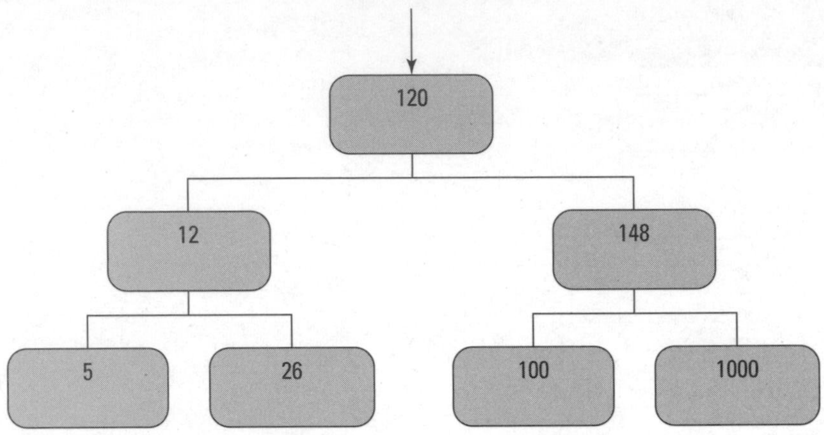

Figure 4-5: B-Tree example

Indexes can be created to be either unique or nonunique. Unique indexes are implicitly created on columns for which a `PRIMARY KEY` or a `UNIQUE` constraint is specified. Duplicate values are not permitted. Nonunique indexes can be created on any column or combination of columns without any regard to duplicates.

Indexes can be created on one column or on multiple columns. The latter can be useful if the columns are often used together in `WHERE` clauses. For example, if some frequently used query looks for a certain customer's orders created on a certain date, you may create a nonunique index on the `ORDHDR_CUSTID_FN` and `ORDHDR_CREATEDATE_D` columns of the `ORDER_HEADER` table.

SQL99 does not specify any standards for indexes (or even require their existence at all), but practically all database vendors provide mechanisms to create indexes, because without them any production database would be unbearably slow.

There is no universal rule on when to create indexes, but some general recommendations can be given.

✦ It usually does not make much sense to create indexes on small tables — they can degrade performance rather than improve it. If the table is only, say, 50 rows long, it might be faster to scan it than to use the B-Tree algorithm.

✦ On large tables, indexes should be created only if the queries that involve indexed column(s) retrieve a small percentage of rows (usually under 15 percent).

✦ Indexes are usually helpful on columns used in table joins. (Primary keys and unique columns are indexed by default; it is often not such a bad idea to index foreign key columns also.)

✦ Indexes slow down DML operations that involve indexed columns — for example, if you update a value on such column, the index column has also to be updated; and if you insert a row, the corresponding index(es) may have to be re-sorted. So if a table is likely to be subjected to frequent updates, inserts, and/or deletes, it is recommended to have fewer indexes.

CREATE INDEX statement

The `CREATE INDEX` statement differs slightly for different implementations. The somewhat simplified syntax is below.

Oracle 9*i*

```
CREATE [UNIQUE | BITMAP] INDEX [<schema>.]<index_name>
ON [<schema>.]<table_name> ({<column> |
                              <column_expression>
                             }[ASC | DESC],...)
[<physical_parameters>];
```

This statement creates a unique index on the `IDX_CUST_NAME` on the `CUST_NAME_S` column of the `CUSTOMER` table with column values stored in descending order:

```
CREATE UNIQUE INDEX idx_cust_name
ON CUSTOMER(cust_name_s DESC)
```

Function-based indexes

Oracle 9*i* also lets you create so-called function-based indexes where instead of a column you can specify a column expression (a deterministic function). For example, you know that customers often query the `CUSTOMER` table using the `LOWER` function in the `WHERE` clause:

```
...
WHERE LOWER(cust_name_s) = 'boswell designs corp.'
...
```

In this situation, a function-based index might make sense:

```
CREATE UNIQUE INDEX idx_cust_name
ON CUSTOMER(LOWER(cust_name_s))
```

Bitmap indexes

The BITMAP keyword indicates that an index is to be created with a bitmap for each distinct key rather than indexing each row. Oracle recommends creating bitmap indexes on columns with low cardinality, that is, columns such as hypothetical GENDER and MARITAL_STATUS columns that would likely have few distinct values.

In the ACME database, order status can be a good candidate for a bitmap index because there are only four possible statuses for an order (COMPLETE, INVOICED, SHIPPED, and CANCELLED). The example below creates bitmap index IDX_ORDHDR_STATUS on the ORDHDR_STATUSID_FN column of the ORDER_HEADER table:

```
CREATE BITMAP INDEX idx_ordhdr_status
ON order_header (ordhdr_statusid_fn)
```

Function-based and bitmap indexes are available in Oracle Enterprise Edition only, so you will get an error if you try to execute the foregoing statement on the Personal or Standard versions.

Physical storage clause

As we mentioned before, you can specify separate tablespaces for table data and table indexes (and it does make sense from the database performance point of view). The syntax is the same as for CREATE TABLE (the example below assumes tablespace INDEX01 exists in your database):

```
CREATE UNIQUE INDEX idx_cust_name
ON CUSTOMER(cust_name_s)
TABLESPACE INDEX01
```

DB2 UDB 8.1

Here is the simplified DB2 syntax to create an index:

```
CREATE [UNIQUE] INDEX [<schema>.]<index_name>
ON [<schema>.]<table_name> (<column_name> [ASC | DESC],...)
```

This statement creates unique index IDX_CUST_NAME_ALS on CUST_NAME_S and CUST_ALIAS_S columns of CUSTOMER table with column values stored in default (ascending) order:

```
CREATE UNIQUE INDEX idx_cust_name_als
ON CUSTOMER(cust_name_s, cust_alias_s)
```

Clustered Indexes

MS SQL Server allows you to create clustered indexes by specifying CLUSTERED keyword. (See the CREATE INDEX syntax described previously.)

The concept is very similar to one with index-organized tables in Oracle—the actual table rows are with the index and the physical order of rows is the same as their indexed order; that is, the rows are re-sorted every time a new one is inserted (or deleted). Only one clustered index is allowed on a table (or view) at a time; thus, you can create a clustered index on a column, drop it later, and create a clustered index on another column, but you can't create two clustered indexes on the same table simultaneously as data in the table can only be physically organized in *one* order.

These statements create the table SALESMAN and unique clustered index on its SALESMAN_CODE_S column.

```
CREATE TABLE SALESMAN
(
    SALESMAN_ID_N          INTEGER         NOT NULL,
    SALESMAN_CODE_S        VARCHAR(2)      NOT NULL,
    SALESMAN_NAME_S        VARCHAR(50)     NOT NULL,
    SALESMAN_STATUS_S      CHAR(1)         DEFAULT 'Y',
    CONSTRAINT CHK_SALESSTATUS CHECK
               (SALESMAN_STATUS_S in ('N', 'Y'))
)

CREATE UNIQUE CLUSTERED INDEX idx_sales_code
ON SALESMAN (salesman_code_s)
```

The default for a CREATE INDEX statement is NONCLUSTERED except for indexes on the primary key columns that are automatically created with CLUSTERED.

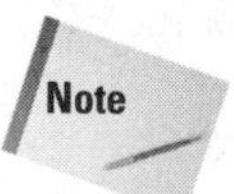

You cannot specify a physical location for the index in a CREATE INDEX statement in DB2; all indexes for a table will be created either in the default tablespace or in a tablespace specified in the CREATE TABLE or ALTER TABLE INDEX IN clause.

MS SQL Server 2000

To create an index in MS SQL Server, use this syntax:

```
CREATE [UNIQUE] [CLUSTERED | NONCLUSTERED] INDEX <index_name>
ON <table_name> | <view_name> ( column [ ASC | DESC ],...)
[ON filegroup]
```

The syntax is very similar to DB2. You can specify a filegroup to create the index on. This statement creates the unique index IDX_CUST_NAME_ALS on the CUST_NAME_S and CUST_ALIAS_S columns of the CUSTOMER table physically stored on filegroup INDEX01 (assuming it exists):

```
CREATE UNIQUE INDEX idx_cust_name_als
ON CUSTOMER(cust_name_s, cust_alias_s)
ON INDEX01
```

In MS SQL Server you can create indexes on views. The view definition must be deterministic and schema bound.

Views

The most common *view* definition describes it as a virtual table. Database users can select rows and columns from a view, join it with other views and tables, limit, sort, group the query results, and so on. Actually, in most cases, users wouldn't even know if they were selecting values from a view or from a table. The main difference is that, unlike tables, views do not take physical disk space. View definitions are stored in RDBMS as compiled queries that dynamically populate data to be used as virtual tables for users' requests.

The details are implementation-specific — RDBMS can create a temporary table behind the scene, populate it with actual rows, and use it to return results from a user's query. The database engine may also combine a user's query with an internal view definition (which is, as you already know, also a query) and execute the resulting query to return data, and so on — from a user's viewpoint, it does not matter at all.

Views are used in many different ways. For example, they can combine data from multiple tables in a more user-friendly form or enforce security rules by making available for users certain horizontal or vertical slices of data (more about security in Chapter 12). In this chapter, you'll learn how to create different types of views.

CREATE VIEW statement

This section explains the CREATE VIEW statement for different RDBMS implementations.

SQL99

Here is the SQL99 syntax for a CREATE VIEW statement:

```
CREATE VIEW <view_name> [(<column_name>,...)]
AS <select_statement>
[WITH [CASCADED | LOCAL] CHECK OPTION]
```

Column names

The column_name list is optional in most cases — if it's skipped, the view columns will be named based on the column names in the SELECT statement; it becomes mandatory though if at least one of the following conditions is true:

✦ Any two columns would otherwise have the same name (ambiguity problem).

✦ Any column contains a computed value (including concatenated strings) and the column is not aliased.

SELECT statement and updatable views

The select_statement can be virtually any valid SELECT statement with some minimal restrictions. For example, the ORDER BY clause cannot be included in view definition, but GROUP BY can be used instead; the view definition cannot be circular; thus, view cannot be referenced in its own select_statement clause, and so on.

Views can be updatable or not updatable. If a view is updatable, that means you can use its name in DML statements to actually update, insert, and delete the underlying table's rows. A view can be updatable only if all these rules hold:

✦ The select_statement does not contain any table joins; that is, the view is based on one and only one table or view. (In the latter case, the underlying view must also be updatable.)

✦ All underlying table's mandatory (NOT NULL) columns are present in the view definition.

✦ The underlying query does not contain set operations like UNION, EXCEPT, or INTERSECT; the DISTINCT keyword is also not allowed.

✦ No aggregate functions or expressions can be specified in the select_statement clause.

✦ The underlying query cannot have a GROUP BY clause.

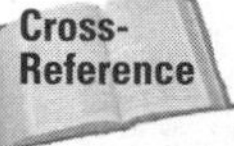

The SELECT statement is covered in detail in Chapters 8 and 9.

View constraints

SQL99 does not allow creating explicit constraints on views, but the CHECK OPTION can be viewed as some kind of a constraint. This clause can only be specified for updatable views and prohibits you from using DML statements on any underlying table's rows that are not visible through the view. The CASCADED option (default) means that if a view is based on another view(s), the underlying view(s) are also checked. The LOCAL keyword would only enforce checking at the level of the view created with this option.

Oracle 9*i*

Oracle has the following syntax to create a view:

```
CREATE [OR REPLACE] [FORCE] VIEW [<schema>.]<view_name>
[(<column_name> <column_constrnt>,... [<view_level_constrnt>])]
AS <select_statement>
[WITH {[READ ONLY | CHECK OPTION [<constrnt name>]]}];
```

The `OR REPLACE` clause (often used when creating many Oracle objects—stored procedures, functions, packages, etc.) basically tells RDBMS to drop the view if it already exists, and then re-create it with the new syntax. This is a very practical feature, but it has to be used with care—if you already have a view with the exact same name, Oracle will just replace the old object definition with the new one without giving you any warning.

The pseudocode for `CREATE OR REPLACE view_name` is:

```
IF EXISTS (view_name) THEN
   DROP VIEW view_name
   CREATE VIEW view_name view_definition
...
END IF
```

For example, this statement creates view `V_CUSTOMER_STATUS` if it does not exist, or replaces the old definition for `V_CUSTOMER_STATUS` if it is present.

```
CREATE OR REPLACE VIEW v_customer_status
(
  name,
  status
)
AS
SELECT  cust_name_s,
        cust_status_s
FROM    customer;
```

The view columns are

```
Name                    Null?      Type
---------------------- --------   ------------
NAME                    NOT NULL   VARCHAR2(50)
STATUS                  NOT NULL   VARCHAR2(1)
```

In the latter case, you would get an error if the OR REPLACE clause is skipped:

```
CREATE VIEW v_customer_status
(
  name,
  status
)
AS
SELECT   cust_name_s,
         cust_status_s
FROM     customer;
ORA-00955: name is already used by an existing object
```

The column names / constraints clause is optional:

```
CREATE OR REPLACE VIEW v_customer_status
AS
SELECT   cust_name_s,
         cust_status_s
FROM     customer;
```

Note that in this case Oracle gives view columns the same names as in underlying table:

```
Name                         Null?       Type
---------------------------- --------    ----------------
CUST_NAME_S                  NOT NULL    VARCHAR2(50)
CUST_STATUS_S                NOT NULL    VARCHAR2(1)
```

Oracle 9*i* allows you to specify integrity constraints on the view column or view as a whole, but does not enforce those constraints, so they are declarative only.

The WITH READ ONLY clause makes the view nonupdatable even if it satisfies all conditions for updatable views listed previously:

```
CREATE OR REPLACE VIEW v_phone_number
(
  phone_id,
  phone_number
)
AS
SELECT   phone_id_n,
phone_phonenum_s
```

```
FROM      phone
WHERE     phone_type_s = 'PHONE'
WITH READ ONLY;
```

```
UPDATE    v_phone_number
SET       phone_number = NULL
WHERE     phone_id = 1;
ORA-01733: virtual column not allowed here
```

The `WITH CHECK` option is basically the same as described for SQL99 except `CASCADE/LOCAL` keywords are not available (the default behavior is always `CASCADE`):

```
CREATE OR REPLACE VIEW v_fax_number
(
  fax_id,
  fax_number
)
AS
SELECT    phone_id_n,
          phone_phonenum_s
FROM      phone
WHERE     phone_type_s = 'FAX'
WITH CHECK OPTION;
```

DB2 UDB 8.1

To create a view in DB2, use this syntax:

```
CREATE VIEW [<schema>.]<view_name>
[(<column_name>,...)]
AS {<select_statement> | <values_statement>}
[WITH [CASCADED | LOCAL] CHECK OPTION]
```

The only clause in DB2's `CREATE VIEW` statement that does not look familiar from the SQL99 standards point of view is the `values_statement`, which allows for creating a view that does not refer to an actual table, but rather contains its own list of values:

```
CREATE VIEW v_exchange_rate
(
 currency_name,
 exchange_rate,
 converted_price
)
AS VALUES
 ('Canadian Dollars', CAST (0.6331458594 AS DECIMAL(20,10)), NULL),
 ('Euro', CAST (0.9761179317 AS DECIMAL(20,10)), NULL),
 ('Japanese Yen', CAST (0.0083339039 AS DECIMAL(20,10)), NULL)
```

```
db2 => SELECT * FROM v_exchange_rate

CURRENCY_NAME         EXCHANGE_RATE      CONVERTED_PRICE
----------------      --------------     ---------------
Canadian Dollars      0.6331458594                     0
Euro                  0.9761179317                     0
Japanese Yen          0.0083339039                     0

3 record(s) selected.
```

DB2 does not perform implicit data type conversion, so we have to use functions CAST and INTEGER in the foregoing example. More about conversion functions in Chapter 10.

The view created in the foregoing example can be used in a way similar to how temporary tables are used—for example, the CONVERTED_PRICE column can be populated dynamically based on data from other tables or views.

MS SQL Server 2000

MS SQL 2000 syntax is

```
CREATE VIEW [[<database_name>.]<owner>.]<view_name>
[(<column_name>,...)]
[WITH {ENCRYPTION | SCHEMABINDING | VIEW_METADATA,...}]
AS select_statement
[WITH CHECK OPTION]
```

MS SQL provides some additional options with the CREATE VIEW statement.

The WITH ENCRYPTION clause gives you the ability to encrypt the system table columns containing the text of the CREATE VIEW statement. The feature can be used, for example, to hide proprietary code:

```
CREATE VIEW v_phone_number
(
  phone_id,
  phone_number
)
WITH ENCRYPTION
AS
SELECT   phone_id_n,
phone_phonenum_s
FROM     phone
WHERE    phone_type_s = 'PHONE'
WITH CHECK OPTION
```

The WITH SCHEMABINDING clause binds the view to the schema (more about schemas later in this chapter):

```
CREATE VIEW dbo.v_phone_number
(
  phone_id,
  phone_number
)
WITH SCHEMABINDING
AS
SELECT   phone_id_n,
phone_phonenum_s
FROM     dbo.phone
WHERE    phone_type_s = 'PHONE'
```

The WITH VIEW_METADATA clause specifies that SQL Server returns to the calling application that uses OLE DB, ODBC, or DBLIB information about the view rather than about underlying tables.

OLE DB, ODBC, DBLIB programming interfaces (API) are covered in more detail in Chapter 16.

Creating complex views

We already mentioned that you can create a view based on practically any SELECT statement (with some insignificant limitations). The SELECT statement itself is one of the most difficult SQL topics and will be covered in detail in later chapters. Examples below are to illustrate the main concepts used when creating a complex view.

Simulating OR REPLACE Clause in MS SQL Server

We mentioned before that Oracle's `OR REPLACE` clause can be a very useful feature. MS SQL Server does not have it, but it can easily be simulated using this syntax:

```
IF EXISTS (
 SELECT table_name
 FROM   information_schema.views
 WHERE  table_name = 'V_CUSTOMER_STATUS'
)
DROP VIEW V_CUSTOMER_STATUS
GO
CREATE VIEW v_customer_status
(
  name,
  status
)
AS
SELECT cust_name_s,
       cust_status_s
FROM   customer
```

This example uses the MS SQL Server built-in procedural language Transact SQL that is widely used by MS SQL Server developers but is not a part of standard SQL (which is non-procedural by definition).

Another option (for all "big three" databases) is to use `ALTER VIEW` statement described in Chapter 5.

Join view with GROUP BY clause and aggregate function

`V_CUSTOMER_TOTALS` displays the total calculated order price grouped by the `CUSTOMER_NAME` and then by `ORDER_NUMBER` fields:

```
CREATE VIEW v_customer_totals
(
   customer_name,
   order_number,
   total_price
)
AS
(
 SELECT   customer.cust_name_s,
          order_header.ordhdr_nbr_s,
          sum(product.prod_price_n * order_line.ordline_ordqty_n)
 FROM     customer,
          order_header,
          order_line,
          product
```

```
WHERE    customer.cust_id_n = order_header.ordhdr_custid_fn
AND      order_header.ordhdr_id_n = order_line.ordline_ordhdrid_fn
AND      product.prod_id_n = order_line.ordline_prodid_fn
AND      order_line.ordline_ordqty_n IS NOT NULL
GROUP BY customer.cust_name_s,
         order_header.ordhdr_nbr_s
)
```

View based on another view example

The V_CUSTOMER_TOTALS_OVER_15000 view displays the same data as its underlying view V_CUSTOMER_TOTALS but only for orders with a total price over $15,000:

```
CREATE VIEW    v_customer_totals_over_15000
AS
SELECT         *
FROM           v_customer_totals
WHERE          total_price > 15000
```

View with UNION example

The V_CONTACT_LIST view displays the combined list of customers and salesmen with their phone numbers and contact types (customer or salesman):

```
CREATE VIEW v_contact_list
(
 name,
 phone_number,
 contact_type
)
AS
SELECT   cust_name_s,
         phone_phonenum_s,
         'customer'
FROM     customer,
         phone
WHERE    cust_id_n = phone_custid_fn
AND      phone_type_s = 'PHONE'
UNION
SELECT   salesman_name_s,
         phone_phonenum_s,
         'salesperson'
FROM     salesman,
         phone
WHERE    salesman_id_n = phone_salesmanid_fn
AND      phone_type_s = 'PHONE'
```

UNION is one of the set operators used to combine the results of two or more SQL queries. The theoretical aspect of the set operators is covered in detail in Appendix L; the practical part is discussed in Chapter 7.

View with subquery

V_WILE_BESS_ORDERS displays orders for customer WILE BESS COMPANY:

```
CREATE VIEW v_wile_bess_orders
(
 order_number,
 order_date
)
AS
SELECT    ordhdr_nbr_s,
          ordhdr_orderdate_d
FROM      order_header
WHERE     ordhdr_custid_fn IN
   (
    SELECT  cust_id_n
    FROM    customer
    WHERE   cust_name_s = 'WILE BESS COMPANY'
   )
```

The foregoing examples will work in all our three RDBMS. Some of the SELECT statements used to create the views will be covered in Chapters 8 and 9.

Aliases and Synonyms

Different databases are organized in quite different ways. Even the word *database* itself has completely different meanings in different RDBMS implementations. For example, an Oracle database is a totally self-contained and independent entity with its own set of users, tables, indexes, and other objects invisible to other databases. Each Oracle database user can have his/her own tables, views, indexes, and so on. (In Oracle terms USER and SCHEMA are often used as synonyms which adds confusion.) To access objects that belong to another user (or are within another schema), you have to be granted appropriate permissions (see Chapter 12) and you also have to use *fully qualified names* (schema_name.object_name). For example, if USER1 wants to select records from SHIPMENT table that belongs to USER3, the query would look like this:

```
SELECT *
FROM USER3.SHIPMENT;
```

Assuming `SHIPMENT` *always* means `USER3.SHIPMENT` for `USER1`, typing fully qualified name makes queries longer and less readable.

The synonyms are especially important when users who don't own objects need to access the database using an application with embedded SQL (discussed in Chapter 15). The programming effort to make such applications work properly without synonyms would increase tremendously.

Figure 4-6 illustrates Oracle's database organization.

DATABASE

USER1	USER2	USER3		USERn
CUSTOMER	ORDER	SHIPMENT		EMPLOYEE
ADDRESS	PRODUCT	VIEW1		SALARY
PHONE	VIEW1	VIEW2	...	PAYROLL
VIEW1	VIEW2	VIEW3		VACATION
...	...	...		...

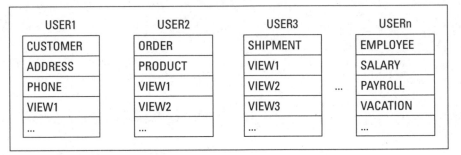

Figure 4-6: Database organization in Oracle

The Oracle RDBMS lets you to create synonyms to deal with the problem. A *synonym* is a name that translates into another name whenever it is referenced. In other words, we can say that a synonym is an alternative name for a database object. You can create the synonym `SHIPMENT` for `USER3.SHIPMENT` and use it any time you need to access the `USER3.SHIPMENT` table.

DB2 UDB organization is quite similar; a database object that is simply a different name for another database object is called `ALIAS`.

The structure of MS SQL Server is different. There can be many databases within a single SQL Server. Users (or *logins*) are created on the server level and can have access to many databases while the database objects belong to a single owner (usually called *dbo*). See Figure 4-7.

SQL99

Synonyms and aliases are not a part of SQL99 standards.

SQL SERVER

DATABASE USERS

USER1	USER2	USER3	...	DBO

USER DATABASES

DATABASE1	DATABASE2	DATABASE3		DATABASEn
CUSTOMER	ORDER	SHIPMENT		EMPLOYEE
ADDRESS	PRODUCT	VIEW1		SALARY
PHONE	VIEW1	VIEW2	...	PAYROLL
VIEW1	VIEW2	VIEW3		VACATION
...	...	...		...

SYSTEM DATABASES

MASTER	MODEL	TEMPDB
SYSTABLE1	SYSTABLE1	SYSTABLE1
SYSTABLE2	SYSTABLE2	SYSTABLE2
...	...	...
SYSVIEW1	SYSVIEW1	SYSVIEW1
...	...	...

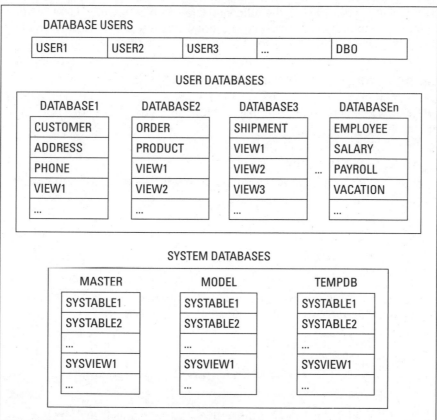

Figure 4-7: Database organization in MS SQL Server

Oracle 9*i* CREATE SYNONYM statement

The syntax for the `CREATE SYNONYM` statement is

```
CREATE [PUBLIC] SYNONYM [<schema>.]<synonym_name>
FOR [<schema>.]<object_name>[@<dblink>];
```

Public versus private synonyms

In Oracle, you can create public synonyms accessible to all database users or private ones visible only to their owners. Use keyword `PUBLIC` if you want to create a public synonym or skip it otherwise. (Keyword `PRIVATE` is invalid.)

Types of objects you can create synonyms for

You can create synonyms for the following Oracle objects: table, view, sequence, stored procedure, function, package, materialized view, and Java class schema object. You can also create a synonym for another synonym.

Creating synonyms for remote database objects

You can create synonyms for objects located in remote databases assuming a *database link* exists for those databases. More about database links later in this chapter.

CREATE SYNONYM examples

The following example creates the public synonym SHIPMENT for a hypothetical table USER3.SHIPMENT:

```
CREATE PUBLIC SYNONYM shipment
FOR user3.shipment;
```

The next statement illustrates the creation of private synonym EMP for a USERn.EMPLOYEE table in USER2 schema:

```
CREATE SYNONYM user2.emp
FOR usern.employee;
```

Note that you could skip USER2 if the above statement was issued by USER2 him/herself; it is mandatory though if the synonym EMP is being created by, say, the database administrator for USER2.

Even though synonyms can be very useful, they also can cause lots of confusion. The most typical situation is when a user has objects in his/her schema with exactly the same names as public or private synonyms. Oracle tries to resolve names looking in the users' schema first, and if the name is found, RDBMS assumes that's the one to use. So, if there are views USER1.VIEW1 and USER2.VIEW1 in the database, and there is also public synonym VIEW1 for USER2.VIEW1 that is supposed to be used in all user queries, USER1 might have serious program errors (if the columns of his/her VIEW1 are different from USER2.VIEW1). Or, which is sometimes even worse because it's more difficult to notice, incorrect results (if the column definitions are identical, but the views use different underlying tables or join them in a different way).

In Oracle you can create synonyms for nonexistent objects; if the objects are created later they can be referred using those synonyms. You can also create synonyms for objects you don't have privileges to access, but doing so *will not* give you an access to those objects.

DB2 UDB 8.1 CREATE ALIAS/SYNONYM statement

You can use either the CREATE SYNONYM or the CREATE ALIAS statement. Aliases can be created for tables, views, or other aliases. The syntax is

```
CREATE {ALIAS | SYNONYM} <alias_name>
FOR <object_name>
```

In DB2, you cannot create an alias with a name identical to one of a table, view, or another alias that already exists in the current database. That resolves the problem described in the previous section about Oracle's synonyms, but makes using aliases in DB2 less flexible.

Here are examples that create aliases in DB2:

```
CREATE ALIAS shipmt
FOR user3.shipment
```

```
CREATE ALIAS emp
FOR usern.employee
```

Note that the following statement returns an error (assuming you are using objects shown in Figure 4-6) because the table named SHIPMENT exists in schema USER3:

```
CREATE PUBLIC SYNONYM SHIPMENT
FOR USER3.SHIPMENT;
```

Like Oracle, DB2 allows you to create synonyms for objects that do not yet exist, though a warning will be issued.

MS SQL Server 2000

MS SQL Server does not let you create aliases or synonyms. This limitation is justified by its database structure (Figure 4-7).

Schemas

A *schema* is a logical database object holder. SQL99 defines a schema as a named group of related objects. Creating schemas can be useful when objects have *circular* references, that is, when we need to create two tables each with a foreign key referencing the other table. Different implementations treat schemas in slightly different ways.

CREATE SCHEMA statement

The CREATE SCHEMA statement has different meanings in SQL99, Oracle, DB2, and MS SQL Server.

SQL99

SQL99 states that the CREATE SCHEMA statement creates a group of objects that somehow logically relate to each other; the group has a name that is called *schema name*. Also, you can grant privileges on these objects within the CREATE SCHEMA statement. The syntax is

```
CREATE SCHEMA
  {<schema_name> |
   AUTHORIZATION <authorization_id> |
   <schema_name> AUTHORIZATION <authorizat_id>
  }
<create_object_statement>,...
<grant_privilege_statement>,...
```

The schema creator usually owns the objects within the schema unless otherwise specified by using a different authorization_id.

Objects that can be created as a part of a schema include tables, views, domains, assertions, character sets, collations, and translations; you can grant any valid privileges within the grant_privilege_statement clause.

Creation of domains, assertions, character sets, collations, and translations are not valid operations in all our three major databases even though they are all part of SQL99 standards.

The GRANT PRIVILEGE statement is covered in Chapter 12 (SQL and RDBMS Security).

Oracle 9*i*

We already mentioned that in Oracle terminology the word *schema* is almost identical to *user*. You still can use the CREATE SCHEMA statement in Oracle, but the only use for that operation would be to create multiple objects in a single transaction.

The CREATE SCHEMA statement *does not* actually create a schema in Oracle. The schema is automatically created when you create a user (see Chapter 12).

The syntax for CREATE SCHEMA is

```
CREATE SCHEMA AUTHORIZATION <schema=your_user_name>
<create_object_statement>,...
<grant_privilege_statement>,...
;
```

The schema name must be the same as your Oracle user ID, otherwise the statement will fail. The valid objects to create include tables and views; you can grant any valid object privileges on them to anybody. The following example creates two tables in hypothetical schema ACMETEST (i.e., we assume that the statement is run by user ACMETEST that does not exist in the ACME test database) and gives permissions on them to user ACME:

```
CREATE SCHEMA AUTHORIZATION ACMETEST
CREATE TABLE address
(
    addr_id_n           INT CONSTRAINT pk_addrprimary PRIMARY KEY,
    addr_custid_fn      INT,
    addr_salesmanid_fn INT CONSTRAINT fk_addr_salesman
                            REFERENCES salesman (salesman_id_n)
                            ON DELETE CASCADE,
    addr_address_s      VARCHAR2(60),
    addr_type_s         VARCHAR2(8) CONSTRAINT chk_addr_type
                                  CHECK
                                  (addr_type_s IN ('BILLING', 'SHIPPING')),
    addr_city_s         VARCHAR2(18) CONSTRAINT nn_addr_city   NOT NULL,
    addr_state_s        CHAR(2),
    addr_zip_s          VARCHAR2(10)    NOT NULL,
    addr_country_s      CHAR(3)
 )
CREATE TABLE salesman
(
  salesman_id_n       INT  CONSTRAINT pk_salesmanprim PRIMARY KEY,
  salesman_code_s     VARCHAR2 (2)  CONSTRAINT uk_salescode UNIQUE,
  salesman_name_s     VARCHAR2 (50)  NOT NULL,
  salesman_status_s   CHAR (1)   CONSTRAINT chk_salesstatus
                                 CHECK
                                 (salesman_status_s in ('N', 'Y'))
)
GRANT ALL ON salesman TO ACME
GRANT ALL ON address TO ACME
;
```

The first CREATE TABLE statement will fail if you didn't create the two tables *as a part of one transaction* because it refers to the nonexistent SALESMAN table (constraint FK_ADDR_SALESMAN).

If any statement within CREATE SCHEMA fails, all other statements are also ignored.

DB2 UDB 8.1

The DB2 CREATE SCHEMA statement seems to be closer to SQL99 standards. The syntax is

```
CREATE SCHEMA {<schema_name> |
               AUTHORIZATION <authorization_id> |
               <schema_name> AUTHORIZATION <authorization_id>
              }
<create_object_statement>,...
<grant_privilege_statement>,...
```

The valid objects to create within the create_object_statement clause are tables, views, and indexes. The owner of the schema is either authorization_id or (if not specified) the user who issued the CREATE SCHEMA statement:

```
CREATE SCHEMA ACMETEST AUTHORIZATION ACMETEST
CREATE TABLE address
(
    addr_id_n           INT NOT NULL CONSTRAINT
                                     pk_addrprimary PRIMARY KEY,
    addr_custid_fn      INT,
    addr_salesmanid_fn  INT CONSTRAINT fk_addr_salesman
                            REFERENCES salesman (salesman_id_n)
                            ON DELETE CASCADE,
    addr_address_s      VARCHAR(60),
    addr_type_s         VARCHAR(8) CONSTRAINT chk_addr_type
                        CHECK
                        (addr_type_s IN ('BILLING', 'SHIPPING')),
    addr_city_s         VARCHAR(18) CONSTRAINT nn_addr_city   NOT NULL,
    addr_state_s        CHAR(2),
    addr_zip_s          VARCHAR(10)    NOT NULL,
    addr_country_s      CHAR(3)
 )
CREATE TABLE salesman
(
  salesman_id_n       INT  NOT NULL  CONSTRAINT
                                     pk_salesmanprim PRIMARY KEY,
  salesman_code_s     VARCHAR (2)  NOT NULL CONSTRAINT uk_salescode UNIQUE,
  salesman_name_s     VARCHAR (50)  NOT NULL,
  salesman_status_s   CHAR (1)   CONSTRAINT chk_salesstatus
                                 CHECK
                                 (salesman_status_s in ('N', 'Y'))
)
GRANT ALL ON salesman TO ACME
GRANT ALL ON address TO ACME
```

MS SQL Server 2000

MS SQL Server provides this syntax to create a schema:

```
CREATE SCHEMA AUTHORIZATION <owner>
<create_object_statement>,...
<grant_privilege_statement>,...
```

The owner must have a valid security account in the database. The statement below assumes the existence of account ACMETEST:

```
CREATE SCHEMA AUTHORIZATION ACMETEST
CREATE TABLE address
(
    addr_id_n           INT CONSTRAINT pk_addrprimary PRIMARY KEY,
    addr_custid_fn      INT,
    addr_salesmanid_fn  INT CONSTRAINT fk_addr_salesman
                            REFERENCES salesman (salesman_id_n)
                            ON DELETE CASCADE,
    addr_address_s      VARCHAR(60),
    addr_type_s         VARCHAR(8) CONSTRAINT chk_addr_type
                                   CHECK
                                   (addr_type_s IN ('BILLING', 'SHIPPING')),
    addr_city_s         VARCHAR(18) CONSTRAINT nn_addr_city   NOT NULL,
    addr_state_s        CHAR(2),
    addr_zip_s          VARCHAR(10)    NOT NULL,
    addr_country_s      CHAR(3)
 )
CREATE TABLE salesman
(
  salesman_id_n       INT  CONSTRAINT pk_salesmanprim PRIMARY KEY,
  salesman_code_s     VARCHAR (2)  not null CONSTRAINT uk_salescode UNIQUE,
  salesman_name_s     VARCHAR (50)  NOT NULL,
  salesman_status_s   CHAR (1)   CONSTRAINT chk_salesstatus
                                 CHECK
                                 (salesman_status_s in ('N', 'Y'))
)
GRANT ALL ON salesman TO ACME
GRANT ALL ON ADDRESS TO ACME
```

Other SQL99 and Implementation-Specific Objects

By now you probably realize that SQL standards exist more in theory than in real life. SQL99 defines many objects that are implemented in none of our three major databases. In its turn, every vendor has its own unique set of database object types not used in other RDBMS implementations and/or not described in SQL99 standards.

Domains (SQL99)

A *domain* is a database object that can be used as an alternative to a data type when defining table columns. In addition to a data type, it can optionally specify a default value, a collation, and a set of constraints. The syntax is

```
CREATE DOMAIN <domain_name> [AS] <datatype>
[DEFAULT <default_value>]
[<constraint_definition>,...]
[COLLATE <collation_name>]
```

As we mentioned before, domains are not implemented by Oracle, DB2, or MS SQL Server, though they all have some kind of functionality to achieve similar goals. (For example, CREATE DISTINCT TYPE in DB2, CREATE RULE in MS SQL Server, and so on. See examples in Chapter 3.)

Domains are implemented in Sybase, PostgreSQL, InterBase, Borland, and some other RDBMS vendors.

Tablespaces and filegroups

We already mentioned tablespaces while discussing the process of creating tables and indexes. The concept of tablespace is not particularly intuitive—it's a *logical* structure for *physical* storage. In other words, tablespace is something you refer in your SQL code when you want to specify a physical location of a database object. Tablespace can consist of one or more *datafiles*—special system files where table, index, or any other physical data is stored in binary form. One datafile can only belong to one tablespace. Figure 4-8 shows the relationship between tablespace and datafile.

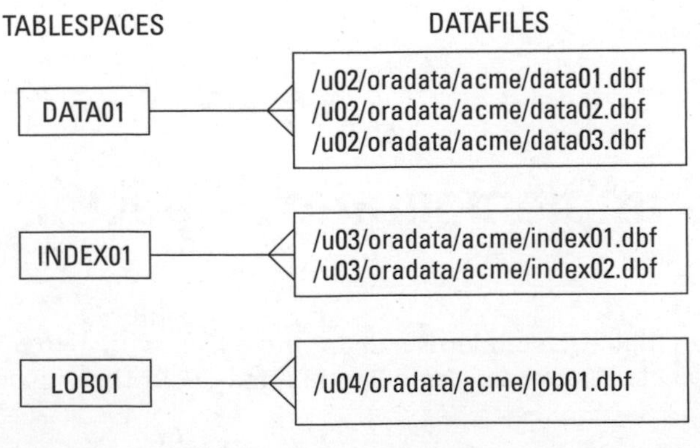

Figure 4-8: Relationship between tablespace and datafile (one-to-many).

When users create tables in, say, the DATA01 tablespace, they have no control over which datafile this table's rows will physically reside: data01, data02, data03, or spread across all three of them. RDBMS will manage that by itself. (Actually, in most cases, users do not need to specify even the tablespace; objects are created in their default tablespaces, i.e., tablespaces assigned to them by the database administrator.)

Note that datafiles are binary files, you can't edit them manually or open them to see table data. Only the RDBMS "knows" their internal proprietary structure and can work with those files.

Oracle 9*i*

Tablespaces in Oracle are created using the CREATE TABLESPACE command. The simplified syntax is

```
CREATE TABLESPACE <tablespace_name>
DATAFILE <file_path_and_name> SIZE <size>[K|M] [REUSE]
[<default_storage_clause>]
```

SIZE is an integer concatenated with letter K (for kilobytes) or M (for megabytes). The default storage specifies the default physical characteristics for objects created in this particular tablespace.

Creating tablespaces in Oracle is not a simple task and is usually handled by the database administrator. They have many optional clauses that are beyond the scope of this book.

The following example creates tablespace DATA01 with one datafile of size one megabyte (assuming standard Oracle9*i* installation on Windows):

```
CREATE TABLESPACE DATA01
DATAFILE 'C:\oracle\ora92\oradata\acme\data01.dbf' SIZE 1M;
```

Oracle creates file data01.dbf in directory C:\oracle\ora92\oradata\acme formatted in Oracle blocks. You will get an error if the file already exists unless the REUSE clause is specified. Now you can try the example from the beginning of this chapter that creates table PHONE in tablespace DATA01.

DB2 UDB 8.1

The CREATE TABLESPACE statement in DB2 is also fairly complex and is normally used by DBA only. The basic syntax is

```
CREATE [REGULAR | LONG] TABLESPACE <tablespace_name>
MANAGED BY [SYSTEM  | DATABASE]
```

```
USING ([FILE | DEVICE] <file_or_device_name> [<size> K|M|G],
...)
[<storage_clause>]
```

The REGULAR clause is the default; you would only create LONG tablespace to store LOB objects.

System-managed tablespace requires less maintenance than database-managed tablespace. Database-managed tablespace in its turn gives more flexibility to an experienced DBA. You cannot use FILE | DEVICE or specify size when creating a system-managed tablespace.

The following code creates regular system-managed tablespace USERDATA01 in directory C:\DB2\DATA01 (assuming the default installation):

```
CREATE TABLESPACE USERDATA01
MANAGED BY SYSTEM
USING ('C:\DB2\DATA01')
```

MS SQL Server 2000

There is no such thing as tablespace in MS SQL Server, but you can create filegroups and add files to them, which is exactly the same concept as using tablespaces in Oracle and DB2. This is simply different terminology and slightly different syntax: you actually use the ALTER DATABASE statement to add filegroups and/or files to a database.

Here is the syntax:

```
ALTER DATABASE
ADD FILEGROUP <filegroup_name>
```

```
ALTER DATABASE
ADD FILE
(
 NAME = <logical_file_name>
 [, FILENAME = <os_file_name>]
 [, SIZE = <size> KB|MB|GB|TG]
 [, <other_physical_parameters>]), ...
 [  TO FILEGROUP <filegroup_name> ]
```

As you can see, the idea is not much different from what you already learned: MS SQL Server *filegroup* is a logical structure, just like tablespace in Oracle and DB2, and a file is an element of physical storage.

Few minor variations to mention here: you can create logical names that are different from their physical OS names; size can be indicated in terabytes in addition to kilobytes, megabytes, and gigabytes, and so on. The following code creates filegroup DATA01 and then adds a file with logical name DATA0101 to it of size 1M:

```
ALTER DATABASE acme
ADD FILEGROUP DATA01

GO

ALTER DATABASE acme
ADD FILE
(
 NAME = DATA0101,
 FILENAME ='C:\Program Files\Microsoft SQL Server\MSSQL\Data\data0101.ndf',
 SIZE = 1MB
)
TO FILEGROUP DATA01
```

Sequences

A *sequence* is a database object with functionality similar to that of identity (discussed previously in this chapter). The main difference is that identity is tied to a table column, and sequence is totally independent from other database objects; thus, multiple users can generate unique numeric values from a sequence and use them for different purposes. The most typical use is to generate primary key values for a table (or for multiple tables).

You can use one sequence to generate primary keys for two or more tables. If you employ the concept of meaningless primary keys, then you don't really care that out of integers from 1 to 10 numbers 1, 2, and 5 will be used to populate primary keys in TABLE1; 3, 7, and 10 will be used for TABLE2; 4, 6, and 8 will become primary key values for TABLE3, and 9 is not used at all as illustrated on Figure 4-9. Still, a more typical approach would be to create a separate sequence for each table's primary key.

In general, a sequence is more flexible than an identity column because it is an independent database object, whereas an identity column is a part of a table definition. For example, sequences can be much more convenient than identity columns when used in a procedural program (C, Java, COBOL, etc.) that populates records for parent/child tables.

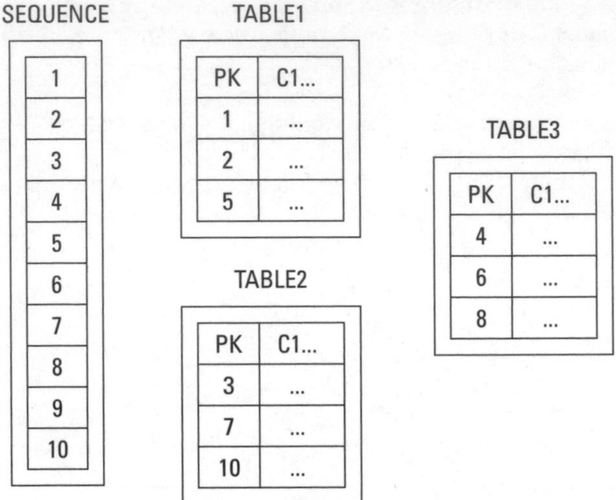

Figure 4-9: Using sequence-generated numbers to populate primary keys in multiple tables

Sequences in Oracle 9*i*

The syntax to create a sequence in Oracle is

```
CREATE SEQUENCE [<schema>.]<sequence_name>
[START WITH <start_value>]
[INCREMENT BY <increment_value>]
[MAXVALUE <max_value> | NOMAXVALUE]
[MINVALUE <min_value> | NOMINVALUE]
[CYCLE | NOCYCLE ]
[CACHE <value> | NOCACHE]
[ORDER | NOORDER]
```

As you probably noticed, most clauses in the CREATE SEQUENCE statement are optional. If you just want to create a sequence that starts with 1 and generates sequential values (2, 3, 4,...) all the way until it reaches the largest possible integer in Oracle (10^{27}), this statement will do:

```
CREATE SEQUENCE my_sequence1;
```

If you need something more complicated, here is what you can do:

Creating ascending and descending sequences

You can create a sequence that starts with a certain value (START WITH clause) and then each next sequence value gets populated according to the value specified in the INCREMENT BY clause. To create a descending sequence, use a negative increment. You would also have to specify the maximum and the minimum sequence values:

```
CREATE SEQUENCE my_sequence2
START WITH 500
INCREMENT BY -10
MAXVALUE 500
MINVALUE 0;
```

Creating cycling sequences

In the previous example, my_sequence2 will generate values 500, 490, 480, 470,...0. After that, you will get an error saying that your sequence goes below the MINVALUE and cannot be instantiated. What you can do is to create a sequence that cycles; that is, after it reaches its maximum (or minimum in the case with a descending sequence), it will simply start over. In the next example sequence, my_sequence3 will restart with 500 again after reaching its minimum value:

```
CREATE SEQUENCE my_sequence3
START WITH 1000
INCREMENT BY -10
MAXVALUE 1000
MINVALUE 0
CYCLE;
```

It's often difficult to understand the difference between START WITH and MINVALUE (or MAXVALUE for descending sequences) clauses. Actually, the difference is only important for cycling sequences. For example, you may want your sequence to start with 100 and then when it reaches its maximum value (for example, 10,000) start over again, but this time not with 100, but rather with 10. In this case, you specify 100 for the START WITH clause and 10 for the MINVALUE clause:

```
CREATE SEQUENCE my_sequence4
START WITH 100
INCREMENT BY 1
MINVALUE 10
MAXVALUE 10000
CYCLE;
```

Caching sequence values

By default, Oracle caches 20 consecutive sequence values in memory for faster access. You can override the default behavior either by specifying a different number of values to cache (10, 100, 1000, or whatever you prefer) or by using the NOCACHE clause that guarantees you sequential values every time you generate values using the sequence. Otherwise the values in memory would be wiped out if, for example, the database has been restarted.

For sequences that cycle, the number of values to cache must be less than the number of values in the cycle.

Guaranteeing the order of sequence values

You may want to guarantee that sequence numbers are generated in order (for example, if you are using them as timestamps) by specifying an ORDER clause. The default is NOORDER.

Oracle does not have identity columns, so sequences are the only option to generate sequential numbers.

Accessing sequences in Oracle

You can generate new sequence values by using SEQUENCE_NAME.NEXTVAL in your SQL code. To access the current sequence value (i.e., the last generated sequence number) use SEQUENCE_NAME.CURRVAL:

```
SQL> SELECT my_sequence4.NEXTVAL
  2  FROM dual;

   NEXTVAL
----------
       102

SQL> SELECT my_sequence4.CURRVAL
  2  FROM dual;

   CURRVAL
----------
       102

SQL> SELECT my_sequence4.CURRVAL
  2  FROM dual;

   CURRVAL
----------
       102
```

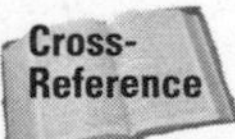

The example above uses a dummy table DUAL that is used in Oracle to select values from "nothing." For more information, see Chapter 10.

To be able to access CURRVAL, you have to generate the sequence value at least once during the current session, or an error will be generated. In a sense, DB2's PREVVAL name is more accurate—you are actually accessing the previously generated value.

DB2 UDB 8.1

The syntax to create a sequence in DB2 is

```
CREATE SEQUENCE <sequence_name> [AS SMALLINT |
                                    INTEGER |
                                    BIGINT |
                                    DECIMAL
                                ]
[START WITH <start_value>]
[INCREMENT BY <increment_value>]
[MAXVALUE <max_value> | NOMAXVALUE]
[MINVALUE <min_value> | NOMINVALUE]
[CYCLE | NOCYCLE]
[CACHE <value> | NOCACHE]
[ORDER | NOORDER]
```

As you can see, it's almost identical to the Oracle syntax; all examples from the previous section would work in DB2. There are a couple of minor differences:

✦ You can specify the data type you want the sequence values to be populated of—it's mainly the precision metter. The default is INTEGER; if you specify DECIMAL data type, the scale must be zero. Oracle always assumes the NUMBER data type.

✦ In DB2, you can create static sequences that would always populate the same value (it's very difficult to imagine why you would need something like that) either by specifying INCREMENT BY 0 or by using same values for MINVALUE and MAXVALUE. Oracle requires that INCREMENT TO be a positive or a negative integer, zero is not permitted; MAXVALUE must be greater than MINVALUE.

Accessing sequences in DB2

You can retrieve either current or previous sequence value using the NEXTVAL and PREVVAL keywords. NEXTVAL is not different from NEXTVAL in Oracle; PREVVAL is an equivalent to Oracle's CURRVAL. The access to the sequence values is slightly different:

```
db2 => SELECT NEXTVAL FOR my_sequence4 AS NETVAL \
db2 (cont.) FROM SYSIBM.SYSDUMMY1

NEXTVAL
------------
```

```
          102

  1 record(s) selected.

db2 => SELECT PREVVAL FOR my_sequence4 AS PREVVAL \
db2 (cont.) FROM SYSIBM.SYSDUMMY1

PREVVAL
-----------
          102

  1 record(s) selected.

db2 => SELECT PREVVAL FOR my_sequence4 AS PREVVAL \
db2 (cont.) FROM SYSIBM.SYSDUMMY1

PREVVAL
-----------
          102

  1 record(s) selected.
```

The SYSIBM.SYSDUMMY1 table in DB2 is an equivalent to Oracle's DUAL. See Chapter 10 for more details.

Materialized views (Oracle 9*i*)

A MATERIALIZED VIEW is yet another Oracle object that contains data and occupies physical space. The name is a bit confusing—you already know that a view is just a compiled query, but the materialized views are more like tables—they have actual rows with data that could be updated dynamically. The closest analogy is summary tables in DB2; although in addition to data aggregation materialized views can be used in many different ways (data warehousing, data replication, and more). In addition to that, materialized views have fewer limitations than DB2 summary tables—most select statements that work with the CREATE VIEW statement can be used to create a materialized view.

The CREATE MATERIALIZED VIEW syntax is quite complex; most clauses are of the database administrator's concern only and require special database security privileges most users don't have. For example, the CREATE MATERIALIZED VIEW privilege allows users to create materialized views; QUERY REWRITE permits users to create materialized views used in query rewrites by optimizer, and so on.

QUERY REWRITE transforms a SQL statement expressed in terms of tables or views into a statement accessing one or more materialized views that are defined on the detail tables. This feature can significantly improve database performance when used properly.

The following examples illustrate a few possible uses for materialized views.

Materialized view refreshed on demand

Materialized view VRM_ORDERLINE_SUMMARY is analogous to the DB2 ORDERLINE_SUMMARY summary table we talked about earlier in the chapter. It summarizes ordered and shipped product quantities by order on demand:

```
CREATE MATERIALIZED VIEW vrm_orderline_summary
BUILD IMMEDIATE
REFRESH FAST ON DEMAND
AS
(
 SELECT    ordline_ordhdrid_fn,
           SUM(ordline_ordqty_n) AS ord_qty_summary,
           SUM(ordline_shipqty_n) AS ship_qty_summary,
           COUNT (*) AS rowcount
 FROM      order_line
 GROUP BY ordline_ordhdrid_fn
);
```

Materialized view refreshed periodically with no user interaction

Materialized view VRM_CONTACT_LIST uses the same select_statement as V_CONTACT_LIST view. The snapshot of records is taken at the moment of the materialized view creation and is refreshed daily at 6 AM:

```
CREATE MATERIALIZED VIEW TEST2
REFRESH START WITH SYSDATE
NEXT (TRUNC(SYSDATE + 1)) + 6/24
AS SELECT    cust_name_s,
             phone_phonenum_s,
             'CUSTOMER' CONTACT
FROM         customer,
             phone
WHERE        cust_id_n = phone_custid_fn
AND          phone_type_s = 'PHONE'
UNION
SELECT       salesman_name_s,
             phone_phonenum_s,
             'SALESPERSON'
FROM         salesman,
             phone
WHERE        salesman_id_n = phone_salesmanid_fn
AND          phone_type_s = 'PHONE';
```

The statement `NEXT (TRUNC(SYSDATE + 1)) + 6/24` in the previous statement adds one day to SYSDATE, truncates the result to get "12 AM tomorrow," and adds 6 hours to it which gives us 6 AM of the following day. More information about the TRUNCATE function and date arithmetic is in Chapter 10.

This materialized view can be used in situations when the use of a regular view is inappropriate, for example, when underlying tables are too large and data retrieval becomes too slow; or when tables used in the `select_statement` physically reside on a remote database and must be transferred over a network; a materialized view can refresh data during off-load time.

The previous examples assume you have the `CREATE MATERIALIZED VIEW` privilege granted to you by a database administrator with the following statement:

```
GRANT CREATE [ANY] MATERIALIZED VIEW TO user_name;
```

More about privileges in Chapter 12.

Database links (Oracle 9*i*)

A *database link* is an object in the local database that enables you to access remote database objects. The remote database does not have to be an Oracle database—you can directly connect to DB2, MS SQL Server, Sybase, or any other RDBMS that supports ODBC or OLE DB protocols. You can refer to a remote table or view in a SQL statement by appending `@<dblink>` to the table or view name (where `<dblink>` is the name of a previously created database link).

CREATE DATABASE LINK statement

The syntax for `CREATE DATABASE LINK` is

```
CREATE [SHARED] [PUBLIC] DATABASE LINK <dblink>
CONNECT TO {[CURRENT_USER |
            <user_name> IDENTIFIED BY <password>]
          }
USING '<connect_string>';
```

The `SHARED` keyword specifies that a single network connection can be used by multiple users; `PUBLIC` means the database link is available to all users, not only to its creator. `CURRENT_USER` can be specified if the remote database user and password are identical to those of whoever is using the database link; otherwise, remote user name and password have to be specified.

The `connect_string` parameter must be a valid service name. (See Oracle's *Net Services Administrator's Guide* for setting service names.) It has to be enclosed by single quotes.

The following command creates database link named DBL_SALES assuming you have a valid service name SALES and pointing to a database where user SALES_MANAGER exists:

```
CREATE DATABASE LINK dbl_sales
CONNECT TO sales_manager IDENTIFIED BY sales123
USING 'SALES';
```

Both DB2 and MS SQL Server also allow you to connect to remote databases. DB2 uses NICKNAMES, and MS SQL Server features Linked Servers and Remote Servers. See vendor-specific documentation for details.

CREATE Statement Cross-Reference

Table 4-1 provides the full list of all objects you can create in the "big three" databases as well as SQL99 CREATE statement standards. Some of the statements were covered in this chapter; some others will be covered later in this book. For example, we'll talk about CREATE USER, CREATE ROLE, and CREATE PROFILE statements in Chapter 12.

Many CREATE statements are for database administrators use only, so you will not find their detailed explanation in the book; refer to vendor-specific documentation for more information.

Table 4-1
Valid CREATE Statements Cross-Reference

Statement	*SQL99*	*Oracle 9i*	*DB2 UDB 8.1*	*MS SQL Server 2000*
CREATE ALIAS			✓	
CREATE ASSERTION	✓			
CREATE BUFFERPOOL			✓	
CREATE CHARACTER SET	✓			
CREATE CLUSTER		✓		
CREATE COLLATION	✓			
CREATE CONTEXT		✓		
CREATE CONTROLFILE		✓		

Continued

Table 4-1 *(continued)*

Statement	*SQL99*	*Oracle 9i*	*DB2 UDB 8.1*	*MS SQL Server 2000*
CREATE DATABASE		✓	✓	✓
CREATE DATABASE LINK		✓		
CREATE DEFAULT				✓
CREATE DIMENSION		✓		
CREATE DIRECTORY		✓		
CREATE DISTINCT TYPE			✓	
CREATE DOMAIN	✓			
CREATE EVENT MONITOR			✓	
CREATE FUNCTION		✓	✓	✓
CREATE FUNCTION MAPPING			✓	
CREATE INDEX		✓	✓	✓
CREATE INDEX EXTENSION			✓	
CREATE INDEXTYPE		✓		
CREATE JAVA		✓		
CREATE LIBRARY		✓		
CREATE MATERIALIZED VIEW		✓		
CREATE MATERIALIZED VIEW LOG		✓		
CREATE METHOD			✓	
CREATE NICKNAME			✓	
CREATE NODEGROUP			✓	
CREATE OPERATOR		✓		
CREATE OUTLINE		✓		
CREATE PACKAGE		✓	✓	
CREATE PACKAGE BODY		✓		
CREATE PFILE		✓		
CREATE PROCEDURE		✓	✓	✓
CREATE PROFILE		✓		
CREATE ROLE	✓	✓		
CREATE ROLLBACK SEGMENT		✓		

Statement	*SQL99*	*Oracle 9i*	*DB2 UDB 8.1*	*MS SQL Server 2000*
CREATE RULE				✓
CREATE SCHEMA	✓	✓	✓	✓
CREATE SEQUENCE		✓	✓	
CREATE SERVER			✓	
CREATE SPFILE		✓		
CREATE STATISTICS				✓
CREATE SYNONYM		✓		
CREATE TABLE	✓	✓	✓	✓
CREATE TABLESPACE		✓	✓	
CREATE TEMPORARY TABLESPACE		✓		
CREATE TRANSFORM			✓	
CREATE TRANSLATION	✓			
CREATE TRIGGER		✓	✓	✓
CREATE TYPE	✓	✓	✓	
CREATE TYPE BODY		✓		
CREATE TYPE MAPPING			✓	
CREATE USER		✓		
CREATE USER MAPPING			✓	
CREATE VIEW	✓	✓	✓	✓
CREATE WRAPPER			✓	

Summary

One of the definitions of a database is "a collection of objects and processes for their manipulation." In a relational database, the objects are created through either standard SQL99 or vendor-specific SQL. The CREATE <object> syntax can be very complicated and usually belongs to the database administrator's domain; nevertheless, understanding how database objects are created is important.

The most important objects introduced in this chapter include table, index, view, materialized view, synonym, schema, and sequence. This list by all means does not cover all objects that could be created within RDBMS using SQL.

The central and most important database object is *table*—a logical concept of a data holder implemented in a database file structure. Tables can be temporary or permanent, according their life span within an RDBMS. Even such a basic concept can be implemented differently by the different vendors. Most differences occur in the context of the `CREATE` syntax employed in temporary tables, whereas the syntaxes used in permanent tables tend to adhere more closely to the SQL standard.

Indexes are not part of the SQL standard specification and are hidden from users. The purpose of an index is to speed up data retrieval from a table. A *view* differs from a table by being populated with data on demand from its base tables (with the exception of materialized views); views are defined by an SQL `SELECT` query and are dependent on the tables this query specifies. Views are used for many reasons, explained in the chapter.

Synonyms are used to facilitate database object referencing by replacing long, fully qualified names with easy-to-use names.

Some other database objects mentioned in the chapter are *domains*, *tablespaces*, *filegroups*, and *constraints*.

Each vendor has chosen to implement a different subset of database objects in its RDBMS software; some of these objects are not part of the standard SQL, and some of the higher-level standard-mandated objects are not implemented. Syntax for creating these objects also differs among the vendors and should be checked against vendors' documentation.

✦ ✦ ✦

CHAPTER 5

Altering and Destroying RDBMS Objects

✦ ✦ ✦ ✦

In This Chapter

Modifying and removing tables

Modifying and removing indexes

Modifying and removing views

Modifying and removing other database objects

✦ ✦ ✦ ✦

Objects created within a database are not cast in stone. The ability to easily change database objects gives an RDBMS a big advantage over nonrelational models because flexibility is built into the relational database concept. This includes the ability to create, modify, and destroy database objects. Needless to say, all our three major vendors provide this ability so as to incur minimal impact on other database entities.

Examples in this chapter assume incremental buildup of the ACME database started in Chapter 4. Constraints implemented in the database scripts included with the CD-ROM may prevent some of the statements from successful execution.

Tables

You already know that the table is the central RDBMS object. In a perfect world you would never have to change anything in a table's structure after it was created. In real life though you need to modify table definitions quite often. Changing business rules are usually the main reason; incorrect initial design is also not uncommon, especially in test environments. The whole idea behind the `ALTER TABLE` statement is to make the table definition changes as fast and as painless as possible. The `DROP TABLE` statement is used to remove a table (both its data and definition) from the database.

ALTER TABLE statement

We are now going to explain how ALTER TABLE is implemented by different vendors.

SQL99

The SQL99 ALTER TABLE syntax is:

```
ALTER TABLE <table_name>
{[ADD [COLUMN] <column_definition>] |
 [ALTER [COLUMN] <column_name> {SET DEFAULT <default> | DROP DEFAULT}] |
 [DROP [COLUMN] <column_name> RESTRICT | CASCADE] |
 [ADD <table_constraint>] |
 [DROP CONSTRAINT <constraint_name> RESTRICT | CASCADE]
};
```

Basically this code defines the syntax for adding or deleting a table column or a default value for a column as well as for dropping a table constraint.

Oracle 9*i*

The ALTER TABLE statement has even more options in Oracle than CREATE TABLE does. The following syntax lists only the ones most important in the context of this book:

```
ALTER TABLE [<qualifier>.]<table_name>
{[<change_physical_attributes>] |
 [ADD <column_name> <datatype> [<size1>[,<size2>]]
     [DEFAULT <default_value>] [<column_constraint>,...]
 ]..., |
 [MODIFY <column_name> <datatype> [<size1>[,<size2>]] |
     [DEFAULT <default_value>] [NULL | NOT NULL]
 ]..., |
 [DROP {COLUMN <column_name> | (<column_name>,...)}
     [CASCADE CONSTRAINTS]
 ] |
 [MODIFY CONSTRAINT <constraint_name> <constraint_state>] |
 [ADD {PRIMARY KEY (<column_name>,...) |
       UNIQUE (<column_name>,...) |
       CONSTRAINT <constraint_name> <constraint_definition>
      }
 ] |
 [DROP {PRIMARY KEY |
        UNIQUE (<column_name>,...) |
        CONSTRAINT <contraint_name> [CASCADE]
       }
 ] |
```

```
  [DISABLE | ENABLE {PRIMARY KEY |
                     UNIQUE (<column_name>,...) |
                     CONSTRAINT <constraint name> |
                     ALL TRIGGERS
                     }
  ] |
  [RENAME TO <new_table_name>]
}
```

Changing physical attributes

Many different physical attributes of a table can be changed in Oracle using the ALTER TABLE statement. For example, it would be very easy to fix once you realized that your table was created in a wrong tablespace. The following example assumes the existence of tablespace DATA01:

```
ALTER TABLE SALESMAN
MOVE TABLESPACE DATA01;
```

In our sample ACME database, all objects were created without explicitly specifying a tablespace. Also, user ACME was created without specifying a default tablespace. That means all tables and indexes are created in SYSTEM tablespace by default, which is absolutely unacceptable in a production database. You now know how to correct it using the ALTER TABLE statement.

See the Oracle documentation for more information on changing table physical attributes.

Adding columns

Often you will need to add a column to an existing table. For example, our ACME database can easily handle situations when a customer has more than one phone number. But now imagine we have a new set of business rules saying that if a customer or a salesman has more than one phone, we need a way to know which number is primary and what kind of phone it is (business, mobile, home, etc.). So, we want to add two new columns to PHONE: PHONE_PRIMARY_S with a default value of Y and PHONE_CATEGORY_S. We also want to specify the range of valid values for PHONE_PRIMARY_S (Y and N). The task is quite simple to implement:

```
ALTER TABLE PHONE
ADD PHONE_PRIMARY_S CHAR(1) DEFAULT 'Y'
    CHECK (PHONE_PRIMARY_S IN ('Y', 'N'))
ADD PHONE_CATEGORY_S CHAR(15);
```

As you can see from this example, Oracle allows you to use one ALTER TABLE statement to add multiple columns at the same time. You can drop multiple columns within one ALTER TABLE statement as well.

If you add a column with a default value to an existing table, each row in the new column is automatically updated with the value specified for DEFAULT.

Modifying existing columns

You can modify columns in a couple of different ways. You can change the column's data type; increase or decrease the size of a CHARACTER or a RAW column (or precision of a NUMERIC column). You can also specify a new default for an existing column and/or add a NOT NULL constraint to it.

As usual, certain restrictions apply. You can decrease the size or precision of a column only if it's empty, that is, if it contains all NULLs. (You can decrease the size and precision with no limitations though.) You also can't add NOT NULL constraint to a column that contains NULLs. (Again, you can do it the other way around.) You can change a column's data type to a compatible data type only (for example, CHAR can be changed to VARCHAR) if the column is not empty; no limitations exist for empty columns.

Only the NOT NULL constraint can be added to a table column using the MODIFY clause of the ALTER TABLE statement. All other constraints can be added, dropped, modified, and disabled using ADD, DROP, DISABLE, ENABLE, and MODIFY CONSTRAINT clauses.

Here are some examples. The column PHONE_CATEGORY_S that we added to PHONE table in our recent example is CHAR(15). We are aware that the CHAR data type is best used when we know exactly how many characters will be stored in the column; otherwise VARCHAR2 is a better choice. Also, we decided to increase the maximum column size to 20 characters because we might want to store larger strings there; but for now we want the default string BUSINESS to be populated in this column for all new rows. We also decided we don't want any NULL values in the PHONE_PRIMARY_S column.

The following statement successfully accomplishes this task:

```
ALTER TABLE PHONE
MODIFY PHONE_PRIMARY_S CHAR(1) NOT NULL
MODIFY PHONE_CATEGORY_S  VARCHAR2(20) DEFAULT 'BUSINESS';
```

This statement works because when we added PHONE_PRIMARY_S column we also specified the default value of Y, so it does not contain any NULL values. Unlike ALTER TABLE ... ADD the above ALTER TABLE ... MODIFY statement does not populate default values for existing columns.

Removing table columns

Now imagine the business rules have changed again, and the columns you added and modified in previous examples are no longer needed. The following statement removes PHONE_PRIMARY_S and PHONE_CATEGORY_S columns from PHONE table:

```
ALTER TABLE PHONE
DROP (PHONE_PRIMARY_S, PHONE_CATEGORY_S);
```

When you drop a column all indexes and/or constraints associated with the column (if any) are also dropped. If the column to be dropped is a parent key of a nontarget column or if a check constraint references both the target and nontarget columns, CASCADE CONSTRAINTS must be specified, or Oracle generates an error.

Modifying constraints

The MODIFY CONSTRAINT clause enables you to change the existing column or table constraints' status of INITIALLY IMMEDIATE to INITIALLY DEFERRED assuming the constraints were created with keyword DEFERRABLE. Assuming Chapter 4 examples, it would probably make sense to issue the following command after the data load is complete:

```
ALTER TABLE SALESMAN
MODIFY CONSTRAINT chk_salesstatus INITIALLY IMMEDIATE;
```

The constraint behavior is now indistinguishable from one of a nondeferrable constraint; that is, the constraint is checked after each DDL statement. When you want to perform another data load, the following statement changes the constraint's behavior again:

```
ALTER TABLE SALESMAN
MODIFY CONSTRAINT chk_salesstatus INITIALLY DEFERRED;
```

Creating new constraints

As with new columns, you might need to create new constraints on the existing table. The situations are usually similar to those when you might need new table columns — for example, when implementing new business rules or amending bad initial designs. For example, you might have realized the salesman's code in the SALESMAN table must be unique. The following statement accomplishes the task:

```
ALTER TABLE salesman
ADD CONSTRAINT uk_salesmancode UNIQUE (salesman_code_s);
```

And here are examples of implementing referential integrity constraints on tables created in Chapter 4:

```
ALTER TABLE customer ADD CONSTRAINT fk_cust_payterms
FOREIGN KEY (cust_paytermsid_fn)
REFERENCES payment_terms (payterms_id_n);
```

```
ALTER TABLE customer ADD CONSTRAINT fk_cust_salesman
FOREIGN KEY (cust_salesmanid_fn)
REFERENCES salesman (salesman_id_n);
```

```
ALTER TABLE order_line ADD CONSTRAINT fk_ordline_ordhdr
FOREIGN KEY (ordline_ordhdrid_fn)
REFERENCES order_header (ordhdr_id_n);
```

```
ALTER TABLE order_line ADD CONSTRAINT fk_ordline_product
FOREIGN KEY (ordline_prodid_fn)
REFERENCES product (prod_id_n);
```

For the full list of ACME tables, indexes, and constraints, refer to Appendix B.

Removing constraints

ALTER TABLE enables you to remove column or table constraints. For example, to remove the unique constraint you just created, use

```
ALTER TABLE SALESMAN
DROP CONSTRAINT uk_salesmancode;
```

Disabling and enabling constraints

In some situations you might want to be able to defer constraint's action:

```
ALTER TABLE SALESMAN
DISABLE CONSTRAINT chk_salesstatus;

Some data load action here...

ALTER TABLE SALESMAN
ENABLE CONSTRAINT chk_salesstatus;
```

As you already know, you can disable/enable constraints only if your table was created with DEFERRABLE constraints. Otherwise you would have to drop and re-create constraints or do some other workarounds described in Chapter 4.

You can also enable or disable all triggers (special database objects discussed in Chapter 14) associated with the specified table using ENABLE | DISABLE ALL TRIGGERS clause.

Renaming a table

You can change the name of a table using a RENAME TO clause. For example, if you (or your boss) decided that name SALESMAN is not politically correct, you can change it to SALESPERSON using this command:

```
ALTER TABLE SALESMAN
RENAME TO SALESPERSON;
```

Please keep in mind that any programs (including your PL/SQL procedures, functions, packages, and triggers that refer the renamed table) will no longer be valid after this change. You would have to find and change all references to the SALESMAN table in your code and recompile the programs.

So, you've found out that's too much of an effort, so you decided to change the name back. No problem:

```
ALTER TABLE SALESPERSON
RENAME TO SALESMAN;
```

DB2 UDB 8.1

The DB2 ALTER TABLE statement allows you to add columns to a table, add or drop constraints, change the length of a column (VARCHAR only), modify identity column properties and summary table options, alter physical attributes, and more. The syntax (simplified for the purpose of this book) is:

```
ALTER TABLE [<qualifier>.]<table_name>
[ADD COLUMN <column_definition>],... |
[ALTER COLUMN [SET DATATYPE VARCHAR <newlength_gt_existinglength>] |
              [<identity_column_options>]
] |
[ADD CONSTRAINT <constraint_definition>] |
[DROP {PRIMARY KEY |
        [FOREIGN KEY | UNIQUE | CHECK | CONSTRAINT] <constraint_name>
      }
] |
[<physical_options>] |
[SET SUMMARY AS {DEFINITION ONLY | <summary_table_definition>}]
```

Adding new columns to a table

The statement below adds two new columns to PHONE:

```
ALTER TABLE PHONE
ADD PHONE_PRIMARY_S  CHAR(1) DEFAULT 'Y'
                     CHECK (PHONE_PRIMARY_S IN ('Y', 'N'))
ADD PHONE_CATEGORY_S CHAR(15);
```

Increasing VARCHAR column size

DB2 has very limited options for modifying existing columns. Virtually all you can do is to increase the size of an existing VARCHAR column:

```
ALTER TABLE CUSTOMER
ALTER COLUMN CUST_ALIAS_S SET DATA TYPE VARCHAR (20)
```

The statement above increases the size of CUST_ALIAS_S from VARCHAR(15) to VARCHAR(20).

DB2 would not let you decrease the size of a VARCHAR column as well as altering the size of any other data type columns or changing a column data type.

Modifying identity column options

You can modify the options for an existing identity column. Assuming you've created the table PAYMENT_TERMS with PAYTERMS_ID_N as an identity column (see Chapter 4), the following statement alters the identity column option in such a way so it would cycle starting with 100 after the maximum value of 500 is reached:

```
ALTER TABLE payment_terms
ALTER COLUMN payterms_id_n
SET CYCLE
SET MAXVALUE 500
RESTART WITH 100
```

This statement would fail if PAYTERMS_ID_N column was not created as an identity column.

Creating new constraints on an existing table

You can add PRIMARY KEY, UNIQUE, CHECK or referential integrity constraints using the ALTER TABLE statement. Some examples follow:

```
ALTER TABLE salesman
ADD CONSTRAINT uk_salesmancode UNIQUE (salesman_code_s)
```

```
ALTER TABLE customer ADD  CONSTRAINT fk_cust_payterms
FOREIGN KEY (cust_paytermsid_fn)
REFERENCES payment_terms (payterms_id_n)
```

```
ALTER TABLE customer ADD  CONSTRAINT fk_cust_salesman
FOREIGN KEY (cust_salesmanid_fn)
REFERENCES salesman (salesman_id_n)
```

```
ALTER TABLE order_line ADD  CONSTRAINT fk_ordline_ordhdr
FOREIGN KEY (ordline_ordhdrid_fn)
REFERENCES order_header (ordhdr_id_n)
```

```
ALTER TABLE order_line ADD  CONSTRAINT fk_ordline_product
FOREIGN KEY (ordline_prodid_fn)
REFERENCES product (prod_id_n)
```

Removing constraints

The ALTER TABLE ... DROP CONSTRAINT statement deletes an existing constraint. For example, to remove the unique constraint you've just created, use

```
ALTER TABLE SALESMAN
DROP CONSTRAINT uk_salesmancode;
```

Altering summary table options

You can alter summary table options; for example, assuming we created ORDERLINE_SUMMARY table (Chapter 4), this statement changes it from INITIALLY DEFERRED REFRESH DEFERRED to DEFINITION ONLY:

```
ALTER TABLE orderline_summary
SET SUMMARY AS DEFINITION ONLY;
```

MS SQL Server 2000

MS SQL Server allows you to change a data type and collation sequence for existing columns, add new and drop existing columns, add or drop constraints, and disable or enable table triggers:

```
ALTER TABLE [<qualifier>.]<table_name>
(
  [ALTER COLUMN <column_name>
                <new_datatype> [<size1>[,<size2>]
  ]
  [COLLATE <collation_name>] |
  [ADD <new_column_definition> [<column_constraint>,...]] |
  [DROP COLUMN <column_name>,...]
  [ADD <table_constraint>,...] |
  [DROP CONSTRAINT <constraint_name>] |
  [{ENABLE | DISABLE} TRIGGER {ALL | <trigger_name>,...}]
)
```

Triggers are explained in Chapter 14.

Adding new columns to a table

You can add new columns to a table using the same syntax for column definitions as in MS SQL Server's CREATE TABLE statement. Collation sequences, defaults, identity properties, and constraints can also be specified. The statement below adds two new columns to PHONE:

```
ALTER TABLE PHONE
ADD PHONE_PRIMARY_S    CHAR(1) DEFAULT 'Y'
                       CONSTRAINT chk_phoneprim
                       CHECK (PHONE_PRIMARY_S IN ('Y', 'N')),
PHONE_CATEGORY_S  CHAR(15)
```

Modifying existing columns

The rules of modifying existing columns in MS SQL Server are different from what either Oracle or DB2 would allow you to do. For example, you cannot change the data type of a column on which a constraint is based or give it a default value. You also are unable to alter columns with TEXT, NTEXT, IMAGE, or TIMESTAMP data types. Some more restrictions apply; see vendor's documentation for details.

Unlike in Oracle, you can decrease the size of a nonempty column as long as all existing data fits the new size. For example, MS SQL Server would let you decrease the size of the PHONE_TYPE_S column from VARCHAR(20) to VARCHAR(10) or even

VARCHAR(5) because the longest string stored in this column PHONE is only five characters long:

```
ALTER TABLE PHONE
ALTER COLUMN PHONE_TYPE_S VARCHAR(5)
```

However, the RDBMS returns an error if you try to decrease the column size to maximum four characters:

```
ALTER TABLE PHONE
ALTER COLUMN PHONE_TYPE_S VARCHAR(4)

Server: Msg 8152, Level 16, State 9, Line 1
String or binary data would be truncated.
The statement has been terminated.
```

MS SQL Server behaves similarly with numeric columns. You can decrease the scale, but only down to the size of the biggest column value. The following statement changes the data type of the ORDLINE_ORDQTY_N column from INTEGER to NUMERIC(3):

```
ALTER TABLE ORDER_LINE
ALTER COLUMN ORDLINE_ORDQTY_N NUMERIC(3)
```

But changing it to NUMERIC(2) is not going to work because the largest current value in this column happens to be 700 in our ACME database:

```
ALTER TABLE ORDER_LINE
ALTER COLUMN ORDLINE_ORDQTY_N NUMERIC(2)

Server: Msg 8115, Level 16, State 8, Line 1
Arithmetic overflow error converting numeric to data type
numeric. The statement has been terminated.
```

Removing table columns

Removing table columns in MS SQL Server is more restrictive than in Oracle. For example, a column cannot be dropped if it is used in an index or in a constraint; associated with a default; or bound to a rule. The statement below fails because the column PHONE_PRIMARY_S is used in check constraint CHK_PHONEPRIM and is also associated with a default:

```
ALTER TABLE PHONE
DROP COLUMN PHONE_PRIMARY_S, PHONE_CATEGORY_S

Server: Msg 5074, Level 16, State 1, Line 1
The object 'DF__PHONE__PHONE_PRI__3B0BC30C' is dependent on
column 'PHONE_PRIMARY_S'.
Server: Msg 5074, Level 16, State 1, Line 1
The object 'chk_phoneprim' is dependent on column
'PHONE_PRIMARY_S'.
Server: Msg 4922, Level 16, State 1, Line 1
ALTER TABLE DROP COLUMN PHONE_PRIMARY_S failed because one or
more objects access this column.
```

The following statement nonetheless succeeds because the PHONE_CATEGORY_S column alone is not the subject for any of the previous limitations:

```
ALTER TABLE PHONE
DROP COLUMN PHONE_CATEGORY_S
```

Creating and removing constraints

The syntax to create new constraints or remove existing constraints in MS SQL Server is no different from one in Oracle's and DB2:

```
ALTER TABLE salesman
ADD CONSTRAINT uk_salesmancode UNIQUE (salesman_code_s);
```

```
ALTER TABLE SALESMAN
DROP CONSTRAINT uk_salesmancode;
```

DROP TABLE statement

Because tables occupy physical space, for the sake of efficiency it is important to be able to get rid of them as soon as they are no longer needed. The DROP TABLE statement works pretty much the same way in all "big three" databases. It releases the physical storage for the deleted table as well as for any indexes on its columns. The definitions for the table, its related indexes, integrity constraints, and triggers are removed from the database data dictionary. All views become invalid and have to be either changed to delete all references to the removed table or manually deleted from the database.

Caution

DROP TABLE is a part of DDL and is therefore irreversible. Specifically, it is committed to the database immediately without possibility of a rollback. Use it with extreme care.

Following is the syntax for the DROP TABLE statement.

Oracle 9*i*

```
DROP TABLE [<qualifier>.]<table_name> [CASCADE CONSTRAINTS];
```

The optional CASCADE CONSTRAINTS clause lets you drop a table with enforced referential integrity constraints; the constraints will also be dropped. If the clause is omitted and such referential integrity constraints exist, Oracle generates an error and the table would not be dropped:

```
SQL> DROP TABLE CUSTOMER;
DROP TABLE CUSTOMER
           *
ERROR at line 1:
ORA-02449: unique/primary keys in table referenced by foreign keys
```

The problem is that CUSTOMER table is referenced by ADDRESS, PHONE, and ORDER_HEADER tables (constraints FK_ADDR_CUST, FK_PHONE_CUST, and FK_ORDHDR_CUSTOMER). To drop CUSTOMER table and the above constraints you could use this SQL statement:

```
SQL> DROP TABLE customer CASCADE CONSTRAINTS;

Table dropped.
```

DB2 UDB 8.1

```
DROP TABLE [<qualifier>.]<table_name>
```

In addition to all objects listed here (indexes, constraints, and triggers), all summary tables referencing the table to be removed are also dropped as well as all related referential integrity constraints:

```
db2 => DROP TABLE customer
DB20000I  The SQL command completed successfully.
```

This unforgiving behavior could spell a disaster resulting in unintentional loss of data, so be especially cautious when working with the DROP TABLE statement in DB2.

MS SQL Server 2000

```
DROP TABLE [<qualifier>.]<table_name>
```

Unlike Oracle, MS SQL Server would not let you drop a table in which a primary key is referenced by any foreign key. To drop the table CUSTOMER you would have to drop the referential integrity constraints FK_ADDR_CUST, FK_PHONE_CUST, and FK_ORDHDR_CUSTOMER first:

```
1> DROP TABLE CUSTOMER
2> GO
Msg 3726, Level 16, State 1, Server PD-TS-TEST1, Line 1
Could not drop object 'CUSTOMER' because it is referenced by a FOREIGN KEY
constraint.
1> ALTER TABLE address
2> DROP CONSTRAINT fk_addr_cust
3> ALTER TABLE phone
4> DROP CONSTRAINT fk_phone_cust
5> ALTER TABLE order_header
6> DROP CONSTRAINT FK_ORDHDR_CUSTOMER
7> GO
1> DROP TABLE CUSTOMER
2> GO
1>
```

Indexes

As we already know, indexes are invisible for most database users, so in most cases they would not need to change indexes. Also, you can always drop and re-create an index rather than modify it. Out of our three database vendors only Oracle provides the ALTER INDEX statement to change the physical definition of an index. The DROP INDEX statement is used to remove indexes; it's available in all three databases.

As discussed in Chapter 4, indexes are not part of SQL99.

ALTER INDEX statement in Oracle 9*i*

As usual, we are not going to concentrate on details of the ALTER INDEX statement and will rather refer you to Oracle documentation for more information, and we'll illustrate only a couple of clauses that might be interesting for us in the course of this book:

```
ALTER INDEX <index_name>
{[RENAME TO <new_name>] |
 [REBUILD TABLESPACE <tablespace_name>]
};
```

Renaming indexes

The RENAME clause can be useful if your indexes were created with system-generated names (that is, if you did not name them specifically on object creation). For instance, suppose you created table SALESMAN with the following statement:

```
CREATE TABLE salesman
(
   salesman_id_n         NUMBER          PRIMARY KEY,
   salesman_code_s       VARCHAR2(2)     UNIQUE,
   salesman_name_s       VARCHAR2(50)    NOT NULL,
   salesman_status_s     CHAR(1)         DEFAULT 'Y',
   CONSTRAINT chk_salesstatus CHECK
            (salesman_status_s in ('N', 'Y'))
);
```

Oracle will automatically create indexes on both the SALESMAN_ID_N and SALESMAN_CODE_S columns (remember, indexes are always created on primary key or unique columns), but the names will be rather nondescriptive; something like SYS_C003521 and SYS_C003522. If your database has some kind of naming conventions similar to those described in Appendix B (which is not a bad idea), you might want to change the names of the indexes to something more descriptive later:

```
ALTER INDEX SYS_C003521
RENAME TO IDX_SALESMAN_ID;
```

```
ALTER INDEX SYS_C003522
RENAME TO IDX_SALESMAN_CODE;
```

Rebuilding indexes into a different tablespace

Another frequent mistake while creating Oracle indexes is to create them in a wrong tablespace. This happens even more often than with tables because Oracle does not provide a default index tablespace option. Specifically, regardless if a user has an assigned default data tablespace (DATA01 for example), all physical objects (including indexes) are created in this tablespace by default if otherwise was not specified. That is not always the desirable behavior, especially in a production environment where data and index tablespaces are usually located on separate physical devices (hard disks); creating indexes in wrong tablespaces can significantly degrade performance.

The ALTER INDEX command can be used to fix the problem:

```
ALTER INDEX IDX_SALESMAN_ID
REBUILD TABLESPACE INDEX01;

ALTER INDEX IDX_SALESMAN_CODE
REBUILD TABLESPACE INDEX01;
```

This example assumes the existence of the tablespace INDEX01.

DROP INDEX statement

Similar to the DROP TABLE statement, DROP INDEX releases the allocated space and removes the index definition from the database information schema. You cannot drop indexes created to implement PRIMARY KEY or UNIQUE constraints using DROP TABLE; ALTER TABLE ... DROP CONSTRAINT statement would have to be used instead.

The database information schema is discussed in Chapter 13.

Oracle 9*i*

The syntax is

```
DROP INDEX [<qualifier>.]<index_name>;
```

The first statement returns an error because PK_ORDHDRPRIM is the primary key on table ORDER_HEADER, but the second one works just fine:

```
SQL> DROP INDEX pk_ordhdrprim;
DROP INDEX pk_ordhdrprim
           *
ERROR at line 1:
ORA-02429: cannot drop index used for enforcement of unique/primary key
```

```
SQL> DROP INDEX idx_phone_cust;

Index dropped.
```

When an index is dropped, all objects dependent on the *underlying* table are invalidated.

DB2 UDB 8.1

Use the same syntax as in Oracle:

```
DROP INDEX [<qualifier>.]<index_name>
```

Assume you want to drop index `IDX_PHONE_CUST` on `PHONE_CUSTID_FN` column of the `PHONE` table:

```
DROP INDEX idx_phone_cust
```

DB2 invalidates packages that have dependency on the dropped index.

MS SQL Server

You have to specify both the table name in which the indexed column is located and the index name:

```
DROP INDEX <table_name>.<index_name> [,...]
```

For example

```
DROP INDEX phone.idx_phone_cust
```

You can drop multiple indexes within one `DROP INDEX` statement. The names must be comma-separated.

Views

Views can be changed or dropped using the `ALTER VIEW` and `DROP VIEW` statements correspondingly.

ALTER VIEW statement

Oracle 9*i*, DB2 UDB, and MS SQL Server all have an `ALTER VIEW` statement, but its syntax and functionality is quite different.

Oracle 9*i*

The two main uses of ALTER VIEW in Oracle are either to recompile a view invalidated because of underlying table(s) DDL changes or to add, modify, or drop view constraints. The syntax is

```
ALTER VIEW [<qualifier>.]<view_name>
{[COMPILE] |
 [ADD CONSTRAINT <view_constraint_definition>] |
 [MODIFY CONSTRAINT <constraint_name>] |
 [DROP {CONSTRAINT <constraint_name> | PRIMARY KEY}]
};
```

For example, you might want to recompile view V_FAX_NUMBER because its underlying table (PHONE) has been modified:

```
ALTER VIEW v_fax_number
COMPILE;
```

You don't actually have to recompile Oracle views invalidated when their underlying tables have been changed. The invalidated view will be automatically recompiled when referred by SQL code; the main reason to recompile views manually is for performance improvement.

The next example adds the UNIQUE constraint to the view V_CONTACT_LIST:

```
ALTER VIEW v_contact_list
ADD CONSTRAINT vpk_contactlist UNIQUE (name, phone_number)
DISABLE;
```

To drop this constraint, issue the following statements:

```
ALTER VIEW v_contact_list
DROP CONSTRAINT vpk_contactlist;
```

Oracle's ALTER VIEW statement cannot alter the view definition; if you need to add or drop view columns, change data types or the underlying query, etc., you have to use CREATE OR REPLACE VIEW statement (or, alternatively, use DROP VIEW and CREATE VIEW statements).

DB2 UDB 8.1

DB2 allows you to use the ALTER VIEW statement to alter a reference type column to add a scope. The functionality is an advanced topic and is not covered in this book.

MS SQL Server 2000

The ALTER VIEW in MS SQL Server enables you to change view columns, underlying select statements, and other view options without affecting dependent database objects or changing permissions (which would be different had you used DROP VIEW and CREATE VIEW statements). The syntax is practically the same as for CREATE VIEW:

```
ALTER VIEW [<qualifier>.]<view_name>
[(<column_name>,...)]
[WITH {ENCRYPTION|SCHEMABINDING|VIEW_METADATA}]
AS <select_statement>
[WITH CHECK OPTION]
```

See Chapter 4 examples for CREATE VIEW.

SQL99 does not specify any rules for altering views.

DROP VIEW statement

DROP VIEW statement removes view definition from the system catalog. The dependent objects become invalid.

Oracle 9*i*

The syntax is

```
DROP VIEW view_name [CASCADE CONSTRAINTS];
```

For example

```
DROP VIEW v_phone_number;
```

The optional CASCADE CONSTRAINTS clause removes all referential integrity constraints that refer to primary and unique keys in the view to be dropped. See Oracle's DROP TABLE statement described previously.

DB2 UDB 8.1

DB2 uses syntax as follows:

```
DROP VIEW [<qualifier>.]<view_name>
```

MS SQL Server

You can drop multiple views using the MS SQL Server `DROP VIEW` statement:

```
DROP VIEW <view_name> [,...]
```

The following statement drops three views (`V_PHONE_NUMBER`, `V_CUSTOMER_TOTALS`, and `V_WILE_BESS_ORDERS`) at once:

```
1> DROP VIEW v_phone_number, v_customer_totals, v_wile_bess_orders
2> Go
1>
```

Aliases and Synonyms

You cannot modify aliases or synonyms in Oracle and DB2. If the definition of a synonym (alias) must be changed, you can drop and re-create it using `DROP SYNONYM` (`ALIAS`) and `CREATE SYNONYM` (`ALIAS`).

Oracle 9*i*

The syntax to destroy an Oracle synonym is

```
DROP [PUBLIC] SYNONYM <synonym_name>;
```

You must use the `PUBLIC` keyword if the synonym you are going to remove was created as a public synonym. Assuming the examples from Chapter 4,

```
DROP PUBLIC SYNONYM SHIPMENT;
```

Oracle does not invalidate any objects that the dropped synonym was referring to except for materialized views.

DB2 UDB 8.1

The syntax to remove an alias in DB2 is

```
DROP {ALIAS | SYNONYM} <alias_name>
```

For example

```
DROP ALIAS SHIPMT
```

All tables, views, and triggers that reference the dropped alias become inoperative.

Schemas

None of our "big three" vendors has syntax to change a schema; only DB2 allows you to drop schema. Here is the syntax to do this:

```
DROP SCHEMA <schema_name> RESTRICT
```

The schema must be empty (i.e., no objects can be defined in it) for the schema to be deleted from the database. The following statement would fail unless you dropped the ACMETEST.ADDRESS and ACMETEST.SALESMAN tables (assuming examples from Chapter 4):

```
DROP SCHEMA acmetest RESTRICT

The object type "SCHEMA" cannot be dropped because there is an
object "ACMETEST.ADDRESS" of type "TABLE" which depends
on it. SQLSTATE=42893
```

```
DROP TABLE ACMETEST.ADDRESS
DB20000I  The SQL command completed successfully.
```

```
DROP TABLE ACMETEST.SALESMAN
DB20000I  The SQL command completed successfully.
```

```
DROP SCHEMA acmetest RESTRICT
DB20000I  The SQL command completed successfully.
```

Other Implementation-Specific Objects

In this section you'll learn how to change and destroy some implementation-specific objects discussed in Chapter 4.

Tablespaces

Both Oracle and DB2 allow you to change or remove existing tablespaces.

ALTER TABLESPACE statement

Several options are available to modify an existing tablespace.

Oracle 9*i*

The most common action on a tablespace is to add a new file to an existing tablespace:

```
ALTER TABLESPACE <tablespace_name>
ADD DATAFILE <file_path_and_name> SIZE size K|M;
```

The following command adds a new data file, `C:\oracle\ora92\oradata\acme\data01.dbf` ,of size 1 megabyte to tablespace `DATA01`:

```
ALTER TABLESPACE DATA01
ADD DATAFILE C:\oracle\ora92\oradata\acme\data01.dbf SIZE 1M;
```

Many more options are available with the `ALTER TABLESPACE` statement in Oracle, but they are mostly for database administrators' use and are not covered in this book.

DB2 UDB 8.1

Similar to Oracle, the `ALTER TABLESPACE` statement in DB2 is primarily for DBAs. For example, you can add a container to a tablespace created with the `MANAGED BY DATABASE` option or increase its size.

You already know from Chapter 4 that MS SQL Server 2000 uses *filegroups* in a way similar to how Oracle and DB2 use tablespaces. The `ALTER DATABASE ... ADD FILE` command is covered in Chapter 4.

DROP TABLESPACE statement

Again, usually only database administrators have the necessary privileges to drop existing tablespaces. Please keep in mind that dropping a tablespace drops all objects defined in the tablespace; proceed with caution.

Oracle 9*i*

In Oracle you can specify several options with the DROP TABLESPACE statement:

```
DROP TABLESPACE <tablespace_name>
[INCLUDING CONTENTS [AND DATAFILES]]
[CASCADE CONSTRAINTS];
```

If you want to drop a tablespace that contains objects, you would have to specify INCLUDING CONTENTS or Oracle generates an error. By default the actual operating files are *not deleted*; you have to specify an AND DATAFILES clause unless you want to remove them manually. Specify CASCADE CONSTRAINTS to drop all referential integrity constraints from tables *outside* tablespace that refer to primary and unique keys of tables inside tablespace.

If the tablespace is Oracle-managed, you don't need the AND DATAFILES clause; the OS files will be deleted automatically.

DB2 UDB 8.1

The syntax for DB2 is

```
DROP TABLESPACE[S] <tablespace_name>,...
```

You can delete multiple tablespaces within one DROP TABLESPACE statement. All OS files for the tablespace(s) managed by the system will be removed; containers created by users are not deleted.

Sequences

Sequences can be modified or dropped both in Oracle and DB2; as you know from Chapter 4, MS SQL Server has no sequence objects.

ALTER SEQUENCE statement

Almost all options for sequences that you can use with the CREATE SEQUENCE statement (Chapter 4) can also be used with ALTER SEQUENCE.

Oracle 9*i*

You can change the increment, minimum, and maximum values, cached numbers, and behavior of an existing sequence. Only the future sequence numbers are affected. The only clause you cannot modify for existing sequences is START WITH.

```
ALTER SEQUENCE [<qualifier>.]<sequence_name>
[INCREMENT BY <increment_value>]
[MAXVALUE <max_value> | NOMAXVALUE]
[MINVALUE <min_value> | NOMINVALUE]
[CYCLE | NOCYCLE ]
[CACHE <value> | NOCACHE]
[ORDER | NOORDER]
```

The following statement changes MY_SEQUENCE4 in such a way that it no longer has a maximum value and does not cycle:

```
CREATE SEQUENCE my_sequence4
INCREMENT BY 1
NOMAXVALUE
NOCYCLE;
```

DB2 UDB 8.1

DB2 allows you to restart the sequence, to change its increment (for future values only), to set or eliminate the minimum or maximum values, to change the number of cached values, and more:

```
ALTER SEQUENCE <sequence_name>
[RESTART WITH <start_value>]
[INCREMENT BY <increment_value>]
[MAXVALUE <max_value> | NOMAXVALUE]
[MINVALUE <min_value> | NOMINVALUE]
[CYCLE | NOCYCLE ]
[CACHE <value> | NOCACHE]
[ORDER | NOORDER]
```

For example

```
CREATE SEQUENCE my_sequence4
RESTART WITH 1
INCREMENT BY 1
NOMAXVALUE
NOCYCLE;
```

DROP SEQUENCE statement

Sequences can be dropped with the DROP SEQUENCE statement.

Oracle 9*i*

```
DROP SEQUENCE [<qualifier>.]<sequence_name>;
```

No dependencies exist (i.e., no database objects would prevent a sequence from being dropped; also, no objects would be invalidated). The statement below removes sequence MY_SEQUENCE1:

```
DROP SEQUENCE <my_sequence1>;
```

DB2 UDB 8.1

```
DROP SEQUENCE <sequence_name> RESTRICT -- restrict is a required keyword
```

You cannot drop a sequence used in a trigger. This example is an equivalent to Oracle's syntax from the previous example:

```
DROP SEQUENCE my_sequence1 RESTRICT
```

ALTER and DROP Statements Cross-Reference

Table 5-1 provides the full list of all objects you can change in the "big three" databases using ALTER statement.

Table 5-1
Valid ALTER Statements Cross-Reference

Statement	*SQL99*	*Oracle 9i*	*DB2 UDB 8.1*	*MS SQL Server 2000*
ALTER BUFFERPOOL			✓	
ALTER CLUSTER		✓		
ALTER DATABASE		✓	✓	✓
ALTER DIMENSION		✓		
ALTER DOMAIN	✓			
ALTER FUNCTION		✓		✓
ALTER INDEX		✓		
ALTER INDEXTYPE		✓		

Continued

Table 5-1 (continued)

Statement	SQL99	Oracle 9i	DB2 UDB 8.1	MS SQL Server 2000
ALTER JAVA		✓		
ALTER MATERIALIZED VIEW		✓		
ALTER MATERIALIZED VIEW LOG			✓	
ALTER NICKNAME			✓	
ALTER NODEGROUP			✓	
ALTER OUTLINE		✓		
ALTER PACKAGE		✓		
ALTER PROCEDURE		✓		
ALTER PROFILE		✓		
ALTER RESOURCE COST		✓		
ALTER ROLE		✓		
ALTER ROLLBACK SEGMENT		✓		
ALTER SEQUENCE		✓	✓	
ALTER SERVER			✓	
ALTER SESSION		✓		
ALTER SPFILE		✓		
ALTER SYNONYM		✓		
ALTER SYSTEM		✓		
ALTER TABLE	✓	✓	✓	✓
ALTER TABLESPACE		✓	✓	
ALTER TRANSLATION	✓			
ALTER TRIGGER		✓		✓
ALTER TYPE	✓	✓	✓	
ALTER USER		✓		
ALTER USER MAPPING			✓	
ALTER VIEW	✓	✓	✓	✓

Table 5-2 provides the full list of all objects you can remove using a DROP statement.

Table 5-2
Valid DROP Statements Cross-Reference

Statement	*SQL99*	*Oracle 9i*	*DB2 UDB 8.1*	*MS SQL Server 2000*
DROP ALIAS			✓	
DROP ASSERTION	✓			
DROP BUFFERPOOL			✓	
DROP CHARACTER SET	✓			
DROP CLUSTER		✓		
DROP COLLATION	✓			
DROP CONTEXT		✓		
DROP DATABASE			✓	✓
DROP DATABASE LINK		✓		
DROP DEFAULT				✓
DROP DIMENSION		✓		
DROP DIRECTORY		✓		
DROP DISTINCT TYPE			✓	
DROP DOMAIN	✓			
DROP EVENT MONITOR			✓	
DROP FUNCTION		✓	✓	✓
DROP FUNCTION MAPPING			✓	
DROP INDEX		✓	✓	✓
DROP INDEX EXTENSION			✓	
DROP INDEXTYPE		✓		
DROP JAVA		✓		
DROP LIBRARY		✓		
DROP MATERIALIZED VIEW		✓		
DROP MATERIALIZED VIEW LOG		✓		
DROP METHOD			✓	
DROP NICKNAME			✓	
DROP NODEGROUP			✓	

Continued

Table 5-2 *(continued)*

Statement	*SQL99*	*Oracle 9i*	*DB2 UDB 8.1*	*MS SQL Server 2000*
DROP OPERATOR		✓		
DROP OUTLINE		✓		
DROP PACKAGE		✓	✓	
DROP PROCEDURE		✓	✓	✓
DROP PROFILE		✓		
DROP ROLE	✓	✓		
DROP ROLLBACK SEGMENT		✓		
DROP RULE				✓
DROP SCHEMA	✓		✓	
DROP SEQUENCE		✓	✓	
DROP SERVER			✓	
DROP STATISTICS				✓
DROP SYNONYM		✓		
DROP TABLE	✓	✓	✓	✓
DROP TABLESPACE		✓	✓	
DROP TABLE HIERARCHY			✓	
DROP TRANSFORM			✓	
DROP TRANSLATION	✓			
DROP TRIGGER		✓	✓	✓
DROP TYPE	✓	✓	✓	
DROP TYPE BODY		✓		
DROP TYPE MAPPING			✓	
DROP USER		✓		
DROP USER MAPPING			✓	
DROP VIEW	✓	✓	✓	✓
DROP VIEW HIERARCHY			✓	
DROP WRAPPER			✓	

Summary

Every object in a database has a lifespan. Objects can be created, modified, and destroyed. In the RDBMS world this is achieved through SQL statements that don't always comply with the SQL standards. Some vendors provide more functionality and control than others, and compliance levels vary greatly among them. Virtually every object that could be created within a database could be altered or destroyed.

In most cases the ability to modify database objects is optional, that is, you can always use a set of alternative statements (like DROP and CREATE) to achieve the same results.

The ability to remove database objects is also very important. It releases space for physical objects that are no longer in use and can also be used to change objects that cannot be altered (by dropping and re-creating them).

✦ ✦ ✦

P A R T

Data Manipulation and Transaction Control

✦ ✦ ✦ ✦

In This Part

✦ ✦ ✦ ✦

Data Manipulation Language (DML)

In This Chapter

Inserting new records

Updating table records

Deleting table records

Merge statement

Truncate statement

Chapters 4 and 5 discussed an important part of SQL called the data definition language (DDL) that enables you to create, alter, and destroy various database objects. We emphasized the fact that tables are the most important database objects because they store data, and data is what databases are all about. This chapter deals with the data manipulation language (DML) that allows you to add data to the database, modify it as necessary, and destroy it when it is no longer needed.

"Classical" DML consists of three statements: INSERT, UPDATE, and DELETE. Oracle 9*i* introduces yet another DML statement, MERGE, that combines the functionality of INSERT and UPDATE.

Examples in this chapter assume incremental buildup of the ACME database started in Chapter 4 and Chapter 5. Constraints implemented in the database scripts included with the CD-ROM may prevent some of the statements from successful execution.

INSERT: Populating Tables with Data

As you know, tables in a relational database denote entities — or at least they should. For example, each row in the CUSTOMER table holds information about a specific customer; a row in ORDER_HEADER represents a definite order, and so on. Usually, the appearance of a new "real-life" entity calls for inserting a new row. For example, you would need a new row in CUSTOMER table if ACME, Inc. obtained a new customer; you need to insert a row into ORDER_HEADER table when a customer makes an order; a new row has to be added to the PRODUCT table if ACME starts selling a new product, and so on.

The INSERT statement is used to add rows to a table, either directly or through an updateable view. The syntax differs slightly among SQL99, Oracle 9*i*, DB2 UDB 8.1, and MS SQL Server 2000, but it is possible to come up with some kind of a generic INSERT syntax that works with all our "big three" databases:

```
INSERT INTO <table_or_view_name>
[(<column_name>,...)]
{ {VALUES (<literal> |
          <expression> |
          NULL |
          DEFAULT,...)} |
  {<select_statement>} }
```

We are going to concentrate on the generic INSERT functionality first, and then describe some of its SQL99 and vendor-specific only features.

Common INSERT statement clauses

One would typically insert values into one table at a time within one INSERT statement. (Oracle 9*i* allows you to perform multitable inserts, but that is rather advanced functionality not covered in this book.) The name of the table is provided in the table_or_view_name clause. (An updateable view name can be given instead of a table name.)

The column_name clause is optional; it determines the order in which column values of the row to be inserted are populated. It also allows you to skip values for columns you don't want to populate at that particular moment; such columns would either have NULL values or would be populated with column defaults specified with a CREATE (ALTER) TABLE statement.

You cannot skip any NOT NULL columns in your column_name clause; otherwise the RDBMS will give you an error.

The values to insert can either be specified using the VALUES clause or the resulting set from the select_statement clause (also called *subquery*). In the first case, usually only one row is inserted (exception is DB2 where you can specify multiple VALUES clauses within one INSERT statement; more about that in this chapter's section about DB2); in the second case, the RDBMS inserts as many rows as were returned by the select_statement — it can be zero, one, ten, or one thousand.

You have to list values for *all* table columns in the VALUES clause in the exact same order they are specified in the table definition if the column_name list was omitted.

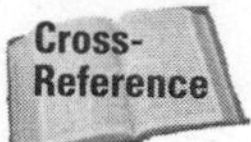

Obtaining information about the internal structure of database objects is discussed in Chapter 13.

If the column_name list is present, you have to specify a corresponding value for each column listed.

If the select_statement clause was used rather than the VALUES clause, its resulting set has to be organized either in table definition order (if column_list is not specified) or in column_list order.

Inserting values for specified columns

The situation when you want to insert a row with NULL values for certain columns is not unusual. As you know, NULL is used when value is unknown or nonapplicable. For example, suppose you know ACME starts selling a new product SPRUCE LUMBER 30×40×50, but certain properties of this product (price and weight) are still unknown. We can add a record to the PRODUCT table using the following INSERT statement:

```
INSERT INTO product
(
 prod_id_n,
 prod_num_s,
 prod_description_s,
 prod_status_s,
 prod_brand_s,
 prod_pltwid_n,
 prod_pltlen_n
)
VALUES
(
 990,
 '990',
 'SPRUCE LUMBER 30X40X50',
 'N',
 'SPRUCE LUMBER',
 4,
 6
)
```

The following two statements insert two records into the PAYMENT_TERMS table (we'll use them later in our examples):

```
INSERT INTO payment_terms
(
 payterms_id_n,
 payterms_code_s,
 payterms_desc_s,
 payterms_discpct_n,
 payterms_daystopay_n
```

```
)
VALUES
(
 27,
 'N21531',
 '2% 15 NET 30',
 0.02,
 31
)
```

```
INSERT INTO payment_terms
(
 payterms_id_n,
 payterms_code_s,
 payterms_desc_s,
 payterms_discpct_n,
 payterms_daystopay_n
)
VALUES
(
 28,
 'N21530',
 '2% 15 NET 30',
 0.02,
 30
)
```

If any of skipped columns has a default value, RDBMS uses this value rather than NULL:

```
INSERT INTO salesman
(
 salesman_id_n,
 salesman_code_s,
 salesman_name_s
)
VALUES
(
 23,
 '02',
 'FAIRFIELD BUGS ASSOCIATION'
)
```

Because the SALESMAN_STATUS_S column of the SALESMAN table has the default value of Y, the inserted row looks like that:

```
SELECT *
FROM salesman
WHERE salesman_code_s = '02'

SALESMAN_ID_N SALESMAN_CODE_S SALESMAN_NAME_S              SALESMAN_STATUS_S
----------------------------------------------------------------------------
           23 02              FAIRFIELD BUGS ASSOCIATION  Y
```

Here is another example using the CUSTOMER table:

```
INSERT INTO customer
(
 cust_id_n,
 cust_paytermsid_fn,
 cust_salesmanid_fn,
 cust_name_s,
 cust_alias_s,
 cust_credhold_s
)
VALUES
(
 1,
 27,
 24,
 'WILE SEAL CORP.',
 'MNGA71396',
 'Y'
)
```

Since the CUST_STATUS_S field has the default value of Y, the value for the column gets populated implicitly:

```
SELECT cust_status_s
FROM customer
WHERE cust_alias_s = 'MNGA71396'

CUST_STATUS_S
------------
Y
```

Inserting values for all columns

Assuming you have all the necessary values and want to populate all columns by the time you are ready to insert a row, you have a choice. You can either still list *all* column names with corresponding values, or the `column_name` clause can be completely skipped. The two statements below produce identical results:

```
INSERT INTO product
(
 prod_id_n,
 prod_price_n,
 prod_num_s,
 prod_description_s,
 prod_status_s,
 prod_brand_s,
 prod_pltwid_n,
 prod_pltlen_n,
 prod_netwght_n,
 prod_shipweight_n
)
VALUES
(
 1880,
 33.28,
 '1880',
 'STEEL NAILS 6''''',
 'Y',
 'STEEL NAILS',
 5,
 4,
 38.39148,
 42.39148
)
```

```
INSERT INTO product
VALUES
(
 1880,
 33.28,
 '1880',
 'STEEL NAILS 6''''',
 'Y',
 'STEEL NAILS',
 5,
 4,
 38.39148,
 42.39148
)
```

Note that the latter syntax requires values to be in exact order to match the column list.

Tip

Even though the second syntax is faster to type, the first one is easier to understand and maintain, so it makes more sense to use column names in your production code.

Inserting NULL and default values explicitly

In the examples above we insert literals; when a column name is skipped, the column is populated with NULL or with the column default value implicitly. But sometimes you may want to explicitly insert a NULL value into a column or make the RDBMS use the column's default value. That can be accomplished by using keywords NULL or DEFAULT, correspondingly. The statement below populates NULL in the PROD_PRICE_N column of the newly inserted row:

```
INSERT INTO product
(
 prod_id_n,
 prod_price_n,
 prod_num_s,
 prod_description_s,
 prod_status_s,
 prod_brand_s,
 prod_pltwid_n,
 prod_pltlen_n,
 prod_netwght_n,
 prod_shipweight_n
)
VALUES
(
 5786,
 NULL,
 '5786',
 'CRATING MATERIAL 12X48X72',
 'Y',
 'CRATING MATERIAL',
 5,
 6,
 20.37674,
 23.37674
)
```

Here is another statement that inserts a row into the ORDER_HEADER table, explicitly populating multiple columns with nulls:

```
INSERT INTO order_header
VALUES
(
 30670,
```

```
    28,
    NULL,
    1,
    24,
    '523783',
    NULL,
    NULL,
    NULL,
    NULL,
    'N',
    'Y',
    NULL,
    'RR',
    NULL
   )
```

Later, the NULL fields (for invoice number, notes, multiple dates, etc.) can be populated with the actual data using the UPDATE statement.

This statement creates a record in the SALESMAN table explicitly specifying to use a default value for the SALESMAN_STATUS_S column:

```
INSERT INTO salesman
VALUES
(
 24,
 '03',
 'AMERICA GONZALES LIMITED',
 DEFAULT
)
```

Inserting values selected from other tables

A typical (but not the only) situation when you may want to insert values selected from other tables is when archiving on a periodic basis. For example, a table that holds shipments for a large company can grow dramatically over long periods. Assume a company that has a business rule stating it usually does not need any information about shipments that are older than 180 days on a regular basis, but still may need the old shipment data occasionally for special cases like auditing, etc. To improve performance, we can create the table SHIPMENT_ARCHIVE with exactly the same columns as in SHIPMENT (see Chapter 4 for details), and then, say once a month, insert into SHIPMENT_ARCHIVE all rows from SHIPMENT that are older than 180 days. The old records can then be removed from the SHIPMENT table using the DELETE statement (discussed later in this chapter). This statement archives shipment records older than 180 days using Oracle syntax:

```
INSERT INTO shipment_archive
SELECT *
FROM shipment
WHERE TRUNC(shipment_createdate_d) < TRUNC(SYSDATE) - 180;
```

DB2 UDB and MS SQL Server have their own methods and functions to work with dates. See Chapter 10 for details.

Archiving Based on Complex Business Rules

The business rules set could be much more complicated than the one described in our archiving example; for instance, you may want to archive certain order information that is older than 90 days and is logically stored in two tables, ORDER_HEADER and ORDER_LINE. Assuming you need to archive order number, order date, customer id, product id, and shipped quantity, you create the archive table with appropriate columns first and then use the INSERT statement with a subquery to archive data (subqueries are discussed in Chapter 8):

```
CREATE TABLE order_archive
AS
(SELECT  ordhdr_nbr_s,
         ordhdr_orderdate_d,
         ordhdr_custid_fn,
         ordline_prodid_fn,
         ordline_shipqty_n
FROM     order_header JOIN order_line
ON       ordhdr_id_n = ordline_ordhdrid_fn)
DEFINITION ONLY

INSERT   INTO order_archive
SELECT   ordhdr_nbr_s,
         ordhdr_orderdate_d,
         ordhdr_custid_fn,
         ordline_prodid_fn,
         ordline_shipqty_n
FROM     order_header JOIN order_line
ON       ordhdr_id_n = ordline_ordhdrid_fn
WHERE    ordhdr_createdate_d < (CURRENT DATE - 90 DAYS)
```

This example is using DB2 syntax to create table ORDER_ARCHIVE that is slightly different from the other two RDBMS; please refer to Chapter 4 on how to create a table based on columns from other tables.

INSERT statement and integrity constraints

Inserting rows into a table obeys certain rules and restrictions. For example, all column values have to be of same or at least compatible data types and sizes with corresponding column definitions. There are some implementation-specific variations — for example, Oracle performs implicit conversions whenever possible (from character string data types to numeric, from dates to strings, etc.), and in DB2 you always have to explicitly convert values to a compatible data type — but in general there is no RDBMS that would allow you to insert a customer name into a numeric or date column. An error will be generated and the whole row (or even multiple rows) is rejected.

The problem with "one bad row" while performing a subquery-based insert is quite typical (and is usually quite annoying). Just imagine the situation where you have to select ten thousand rows, twenty columns in each, from multiple tables and insert the result into your destination table. Just one value in one row can cause the whole insert to fail if the value is bigger than the column definition allows. For example, if your destination table column is NUMERIC(5), an attempt to insert into this column any value greater than 99,999 will fail – as well as the whole INSERT statement that might have been running for a couple of hours before it did. The conclusion is simple: Be careful when designing your INSERT statements.

A similar problem happens when you try to insert a value that violates an integrity constraint. You cannot insert NULL values into NOT NULL columns; duplicate values will be rejected for UNIQUE and PRIMARY KEY columns, and so on. For example, the following statement would fail because of the CHECK constraint violation:

```
INSERT INTO salesman
(
  salesman_id_n,
  salesman_code_s,
  salesman_name_s,
  salesman_status_s
)
VALUES
(
  26,
 '07',
 'ELMERSON INDUSTRIES INCORPORATED',
 'A'
)
```

The check constraint on SALESMAN_STATUS_S says the only two valid values for this column are Y and N, and we are trying to insert A. Simply change it to Y to make this statement work.

RDBMS error messages

Each vendor has its own specific set of error messages for certain events. The wording is different; what is common though—all our "big three" vendors mention the name of the violated constraint.

Oracle

```
ORA-02290: check constraint (ACME.CHK_SALESSTATUS) violated
```

DB2

```
SQL0545N The requested operation is not allowed because
a row does not satisfy the check constraint
"ACME.SALESMAN.CHK_SALESSTATUS".
```

MS SQL Server

```
INSERT statement conflicted with COLUMN
CHECK constraint 'CHK_SALESSTATUS'.
```

It is much easier to identify and fix a problem fast if the constraint name is *descriptive*, that is, if it tells you right away which column in what table caused the problem.

INSERT statement vendor-related specifics

The generic INSERT statement syntax given at the beginning of this chapter includes the most important clauses common for our "big three" RDBMS as well as for SQL99 syntax. In this section, we will talk about some vendor-specific differences.

SQL99

The main difference between our generic syntax and one used as SQL99 standard is that SQL99 has an additional DEFAULT VALUES clause:

```
INSERT INTO <table_or_view_name>
[(<column_name>,...)]
{ {VALUES (<literal> |
           <expression> |
           NULL,...)} |
  {<select_statement>} |
  {DEFAULT VALUES}}
```

The DEFAULT VALUES clause is explained in the "MS SQL Server" section of this chapter.

Abstract Data Types (ADT)–related clauses are intentionally excluded from the syntax above; abstract data types are discussed in Chapter 17.

Oracle 9*i*

The INSERT statement in Oracle has many optional clauses. For example, it can return rows and store them in predeclared variables. (UPDATE and DELETE also have this functionality.) Also, you can perform multitable inserts (i.e., insert values derived from the returned rows into multiple tables within one insert statement) that can also be conditional—for example, rows that satisfy *condition1* are inserted into TABLE1; rows that suit *condition2* go to TABLE2, and so on. And you can use sequences in your INSERT statements, work with partitioned tables, and more.

Tables (and indexes) in Oracle can be partitioned. A partitioned table consists of a number of parts called partitions, all of which have the same logical attributes. For example, all partitions in a table share the same column and constraint definitions, but may reside on different logical and/or physical devices. Partitioning is usually done by a DBA for performance improvement; see Oracle technical documentation for details.

Most of the options listed above are advanced and vendor-specific and therefore are out of the scope of this book. Using sequences in the INSERT statement, however, is quite typical for Oracle (primarily for populating the primary keys or other unique values).

The following example illustrates inserting a row into an ADDRESS table using sequence SEQ_ADDR:

```
CREATE SEQUENCE seq_addr;

INSERT INTO address
(
 addr_id_n,
 addr_custid_fn,
 addr_salesmanid_fn,
 addr_address_s,
 addr_type_s,
 addr_city_s,
 addr_state_s,
 addr_zip_s,
 addr_country_s
)
VALUES
(
 SEQ_ADDR.NEXTVAL,
 NULL,
 23,
 '223 E FLAGLER ST.',
 NULL,
 'MIAMI',
```

```
 'FL',
 '33131',
 'USA'
);
```

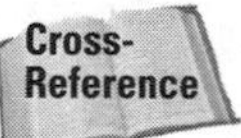

Sequences are discussed in Chapters 4 and 5.

DB2 UDB 8.1

The main difference between DB2's INSERT and our generic syntax is the ability to insert multiple rows within a single VALUES clause of the INSERT statement. The following statement inserts four rows into STATUS table at once:

```
INSERT INTO status
(
  status_id_n,
  status_code_s,
  status_desc_s
)
VALUES
 ( 2, '20', 'COMPLETE'),
 ( 6, '60', 'SHIPPED'),
 ( 8, '70', 'INVOICED'),
 ( 9, '80', 'CANCELLED')
```

You can also use sequences in your INSERT statements (using syntax slightly different than in Oracle):

```
CREATE SEQUENCE seq_addr

INSERT INTO address
(
 addr_id_n,
 addr_custid_fn,
 addr_salesmanid_fn,
 addr_address_s,
 addr_type_s,
 addr_city_s,
 addr_state_s,
 addr_zip_s,
 addr_country_s
)
VALUES
(
 NEXTVAL FOR SEQ_ADDR,
 NULL,
 23,
```

```
  '223 E FLAGLER ST.',
  NULL,
  'MIAMI',
  'FL',
  '33131',
  'USA'
)
```

The last thing to mention is identity columns (discussed in Chapter 4). When a row is inserted into a table that has an identity column, DB2 generates a value for the identity column. This value is always generated for a `GENERATED ALWAYS` identity column — in fact, if you explicitly try to insert a value (other than `DEFAULT`) into such column, an error will be generated. For a `GENERATED BY DEFAULT` column, DB2 generates a value only if it is not explicitly specified with a `VALUES` clause or with a subquery.

MS SQL Server 2000

In addition to the generic `INSERT` syntax clauses, MS SQL Server allows you to use the `DEFAULT VALUES` clause and to manipulate with identity columns.

The `DEFAULT VALUES` clause can be used to insert into a table with each column having a value that can be used when no explicit value is specified (`DEFAULT`, `IDENTITY`, `NULL` OR `TIMESTAMP`). In other words, the `DEFAULT VALUES` option is used to add rows without supplying explicit values:

```
1> CREATE TABLE defaults
2> (
3>   c1 int identity,
4>   c2 varchar(30) DEFAULT ('column default'),
5>   c3 timestamp,
6>   c4 int NULL
7> )
8>
9> INSERT INTO defaults
10> DEFAULT VALUES
11>
12> SELECT *
13> FROM defaults
14>
15> GO
(1 row affected)
 c1          c2             c3                 c4
 ----------- -------------- ------------------ ------------
           1 column default 0x00000000000002A9         NULL

(1 row affected)
```

Trying to explicitly insert values into an identity column generates an error unless you override the identity property of the column using Transact-SQL syntax (see below). In addition, you have to use the `column_name` list in your `INSERT` statement.

The following example illustrates this concept using the `PAYMENT_TERMS` table created with `PAYTERMS_ID_N` as an identity column (see Chapter 4):

```
-- Trying to insert with IDENTITY_INSERT option off fails
1> INSERT INTO payment_terms
2> (
3>  payterms_id_n,
4>  payterms_code_s,
5>  payterms_desc_s,
6>  payterms_discpct_n,
7>  payterms_daystopay_n
8> )
9> VALUES
10> (
11>  26,
12>  'N30',
13>  'NET 30',
14>  0,
15>  30
16> )
17> GO

Msg 544, Level 16, State 1, Server PD-TS-TEST1, Line 1 Cannot
insert explicit value for identity column in table
'payment_terms' when IDENTITY_INSERT is set to OFF.
```

```
-- Set IDENTITY_INSERT option on; insert succeeds.
1> SET IDENTITY_INSERT payment_terms ON
2> GO

1> INSERT INTO payment_terms
2> (
3>  payterms_id_n,
4>  payterms_code_s,
5>  payterms_desc_s,
6>  payterms_discpct_n,
7>  payterms_daystopay_n
8> )
9> VALUES
10> (
11>  26,
12>  'N30',
13>  'NET 30',
```

```
14>  0,
15>  30
16> )
17> GO

(1 row affected)
```

UPDATE: Modifying Table Data

The UPDATE statement serves the purpose of modifying existing database information. We can emphasize two general situations when we need to change data.

Sometimes when you insert rows into a table, you don't know all information yet (that's where NULL values come in handy); later on, when the information becomes available, you can update the appropriate row(s). For example, you may want to create a new customer before you know who the customer's salesperson is going to be, or generate a new order line entry with an unknown shipped quantity. (There is no way to know what this quantity is before the order is actually shipped.)

Another case when you may need to change database information is when you have to reflect some changes in the "real world." For example, a customer could cancel an order, so you would have to change the order status from COMPLETE to CANCELLED; a customer might accumulate "bad debt," so you would want to put his credit on hold. (In the ACME database that would mean to change CUST_CREDHOLD_S field to Y.)

The UPDATE statement is used to modify table data; again, as with the INSERT statement discussed earlier, either directly or through an updateable view. Here is the generic syntax for our "big three" databases:

```
UPDATE <table_or_view_name>
SET {<column_name> = <literal> |
                       <expression> |
                       (<single_row_select_statement>) |
                     NULL |
                     DEFAULT,...}
[WHERE <predicate>]
```

The UPDATE statement allows you to update one table at a time. Other than that, it provides great flexibility on what set of values you are updating. You could update single or multiple columns of a single row or multiple rows, or (though it is rarely employed) you could update each and every column of all table rows. The granularity is determined by different clauses of the UPDATE statement.

The situation when no rows were updated because there were no rows in the table that satisfied the WHERE clause condition is not considered an error by RDBMS. The same stands for the DELETE statement (discussed in the next section). When no rows satisfy the WHERE clause, no rows are updated and no error is generated.

We are now going to discuss the most common clauses of the generic UPDATE.

Common UPDATE statement clauses

The name of the table (or an updateable view) to be updated is provided in the table_or_view_name clause.

In the SET clause, you specify the name of the column to update and the new value to be assigned to it. You can specify multiple corresponding column/value pairs separated by commas. The assignment values could themselves be the same as in the VALUES clause of the INSERT statement (i.e., literals, expressions, nulls, defaults, etc.).

The WHERE clause sets your "horizontal" limits—if in the SET clause you specified what columns to update, now you have to define a condition upon which some rows need to be updated.

Dangers of the WHERE Clause

The WHERE clause is very important and has to be handled with care. If you accidentally skipped it or based it on an incorrect assumption, it could update *all* rows in your table with the same value, and that's usually not what you want. For example, you might want to change the price from $33.28 to $34.76 for product 1880 (STEEL NAILS 6"). You start thinking—well, may be something like the following will do:

```
UPDATE product
SET prod_price_n = 34.76
```

But if you forgot about the WHERE clause, the result would be rather disastrous—all products in the ACME database now cost $34.76! The correct syntax to use would be:

```
UPDATE product
SET prod_price_n = 34.76
WHERE prod_num_s = '1880'
```

Note that even if you remembered about the WHERE clause but just made a typo, e.g., > instead of =, the result is not much better—all products with product numbers greater than '1880' will be erroneously updated.

Updating a single column of a single row

One of the most common update situations is when you need to modify just one column of a single row. Assigning a salesperson to a recently created customer, canceling an order, changing a product price—these are all examples of such a procedure. The following example assigns a price to product 990 that we previously created when we discussed INSERT in this chapter:

```
UPDATE product
SET prod_price_n = 18.24
WHERE prod_id_n = 990
```

Using primary key or column(s) with UNIQUE constraint in the UPDATE statement's WHERE clause ensures you are only updating one row uniquely identified by the value in the column.

Updating multiple columns

Sometimes you might want to update more than one column within one UPDATE statement. For example, imagine the manufacturer has changed the packaging for its product 990, so the dimensions are now 5×7 instead of 4×6. This update statement synchronizes the database information with the real-world change:

```
UPDATE product
SET prod_pltwid_n = 5,
    prod_pltlen_n = 7
WHERE prod_id_n = 990
```

Updating a column in all rows

Even though updating all table rows is not very typical (and often undesirable), sometimes you might want to perform such an operation. Giving all employees a 5 percent raise, inactivating all customers, setting all column values to NULL—these are a few common examples. As you could have noticed, the keyword here is "all." In other words, we would only want to omit the WHERE clause intentionally if we wanted to update each and every single row in the target table.

The UPDATE statement below increases all product prices by 10 percent (ACME, Inc. struggles with the increased operation costs):

```
UPDATE product
SET prod_price_n = prod_price_n * 1.1
```

Using operators in SQL queries is explained in Chapter 11.

Updating column using a single-row subquery

You can use the result of a `SELECT` statement (subquery) as an assignment value in an `UPDATE` statement. The main thing to remember is that your subquery must return no more than one row. (If no rows are returned, the `NULL` value will be assigned to the target column.) Also, according to SQL99 standards, only one expression can be specified in the select list.

Oracle and DB2 allow you to specify multiple values in the select list of a single row subquery; the details are given later in this chapter.

You can concatenate two or more columns or perform math operations on them, but you can not list multiple columns separated with commas. Thus, `SET my_col = (SELECT col1 + col2 ...)` is valid, but `SET my_col = (SELECT col1, col2 ...)` is not.

Deriving the assignment value from another value

There are many situations when using a subquery as an assignment value is beneficial. For example, you want to change the payment terms for order 30670 to be `N21531` in the ACME database. The problem is, in our relational database we do not store the actual value `N21531` in an `ORDER_HEADER` table column; instead, we use the foreign key, which is a meaningless integer, from the `PAYMENT_TERMS` table. Using a subquery helps us to accomplish the task:

```
UPDATE order_header
SET ordhdr_payterms_fn =
      (SELECT payterms_id_n
       FROM payment_terms
       WHERE payterms_code_s = 'N21531')
WHERE ordhdr_id_n = 30670
```

Figure 6-1 illustrates the above example.

ORDER_HEADER

ORDHDR_ID_N	ORDHDR_PAYTERMS_FN
...	...
30670	?
...	...

PAYMENT_TERMS

PAYTERMS_ID_N	PAYTERMS_CODE_S
...	...
27	N21531
...	...

Figure 6-1: Using data from other table as an assignment value

The statement above has two WHERE clauses, but don't be confused: the first one belongs to the SELECT statement — as indicated by the surrounding parentheses, limiting the resulting set to one value — the primary key for the row where the value of payterms_code_s column is equal to N21531; the second WHERE clause belongs to the UPDATE statement and ensures that only one row of ORDER_HEADER with ordhdr_id_n equal to 30670 is updated.

Update with correlated subquery

The previous example was relatively straightforward — you derived the value you needed for the update from another given value. But sometimes conditions are more complicated. For example, imagine that ACME's business rules have changed and no longer allow orders to have payment terms different from the default payment terms of a customer who placed the order. You can relate (join) a table from the UPDATE clause with tables specified in the assignment subquery — that pretty much overrides the "single-row" rule because the assignment will be done on a row-by-row basis:

```
UPDATE order_header
SET ordhdr_payterms_fn =
     (SELECT payterms_id_n
      FROM   payment_terms,
             customer
      WHERE  payterms_id_n = cust_paytermsid_fn
      AND    ordhdr_custid_fn = cust_id_n)
```

The very last line of this syntax joins the ORDHDR_CUSTID_FN field of the ORDER_HEADER table (UPDATE statement) with the CUST_ID_N table of the CUSTOMER table (nested subquery); in other words, the customer id field is the link between the UPDATE statement and the subquery that *correlates* them.

You don't have to use table aliasing here because of the special notation rules you used when the ACME database was created. Each column is already prefixed with its table name abbreviation, so there are no ambiguous column names.

More discussion about table aliasing can be found in Chapters 8 and 9.

For each row in ORDER_HEADER you must find the corresponding value in the resulting set of the subquery and use it as an assignment value. The concept is illustrated in Figure 6-2.

ORDER_HEADER

ORDHDR_ID_N	ORDHDR_CUSTID_FN	ORDHDR_PAYTERMS_FN
...	...	...
30618	152	?
30619	152	?
30620	7	?
...	...	...

CUSTOMER

CUST_ID_N	CUST_PAYTERMSID_FN
...	...
7	42
152	27
...	...

PAYMENT_TERMS

PAYTERMS_ID_N	PAYTERMS_CODE_S
...	...
27	N21531
42	N120
...	...

Figure 6-2: Updating multiple rows using correlated subquery

Note

This syntax uses "old" join notation, which is recognized by all our "big three" databases. We used it here because in our opinion it better illustrates the correlated query concept. The SQL99-compliant equivalent syntax would be:

```
UPDATE order_header
SET    ordhdr_payterms_fn =
        (SELECT payterms_id_n
         FROM payment_terms
         JOIN customer
         ON payterms_id_n = cust_paytermsid_fn
         JOIN order_header
         ON ordhdr_custid_fn = cust_id_n)
```

The main differences between the "old" and the "new" join syntaxes are discussed in Chapter 9.

Note

Subqueries can also be used in the `WHERE` clause of the `UPDATE` statement in a similar way to the `WHERE` clause of the `SELECT` statement. We are going to discuss subqueries in general and correlated subqueries in particular in Chapter 8.

UPDATE statement and integrity constraints

Updating table rows obeys rules and restrictions similar to ones with `INSERT` statement. All column values have to be of the same or compatible data types and sizes with corresponding column definitions and no integrity constraints should be violated. There is a slight difference in behavior with the referential integrity constraints — when constraint is specified with `ON UPDATE CASCADE` or `ON UPDATE SET NULL`, RDBMS successfully performs an update of the target table; child tables' columns are also updated with the corresponding values.

Constraints are discussed in Chapter 4.

Vendor-specific UPDATE statement details

Like the INSERT statement, UPDATE also has some vendor-specific features. This section briefly discusses the most important ones.

Oracle 9*i* and DB2 8.1

The main thing that differs between Oracle and DB2's UPDATE syntax and that of our generic one is the option to specify values enclosed into the brackets and separated with commas in the SET clause and specify multiple corresponding assignment values for them. The syntax is

```
SET (col1, col2,... colN) = (value1, value2,... valueN)
```

The advantage of this syntax is in ability to use a multicolumn subquery instead of the list of values:

```
SET (col1, col2,... colN) =
      (SELECT value1, value2,... valueN
       FROM...)
```

The subquery still has to return no more than one row.

Subqueries are explained in Chapter 8.

MS SQL Server 2000

The UPDATE statement has an optional FROM clause in MS SQL Server. It specifies the table(s) to be used to provide the criteria for the update operation and can be used in a very similar way to the previously discussed correlated query. The following example performs virtually the same task as the correlated query from the previous section; the only difference is that when you use the former syntax, each and every row of ORDER_HEADER is updated unconditionally, whereas MS SQL Server syntax excludes columns with nulls unless the OUTER JOIN was used (more about joins in Chapter 9):

```
UPDATE order_header
SET    ordhdr_payterms_fn = payterms_id_n
FROM   payment_terms JOIN   customer
ON     payterms_id_n = cust_paytermsid_fn JOIN order_header
ON     ordhdr_custid_fn = cust_id_n
```

DELETE: Removing Data from Table

Believe it or not, there is such a thing as too much data. Since computerized databases were introduced, humankind had accumulated pentabytes of data. We are drowning in it, and DELETE provides a way to get rid of the information that is no longer needed. Deleting database rows is usually necessary when the entity these rows correspond to becomes irrelevant or completely disappears from the real world. For example, an employee quits, a customer does not make orders any more, or shipment information is no longer needed.

Quite often the entity information is not removed from the database right away. When an employee quits, the HR department still keeps the historical information about this employee; when a customer is inactive for a long time, it is sometimes more logical to "inactivate" him rather than delete – in the relational database deleting a customer usually involves much more than just removing one CUSTOMER table record – it would normally have referential integrity constraints from other tables, the other tables in their order would be referenced by more tables, and so on. There is a way to simplify the process by using the ON DELETE CASCADE clause, but that's not always exactly what you want. Even when you don't need, say, information for a certain customer any more, you still may want to be able to access the data about orders and invoices for this customer, and so on.

You may also want to delete rows when they were inserted by mistake — for example, an order was taken twice, or a duplicate customer record was created. Situations like those are not atypical at all, especially for large companies where dozens of clerks take orders and create new customers.

Good database design can help to reduce the number of human errors. For example, putting unique constraint on the customer name field could help in preventing duplicate customers (not completely foolproof, though, because RDBMS would still treat "ACME, INC." and "ACME INC." as two distinct strings).

The DELETE statement removes rows from a single table (either directly or through an updateable view). The generalized syntax is

```
DELETE FROM <table_or_view_name>
WHERE <predicate>
```

The FROM keyword is optional in Oracle and MS SQL Server but is required for DB2 syntax and compliant with SQL99 standards.

DELETE removes rows from one table at a time. You can delete one or many rows using a single DELETE statement; when no rows in the table satisfy the condition specified in the WHERE clause, no rows are deleted, and no error message is generated.

Common DELETE statement clauses

The DELETE statement is probably the simplest out of all DML statements. All you need to specify is the table you want to remove rows from and (optionally) upon what criteria the rows are to be deleted. The syntax simplicity should not mislead you — DELETE statements can be quite complicated and require caution. If the WHERE clause is omitted or malformed, valuable information could be deleted from the target table. Quite often the results are not exactly what you wanted, and the data restoration process could be painful and time consuming.

The statement below deletes a salesman record from the SALESMAN table:

```
DELETE FROM salesman
WHERE salesman_code_s = '02'
```

This statement deletes all records from PHONE table:

```
DELETE FROM phone
```

DELETE statement and integrity constraints

The DELETE statement is not as restrictive as INSERT and UPDATE in terms of integrity constraints. PRIMARY KEY, UNIQUE, NOT NULL, or CHECK constraints would not prevent you from deleting a row. The referential integrity constraints are a different story — you would not be able to delete a row that contains a column referenced by another column unless the referential integrity constraint has the ON DELETE CASCADE option (SQL99 standard implemented by all "big three" RDBMS vendors). In that case DELETE would succeed; all rows in any tables that referenced the constrained column would also be deleted. This behavior can be extremely dangerous, especially in combination with a badly constructed WHERE clause, so it is considered to be a good practice to use ON DELETE CASCADE with care. Imagine the situation where you have a table CUSTOMER referenced by a table ORDER, which is its order referenced by a table SHIPMENT. If ON CASCADE DELETE is used in both relationships, when you delete a customer record, all related order and shipment records are also gone. Just imagine what would happen if you also skipped the WHERE clause! Figure 6-3 illustrates this example.

Another (slightly less dangerous) referential constraint option is ON DELETE SET NULL (SQL99 standard implemented by Oracle and DB2). No records from the referencing tables will be deleted, but the values for the foreign key columns will be set to nulls as illustrated in Figure 6-4.

DELETE FROM customer

CUSTOMER

CUST_ID	NAME	ADDRESS
...	...	...
1023	ACME, INC.	
...	...	...

ORDER

ORD_ID	CUST_ID_FK	...
...	...	...
100234	1023	...
100345	1023	...
...	...	...

SHIPMENT

SHIP_ID	ORD_ID_FK	...
...	...	...
200345	100234	...
200346	100234	...
200577	100345	...
200578	100345	...
200579	100345	...
...	...	...

Figure 6-3: Deleting from table referenced by ON DELETE CASCADE constraints

DELETE FROM customer

CUSTOMER

CUST_ID	NAME	ADDRESS
...	...	...
1023	ACME, INC.	
...	...	...

ORDER

ORD_ID	CUST_ID_FK	...
...	...	...
100234	NULL	...
100345	NULL	...
...	...	...

SHIPMENT

SHIP_ID	ORD_ID_FK	...
...	...	...
200345	100234	...
200346	100234	...
200577	100345	...
200578	100345	...
200579	100345	...
...	...	...

Figure 6-4: Deleting from table referenced by ON DELETE SET NULL constraints

If a referential integrity constraint exists on a column with default (NO ACTION) options, and the column is referenced, the DELETE would fail. The error messages vary between different vendors. The example below is for Oracle:

```
SQL> DELETE FROM CUSTOMER;
DELETE FROM CUSTOMER
*
ERROR at line 1:
ORA-02292: integrity constraint(ACME.FK_ORDHDR_CUSTOMER)
violated - child record found
```

Using subqueries in DELETE statement WHERE clause

Similarly to UPDATE statement, in addition to comparison operators, literals, and expressions, the WHERE clause in DELETE statements can contain a subquery to allow the selection of rows to be deleted based on data from other tables. The idea is very similar to one explained in section about the SET clause of the insert value — using a subquery you derive value(s) based on some known value(s). For example, you want to delete all orders for customer WILE SEAL CORP., but we don't know the value of its primary key (which is a foreign key in the ORDER_HEADER). You can accomplish the task using the appropriate subquery in the WHERE clause:

```
DELETE FROM order_header
WHERE ordhdr_custid_fn =
                        (SELECT cust_id_n
                         FROM customer
                         WHERE cust_name_s = 'WILE SEAL CORP.')
```

Tip

Correlated subqueries can also be used with the DELETE statement in a way similar to one discussed in the UPDATE section.

Vendor-specific DELETE statement clauses

The vendor-specific DELETE statement variations are rather insignificant. The brief explanation follows.

Oracle 9*i*

The only significant difference between Oracle and generic DELETE syntax is that the FROM keyword is optional and can be skipped.

MS SQL Server 2000

MS SQL Server recognizes our generic syntax that uses a subquery in the WHERE clause; in addition, it provides its own proprietary syntax using the FROM clause with different meaning. This is the equivalent to our "standard" syntax to delete all orders for WILE SEAL CORP.:

```
DELETE order_header
FROM order_header JOIN customer
ON ordhdr_custid_fn = cust_id_n
WHERE cust_name_s = 'WILE SEAL CORP.'
```

Other SQL Statements to Manipulate Data

Two more vendor-specific SQL statements to manipulate table data are MERGE and TRUNCATE

MERGE statement

Oracle 9*i* introduces the MERGE statement that could be thought of as a combination of INSERT and UPDATE. MERGE inserts a row if it does not yet exist and updates specified columns based on given criteria if the target row has previously been inserted. The syntax for the statement is

```
MERGE INTO [<qualifier>.]<table_name1>
USING [<qualifier>.]<table_name2> ON (<condition>)
WHEN MATCHED THEN
UPDATE SET {<column> = {<expression> | DEFAULT},...}
WHEN NOT MATCHED THEN
INSERT [(<column>,...)] VALUES (<expression> | DEFAULT,...);
```

The statement could be practical in many different situations; for example, imagine ACME, INC. has a central database and a local database for each warehouse. Each location has its own LOCAL_PRODUCT table that structurally is a copy of the PRODUCT table:

```
CREATE TABLE LOCAL_PRODUCT
(
  PROD_ID_N            NUMBER          NOT NULL,
  PROD_PRICE_N         NUMBER,
  PROD_NUM_S           VARCHAR2 (10),
  PROD_DESCRIPTION_S   VARCHAR2 (44)   NOT NULL,
  PROD_STATUS_S        CHAR (1)        DEFAULT 'Y',
  PROD_BRAND_S         VARCHAR2 (20)   NOT NULL,
  PROD_PLTWID_N        NUMBER          NOT NULL,
  PROD_PLTLEN_N        NUMBER          NOT NULL,
  PROD_NETWGHT_N       NUMBER,
  PROD_SHIPWEIGHT_N    NUMBER,
  CONSTRAINT CHK_LPRODSTATUS
             CHECK (PROD_STATUS_S in ('N', 'Y')),
  CONSTRAINT PK_LPRODUCTPRIM PRIMARY KEY ( PROD_ID_N ) );
```

You can use the MERGE statement to synchronize the contents of LOCAL_PRODUCT with data in PRODUCT. Most likely you don't have to synchronize all columns because some of them are static, i.e., data in these fields changes rarely, if ever. Assuming the values that could change are price, active status, packaging dimensions, and shipping weight your MERGE statement would be

```
MERGE INTO local_product lp
USING product p ON (lp.prod_id_n = p.prod_id_n )
WHEN MATCHED THEN UPDATE
SET      lp.prod_price_n = p.prod_price_n,
         lp.prod_status_s = p.prod_status_s,
         lp.prod_pltwid_n = p.prod_pltwid_n,
         lp.prod_pltlen_n = p.prod_pltlen_n,
         lp.prod_shipweight_n = p.prod_shipweight_n
WHEN NOT MATCHED THEN INSERT
```

```
VALUES    (p.prod_id_n,
           p.prod_price_n,
           p.prod_num_s,
           p.prod_description_s,
           p.prod_status_s,
           p.prod_brand_s,
           p.prod_pltwid_n,
           p.prod_pltlen_n,
           p.prod_netwght_n,
           p.prod_shipweight_n)
```

Now, when you run this statement for the first time when LOCAL_PRODUCT is empty, all rows from PRODUCT will be inserted into your local table. If scheduled to run on a permanent basis (for example, every hour) the MERGE statement will trace all possible changes in the PRODUCT table and will either update existing rows of LOCAL_PRODUCT appropriately or insert new rows.

TRUNCATE statement

In addition to the standard DML statements described in this chapter, Oracle and MS SQL Server also introduce a TRUNCATE statement that is functionally identical to DELETE without a WHERE clause—it removes all rows from the target table. The difference is that TRUNCATE is much faster and uses fewer system resources than DELETE. The main limitation of TRUNCATE is that you cannot use it on a table referenced by an enabled FOREIGN KEY constraint.

Tip Sometimes dropping referential integrity constraints, truncating table, and then re-creating constraints is still more efficient than using DELETE; also in Oracle you can disable and then re-enable constraints (see Chapter 5).

The syntax for TRUNCATE is simple:

```
TRUNCATE TABLE <table_name>
```

This example illustrates the use of TRUNCATE statement using Oracle:

```
-- TRUNCATE fails because PRODUCT is referenced
-- by foreign key FK_ORDLINE_PRODUCT
SQL> TRUNCATE TABLE PRODUCT;
TRUNCATE TABLE PRODUCT
               *
ERROR at line 1:
ORA-02266: unique/primary keys in table referenced by enabled foreign keys

-- Disable the constraint and try again
```

```
SQL> ALTER TABLE ORDER_LINE DISABLE CONSTRAINT FK_ORDLINE_PRODUCT;

Table altered.

SQL> TRUNCATE TABLE PRODUCT;

Table truncated.

-- Re-enable the constraint
SQL> ALTER TABLE ORDER_LINE ENABLE CONSTRAINT FK_ORDLINE_PRODUCT;

Table altered.
```

DB2 does not have TRUNCATE statement in its syntax.

Differences between Oracle and MS SQL Server TRUNCATE statements

The main difference is that in Oracle TRUNCATE is irreversible; in other words, you cannot undo it using the ROLLBACK statement. Moreover, Oracle treats TRUNCATE as a DDL statement, which means TRUNCATE, like any other DDL statement in Oracle, always ends transactions performing implicit COMMIT. That means if you issued five INSERT statements, ten updates, and three deletes on some tables, and then performed TRUNCATE for a yet another table within a single transaction, all your changes will be committed right away and the transaction will be ended.

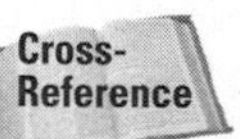

Transactional control terms and commands such as session, transaction, COMMIT, and ROLLBACK are covered in detail in Chapter 7.

MS SQL Server's transactional control differs from Oracle's one significantly, so the TRUNCATE behavior is also different. It is reversible by ROLLBACK statement within explicitly started transaction and does not perform the implicit COMMIT.

Summary

The three classical DML statements are INSERT, UPDATE, and DELETE.

RDBMS data is dynamic by definition because it represents real-world entities that often change. When a new entity emerges that is relevant to your database, you create new row(s) of data in one or more tables that represent this entity using an INSERT statement. When an entity already exists in the database changes in real world, you modify database information about this entity using an UPDATE statement. When an entity is no longer relevant to your database or disappears from the real world completely, you remove information about it from your database using a DELETE statement.

DML statements have different granularity. The smallest unit you can `INSERT` or `DELETE` is one row; `UPDATE` can perform changes on a singe column of a single row. Even though you might say you are deleting values from a column or inserting values into a column, you would actually use an `UPDATE` statement to set the column values to nulls or to certain values, correspondingly.

It is critical to understand the importance of the `WHERE` clause of `UPDATE` and `DELETE` statements. When the `WHERE` clause is omitted, all target table rows are affected (modified or removed).

Some vendors have additional statements that perform similar functions to the classical DML statements. In this chapter, we described Oracle 9*i*'s `MERGE` statement that combines the functionality of `INSERT` and `UPDATE` statements. The `TRUNCATE` statement supported by Oracle and MS SQL Server was also discussed; it works in a way like the `DELETE` statement without a `WHERE` clause.

✦ ✦ ✦

CHAPTER 7

Sessions, Transactions, and Locks

In This Chapter

Sessions

Database transactions

Introducing locks

In an ideal world, a database is accessed by one and only one user, changes are made and saved in a proper order, and malicious intrusion is an unheard of concept. Unfortunately, it doesn't happen like that in the real world. Frequently data must be shared; it might come from different sources, sometimes at unusual times; and rarely, if ever, would a database server be accessed by one user at a time.

Relational databases were designed to work in a multiuser environment. When more than one user accesses the same set of data, a completely different set of problems appears: What data should be visible for the users? Which modification should take the precedence? What is the guarantee that the data changes will not be lost during execution of a lengthy database procedure? The answer to these and many other problems comes in terms of sessions, transactions, and locks.

The transaction is a solution to potential data consistency problems (discussed in detail later in the chapter), while locks deal with data concurrency problems. The session represents the context in which — along with some other things — transactions and locks take place.

Sessions

Whatever happens in terms of communication between an RDBMS server and a user accessing it happens in the context of a *session*. In a multiuser environment, one of the primary concerns is data integrity. When a client application establishes a connection to an RDBMS server, it is said that it *opens a session*. The session becomes this application's private communication channel. The user of the application may change some preferences within the session (for example, default language or default date format); these settings would affect only the session environment and remain valid only for the duration of the session. The details of the implementation and default behavior of the sessions might differ among the RDBMS, but these basic principles always remain the same.

By now, you ought to be acquainted with at least one of the tools provided by Oracle, IBM, or Microsoft to access their respective databases. Each RDBMS package is a resource intensive piece of software, and in general it is recommended not to install all of them onto the same machine. Once you've installed your RDBMS of choice, you could run multiple instances of Oracle's SQL Plus to access Oracle 9*i* RDBMS, Microsoft's OSQL (if you've selected MS SQL Server 2000), or IBM's Command Line Processor for IBM DB2 UDB from the same computer where your RDBMS is installed, and each instance will open its own session, which would be isolated from every other session established to the RDBMS server.

The SQL standard specifies a number of parameters that could be set in a session (listed in Table 7-1). None of these are implemented directly by the RDBMS, though some elements made it into proprietary syntax, ditching the letter, preserving the spirit.

Table 7-1
SQL Standard SET Statements

SQL Statement	*Description*
`SET CONNECTION`	If more than one connection is opened by a user to an RDBMS, this statement allows that user to switch between the connections.
`SET CATALOG`	This statement defines the default catalog for the session.
`SET CONSTRAINTS MODE`	Changes the constraints mode between `DEFERRED`, and `IMMEDIATE`.
`SET DESCRIPTOR`	Stores values in the descriptor area.
`SET NAMES`	Defines the default character set for the SQL statements.
`SET SCHEMA`	Sets the schema to be used as a default qualifier for all unqualified objects.
`SET SESSION AUTHORIZATION`	Sets the authorization ID for the session, no other IDs can be used.
`SET TIME ZONE`	Sets the default time zone for the session.

In Oracle, a user must have a system privilege CREATE SESSION in order to establish a database connection. Initially, all the default parameter values for the session are loaded from a special Oracle configuration file; the file could be modified only by a database administrator, or someone who has the necessary privileges. Once the connection is established (a session is created), a user can alter the session according to his/her preferences and job requirements.

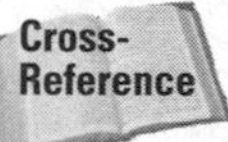

See Chapter 12 for more information on privileges.

The session parameters in Oracle can be modified using an ALTER SESSION statement. The syntax of the statement is relatively complicated and usually belongs to advanced database topics. Even the parameters that can be changed with this statement are somewhat irrelevant to SQL programming, like DB_BLOCK_CHECKING, HASH_JOIN_ENABLED, or MAX_DUMP_FILE_SIZE. These statements deal more with RDBMS administration and optimization, and belong to an advanced Oracle book.

We recommend *Oracle Administration and Management* by Michael Ault (Wiley, 2002).

Here we are going to demonstrate the concept of altering the session to suit your particular needs using one of the parameters NLS_DATE_FORMAT.

You can use this parameter to alter date format returned by your SQL query, as it specifies the default date format returned by the TO_CHAR and TO_DATE functions.

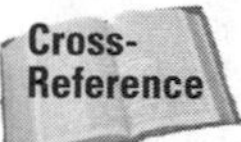

Read more about NLS_DATE_FORMAT in Chapter 10.

```
SQL> SELECT TO_CHAR(SYSDATE) nls_date
     FROM   dual;

NLS_DATE
------------------
06 - 10 - 03
```

The format in which the output of the TO_CHAR function appears is determined by the initialization parameter NLS_DATE_FORMAT, which is the default for each new session. After the session is altered, the format of the displayed date is changed:

```
SQL> ALTER SESSION
            SET NLS_DATE_FORMAT = 'DD-MON-YYYY HH24:MI:SS';

Session altered.

SQL > SELECT TO_CHAR(SYSDATE) nls_date
            FROM      dual;
```

```
NLS_DATE
------------------------------
06-OCT-2003 10:33:44
```

Setting SQL*Plus Session Parameters

Oracle's command-line utility SQL*Plus has its own parameters that can be set within the session initiated through it. These parameters affect the way data is fetched, manipulated, and displayed—in the SQL*Plus utility. The following is a short list of some options that could be SET in SQL *plus.

SET Option	***Description***
AUTO[COMMIT] {ON | OFF | IMMEDIATE}	This command sets up default behavior for the pending data changes in the database. Setting it to OFF (default value) requires users to commit changes manually, issuing the COMMIT statement.
[LIN]ESIZE n	This option sets up the maximum number of the characters that SQL*Plus can display on one line; range is from 1 to a system-dependent maximum.
NULL <text>	This option sets up the text you'd like to be displayed when data containing NULL is returned.
[PAGES]IZE n	Sets up the maximum number of lines per page for displaying the results of a query.
[WRA]P (WRA) {N | OFF}	This command determines how the output data is displayed: ON enables a returned row that is longer than the current setting to be wrapped to the next line, OFF truncates it to the size of the line.

All these options (and many more, not listed here) could be SET within the SQL*Plus environment using the standard syntax:

```
SET <option> [<value>]
```

The options set up during the session are usually lost once the session is ended. You can save these custom options into a script file, that later could be conveniently loaded into SQL*Plus to restore your custom session environment.

To view all parameters set for any given session, the SHOW ALL command is used:

```
SQL> show all
appinfo is ON and set to "SQL*Plus"
arraysize 15
autocommit OFF
autoprint OFF
autorecovery OFF
autotrace OFF
blockterminator "." (hex 2e)
btitle OFF and is the first few characters of the next SELECT
statement
cmdsep OFF
colsep " "
compatibility version NATIVE
concat "." (hex 2e)
copycommit 0
. . .
underline "-" (hex 2d)
USER is "ACME"
verify ON
wrap : lines will be wrapped
```

There are many more parameters than are shown here. Refer to the Oracle documentation for more information.

The changes made with an ALTER SESSION statement are valid for the duration of the session. To make changes permanent, the ALTER SYSTEM statement should be used.

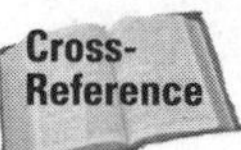

You may also control privileges afforded to the session by issuing a SET ROLE statement. Refer to Chapter 12 for more information.

IBM DB2 UDB provides surprisingly little control for the user over the session environment. It lists the keyword SESSION as reserved for future use, alongside with SESSION_USER.

The closest it comes to providing session control is with the SET PASSTHRU statement, which opens and closes a session for submitting SQL data directly to the database. Also, a global temporary table created during the session may be qualified with the SESSION component as a schema. (It is used to prevent ambiguity in accessing the table, when the temporary table name is the same as some persistent table, and in some other just as obscure cases.)

Microsoft SQL Server 2000 has a number of statements that you can specify to alter the current session (some of them are shown in Table 7-2 and Table 7-3). These statements are not part of SQL standard, being rather part of the Transact-SQL dialect. They can be grouped in several categories: statements that affect date and time settings, query execution statements, statistics statements, locking and transaction statements, SQL-92 settings statements, and — the all-time favorite — miscellaneous settings.

While detailed discussion of these settings and their implications are well beyond the scope of our SQL topic, nevertheless, we are going to discuss some of the most important statements and how they may affect your SQL statements executed against Microsoft SQL Server 2000.

Table 7-2
Microsoft SQL Server 2000 SQL-92 Settings

SET Statement	*Description*
`SET ANSI_DEFAULTS {ON | OFF}`	Specifies that all the defaults used for the duration of the session should be these of ANSI defaults. This option is provided for compatibility with SQL Server 6.5 or later
`SET ANSI_NULL_DFLT_OFF {ON | OFF}`	Specifies whether columns could contain `NULL` value by default. If set to `ON`, the new columns created would allow `NULL` values (unless `NOT NULL` is specified); otherwise it would raise an error. It has no effect on the columns explicitly set for `NULL`. It is used to override default nullability of new columns when the `ANSI` null default option for the database is `TRUE`.
`SET ANSI_NULL_DFLT_ON {ON | OFF}`	Essentially, the same as the statement above, with one exception: it is used to override default nullability of new columns when the ANSI null default option for the database is `FALSE`.
`SET ANSI_NULLS {ON | OFF}`	Specifies the SQL-92 compliant behavior when comparing values using operators `EQUAL` (=) and `NOT EQUAL` (< >).

SET Statement	***Description***
SET ANSI_PADDING {ON | OFF}	Specifies how the values that are shorter than the column size for CHAR, VARCHAR, BINARY, and VARBINARY data types are displayed.
SET ANSI_WARNINGS {ON | OFF}	Specifies whether a warning should be issued when any of the following conditions occur: presence of NULL values in the columns evaluated in the aggregate functions (like SUM, AVG,COUNT, etc.); divide-by-zero and arithmetic overflow errors generate an error message and the statement rolls back when this option is set to ON; specifying OFF would cause a NULL value to be returned in the case.

Here is an example of how setting ANSI_NULLS affects the output in the current session. The SQL-92 standard mandates that the comparison operations involving NULL always evaluate to FALSE. The following statement is supposed to bring all the records from the PHONE table of the ACME database when the PHONE_SALESMANID_FN filed is not NULL.

```
1> SET ANSI_NULLS ON
2> GO
1> SELECT phone_phonenum_s
2> FROM   phone
3> WHERE  phone_salesmanid_fn <> NULL
4> GO

PHONE_PHONENUM_S
--------------------
 (0 row(s) affected)
```

The query returns zero records in spite of the fact that there are supposed to be 12 records satisfying this criterion. Setting the ANSI_NULLS OFF changes the situation (valid in Microsoft SQL Server only; neither Oracle nor IBM DB2 UDB supports this feature):

```
1> SET ANSI_NULLS OFF
2> GO
1> SELECT phone_phonenum_s
2> FROM   phone
3> WHERE  phone_salesmanid_fn <> NULL
```

```
4> GO

PHONE_PHONENUM_S
--------------------
(305) 555-8502
(626) 555-4435
(717) 555-5479
(718) 555-7879
(718) 555-5091
(814) 555-0324
(305) 555-8501
(626) 555-4434
(717) 555-5478
(718) 555-7878
(718) 555-5091
(814) 555-0323

(12 row(s) affected)
```

This situation could be completely avoided if the IS NULL syntax is used. The query

```
SELECT phone_phonenum_s
FROM   phone
WHERE  phone_salesmanid_fn IS NULL
```

would return correct results in all three RDBMS. Since NULL is not a specific value, it has to be treated differently. Neither Oracle 9*i* nor IBM DB2 UDB have such a setting as ANSI_NULLS. Refer to Chapter 3 for more information about NULL.

Table 7-3
Microsoft SQL Server 2000 SET Statements

SET Statement	***Description***
SET DATEFORMAT {<format> | @<format ID>}	Specifies the order of the date parts for DATETIME and SMALLDATETIME input.
SET CONCAT_NULL_YIELDS_NULL {ON | OFF}	Specifies what would be the result of concatenation of the column values (or expressions) should any or both of them contain NULL.
SET LANGUAGE { <language> | @<language ID>}	Specifies the default language for the session. This setting affects the datetime format, and system messages returned by SQL Server.

SET Statement	*Description*
SET NOCOUNT {ON | OFF}	SQL Server usually returns a message indicating how many rows were affected by any given statement. Issuing this command would stop this message.
SET NUMERIC_ROUNDABORT {ON | OFF}	Specifies the severity of an error that results in loss of precision; if set to OFF the rounding generates no error; when it is set to ON, then an error will be generated and no results returned. Depending on some other settings, a NULL might be returned.
SET ROWCOUNT <integer>	If this statement is used, Microsoft SQL Server stops processing a query after the required number of rows (specified in the SET statement) is returned.

It is possible to specify multiple options with ON or OFF settings, using one SET statement. For example, the following statement will set two options at the same time.

```
1> SET NOCOUNT,  ANSI_DEFAULTS ON
2> GO
```

To check the options set for your session, use the following statement. It returns all the active options that have been set for this particular session within which you execute this statement

```
1> DBCC USEROPTIONS

Set Option                    Value
--------------------------    ---------------------
textsize                      64512
language                      us_english
dateformat                    mdy
datefirst                     7
quoted_identifier             SET
arithabort                    SET
ansi_null_dflt_on             SET
ansi_defaults                 SET
```

```
ansi_warnings                     SET
ansi_padding                      SET
ansi_nulls                        SET
concat_null_yields_null           SET

(12 row(s) affected)

DBCC execution completed. If DBCC printed error messages,
contact your system administrator.
```

The DataBase Console Command (DBCC) package is a toolbox of all the DBA utilities, with some options accessible to a user. There are over 60 DBCC commands that handle various aspects of SQL Server configuration, administration, status checking, and so on.

If the SET statement is set in the stored procedure, it is valid within the session for the duration of the stored procedure execution, and reverts to its previous value once the execution stops. When using Dynamic SQL (see Chapter 15), the SET statement affects only the batch it is specified in; subsequent statements will not be affected by this setting.

Some other SET statements pertaining to transactions and locks will be discussed in the corresponding paragraphs of this chapter.

When a client terminates a session—either voluntarily or abnormally—all values set for various session parameters disappear. In addition, for all pending transactions, an implicit commit will be issued in the case of voluntary termination or rolled back when the session has terminated abnormally. The session can be killed or disconnected by a DBA; syntax for the statements vary among RDBMS.

Orphaned Sessions

Orphaned sessions occur when a client application terminates abruptly without the ability to terminate its open session to RDBMS server. Usually, it is the responsibility of the operating system to detect that the client exited, and notify the server. (In some implementations, the server would query the client whether it is still present after some period of inactivity.) Certain situations, however, might prevent a proper client exit (e.g., sudden network failure). If the session was active (i.e., RDBMS was processing some command at the time), it will detect the absence of the client automatically and terminate the session. However, if the session was inactive, waiting for command from the client, such a session remains valid for the server.

Such sessions consume system resources and should be cleaned up. Usually it is done automatically after a certain interval configured for the server; or these sessions may be resolved manually by the DBA.

Transactions

A transaction is one of the mechanisms provided within SQL to enforce database integrity and maintain data consistency. The details of implementation differ among the RDBMS vendors, though the SQL92/99 spirit is generally preserved.

What is a transaction?

A transaction complements the concept of the session with additional granularity — it divides every operation that occurs within the session into logical units of work. In this way, database operations — those involving data and structure modifications — are performed step-by-step and can be rolled back at any time, or committed if every step is successful. The idea of the transaction is to provide a mechanism for ensuring that a multistep operation is performed as a single unit. If any of the steps involved in a transaction fails, the whole transaction is rolled back. If all steps have been completed successfully, the transaction can be either committed (to save all the changes into a database) or rolled back to undo all the changes.

The SQL standard defined transactions from the very beginning and enhanced the concept during subsequent iterations. According to the standard, a transaction is started automatically by RDBMS and continues until `COMMIT` or `ROLLBACK` statements are issued; the details were left for the vendors to implement.

A transaction must pass the ACID test:

- ✦ **Atomicity.** Either all the changes are made or none.
- ✦ **Consistency.** All the data involved into an operation must be left in a consistent state upon completion or rollback of the transaction; database integrity cannot be compromised.
- ✦ **Isolation.** One transaction should not be aware of the modifications made to the data by any other transaction unless it was committed to the database. Different isolation levels can be set to modify this default behavior.
- ✦ **Durability.** The results of a transaction that has been successfully committed to the database remain there.

One of the classic real-life example of a transaction involves an ATM (bank machine) withdrawal operation. Suppose you need $20 and you decide to withdraw this money from the nearest bank machine; you put in your bank card (User ID) and enter your PIN (personal identification number) to initiate the session. Once the bank confirms your identity, you are allowed to proceed; you ask for a money withdrawal operation in the amount of $20. That's where the transaction begins. There are several operations involved: the machine needs to check your account to verify that you have enough money to cover the transaction, subtract the money from your account, and release the money to you. If any of these steps (and some others, depending on the given bank policies) fails, the transaction must be aborted, and everything must revert to a state where it was before the transaction even began.

Explicit and Implicit Transactions

An implicit transaction has been chosen as the default in SQL92/99 standard. Whenever certain statements (of DDL and DML type) are executed within a session, they start (or continue) a transaction. A transaction is terminated by issuing either a `COMMIT` statement or a `ROLLBACK` statement.

An explicit transaction is started by the client application with a `BEGIN TRANSACTION` statement and is terminated in a manner similar to the implicit transaction protocol. This is a Microsoft SQL Server 2000–only feature, which is the default setting. Microsoft SQL Server 2000 provides a statement `SET IMPLICIT_TRANSACTIONS {ON | OFF}` to configure the default behavior of the transaction. When the option is `ON`, the SQL Server automatically starts a transaction when one of the following statements is specified: `ALTER TABLE`, `CREATE`, `DELETE`, `DROP`, `FETCH`, `GRANT`, `INSERT`, `OPEN`, `REVOKE`, `SELECT`, `TRUNCATE TABLE` and `UPDATE`. The transaction must be explicitly committed or rolled back, though; a new transaction is started once any of the listed statements gets executed. Turning the `IMPLICIT_TRANSACTIONS` option `OFF` returns the transaction to its default autocommit transaction mode.

While not required by the SQL standard, in every RDBMS implementation `COMMIT` is issued implicitly before and after any DDL statement.

This means that you cannot get your cash, unless it was subtracted from your balance; the bank cannot subtract the money from your balance unless you have enough money to cover the transaction and you actually received your cash.

The transaction model, as it is defined in the ANSI/ISO standard, utilizes the implicit start of a transaction, with an explicit `COMMIT`, in the case of successful execution of all transactions logical units, or an explicit `ROLLBACK`, when the noncommitted changes need to be rolled back (e.g., when program terminates abnormally). Most vendors follow this model, while some — Microsoft SQL Server 2000 is one example — allow for explicit start of a transaction.

Transactions COMMIT and ROLLBACK

The `COMMIT` statement ends the current transaction and makes all changes made to the data during transaction permanent. The syntax is virtually identical for all three RDBMS vendors, as well as for the SQL99 standard, and is very straightforward:

```
COMMIT [WORK]
```

The keyword `WORK` is not required, though it might be added for clarity; a simple `COMMIT` is usually all that is required.

Oracle 9*i* syntax looks like follows

```
COMMIT [WORK] [COMMENT (<text>)] [FORCE (<text>), [<int>]] ;
```

Here the COMMENT clause enables you to specify a comment (up to 255 bytes long) that is recorded for every pending transaction and can be viewed through DBA2_PC_PENDING dictionary view (see Chapter 13 for more information on system catalogs). The FORCE clause allows you to commit an in-doubt *distributed* (see more about distributed transactions later in the chapter) transaction manually; it commits only a named transaction and has no effect on all other transactions.

The IBM DB2 UDB syntax is identical to the standard. In IBM terminology, transaction is a unit of work (UOW). No authorization is required to issue the statement; all locks held by the transaction are released. Named transactions are not supported.

The following syntax will work both for Oracle 9*i* and IBM BDF2 UDB:

```
UPDATE customer
SET cust_status_s = 'N';

COMMIT;
```

Microsoft SQL Server 2000 does support the SQL99 standard syntax—in addition to its own. The Microsoft syntax allows for committing named transaction whereas the standard one does not.

```
COMMIT [ TRAN [ SACTION ] [<transaction name>]]
```

As you can see, only COMMIT is required, everything else is optional, and the keywords can be shortened (i.e., TRAN instead of TRANSACTION). Alternatively COMMIT WORK can be used.

The following example illustrates the COMMIT statement using Microsoft SQL Server 2000 explicit transactions mode.

```
BEGIN TRAN
    SELECT * FROM customer
    UPDATE customer
    SET cust_status_s = 'N'
COMMIT TRAN
```

No changes are taking place until the last COMMIT is executed. Only Microsoft requires a BEGIN TRANSACTION statement to start an explicit transaction; in both Oracle and DB2 UDB, transaction are always started implicitly for every DML or DDL statement.

Nested Transactions

Named transactions are especially handy for nested transactions. This concept is not implemented by either Oracle or IBM DB2UDB. The idea is to have a transaction within a transaction within a transaction—ad infinitum. At any time you can check the total number of pending transactions using the @@TRANSCOUNT unary function. Nested transactions in Microsoft SQL Server 2000 are introduced for readability purposes only; committing an internal transaction does not really commit anything, only the outermost COMMIT actually commits the changes; all other commits just decrement the transaction counter. Here is an example illustrating the concept:

```
BEGIN TRANSACTION trans1
-- the transaction counter @@TRANSCOUNT = 1
INSERT INTO <table> VALUES <values>
BEGIN TRANSACTION trans2
-- the transaction counter @@TRANSCOUNT = 2
INSERT INTO <table> VALUES <values>
BEGIN TRANSACTION trans3
-- the transaction counter @@TRANSCOUNT = 3
INSERT INTO <table> VALUES <values>
COMMIT TRANSACTION  trans3
-- Nothing committed at this point but the transaction
-- counter is decremented by 1; @@TRANSACOUNT = 2
COMMIT TRANSACTION trans2
-- Nothing committed at this point but the transaction counter
-- is decremented by 1; @@TRANSACOUNT = 1
COMMIT TRANSACTION trans1
-- All INSERTs are committed to the database
-- the transaction counter is decremented by 1; @@TRANSACOUNT =0
```

In this case, three transactions were initiated to insert three records into a table; only the very last COMMIT actually made the changes to the table.

When COMMIT is executed, SQL Server must start a transaction either implicitly or explicitly for another COMMIT to execute successfully; if no transaction is started, issuing this command will result in an error:

```
Server: Msg 3902, Level 16, State 1, Line 1
The COMMIT TRANSACTION request has no corresponding BEGIN TRANSACTION.
```

Neither Oracle nor DB2 UDB will complain, no matter how many times you execute COMMIT.

When changes made to the data in the databases need to be "undone" the ROLLBACK should be used. It may be issued anytime before the last COMMIT and results in automatic rollback of all changes made since the controlling transaction had started.

The syntax is identical in all RDBMS and SQL99 standards (see Table 7-4), save for using named transactions in Microsoft SQL Server 2000 and some Oracle-specific optional clauses. The following statement will attempt to update column CUST_STATUS_S in the CUSTOMER table of the ACME database, but all changes will be rolled back:

```
UPDATE customer
SET    cust_status_s = 'N'

ROLLBACK WORK
```

As with a COMMIT statement, all the locks are released if the ROLLBACK command is issued.

Table 7-4
Vendor-Specific ROLLBACK Statements

RDBMS	*ROLLBACK Syntax*
Oracle 9*i*	ROLLBACK [WORK] [TO SAVEPOINT <savepoint name>] | [FORCE <text>]
IBM DB2 UDB	ROLLBACK [WORK] [TO SAVEPOINT <savepoint name>]
Microsoft SQL Server 2000	ROLLBACK [TRAN[SACTION]] [<transaction name>] [<savepoint name>]

The Oracle 9*i* WORK clause is optional and the TO SAVEPOINT clause is explained later in this chapter; the FORCE clause pertains to distributed transactions, acting very much the same as in the COMMIT transaction case; Microsoft SQL Server has an optional transaction name clause.

Because certain statements (like DDL) automatically issue a COMMIT before and after, every change to data that happened prior to the DDL statement would be committed as well.

Here is an example that is valid for all three RDBMS (assuming the IMPLICIT_TRANSACTIONS option is set to ON in Microsoft SQL Server 2000):

```
UPDATE customer
SET    cust_status_s = 'N'
```

```
WHERE  cust_id_n = 1

DELETE customer
WHERE  cust_id_n = 1

ROLLBACK WORK
```

Neither UPDATE nor DELETE will be committed to the database, as the whole transaction is rolled back.

Usually, a transaction consists of more than one SQL statement that you may want to either COMMIT or ROLLBACK. To add granularity to the transaction processing, the SAVEPOINT concept was introduced. It allows you to specify a named point within the transaction, usually after the last successful statement, and, if any error occurs after that, roll all the changes back not to the beginning of the transaction but to that particular SAVEPOINT. An explicit (or implicit, like the one issued after a DDL statement) COMMIT releases all SAVEPOINTs declared within a transaction.

Oracle 9*i* has the most straightforward syntax for the SAVEPOINT:

```
SAVEPOINT <savepoint name>;
```

Here is an example of using the SAVEPOINTs in Oracle:

```
UPDATE customer
SET    cust_status_s = 'N'
WHERE  cust_id_n = 1;

SAVEPOINT first_upadate;

DELETE customer
WHERE  cust_id_n = 2;

SAVEPOINT first_delete;

DELETE customer
WHERE  cust_id_n = 10;

ROLLBACK first_update;

COMMIT;
```

In the example above, only UPDATE gets committed to the database, all DELETEs are rolled back, and the SAVEPOINT first_delete is erased.

The savepoint name must be unique within the current transaction; if a new savepoint uses the same name, the previous savepoint is destroyed.

Here is the IBM DB2 UDB syntax for SAVEPOINT:

```
SAVEPOINT <savepoint name > [UNIQUE]
[ON ROLLBACK RETAIN CURSORS]
[ON ROLLBACK RETAIN LOCKS]
```

Several optional clauses can be specified with the standard SAVEPOINT statement. The UNIQUE clause indicates that the session does not intend to reuse the name, rendering it therefore unique; if this statement is omitted and the same name is used later in the transaction, the previous SAVEPOINT with that name will be destroyed and a new one created.

The ON ROLLBACK RETAIN CURSORS clause specifies what the system will do with implicit or explicit cursors opened after the SAVEPOINT statement in the case of a rollback; the last clause — ON ROLLBACK RETAIN LOCKS — changes the default behavior that instructs RDBMS not to release locks acquired after the SAVEPOINT statement.

See Chapter 14 for more information on explicit cursors. Both IBM and Oracle employ a concept of an implicit cursor – a special structure for manipulating data, when virtually every select statement opens one. The discussion of implicit cursors is beyond the scope of this book.

DB2 UDB also has RELEASE SAVEPOINT statement that destroys all the SAVEPONTS created after that named savepoint.

Microsoft SQL Server 2000 has the most unorthodox syntax, when it comes to establishing the SAVEPOINTs.

```
SAVE TRAN[SACTION] <savepoint name>
```

When rolling back to a specific SAVEPOINT, all data changes become undone, but all the locks are held until COMMIT or full ROLLBACK commands are issued. The SAVE TRAN [SACTION] statement is not supported in distributed transactions.

Here is an example illustrating use of the SAVE TRANSACTION statement in Microsoft SQL Server 2000:

```
BEGIN TRANSACTION trans1

UPDATE customer
SET    cust_status_s = 'N'
```

```
WHERE  cust_id_n = 1

SAVE TRANSACTION cust_1

UPDATE customer
SET    cust_status_s = 'N'
WHERE  cust_id_n = 2

ROLLBACK TRANSACTION cust_1

COMMIT TRANSACTION
```

Distributed Transactions

Transactions that involve more than one database are referred to as *distributed transactions*. Such transactions are by their very nature complex and require advanced skills and knowledge.

In Oracle 9*i*, a distributed query uses *dblinks* to qualify the object, and there are several restrictions for such transactions. The RDBMS server manages these transactions and ensures data consistency; a special `ADVISE` statement issued within the session determines whether the transaction needs to be rolled back or committed whenever its status is set in doubt by the database.

IBM DB2 UDB labels distributed transactions as `DUOW` (Distributed Unit Of Work) and uses the Database Manager to coordinate distributed transactions.

In Microsoft SQL Server 2000, the task of managing the distributed transactions belongs with MSDTC (Microsoft Distributed Transaction Coordinator). (Other transaction managers complying to the X/Open XA specification could be employed instead.) The transaction can be explicitly started with the `BEGIN DISTRIBUTED TRANS[ACTION]` statement.

A distributed transaction must minimize the risk of data loss in case of a network failure. The two-phase commit protocol is employed in distributed transactions, and while details of the implementation are different between the vendors, they generally follow the same phases.

- ✦ **Prepare Phase.** When the transaction manager receives a `COMMIT` request, it communicates it to all resource managers involved in the transaction, and they prepare to do a `COMMIT`
- ✦ **Commit Phase.** In this phase, they actually issue `COMMIT` and report to the coordinator; when all `COMMIT`s are successful, the coordinator sends notification to the client application. If any of the resource managers fails to notify the coordinator, a `ROLLBACK` command is issued to all resource managers. To perform a `ROLLBACK` after a `COMMIT` is executed, log files are normally used.

This code begins a named transaction TRANS1, updates field CUST_STATUS_S for the customer whose ID is 1, then creates a SAVEPOINT with the name CUST_1. It then proceeds to update another customer's status, and then it rolls back the changes made for customer 2 by rolling back the transaction to the savepoint. The transaction is finally committed, and only the first update actually takes place.

Transaction isolation levels

There are different transaction isolation levels. Isolation levels refer to the ability of the transaction to see the world (data) outside its own scope, i.e., data modified by any other transaction. The SQL99 standard isolation levels are listed in Table 7-5.

Table 7-5
SQL99 Transaction Isolation Levels

Isolation Level	*Description*
READ UNCOMMITED	This level is the lowest of all isolation levels, permitting *dirty reads* (i.e., able to see uncommitted data). No locks are issued, none honored.
READ COMMITED	This level specifies that shared locks will be held while data is being read. No *dirty reads* (containing uncommitted data) are permitted; though *phantom reads* (when row number changes between the reads) may occur.
REPEATABLE READ	No changes will be allowed for the data selected by a query (locked for updates, deletes, etc.), but phantom rows may appear.
SERIALIZABLE	The highest level of transaction isolation; places a lock for the whole dataset; no modifications from outside are allowed until the end of the transaction.

Oracle 9*i* has two transaction isolation levels — SERIALIZABLE and READ COMMITED. The SET TRANSACTION syntax for Oracle can be complicated:

```
SET TRANSACTION
    [READ ONLY] | [READ WRITE]
    [ISOLATION LEVEL [SERIALIZABLE | READ COMMITTED]]
    [USE ROLLBACK SEGMENT &lt;segment name&gt;]
    [NAME <transaction  name>]
```

As you can see, the statement can be used to set many parameters, though it cannot be done all at once. To set a transaction as READ ONLY, the following statement could be used:

```
SET TRANSACTION READ ONLY NAME 'trans1';

SELECT  *
FROM    CUSTOMER ;

COMMIT;
```

After the transaction was set as READ ONLY, you cannot modify any data within this transaction either with UPDATE or INSERT statements.

Oracle is the only one among the "big three" RDBMS that provides for READ ONLY mode of a transaction. In full compliance with the SQL99 standard, this clause sets the transaction for read-only mode, and an error is generated if an attempt to change data is made. It establishes statement-level behavior, which becomes the default for the session.

There is some terminology confusion in how DB2 UDB defines transaction isolation levels. What SQL99 specifies as SERIALIZABLE, it names REPEATABLE READ (RR), which is the highest isolation level in DB2 UDB.

SQL99 REPEATABLE READ becomes READ STABILITY (RS), and a new level—CURSOR STABILITY—is introduced.

The last one, CURSOR STABILITY (CS), is the default for IBM DB2 UDB and resembles the READ COMMITTED level of the SQL99 standard. Essentially, it guarantees that a row of data will remain unchanged.

The UNCOMMITED READ (UR) level is the same as it is defined by the standard: no locks are acquired, so dirty reads are possible.

DB2 UDB also has NO COMMIT (NC) as the isolation level, which is not supported by its mainframe big brother DB2.

When establishing connection from within an application, the isolation level can be specified using PREP or BIND API directives, from the command-line processor the following statement may be used:

```
db2 => CHANGE ISOLATION TO UR
DB20000I The CHANGE ISOLATION command completed successfully
```

Tip

You cannot change isolation levels while connected to DB2 UDB; the isolation level is specified before the connection is established. Use the `TERMINATE` command to disconnect from the DB2 UDB database.

Microsoft SQL Server 2000 supports all four levels of isolation. The isolation level is set for the whole session, not just a single transaction. To specify a level within the session, the following statement is used:

```
SET TRANSACTION ISOLATION LEVEL <level>
```

Here is an example, illustrating the importance of the transaction isolation level to manipulate consistent data using Microsoft SQL Server 2000. (The example, with minor modifications, is applicable to Oracle and DB2 UDB as well.) This example performs an update, selects the updated value, and then rolls back the transaction (OSQL interface, see Appendix E for more information):

```
1> SELECT cust_status_s
2> FROM   customer
3> WHERE  cust_id_n = 1
4> GO

 cust_status_s
 -------------
 N
(1 row affected)
1> SET TRANSACTION ISOLATION LEVEL READ COMMITTED
2> GO
1> BEGIN TRAN TRAN1
2> UPDATE customer
3> SET    cust_status_s = 'Y'
4> WHERE  cust_id_n = 1
5> GO

(1 row affected)

1> SELECT cust_status_s
2> FROM   customer
3> WHERE  cust_id_n = 1
4> GO

 cust_status_s
 -------------
 Y

(1 row affected)

1> ROLLBACK TRAN TRAN1
2> GO
1> SELECT cust_status_s
2> FROM   customer
```

```
3> WHERE  cust_id_n = 1
4> GO

 cust_status_s
 -------------
 N

(1 row affected)
```

The transaction TRANS1 updates the field CUST_STATUS_S, changing it from Y to N, and then issues a SELECT statement that shows the changed data. The transaction isolation level for the session is READ COMMITED, so only changes committed to the database are supposed to be selected. Since the SELECT was issued within the same transaction, it will be able to see uncommitted changes made by this transaction update. The data changes will be visible to other transactions that attempt to select it within the sessions with transaction isolation level set to READ UNCOMMITED; but they are invisible for transactions with other levels of isolation—if they were issued prior to the ROLLBACK TRANSACTION statement. The example also shows that the data, after the transaction was rolled back, remain unchanged.

Understanding Locks

Concurrency is one of the major concerns in a multiuser environment. When multiple sessions write or read data to and from shared resources, a database might loose its integrity. To prevent this from happening, every RDBMS worth its salt implements a concurrency control mechanisms. In the case of RDBMS servers, the concurrency is managed through various locking mechanisms. All three leading RDBMS vendors have implemented sophisticated mechanisms for concurrency management.

Oracle has probably the most evolved and complex locking schema. It follows the rule that reading and writing processes cannot block each other, even if working on the same (or a close) set of data. Each session receives a read-consistent image of the data. Thus, even if some other process has begun modifying data in the set but did not commit the changes, every subsequent session will be able to read the data just as it was before; once the changes are committed in the first session, every other session is able to see it. The locks are acquired only when the changes are being committed to the database. Oracle automatically selects the least-restrictive lock. User can choose to manually lock a resource (a table, for example). In this case, other users still might be able to access the data, depending on the type of lock deployed.

IBM DB2 UDB and Microsoft SQL Server 2000 both employ locks that can enable a reader to block a writer and vice versa. The problem of concurrent access to the data is somewhat alleviated by the granularity of the locking—table, page, row, and so on. There are locks acquired by read-only queries, DDL statements, DML queries, and so on. There are different lock types for each scenario, which we're going to discuss in more detail.

Most of the time, a user does not have to worry about locking, as RDBMS automatically select the most appropriate lock (or locks) for a particular operation; only if this programmed logic fails should you attempt to specify the locks manually, using the SQL statements.

Locking modes

There are two broad categories of concurrency—optimistic and pessimistic. The names are self-explanatory. Transactions with optimistic concurrency work on the assumption that resource conflicts—when more than one transaction works on the same set of data—are unlikely (though possible). Optimistic transactions check for potential conflicts when committing changes to a database and conflicts are resolved by resubmitting data. Pessimistic transactions expect conflicts from the very beginning and lock all resources they intend to use. Usually RDBMS employ both optimistic and pessimistic transactions, and users can instruct their transactions to use either.

Locking granularity has a significant effect on system performance. Row-level locking increases concurrency (i.e., does not block other transactions from accessing a table) but usually incurs overhead costs of administration. A full table lock is much less expensive in terms of system resources but comes at the price of concurrency. This is something to keep in mind when designing database applications.

Locks are used to implement pessimistic transactions, and each RDBMS has its own levels of locking, though there are some similarities. In general, there are either share locks or exclusive locks, which refer to the way a resource (e.g., a table) is being used.

In Oracle, when a client process accesses a resource, it can explicitly lock the resource using one of the lock types specified in Table 7-6. Such a lock overrides any automatic lock settings.

Table 7-6
Oracle 9*i* Lock Modes

Lock Mode	***Description***
EXCLUSIVE	Allows a SELECT query on the locked table, all other operations (i.e., UPDATE, DELETE, etc.) are prohibited to other transactions.
SHARE	Allows concurrent queries, but updates are prohibited for all transactions.
ROW SHARE	Allows concurrent access to the table, but no other users can acquire an exclusive lock on the table. Also, the SHARE UPDATE mode is provided for backward compatibility.
ROW EXCLUSIVE	Is essentially the same as ROW SHARE but also prevents locking in SHARE mode.
SHARE ROW EXCLUSIVE	Locks the whole table; queries are allowed but no other transaction can acquire any lock on the table.

For example, the following statement locks table CUSTOMER of the ACME database in exclusive mode:

```
LOCK TABLE customer
IN EXCLUSIVE MODE;
```

The transaction that issues this statement will attempt to lock the table for its exclusive use, subject to the restrictions specified in Table 7-6. If any other process keeps a lock on the table, the transaction will be put in a queue, and the lock will be acquired in priority received. The lock will be in place for the duration of the transaction (i.e., until COMMIT is executed). A deadlock situation might occur (see next paragraph) if the transaction that already holds a lock on the table attempts to acquire a lock on a resource that the second transaction has a lock on. The clause NOWAIT instructs a transaction to move on if a table it tries to lock is already locked.

```
LOCK TABLE customer
IN EXCLUSIVE MODE NOWAIT;
```

If the lock command is issued for a view, Oracle will attempt to lock the base tables for the view. Certain types of operations require locking. Oracle will allow you to perform DDL operations on a table only if that table can be locked. (It is possible to use this statement to lock some other types of objects in Oracle, e.g., *dblink*).

Oracle allows specifying a special clause in CREATE and ALTER TABLE statements that either allows or disallows locking for the table. Disabling locking for the table effectively prevents any DDL operation against such a table.

Oracle provides several hints for performance optimization; some of these would affect the locking used by Oracle. The hints, while being very important for Oracle database tuning and optimization, are beyond the scope of this book; please refer to the vendor's documentation for more information.

In IBM DB2 UDB, the custom locking control is somewhat similar to that in Oracle, though less granular. A user can specify two modes of table locking — SHARE or EXCLUSIVE. For example:

```
db2=>LOCK TABLE customer IN EXCLUSIVE MODE

DB20000I The SQL command completed successfully.
```

The SHARE mode prevents any other transaction from executing any type of operation on the locked table, except for a read-only SELECT; also, no other transaction can acquire a lock to that table The EXCLUSIVE mode prevents any operation on the table, including read-only operations.

The lock is held for the duration of the transaction and is released once a COMMIT statement is issued. Except for these two modes, the locking for operations in DB2 UDB databases is governed by isolation levels set for the transactions (described earlier in the chapter).

All other locks are at the discretion of the RDBMS. Default locking is row-level, and a lock may escalate to a table-level lock (there is no page-level locking in DB2 UDB); the lock escalation may be avoided using the LOCK TABLE statement from above. The escalation thresholds are configurable by the DBA through a number of parameters (i.e., *maxlocks*, *locksize,* etc.).

Microsoft SQL Server 2000 provides several lock options to be specified for the transactions (Table 7-7). These represent categories of locks that further could be divided by specific lock HINTS, some of which are presented in Table 7-8.

Table 7-7
Microsoft SQL Server 2000 Lock Modes

Lock Mode	*Description*
`SHARED (S)`	This type of lock is used for read-only operations.
`UPDATE (U)`	This lock is used whenever the data is updated.
`EXCLUSIVE (X)`	Prevents all other transactions from performing `UPDATE`, `DELETE` or `INSERT`.
`INTENT`	This is used to establish a hierarchy of locking: intent, shared intent, exclusive, and shared with intent exclusive. An intent lock indicates that SQL Server wants to acquire a shared or exclusive lock on some resources down in the hierarchy (e.g., table—page—row); at the very least the intent lock prevents any transactions from acquiring an exclusive lock on the resource.
`SCHEMA`	This lock type is used when a DDL operation is performed.
`BULK UPDATE (BU)`	These locks are used when bulk copying is taking place.

The lock mode is either selected by the SQL Server itself, or based on the type of operation performed. To manually specify the locking mode, one should use the table-level locking hints that fall into one of the categories listed in Table 7-7. These locking hints override the transaction isolation level and should be used judiciously. The hints in the Table 7-8 provide just a sampling of what is available, and the list is by no means complete.

Table 7-8
Microsoft SQL Server 2000 Locking Hints

Locking Hint	*Description*
`NOLOCK`	This hint issued in a `SELECT` statement specifies that no shared locks should be used and no exclusive locks should be honored; this means that the `SELECT` statement could potentially read uncommitted transactions (dirty reads).
`UPDLOCK`	Instructs SQL Server to use `UPDATE` locking (as opposed to shared locks) while reading data; makes sure that data has not changed if an `UPDATE` statement follows next.
`XLOCK`	Places an exclusive lock until the end of a transaction on all data affected by the transaction. Additional levels of granularity can be specified with this lock.
`ROWLOCK`	Specifically instructs SQL Server to use row-level locks (as opposed to page and table-level).

For example, to specify row-level locking for the transaction in a SELECT statement, the following syntax may be used:

```
SELECT  *
FROM    customer
WITH    (ROWLOCK)
```

There is a penalty to pay for the high granularity — it degrades performance as SQL Server allocates more resources for row-level locking operations.

In addition to the visual interface of the Enterprise manager, Microsoft SQL Server provides stored procedure sp_locks, which return information about all active locks on the system; sufficient privilege-levels are required.

SQL Server deploys different locks at its own discretion based on cost decisions: the default is a row-level lock, which may escalate to a page-level lock, and in turn to a table-level lock, when a transaction exceeds its escalation threshold. This parameter is not configurable and is determined by SQL Server itself in each situation.

Dealing with deadlocks

The classic deadlock situation arises when two (or more) sessions are waiting to acquire a lock on a shared resource, and none of them can proceed because a second session also has a lock on some other resource that is required by the first session. Imagine a situation, in which Session 1 holds resource A, while trying to access resource B; at the same time Session 2 holds resource B while trying to access resource A.

Usually RDBMS resolves situations like this automatically by killing one of the processes and rolling back all the changes it may have made.

Oracle implements a sophisticated mechanism enforcing the rule "reader and writer processes cannot block each other." The idea behind this rule is to present each process with a consistent image of data without noncommitted changes. Nevertheless, deadlocks do occur in Oracle and usually are resolved by the RDBMS itself; in some rare cases, manual resolution — choosing the deadlock "victim" process — is required. The most common deadlock types are ORA-00060 (en queue deadlocks) and ORA-04020 (library cache deadlocks). It is possible to specify the NOWAIT clause or set up session timeouts to avoid deadlocks, some other techniques involve explicit locking and use of the isolation levels within the transaction. A deadlock may also be resolved manually through Oracle's interfaces.

IBM DB2 runs a background process, called Deadlock Detector, to find and resolve the deadlock situation. The session chosen as a deadlock victim is rolled back, and a special error is generated (SQLCODE-901, SQLSTATE 40001). The read-only process is a prime candidate for the deadlock victim, and beyond that, DB2 employs "least cost" criteria to select the session to be killed. If deadlocks ever become a problem, IBM recommends using system monitoring tools to collect information about the deadlock situations and either optimize the system or redesign any applications involved.

Microsoft SQL Server 2000 employs a proprietary algorithm for detecting deadlocks and resolves them in a way similar to that implemented by Oracle or DB2 UDB: deadlocks are resolved automatically or manually through the Enterprise Manager Console. It is possible to volunteer a session to become a deadlock victim by setting the DEADLOCK_PRIORITY parameter within that session (see paragraph about sessions earlier in the chapter).

```
SET DEADLOCK_PRIORITY LOW
```

Another way of dealing with the situation would be setting LOCK_TIMEOUT for the session. Setting the timeout means that the session will hold the resource under the lock no longer than a specified interval. Once the time set for locking expires, SQL Server returns an error and the transaction is rolled back. The resolution of the situation will be similar to that for every other RDBMS: handle the situation in which an error indicating a deadlock situation is returned (Error 1205 for SQL Server, SQLSTATE 40001) by re-running the transaction, redesigning the application to decrease or eliminate the deadlock possibility, and so on.

Summary

All communications with RDBMS happen within the context of a session. When a session between a client program and RDBMS is established, it possesses certain default properties that determine its behavior. Some of these can be changed for the duration of the session, and the database administrator can change the defaults. Some parameters may be changed through use of SQL statements; some are client-dependent and must be set in the client's environment.

The next level of granularity is transactions — when one or more SQL statements comprise a single logical unit of work. Within the session, an SQL statement runs as a transaction — by the SQL standard definition. RDBMS implementations may treat it differently, some starting an implicit transaction by default, and some requiring explicit statements to begin a transaction. Transactions must satisfy certain criteria (the so-called ACID test) to comply with these standards, but these details are usually taken care of by the RDBMS itself.

Transactions accessing shared resources must implement some concurrency control. One of a transaction's properties is its isolation level established for the transaction. The isolation level regulates what this transaction may access, and what data it is allowed to "see."

There are four isolation levels defined by the SQL standard and some RDBMS (Microsoft SQL Server 2000 and IBM DB2 UDB) have implemented all of them, while some (Oracle 9*i* being one example) have implemented only two.

Some RDBMS implement intricate locking systems to address the concurrency issue, though locks are not part of the SQL standard. The locks might be of different types; they can be specified within the SQL statement itself, or they may be specified properties of the session. A deadlock situation may occur in a high-volume of transactions or improperly designed systems. Deadlocks may be resolved automatically by the RDBMS or manually by database administrators.

✦ ✦ ✦

Retrieving and Transforming Data

P A R T

IV

✦ ✦ ✦ ✦

In This Part

✦ ✦ ✦ ✦

Understanding SELECT Statement

✦ ✦ ✦ ✦

In This Chapter

Single table select

Select statement required and optional clauses

Using literals, functions, and calculated columns

Using subqueries in different select statement clauses

Compound operators in select statement

Combining results of multiple queries

✦ ✦ ✦ ✦

This chapter covers selecting data from the RDBMS tables using the SELECT statement. As the name implies it deals with selecting data from the RDBMS objects — tables or views — either to be presented to the users, or for some internal purpose. This is the only statement of the data query language (DQL) group.

The use of this statement within a SELECT query is relatively simple, but the SELECT statement rarely executes without clauses, and that's where the fun begins. The select query clauses are probably the most confusing in the SQL and have to be dealt with accordingly. This chapter introduces the topic, covering use of subqueries, compound operators, and aggregate function clauses.

Single Table SELECT Statement Syntax

Here is the generic SELECT statement, as it is defined by the SQL99 standard, for selecting data from a single table. The query includes the SELECT command, followed by the list of identifiers (table or view columns); then comes the mandatory FROM clause that contains names of the tables, from which these columns are selected. The rest of the clause is optional, used to increase selectiveness of the query, as well as add some ordering capabilities. All of these pieces make up the complete SELECT statement.

```
SELECT [DISTINCT] [<qualifier>.]<column_name> |
                  * |
                  <expression>
                   [AS <column_alias>],...
FROM  <table_or_view_name> |
      <inline_view>
       [[AS] <table_alias>]
[WHERE <predicate>]
[GROUP BY [<qualifier>.]<column_name>,...
 [HAVING <predicate>]
]
[ORDER_BY <column_name> |
          <column_number>
           [ASC | DESC],...
];
```

Of course, the statements that you would run against the three leading RDBMS do differ, both in syntax and usage.

SELECT Clause: What Do We Select?

In the relational databases the `SELECT` statement selects values in the columns, literal values, or expressions. The returned values themselves could be of any valid data types. These values can be displayed in the client application, or written into a file, used in the intermediate calculations, or entered into database tables.

Prior in this chapter, we've mentioned that the `FROM` clause of the `SELECT` statement is mandatory, whereas all other clauses are optional. This still holds true for the SQL99 standard, though the rules are somewhat more relaxed with the vendor-specific implementations.

Single-column select

You can select as many or as few columns as you wish from a table (or a view) for which you have `SELECT` privileges (see Chapter 12 on SQL security). The following example selects only a customer name (column `CUST_NAME_S` from the table `CUSTOMER` in the ACME database).

```
SELECT cust_name_s
FROM   customer

CUST_NAME_S
--------------------------------------------------
DLH INDUSTRIES
FAIR AND SONS AIR CONDTNG
```

```
KILBURN GLASS INDUSTRIES
BOSWELL DESIGNS CORP.
WILE ELECTROMATIC INC.
FABRITEK INC.
...
DALCOMP INC.
INTEGRATED POWER DESIGNS
GUARDIAN MANUFACTURING INC.
WILE BESS COMPANY
```

The return result is a set of the CUST_NAME_S column values from all rows in the CUSTOMER table. The values in the set are not ordered in any way; it is possible to order the returned values though; see later in the chapter for information on ordering data in the resultset (section on GROUP BY clause).

The syntax is identical across all three RDBMS products as well as for the SQL99 standard.

Multicolumn SELECT

A single column SELECT, while useful, is certainly not the limit of the SQL capabilities. It's very likely that you'll be selecting more than one column at a time in your queries.

Selecting several columns

The following query selects three columns at the same time from the same CUSTOMER table in the ACME database:

```
SELECT   cust_id_n,
         cust_status_s,
         cust_name_s
FROM     customer

CUST_ID_N  C CUST_NAME_S
---------- - --------------------------------------------------
        51 Y DLH INDUSTRIES
         5 Y FAIR AND SONS AIR CONDTNG
        12 Y KILBURN GLASS INDUSTRIES
        61 Y BOSWELL DESIGNS CORP.
        55 Y WILE ELECTROMATIC INC.
         6 Y FABRITEK INC.
...
        16 Y DALCOMP INC.
        89 Y INTEGRATED POWER DESIGNS
        85 Y GUARDIAN MANUFACTURING INC.
       152 Y WILE BESS COMPANY
```

As in the case with a single column SELECT, the result returned is a set of values, with a distinction that it is rather a set of sets — one set for each column mentioned in the SELECT statement. The sequence in which these sets appear directly corresponds to the sequence in which the column names were mentioned in the SELECT clause.

It is possible to select a column more than once within a single query. The result will simply be duplicate sets of values.

The syntax is identical across all three RDBMS products as well as for the SQL99 standard.

Selecting all columns

Selecting all columns in the table could be achieved by listing every single column from the table in the SELECT clause of the query, or using the convenient shortcut — asterisk (*) — provided by the SQL99 standard and implemented by virtually every RDBMS on the planet.

```
SELECT *
FROM status

STATUS_ID_N ST STATUS_DESC_S
----------- -- ------------------------------
          6 60 SHIPPED
          2 20 COMPLETE
          8 70 INVOICED
          9 80 CANCELLED
```

As with any multirow query, the returned result comprises the sets of the selected values of all rows for each column. The sequence in which columns appear in the resultset is exactly the same as in the underlying table (view).

Selecting all columns plus an extra column

In a relatively rare case where you need to select all the columns from the table and a duplicate of a column(s), you may do so in all three RDBMS, but this is where vendor's implementations differ from the SQL99 standard as well as from each other.

Oracle and DB2 require the asterisk to be prefixed by a table name or a table alias (the order in which asterisk is listed in relation to other columns is not important):

```
SQL>  SELECT status.*, status_desc_s
2     FROM status;

STATUS_ID_N ST STATUS_DESC_S                  STATUS_DESC_S
----------- -- ------------------------------ -------------
          6 60 SHIPPED                        SHIPPED
          2 20 COMPLETE                       COMPLETE
```

```
          8 70 INVOICED                                INVOICED
          9 80 CANCELLED                               CANCELLED

4 rows selected.
```

This full name qualification is not required in MS SQL Server:

```
1>  SELECT *, status_desc_s  FROM status
2>  GO

 STATUS_ID_N STATUS_CODE_S STATUS_DESC_S   STATUS_DESC_S
 ----------- ------------- --------------- --------------
           2 20            COMPLETE        COMPLETE
           6 60            SHIPPED         SHIPPED
           8 70            INVOICED        INVOICED
           9 80            CANCELLED       CANCELLED

(4 rows affected)
```

This may seem a superfluous feature, but imagine a situation when you need to see all 200 rows in the table and wish to change the default sequence in which the columns appear in the final resultset. You have an option to list all the columns in the desired order (i.e., typing in all the columns in the SELECT clause of your query) or to do it the easier way at the expense of having a duplicate set of values — *but in the place where you would rather see it.* Of course, you may combine all/any rows in the table into a single resultset more than once.

Selecting distinct values

As you become more selective in terms of what data is expected to be returned by a query, the need may arise to eliminate duplicates. The SQL99 standard provides an easy and elegant way to eliminate any duplicate values from the final resultset.

The table PAYMENT_TERMS in the ACME database contains data about discounts, in terms of percentages, given to customers. While the particulars of each discount might differ, it is quite conceivable that the actual percentage might be the same.

The following example selects all the rows for the PAYTERMS_DISCPCT_N column from that table:

```
SELECT payterms_discpct_n
FROM   payment_terms

PAYTERMS_DISCPCT_N
------------------
               .00
               .02
```

```
                 .02
                 .00
                 .00
                 .00
                 .00
                 .00
                 .00
                 .00
                 .02

(11 rows affected)
```

As you can see, there are quite a few duplicates among these 11 records. If the goal is to find out what are the percentage rates used within the company, the DISTINCT keyword might be used.

```
SELECT DISTINCT payterms_discpct_n
FROM            payment_terms

PAYTERMS_DISCPCT_N
------------------
                 0
               .02

2 rows selected.
```

Now, all the duplicate values have been eliminated and the resultset contains only two distinct values.

It is important to understand that DISTINCT refers to the *entire* row, not just a single column; if DISTINCT precedes multiple columns the entire set — row values in all columns — needs to be distinct. Here is an example run in MS SQL Server 2000 (applicable to Oracle and DB2 UDB as well):

```
SELECT DISTINCT payterms_discpct_n,
                payterms_code_s
FROM            payment_terms

PAYTERMS_DISCPCT_N PAYTERMS_CODE_S
------------------ ---------------
.00                N10
.00                N120
.00                N15
.00                N20
.00                N30
.00                N45
```

```
.00                N60
.00                N90
.02                CADV
.02                N21530
.02                N21531

(11 row(s) affected)
```

By adding the PAYTERMS_CODE_S column to PAYTERMS_DISCPCT_N, we've made the *pair* of the columns to be distinct. As a result, duplicate values in a single column are allowed as long as the pair of the values is distinct.

Using literals, functions, and calculated columns

Columns are not the only things that you can select in the relational database world, and the SELECT statement does not always involve a table. Selecting columns from a table is a very straightforward concept, much more so than selecting expressions and literals.

When a value we are after does not exist up to the moment we call it, because it is returned by a function, or being calculated on the fly, you still need to SELECT from somewhere. This "somewhere" could be any table existing within the database and to which you have select privilege (see Chapter 12 for more information on the privileges), but it would be rather inconvenient, and hard to maintain, as the user must know what tables are present in the database, and change the query every time the table in use is dropped or renamed; besides, if you SELECT a literal or an expression from an actual table, the resultset will have as many rows as there are in the table.

Oracle supports the SQL99 standards to the extent of providing a special table, DUAL, when there is no physical object (view or table) to select from. Suppose you need to find out a system time of your Oracle database; the RDBMS provides you with a function SYSDATE (more about the functions in Chapter 10), which returns this information. While not being SQL99 standard compliant, this function is a legitimate Oracle 9*i* SQL dialect statement and must be treated as such. Since all queries must start with SELECT, you would start with it, but the information is not stored anywhere in the database — it is generated dynamically at the request's moment. That's where the table DUAL comes in handy — you can "select" virtually anything from this table.

```
SQL> SELECT SYSDATE FROM dual;

SYSDATE
---------
21-OCT-03
```

The DUAL table itself has only one column (not without irony named DUMMY) and one row containing value X.

The DUAL table was introduced by Chuck Weiss of Oracle as an underlying object in the Oracle Data Dictionary. It was never meant to be seen by itself, but rather to be used in some complex JOIN operations (discussed Chapter 9); it logically fits the SELECT notion as it implies that the FROM clause is to be used with each statement.

For selecting noncolumn values, DB2 UDB 8.1 has essentially the same concept—table SYSDUMMY1, located in the SYSIBM system schema. This table has a single column called IBMREQD, and a single row containing value Y. The following example demonstrates using this table for calculating the sum of two numbers:

```
db2=> SELECT (5+5) FROM sysibm.sysdummy1

1
---------
       10

1 record(s) selected.
```

The sum of these numbers is not stored anywhere, but it has to be *selected* following the SQL99 standard rules. This becomes more important, when SQL functions (Chapter 10) are used in the procedural language (like PL/SQL or Transact-SQL).

Microsoft SQL Server 2000 actually allows you to forgo the FROM clause altogether in the situation like this. Here is an example:

```
SELECT (5+5) num_sum
num_sum
-----------
10
```

The "dummy" tables, as well as ability to select from nothing, is not a part of the SQL standard, but rather manifests of vendors' ingenuity in customers' satisfaction quest.

In the most recent example we've used alias NUM_SUM as the name for the non-existent column. This is *alias* – a standard feature, supported by all three RDBMS vendors as well as mandated by the SQL standard. The idea behind alias is very simple—giving columns selected in the SQL query more descriptive names as they appear in the final result set. Every single SELECT example in this book could be rewritten with the column names substituted by aliases. For instance, the example from above that selects a distinct value of the PAYTERMS_DISCPCT_N, could be written as follows

```
SELECT DISTINCT payterms_discpct_n AS discount_percent
FROM            payment_terms

discount_percent
------------------
                 0
               .02
```

The new name, while not being shorter, is significantly more descriptive for the user, just as the column name is more informative for the programmer (as it tells what data type the column contains — N — for NUMERIC). The use of the 'AS' operator is optional, and the syntax (either with or without 'AS') is valid in all three databases.

The aliasing becomes even more useful when literals and expressions are selected. An example of selecting an expression (5 + 5) was given previously in the chapter; here is the SELECT statement involving literals:

```
SELECT cust_name_s,
       100 AS NUMERIC_CONSTANT,
       'ABC' AS STRING_CONSTANT
FROM   customer

CUST_NAME_S                   NUMERIC_CONSTANT STRING_CONSTANT
----------------------------- ---------------- ---------------
WILE SEAL CORP.                            100 ABC
WILE ELECTRONICS INC.                      100 ABC
WILE ELECTROMUSICAL INC.                   100 ABC
WILE ELECTROMATIC INC.                     100 ABC
WILE BESS COMPANY                          100 ABC
MAGNETOMETRIC DEVICES INC.                 100 ABC
MAGNETICS USA INC.                         100 ABC
. . .                                      . . .
BURNETTE WILLIAM CORP.                     100 ABC
BOSWELL DESIGNS CORP.                      100 ABC

37 record(s) selected.
```

In the default behaviour, if no alias is specified for the constructed column — be it a literal, expression, or a function — Oracle will use the literal itself or an expression in the place of the alias; IBM DB2 UDB will number the columns starting with 1; and Microsoft SQL Server simply leaves the name blank.

Literals can be a part of a "standard" SELECT query, where they are listed together with the column names, as in the example above.

Aliasing is very convenient when a resulting value combines different sources — a column, a function, an expression, or a literal. Here is an example in Oracle and DB2 UDB syntax that concatenates product ID (column PROD_ID_N) from the PRODUCT table of the ACME database with an empty space and product brand (column PROD_BRAND_N) into a single value:

```
SELECT CAST(prod_id_n AS CHAR(5)) || ' ' || prod_brand_s
 AS ID_AND_BRAND
FROM   product

ID_AND_BRAND
--------------------------
990   SPRUCE LUMBER
1880  STEEL NAILS
2871  STOOL CAPS
3045  STOOL CAPS
4000  HAND RAILS ROUNDS
4055  GAZEBOS
4761  BAR RAILS
4906  BAR RAILS
4964  BASES
5786  CRATING MATERIAL


10 record(s) selected.
```

Concatenation operators and functions are covered in detail in Chapters 11 and 10, respectively.

To run this query in MS SQL Server, replace the concatenation (||) operator to a plus (+) operator.

See Chapter 11 for more about operators.

As a part of the SELECT statement, the functions or expressions could be used for insert or update purposes. Imagine that you would like to keep track of every insert and update with a date/time stamp, using a SELECT query as an input (see INSERT and UPDATE statements in Chapter 6); the following Oracle 9*i* syntax provides this functionality using SYSDATE and USER functions. (See Chapter 10 for equivalent DB2 UDB and Microsoft SQL Server 2000 syntax.)

```
SELECT  salesman_code_s,
        salesman_name_s,
        sysdate,
        user
```

```
FROM    salesman;

SA SALESMAN_NAME_S                         SYSDATE   USER
-- ------------------------------------ --------- -------
02 FAIRFIELD BUGS ASSOCIATION          15-OCT-03ACME
03 AMERICA GONZALES LIMITED            15-OCT-03 ACME
04 HUNTER COMPONENTS                   15-OCT-03 ACME
07 ELMERSON INDUSTRIES INCORPORATED 15-OCT-03 ACME
09 SAM KRISTEL INC                     15-OCT-03 ACME
10 HENERY INCORPORATED                 15-OCT-03 ACME

6 rows selected.
```

Using subqueries in a SELECT clause

The concept of a subquery is simple — it is a query within a query that supplies necessary values for the first query. A SELECT query could have an embedded subquery as a way to retrieve unknown values, and the nesting level (how many subqueries you could have within each other) is limited only by the RDBMS capability.

To illustrate the concept, some preliminary work is required (since the required table is not within the ACME database). Let's say that in full accordance with database design guidelines you have created a table that contains state tax amounts for each state, as well as each state's full name and two-letter postal abbreviation.

First you need to create a table:

```
CREATE TABLE sales_tax
(
  stax_id_n     INTEGER NOT NULL,
  stax_amt_n    DECIMAL(6,3),
  stax_state_s  CHAR(2),
  CONSTRAINT pk_sales_tax PRIMARY KEY (stax_id_n )
)
```

The next step is to insert some meaningful data into your new table.

```
INSERT INTO sales_tax
(
 stax_id_n,
 stax_amt_n,
 stax_state_s
)
VALUES (1, 8.5,'WA')
```

When you wish to produce a report that would contain a product ID and price, and the amount of tax applied to unit of the product in the state of Washington, the following query would be useful:

```
SELECT prod_num_s,
       prod_price_n,
       (SELECT stax_amt_n
        FROM sales_tax
        WHERE stax_state_s = 'WA') AS TAX_RATE,
       prod_price_n *
       (SELECT stax_amt_n
        FROM sales_tax
        WHERE stax_state_s = 'WA')/100 AS SALES_TAX
FROM    product

prod_num_s prod_price_n TAX_RATE SALES_TAX
---------- ------------ -------- -----------------------
990        18.32          8.500    1.557200000
1880       34.09          8.500    2.897650000
2871       26.92          8.500    2.288200000
3045       15.98          8.500    1.358300000
4000       11.84          8.500    1.006400000
4055       16.09          8.500    1.367650000
4761       23.20          8.500    1.972000000
4906       27.10          8.500    2.303500000
4964       23.20          8.500    1.972000000
5786       17.98          8.500    1.528300000

(10 row(s) affected)
```

This example uses the state abbreviation (WA) as a parameter to find the amount of the applicable state tax and calculates the necessary values on the fly using subquery to extract this value from the SALES_TAX table; note that the data retrieval is conducted for each and every row in the resulting set.

FROM Clause: Select from What?

The FROM clause is mandatory for every SELECT statement—with the exception of the MS SQL Server case discussed earlier in this chapter. The database objects you should be able to select from are tables and views. These come in many flavors—temporary tables, inline views, materialized views, to name just a few—but the truth is that there is nothing else in the RDBMS world to select from.

Selecting from tables and views

We've used tables and views as "selectable from" objects in the examples given earlier in this chapter (and all previous chapters). In fact, the only truly selectable object in RDBMS is a table, while view is a query that is based on some table (or tables). Unlike a table, view, by definition, does not contain data but rather collects it from the base tables whenever a SELECT query is executed against the view.

Oracle also sports the concept of a materialized view. The regular view is based on some query that extracts data from the underlying tables; this query executes the very moment as the SELECT statement is executed against the view. To speed up the selection process, it is possible to create a materialized view that actually contains a snapshot of the data it's supposed to fetch. Such a view does not differ much from a table. The thing to remember here is that the data in a materialized view might not be up-to-date, and needs refreshing to ensure it.

Using aliases in a FROM clause

It is possible to alias the table names listed in the FROM clause of a SELECT query to shorten notation and make it more visual by prefixing the columns in a different clause with the table alias. Here is an example of selecting three columns from a STATUS table in the ACME database where the table is aliased with s:

```
SELECT status_id_n,
       s.status_code_s,
       s.status_desc_s
FROM   status s
```

The columns in the SELECT clause may or may not be prefixed with the table's alias (or table name); moreover, the columns themselves could be aliased for readability purposes, replacing somewhat cryptic column names with more meaningful ones (see paragraph earlier in this chapter). If such prefixes are used, they follow <object>.<property> notation, shown in the example above.

While not being very useful in the case of a single table selection, it simplifies queries when more than one table is involved, and helps to remove confusion should two or more tables have identically named columns. Please refer to Chapter 9 for more information on multitable queries.

Using alias for the tables in the FROM clause of the SELECT query is not the same as CREATE ALIAS statement, described in Chapter 4. The latter creates a database object that subsequently could be used to refer to the object (not necessarily a table) by some other, usually more convenient way. The alias in the SELECT query serves somewhat the same purpose—shortening the calling notation—but is radically different because it only refers to a table (or view) and exists only for the time the query is running, and disappears afterward.

There are certain rules on using the aliases in the other clauses that comprise the SELECT query. The table that was aliased in the FROM clause could be referred to by this alias throughout the whole query: SELECT, WHERE, GROUP BY, ORDER BY, and so on. Though it is possible to use column names in these clauses without qualifying them by the table name (or alias), it is recommended to use aliases (if specified) to prevent ambiguity.

Using subqueries in a FROM clause (inline views)

We have discussed the VIEW database object in Chapter 4 and Chapter 5. Here we are going to introduce so-called *inline views*. Unlike the VIEW object, the inline views do not exist outside the query that contains them, and may or may not have a proper name for themselves. Consider the following statement that selects customer's ID, name, and status from an inline view CUST:

```
SELECT  cust.id,
        cust. cust_name_s,
        cust.active
FROM    (SELECT cust_id_n AS id,
                cust_status_s AS active,
                cust_name_s,
                cust_alias_s AS alias,
                cust_credhold_s AS hold
         FROM   customer) cust

ID          CUST_NAME_S                      ACTIVE
----------- -------------------------        ------
51 DLH INDUSTRIES                            Y
5 FAIR AND SONS AIR CONDTNG                  Y
12 KILBURN GLASS INDUSTRIES                  Y
61 BOSWELL DESIGNS CORP.                     Y
55 WILE ELECTROMATIC INC.                    Y
6 FABRITEK INC.                              Y
   ...
16 DALCOMP INC.                              Y
89 INTEGRATED POWER DESIGNS                  Y
85 GUARDIAN MANUFACTURING INC.               Y
152 WILE BESS COMPANY                        Y

37 record(s) selected.
```

Note that the outer SELECT clause refers to the columns selected from the inline view by their alias — because of the way these columns are exposed to it; replacing CUST.ID with CUST. CUST_ID_N would generate an Invalid column name error, since that is not the name that outer query could reference. At the same time, the column CUST_NAME_S could be used the way it is mentioned in the subquery because it was not aliased.

WHERE Clause: Setting Horizontal Limits

While selecting everything a table or view could contain might be of value for some operations, most of the time you will be looking for specific information — a person with a particular phone number, data falling into a certain date range, and so on. The table might contain several million rows, and you simply have no time to search for the information all by yourself. The SQL WHERE clause provides a mechanism for setting horizontal limits; specifically, it allows you to limit the number of rows in resultsets returned by a query through specifying some condition or set of conditions. Depending on what conditions you have specified with your query, there might be zero, one, or more records (rows) returned. The search criteria specified in the WHERE clause evaluate to TRUE or FALSE, and all the rules of Boolean algebra are fully applicable there.

See Appendix L for information on Boolean algebra.

Using comparison operators

To specify conditions in the WHERE clause, SQL employs a number of *operators*. These are discussed in detail in Chapter 11. Here, we are going to touch them only briefly.

Consider the following query run against the ACME database in Microsoft SQL Server (the syntax and results would be identical in all "big three" databases). It returns some information about a particular customer, uniquely identified by the customer ID field CUST_ID_N. The uniqueness of the customer ID (not that of the address record) value is enforced by the primary key constraint as well as a UNIQUE constraint placed onto the column in the table CUSTOMER. (There could be only one customer associated with any given ID.)

```
SELECT cust_id_n,
       cust_name_s,
       cust_status_s
FROM   customer
WHERE  cust_id_n = 7

CUST_ID_N   CUST_NAME_S             CUST_STATUS_S
---------- ---------------------- -------------
7          WILE ELECTRONICS INC.   Y

(1 row(s) affected)
```

You were able to pinpoint the record because only one record satisfied your condition.

Now, nothing prevents a customer from having one or more addresses, which is illustrated by the following query requesting all address records for a customer with a customer ID equal to 7:

```
SELECT  addr_address_s,
        addr_city_s,
        addr_state_s,
        addr_zip_s
FROM    address
WHERE   addr_custid_fn = 7

addr_address_s     addr_city_s        addr_state_s addr_zip_s
------------------ ------------------ ------------ ----------
411 S LONDON AVE   EGG HARBOR CITY    NJ           08215
232 EEL ST.        EGG HARBOR CITY    NJ           08215
454 OAK ST.        EGG HARBOR CITY    NJ           08215
456 WILLOW ST.     EGG HARBOR CITY    NJ           08215
678 MAPLE AVE.     EGG HARBOR CITY    NJ           08215
. . .               . . .             . . .        . . .
865 CEDAR AVE.     EGG HARBOR CITY    NJ           08215
911 MYRTLE ST.     EGG HARBOR CITY    NJ           08215
777 SITKA AVE.     EGG HARBOR CITY    NJ           08215
999 ELK AVE.       EGG HARBOR CITY    NJ           08215

 (11 row(s) affected)
```

This query yields 11 records, containing all the addresses under which customer number 7 conducts its business.

Comparison operators could also determine a range of values. When you want to know what products in your database are selling for more than $20, use the following query:

```
SELECT  prod_description_s,
        prod_price_n
FROM    product
WHERE   prod_price_n > 20

PROD_DESCRIPTION_S                          PROD_PRICE_N
------------------------------------------- ------------
STEEL NAILS 6''                                    33.28
STOOL CAPS 5''                                     26.82
BAR RAILS 24X48X128                                23.10
BAR RAILS 30X45X60                                 27.00
BASES 30X45X60                                     23.10

(5 rows affected)
```

This query returns information for all products whose price is over $20.

Compound operators: Using AND and OR

There could be more than one criterion specified with the query. For example, you may want to retrieve all the phone salespersons in your company that are not assigned to a customer. In the table, there are phone numbers and fax numbers; to eliminate the latter, the following query could be used:

```
SQL> SELECT  phone_salesmanid_fn,
             phone_phonenum_s,
             phone_type_s
FROM         phone
WHERE        phone_custid_fn IS NULL
AND          phone_type_s = 'PHONE'

PHONE_SALESMANID_FN PHONE_PHONENUM_S     PHONE_TYPE_S
------------------- -------------------- --------------------
                 23 (305) 555-8502       PHONE
                 24 (626) 555-4435       PHONE
                 25 (717) 555-5479       PHONE
                 26 (718) 555-7879       PHONE
                 27 (718) 555-5091       PHONE
                 28 (814) 555-0324       PHONE

6 record(s) selected.
```

Only records where column PHONE_CUSTID_FN contains NULL *and* the type of the numbers is PHONE made it to the final resultset.

The records could be selected using the OR compound operator. In the following example, only records for the orders that were placed by customer 63 or that have an order ID equal to 30661 are taken into consideration.

```
SELECT ordhdr_id_n,
       ordhdr_custid_fn
FROM   order_header
WHERE  ordhdr_id_n = 30661
OR     ordhdr_custid_fn = 63

ORDHDR_ID_N ORDHDR_CUSTID_FN
----------- ----------------
30613       63
30614       63
30615       63
30661       1

4 records(s) selected.
```

This provides you with the functionality to specify disparate selection criteria: the customer ID of the customer who had placed order 30661 is not 7, nevertheless it is present on the list of the records because you've specified that you are interested in the orders placed by customer 63 OR the order #30661, regardless of the customer ID. Using AND in this case would yield no results since order 30661 was not placed by customer 7, and no record satisfying both criteria at the same time would be found.

Using the BETWEEN operator

While it is possible to use a combination of => (greater than or equal to) and <= (less than or equal to) operators to achieve exactly the same results, the BETWEEN operator provides a more convenient (and often more efficient) way for selecting a range of values.

```
SELECT  prod_description_s,
        prod_price_n
FROM    product
WHERE   prod_price_n BETWEEN 23.10 AND 30

PROD_DESCRIPTION_S                           PROD_PRICE_N
-------------------------------------------- ------------
STOOL CAPS 5''                                      26.82
BAR RAILS 24X48X128                                 23.10
BAR RAILS 30X45X60                                  27.00
BASES 30X45X60                                      23.10

4 record(s) selected.
```

Note that the range of the values is inclusive, that is, the values used in specifying the range are included into the final resultset. This behavior is number-specific, if other database types (e.g., characters, dates, etc.) are used for criteria, results might differ. The operator could be used with virtually any data type: dates, characters, numbers, and so on. (See Chapter 11 for more information.)

Using the IN operator: Set membership test

When there is more than one exact criterion for the WHERE clause, and these criteria do not fit any range of values, you may use an OR statement. Consider the following query:

```
SELECT  cust_name_s,
        cust_credhold_s
FROM    customer
WHERE   cust_alias_s = 'MNGA71396' OR
        cust_alias_s = 'MNGA71398' OR
```

```
        cust_alias_s = 'MNGA71400'

CUST_NAME_S                           CUST_CREDHOLD_S
------------------------------------- ---------------
WILE SEAL CORP.                       Y
MAGNETICS USA INC.                    N
MAGNETOMETRIC DEVICES INC.            N

3 record(s) selected.
```

Any records that correspond to either of the three specified criteria make it into the final resultset. The same result is easier achieved using an `IN` operator:

```
SELECT  cust_name_s,
        cust_credhold_s
FROM    customer
WHERE   cust_alias_s IN
        ('MNGA71396', 'MNGA71398', 'MNGA71400')

CUST_NAME_S                           CUST_CREDHOLD_S
------------------------------------- ---------------
WILE SEAL CORP.                       Y
MAGNETICS USA INC.                    N
MAGNETOMETRIC DEVICES INC.            N

3 record(s) selected.
```

The `IN` operator makes your life easier by replacing numerous `OR` statements and speeding up the query execution along the way. All values specified within an `IN` operator must be of the same data type as they refer to one column.

The NOT operator

The `NOT` operator negates results of the operator by making it perform a search for the results exactly opposite to those specified. Any of the operators and queries discussed to this point could have produced opposite results if `NOT` was used. The following example returns all the results that *do not* match the specified criteria—having the name with the second letter I, third L, and fourth E; only records that *do not* have such a sequence starting from the second position within the company name are selected:

```
SQL> SELECT  cust_name_s
     FROM    customer
     WHERE  cust_name_s  NOT LIKE  '_ILE%'

cust_name_s
```

```
--------------------------------------------------
MAGNETICS USA INC.
MAGNETOMETRIC DEVICES INC.
FAIR PARK GARDENS
FAIR AND SONS AIR CONDTNG
. . .
KILBURN GLASS INDUSTRIES
CARLTONBATES COMPANY
DABAH BROS INC.
. . .
INSULECTRO INC.
INTEGRATED POWER DESIGNS
EASTERN SATELLITE COMPANY

32 record(s) selected
```

Using the IS NULL operator: Special test for NULLS

We have mentioned before that relational databases are using a special value to signify the absence of the data in the database table column — NULL. Since this value does not comply with the rules that all the other values follow (e.g., comparison, operations, etc.), they cannot be detected with the equation/comparison operator =; i.e., the syntax WHERE <column_name> = NULL, while being technically valid in Oracle or DB2 UDB (and valid in Microsoft SQL Server 2000 under certain circumstances), would never yield any data because the equation will always evaluate to FALSE.

The test for NULL is performed with the IS keyword, as in the example below, which retrieves information about salesmen that have customers without a PHONE_CUSTID_FN number.

```
SELECT  phone_salesmanid_fn,
        phone_phonenum_s,
        phone_type_s
FROM    phone
WHERE   phone_custid_fn IS NULL

PHONE_SALESMANID_FN PHONE_PHONENUM_S     PHONE_TYPE_S
------------------- -------------------- --------------------
                 23 (305) 555-8502       PHONE
                 24 (626) 555-4435       PHONE
                 25 (717) 555-5479       PHONE
                 26 (718) 555-7879       PHONE
                 27 (718) 555-5091       PHONE
                 28 (814) 555-0324       PHONE
                 23 (305) 555-8501       FAX
                 24 (626) 555-4434       FAX
```

```
            25 (717) 555-5478          FAX
            26 (718) 555-7878          FAX
            27 (718) 555-5091          FAX
            28 (814) 555-0323          FAX

12 record(s) selected.
```

In Microsoft SQL Server 2000 Transact-SQL, a NULL is never equal to another NULL unless you specifically instruct SQL Server to do so by issuing command SET ANSI_NULLS OFF; setting this parameter OFF within the session would allow you to compare a NULL value with another NULL value, setting it back ON (default) brings back the SQL99 standard behavior.

Just as easily, you may test for the absence of the NULL value in the specified column using the NOT operator. The IS NULL test returns FALSE or TRUE, depending on whether the value in the column is or is not a NULL. The syntax follows that of the English language: you cannot use NOT IS NULL (produces error), but IS NOT NULL yields the desired results. The following query produces the records for the salesmen whose customers do have phones (therefore the value in the field PHONE_CUSTID_FN is NOT a NULL):

```
SELECT   phone_custid_fn,
         phone_phonenum_s,
         phone_type_s
FROM     phone
WHERE    phone_custid_fn IS NOT NULL

PHONE_CUSTID_FN PHONE_PHONENUM_S     PHONE_TYPE_S
--------------- -------------------- --------------------
              1 (909) 555-9957       PHONE
              1 (909) 555-9956       FAX
              2 (501) 555-5702       PHONE
              2 (501) 555-5701       FAX
...
            152 (541) 555-8979       PHONE
            152 (541) 555-8978       FAX

  74 records
```

Using subqueries in a WHERE clause

As in the SELECT clause, the subqueries could be used with the WHERE clause to provide missing values (or a set of values). For example, you cannot find information from the ORDER_HEADER table using a customer's name only, because the

ORDER_HEADER table contains customer IDs, not the names; thus, the customer ID could be found in the table CUSTOMER using the customer name as a criterion, and then used to select values from the ORDER_HEADER table:

```
SELECT  ordhdr_nbr_s,
        ordhdr_orderdate_d
FROM    order_header
WHERE   ordhdr_custid_fn =
(SELECT cust_id_n
 FROM   customer
 WHERE  cust_name_s = 'WILE ELECTRONICS INC.')

ordhdr_nbr_s     ordhdr_orderdate_d
------------- ---------------------------
523733          2002-08-15 00:00:00.000
523734          2002-08-15 00:00:00.000
523735          2002-08-15 00:00:00.000

(3 row(s) affected)
```

The subquery executes first, thus providing the outer query with a set of values to select from. In this case, a single matching value is expected. If for some reason the subquery returns more than one row (and therefore more than one value could match the ORDHDR_CUSTID field), an error will be generated.

Any of the operators discussed earlier in this chapter could be used with the subqueries, though one has to pay attention to the kind of data required by them: the IN operator would accept a range of values, while LIKE requires a single value to function. For example, the following query uses the IN operator for several values returned by the subquery:

```
SELECT   phone_phonenum_s,
         phone_type_s
FROM     phone
WHERE    phone_salesmanid_fn IN
(SELECT salesman_id_n
 FROM   salesman
 WHERE  salesman_code_s BETWEEN '07' and '10')

PHONE_PHONENUM_S      PHONE_TYPE_S
-------------------- --------------------
(718) 555-7879        PHONE
(718) 555-5091        PHONE
(814) 555-0324        PHONE
(718) 555-7878        FAX
(718) 555-5091        FAX
(814) 555-0323        FAX

6 record(s) selected.
```

When the subquery returns a set of possible values, and the outer query employs some operator that compares them, how would this query distinguish between these values? SQL introduces two operators ANY and ALL to accomplish this distinction.

There is a view in the ACME database that contains order totals for a single company—WILE BESS COMPANY. The view was created to illustrate the usage of these two operators. Consider the following query:

```
SELECT     v_total.customer_name,
           v_total.total_price
FROM       v_customer_totals  v_total
WHERE      v_total.total_price >
  ANY (SELECT vctw.total_price
       FROM   v_customer_totals_wilebess)
ORDER BY  total_price ASC

CUSTOMER_NAME                            TOTAL_PRICE
---------------------------------------- -----------
WILE ELECTROMATIC INC.                   7511.00
WILE BESS COMPANY                        7511.00
WILE ELECTROMATIC INC.                   7799.20
WILE BESS COMPANY                        8390.00
WILE BESS COMPANY                        8390.00
. . .                                    . . .
WILE SEAL CORP.                          15456.80
WILE ELECTRONICS INC.                    15456.80

29 rows selected.
```

It is looking for orders with a total greater than ANY order by WILE BESS COMPANY (i.e., greater than any amount present in the set returned by the subquery). That means that records selected by the outer query should be greater than any of the values—effectively meaning that they should be greater than the smallest of the values returned by the subquery (which is 6608.00). The resultset was sorted in ascending order to help you visualize the situation. Here is a query that would produce identical results:

```
SELECT   v_total.customer_name,
         v_total.total_price
FROM     v_customer_totals v_total
WHERE    v_total.total_price >
   (SELECT   MIN(vctw.total_price)
    FROM     v_customer_totals_wilebess)
    ORDER BY total_price ASC);
```

The subquery here returns a single value—the minimal TOTAL_PRICE, which could be compared with a single value from the outer query.

Deploying the ALL operator brings up completely different records. It will instruct the outer query to select records whose TOTAL_PRICE is greater than all the values—meaning greater than the greatest value returned by the subquery. The results are arranged in ascending order, to underscore the point that the lowest TOTAL_PRICE column from the view V_CUSTOMER_TOTAL value returned by the outer query is bigger than the greatest:

```
SELECT  v_total.customer_name,
        v_total.total_price
FROM    v_customer_totals v_total
WHERE   v_total.total_price >
   ALL (SELECT vctw.total_price
        FROM v_customer_totals_wilebess vctw)
ORDER BY total_price DESC

CUSTOMER_NAME                        TOTAL_PRICE
------------------------------------ -----------
WILE ELECTRONICS INC.                15456.8
WILE SEAL CORP.                      15456.8

2 rows selected.
```

The same results could be achieved employing MAX function in the subquery, which ensures that only a single value (i.e., 15402.20) would be returned for comparison purposes:

```
SELECT  customer_name,
        total_price
FROM    v_customer_totals
WHERE   total_price > (SELECT MAX(total_price)
                       FROM v_customer_totals_wilebess)
ORDER BY total_price DESC;
```

Nested subqueries

The subquery could host a subquery in its turn. This is called nested subqueries. There is no theoretical limit on the nesting level—i.e., how many times there could be a query within a query—though some vendors limit it. Subquery is an expensive way (in computer resources terms) to find out information and should be used judiciously.

For example, to find all customers that ever ordered a product called CRATING MATERIAL 12X48X72, you could use the following query:

```
SELECT cust_name_s,
       cust_alias_s
```

```
FROM    customer
WHERE   cust_id_n IN
  (SELECT ordhdr_custid_fn
   FROM order_header
   WHERE ordhdr_id_n in
    (SELECT ordline_ordhdrid_fn
     FROM order_line
     WHERE ordline_prodid_fn =
      (SELECT prod_id_n
       FROM product
       WHERE prod_description_s = 'CRATING MATERIAL 12X48X72'
       )
    )
  )
CUST_NAME_S                                   CUST_ALIAS_S
--------------------------------------------- ---------------
WILE ELECTROMATIC INC.                          ECEL71460
WILE BESS COMPANY                               BSSE71641

2 rows selected.
```

The first query to be executed would be that with the highest nesting level — three in this case, then the second, then the first, and finally, when all necessary information is gathered, the main query would be executed.

There are also special cases of subquery called *correlated subquery*. The difference in regular and correlated subqueries is that the values from the outer subquery (host query) can be used as a parameter in the inner subquery. The correlated subqueries will be explained further in the chapter, in the section dealing with combining resultsets of the queries — namely, dealing with INTERSECT and MINUS keywords.

GROUP BY and HAVING Clauses: Summarizing Results

Grouping records in the resultset based on some criteria could provide a valuable insight into data that has accumulated in the table. For example, you would like to see the final resultset of your orders (where there could be one or more order items per order) not in the random order they were entered in, but rather in groups of items that belong to the same order:

```
SELECT    ordline_ordhdrid_fn,
          ordline_ordqty_n AS QTY_PER_ITEM
FROM      order_line
```

```
GROUP BY ordline_ordhdrid_fn,
         ordline_ordqty_n;

ordline_ordhdrid_fn QTY_PER_ITEM
------------------- ------------
30607               90
30607               500
30608               275
30608               340
30609               560
. . .               . . .
30666               560
30667               560
30668               72
30668               90
. . .               . . .
30669               120
30669               480
. . .               . . .
30670               126
30670               450

97 records selected.
```

Note the repeating values (groups) in the ORDLINE_ORDHDRID_FN field, representing the order header ID for which there could be one or more order items and for which there are different quantities. This information might become more concise with the use of aggregate functions that could sum the quantity for the order or calculate the average, and so on (see the example in this paragraph using SUM function).

All columns specified in a SELECT clause list, with the exception of aggregate columns (these used as an argument for an aggregate function), must be listed in the GROUP BY clause as well.

The GROUP BY clause is mostly (but not always) used in conjunction with aggregate functions, which are introduced in Chapter 10. The aggregate functions return a single value as a result of an operation conducted on a set of values. The set is grouped to provide a series of sets for use with the aggregate functions.

Table 10-7 in Chapter 10 lists five aggregate functions alongside their descriptions and particulars of implementation across all three RDBMS. For examples of the specific function usage, please refer to Chapter 10; here we're going to discuss the concept of aggregation and how it refers to the GROUP BY clause within a SELECT query.

To calculate the total sum of an ordered quantity for all orders (and one order could have one or more items) in the table ORDER_LINE you could use the SUM aggregate function:

```
SELECT
         SUM(ordline_ordqty_n) AS TOT_QTY_PER_ORDER
FROM     order_line;

TOT_QTY_PER_ORDER
-----------------
31847

1 record selected.
```

The single value that summed up all ordered quantities for all the records in the table was returned. While useful, this information could be more valuable if the ordered quantity is summed up per order—you would know how many items were ordered in each and every order. Here is the query that accomplishes this task:

```
SELECT   ordline_ordhdrid_fn,
         SUM(ordline_ordqty_n) AS TOT_QTY_PER_ORDER
FROM     order_line
GROUP BY ordline_ordhdrid_fn

ORDLINE_ORDHDRID_FN   TOT_QTY_PER_ORDER
-------------------   -----------------
              30607                 590
              30608                 615
              30609                 560
              ...                   ...
              30669                 600
              30670                 720

51 rows selected.
```

Here we have much more detailed information, as the quantities were grouped by order and then summed up for each order, producing a single value for each order (as opposed to producing it for a whole resultset).

Here is an example of another aggregate function AVG, which calculates the average of the values. In this case, you are going to calculate the average quantity per order.

```
SELECT   ordline_ordhdrid_fn,
         AVG(ordline_ordqty_n) AS AVG_QTY_PER_ORDER
FROM     order_line
```

```
GROUP BY ordline_ordhdrid_fn
ORDLINE_ORDHDRID_FN AVG_QTY_PER_ORDER
------------------- -----------------
              30607               295
              30608             307.5
              30609               560
                ...               ...
              30669               300
              30670               180

51 rows selected.
```

For order #30608, the average quantity is 307.5 in Oracle, but MS SQL Server and DB2 would round the value to 307 because the field is of INTEGER data type, whereas Oracle uses the NUMBER data type able to accommodate decimals. Refer to Chapter 3 for more information on data types.

The HAVING clause used exclusively with the GROUP BY clause provides a means of additional selectivity. Imagine that you need to select not all records in your GROUP BY query but only those that would have their grouped value greater than 750. Adding additional criterion to the WHERE clause would not help, as the value by which we could limit the records is calculated using GROUP BY and is unavailable outside it before the query has completed execution. The HAVING clause used within the GROUP BY clause allows us to add this additional criterion to the results of the GROUP BY operation. For example, to display orders with a total quantity greater than 750, the following query could be used:

```
SELECT    ordline_ordhdrid_fn,
          SUM(ordline_ordqty_n) TOT_QTY_PER_ORDER
FROM      order_line
GROUP BY  ordline_ordhdrid_fn
HAVING   SUM(ordline_ordqty_n) > 750

ORDLINE_ORDHDRID_FN TOT_QTY_PER_ORDER
 ------------------- -----------------
              30628               789
              30668               789

2 records selected.
```

As you can see, only 2 records among 51 from the previous query had satisfied this additional restriction.

We could have used a column ORDLINE_ORDHDRID_FN, without the SUM aggregate function in the HAVING clause to restrict the returned records by some other criteria, but we cannot use just any column from the SELECT clause: It also has to be listed in the GROUP BY clause to be used with HAVING. Here is a query example that sums up order quantities grouped by order header ID only if they fall into a specified list of orders:

```
SELECT    ordline_ordhdrid_fn,
          SUM(ordline_ordqty_n) TOT_QTY_PER_ORDER
FROM      order_line
GROUP BY ordline_ordhdrid_fn
HAVING    ordline_ordhdrid_fn IN (30607,30608,30611,30622)

ordline_ordhdrid_fn TOT_QTY_PER_ORDER
------------------- -----------------
30607                   590
30608                   615
30611                   625
30622                   726

4 records selected.
```

While GROUP BY would consider the null values in the columns by which the grouping is performed a valid group, this is not the way the NULLs are treated by the aggregate functions. Aggregate functions simply exclude the NULL records—they will not make it to the final result. See Chapter 10 for more information.

ORDER BY Clause: Sorting Query Output

The query returns results matching the criteria unsorted—i.e., in the order they've been found in the table. To produce sorted output—alphabetically or numerically—you would use an ORDER BY clause. The functionality of this clause is identical across all "big-three" databases.

The following query sorts the output by the customer name alphabetically in ascending order:

```
SQL> SELECT cust_name_s,
            cust_alias_s,
            cust_status_s
FROM        customer
ORDER BY    cust_name_s;

cust_name_s                      cust_alias_s    cust_status_s
-------------------------------- --------------- -------------
BOSWELL DESIGNS CORP.            BWS071471       Y
BURNETTE WILLIAM CORP.           BNRU71477       Y
CARLTONBATES COMPANY             CLRA71445       Y
CHGO SWITCHBOARD INC.            COGH71478       N
COFFMAN DOUGLAS                  CFF071482       Y
```

```
. . .
WILE ELECTRONICS INC.             ISCC71419        Y
WILE SEAL CORP.                   MNGA71396        Y

37 rows selected.
```

The results could be sorted in either ascending or descending order. To sort in descending order, you must specify keyword DESC after the column name; to sort in ascending order you may use ASC keyword (or omit it altogether, as it is done in the above query, since ascending is the default sorting order).

The column used in the ORDER BY clause does not have to appear in the SELECT clause, though it must be present in the table:

```
SELECT   cust_name_s,
         cust_alias_s
FROM     customer
ORDER BY cust_status_s
```

In this query, results are sorted by CUST_STATUS_S — a column that is not among those selected for display.

It is possible to sort by more than one column at the same time, though results might not be as obvious. The precedence of the columns in the ORDER BY clause is of importance here: First results are sorted by the values of the first column, then — within the order established by the first column — the results will be sorted by the second column values.

It is even possible to specify different orders — ascending or descending for the different columns listed in the ORDER BY clause. The following example orders the records from the PRODUCT table first by the price in ascending order, then by the net weight — in descending order *for each price value:*

```
SELECT   prod_id_n,
         prod_price_n,
         prod_netwght_n
FROM     product
ORDER BY prod_price_n ASC,
         prod_netwght_n DESC

PROD_ID_N   prod_price_n prod_netwght_n
----------- ------------ --------------
4000        11.80        15.194
. . .       . . .        . . .
990         18.24        21.226
4964        23.10        18.480
4761        23.10        10.032
```

```
2871          26.82          34.552
4906          27.00          22.000
1880          33.28          38.391

10 rows selected
```

Among the results returned by the query (which are sorted by the price in ascending order) there are two products (PROD_ID_N = 4964 and PROD_ID_N = 4761) that happen to have an identical price—$23.10. You can see that the values of the column PROD_NETWGHT_N for these products IDs are sorted in descending order.

If any of the column values contain NULLs, they would appear last on the ascending list, as NULLs by definition have ASCII number greater than any printable character.

Both Oracle and Microsoft SQL Server 2000 allow using ordinal numbers in the ORDER BY clause—i.e., instead of the column name you may use a number referring to the order in which this column appears in the SELECT part of the query. Following these rules, the above query could be rewritten as

```
SELECT   prod_id_n,
         prod_price_n,
         prod_netwght_n
FROM     product
ORDER BY 2 ASC,
         3 DESC
```

When ordinals are used instead of the column names in the ORDER BY clause, all these columns must appear in the SELECT statement (compare with the previous paragraph).

The ORDER BY clause is commonly used in conjunction with the GROUP BY expression, and the ordering could be performed by a computed column. The next query demonstrates this; it also uses a computed aliased AVG value for sorting purposes:

```
SELECT   ordline_ordhdrid_fn,
         AVG(ordline_ordqty_n) AS AVG_QTY_PER_ORDER
FROM     order_line
GROUP BY ordline_ordhdrid_fn
ORDER BY AVG_QTY_PER_ORDER DESC
ORDLINE_ORDHDRID_FN AVG_QTY_PER_ORDER
------------------- -----------------
              30610               700
              30619               700
              30650               700
              ...
```

```
           30668                157.8
           30622                145.2
           30662                145.2

51 rows selected.
```

The GROUP BY and ORDER BY clauses have certain similarities in both syntax and usage. They both are dealing with the ordering of data, and sometimes it is possible to use a GROUP BY clause in place of an ORDER BY clause. (That might be useful; for example, in the view creation process when the ORDER BY clause is illegal.) However, GROUP BY used for this purpose would have some disadvantages: You must list all nonaggregate columns listed in the SELECT clause in the GROUP BY clause, and you cannot use numbers to designate columns.

Combining the Results of Multiple Queries

It is possible to produce a single result combining the results of two or more queries. The combined resultset might be a simple aggregation of all records from the queries; or some operation related to the theory of sets (see Appendix L) could be performed before the final resultset was returned.

The SQL99 standard supports UNION, INTERSECT, and EXCEPT clauses that could be used to combine the results of two or more queries.

UNION

The following query returns all the records containing some information about customers that do not yet have an assigned salesman:

```
SELECT   phone_custid_fn OWNER_ID,
         'CUSTOMER PHONE' PHONE_TYPE,
         phone_phonenum_s
FROM     phone
WHERE    phone_type_s = 'PHONE'
AND      phone_salesmanid_fn IS NULL

OWNER_ID    PHONE_TYPE     phone_phonenum_s
----------- -------------- --------------------
51          CUSTOMER PHONE (817) 555-5524
5           CUSTOMER PHONE (847) 555-2924
12          CUSTOMER PHONE (508) 555-5224
61          CUSTOMER PHONE (541) 555-3091
. . .       . . .          . . .
16          CUSTOMER PHONE (201) 555-9302
89          CUSTOMER PHONE (908) 555-3779
```

```
85            CUSTOMER PHONE (281) 555-2835
152           CUSTOMER PHONE (541) 555-8979

37 records selected
```

This query returns a total of 37 records. Now, assume that you also would like to include in the resultset the list of salesmen's phones who do not have a customer assigned to them yet. Here is the query to find these salesmen; it returns six records:

```
SELECT      phone_salesmanid_fn,
            'SALESMAN PHONE',
            phone_phonenum_s
FROM        phone
WHERE       phone_type_s = 'PHONE'
AND         phone_custid_fn IS NULL

phone_salesmanid_fn                  phone_phonenum_s
------------------- -------------- --------------------
23                  SALESMAN PHONE (305) 555-8502
24                  SALESMAN PHONE (626) 555-4435
25                  SALESMAN PHONE (717) 555-5479
26                  SALESMAN PHONE (718) 555-7879
27                  SALESMAN PHONE (718) 555-5091
28                  SALESMAN PHONE (814) 555-0324

6 records selected
```

To combine these records into a single resultset, you would use the `UNION` statement:

```
SELECT            phone_custid_fn OWNER_ID,
                  'CUSTOMER PHONE' PHONE_TYPE,
                  phone_phonenum_s
FROM              phone
WHERE             phone_type_s = 'PHONE'
AND               phone_salesmanid_fn IS NULL
UNION
SELECT            phone_salesmanid_fn,
                  'SALESMAN PHONE',
                  phone_phonenum_s
FROM              phone
WHERE             phone_type_s = 'PHONE'
AND               phone_custid_fn IS NULL
ORDER BY    2, 1

  OWNER_ID PHONE_TYPE     PHONE_PHONENUM_S
---------- -------------- --------------------
         1 CUSTOMER PHONE (909) 555-9957
```

```
 2 CUSTOMER PHONE (501) 555-5702
 3 CUSTOMER PHONE (520) 555-5513
 4 CUSTOMER PHONE (802) 555-2091
...
26 SALESMAN PHONE (718) 555-7879
27 SALESMAN PHONE (718) 555-5091
28 SALESMAN PHONE (814) 555-0324

43 rows selected.
```

Now you have a full list that includes all records from the query about customers, combined with the results brought by the query about salesmen. You may visualize this as two resultsets glued together. All queries in an SQL statement containing a `UNION` operator must have an equal number of expressions in their lists. In addition, these expressions (which could be columns, literals, results of functions, etc.) must be of compatible data types: For example, if the expression evaluates to a character string in one query, it cannot be a number in the second query that is joined to the first by the `UNION` operator.

The results of `UNION` could be ordered (as we can see in the `UNION` query above) but the `ORDER BY` clause could be used only with the final resultset—that is, it can refer to the result of the `UNION`, not to particular queries used in it.

If the queries potentially could bring duplicate records, you may want to filter the duplicates, or, conversely, make sure that they all are present. By default, the `UNION` operator excludes duplicate records; specifying `UNION ALL` makes sure that your final resultset has all the records returned by all the queries participating in the `UNION`.

Here is a simple query returning status code and description from the `STATUS` table of the ACME database:

```
SELECT status_code_s,
       status_desc_s
FROM   status

ST STATUS_DESC_S
-- ------------------------------
60 SHIPPED
20 COMPLETE
70 INVOICED
80 CANCELLED

4 rows selected.
```

You can use exactly the same query to produce a resultset containing the duplicate rows, and combine the resultsets together using `UNION`:

```
SELECT status_code_s,
       status_desc_s
FROM   status
UNION
SELECT status_code_s,
       status_desc_s
FROM   status

ST STATUS_DESC_S
-- ------------------------------
20 COMPLETE
60 SHIPPED
70 INVOICED
80 CANCELLED

4 rows selected.
```

As you can see, the duplicates (i.e., the record where each corresponding column matched in both queries) were excluded, and the final record count is still 4, which is what you could have gotten from the one query only. This behaviour is in full compliance with the Set Theory. Running the same queries combined with the `UNION ALL` operator (which overrides this behaviour) returns all records from both queries, no duplicates are excluded:

```
SELECT   status_code_s,
         status_desc_s
FROM     status
UNION ALL
SELECT   status_code_s,
         status_desc_s
FROM     status

ST STATUS_DESC_S
-- ------------------------------
60 SHIPPED
20 COMPLETE
70 INVOICED
80 CANCELLED
60 SHIPPED
20 COMPLETE
70 INVOICED
80 CANCELLED

8 records selected.
```

The ALL keyword in the UNION operator brings the business world into our discussion: UNION ALL does not comply with set theory, where Idempotent Law A U A = A (see Appendix L) simply states that union of a set with itself is the same union. It is more intuitive from a business point of view to expect all records from constituent queries combined in the final resultset.

INTERSECT

The INTERSECT operator is used to evaluate results returned by two queries but includes only the records produced by the first query that have matching ones in the second. This operator is implemented in Oracle and IBM DB2 UDB but not in Microsoft SQL Server 2000, which uses EXISTS operator for this purpose.

Consider the query that selects customer IDs (field CUST_ID_N) from the CUSTOMER table of the ACME database and intersects them with results returned by a second query, producing a resultset of customer's IDs who placed an order:

```
SELECT  cust_id_n
FROM    customer
INTERSECT
SELECT  ordhdr_custid_fn
FROM    order_header

CUST_ID_N
----------
         1
         7
        55
        63
       152

5 records selected
```

The same results are achievable in a variety of ways. Here is an example, using a subquery and an IN operator:

```
SELECT cust_id_n
FROM   customer
WHERE  cust_id_n IN
 (SELECT ordhdr_custid_fn
  FROM   order_header)

CUST_ID_N
----------
         1
         7
        55
```

```
        63
       152

5 records selected
```

MS SQL Server does not have INTERSECT, offering the EXISTS operator instead. The following query could be rewritten in SQL Sever syntax using this operator and a correlated query:

```
SELECT  cust_id_n
FROM    customer
WHERE EXISTS
   (SELECT ordhdr_custid_fn
    FROM   order_header
    WHERE  ordhdr_custid_fn = cust_id_n)

cust_id_n
-----------
1
7
55
63
152
(5 row(s) affected)
```

The EXISTS keyword is common for all our "big three" databases, so this query would work for all of them.

While INTERSECT could be replaced with a combination of other SQL methods, it contributes to the clarity of the SQL code and speeds up its execution because it is more optimized than a subquery.

EXCEPT (MINUS)

When combining the results of two or more queries into a single resultset, you may want to exclude some records from the first query based on what was returned by the second. This keyword is implemented in IBM DB2 UDB only, whereas Oracle uses the MINUS keyword and Microsoft SQL Server 2000 uses EXISTS for the same purpose. The operation's functionality directly follows the rules of set theory, covered in Appendix L.

Consider the following two queries; both select some information about a customer. Here is the resultset returned by the first query:

```
SELECT cust_id_n
FROM   customer

cust_id_n
-----------
61
64
14
65
. . .
152
. . .
6
7
1

37 rows selected
```

The first query returns 37 rows. And here are the results of the second query:

```
SELECT ordhdr_custid_fn
FROM   order_header

ordhdr_custid_fn
----------------
NULL
NULL
1
1
. . .
1
7
7
. . .
152

(51 row(s) affected)
```

The `EXCEPT` result will be all the records from the first *minus* those returned by the second.

```
SELECT  cust_id_n
FROM    customer
MINUS
```

```
SELECT  ordhdr_custid_fn
FROM    order_header;

cust_id_n
-----------
61
. .
68
69
15
. . .
9
12
. . .
2
3

(32 row(s) affected)
```

And the MINUS operation brings 32 records. Five of the records from the second query were excepted from the records returned by the first query. We've shortened the output of all three queries to fit the page, but you may run the query yourself on the RDBMS of your choice; with any luck the results would match these described in the paragraph.

Oracle's name for this operator is MINUS, while DB2 UDB retains the SQL99 standard—EXCEPT.

The DB2 UDB syntax for this query would be identical save for the use of the EXCEPT operator:

```
SELECT cust_id_n
FROM   customer
EXCEPT
SELECT ordhdr_custid_fn
FROM   order_header
```

Microsoft SQL Server 2000 offers the NOT EXISTS operator instead; surprisingly this syntax, while not part of the SQL99 standard, is common to all "big-three" databases. To get the results with the NOT EXISTS operator you need to use a *correlated* subquery. A correlated subquery differs from a regular subquery in that it accepts a parameter from the outer query as a criterion in the WHERE clause:

```
SELECT  cust_name_s,
        cust_alias_s,
        cust_status_s
```

```
FROM    customer cust
WHERE NOT EXISTS (SELECT *
                  FROM order_header
                  WHERE ordhdr_custid_fn = cust.cust_id_n)

cust_name_s                        cust_alias_s   cust_status_s
---------------------------------- -------------- -------------
MAGNETICS USA INC.                                MNGA71398      Y
MAGNETOMETRIC DEVICES INC.                        MNGA71400      Y
FAIR PARK GARDENS                                 NULL           Y
FAIR AND SONS AIR CONDTNG                         FRIA71406      Y
. . .                                             . . .          ...
INSULECTRO INC.                                   IUSN71521      Y
INTEGRATED POWER DESIGNS                          IETN71523      Y
EASTERN SATELLITE COMPANY                         ETSA71626      Y

(32 row(s) affected)
```

In this case, we used the CUST_ID_N field of the CUSTOMER table as a criterion for the subquery to limit the number of the potential records. If there is a record for a customer ID (ORDHDR_CUSTID_FN = CUST.CUST_ID_N) in the ORDER_HEADER table, the record will be excluded from the outer query final resultset; only records for customers that have not placed orders will be returned.

Summary

The SELECT statement is arguably the most important statement in the whole Structured Query Language. It is the only statement of the data query language (DQL) and provides the means for extracting data.

This chapter introduces the important concepts of a single table SELECT query and all its component clauses — SELECT, FROM, and WHERE.

The query only extracts data and modifies the extract, it never modifies the data in the underlying tables. The operations on the resultsets generally follow the rules of the mathematical set theory, the basic knowledge of which is beneficial for understanding the results.

The queries could be combined into a single resultset using the UNION, INTERSECT, or EXCEPT operations. Some of these results are implemented differently by different RDBMS vendors.

Subqueries can be used as a part of a general SELECT query and can be nested in order to dynamically retrieve information that is difficult or impossible to obtain otherwise.

✦ ✦ ✦

CHAPTER 9

Multitable Queries

✦ ✦ ✦ ✦

In This Chapter

Simple inner join

Cross join

Natural join

Self join

Right, left, and full outer joins

Union join

Joins involving inline views and correlated queries

Improving multitable query performance

✦ ✦ ✦ ✦

In the previous chapter we introduced the simple, or single-table query. However, you can hardly find a relational database with just one table — that contradicts the whole idea of RDBMS and normalization rules. To achieve meaningful results you usually have to retrieve information from multiple tables within a single query. All RDBMS allow you to join data from two or more tables based on a common column (or multiple columns), i.e., when this column(s) appears in both tables — under the same or a different name; for example (having ACME database in mind), ORDER_HEADER table could be joined with CUSTOMER using the ORDHDR_CUSTID_FN and CUST_ID_N columns.

Note

The rule above is only enforced logically; for example, nothing prevents you from joining two tables based on unrelated columns (for example, ORDER_HEADER and PRODUCT using ORDHDR_ID_N and PROD_ID_N correspondingly), but the result of such a join would be completely meaningless nonsense.

All joins can generally be divided into two large groups — inner joins and outer joins.

Inner Joins

In this section we'll be talking about inner joins, which only return rows with matching values from both joined tables excluding all other rows.

Two syntaxes for inner joins

There are two different syntaxes for table joins in SQL, one introduced in 1992 by the SQL standards committee, and the "old" one, used before this date but which still persists. The new standard syntax began to take a foothold in the late 1990s with introduction of Microsoft SQL Server 7.0, IBM DB2 UDB 7.1, and eventually Oracle joining the club with its 9*i* version, which supports the standard "new" SQL syntax in addition to the old one.

SQL99

SQL99 defines syntax that uses FROM clause of the SELECT statement to join tables:

```
...
FROM  <table1>
[INNER | NATURAL | CROSS] JOIN
      <table2>
[ON <condition>] | [USING <column_name>,...],...
...
```

The actual examples are given later in this chapter; for now let's clarify what all the optional clauses stand for.

Inner join options

With an inner join, you have these options:

- ✦ Keyword INNER is optional; it could be used for clarity to distinguish between inner and outer joins.
- ✦ Keyword NATURAL is used to specify a natural join between two tables, i.e., join them by column(s) with identical names. You cannot invoke either the ON or USING clause along with the NATURAL keyword. Out of all our "big three" RDBMS, it is available only in Oracle 9*i*. The natural join is discussed in more detail later in this chapter.
- ✦ Keyword CROSS is used to produce a cross join, as discussed later in this chapter. The keyword is valid for Oracle 9*i* and MS SQL Server 2000 syntax but is not recognized by DB2 UDB 8.1.

ON and USING clauses

The ON clause is to specify the join condition (equijoin or nonequijoin, explained later in the chapter); all our "big three" databases have it in their syntax.

When you are specifying an equijoin of columns that have the same name in both tables, a USING clause can indicate the column(s) to be used. You can use this clause only if the join columns in both tables have the same name. The USING clause could be used when the NATURAL join would not work properly, i.e., tables have more identically named columns than you would actually want to use in your join. For example, if hypothetical tables A and B have common fields CUST_ID, PROD_ID, and ORDER_ID, but you only want to join them by CUST_ID and PROD_ID, you could specify

```
...
FROM A JOIN B
USING (CUST_ID, PROD_ID)
...
```

The column names in USING clause should not be qualified by table names.

The USING clause is only supported by Oracle 9*i* out of our three vendors, but the same results could easily be achieved with ON clause:

```
...
FROM A JOIN B
ON A.CUST_ID = B.CUST_ID
AND A.PROD_ID = B.PROD_ID
...
```

Old syntax

The other syntax, which is commonly used by virtually everyone (Oracle only recognized the "standard" syntax starting version 9*i*, and Microsoft SQL Server introduced it in version 7.0), performs joins in the WHERE clause:

```
...

  WHERE [<qualifier>.]<column_name>
         <join_condition>
        [<qualifier>.]<column_name>
  [AND  [<qualifier>].<column_name>
         <join_condition>
        [<qualifier>.]<column_name>],...
  ...
```

The join_condition can be the "equal" sign ('=') for equijoin or "not equal," "greater than," "less than," "greater than or equal," or "less than or equal" signs (<>, >, <, >=, <=) for non-equijoin. The explanation of terms "equijoin" and non-equijoin" follows.

Equijoin

Equijoin, which is the most popular type of table join, uses exact matching between two columns. For example, in the ACME database the CUSTOMER table does not contain any information about customer phone numbers; the PHONE table has the field PHONE_CUSTID_FN, which is the foreign key to CUSTOMER table. To display information from both tables, use equijoin as shown in Figure 9-1.

CUSTOMER

cust_name_s	cust_id_n
WILE SEAL CORP.	1
MAGNETICS USA INC.	2
MAGNETOMETRIC DEVICE. . .	3
FAIR PARK GARDENS	4
FAIR AND SONS AIR CO. . .	5

PHONE

phone_custid_fn	phone_phonenum_s	phone_type_s
1	(909) 394-9957	PHONE
1	(909) 394-9956	FAX
2	(501) 674-5702	PHONE
2	(501) 674-5701	FAX
3	(520) 885-5513	PHONE
3	(520) 885-5512	FAX
4	(802) 888-2091	PHONE
4	(802) 888-2091	FAX
5	(847) 885-2924	PHONE
5	(847) 885-2923	FAX

CUSTOMER JOIN PHONE ON CUST_ID_N = PHONE_CUSTID_FN

cust_id_n	cust_name_s	phone_phonenum_s	phone_type_s
1	WILE SEAL CORP.	(909) 394-9957	PHONE
1	WILE SEAL CORP.	(909) 394-9956	FAX
2	MAGNETICS USA INC.	(501) 674-5702	PHONE
2	MAGNETICS USA INC.	(501) 674-5701	FAX
3	MAGNETOMETRIC DEVICE. . .	(520) 885-5513	PHONE
3	MAGNETOMETRIC DEVICE. . .	(520) 885-5512	FAX
4	FAIR PARK GARDENS	(802) 888-2091	PHONE
4	FAIR PARK GARDENS	(802) 888-2091	FAX
5	FAIR AND SONS AIR CO. . .	(847) 885-2924	PHONE
5	FAIR AND SONS AIR CO. . .	(847) 885-2923	FAX

Figure 9-1: Simple inner join

SQL99 standard syntax

The SQL99-compliant syntax to produce the output shown on the bottom of Figure 9-1 is given here:

```
SELECT          cust_id_n,
                cust_name_s,
                phone_phonenum_s,
                phone_type_s
FROM            customer JOIN phone
ON              cust_id_n = phone_custid_fn
```

Natural join

Natural join is a special case of equijoin performed by RDBMS on the following assumption: "Always join tables using a column (or multiple columns) if they share the same name(s)." In other words, you don't have to specify the columns explicitly in the `ON` subclause of the `SELECT` statement's `FROM` clause. The `ON` subclause is omitted completely.

The idea of natural join contradicts the quasi-"Hungarian" notation concept (see Appendix B). In the ACME database, every column is prefixed with its abbreviated table name, so every column name in the database is unique and as such the natural join cannot be used at all. There are different opinions on whether the primary and the foreign keys should share the same name. The possibility to perform natural joins seems to be the only advantage in this case (and only if you are using Oracle), so in our ACME database we decided to use the notation consistently.

The naming conventions for the ACME database are described in Appendix B.

The natural join can make the query writing process easier, but only assuming the database structure and the query itself are simple enough; otherwise undesirable joins and incorrect query output could result.

Fully Qualified Column Names

If two or more tables share one or more column names referenced in your query, you must prefix column names with either names of tables or with table aliases; otherwise the RDBMS will not be able to resolve the ambiguity and an error message will be generated.

It is considered to be a good practice to qualify column references explicitly; however, as we mentioned before, in our ACME sample database each and every column name is unique (i.e., is already fully qualified, in a way), which makes the use of the fully qualified names unnecessary. The following example illustrates the use of the qualified names with the same query as in the previous example:

```
SELECT          customer.cust_id_n,
                customer.cust_name_s,
                phone.phone_phonenum_s,
                phone.phone_type_s
FROM            customer JOIN phone
ON              customer.cust_id_n = phone.phone_custid_fn
```

We'll use the fully qualified names randomly in our further examples.

Old syntax

The old syntax joins tables in the WHERE clause of the SELECT statement. The syntax has its defenders and opponents. The main argument against it is that the WHERE clause should not mix joins and predicates — its only purpose should be setting the "vertical" limits on the produced resultset. The major point for it is that in queries that join dozens of tables the old syntax is more readable. Another big point is code legacy, especially for Oracle where the standard syntax was not available until version 9*i*. It is your choice which syntax to use (we would suggest the SQL99-compliant one for all new developments), but it is definitely not a bad idea to be familiar with both.

The following statement is the equivalent to one given in the previous section; the old syntax being the only difference:

```
SELECT          c.cust_id_n,
                c.cust_name_s,
                p.phone_phonenum_s
FROM            customer c,
                phone p
WHERE           c.cust_id_n = p.phone_custid_fn
```

Nonequijoin

Sometimes you need to join tables based on criteria other than equality. While the most typical use of equijoin deals with primary/foreign key relationships, that is not usually the case with nonequijoins — such a join would usually populate the resulting set in a way that does not make much sense at all. For example, if you replace the = (equals) operator in the query from the last section with <> (not equal), the resulting query will return every possible combination of customers and phone numbers except the ones that actually represent the valid customer/phone listings (Figure 9-2); in other words, the result will be somehow similar to the Cartesian product (CROSS JOIN) discussed later in this chapter.

In some situations though, nonequijoins appear to be quite useful. For example, imagine ACME, INC. has the following set of business rules. There is no discount for orders under $10,000; a 2 percent discount is given to all orders with total amount between $10,000 and $14,999; the orders with a total amount between $15,000 and $19,999 receive a 3 percent discount; and, finally, the orders that are $20,000 or more are eligible for a 4 percent discount.

One of the ways to implement such business rules is to have a table that stores minimum and maximum order amount along with the corresponding discount percentage as shown in Figure 9-3.

CUSTOMER JOIN PHONE ON CUST_ID_N <> PHONE_CUSTID_FN

cust_id_n	cust_name_s	phone_phonenum_s	phone_type_s
1	WILE SEAL CORP.	(817) 236-5524	PHONE
1	WILE SEAL CORP.	(847) 885-2924	PHONE
1	WILE SEAL CORP.	(508) 761-5224	PHONE
1	WILE SEAL CORP.	(541) 994-3091	PHONE
1	WILE SEAL CORP.	(541) 336-3246	PHONE
1	WILE SEAL CORP.	(305) 822-8802	PHONE
1	WILE SEAL CORP.	(760) 355-2335	PHONE
1	WILE SEAL CORP.	(619) 424-6635	PHONE
...	...	...	...
1	WILE SEAL CORP.	(847) 885-2923	FAX
1	WILE SEAL CORP.	(508) 761-5223	FAX
1	WILE SEAL CORP.	(541) 994-3091	FAX
1	WILE SEAL CORP.	(541) 336-3245	FAX
1	WILE SEAL CORP.	(305) 822-8801	FAX
1	WILE SEAL CORP.	(760) 355-2334	FAX
1	WILE SEAL CORP.	(619) 424-6634	FAX
...	...	...	...
152	WILE BESS COMPA	(847) 885-2924	PHONE
152	WILE BESS COMPA	(508) 761-5224	PHONE
152	WILE BESS COMPA	(541) 994-3091	PHONE
152	WILE BESS COMPA	(541) 336-3246	PHONE
152	WILE BESS COMPA	(305) 822-8802	PHONE
152	WILE BESS COMPA	(760) 355-2335	PHONE
...	...	...	...

Figure 9-2: Primary/foreign key nonequijoin

DISCOUNT

DISC_MINAMOUNT_N	DISC_MAXAMOUNT_N	DISC_PCT
0	9999	0
10000	14999	2
15000	19999	3
20000	1000000000	4

Figure 9-3: The contents of DISCOUNT table

It is always a good practice to store values that potentially could change (for example, the discount for orders over $20,000 might change from 4 to 3.5 percent) in a RDBMS table rather than to hardcode them in the application. Should business rules change, you only need to update the table value(s) — which is fast and painless in comparison with changing the application code, recompiling the application, and so on.

In the following example, the nonequijoin between view V_CUSTOMER_TOTALS (that displays the dollar amount totals per order calculated using the order line amounts) and table DISCOUNT is shown. The query calculates the appropriate discount for each dollar amount (TOTAL_DISCOUNT) by multiplying the order total amount by the appropriate percent discount found based on the rules described above.

SQL99 standard syntax

```
SELECT  ct.order_number,
        ct.total_price,
        ct.total_price * d.disc_pct / 100 AS total_discount
FROM    v_customer_totals ct
   JOIN
        discount d
   ON   ct.total_price > d.disc_minamount_n
   AND
        ct.total_price < d.disc_maxamount_n

ORDER_NUMBER                   TOTAL_PRICE TOTAL_DISCOUNT
------------------------------ ----------- --------------
523774                                6608              0
523778                                6608              0
...
523777                               10010          200.2
523737                               10010          200.2
523730                             10915.8        218.316
...
523781                             15402.2        462.066
523741                             15402.2        462.066
523775                             15456.8        463.704
523735                             15456.8        463.704

51 rows selected.
```

Old syntax

```
SELECT  order_number,
        total_price,
        total_price * disc_pct / 100 AS total_discount
FROM    v_customer_totals ct,
        discount d
WHERE   ct.total_price > d.disc_minamount_n
AND     ct.total_price < d.disc_maxamount_n
```

Tables can be joined by more than one column. In this example we join the V_CUSTOMER_TOTALS column TOTAL_PRICE with both the DISC_MINAMOUNT_N and DISC_MAXAMOUNT_N columns of the DISCOUNT table to find the appropriate discount percentage for the specified range. Another typical example of multicolumn joins is when you have to join composite primary/foreign keys.

Self-join

The idea of self-join is probably one of the most unintuitive SQL concepts. Even though it sounds very simple — a table is joined with itself rather than with another table — sometimes it causes lots of confusion.

One important thing to understand here is that despite the fact that you are joining the table with itself, you are still dealing with *two instances* of the same table, or with two identical tables rather than with just one table, so the self-join should be considered as a special case of the multitable join.

The understanding of the difference between a table and its instance is also very important. Two table instances could be thought of as the table data loaded twice into two different memory locations completely separate from each other.

Imagine if ACME, INC. decided to implement some kind of multilevel marketing. It starts selling products to resellers, who in their turn either sell the products to a lower-level reseller or directly to a customer. That means any of ACME's customers now could be a reseller (the one who buys and resells products) or a supplier (the one whom products are bought from), or both. The relationship has been implemented in the RESELLER table. ACME, INC. has NULL in the RESELLER_SUPPLIER_ID column because it's on the top of the tree and so it does not have a supplier. Everybody else has another entity's (from the RESELLER table) primary key in this field.

Figure 9-4 illustrates this concept as well as the idea of multiple table instances.

SQL99 standard syntax

The following query uses self-join to retrieve the reseller id and name along with its supplier id and name (for each entity in RESELLER table) using SQL99-compliant syntax:

```
SELECT  r.reseller_id_n    AS res_id,
        r.reseller_name_s  AS res_name,
        s.reseller_id_n    AS sup_id,
        s.reseller_name_s  AS sup_name
FROM    reseller r JOIN reseller s
  ON    r.reseller_supplier_id = s.reseller_id_n

RES_ID RES_NAME                    SUP_ID SUP_NAME
------ --------------------------- ------ -------------------------
     2 MAGNETICS USA INC.          1      ACME, INC
     3 MAGNETOMETRIC DEVICES INC.  1      ACME, INC
     4 FAIR PARK GARDENS           2      MAGNETICS USA INC.
     5 FAIR AND SONS AIR CONDTNG   2      MAGNETICS USA INC.
     6 FABRITEK INC.               2      MAGNETICS USA INC.
     7 WILE ELECTRONICS INC.       3      MAGNETOMETRIC DEVICES INC.
     8 INTEREX USA                 3      MAGNETOMETRIC DEVICES INC.
     9 JUDCO MANUFACTURING INC.    4      FAIR PARK GARDENS
    10 ELECTRO BASS INC.           5      FAIR AND SONS AIR CONDTNG

(9 rows affected)
```

RESELLER TABLE STRUCTURE

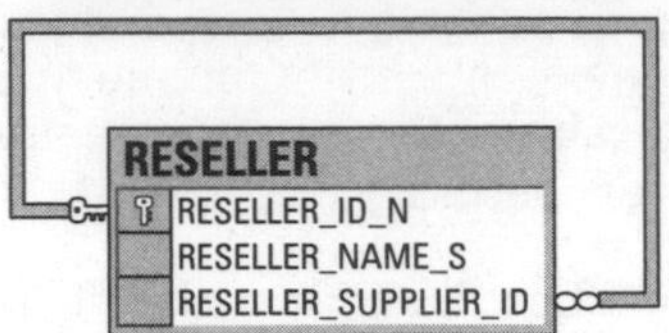

RESELLER R
(FIRST INSTANCE)

RESELLER_ID_N	RESELLER_NAME_S	RESELLER_SUPPLIER_ID
1	ACME, INC	NULL
2	MAGNETICS USA INC.	1
3	MAGNETOMETRIC DEVICE. . .	1
4	FAIR PARK GARDENS	2
5	FAIR AND SONS AIR CO. . .	2
6	FABRITEK INC.	2
7	WILE ELECTRONICS INC.	3
8	INTEREX USA	3
9	JUDCO MANUFACTURING INC.	4
10	ELECTRO BASS INC.	5

RESELLER S
(SECOND INSTANCE)

RESELLER_ID_N	RESELLER_NAME_S	RESELLER_SUPPLIER_ID
1	ACME, INC	NULL
2	MAGNETICS USA INC.	1
3	MAGNETOMETRIC DEVICE. . .	1
4	FAIR PARK GARDENS	2
5	FAIR AND SONS AIR CO. . .	2
6	FABRITEK INC.	2
7	WILE ELECTRONICS INC.	3
8	INTEREX USA	3
9	JUDCO MANUFACTURING INC.	4
10	ELECTRO BASS INC.	5

Figure 9-4: Self-join

The information is to be interpreted this way: ACME, INC. sells directly to MAGNETICS USA INC. and MAGNETOMETRIC DEVICES INC. MAGNETOMETRIC DEVICES INC. buys products from ACME, INC. and sells them to WILE ELECTRONICS INC. and INTEREX USA, and so on.

Old syntax

The following statement is the old syntax equivalent of the same query:

```
SELECT  r.reseller_id_n   AS res_id,
        r.reseller_name_s AS res_name,
        s.reseller_id_n   AS sup_id,
        s.reseller_name_s AS sup_name
FROM    reseller r,
        reseller s
WHERE   r.reseller_supplier_id = s.reseller_id_n
```

Cross join (Cartesian product)

Cross join, or the Cartesian product of two tables, can be defined as another (rather virtual) table that consists of all possible pairs of rows from the two source tables. Returning to our customer phone example in the nonequijoin section of this chapter, the cross join of the CUSTOMER and PHONE tables returns results very similar to what we've got on Figure 8-2 except it would also return the valid customer/phone combinations, excluded from the previously mentioned nonequijoin.

SQL99 standard syntax

This query will return all possible combinations of customer names and phone numbers by performing cross join of CUSTOMER and PHONE tables:

```
SELECT  cust_name_s,
        phone_phonenum_s
FROM    customer CROSS JOIN
        phone

CUST_NAME_S                                        PHONE_PHONENUM_S
-------------------------------------------------- --------------------
DLH INDUSTRIES                                     (817) 555-5524
FAIR AND SONS AIR CONDTNG                          (817) 555-5524
KILBURN GLASS INDUSTRIES                           (817) 555-5524
BOSWELL DESIGNS CORP.                              (817) 555-5524
WILE ELECTROMATIC INC.                             (817) 555-5524
FABRITEK INC.                                      (817) 555-5524
...                                                ...
DLH INDUSTRIES                                     (847) 555-2924
FAIR AND SONS AIR CONDTNG                          (847) 555-2924
KILBURN GLASS INDUSTRIES                           (847) 555-2924
BOSWELL DESIGNS CORP.                              (847) 555-2924
WILE ELECTROMATIC INC.                             (847) 555-2924
FABRITEK INC.                                      (847) 555-2924
...                                                ...
DLH INDUSTRIES                                     (814) 555-0323
FAIR AND SONS AIR CONDTNG                          (814) 555-0323
KILBURN GLASS INDUSTRIES                           (814) 555-0323
```

```
BOSWELL DESIGNS CORP.                    (814) 555-0323
WILE ELECTROMATIC INC.                   (814) 555-0323
FABRITEK INC.                            (814) 555-0323
...                                      ...

3182 rows selected.
```

Old syntax

The old syntax for cross join simply omits the WHERE clause in a multitable join:

```
SELECT  cust_name_s,
        phone_phonenum_s
FROM    customer,
        phone
```

Cross join could be a very costly operation, especially when it happens as the result of a human error and involves large tables with hundreds of thousands or even millions of rows. Since the resulting set of a Cartesian product is every possible combination of all rows in both tables, if the first table is, say, one hundred thousand rows and the second one is two hundred thousand rows, the query returns twenty billion rows (100,000 * 200,000 = 20,000,000,000) — quite enough to cause considerable database server slowdown that would affect all users that are currently logged on.

Thus, the Cartesian product should be handled with care, especially because it is not something that a typical SQL user uses a lot. Cross joins can be useful to generate test data or in educational purposes (for example, to demonstrate the idea that all equijoins and nonequijoins are simply a subset of a cross join that meets certain conditions), but one would hardly need, say, all possible combinations of customer names and phone numbers. In most real-life situations a Cartesian product is simply the result of a human error that would have to be fixed by the DBA (probably by killing the user's session; more on the sessions in Chapter 7).

Joining more than two tables

In a relational database quite often you need to retrieve data from many tables simultaneously within a single query to get all necessary information. Thus, in real life a multitable query could easily mean a dozen-table query or even a hundred-table query. Probably 90 percent of the SQL programming art is the talent to properly join multiple tables based on the knowledge of the internal database objects' structure plus the ability to apply this knowledge.

The concept is simple. The result of joining two tables could be considered as a new virtual table, which, in its turn, could be joined with the next table in the query, producing yet another virtual table, and so on. For example, if you needed to know what customers ordered which products, your query would have to join four tables: CUSTOMER, ORDER_HEADER, ORDER_LINE, and PRODUCT:

```
SELECT DISTINCT  customer.cust_name_s,
                 product.prod_description_s
FROM             customer
   JOIN          order_header
   ON            customer.cust_id_n = order_header.ordhdr_custid_fn
   JOIN          order_line
   ON            order_header.ordhdr_id_n =  order_line.ordline_ordhdrid_fn
   JOIN          product
   ON            product.prod_id_n = order_line.ordline_prodid_fn
```

You could envision this query as a sequence of joins. First, join CUSTOMER and ORDER_HEADER using the appropriate columns; then join the resulting set of rows with the ORDER_LINE table; and, finally, join your result with the PRODUCT table as illustrated in Figure 9-5.

Also note that even though you might not need any columns either from ORDER_HEADER or from ORDER_LINE tables, you have to use them in your query joins because there is no direct relationship between the CUSTOMER and PRODUCT tables.

Number of joins

One important rule to remember is that there should be at least (n – 1) joins in an n-table query, thus, at least two joins for a three-table query, at least three joins for query that involves four tables, and so on. The words "at least" are important—there could be more than (n – 1) joins in a nonequijoin query or in a query that joins tables using composite primary/foreign keys, but if your multitable query has less than (n – 1) joins, the result will be a Cartesian product.

The most common (and the most dangerous) type of a cross join happens in queries that involve more than two tables. In that situation you don't even have to omit the WHERE clause—it would be sufficient to simply skip a join between two tables out of a dozen. Also, the more tables are joined within a single query, the bigger the resulting set could be—the Cartesian product of five tables, with only one hundred rows each, produces ten billion rows.

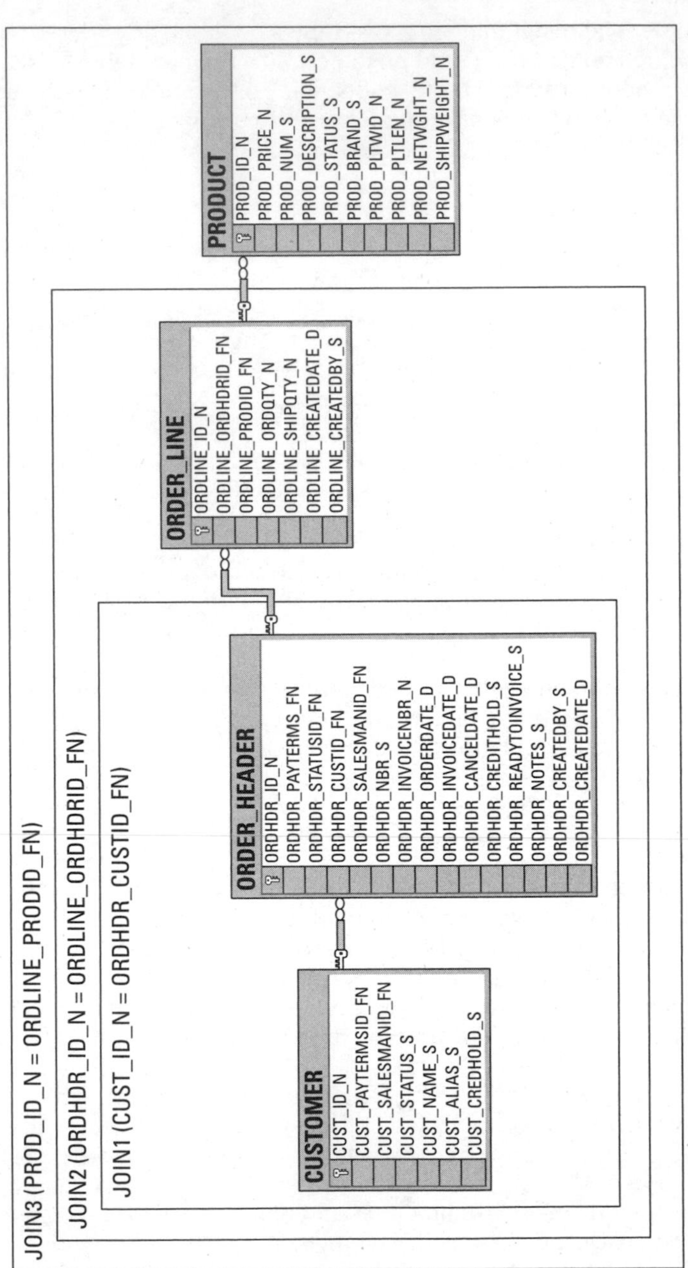

Figure 9-5: Four tables join

SQL99 standard syntax

The query in the previous example uses SQL99-compliant syntax. The query that follows also uses SQL99-compliant syntax to join the CUSTOMER, ORDER_HEADER, and STATUS tables and return customer name, order number, and order status:

```
SELECT cust_name_s,
       ordhdr_nbr_s,
       status_desc_s
FROM   customer
   JOIN
       order_header
   ON  cust_id_n = ordhdr_custid_fn
   JOIN
       status
   ON  status_id_n = ordhdr_statusid_fn

CUST_NAME_S                ORDHDR_NBR_S      STATUS_DESC_S
------------------------   ------------      -------------
WILE BESS COMPANY          523731             COMPLETE
WILE BESS COMPANY          523732             COMPLETE
WILE ELECTRONICS INC.      523733             COMPLETE
WILE ELECTRONICS INC.      523734             COMPLETE
WILE ELECTRONICS INC.      523735             COMPLETE
WILE BESS COMPANY          523736             COMPLETE
...                        ...                ...
WILE BESS COMPANY          523738             CANCELLED
WILE BESS COMPANY          523742             CANCELLED
WILE BESS COMPANY          523743             CANCELLED

51 rows selected.
```

Old syntax

Here is the old syntax equivalent of the previous query:

```
SELECT   cust_name_s,
         ordhdr_nbr_s,
         status_desc_s
FROM     customer,
         order_header,
         status
WHERE    cust_id_n = ordhdr_custid_fn
AND      status_id_n = ordhdr_statusid_fn
```

Outer Joins: Joining Tables on Columns Containing NULL Values

You probably noticed in the RESELLER table presented earlier in this chapter that the query returns all table records except one for ACME, INC. This is because the ACME, INC. record in the RESELLER table has NULL in the RESELLER_SUPPLIER_ID column, so an RDBMS cannot find the corresponding value in the table you are trying to join (in this case, the other instance of RESELLER table). As the result, the query returns nine rows even though the table contains ten records. That's just the way the standard (inner) join works. Sometimes, however, you want a query to return *all* rows from table A and the corresponding rows from table B — if they exist. That's where you use outer joins.

Two syntaxes for outer joins

Like inner joins, the outer joins also have two different syntaxes.

SQL99

The SQL99-compliant syntax indicates outer join in the FROM clause of the SELECT statement:

```
...
FROM  <table1>
  {LEFT | RIGHT | FULL [OUTER]} | UNION JOIN
      <table2>
  [ON <condition>] | [USING <column_name>,...],...
...
```

The syntax is generally supported by all our three RDBMS vendors. The exceptions are the USING clause that is implemented only by Oracle and the UNION clause (discussed later in this chapter) that is not a part of any of the "big three" databases syntax.

Old syntax

The old syntax uses the WHERE clause and is different for Oracle and MS SQL Server. (DB2 does not have any "old" syntax for outer joins at all; it was using the SQL99-compliant syntax from the very beginning. In fact, the latter syntax has originated from DB2 standards.)

Oracle 9*i*

The old right or left outer join syntax is denoted by the plus operator (+) placed after the name of the table with no matching rows on the corresponding side of the

= sign. The full outer join can be only specified with the SQL99-compliant syntax. The old Oracle syntax for right and left outer joins is shown below:

Syntax for right outer join

```
...
WHERE [<qualifier>.]<column_name> =
      [<qualifier>.]<column_name> (+)
[AND  [<qualifier>.]<column_name> =
      [<qualifier>.]<column_name> (+)
],...
...
```

Syntax for left outer join

```
...
WHERE [<qualifier>.]<column_name> (+) =
      [<qualifier>.]<column_name>
[AND  [<qualifier>.]<column_name> (+) =
      [<qualifier>.]<column_name>
],...
...
```

MS SQL Server 2000

The right or left outer join is denoted by the asterisk (*) placed on the appropriate (right or left) side of the equals sign (=). The full outer join is unavailable in the old syntax. The following old syntax could be used in MS SQL Server for right and left outer joins:

Syntax for right outer join

```
...
WHERE [<qualifier>.]<column_name> =*
      [<qualifier>.]<column_name>
[AND  [<qualifier>.]<column_name> =*
      [<qualifier>.]<column_name>
],...
...
```

Syntax for left outer join

```
...
WHERE [<qualifier>.]<column_name> *=
      [<qualifier>.]<column_name>
[AND  [<qualifier>.]<column_name> *=
```

```
      [<qualifier>.]<column_name>
   ],...
   ...
```

Left outer join

In fact, the term "left outer join" is just a convention used by SQL programmers. You can achieve identical results using left or right outer joins as we will demonstrate later in this chapter. The whole idea behind an outer join is to retrieve all rows from table A (left) or table B (right), even though there are no matching columns in the counterpart table, so the join column(s) is NULL. A left (or right) outer join also returns nulls for all unmatched columns from the joined table (for rows with NULL join columns only).

SQL99 standard syntax

The following query illustrates how to produce the resulting set containing all ten rows from RESELLER table using SQL99-compliant left outer join:

```
SELECT            r.reseller_id_n   AS res_id,
                  r.reseller_name_s AS res_name,
                  s.reseller_id_n   AS sup_id,
                  s.reseller_name_s AS sup_name
FROM              reseller r
  LEFT OUTER JOIN
                  reseller s
  ON              r.reseller_supplier_id = s.reseller_id_n

RES_ID RES_NAME                     SUP_ID SUP_NAME
------ ---------------------------- ------ --------------------------
     1 ACME, INC.                   NULL   NULL
     2 MAGNETICS USA INC.           1      ACME, INC
     3 MAGNETOMETRIC DEVICES INC.   1      ACME, INC
     4 FAIR PARK GARDENS            2      MAGNETICS USA INC.
     5 FAIR AND SONS AIR CONDTNG    2      MAGNETICS USA INC.
     6 FABRITEK INC.                2      MAGNETICS USA INC.
     7 WILE ELECTRONICS INC.        3      MAGNETOMETRIC DEVICES INC.
     8 INTEREX USA                  3      MAGNETOMETRIC DEVICES INC.
     9 JUDCO MANUFACTURING INC.     4      FAIR PARK GARDENS
    10 ELECTRO BASS INC.            5      FAIR AND SONS AIR CONDTNG

(10 rows affected)
```

One more example. Assume we need to retrieve customer name and all order numbers for customer 152. The following (inner) join will do:

```
SELECT  cust_name_s,
        ordhdr_nbr_s
FROM    customer
  JOIN
        order_header
ON      cust_id_n = ordhdr_custid_fn
WHERE   cust_id_n = 152

CUST_NAME_S        ORDHDR_NBR_S
------------------ ------------
...                ...
WILE BESS COMPANY  523731
WILE BESS COMPANY  523732
...                ...

31 rows selected.
```

Now we need very similar results except that we also want corresponding payment terms for each order. We assume we could simply modify our query by joining PAYMENT_TERMS table to it:

```
SELECT  cust_name_s,
        ordhdr_nbr_s,
        payterms_desc_s
FROM    customer
  JOIN
        order_header
  ON    cust_id_n = ordhdr_custid_fn
  JOIN
        payment_terms
  ON    payterms_id_n = ordhdr_payterms_fn
WHERE   cust_id_n = 152;

CUST_NAME_S        ORDHDR_NBR_S PAYTERMS_DESC_S
------------------ ------------ ---------------
...                ...          ...
WILE BESS COMPANY  523732       2% 15 NET 30
...                ...          ...

30 rows selected.
```

To our surprise, the query now returns thirty rows instead of thirty one. The reason is order 523731 for WILE BESS COMPANY has NULL in the ORDHDR_PAYTERMS_FN column, so the row is completely excluded from the resultset if we use inner join. The solution is to use outer join:

```
SELECT  cust_name_s,
        ordhdr_nbr_s,
        payterms_desc_s
FROM    customer
  JOIN
        order_header
  ON    cust_id_n = ordhdr_custid_fn
  LEFT OUTER JOIN
        payment_terms
  ON    payterms_id_n = ordhdr_payterms_fn
WHERE   cust_id_n = 152;

CUST_NAME_S        ORDHDR_NBR_S PAYTERMS_DESC_S
------------------ ------------ ---------------
...                ...          ...
WILE BESS COMPANY  523731       NULL
WILE BESS COMPANY  523732       2% 15 NET 30
...                ...          ...

31 rows selected.
```

Old syntax

The old syntax for outer joins varies from vendor to vendor.

Oracle 9*i*

Oracle did not become compliant with SQL99 syntax for outer joins until version 9*i*. If you use an earlier version of Oracle, an outer join would be announced by the plus sign enclosed by parentheses, `(+)`, placed after the table name that does not have matching rows. The query producing results identical to the previous example would be as follows:

```
SELECT  cust_name_s,
        ordhdr_nbr_s,
        payterms_desc_s
FROM    customer,
        order_header,
        payment_terms
WHERE   cust_id_n = ordhdr_custid_fn
AND     ordhdr_payterms_fn = payterms_id_n (+)
AND     cust_id_n = 152
```

The confusion is compounded by the fact that in Oracle the join is usually called a "right outer join" — because the `(+)` sign is on the right side of the = sign.

DB2 UDB 8.1

DB2 uses only the standard SQL99 syntax for left outer join.

MS SQL Server 2000

The old MS SQL Server syntax for left outer join is to put an asterisk on the left side of the equals sign in the WHERE clause. The left outer join that produces results identical to those with SQL99 syntax is

```
SELECT  cust_name_s,
        ordhdr_nbr_s,
        payterms_desc_s
FROM    customer,
        order_header,
        payment_terms
WHERE   cust_id_n = ordhdr_custid_fn
AND     ordhdr_payterms_fn *= payterms_id_n
AND     cust_id_n = 152
```

Right outer join

As we mentioned before, the only difference between left and right outer joins is the order in which the tables are joined in the query. To demonstrate that we'll use queries that produce exactly same output as in the previous section.

SQL99 standard syntax

As you can see, the resulting set of the inner join of ORDER_HEADER and CUSTOMER is on the right-hand side from the PAYMENT_TERMS table:

```
SELECT  cust_name_s,
        ordhdr_nbr_s,
        payterms_desc_s
FROM    payment_terms
  RIGHT OUTER JOIN
        order_header
  ON    payterms_id_n = ordhdr_payterms_fn
  JOIN
        customer
ON      cust_id_n = ordhdr_custid_fn
WHERE   cust_id_n = 152

CUST_NAME_S         ORDHDR_NBR_S
------------------- ------------
...                 ...
WILE BESS COMPANY   523731
WILE BESS COMPANY   523732
...                 ...

31 rows selected.
```

Old syntax

We already explained the old syntax for left outer join in previous section; the syntax for right outer join is very similar.

Oracle 9*i*

As we mentioned in the section about left outer join, the old definition of left and right outer joins in Oracle is vague. The equivalent to the above query using the old syntax is

```
SELECT  cust_name_s,
        ordhdr_nbr_s,
        payterms_desc_s
FROM    customer,
        order_header,
        payment_terms
WHERE   cust_id_n = ordhdr_custid_fn
AND     payterms_id_n (+) = ordhdr_payterms_fn
AND     cust_id_n = 152
```

The (+) sign has moved to the left along with the column name from the PAYMENT_TERMS table (PAYTERMS_ID_N) that does not have matching rows. The output is identical to what all other "identical" queries produce; this type of join is called "left outer join" in Oracle.

Many Oracle users are confused by the "new" SQL99 outer join syntax. The problem is, they used to call an outer join "left" or "right" depending on what side of the equals sign, =, the outer join sign, (+), was located. The "new" syntax takes a different approach—the term "left" or "right" identifies the relational position of the table from which you want to retrieve all rows, no matter if the other table that participates in the join operation has matching rows or not.

DB2 UDB 8.1

DB2 uses only the standard SQL99 syntax for right outer join.

MS SQL Server 2000

The old MS SQL Server syntax for right outer join is to put an asterisk on the right side of the equal sign in the WHERE clause. The right outer join that produces results identical to ones from SQL99 syntax is

```
SELECT  cust_name_s,
        ordhdr_nbr_s,
        payterms_desc_s
FROM    customer,
        order_header,
        payment_terms
```

```
WHERE   cust_id_n = ordhdr_custid_fn
AND     payterms_id_n =* ordhdr_payterms_fn
AND     cust_id_n = 152
```

Full outer join

Full outer join is the combination of left and right outer join. It returns all rows from both "left" and "right" tables, no matter if the counterpart table has matching rows or not. For example, in the ACME database there are some customers that did not place any orders yet — as well as some orders with no customers assigned to them.

An order without a customer may sound unusual, but think of a situation in which customers A and B make very similar orders on a weekly basis. Customer service personnel create a few "barebones" orders when they have spare time and leave the customer number field blank (as well as some other fields), so when a customer actually calls to place the order, it takes less time to process the request.

The query that retrieves all customers without orders as well as all orders with no customer assigned to them is shown below:

```
SELECT  customer.cust_name_s,
        order_header.ordhdr_nbr_s
FROM    customer
   FULL OUTER JOIN
        order_header
   ON customer.cust_id_n = order_header.ordhdr_custid_fn

CUST_NAME_S                                    ORDHDR_NBR_S
----------------------------------------       -------------
...
WILE SEAL CORP.                                       523774
WILE SEAL CORP.                                       523775
WILE SEAL CORP.                                       523776
WILE SEAL CORP.                                       523777
WILE SEAL CORP.                                       523778
...                                                   ...
WILE BESS COMPANY                                     523730
NULL                                                  523727
NULL                                                  523728
MAGNETICS USA INC.                                    NULL
MAGNETOMETRIC DEVICES INC.                            NULL
FAIR PARK GARDENS                                     NULL
...

  83 record(s) selected.
```

The above syntax is SQL99-compliant and is the only one available for full outer join in all our "big three" databases. It would be logical to suggest something like (+) = (+) for Oracle and *=* for MS SQL Server, but these are not valid.

Union join

The UNION join (not to be confused with the UNION operator) could be thought of as the opposite of an inner join—its resulting set only includes those rows from both joined tables for which no matches were found; the columns from the table without matching rows are populated with nulls.

Applying set theory basics, covered in Appendix L, you could say that A UNION JOIN B = (A FULL OUTER JOIN B) DIFFERENCE (A INNER JOIN B).

Joins Involving Inline Views

As we already mentioned in this chapter, a query that involves table joins could be quite complicated. You can join tables with other tables, views, or any other RDBMS-specific objects you can select rows from to produce the resulting set.

Another type of object that can participate in a join is an inline view (which simply is a nested query in the FROM clause).

An inline view could be useful to produce a resulting set that is used in only one single query as an alternative to creating a regular view. Unlike regular views, inline view definitions do not exist in the database information schema and require no maintenance at all. You could consider using inline views in your queries if you know for sure you (or somebody else) are not going to use its results anywhere else.

The query below returns phone numbers for salesmen who have associated customers with more than five orders using inline query results in SQL99 standard join. The inline view counts the number of orders per customer, limits the result with only those who have more than five orders, and returns the salesmen id's for those customers. The results are then joined with SALESMAN table to get the appropriate salesmen names; the resulting set in its order is joined with PHONE table to retrieve the salesmen phone numbers:

```
SELECT s.salesman_name_s,
       p.phone_phonenum_s
FROM   salesman s
    JOIN
       (SELECT   cust_id_n,
                 cust_salesmanid_fn,
                 COUNT(ordhdr_nbr_s) cnt
```

```
            FROM      customer
               JOIN
                      order_header
               ON     cust_id_n = ordhdr_custid_fn
            GROUP BY cust_id_n,
                      cust_salesmanid_fn
            HAVING  COUNT(ordhdr_nbr_s) > 5) c
    ON          s.salesman_id_n = c.cust_salesmanid_fn
    JOIN        phone p
    ON          p.phone_salesmanid_fn = s.salesman_id_n
WHERE           p.phone_type_s = 'PHONE'

SALESMAN_NAME_S          PHONE_PHONENUM_S
------------------------ --------------------
HUNTER COMPONENTS        (717) 555-5479
HENERY INCORPORATED      (814) 555-0324

  2 record(s) selected.
```

Note that in this example you have joins in both the main query and the nested query (inline view); the joins in the inline view are performed first and the resulting set is later used in the main query.

Multitable Joins with Correlated Queries

One important rule to remember is never to combine the new syntax with the old one within a single query. First, such syntax may not work properly, and also it would definitely look confusing.

However, if you need to create a correlated query, the SQL99 syntax simply will not work, so the general recommendation is to either use the old syntax or replace correlated query with something else.

The following statement uses a correlated query to retrieve all customer names and phone numbers for customers who have orders:

```
SELECT
DISTINCT c.cust_name_s,
         p.phone_phonenum_s
FROM     customer c,
         phone p
WHERE    c.cust_id_n = p.phone_custid_fn
AND EXISTS (SELECT *
            FROM order_header oh
```

```
            WHERE oh.ordhdr_custid_fn = c.cust_id_n)
AND       p.phone_type_s = 'PHONE'

CUST_NAME_S                   PHONE_PHONENUM_S
----------------------------- ----------------
WILE BESS COMPANY             (541) 555-8979
WILE ELECTROMATIC INC.        (541) 555-3246
WILE ELECTROMUSICAL INC.      (503) 555-0502
WILE ELECTRONICS INC.         (609) 555-4091
WILE SEAL CORP.               (909) 555-9957

  5 record(s) selected.
```

The equivalent query that does not involve correlated queries is

```
SELECT
DISTINCT c.cust_name_s,
         p.phone_phonenum_s
FROM     customer c
   JOIN
         order_header oh
   ON    c.cust_id_n = oh.ordhdr_custid_fn
   JOIN
         phone p
   ON    c.cust_id_n = p.phone_custid_fn
WHERE    p.phone_type_s = 'PHONE'
```

As you can see, it is usually possible to avoid correlated queries in a `SELECT` statement; `UPDATE` and `DELETE` statements could be trickier, especially in Oracle and DB2. (MS SQL has a special `FROM` clause in `UPDATE` and `DELETE` statements as described in Chapter 6.)

Improving Efficiency of Multitable Queries

Each RDBMS has its own algorithms to translate an SQL query into a set of binary instructions that could be further interpreted by the RDBMS engine to create the execution plan for the query. This plan indicates the order in which tables are joined, the `WHERE` clause conditions that are applied, whether the indexes are used, and so on.

The order of joins and WHERE clause conditions can seriously affect query performance. For example, assume a goal to join tables CUSTOMER and ORDER_HEADER and then get all orders for customer FAIR PARK GARDENS only. It is obvious that the operation will take less time if we limit the row set from the CUSTOMER table first (WHERE customer.cust_name_s = 'FAIR PARK GARDENS') and then perform the join of the resulting set with the ORDER_HEADER table, because in that case you only perform the join for one row. Also, indexes on both CUST_NAME_S and the columns participating in the join operation could be useful.

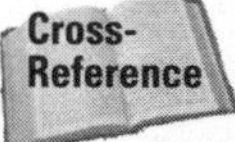

See Chapter 4 for index creation recommendations.

All modern RDBMS have special mechanisms called optimizers that create execution plans for queries based on certain information accumulated in the information schema. That — in theory — makes complex query writing rules (that are different for all vendors and are beyond the scope of this book) obsolete. SQL developers no longer have to specify tables and columns in a certain order in FROM and WHERE clauses of the SELECT statement to achieve acceptable query performance — the optimizer will do the job.

The words "in theory" were not used here by accident. Sometimes (usually for complex queries that join large number of tables) optimizers simply cannot find the "optimal" way to parse a query. In situations like that, you can give the query a hint, using a predefined vendor-specific set of keywords that overrides the optimizer's algorithm and perform actions in the order specified by the programmer. In general, hints can tell RDBMS which tables to join first, whether or not to use an index or to perform full table scan, and so on.

Hints are instructions in the SQL code that direct the RDBMS optimizer to use specific methods when creating the execution plan.

You know from Chapter 4 that you would not always benefit from using indexes. For example, the STATUS table is very small, so the full table scan does a better job. The following syntax overrides the index on the STATUS_ID_N column and forces the optimizer to perform the full table scan (using Oracle syntax):

```
SELECT /*+ FULL(status)*/ status_id_n,
                          status_code_s,
                          status_desc_s
FROM                      status
```

Summary

The multitable query is the bread and butter of every RDBMS operation. It combines data in a variety of ways into a single resultset, sometimes incorporating convoluted business logic.

Joining tables is one of the most important concepts to learn in the entire SQL world, and should not be taken lightly.

There are several different types of joins, which could be divided into two broad categories — inner join and outer join. The conditions on which tables could be joined fall into either equijoin or nonequijoin, depending on how columns that are used to join the tables are compared (equal, greater, less than, etc.).

The tables are not the only objects that could be joined in the query. Other objects can be views, or even inline views. A rich arsenal of the SQL language — operators, functions, subqueries — can be used to produce a join query resultset.

To improve database performance when running queries involving complex `JOIN` statements, a system of hints can be employed. The hints are strictly RDBMS implementation-specific, and are not part of the SQL standard.

✦ ✦ ✦

CHAPTER 10

SQL Functions

In This Chapter

SQL functions and their classification

Functions for every season

SQL standards and vendor-specific implementations

SQL functions exist to make your life easier when you need to manipulate data retrieved from a table. While SQL query, which is composed of the statements, is busy retrieving some data for you, the functions used within that query are validating, converting, calculating, getting the system information, and much more.

Think of the SQL functions as tools designed to accomplish a single well-defined task, for example, calculating square root or converting lowercase letters into uppercase. You invoke a function within SQL query by name (usually a single keyword). Some functions accept arguments and some do not, but what differentiates a function from every other executable module in RDBMS is that it always returns value.

While SQL itself is not a procedural language — that is, it lacks procedural features such as flow control structures and loops — using functions allows you, to a certain extent, to alleviate problems stemming from this deficiency.

All functions could be divided into two broad categories: *deterministic* functions and *nondeterministic* functions. Deterministic functions always return the same result if you pass into the same arguments; nondeterministic functions might return different results, even if they are called with exactly the same arguments. For example function `ABS`, which returns the absolute value of a number passed to it as an argument, is a deterministic function — no matter how many times you call it with, say argument, -5, it will always return 5 as a result. For example, the Microsoft SQL Server function `GETDATE()` — when it accepts no arguments and returns only the current date and time on the RDBMS server — is an example of a nondeterministic function: each time you call it a new date and time is returned, even if the difference is one second.

Some RDBMS restrict use of the nondeterministic function in database objects such as `INDEX` or `VIEW`. For example, the MS SQL Server disallows use of such functions for indexed computed columns and indexed views; the IBM DB2 UDB does not allow nondeterministic functions in the join condition expression, and you cannot use these function in Oracle's function-based index.

Virtually every database vendor provides procedural extensions for use with their database products. Oracle has built-in PL/SQL, Microsoft uses its own dialect of Transact-SQL, and DB2 UDB uses IBM SQL (which is similar to Transact-SQL). Unlike SQL, these procedural extensions allow for creating full-fledged programs within their respective host environments. User-defined custom functions are usually created using one of their procedural languages.

The list of SQL functions available for use within a particular RDBMS implementation grows with every new release, and some vendors are allowing users to define their own custom functions to perform nonstandard tasks. In this chapter we provide only a short list of the most helpful functions and their uses. Differences between vendor-specific implementations are highlighted.

The portability problem with using functions in a query is the possibility that the query might not run properly with competitors' products. Some functions are identical in name and usage, some have only a different name, and some exist only within a particular RDBMS implementation.

Not all of these functions (some would say most of them are not) are part of the SQL standard — be it SQL89 (SQL1), SQL92 (SQL2), or even SQL99 (SQL3). In fact, all of these standards specify only a handful of functions as a requirement for conformance to a specific level (entry, intermediate, or full). The old saying that you cannot program a standard still keeps true. The list of the functions specified in the SQL2 standard is given in Table 10-1.

Table 10-1
Standard SQL2 Functions

SQL Function	***Description***
BIT_LENGTH (expression)	Returns the length of the expression, usually string, in bits.
CAST (value AS data type)	Converts supplied value from one data type into another *compatible* data type.
CHAR_LENGTH (expression)	Returns the length of the expression, usually string, in characters.
CONVERT (expression USING conversion)	Returns string converted according to the rules specified in the conversion parameter.
CURRENT_DATE	Returns current date of the system.
CURRENT_TIME (precision)	Returns current time of the system, of the specified precision.
CURRENT_TIMESTAMP (precision)	Returns current time *and* the current date of the system, of the specified precision.
EXTRACT (part FROM expression)	Extracts specified named part of the expression.

SQL Function	Description
LOWER (expression)	Converts character string from uppercase (or mixed case) into lowercase letters.
OCTET_LENGTH (*expression*)	Returns the length of the expression in *bytes* (each byte containing 8 bits).
POSITION (*char expression* IN *source*)	Returns position of the char expression in the source.
SUBSTRING (*string expression, start, length*)	Returns the string part of a *string expression*, from the *start* position up to specified *length*.
TRANSLATE (*string expression* USING *translation rule*)	Returns string translated into another string according to specified rules.
TRIM(LEADING | TRAILING | BOTH *char expression* FROM *string expression*)	Returns string from a string expression where *leading, trailing,* or *both* char expression characters are removed.
UPPER (*expression*)	Converts character string from lowercase (or mixed case) into uppercase letters.

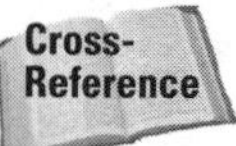

For obvious reasons, it would be very beneficial to have a clear picture of what functions are available in the most popular RDBMS as well as mapping of those functions between different implementations. In Appendix D, we've attempted to provide list of all functions, their respective mapping to each other, and brief explanations for the "big three" — Oracle 9*i*, IBM DB2 UDB 8.1, and Microsoft SQL Server 2000.

Every vendor has its own classifications of the functions supported in its database product. IBM groups its DB2 UDB functions into *column functions, scalar functions, row functions and table functions;* whereas Oracle uses terms like *single-row functions, aggregate functions, analytic functions, and object-reference functions;* and Microsoft sports the most detailed classifications of *configuration functions, cursor, date and time, mathematical functions, aggregate functions, metadata, security, string, system functions, and system statistical functions,* as well as *text and image functions, and rowset functions.*

Note

IBM makes a distinction between SYSIBM and SYSFUN schema functions; they differ in the way they handle data; for example, sometimes one is handling numeric input while the other handling character input. Consider it an IBM implementation of function overloading where a different task is expected of a function based on the argument data types passed into the function.

This chapter concentrates on the functions that could be used in any implementation context, leaving out many proprietary extensions. The XML-related functions are discussed in Chapter 17, security functions are in Chapter 12, and metadata functions are in Chapter 13.

All the examples, unless otherwise stated, use the ACME database. You could run them directly against this database installed in the RDBMS of your choice.

Refer to Appendix F on instructions for installing ACME database, and Appendix E for how to start a command line or visual interface for the RDBMS of your choice.

Numeric functions

We grouped some functions into numeric functions because they are operating with numbers—both input and output parameters are usually numeric: INTEGER, DECIMAL, and so on. The list of most common numeric functions is given in Table 10-2.

Table 10-2
Numeric Functions

Oracle 9i	*IBM DB2 UDB 8.1*	*MS SQL Server 2000*	*Description*
ABS (n)	ABSs (n)	ABS (n)	Returns absolute value of a number *n*.
CEIL (n)	CEIL[ING] (n)	CEILING (n)	Returns smallest integer that is greater than or equal to *n*.
EXP (n)	EXP (n)	EXP (n)	Returns exponential value of *n*.
FLOOR (n)	FLOOR (n)	FLOOR (n)	Returns the largest integer less than or equal to *n*.
MOD.(n,m)	MOD.(n,m)	Operator %	Returns remainder of *n* divided by *m*.
POWER.(m,n)	POWER.(m,n)	POWER.(m,n)	Returns value of *m* raised into n^{th} power.
N/A	RAND.(n)	RAND.(n)	Returns a random number between 0 and 1.
ROUND(n,[m])	ROUND (n,[m])	ROUND (n,m,[0])	Returns number *n* rounded to *m* decimal places. For MS SQL Server, the last argument—zero—is a default.
SIGN(n)	SIGN(n)	SIGN(n)	Returns -1, if *n* is a negative number, 1 if it is a positive number, and 0 if the number is zero.
TRUNC (n,[m])	TRUNC[ATE] (n,[m])	ROUND (n,m,<>0)	Returns *n* truncated to *m* decimal places. For MS SQL Server, when the last argument has a value other than zero, the result of the function is truncation.

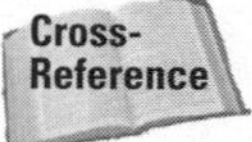

See Chapter 3 for more information on data types.

CEIL

By definition, function `CEIL` returns the *least* integer of the argument passed; that means that the function rounds the values up. The syntax and usage are identical for all three databases.

The argument could be a number or a column value; the output is shown underneath the query:

```
SELECT
    CEILING (prod_price_n) ceil_price,
    prod_price_n
FROM product;

ceil_price   prod_price_n
------------ ------------
19           18.24
34           33.28
27           26.82
```

The `FLOOR` function acts in a very similar fashion, rounding *down.* The syntax is identical across all three databases:

```
SELECT
    FLOOR (prod_price_n) floor_price,
    prod_price_n
FROM product;

floor_price  prod_price_n
------------ ------------
18           18.24
33           33.28
26           26.82
```

The command line interface is different in all three implementations. Oracle uses SQL*Plus, Microsoft uses the OSQL utility, and IBM the command line processor. To execute an SQL command (after connection is established), type the command into the window of the utility (DOS window on the Windows platform, command prompt on UNIX/LINUX), and press Enter for DB2 UDB or type in a semicolon (`;`) and Enter for Oracle, or type `GO` and press Enter for the MS SQL Server. Each of these interfaces is customizable, and you could "teach," for instance, the MS SQL Server to accept a semicolon in lieu of `GO` statement.

ROUND

One might wonder how that is different from the TRUNC function. This function rounds a number to a specific length or precision, and works almost identically in all three RDBMS implementations.

In the following example, all the values of the PROD_PRICE_N column from the table PRODUCT are rounded to 1 decimal digit of precision:

```
SELECT
    ROUND(prod_price_n,1) round_price,
    prod_price_n
FROM product;

round_price  prod_price_n
------------ ------------
18.20        18.24
33.30        33.28
26.80        26.82
```

Since our query requested precision 2, the numbers were rounded *up* and *down*—depending on the number itself: 33.28 was rounded to 33.30, and 18.24 was rounded to 18.20.

The Microsoft SQL Server's version of the ROUND function behaves somewhat differently than its equivalents in Oracle and DB2 UDB—it has a third optional argument (function) that by default is 0. When this argument is omitted or explicitly set to 0, the result is rounding—exactly as seen in the foregoing example; when the value is other than 0, the result will be truncated.

The second integer argument could be negative to round numbers on the left of the decimal point, the integral part of the number:

```
SELECT
    ROUND (prod_price_n,1) round_price_right,
    ROUND (prod_price_n,-1) round_price_left,
    prod_price_n
FROM product;

round_price_right round_price_left prod_price_n
----------------- ---------------- ------------
18.30             20.00            18.32
34.10             30.00            34.09
26.90             30.00            26.92
16.00             20.00            15.98
```

Here, specifying -1 as the second argument of the - function, we are getting the result of a rounded value for the digits on the left side of the decimal point.

TRUNC

Function TRUNC returns its argument truncated to the number of decimal places specified with the second argument. The example shown applies to Oracle and IBM DB2 UDB; the MS SQL Server uses the ROUND function to truncate:

```
SELECT
    TRUNC(prod_price_n, 1) trunc_price,
    prod_price_n
FROM product;

trunc_price  product_price_n
-----------  ------------
18.2         18.24
33.2         33.28
26.8         26.82
```

There is a special case where function TRUNC is used to truncate dates in Oracle. It produces the midnight value for the date argument, that is, it truncates off all the hours, minutes, and seconds:

```
SELECT
    SYSDATE,
    TRUNC(SYSDATE) truncated
FROM dual;

SYSDATE                  TRUNCATED
----------------------   ----------------------
9/22/2003 10:53:36 AM    9/22/2003 00:00:00 AM
```

RAND

The RAND function is used to generate some random numbers at runtime. The syntax and usage are almost identical for DB2 UDB and the MS SQL Server 2000. (There is no analog function in Oracle, although it could be emulated through use of PL/SQL packages.) It accepts an optional seed argument (integer) and would produce a random float number in the range between 1 and 0 (inclusive).

The MS SQL Server 2000 syntax is:

```
SELECT RAND(1) random_number

random_number
----------------------
0.71359199321292355
```

The DB2 UDB Syntax produces analogous results in somewhat different format:

```
SELECT
    RAND(5)
FROM sysibm.sysdummy1

random_number
----------------------
+1.64799951170385E-03
```

There are some nuances to `RAND` function usage: called several times within a session with the same seed value, it will produce exactly the same output. To get different pseudo-random numbers you need to specify different seed values, or use different sessions.

Getting Random Numbers in a Different Range

What do you do when random numbers of a range different from 0 to 1 are required? In this case you could multiply the output of the - function by the range factor, and then TRUNCATE or ROUND the result. Here is an example of producing a set of pseudo-random values in the range of 0 to 10000 in MS SQL Server 2000 syntax:

```
SELECT ROUND((RAND(15)* 10000),0) from_zero_to_10000

from_zero_to_10000
--------------------------
7139.0
```

Encapsulating this functionality in a custom-made function would be the most rational solution. All three vendors provide the ability to create user-defined functions in their RDBMS software.

SIGN

The SIGN function works exactly the same way in all three implementations. It is used to determine the sign of the numeric expression argument: if the number is positive, then the function returns 1; if the number is negative (the result will be -1, if the argument is zero), then 0 is returned. In our example all 1s were returned since the price is expressed in positive numbers:

```
SELECT
    SIGN (prod_price_n) sign_price,
    prod_price_n
FROM product;

sign_price   prod_price_n
------------ ------------
118.24
1            33.28
1            26.82
```

You could use just a literal number in place of the value from a table's column. Since all implementations use SELECT as the keyword to execute a function, you need something to select from.

The DUAL table was introduced by Chuck Weiss of Oracle as an underlying object in the Oracle Data Dictionary. It was never meant to be seen by itself, but rather to be used in some complex JOIN operations (discussed in Chapter 9); it logically fits the SELECT notion as it implies that the FROM clause is to be used with each statement.

String functions

String functions are grouped together because they perform some operations specifically pertaining to strings characters — that is, manipulation of the strings: changing the letter case, changing alignment, finding ASCII codes, and so on. Usually, but not always the output of such functions is a string. Some of the most common string functions are listed in Table 10-3.

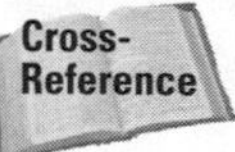

Refer to Appendix G for a comprehensive list of vendor-specific functions.

Table 10-3
String Functions

ORACLE 9i	IBM DB2 UDB 8.1	MS SQL Server 2000	Description
ASCII (string)	ASCII (string)	ASCII (string)	Returns ASCII code of the first character of a string.
CHR (number)	CHR (number)	CHAR (number) NCHAR (number)	Returns character for the ASCII code.
CONCAT (string1, string2)	CONCAT (string1, string2)	operator '+'	Returns result of concatenation of two strings.
INSTR (string, substring, start position, occurrence)	LOCATE (string1, string2, n) POSSTR (string1, string2, n)	CHARINDEX (string1,string2, n) PATINDEX (<pattern>, <string>)	Returns position of an occurrence of a substring within the string. The POSSTR test is case sensitive.
SUBSTR (1,n)	LEFT (string, n)	LEFT (string, n)	Returns *n* number of characters starting from the left.
LENGTH (string)	LENGTH (string)	LEN (string)	Returns number of characters in a string.
LENGTHB (expression)	LENGTH (expression)	DATALENGTH (expression)	Returns number of bytes in the expression, which could be any data type.
LOWER (string)	LOWER (string) LCASE (string)	LOWER (string)	Converts all characters in a string to lowercase.
LPAD (string1,n, string 2)	REPEAT (char expression, integer) SPACE (integer)	REPLICATE (char expression, integer) SPACE(integer)	Returns *string1* padded from the left with *string2 n* times.
LTRIM (string, set)	LTRIM (string)	LTRIM (string)	Returns string with leading blank characters removed.
REPLACE (string1, string2, string3)	REPLACE (string1, string2, string3)	REPLACE (string1, string2, string3)	Replaces all occurrences of *string1* within *string2* with *string3*.
RPAD (string1,n, string2)	SPACE (integer)	SPACE (integer)	Returns *string1* padded from the left with *string2 n* times.

ORACLE 9i	IBM DB2 UDB 8.1	MS SQL Server 2000	Description
LPAD/RPAD combination	REPEAT (string, n)	REPLICATE (string, n)	Returns string consisting of the argument repeated *n* times.
RTRIM (string, set)	RTRIM (string)	RTRIM (string)	Returns string with trailing blank characters removed.
TO_CHAR (expression)	CHAR (expression)	STR (expression)	Converts argument expression into a character string.
SUBSTR (string, n, m)	SUBSTR (string, n, m)	SUBSTRING (string, n, m)	Returns a part of a string starting from n^{th} character for the length of *m* characters.
TRANSLATE (string1, string2, string3)	TRANSLATE (string1, string2, string3) INSERT (works similar to STUFF)	STUFF (<char_expression1>, <start>, <length>, <char_expression1>)	Replaces all occurrences of *string1* within *string2* *translated* into *string3*. Functions STUFF and INSERT add/replace strings within strings.
TRIM (string)	LTRIM (RTRIM (string))	LTRIM (RTRIM (string))	Trims leading or trailing spaces off the string, or both.
UPPER (string)	UPPER (string) UCASE (string)	UPPER (string)	Converts all characters of a string into uppercase.

String functions are arguably the most widely used and the most confusing of the SQL functions. Here we are giving the examples of some we are using daily.

CONCAT

The CONCAT function simply concatenates two strings. This function could be replaced with an operator — + for SQL Server, and || for Oracle and DB2 UDB.

You could use output of one function to be an input for another — this is not RDBMS- or even SQL-specific; it is a general programming concept.

Here is a concatenation example in Oracle 9*i* syntax:

```
SELECT
    CONCAT( '$', TO_CHAR(prod_price_n)) display_price
FROM product;
```

```
display_price
---------------------------------
$18.24
$33.28
$26.82
```

For DB2 UDB the syntax will be:

```
SELECT
    '$' || CHAR(prod_price_n) display_price
FROM product;

display_price
-------------
$00000018.24
$00000033.28
$00000026.82
```

That CHAR function converts numeric data into a fixed-length string, and the final result will be padded with zeroes from the left. The number of zeroes depends on the numeric data type converted. You could use additional formatting/conversion functions to produce results identical to these produced by Oracle or the MS SQL Server.

Here is an equivalent MS SQL Server 2000 syntax:

```
SELECT
    '$' + CONVERT(varchar, prod_price_n) display_price
FROM product;
```

We used conversion functions CHAR, TO_CHAR, and CONVERT to convert a numeric expression into a string data type to combine two different types. Some implementations would implicitly convert compatible data types; some require explicit conversion to take place. It is usually a good idea not to rely on implicit conversions but rather explicitly convert the values. There is more on conversion later in this chapter.

CHARINDEX, INSTR, LOCATE, and POSSTR

SQL is a language specifically designed to handle information. As such it has a rich toolset for manipulating strings and characters. The three functions INSTR, LOCATE, and CHARINDEX are used to determine the position of a specific character (or combination of characters) within a string; based on this information, you can slice and dice text information in a number of ways.

For example, to locate the position of the end of the first word, use a blank space to separate the words in the description (assuming that every value in the column PROD_DESCRIPTION_S would have at least one blank space).

In MS SQL Server 2000 syntax, the blank space is indicated as ' '. You can use ASCII code 32 to specify blank space — CHAR (32). The following two statements are equivalent and produce identical results:

```
SELECT
    CHARINDEX(' ', prod_description_s, 1)
FROM product;

SELECT
    CHARINDEX(CHAR(32),
    prod_description_s, 1) char_position
FROM product;

char_position
-------------
7
6
6
6
5
8
4
4
6
8

(10 row(s) affected)
```

Oracle's INSTR function syntax is slightly different — Oracle allows you to specify occurrence of the string within a string — first, second, and so on. Most of the arguments are optional.

This query, executed in Oracle 9i SQL*Plus, looks for a *second* occurrence of the blank space within the string:

```
SELECT
    INSTR(PROD_DESCRIPTION_S, CHAR(32),1,2) char_position
FROM product;
```

The following query executed in IBM DB2 UDB produces a result identical to that shown for MS SQL Server: it finds the first occurrence of a blank space in the string (both starting char and occurrence are optional arguments, if omitted defaults to 1):

```
SELECT
    LOCATE(' ',PROD_DESCRIPTION_S) char_position
FROM product;
```

To use IBM DB2 UDB function POSSTR you would need to change order of arguments:

```
SELECT
    POSSTR(PROD_DESCRIPTION_S,' ') char_position
FROM product;
```

The results of the both queries will be identical, and match that produced for MS SQL Server.

Optional arguments are the arguments that have some predefined default value that is assumed if the argument is missing from the list. Since the order of arguments is fixed, you must enter all the arguments prior to the one that you decided to specify; in the foregoing example, once you've specified occurrence value (fourth argument) you no longer can omit starting position (third argument).

SUBSTR and SUBSTRING

The `SUBSTR` (`SUBSTRING` on MS SQL Server) function returns part of an argument string, which is designated by starting position and required character length. Here is a query example using the function to return only the first three characters of the column *prod_description_s* value:

```
SELECT
    SUBSTR(prod_description_s,1,3)
FROM product;
```

The third argument, specifying the required length, is optional for Oracle and DB2 UDB, and is mandatory for MS SQL Server's `SUBSTRING` function. If the third argument is omitted, the function would return all characters after the starting position in Oracle and DB2 UDB; for SQL Server to simulate this behavior, use an `LEN` / `LENGTH` function (see later in the chapter) to determine the total length of the string, or a number large enough to exceed any possible length of the string (no greater than 8000). For example, in the SQL Server this query would return all characters in the column *prod_description_s*, beginning from the second character:

```
SELECT
    SUBSTRING(prod_description_s, 2, LEN(prod_description_s))
FROM product;
```

Let's make our output slightly more complex. Say a user wants results to be mangled in a special way to produce an output that combines product number, product price, and product description in the format `<first word of product description><pound sign><product_number><pound sign><dollar sign>< product_price>` for some company application. This could be done in a number of ways, one of which is the following query below (in MS SQL Server syntax):

```
SELECT
    LEFT(prod_description_s,
    CHARINDEX(CHAR(32),
    prod_description_s, 1)-1) + '#'+ prod_num_s + '#' + '$' +
CONVERT(VARCHAR,prod_price_n) display
FROM product;

display
-------------------------
SPRUCE#990#$18.24
STEEL#1880#$33.28
STOOL#2871#$26.82
STOOL#3045#$15.92
HAND#4000#$11.80
```

In Oracle this result can be produced with this query:

```
SELECT
    SUBSTR(prod_description_s,1
      INSTR(CHAR(32),
      prod_description_s, 1,1)-1) || '#' ||
      prod_num_s || '#' || '$' ||
      TO_CHAR(prod_price_n)display
FROM  product;

display
--------------------------
SPRUCE#990#$18.24
STEEL#1880#$33.28
STOOL#2871#$26.82
STOOL#3045#$15.92
HAND#4000#$11.80
```

IBM DB2 UDB uses the POSSTR (or LOCATE) function in place of Oracle's INSTR function, and function CHR to produce a blank character from ASCII code 32 and converts number to string with the CHAR function (instead of Oracle's TO_CHAR):

```
SELECT
    SUBSTR(prod_description_s,1
    POSSTR(prod_description_s, CHR(32))-1) || '#' ||
prod_num_s || '#' || '$' ||
    CHAR(prod_price_n) display
FROM  product;
display
------------------------------------
SPRUCE#990#$18.24
STEEL#1880#$33.28
STOOL#2871#$26.82
STOOL#3045#$15.92
HAND#4000#$11.80
```

While this query might look a bit scary, there is nothing mysterious about it. The CHARINDEX / INSTR / POSSTR functions find the position of blank space—CHAR(32)—and subtract 1 from that number so a blank space is not included in the final result. We use the position value as input for the function LEFT, specifying from which position it should return the characters (column PROD_DESCRIPTION_S) to the left (Oracle and DB2 UDB use the SUBSTR function; MS SQL Server uses SUBSTRING—which, in a sense, is a more generic version of its own LEFT/RIGHT functions); the rest is a simple concatenation of characters, discussed previously.

You may have noticed that we did not use the available function LEFT in DB2 UDB; this is because this function works differently from the similarly named function in the MS SQL Server. In the IBM DB2 UDB database, function LEFT returns a string consisting of the leftmost *expression2* bytes in *expression1*.

Also, function LOCATE has a third optional argument with which to specify what character the search should start from. (POSSTR always starts at the first character.)

LENGTH

The function LENGTH (LEN for MS SQL Server) returns a number of characters (not a number of bytes!—see Chapter 3 for more details) in the argument. If an argument is not of a character type, it will be implicitly converted into string, and its length will be returned. Oracle also provides a number of variations of the function:

```
SELECT
    LENGTH(prod_description_s) length_of_string
FROM product;
```

To return a number of bytes in the expression, use LENGTHB and DATALENGTH for Oracle and SQL Server, respectively. IBM and Oracle also overload their LENGTH functions — the same function could return length in characters or bytes, depending upon the data type of the argument. These functions do not convert argument into string, but rather give the internal storage size for the data type as it is defined in the RDBMS. For example, the query

```
SELECT
    LENGTHB(SYSDATE)
FROM dual;
```

returns 9 for Oracle (internal storage for current system date). The MS SQL Server equivalent expression

```
SELECT DATALENGTH(GETDATE())
```

reports that 8 bytes are used to store system date. IBM UDB2, for example, uses 4 bytes for date storage and 10 bytes for timestamp:

```
SELECT
    LENGTH(CURRENT DATE) date_length,
    LENGTH(CURENT TIMESTAMP) timestamp_length
FROM sysibm.sysdummy1

date_length          timestamp_length
------------       -----------------
  4     10
```

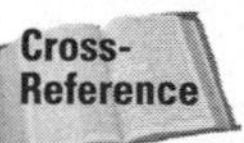

For more information on data types and their internal storage, see Chapter 3.

LOWER and UPPER

The functions LOWER and UPPER are the rare examples of functions mandated by the SQL92/99 standard and implemented across all three RDBMS without modifications. These functions are simple and intuitive to use. They convert string expressions into lowercase or uppercase, respectively:

```
SELECT
    UPPER(prod_description_s) upper_case,
    LOWER(prod_description_s) lower_case
FROM product;

upper_case                  lower_case
------------------------    ------------------------
SPRUCE LUMBER 30X40X50      spruce lumber 30x40x50
```

```
STEEL NAILS 6''          steel nails 6''
STOOL CAPS 5''           stool caps 5''
```

IBM DB2 UDB also contains additional versions of the functions LCASE and UCASE, most probably due to being in business for a long time—you certainly accumulate some baggage after being on the market for over 30 years.

TO_CHAR, CHAR, and STR

These functions fall into the broader range of Conversion Functions, which are discussed later in this chapter. They are used to convert one data type into character data type, for example, a number into a string or date/time data into a string (this might be needed to produce a report that accepts character data only). In addition, these functions allow you to format output when used to convert, for instance, date and time data types.

The usage examples are shown in the CONCAT function above. Since this function accepts only strings, it is necessary to convert all the numbers into strings to avoid an error in IBM DB2 UDB; Oracle 9*i* implicitly converts all concatenated values into strings.

Microsoft function STR differs from Oracle's TO_CHAR and IBM's CHAR in that it accepts only numeric input—no date/time or even string. It has optional arguments that specify total length of the result (including decimal point) as well as number decimal places. For example, the following query converts a float number 123.35 (two decimal places) into a string (MS SQL Server 2000 syntax):

```
SELECT STR(123.35) result
result
----------
       123
```

Since both optional arguments—total length (default 10) and precision (default 0)—were omitted, the result is truncation. The following query takes into account that the expected result should be 7 characters long and have 3 decimal places (specifying 2 decimal places—less than is present—would result in rounding the final output):

```
SELECT STR(123.235,7,3) result

result
-------
123.235
```

REPLACE

The REPLACE function found in IBM DB2 UDB, Oracle, and MS SQL Server returns a string (CHAR data type); every occurrence of an expression2 is replaced with expression3, for example:

```
SELECT
    REPLACE('aabbaabbaa','aa','bb')
FROM dual;

result
-------------
bbbbbbbbbb
```

This query returns a '*bbbbbbbbbb*' string since every occurrence of '*aa*' is replaced with '*bb*'. To run this query against SQL Server, just remove the FROM clause.

REPLICATE and REPEAT

To replicate a character or sequence of characters you may use the REPLICATE and REPEAT functions. These functions pertain to IBM DB2 UDB and the Microsoft SQL Server; in Oracle similar functionality is achieved with a combination of functions LPAD/RPAD. It is a fairly intuitive to use this function because the DB2 UDB syntax produces a string where a word repeat is replicated three times (note the absence of a blank space separator between the words):

```
SELECT
    REPEAT('repeat',3) example
FROM SYSIBM.SYSDUMMY1

example
-------------------------------
repeatrepeatrepeat
```

There is a limit to the total length of the resulting string imposed by the argument's data type—the maximum number of replications must not exceed the upper range of integer values for the system (for 32-bit machines, up to 2,147,483,647). The results from MS SQL Server would be identical with the following syntax:

```
SELECT
    REPLICATE('repeat',3) example

example
-------------------------------
repeatrepeatrepeat
```

Here is an example of using the RPAD function to replicate a string:

```
SELECT
    RPAD('repeat',LENGTH('repeat')*3,'repeat') example
FROM dual;

example
------------------------------
repeatpepeatrepeat
```

The second argument of the function specifies the total length of the resulting string, and the function LENGTH is used to generically determine the length of the initial string. Multiplying it by three specifies that the string is to be repeated three times.

TRANSLATE

This is a smart version of the REPLACE function. It uses pattern matching to find and replace characters within a string; the following query replaces all numbers (from 0 through 9) with 0, and all letters — except K — with an asterisk (*); the letter K is replaced with X:

```
SELECT
    TRANSLATE('2KRW229',
    '0123456789ABCDEFGHIJKLMNOPQRSTUVWXYZ',
    '0000000000**********X***************') translate_example
FROM DUAL;

translate_example
------------------------------
0X**000
```

This function is useful for security purposes: inside the SQL code you can use the exact values (say, credit card numbers), but the produced output is obfuscated. Here is a credit card example, which replaces all numbers with asterisks:

```
SELECT
    TRANSLATE('4526 43567 6091 1506',
   '0123456789',
   '**********') visa_card_number
FROM dual;

visa_card_number
------------------------
**** ***** **** ****
```

The usage is identical in Oracle and DB2 UDB, while the SQL Server does not have a built-in function to do this; its function STUFF removes a specified number of characters at a specific point, and stuffs in another specified string of characters. The first argument is the string itself, the second specifies at what character to start, the third argument tells the function how many characters to remove (0 or greater), and the fourth — the last — argument specifies what characters to insert at this point. In this example an insertion of the bbb string is made at the third character in the argument string, replacing this character in the process:

```
SELECT
    STUFF('aaaaaaaaa', 3, 1, 'bbb') result

result
-----------
aabbbaaaaaa
```

One could use the STUFF function (in conjunction with some other SQL functions) to duplicate Oracle and DB2 UDB functionality by creating customized, user-defined functions. (The creation of user-defined functions, which are mentioned at the end of this chapter, is beyond scope of this book.)

TRIM, LTRIM, and RTRIM

Although it might not be apparent, blank spaces could be a major concern. Usually, blank spaces are not shown in the user interface when typing in some character value, and that could easily cause mistakes. RDBMS requires absolute precision — the string 'user' and the string 'user ' (with a trailing blank space) are never the same.

These functions act similarly in all three RDBMS: they remove leading and/or trailing characters from a string expression. The main difference is that Oracle 9*i* supports more of the SQL standard syntax (TRIM in addition to LTRIM and RTRIM), and allows for trimming characters other than blank spaces; while IBM DB2 UDB and the Microsoft SQL Server use this function for blank spaces only.

Consider the following example, which works in IBM UDB2:

```
SELECT
    LENGTH(LTRIM('   three_blanks'))  ltrimmed,
    LENGTH('   three_blanks')  with_leading_blanks
FROM sysibm.sysdummy1

ltrimmed    with_leading_blanks
----------- -------------------
12          15
```

A similar script in the MS SQL Server produces identical results:

```
SELECT
      LEN(LTRIM('   three_blanks')) ltrimmed,
      LEN('   three_blanks') with_leading_blanks
```

To achieve the same results in Oracle 9*i*, use either the `LTRIM` function or the `TRIM` function. The `LTRIM` example looks almost identical to IBM DB2 UDB (just replace *sysibm.sysdummy1* with *dual*), and therefore is omitted:

```
SELECT
      LENGTH(TRIM(LEADING FROM '   three_blanks'))  ltrimmed,
      LENGTH('   three_blanks')  with_leading_blanks
FROM dual;

ltrimmed    with_leading_blanks
----------- --------------------
12 @code last w/ rule Char:15
```

Note that blank spaces are default for the `TRIM` function. To use this function to trim characters other than blank spaces from a string expression, the following syntax could be used. For example, to remove the letter `M` from both the beginning (leading) and end (trailing) of the string value `M&M or IBM`:

```
SELECT
      TRIM(BOTH 'M' FROM 'M&M or IBM')  trimmed
FROM dual;

trimmed
-----------
&M or IB
```

The argument specifying what letter is to be removed is always case-sensitive.

Date and time functions

The functions grouped in Table 10-4 deal with date and time; they accept a wide range of parameter data types and produce output strings (characters), date/times, and numbers.

Table 10-4
Date and Time Functions

ORACLE 9i	*IBM DB2 UDB 8.1*	*MS SQL Server 2000*	*Description*
ADD_MONTHS (date, n)	DATE + n MONTHS TIME + n	DATEADD (month, number, date)	Returns date plus *n* months (Oracle); returns date plus date partyear, month, day (MS SQL Server).
CURRENT_DATE CURRENT_ TIMESTAMP (precision)	CURRENT DATE CURRENT TIME CURRENT TIMESTAMP	GETDATE** GETUTCDATE** CURRENT_ TIMESTAMP	Returns current date in session's time zone.
TO_DATE (value, format, nls_param)	DATE (value)	CONVERT** CAST**	Returns date from the value according to specific format, national language (Oracle) (**).
EXTRACT (day)	DAY	DAY	Returns DAY part (integer) of the specified datetime expression.
TO_CHAR (date, 'day'/month)	DAYNAME MONTHNAME	DATENAME (date part, datetime)	Returns a name of the requested date part: day or month.
EXTRACT (datetime)	MONTH, DAY, HOUR etc	DATEPART (date part, datetime)	Returns requested date part (day, month, year).
MONTH_BETWEEN	Date arithmetic	DATEDIFF	Calculates difference between two dates.
NEW_TIME	CURRENT TIMEZONE	GETUTCDATE	Returns datetime relative to current datetime on the server.
NEXT_DAY	Date arithmetic	DATEADD (day, n, m)	Calculates what day would be next relative to some other supplied date.
SYSDATE	CURRENT DATE CURRENT TIME	GETDATE	Returns current datetime on the RDBMS server.
EXTRACT (year)	YEAR	YEAR	Returns YEAR part of the specified datetime expression.

GETDATE, SYSDATE, and CURRENT DATE

Keeping a time track of the changes in the database requires access to the system's date and time settings. Oracle implemented SYSDATE pseudo column (which can be considered a function for our purposes) that returns the system's current date and time, the Microsoft SQL Server has function GETDATE (), and IBM DB2 UDB uses a CURRENT DATE clause in the SELECT part of the query. These functions are listed in Table 10-5.

Table 10-5
Getting Current Date Out of RDBMS

ORACLE	*IBM DB2 UDB*	*SQL Server 2000*
SELECT SYSDATE	SELECT CURRENT DATE	SELECT GETDATE()
[FROM DUAL];	[FROM SYSIBM.SYSDUMMY1]	2003-09-05 13:54:18.873
------------------------------	------------------	-----------------
05-SEP-03 9:47:01 PM	9/5/2003	2003-09-05 13:54:18.873

The date output can be formatted using various vendor-specific masks, arguments, or conversion functions. Refer to the RDBMS manual for more information.

Time zone functions

These functions deal with the Earth's different time zones. The "standard" functions always return the time zone in which the machine is located, and sometimes — especially when telecommuting to a central location from a different time zone — it is not what is needed.

The MS SQL server function GETUTCDATE returns current UTC time (Universal Time Coordinate or Greenwich Mean Time). Consider the following query, which returns results from both the GETDATE and GETUTCDATE functions:

```
SELECT
     GETUTCDATE() utc_time,
     GETDATE() local_time

utc_time                      local_time
----------------------------  ------------------------------
2003-09-06 00:06:14.660       2003-09-05 19:04:14.660
```

Oracle's approximate equivalents to this function are TZ_OFFSET and SYS_EXTRACT_UTC, while NEW_TIME returns the time that would be in zone 2 when the date/time in zone 1 is the specified value.

For example, to find out the date and time in New York, NY, when it is September 5, 2002, 7:23:45 p.m. in Seattle, WA, using Oracle RDBMS software, you would run the following query (to force Oracle SQL*Plus to show date/time in the extended format, use ALTER SESSION statement explained later in this chapter):

```
SELECT
    NEW_TIME(TO_DATE('09-05-2003 7:23:45 AM',
    'MM-DD-YY HH:MI:SS PM'
    'PST', 'EST') eastern_time
FROM dual;

eastern_time
---------------------------
05-SEP-2003 10:23:45 PM
```

The function NEW_TIME takes only arguments specified in Table 10-6. The function FROM_TZ could use many more time zones values.

Table 10-6
Valid Range of the Time-Zone Values for Oracle's NEW_TIME Function

Time Zone	*Description*
AST (ADT)	Atlantic Standard (or Daylight Time)
BST (BDT)	Bering Standard (or Daylight Time)
CST (CDT)	Central Standard (or Daylight Time)
EST (EDT)	Eastern Standard (or Daylight Time)
GMT	Greenwich Mean Time
HST (HDT)	Alaska-Hawaii Standard Time or Daylight Time
MST (MDT)	Mountain Standard or Daylight Time
NST	Newfoundland Standard Time
PST (PDT)	Pacific Standard or Daylight Time
YST (YDT)	Yukon Standard or Daylight Time

In DB2 UDB you can use CURRENT TIMEZONE to find out the difference between UTC and your current time zone. In our example it shows 7 hours difference between Pacific Time Zone and UTC (Coordinated Universal Time):

```
SELECT
   HOUR(CURRENT TIMEZONE) utc_difference
FROM sysibm.sysdummy1

utc_difference
--------------
   -7
```

Oracle's function CURRENT_DATE returns the current date of the session, not the server.

UTC is an abbreviation corresponding to Coordinated Universal Time, formerly known as Greenwich Mean Time (GMT). The GMT is based on the time at the zero meridian that crosses Greenwich, England; it became the de-facto standard in the nineteenth century, largely because of the successes of British Navy and English traders. UTC is essentially GMT, only "politically corrected." It uses 24-hour time notation.

The following examples demonstrate this. First, to instruct Oracle to return the extended date/time value format for your SQL*Plus session:

```
SQL> ALTER SESSION SET NLS_DATE_FORMAT='DD-MON-YYYY HH24:MI:SS'

Session altered.
```

To use the function SYSDATE to get the current system date:

```
SELECT
    SYSDATE server_date,
    CURRENT_DATE session_date
FROM dual;

server_datesession_date
--------------------    --------------------
30-SEP-2003 19:05:35    30-SEP-2003 19:05:35
```

As you can see, the session time and the system time are identical. To change the session time, say, for Portugal's time zone ('WET'), eight hours ahead, code:

```
SQL> ALTER SESSION SET TIME_ZONE ='WET';

Session altered.
```

You could specify the time in HH:MI format or supply some predefined TIME_ZONE value set for the system. To find out the list of valid values for this parameter, query Oracle's dynamic performance view V$TIMEZONE_NAMES.

And now our session time is eight hours ahead of our system time:

```
SELECT
    SYSDATE server_date,
    CURRENT_DATE session_date
FROM dual;

server_datesession_date
--------------------    --------------------
30-SEP-2002 19:05:39    01-OCT-2002 03:05:39
```

These examples by far do not exhaust the topic of time zone functions. Refer to the specific RDBMS manuals to learn more.

ADD_MONTHS and DATEADD

The MS SQL Server DATEADD function returns a new datetime value calculated by adding a specified date part on top of the date argument. It is not as straightforward as it may seem.

The following example query returns the date that is exactly five months from date '2002-09-05' (refer to Chapter 3 for more information on this datetime type and its use of literals):

```
SELECT
    DATEADD(month,5,'2003-09-05') months

months
---------------------------
  2003-02-05 00:00:00.000
```

The DATEADD function can also add days, hours, and minutes to a date; Oracle and DB2 UDB use date arithmetic to accomplish this task.

The same results can be produced in Oracle with the following query:

```
SELECT
    ADD_MONTHS(TO_DATE('2003-09-05','YYYY-MM-DD'),5) months
FROM dual;

months
----------------------------
05-FEB-2004
```

Oracle is much less flexible in accepting literals as dates—hence the need for explicit conversion of the literal '2003-09-05' into date type. (See Chapter 3 for literals usage; conversion functions are discussed later in the chapter.) Also, the default output format depends on the machine settings and could be overridden by an application—that is, forward slashes can be replaced with dashes, the year can be put in front followed by month and date.

To add, say, 20 days to a current date, use the following query in Oracle:

```
SELECT
    SYSDATE + 20
FROM DUAL;
```

Oracle 9*i* introduced the INTERVAL data type, which could be used in date/time arithmetic, effectively obliterating the ADD_MONTH function. Refer to Chapter 3 for more information on using interval literals.

IBM DB2 UDB does not have a special function for date and time arithmetic. To add five months to a date you can use the following query:

```
SELECT
    (CURRENT DATE + 5 MONTH)add_months
FROM sysibm.sysdummy1

add_months
----------
  02/05/2003
```

The same syntax serves for adding days, hours, and so on:

```
SELECT
    (CURRENT DATE + 5 DAYS)add_days
FROM sysibm.sysdummy1

add_days
----------
  09/10/2002
```

You may substitute the date value with that from the table in a query, or use a literal.

EXTRACT and DATEPART

Oracle's EXTRACT function returns the value of a specified part of a date/time expression. The acceptable parts are YEAR, MONTH, DAY, HOUR, MINUTE, and SECOND. It also allows you to specify TIMEZONE_HOUR, TIMEZONE_MINUTE, TIMEZONE_REGION, and TIMEZONE_ABBR (for 'abbreviation'); these are added to accommodate time zone differences. This sample query extracts the YEAR part from the current date:

```
SELECT
    EXTRACT(YEAR FROM SYSDATE) year_part
FROM DUAL;

year_part
--------------
          2002
```

The date/time expression must be in correct format; for example, asking for a MINUTE portion of the expression would be meaningless (defaults to 00) if that expression does not have minutes in it.

The Microsoft SQL Server uses the DATEPART function to extract parts of the date/time expression. In addition to the standard arguments like YEAR, MONTH, DAY, HOUR, MINUTE, and SECOND, it also returns milliseconds—if required:

```
SELECT
    DATEPART( month, '09-08-2002') month_part

month_part
--------------
 9
```

DAYNAME, MONTHNAME, and DATENAME

DB2 UDB and the SQL Server have special functions to return the name of the part of the date. Here is an example of such a function in IBM DB2 UDB:

```
SELECT
    DAYNAME(CURRENT DATE) day_name
FROM sysibm.sysdummy1

day_name
--------------
     Saturday
```

The function MONTHNAME would have returned 'September'.

The MS SQL Server has a DATENAME function that encompasses functionality of both DAYNAME and MONTHNAME functions of IBM. The following query returns the name of the month:

```
SELECT
    DATENAME(MONTH, GETDATE()) month_name

month_name
----------------
     September
```

And this function returns the name of the day of the week:

```
SELECT
    DATENAME(WEEKDAY, GETDATE()) day_name

day_name
----------------
     Thursday
```

As said before, Oracle does not have any specific functions to accomplish these tasks, but you can use the conversion function with applied format. This function is similar to the DATENAME function of the SQL Server.

This query returns day name of the today's date:

```
SELECT
TO_CHAR(SYSDATE,'DAY') day_name_upper,
TO_CHAR(SYSDATE,'Day') day_name_mixed
FROM dual;

day_name_upper        day_name_mixed
----------------      ------------------
     THURSDAY         Thursday
```

And this query returns month name of the current date:

```
SELECT
    TO_CHAR(SYSDATE,'MONTH') day_name_upper,
    TO_CHAR(SYSDATE,'month') day_name_lower
FROM dual;

day_name_upperday_name_lower
----------------------------------
     SEPTEMBER          september
```

Note that using a different letter case to specify the date part name in Oracle 9*i* results in different output formatting. This does not apply to either the MS SQL Server, or IBM DB2 UDB v8.1.

MONTHS_BETWEEN and DATEDIFF

The Oracle function MONTHS_BETWEEN returns the number of the months between two dates: if the first date is later than the second, the result is a positive number; if the first date is earlier than the second, the returned number will be negative. When compared dates have the same day portion, the result is always an integer; otherwise, Oracle returns a fractional value based on 31-day month and takes into consideration time portion of the dates:

```
SELECT
    MONTHS_BETWEEN
   (TO_DATE('09-05-2002','MM-DD-YYYY'),
   TO_DATE('11-05-2002','MM-DD-YYYY')) months_in_between
FROM dual;

months_in_between
-----------------
               -2
```

The DATEDIFF function in the MS SQL Server returns a specified date part (or all of them) between the two dates. It obeys the same rules as Oracle's function, but is different in that its return value could represent days, months, minutes, and so on:

```
SELECT
    datediff(month, '09-05-2002','11-05-2002')
months_in_between

months_in_between
-----------------
 2
```

For DB2 UDB, use date arithmetic:

```
SELECT
    (MONTH('09-05-2002') - MONTH('11-05-2002'))
     months_in_between
FROM sysibm.sysdummy1

months_in_between
-----------------
                2
```

In exacltly the same way you can calculate, for example, the number of days, hours, minutes, or seconds, using DAY, HOUR, MINUTE, or SECOND functions, respectively.

Aggregate functions

While aggregate functions (listed in Table 10-7) logically belong with the SELECT statement discussed in Chapter 8 and are thoroughly covered there, it is appropriate to include a brief description in this chapter for reference.

Aggregate functions return a single value based on a specific calculation within a set (group) of values; usually they are tied to the GROUP BY clause of the SELECT statement, though it is not a requirement for some of them. When used with a GROUP BY clause, each aggregate function produces a single value for each group, not to the whole table.

Of course, since aggregate functions are mathematical in nature, they work exclusively with numbers; arguments must be of built-in numeric data types, and the result of the function must be within the range defined for this data type.

Table 10-7
Aggregate Functions

ORACLE 9i	IBM DB2 UDB	MS SQL Server 2000	Description
AVG (number)	AVG (number)	AVG (number)	Calculates average for a range of numeric values.
COUNT (number)	COUNT (integer)	COUNT (integer) COUNT_BIG (bigint)	Returns number of rows in a SELECT statement.
MAX (number)	MAX (number)	MAX (number)	Returns max value among selected values.
MIN (number)	MIN (number)	MIN (number)	Returns min value among selected values.
SUM (number)	SUM (number)	SUM (number)	Calculates sum of the selected values.

SUM

The SUM function sums up all the values in the specified column. If you, for example, needed to know the total amount of all your sales, this query would bring the answer:

```
SELECT
    SUM(total_price) total_sale
FROM  v_customer_totals;

total_sale
---------------
457000.40
```

For the total of all your sales grouped by customer, use the query:

```
SELECT
    customer_name,
    SUM(total_price) total_sale
    FROM  v_customer_totals
GROUP BY customer_name;

customer_name                  total_sale
------------------------------ ----------
WILE BESS COMPANY              276775.60
```

```
WILE ELECTROMATIC INC.       30956.20
WILE ELECTROMUSICAL INC.     19824.00
WILE ELECTRONICS INC.        28672.80
WILE SEAL CORP.              100771.80
```

This query summed up the values contained in the `total_price` column for each customer separately and produced total sales for each customer in the `total_sale` column.

This function can be used with `ALL` or `DISTINCT` predicates. The concept behind these is quite simple: `ALL` counts each and every value found in the column, while `DISTINCT` counts identical values only once (i.e., if there are several sales in the amount of $6608.00, only one of the sales is counted). Consider the following query comparing outcome of the `SUM` functions with and without the `DISTINCT` predicate:

```
SELECT
    SUM(DISTINCT total_price)distinct_price,
    SUM(ALL total_price) total_sale
FROM  v_customer_totals;

distinct_price    total_sale
----------------- --------------------
165405.80         457000.40
```

Comparing results of this query with previous examples, you can see that the `ALL` predicate is specified by default. The syntax for the `SUM` function is identical for all three RDBMS.

You could specify the `WHERE` clause to further restrict the values, for example, to find total sales for the last quarter.

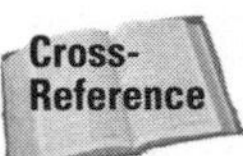

Refer to Chapter 8 for more detailed discussion of the aggregate functions uses, including examples.

COUNT

This function returns the total number of records in the table/view. To find how many orders were placed by customers in the ACME database, all you have to do is query the `V_CUSTOMER_TOTALS` view:

```
SELECT
    COUNT(order_number) total_orders
FROM  v_customer_totals;
```

```
total_orders
------------
51
```

The same result could be achieved by issuing another COUNT query:

```
SELECT
    COUNT(*) total_orders
FROM  v_customer_totals;

total_orders
------------
51
```

The results are dependent on whether the ALL (default) or DISTINCT predicates are applied. ORDER_NUMBER is unique within the view; that's why counting order numbers produces results identical to counting the total number of records in the view. However, if we count customers who placed these orders in the CUSTOMER_NAME column, the results will be different. Here is the query that uses COUNT in the CUSTOMER_NAME column twice — once with the DISTINCT predicate and one with the ALL predicate (default):

```
SELECT
    COUNT(DISTINCT customer_name)total_customers,
    COUNT(ALL customer_name) all_records
FROM  v_customer_totals;

total_customers all_records
--------------- -----------
5               51

(1 row(s) affected)
```

To find out how many orders each customer placed, use the GROUP BY clause. The following query accomplishes this task:

```
SELECT
    customer_name,
    COUNT(order_number) total_orders
FROM  v_customer_totals
GROUP BY customer_name;

customer_name                  total_orders
------------------------------ ----------
WILE BESS COMPANY              31
```

```
WILE ELECTROMATIC INC.       4
WILE ELECTROMUSICAL INC.     3
WILE ELECTRONICS INC.        3
WILE SEAL CORP.              10
```

You could use SQL predicates DISTINCT and ALL with the COUNT function, ALL being the default. In the foregoing example, orders are grouped by CUSTOMER_NAME to get the total orders for a customer; imagine that you are asked, "How many customers do you have?" Obviously, using the COUNT function in the CUSTOMER_NAME column would not produce the desired results because it counts each of the multiple entries of the same company; you need to use the DISTINCT predicate here:

```
SELECT
    COUNT(customer_name) all_records,
    COUNT(DISTINCT customer_name) distinct_records
FROM  v_customer_totals

all_records distinct_records
----------- ----------------
51          5
```

As you can see, only five different customers placed the 51 orders recorded in the view.

NULL and Aggregate Functions

You also should know about the use of NULL in aggregate functions. NULL values are not included for calculations; if all values are NULL, that is what will be returned, not 0. Consider the following query, which returns counts for the column PHONE_SALESMANID_FN:

```
SELECT
    COUNT(phone_salesmanid_fn) count_for_nulls,
    COUNT (*)count_all
FROM phone;

count_for_nulls  count_all
---------------- -----------
12 @SB code last:86
```

Notice that all the NULLs are simply ignored when they are used for calculating averages, sums, and so on. Should you specifically request records "WHERE phone_salesmanid_fn IS NULL" an exact 74 records would be returned, which together with 12 not NULL values make up the total 86.

AVG

This function produces average value of a group of numeric values. For example, if you would like to know the average value of the orders you have in the V_CUSTOMER_TOTALS view, you would issue the following statement:

```
SELECT
    AVG(total_price) average_price
FROM  v_customer_totals;

average_price
----------------
8960.792156
```

What this function did was sum up the total_price value for every record in the view and then divide it by the number of records. You can produce the same result by using a combination of the SUM and COUNT functions:

```
SELECT
    SUM(total_price)/COUNT(order_number) average_price,
FROM v_customer_totals;

average_price
-------------------
8960.792156
```

To get the average order placed per customer, use the GROUP BY clause:

```
SELECT
    customer_name,
    AVG(total_price) average_order
FROM v_customer_totals
GROUP BY customer_name;

customer_name                average_order
---------------------------- -------------
WILE BESS COMPANY            8928.245161
WILE ELECTROMATIC INC.       7739.050000
WILE ELECTROMUSICAL INC.     6608.000000
WILE ELECTRONICS INC.        9557.600000
WILE SEAL CORP.              10077.180000
```

MIN and MAX

These functions select minimum and maximum values from the list of values in the column. The following example finds the biggest and the smallest orders ever placed, looking at all customers:

```
SELECT
    MAX(total_price) max_order,
    MIN(total_price) min_order
FROM v_customer_totals;

max_order       min_order
--------------- -------------
15456.80        6608.00
```

To find out the minimum and maximum orders placed by a particular customer, use the GROUP BY clause in your query:

```
SELECT customer_name,
    MAX(total_price) max_order,
    MIN(total_price) min_order
FROM v_customer_totals
GROUP BY customer_name;

customer_name                 max_order   min_order
----------------------------- ----------- -----------
WILE BESS COMPANY             15402.20    6608.00
WILE ELECTROMATIC INC.        9038.00     6608.00
WILE ELECTROMUSICAL INC.      6608.00     6608.00
WILE ELECTRONICS INC.         15456.80    6608.00
WILE SEAL CORP.               15456.80    6608.00
```

You can also use SQL predicates DISCTINCT and ALL with the MIN and MAX functions.

Oracle 9*i* also uses aggregate functions with the analytic clause OVER. There is no direct equivalent to this functionality in MS SQL Server 2000 and IBM DB2 UDB.

There are more aggregate functions implemented by the vendors in their products. For a comprehensive list of the vendor-specific implementations, refer to Appendix G.

Conversion functions

Sometimes it is necessary to convert one data type into another. In the examples with CONCAT function, we had to convert numbers into string before being able to concatenate then with other string values. As it becoming clearer that English is not the only language on Earth, there is ever-increasing demand for national characters databases: conversion functions provide translation for data so it could be correctly represented in the character set of the native alphabets. Some of the most common conversion functions are listed in Table 10-8.

Table 10-8
Conversion Functions

ORACLE 9i	***IBM DB2 UDB 8.1***	***MS SQL Server 2000***	***Description***
CAST (data type AS data type)	CAST (data type AS data type)	CAST (data type AS data type) CONVERT (into data type, value, format)	Converts one data type into another, compatible data type.
CONVERT	N/A	N/A	Converts character data from one character set into another character set.
TO_CHAR (expression)	CHAR (expression)	CAST (expression as VARCHAR/CHAR (N))	Converts an expression of a compatible data type into a string of characters.
TO_DATE (expression)	DATE (expression)	CAST (expression as DATETIME)	Converts an expression of a compatible data type/format into DATE/DATETIME data type.

Sometimes RDBMS converts data implicitly from one type to another; while this feature might be convenient, it is also something to worry about. One example is the loss of precision when inserting the FLOAT data type intro a column that was declared as INTEGER—the number would lose all decimal numbers because it would be truncated when converted implicitly into INTEGER.

Conversion between different data types

There are two general functions that perform this type of conversion: CAST and CONVERT. These functions convert one data type into another. The function CAST is used almost identically across all three RDBMS. CONVERT, however, is used for conversion from one character set to another Oracle 9*i* (discussed later in this chapter), and in the Microsoft SQL Server it is almost a synonym for the function CAST.

The CAST function syntax is as follows:

```
CAST (<from datatype> AS <into datatype>)
```

There are slight differences in the CAST function's capabilities among the three implementations: the IBM DB2 UDB and the SQL Server can cast any built-in data type into another built-in data type, while Oracle allows collection-based data types (like VARRAY) to be used as valid arguments for this function.

In comparison, the SQL Server's CONVERT function's syntax is more convoluted; it can deal not only with data type but also with how the output is formatted. The parameters *length* and *style* are optional: *length* is used for data types that could have length — like VARCHAR, CHAR, NCHAR, VARBINARY — and *style* is used to convert datetime and smalldatetime into text. (It defines how the resulting string is formatted, e.g., with century or without, with milliseconds or not.) The data type must be system-defined data types; user-defined data types are not permissible:

```
CONVERT ( <data_type> [(length)] , <expression> [,style ])
```

For example, the ACME database view V_CUSTOMER_TOTAL has a column TOTAL_PRICE with a numeric data type; in order to display this data with a preceding dollar sign ($), you must convert a number into a character data type first. (Oracle would perform an implicit conversion in this case, while DB2 UDB and the MS SQL Server would both generate an error.)

Oracle implicitly converts the numeric data types into character string data types when concatenating numbers (values in the TOTAL_PRICE column) and strings ($) as follows:

```
SELECT
    customer_name,
    ('$' || total_price) price
FROM v_customer_totals

customer_name                 price
----------------------------  ----------
WILE BESS COMPANY             $7511.00
WILE BESS COMPANY             $8390.00
WILE ELECTROMUSICAL INC.      $6608.00
```

Here is the SQL Server syntax for the query (the MS SQL Server also could use the CONVERT function to achieve the same result):

```
SELECT
    customer_name,
    '$' + CAST(TOTAL_PRICE as VARCHAR(10)) price
FROM v_customer_totals

customer_name                 price
----------------------------  ----------
WILE BESS COMPANY             $7511.00
```

```
WILE BESS COMPANY              $8390.00
WILE ELECTROMUSICAL INC.       $6608.00
```

A similar result in DB2 UDB is produced with the following query:

```
SELECT
    customer_name,
    CONCAT('$', CAST(total_price as CHAR(32)) price
FROM v_customer_totals

customer_name                  price
----------------------------  ----------
WILE BESS COMPANY              $7511.00
WILE BESS COMPANY              $8390.00
WILE ELECTROMUSICAL INC.       $6608.00
```

DB2 UDB insists on including leading zeroes in the final result, which for the DECIMAL data type is 32 characters long (since the precision is 32 for the TOTAL_PRICE column data type); the result is $000000000000000000000000007511.00. To reduce the number of leading zeroes, the first step is to cast TOTAL_CAST value to a DECIMAL with a different precision:

```
SELECT
    customer_name,
    CONCAT('$',
    CAST(CAST(total_price as DECIMAL(7,2)) AS CHAR(12)) price
FROM v_customer_totals

customer_name                  price
----------------------------  ----------
WILE BESS COMPANY              $07511.00
WILE BESS COMPANY              $08390.00
WILE ELECTROMUSICAL INC.       $06608.00
```

Notice that there is still one leading zero, since specifying, for example, DECIMAL (6, 2) would lead to an overflow error for the values that exceed this precision (while producing correct results for the three result values).

Format templates (models) are literals that define how the date or number would be represented in a string, or how a string is to be interpreted for conversion into date or number. A format template does not change the internal representation of the data; it only affects how it is displayed. Oracle and IBM use format templates, while the MS SQL Server has assigned codes for these.

When using the MS SQL Server CONVERT function, you must correctly format the output results. To display current date in *mon dd yyyy hh:mi:ss:mmmAM (or PM)* format:

```
SELECT
    CONVERT(VARCHAR(25), GETDATE(),109)

formatted_date
--------------------------
Sep 11 2002  3:30:03:037P
```

To format the same output into the Japanese standard YYYY/MM/DD, the following query would be used:

```
SELECT
     CONVERT(VARCHAR(25), GETDATE(),111)

formatted_date
--------------------------
2002/09/11
```

The third parameter in the code above (111) specifies an output format. Some useful formats for the SQL Server CONVERT function are given in Table 10-9. The last column in the table, *Input/Output,* shows *input* when converting into the datetime data type, and shows *output* when converting datetime data into character strings.

Table 10-9
Formatting MS SQL Server CONVERT Function Output for Dates

Standard	*With century (YYYY)*	*Without century (YY)*	*Input/Output*
Default	0 or 100	N/A	MON DD YYYY hh:mi AM/PM
USA	101	1	MM/DD/[YY]YY
ANSI	102	2	[YY]YY.mm.dd
British/ French	103	3	DD/MM/[YY]YY
German	104	4	DD.MM.YY[YY]

Standard	*With century (YYYY)*	*Without century (YY)*	*Input/Output*
Italian	105	5	DD-MM-[YY]YY
N/A	106	6	DD MM [YY]YY
N/A	107	7	MON DD, [YY]YY
N/A	108	8	hh:mm:ss
Default and milliseconds	9 or 109	N/A	MON DD YYYY hh:mi:ss:mmm AM/PM
USA	110	10	MM-DD-[YY]YY
Japan	111	11	[YY]YY/MM/DD
International Standards Organization (ISO)	112	12	[YY]YYMMDD
Europe default and milliseconds	13 or 113	N/A	DD MON YYYY hh:mm:ss:mmm (24 h)
N/A	114	14	hh:mm:ss:mmm (24 h)

Oracle offers a variety of formats for the character-to-number, character-to-date types of conversion. Here are just a few of the most useful formats (shown in Table 10-10).

Character-to-date/date-to-character format templates are accepted by the date-related functions `TO_DATE`, `TO_TIMESTAMP`, `TO_TIMESTAMP_TZ`, `TO_YMINTERVAL`, and `TO_DS_INTERVAL` (see Appendix G for their syntax and brief descriptions). Function `TO_CHAR` also accepts these format templates when converting character data into date type data. The separator characters between these format elements could be dashes (`-`), forward slashes (`/`), commas (`,`), semicolons (`;`), apostrophes (`'`), or colons (`:`). The Example column shows how to use the format template against a current date returned by Oracle's `SYSDATE` function.

Table 10-10
Selected Oracle Datetime Format Templates

Format Element	*Description*	*Example*
AD	AD indicator	`TO_CHAR (SYSDATE,'YYYY AD')`
AM	Meridian indicator (AM/PM)	`TO_CHAR (SYSDATE,'HH:MI:SS AM')`
BC	BC indicator (Before Common era/Before Christ)	`TO_CHAR (SYSDATE,'YYYY BC')`
D	Day of the week (from 1 to 7)	`TO_CHAR (SYSDATE,'D')`
DAY	Name of the day, padded with blank spaces to the total length of 9 characters	`TO_CHAR (SYSDATE,'DAY')`
DD	Day of the month (from 1 to 31)	`TO_CHAR (SYSDATE,'DD')`
DDD	Day of the year (from 1 to 366)	`TO_CHAR (SYSDATE,'DDD')`
DY	Abbreviated name of the day	`TO_CHAR (SYSDATE,'DY')`
HH	Hour of the day (from 1 to 12)	`TO_CHAR (SYSDATE,'HH')`
HH12	Hour of the day (from 1 to 12)	`TO_CHAR (SYSDATE,'HH12')`
HH24	Hour of the day (from 0 to 23)	`TO_CHAR (SYSDATE,'HH24')`
MI	Minute (from 0 to 59)	`TO_CHAR (SYSDATE,'MI')`
MM	Month (from 01 to 12)	`TO_CHAR (SYSDATE,'MO')`
MON	Abbreviated name of the month	`TO_CHAR (SYSDATE,'MON')`
MONTH	Name of the month, padded with blank spaces to the total length of 9 characters	`TO_CHAR (SYSDATE,'MONTH')`
PM	Meridian indicator (AM/PM)	`TO_CHAR (SYSDATE,'PM')`
RM	Roman numeral month (from I to XII)	`TO_CHAR (SYSDATE,'RM')`
RR	Calculates full year given 2 digits	`TO_CHAR (SYSDATE,'RR')`
SS	Second (from 0 to 59)	`TO_CHAR(SYSDATE,'SS')`

Each of these elements can be used in conjunction with all other valid elements in the table. For example, to produce a string representing a current date in format `<date><full day's name><full month name><spelled out year>` this SQL query would help:

```
select
    TO_CHAR(SYSDATE,'DD-DAY-MONTH-YEAR') LONG_DATE
FROM dual;

LONG_DATE
----------------------------------------
12-THURSDAY -SEPTEMBER-TWO THOUSAND TWO
```

The RR date format element needs a little more explanation. It represents an incomplete two-digit year (remember the so-called "Y2K" scare?). If the input for the TO_DATE function is a year with the last two digits less than 50, and the current year's last two digits are equal to or less than 50, then the date will be in the current century:

```
select
    TO_DATE('09/12/49','DD/MM/RR') a_date
FROM dual;

a_date
--------------
  09-DEC-49
```

To make this output more intelligible, we need to see all four digits of the year part of the date. The time zone examples given earlier in this chapter showed how to change output display format by altering a session's settings. Similarly, the following statement displays all four digits in Oracle's SQL*Plus utility:

```
ALTER SESSION
SET  NLS_DATE_FORMAT = 'DD-MON-YYYY';
```

The same query would produce a four-digit year output:

```
SELECT
    TO_DATE('09/12/49','DD/MM/RR') a_date
FROM dual;

a_date
--------------
  09-DEC-2049
```

If supplied date digits are equal to or over 50, and the current year's last two digits are less than or equal to 50, then the resulting date will be from the previous century (current year's first two digits minus 1):

```
SELECT
    TO_DATE('09/12/51','DD/MM/RR') a_date
FROM dual;

a_date
-----------
09-DEC-1951
```

The format templates in Table 10-10 are used to convert numeric data into a character string of specific format. For example, the following query displays the result of a conversion using the TO_CHAR function (see Table 10-11 for the conversion format templates):

```
SELECT
    TO_CHAR(-1234,'9999MI') result
FROM dual;

result
-----------
  1234-
```

Table 10-11
Selected Oracle Number Format Templates

Format element	*Description*	*Example*
$	Returns value with appended dollar sign at the beginning.	TO_CHAR(1234,'$9999')
0	Returns leading and/or trailing zeroes.	TO_CHAR(1234,'09999')
9	Returns value of the specified number of digits, adding leading blank space for positive numbers or leading minus sign for negatives.	TO_CHAR(1234,'9999')

Format element	*Description*	*Example*
B	Returns blanks for the integer of a fixed-point number, where the integer part of the number is zero.	`TO_CHAR(1234,'B9999')`
C	Returns ISO currency symbol (as defined by Oracle's NLS_ISO_CURRENCY parameter) in the requested position.	`TO_CHAR(1234,'C9999')`
D	Returns ISO decimal character (as defined by Oracle's NLS_NUMERIC_CHARACTER parameter) in the requested position.	`TO_CHAR(1234.5,'99D99')`
EEEE	Returns value in scientific notation.	`TO_CHAR(1234,'9.9EEEE')`
FM	Returns value with no leading or trailing blank spaces.	`TO_CHAR(1234,'FM9999')`
MI	Returns negative value with the trailing minus sign; positive values are returned with a trailing blank space.	`TO_CHAR(-1234,'9999MI')`
PR	Returns negative value in the angle brackets, and positive value with leading and trailing blank spaces.	`TO_CHAR(-1234,'9999PR')`
RN / rn	Returns value as a Roman numeral in uppercase/or lowercase.	`TO_CHAR(1234,'RN')`
S	Appends minus or plus signs either in the beginning or at the end of the number.	`TO_CHAR(1234,'S9999')`
X	Returns hexadecimal value of the specified number of digits; noninteger values are rounded.	`TO_CHAR(1234,'XXXX')`

IBM DB2 UDB does not offer multiple formatting options for any of its functions. It solves formatting problems by offering an incredible number of single functions dealing with every imaginable part of a date, for example, functions `DAY`, `YEAR`, `MICROSECOND`, `MINUTE`, and `MIDNIGHT_SECONDS`.

To convert literal strings into a date or time, the string must be in one of the formats listed in Table 10-12 and Table 10-13.

Table 10-12
IBM DB2 UDB Date Strings Formats

Format	*Template*	*Example*
International Standard Organization (ISO) Japanese Industrial Standard Christian Era (JIS)	YYYY-MM-DD	2002-09-12
IBM USA Standard	MM/DD/YYYY	09/12/2002
IBM European Standard	DD.MM.YYYY	12.09.2002
Database Custom Defined	Depends on the database country code	N/A

For example, this query accepts data in any of the formats in the table and converts it into data type `DATE` in the internal IBM format:

```
SELECT
    DATE('2002-09-12') ISO
    DATE('09/12/2002') USA
    DATE('12.09.2002') EUR
FROM sysibm.sysdummy1

ISO          USA          EUR
-----------  -----------  -----------
09/12/2002   09/12/2002   09/12/2002
```

The DB2 UDB `TIMESTAMP/TIMESTAMP_FORMAT` function has only two formats (`YYYY-MM-DD HH:MM:SS` and `YYYY-MM-DD HH:MM:SS:nnnnnn`) to use when either converting a string into a timestamp or a timestamp into a string.

As for the `CHAR` and `VARCHAR` functions that could be used to convert a `DATE` or `TIME` into a string, there are no templates to be applied; the resulting string is always in the system-specified format. You could bypass this deficiency by implementing a custom function for this purpose.

The data type can only be casted/converted into a compatible data type. To make things worse, every database has its own compatibility criteria: compatible types in one RDBMS might be incompatible in another. In the foregoing example, for instance, we cannot cast `DECIMAL` to `VARCHAR` in DB2 UDB as these are incompatible for this RDBMS, while the same operation in the MS SQL Server or Oracle would be perfectly legal.

Table 10-13
IBM DB2 UDB Time String Formats

Format	*Template*	*Example*
International Standard Organization (ISO) Japanese Industrial Standard Christian Era (JIS)	HH.MM.SS	22.45.02
IBM USA Standard	HH:MM AM/PM	10.45 PM
IBM European Standard	HH.MM.SS	22.45.02
Database Custom Defined	Depends on the database country code	N/A

Conversion between different character sets

The Microsoft SQL Server uses functions NCHAR and UNICODE for the conversion purpose. The NCHAR function returns the UNICODE character being given an integer code as defined by the Unicode standard, and the UNICODE function returns the character corresponding to the integer code.

For example, the following operations take the Scandinavian character 'Ø' to find a UNICODE number for it:

```
SELECT UNICODE('Ø') uni_code

uni_code
----------
216
```

It then displays the character again by passing this number into the NCHAR function:

```
SELECT NCHAR(216) uni_character

uni_char
--------
Ø
```

Oracle 9*i* CONVERT, TRANSLATE ... USING and UNISTR

The function TRANSLATE...USING converts text from one database default character set into another. In a sense it works like Oracle's CONVERT function, except that the former deals with strings (as opposed to *text*), which could be NCHAR or NVARCHAR data types.

The following example converts three characters — one is 'A umlaut' (signified by two dots at the top of the letter, found in German and Scandinavian languages), the letter 'Ø' (from the Scandinavian alphabet), and another being just plain 'A' from the ISO 8859-1 West European 8-bit character set into a U.S. 7-bit ASCII character set:

```
SELECT

    CONVERT('Ž A Ø', 'US7ASCII', 'WE8ISO8859P1') translation
FROM dual;

translation
--------------------
A A ?
```

As you can see, the 'A umlaut' is translated into regular 'A' because this character does not exist in the English-based U.S. 7-bit ASCII character set. When no replacement is available, a question mark appears. The replacement character's mapping could be defined in the character set itself.

The `CHAR_CS` value returns Oracle's database character set ID that is specified for the server. Its `NCHAR_CS` equivalent does the same for the national character set.

The function `TRANSLATE ... USING` returns similar results:

```
SELECT
    TRANSLATE('Ž A Ø' USING CHAR_CS) translation
FROM dual;

translation
--------------------
A A ?
```

The function `UNISTR` performs string conversion from any character set into Unicode (see Chapter 2 for more information on Unicode); a backslash in the value is an escape character that signifies the input is a hexadecimal number to be converted into a Unicode character (see Appendix L for more about hexadecimal numbers):

```
SELECT
    UNISTR('\00F5'|| '\00D1')
FROM dual;

UN
---
♀ Ω
```

If you check the number of bytes (using the Oracle function LENGTHB) allocated by Oracle to each of these characters, you will find an interesting fact: a length *in characters* is identical for ASCII and Unicode characters, but the length *in bytes* shows that a Unicode character occupies 2 bytes as opposed to one for ASCII:

```
SELECT
    LENGTHB(unistr('\00F5')) in_bytes,
    LENGTH(unistr('\00F5'))  in_chars,
    LENGTHB('A')             in_bytes,
    LENGTH(unistr('A'))      in_chars
FROM dual;

  IN_BYTES   IN_CHARS   IN_BYTES   IN_CHARS
---------- ---------- ---------- ----------
         2          1          1          1
```

IBM DB2 UDB uses VARGRAPHIC for conversion. The absence of the rich set of functions found in other RDBMS shows the AS/400 legacy. IBM assumes that you set up a database to work in a specific character set and stay there. In the personal edition of DB2 UDB version 8.1 this function is not supported.

Data type specific conversion functions

In addition to the universal CAST function, Oracle has a number of conversion functions specifically for one data type; the same goes for DB2 UDB where data type declarations are conversion functions at the same time.

There is no difference in results produced by either function, and the only reason for using them is convenience.

The use of

```
SELECT
    CAST (SYSDATE AS VARCHAR2(10)) char_date
FROM dual;

char_date
-----------
10-SEP-02
```

is equivalent to Oracle's

```
SELECT
    TO_CHAR(SYSDATE)
FROM dual;

char_date
-----------
10-SEP-02
```

and is identical to IBM DB2 UDB's

```
SELECT
    CHAR(CURRENT DATE) char_date
FROM sysibm.sysdummy1

char_date
-----------
09/10/02
```

The actual format of the displayed string depends on your system settings, and it always could be changed with a formatting function.

Oracle's conversion function for a specific type includes `TO_DATE`, `TO_CHAR`, `TO_NUMBER`, and `TO_CLOB`. For IBM DB2 UDB, as mentioned before, the data type declaration is overloaded with an additional conversion functionality.

For a comprehensive list of vendor-specific functions, see Appendix G.

A data type could be converted into another data type only if the type it is converted into is compatible with the original. Since each RDBMS implements its own data types, the conversion rules are different for each of them. Appendix K contains a matrix table of data conversions for the MS SQL Server, Oracle 9*i*, and IBM DB2 UDB data types.

Miscellaneous functions

With every classification there are always some functions that do not fit into a single well-defined category. We've grouped such functions into a "Miscellaneous" category (Table 10-14).

Table 10-14
Miscellaneous Functions

ORACLE 9i	IBM DB2 UDB 8.1	MS SQL Server 2000	Description
COALESCE (expression1, expression2, expression3 ...)	COALESCE (expression1, expression2, expression3 ...) VALUE	COALESCE (expression1, expression2, expression3 ...)	Returns first argument on the list that is not NULL.
CASE (expression) WHEN <compare value> THEN <substitute value> ELSE END DECODE (expression compare value, substitute value ...)	CASE (expression) WHEN <compare value> THEN <substitute value> ELSE END	CASE (expression) WHEN <compare value> THEN <substitute value> ELSE END	Compares input expression to some predefined values, and outputs a substitute value, either hard coded or calculated.
NULLIF (expression1, expression2)	NULLIF (expression1, expression2)	NULLIF (expression1, expression2)	Compares two expressions; if they are null, returns NULL, otherwise the first expression is returned.
NVL (expression, value)	COALESCE (expression, value)	ISNULL (expression, value)	Checks whether expression is null, and if it is returns specified value.
NVL2 (expression, value1, value2)	N/A	N/A	If the expression is NULL, returns first value, otherwise returns the second one.

DECODE and CASE

CASE is an SQL99 keyword that is implemented as a DECODE function in Oracle. Microsoft and DB2 UDB allow the CASE statement to be used with a standard SELECT statement, and DB2 UDB also uses it as a part of its procedural extension to SQL.

Oracle's DECODE function allows you to modify the output of the SELECT statement depending on certain conditions. It compares an expression (usually a column value) to each search value one by one. If a match is found, the function returns the corresponding result, otherwise it returns the default value; if no match is found and no default specified, the function returns NULL. In addition to DECODE, Oracle 9*i* also has a CASE statement that is identical in usage to that of the other RDBMS discussed.

The CASE statement produces similar results though using somewhat different syntax—and no function is involved.

For example, you can prepare a list where a customer's name is listed alongside its credit status. In our ACME database table CUSTOMER, column CUST_CREDHOLD_S defines whether this particular customer is allowed to order on credit. If it is, the column value is 'Y,' otherwise it displays 'N.' The simple SELECT that fetches two columns looks as follows (the syntax is valid for all three vendors):

```
SELECT
    cust_name_s,
    cust_credhold_s
FROM customer;

cust_name_s                     cust_credhold_s
-----------------------------   ---------------
WILE SEAL CORP.                 Y
MAGNETICS USA INC.              N
MAGNETOMETRIC DEVICES INC.      N
FAIR PARK GARDENS               N
```

While technically correct, such a report requires additional information on how to interpret the somewhat cryptic 'Y' and 'N.' The query that would resolve the problem in Oracle (old syntax) is:

```
SELECT
cust_name_s,
  DECODE(cust_credhold_s, 'Y', 'good credit',
'N', 'on hold', 'undefined')
FROM customer;

cust_name_s
-----------------------------   --------------
WILE SEAL CORP.                 'good credit'
MAGNETICS USA INC.              'on hold'
MAGNETOMETRIC DEVICES INC.      'on hold'
FAIR PARK GARDENS               'on hold'
```

And this example produces identical results in the MS SQL Server 2000, IBM DB2 UDB, and Oracle 9*i:*

```
SELECT
     cust_name_s,
     CASE cust_credhold_s
          WHEN 'Y' THEN 'good credit'
          WHEN 'N' THEN 'on hold'
          ELSE 'undefined'
     END
FROM customer

cust_name_s
----------------------------- ---------------
WILE SEAL CORP.               'good credit'
MAGNETICS USA INC.            'on hold'
MAGNETOMETRIC DEVICES INC.    'on hold'
FAIR PARK GARDENS             'on hold'
```

In plain English the DECODE statement in this query means: if the value in the column CUST_CREDHOLD_S is 'Y,' then replace it in the output with 'good credit' string; if the value is 'N,' then put 'on hold' in its place, if it is neither 'Y' nor 'N,' then replace it with 'undefined.'

Oracle introduced CASE expressions in version 9*i*; previous versions used the DECODE function exclusively, and it is still supported for backward compatibility.

When using CASE expressions with DB2 UDB, you must have the ELSE clause; if there is no action to take and there is no matching case, add ELSE NULL.

You could use both functions in several ways; here we're just showing a few basic examples of how they are used. For instance, usage is not limited to SELECT queries, you also can use them in UPDATE. The column CUST_STATUS_S can only accept values 'Y' and 'N,' but the following query reverses these values, putting 'N' in place of 'Y' and vice versa:

```
UPDATE CUSTOMER
     SET cust_status_s = CASE cust_status_s
          WHEN 'Y' then 'N'
          ELSE 'Y'
     END

(37 row(s) affected)
```

Other uses for the function include the WHERE clause and nested queries. Refer to the vendor's documentation for detailed discussions of these features.

COALESCE and NULLIF

These two functions are special cases of the Oracle DECODE function and the CASE expression, dealing with NULL values exclusively; they are found in all three databases.

IBM DB2 UDB also has a VALUE function that operates in exactly the same way as COALESCE; Oracle's function VALUE has nothing to do with NULLs and belongs to the object-oriented features domain.

The function NULLIF compares two expressions; if they are equal, it returns NULL, otherwise it returns the first expression. For example, in our CUSTOMER table we not only have CUST_CREDHOLD_S information but also a CUST_STATUS_S column that tells us whether or not this customer is active. If CUST_CREDHOLD_S and CUST_STATUS_S *s* contain the same values, we return NULL, otherwise CUST_CREDHOLD_S value. Such a technique might be useful for discovering discrepancies in the company rules. If customer credit is on hold (N), then its status also has to be N;, if NULLs are detected, the conflict must be resolved manually by one of the managers:

```
SELECT
    NULLIF(cust_credhold_s, cust_status_s) compare_stat
FROM customer

compare_stat
------------
NULL
N
N
N
```

The syntax for the NULLIF function is identical across all three RDBMS.

The COALESCE function takes the principle of NULLIF a step further — it returns the very first argument on the list that is not NULL. For example, you've devised several methods for your customers to pay their bills — credit account, direct deposit, and mail-in check. If you are about to send a customer a bill but do not remember which method was approved for this particular customer, this query might help:

```
SELECT
    customer_id,
    COALESCE(visa_account, direct_deposit, check_account)
FROM account_management
```

The ACCOUNT_MANAGEMENT table is not in our ACME database, but this example gives you an idea how to use the COALESCE function. The syntax for this function is identical for all three RDBMS vendors.

NVL, NVL2, and ISNULL

These functions are used to detect NULLs in the fetched values and take action by replacing NULL values with non-NULL values. NVL is Oracle's equivalent of the SQL Server's ISNULL function; DB2 UDB does not have NULL detection functions, but you may use the COALESCE function to achieve similar results.

An example of Oracle's NVL function is:

```
SELECT
    cust_name_s,
    NVL(cust_alias_s, 'undefined')
FROM customer;

cust_name_s                         alias_status
----------------------              -----------------
WILE SEAL CORP.                     MNGA71396
MAGNETICS USA INC.                  MNGA71398
MAGNETOMETRIC DEVICES INC.          MNGA71400
FAIR PARK GARDENS                   undefined
INTEREX USA                         undefined
```

This query will return a list of customer names and their corresponding aliases. For the customers where an alias value is not yet entered (and therefore contains NULL), the resulting list would contain 'undefined.' In the SQL Server's syntax this query would look as follows:

```
SELECT
    cust_name_s,
    ISNULL(cust_alias_s, 'undefined') alias_status
FROM customer

cust_name_s                    alias_status
------------------------------ ---------------
WILE SEAL CORP.                MNGA71396
MAGNETICS USA INC.             MNGA71398
MAGNETOMETRIC DEVICES INC.     MNGA71400
FAIR PARK GARDENS              undefined
INTEREX USA                    undefined
```

As we've mentioned, the DB2 UDB equivalent would use the COALESCE function:

```
SELECT
    cust_name_s,
    COALESCE(cust_alias_s, 'undefined') alias_status
FROM customer

cust_name_s                    alias_status
------------------------------ ---------------
```

```
WILE SEAL CORP.                  MNGA71396
MAGNETICS USA INC.               MNGA71398
MAGNETOMETRIC DEVICES INC.       MNGA71400
FAIR PARK GARDENS                undefined
INTEREX USA                      undefined
```

The result of this query in DB2 UDB and the SQL Server is identical to that shown previously for Oracle 9*i*.

Oracle 9*i* also has a more evolved NVL2 function, which differs in action from the regular `NVL` function. It allows for more than one substitution based on whether the expression is `NULL` or not. If, for instance, you wish to check what customers were assigned aliases and which were not, this query would do the job:

```
SELECT
    cust_name_s,
    NVL2(cust_alias_s, 'alias assigned', 'not assigned' )
alias_status
FROM customer;

cust_name_s                      alias_status
----------------------           -----------------
WILE SEAL CORP.                  alias assigned
MAGNETICS USA INC.               alias assigned
MAGNETOMETRIC DEVICES INC.       alias assigned
FAIR PARK GARDENS                not assigned
INTEREX USA                      not assigned
```

In the above query, if the customer alias column contains `NULL` then 'not assigned' will be included in the final resultset, otherwise 'alias assigned' will be included.

The arguments for *expression2* and *expression3* can be of any data type except `LONG`, the *expression1* can be of any data type.

All three RDBMS have a number of functions that are not covered in this chapter. This refers to Oracle 9*i* cursor, analytical, and object reference functions; IBM DB2 UDB table functions and expressions; as well as Microsoft SQL Server 2000 system functions, text and image functions, rowset functions, and so on. These functions represent vendor-specific extensions and are rarely used; they also require advanced understanding of a particular RDBMS structure. Most of these are mentioned in Appendix G.

Conversion Pitfalls

For every function that substitutes one value for another, it is important to specify data of compatible data types: the substitute value must match that of the column. For example, if instead of 'undefined' we put a number 0, the MS SQL Server and IBM DB2 UDB databases would generate an error complaining about inability to convert `VARCHAR` into `INTEGER`.

Oracle would implicitly convert `NUMBER` into `VARCHAR2`, but not vice versa. The following query demonstrates this distinctive Oracle' behavior:

```
SELECT
 '4'||5 concat_value,
 '4'+ 5 sum_value
FROM dual;

concat_value    sum_value
----------------  -----------
45 @SB code:9
```

Based on the operator's function, Oracle implicitly converted the literal 4 (a character, defined by single quotes) into the `NUMBER` data type for the `SUM_VALUES` (operator +), and for the `CONCAT_VALUE` (operator ||). The number 5 was converted into a string.

User-Defined Functions

User-defined functions extend the built-in functionality provided with RDBMS products. They are not a part of the SQL standard, and as such are out of the scope of this book. The syntax for creating a function within RDBMS (the `CREATE FUNCTION)` is similar across all three vendors; it is created just as any other RDBMS object.

Although not every vendor provides an ability to add custom functions, all "big three" RDBMS vendors provide this capability with their RDBMS, thus enabling code reuse (the same functions could be called by many users/programs).

The user-defined functions are usually implemented in a procedural language, which includes Java and PL/SQL for Oracle, Transact-SQL and C (for extended stored procedures) for the Microsoft SQL Server 2000, and Java and IBM SQL for IBM DB2 UDB 8.1. The syntax vastly differs among these RDBMS.

In addition to the functions created and maintained within RDBMS, all three vendors provide *scripts* and *executables* capabilities for calling external objects maintained by the operating system. The mechanisms for invoking external programs are different, but the principle is the same—provide an ability to communicate with outside OS, without restrictions imposed by RDBMS framework. Such programs could be written in any language supported by OS.

The MS SQL Server 2000 also has the ability to invoke and execute OLE (ActiveX) objects within SQL code inside stored procedures via a special set of system-stored procedures.

Summary

SQL built-in functions complement inherent deficiencies in the nonprocedural language. They perform many tasks, ranging from rounding numbers to strings manipulation to conversion of data types into the sophisticated logic of substitute functions like `DECODE`.

While the number of functions defined in SQL92/99 standards is relatively small, every RDBMS vendor has its own set of these useful tools well in excess of hundreds. Therefore, it should not come as a surprise that functions differ across the vendors — in capability, implementation details, syntax, or simply being included or excluded from the implementation.

This chapter contains a comprehensive overview of the most important functions, as well as the correspondence between the three RDBMS implementations in terms of producing similar outcomes. The function classifications in this chapter are based on the data types of the arguments used by the functions to perform operations (for example, character data, numeric data, date), and on general functionalities (like conversion). Some functions that have advanced or nonstandard features are included in the chapters that discuss topics relevant to those functions: security functions are covered in the security chapter, and XML functions are part of the chapter on latest SQL developments.

✦ ✦ ✦

SQL Operators

In This Chapter

Arithmetic operators

Logical operators

Operators precedence

Assignment operator

Comparison operators

Bitwise operators

User-defined operators

Operators in SQL are defined as symbols and keywords that are used to specify an action to be performed on one or more expression called *operands* or *arguments*.

There are two general types of operators

- **Unary Operators.** Applied to only one operand at the time; the typical format is *<operator><operand>*.
- **Binary Operators.** Applied to two operands at the time; they usually appear in format *<operand><operator> <operand>*.

Arithmetic Operators

These operators, just as the name implies, are used for arithmetic computations. The use of the arithmetic operators is very intuitive (assuming that one did not flunk elementary school), and they can be used in virtually every clause of the SQL statement. The full list of arithmetic operators is given in Table 11-1.

Table 11-1
Arithmetic Operators

Operator	*Description*
+	Addition; adds two numbers or — in the case of MS SQL Server — also concatenates strings. With this exception, the usage is identical across all three databases. Only MS SQL Server overloads the operator, using it both for concatenation and addition.
-	Subtraction; subtracts one numeric value from another. The usage is identical across all three databases. It is also used as a sign identity or unary negation operator.

Continued

Table 11-1 *(continued)*

Operator	*Description*
*	Multiplication; multiplies one number by another. The usage is identical across all three databases.
/	Division; divides one number by another. The usage is identical across all three databases.
||	Concatenation operator; concatenates character strings; valid for Oracle and IBM DB2 UDB only.
%	Modulo; calculates integer remainder of a division. This is an MS SQL Server-only operator. The functionality of this operator is represented by the `MOD` function in both Oracle and IBM DB2 UDB.

While doing arithmetic in SQL is relatively easy, one must pay attention to the data type used in the operations; for numeric values that would mean the precision and scale of the result; for datetime, the range of the resulting values and so on.

Some databases (like Oracle) would perform implicit conversion (whenever possible) if data types are not compatible with operator (e.g., string value used with addition operator); the others (DB2 UDB and SQL Server) would require explicit conversion into a compatible data type to perform an operation.

Here are several examples of arithmetic operator usage. To add two values in Oracle, the following query could be used:

```
SELECT 5 + 5  total_value
FROM   dual;

total_value
-----------
         10
```

The resulting `TOTAL_VALUE` is of a numeric data type; if, instead of the addition operator, the concatenation operator is used, the result would be quite different:

```
SELECT 5 || 5  total_value
FROM   dual;

total_value
-----------
55
```

Here, Oracle implicitly converted numbers into characters and the TOTAL_VALUE is a result of this concatenation of the character data type. DB2 UDB also recognizes the concatenation operator, though it does not perform implicit conversion; this example executed in UDB would generate an error, requiring explicit data type conversion of the numbers into strings.

MS SQL Server works differently—it overloads the addition operator, for example, the addition operator is also used for concatenating strings. The decision to add operands or concatenate them is made based upon the operand's data types: SQL Server will add numbers and concatenate strings. The following examples demonstrate this functionality. This query has two integers as operands, and SQL Server calculates the sum of these (also an integer):

```
SELECT 5 + 5  total_value

total_value
-----------
         10
```

The following query uses two characters (signified by single quotes for literal values), and the result is concatenation (character data):

```
SELECT '5' + '5'  total_value

total_value
-----------
55
```

This operator also is used in date arithmetic. While numerous functions could be employed to add and subtract dates, the same functionality can be achieved with arithmetic operators. Here is an example of adding 10 days to a date in MS SQL Server 2000 (date is given as a literal and is converted to a datetime data type to ensure proper handling):

```
SELECT CAST('09/10/2003 12:00 AM' AS DATETIME) + 10
         AS result_date

result_date
-------------------------
2003-09-20 00:00:00.000
```

The date arithmetic could be very confusing. Oracle allows for extensive use of arithmetic for date manipulation, as does IBM DB2 UDB — whereas Microsoft SQL Server clearly steers users to use date- and time-related functions.

The following are examples of date arithmetic in Oracle. The first query adds a specified number of days to the specified date; the date might come from the table or be requested from the RDBMS:

```
SELECT SYSDATE,
       (SYSDATE) + 10 result_date
FROM   dual;

SYSDATE     result_date
---------- ------------
9/17/2003   9/27/2003
```

For instance, to add two hours, the following operation could be used:

```
SELECT SYSDATE,
       (SYSDATE) + 2/24 result_date
FROM   dual;

SYSDATE                  result_date
----------------------   ----------------------
9/22/2003 11:04:05 AM    9/22/2003 1:04:05 PM
```

By adding 24/24 (evaluating to 1), you are essentially adding 1 day; henceforth 2/24 constitute 2 hours.

The same goes for the minutes and seconds:

```
SELECT SYSDATE ,
       (SYSDATE) + 1/(24*60) result_date
FROM   dual;

SYSDATE                  result_date
----------------------   ----------------------
9/22/2003 11:08:26 AM    9/22/2003 11:09:26 AM
```

The parentheses around the `24*60` are significant. As you will learn in this chapter, the results are dependent on the precedence of operators used in the expression; these brackets make sure that 1 is divided by the product of 24 multiplied by 60 (number of minutes).

Of course, the same manipulations would apply to other operators — as long as the operands are of compatible data types. You cannot multiply or divide dates, for example; only addition and subtraction is allowed. For the regular numeric data types, any arithmetic operator is valid.

For example, if you would like to calculate amount of sales tax (say, 8.5%) imposed on each of your transactions as recorded in the ACME database, view V_CUSTOMER_TOTALS:

```
SELECT order_number,
       total_price,
       total_price * 0.085 tax
FROM   v_customer_totals

order_number         total_price         tax
----------------     -----------   ---------
523720                   7511.00   638.43500
523721                   8390.00   713.15000
523722                   6608.00   561.68000
```

The modulo operator (%) calculates the integer remainder of a division. This is MS SQL Server-specific operator, as both Oracle and IBM use the MOD function instead. The following query calculates modulo of the integer 5 divided by 3 in MS SQL Server:

```
SELECT 5%3 remainder

remainder
---------
        2
```

Which is absolutely identical to the Oracle and IBM DB2 UDB function MOD (where SYSDUMMY1 table is Oracle's equivalent of DUAL):

```
SELECT MOD(5,3) remainder
FROM   sysibm.sysdummy1

remainder
---------
        2
```

SQL Server and Oracle would allow NULLs to be used with arithmetic operators (e.g., `SELECT SYSDATE + NULL FROM DUAL;` the result is NULL). It is important to understand, that for any operator given a NULL operand, the result always will be NULL—no matter what the other operand may be. Oracle excepts the concatenation operator from this rule, whereas IBM DB2 UDB does not allow NULLs in any operator's context.

Logical Operators

These operators are used to evaluate some set of conditions, and the returned result is always of value of TRUE, FALSE or "unknown."

Starting from Oracle 9i RDBMS release, Oracle lists logical operators as *SQL Conditions*. Previous versions refer to Comparison Operators and/or Logical Operators. IBM DB2 UDB uses term *Predicates* instead of *Operators* (which is totally misleading, in our opinion).

Table 11-2 lists all the logical operators supported in SQL.

Table 11-2
SQL Logical Operators

Operator	*Action*
ALL	Evaluates to TRUE if all of a set of comparisons are TRUE.
AND	Evaluates to TRUE if both Boolean expressions are TRUE.
ANY	Evaluates to TRUE if any one of a set of comparisons are TRUE.
BETWEEN	Evaluates to TRUE if the operand is within a range.
EXISTS	Evaluates to TRUE if a subquery contains any rows.
IN	Evaluates to TRUE if the operand is equal to one of a list of expressions.
LIKE	Evaluates to TRUE if the operand matches a pattern.
NOT	Reverses the value of any other Boolean operator.
OR	Evaluates to TRUE if either Boolean expression is TRUE.
SOME	Evaluates to TRUE if some of a set of comparisons are TRUE.

ALL

Compares a scalar value with a single-column set of values. It is used in conjunction with comparison operators and is sometimes classified as a comparison operator. It returns TRUE when specified condition is TRUE for all pairs; otherwise it returns FALSE. The example of its usage is given in Chapter 8, the section "Using Subqueries in a WHERE clause."

ANY | SOME

Compares a scalar value with a single-column set of values. The keywords ANY and SOME are completely interchangeable. The operator returns TRUE if specified condition is valid for any pair; otherwise it returns FALSE. The example of its usage is given in Chapter 8, the section "Using Subqueries in a WHERE clause."

For Microsoft SQL Server and IBM DB2 UDB, operators ANY | SOME could only be used with a subquery; only Oracle allows for the list of scalar values to be used with it.

BETWEEN <expression> AND <expression>

The BETWEEN operator allows for "approximate" matching of the selection criteria. It returns TRUE if the expression evaluates to be greater or equal to the value of the start expression, and is less or equal to the value of the end expression. Used with negation operator NOT, the expression evaluates to TRUE only when its value is *less* than that of the start expression, or *greater than* the value of the end expression.

AND keyword used in conjunction with BETWEEN operator is not the same as the AND operator explained later in the chapter

The following query retrieves data about product ID, product description and product price from the PRODUCT table, where product price is in the range between 15 and 25 dollars.

```
SELECT prod_id_n,
       prod_description_s description,
       prod_price_n price
FROM   product
WHERE  prod_price_n BETWEEN 15 AND 25

prod_id_n description               price
--------- ------------------------- -----
      990 SPRUCE LUMBER 30X40X50    18.24
     3045 STOOL CAPS 9''            15.92
     4055 GAZEBOS 40X
```

```
30X60           16.03
     4761 BAR RAILS 24X48X128          23.10
     4964 BASES 30X45X60               23.10
     5786 CRATING MATERIAL 12X48X72 17.90

(6 row(s) affected)
```

Note that the border values are included into the final result set. The operator works identically across all three databases and could be used with a number of different data types: dates, numbers, and strings.

Though rules for evaluation strings are the same, the produced results are not that straightforward as those with the numbers. The string are evaluated according to the characters in the value, and unless full string is specified, the border limit values are not included. For example, if one wants to get the product's information for a range of descriptions starting with "C" and "S," the following query could be used:

```
SELECT prod_id_n,
       prod_description_s description,
       prod_price_n price
FROM   product
WHERE  prod_description_s BETWEEN 'C' AND 'S'

prod_id_n   description                        price
---------   ------------------------------     -----
     4000   HAND RAILS ROUNDS 48X48X12         11.80
     4055   GAZEBOS 40X30X60                   16.03
     5786   CRATING MATERIAL 12X48X72          17.90

(3 row(s) affected)
```

Note that the product with description 'SPRUCE LUMBER 30X40X50' was not included in spite that it does starts with 'S'; the cut-off criterion 'S' implies that only description consisting of a single 'S' answers the condition; using wildcard characters (see later in the chapter) does not help in this case. To include the product for the above description, the full value must be used, or the first TWO characters of the value next in line (see the query above), and so on

```
SELECT prod_id_n,
       prod_description_s description,
       prod_price_n price
FROM   product
WHERE  prod_description_s BETWEEN 'C' AND 'ST'

prod_id_n    prod_description_s                   prod_price_n
---------    --------------------------------     ------------
      990    SPRUCE LUMBER 30X40X50                      18.24
```

```
     4000    HAND RAILS ROUNDS 48X48X12                  11.80
     4055    GAZEBOS 40X30X60                            16.03
     5786    CRATING MATERIAL 12X48X72                   17.90

(4 row(s) affected)
```

IN

This operator matches any given value to that on the list — either represented by literals, or returned in subquery. The following query illustrates the concept of the IN operator

```
SELECT prod_id_n,
       prod_description_s description,
       prod_price_n price
FROM   product
WHERE  prod_price_n IN (10,15,18.24,16.03)

prod_id_n description                 price
--------- ------------------------    -----
      990 SPRUCE LUMBER 30X40X50      18.24
     4055 GAZEBOS 40X30X60            16.03

(2 row(s) affected)
```

Since we do not have products priced exactly at 10 or 15 dollars, only two matching records were returned.

The data type of the expression evaluated against the list must be correspond to the data type of the list values. Some RDBMS would implicitly convert between compatible data types (e.g. MS SQL Server 2000 and Oracle 9i both would accept the list like follows (10,15,'18.24', 16.03) – mixing numbers with strings, while IBM DB2 UDB would generate an error SQL0415N, SQLSTATE 42825).

The operator IN behavior could be emulated (to a certain extent) by using OR operator. The following query would bring the result set identical to that returned by the query using a list of literals

```
SELECT prod_id_n,
       prod_description_s description,
       prod_price_n price
FROM   product
WHERE  prod_price_n = 10
OR     prod_price_n = 15
```

```
OR      prod_price_n = 18.24
OR      prod_price_n = 16.03

prod_id_n description                      price
--------- ------------------------         -----
      990 SPRUCE LUMBER 30X40X50           18.24
     4055 GAZEBOS 40X30X60                 16.03

(2 row(s) affected)
```

The values on the IN list could be generated dynamically from a subquery. The following query retrieves all descriptions for the products that were sold in quantities of less than 90 items:

```
SELECT prod_description_s
FROM   product
WHERE  prod_id_n IN
    (SELECT ordline_prodid_fn
     FROM   order_line
     WHERE  ordline_ordqty_n < 90)

prod_description_s
------------------------------------------
HAND RAILS ROUNDS 48X48X12
BAR RAILS 24X48X128
BAR RAILS 30X45X60
BASES 30X45X60
CRATING MATERIAL 12X48X72

(5 row(s) affected)
```

Using NOT operator in conjunction with IN would return all records that are not within the specified list of values — either predefined or generated from a subquery.

EXISTS

The EXISTS operator checks for the existence of any rows with matched values in the subquery. The subquery could query the same table, or different table(s), or a combination of both (see Chapter 8 for information on correlated query). The operator acts identically in all three RDBMS implementations

EXISTS usage resembles that of IN operator (normally used with correlated query, discussed in Chapter 8). The following SQL query produces results identical to those produced by the queries in the above examples:

```
SELECT prod_description_s
FROM   product
WHERE  EXISTS(SELECT *
              FROM   order_line
              WHERE  ordline_prodid_fn = product.prod_id_n
              AND    ordline_ordqty_n < 90)

prod_description_s
------------------------------------------
HAND RAILS ROUNDS 48X48X12
BAR RAILS 24X48X128
BAR RAILS 30X45X60
BASES 30X45X60
CRATING MATERIAL 12X48X72

(5 row(s) affected)
```

The use of an additional condition (*ordline_prodid_fn = product.prod_id_n*) is necessary to limit output to those records from PRODUCT to only those that have corresponding records in ORDER_LINE table – i.e., only those products for which there are orders. Without this condition, the query would bring all products from the PRODUCTS table.

While it is possible to specify a nonempty list of values with the EXIST operator, it would always evaluate to TRUE. For example, the following query would return all records from the table PRODUCT, because the subquery always would evaluate to TRUE:

```
SELECT prod_description_s
FROM   product
WHERE  EXISTS (SELECT * FROM DUAL)
```

The EXISTS operator produces results identical to '= ANY' from the examples in the respective sections. Using operator NOT in conjunction with EXISTS results in records when no rows are returned by a subquery.

LIKE

Operator LIKE belongs to the "fuzzy logic" domain. It is used any time when criteria in the WHERE clause of the SELECT query are only partially known. It utilizes a variety of wildcard characters to specify the missing parts of the value (Table 11-3). The pattern must follow the LIKE keyword.

Table 11-3
Wildcard Characters for use with Operator LIKE

Character	*Description*	*Implementation*
%	Matches any string of zero or more characters	Oracle, IBM DB2 UDB, MS SQL Server 2000
_ (underscore)	Matches any single character within a string	Oracle, IBM DB2 UDB, MS SQL Server 2000
[]	Matches any single character within the specified range or set of characters	Microsoft SQL 2000 only
[^]	Matches any single character NOT within specified range or set of characters	Microsoft SQL 2000 only

The following query requests information from the table CUSTOMER of the ACME database, where customer name (field CUST_NAME_S) starts with 'WILE'

```
SELECT cust_id_n,
       cust_name_s
FROM   customer
WHERE  cust_name_s LIKE 'WILE%'

cust_id_n   cust_name_s
--------- --------------------------------
      152 WILE BESS COMPANY
       55 WILE ELECTROMATIC INC.
       63 WILE ELECTROMUSICAL INC.
        7 WILE ELECTRONICS INC.
        1 WILE SEAL CORP.

(5 row(s) affected)
```

Note that blank spaces are considered to be characters for the purpose of the search.

If, for example, we need to refine a search to find a company whose name starts with WILE and has a second part sounding like EAL ("MEAL"? "SEAL"?), the following query would help:

```
SELECT cust_id_n,
       cust_name_s
FROM   customer
```

```
WHERE  cust_name_s LIKE 'WILE% _EAL%'

cust_id_n   cust_name_s
---------   ------------------------------
        1   WILE SEAL CORP.

(1 row(s) affected)
```

In plane English, this query translates as "all records from the table CUSTOMER where field CUST_NAME_S contains the following sequence of characters: the value starts with WILE followed by unspecified number of characters, then blank space, and the second part of the value starts with some letter or number followed by combination EAL; the rest of the characters is unspecified".

In Microsoft SQL Server (and Sybase, as well), you also may use matching pattern that specifies range of characters. The following query retrieves records for the customer whose second part of the name starts with either 'S' or 'B':

```
SELECT cust_id_n,
       cust_name_s
FROM   customer
WHERE  cust_name_s LIKE 'WILE% [S,B]%'

cust_id_n   cust_name_s
---------   -----------------------------------
      152   WILE BESS COMPANY
        1   WILE SEAL CORP.

(2 row(s) affected)
```

ESCAPE clause in conjunction with the LIKE operator allows for inclusion wildcard characters themselves to be included in the search string. It allows you to specify an escape character to be used to identify special characters within the search string that should be treated as "regular" ones. Virtually any character could be designated as an escape character in a query, though caution must be exercised in order not to use characters that might be encountered in the values themselves (e.g., use of the '%' or 'L' as an escape character would result in erroneous results to be returned). The clause is supported by all three major databases and is part of SQL standard.

The following example uses an underscore sign (_) as one of the search characters; it queries INFORMATION_SCHEMA view (Microsoft SQL Server 2000 specific view for accessing information about objects present in the current database; covered in detail in Chapter 13):

```
SELECT table_name,
       table_type
FROM   INFORMATION_SCHEMA.TABLES
WHERE  table_name LIKE 'ORD%/_L%' ESCAPE '/'

table_name      table_type
--------------- ----------
ORDER_LINE      BASE TABLE

(1 row(s) affected)
```

The query requests records from the view where table name starts with 'ORD' followed by unspecified number of characters, has an underscore "_" as part of its name, followed by 'L' and, again, ending with an unspecified number of characters. Since the underscore character has a special meaning as a wildcard character it has to be preceded by an escape character '/'. As you can see, the table name ORDER_LINE uniquely fits these requirements.

Oracle 9*i* specifies four types of LIKE operator: LIKE, LIKEC, LIKE2, and LIKE4. The first evaluates a string as defined by the input value character set, the second (LIKEC) assumes UNICODE complete set, while LIKE2 and LIKE4 subsets use USC2 (fixed-width, 2 bytes/16-bit encoding of the UNICODE characters) and USC4 (4 bytes/32-bit encoding) codepoints, respectively. The term USC refers to Universal Multiple-Octet Coded Character Set.

With a bit of practice one could construct quite sophisticated pattern matching queries. Here is an example: the query that specifies exactly three characters preceding 'E' in the first part of the name, followed by unspecified number of characters, exactly one character preceding letters 'ES' in the second part, followed by unspecified number of characters

```
SELECT cust_id_n,
       cust_name_s
FROM   customer
WHERE  cust_name_s LIKE  '___E% _ES%'

cust_id_n   cust_name_s
---------   ----------------------------------------
       89   INTEGRATED POWER DESIGNS
      152   WILE BESS COMPANY

(2 row(s) affected)
```

The results might be surprising at first glance: why does the resultset include 'INTEGRATED POWER DESIGNS'? To understand the results one should recall that '%' stands for any character, blank spaces included; therefore 'GRATED POWER' string fits the criteria; it is followed by a blank space and a word that includes 'ES' as the second and first characters.

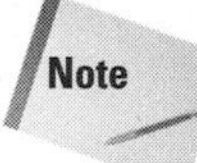

In a search for similarly sounding names use SOUNDEX function, described in Chapter 10.

AND

AND combines two Boolean expressions and returns TRUE when both expressions are TRUE. The following query returns records for the product with a unit price over $20 and whose description starts with 'S':

```
SELECT prod_id_n,
       prod_description_s description,
       prod_price_n price
FROM   product
WHERE  prod_price_n > 20
AND    prod_description_s LIKE 'S%'

prod_id_n  description              price
---------  ------------------------ -----
     1880  STEEL NAILS 6''          33.28
     2871  STOOL CAPS 5''           26.82

(2 row(s) affected)
```

Only records that answer both criteria are selected.

When more than one logical operator is used in a statement, AND operators are evaluated first. The order of evaluation could be changed through use of parentheses.

NOT

This operator negates a Boolean input. It could be used to reverse output of any other logical operator discussed so far in this chapter. Here is a simple example using IN operator.

```
SELECT prod_id_n,
       prod_description_s description,
       prod_price_n price
FROM   product
```

```
WHERE  prod_price_n NOT IN (10,15,18.24,16.03)

prod_id_n   description                        price
---------   ------------------------------     -----
     1880   STEEL NAILS 6''                    33.28
     2871   STOOL CAPS 5''                     26.82
     3045   STOOL CAPS 9''                     15.92
     4000   HAND RAILS ROUNDS 48X48X12         11.80
     4761   BAR RAILS 24X48X128                23.10
     4906   BAR RAILS 30X45X60                 27.00
     4964   BASES 30X45X60                     23.10
     5786   CRATING MATERIAL 12X48X72          17.90

(8 row(s) affected)
```

The query returned information for the products whose price does not match any on the supplied list, i.e., where operator IN returns TRUE (match) it becomes FALSE, while FALSE (no match) translates into TRUE.

OR

Combines two conditions according to the rules of Boolean logic (see Appendix L for more information on Boolean logic). When more than one logical operator is used in a statement, OR operators are evaluated after AND operators. However, you can change the order of evaluation by using parentheses. The example of the usage of the OR operator is given earlier in the chapter, in a paragraph discussing operator IN.

Operator Precedence

Precedence represents the order in which operators from the same expression are being evaluated. When several operators are used together, the operators with higher precedence are evaluated before those with the lower precedence. In general, the operators' precedence follows the same rules as in the high school math, which might be somewhat counterintuitive. The order of the precedence is indicated in Table 11-4.

Table 11-4
Operators Precedence

Operator	*Precedence*
Unary operators, bitwise NOT (MS SQL Server only)	1
Multiplication and division	2
Addition, subtraction, and concatenation	3
SQL conditions	4

The evaluation precedence could dramatically affect results of the query. Consider the following Oracle query, which supposedly calculates value as `TOTAL_PRICE + 4 * 0.085`:

```
SELECT total_price,
       total_price + 4 * 0.085 tax
FROM   v_customer_totals

total_price      tax
-----------  -------
    7538.20  7538.54
    8420.10  8420.44
    6630.40  6630.74
```

Depending on how you are inclined to count, it might mean that you want to increase all your prices by four dollars and then calculate 8.5 percent of the result; or — if operators' precedence rules are taken into consideration — it means that you would like to increase the price by 0.34 cents. Of course, RDBMS would follow the rules of precedence and would first multiply 4 by 0.085 and then add the result to whatever value there is in the `TOTAL_PRICE` column.

You may be wondering how the minus (–) and plus (+) operators are of the first and third precedence at the same time. This is just another example of an operator's overloading: in addition to performing subtraction and addition operations, they also signify the unary operators *negation* and *sign identity* (like –5 or +5). For example, the following expression will evaluate to a negative number rather than a positive one:

```
SELECT
    -2 * 3 + 5 result
FROM   dual;

result
------
    -1
```

Instead of -11, as you might have expected, this expression evaluates to –1 because the sign of the multiplier 2 is taken into consideration before the multiplication. If we employ brackets to apply the minus sign last, the result is different:

```
SELECT
     -(2 * 3 + 5) result
FROM   dual;

result
------
    -11
```

The unary operator + does not affect its operand, while - changes it to negative, as illustrated in the following example (applies to all three RDBMS):

```
SELECT -(+total_price) minus_first,
       +(-total_price) plus_first
FROM   v_customer_totals

minus_first    plus_first
-----------    ----------
-7538.20       -7538.20
-8420.10       -8420.10
. . .          . . .
-6630.40       -6630.40
. . .          . . .
-12138.60      -12138.60
```

Why Operator Precedence Is Important

The issue of operator precedence is not as trivial as it may seem. Take, for example, a ubiquitous computer program such as Microsoft Calculator (or any modern calculator, for that matter), which is bundled with every copy of the Windows operating system. It seems as if this program differentiates between Standard and Scientific types of calculations. When Standard mode is selected from the View menu, the expression `5+4*3`, for example, evaluates to `27`, and if a Scientific mode is selected from the menu, exactly the same expression suddenly gives `17` as an answer; a regular calculator would insist on `27` as a correct answer, no matter what.

For a historical reason—namely, dearth of memory, the first calculators had only two registers (i.e., storage for input numbers) so only two numbers could be placed there and then an operation had to be performed to free up space for the next number. In our example it would look like the following sequence of instructions: put 5 into one register, then put 4 into the second register, perform operation (+), save the result into one of the registers, put number 3 into the second register, perform operation (*), and so on.

The result is calculated after each operator button is pressed. Gradually, as hardware became cheaper, it became possible to use more than two registers—and implement precedence rules that had been established in mathematics for centuries.

By then, there was already a huge amount of calculators out there doing math the "simple" way, and rather than risk consumer revolt, vendors decided on having two types of calculators—one for "normal" people, and one for the "scientific" ones. This, of course, was transferred into software calculators.

As you can see, the order of unary operators did not affect the result it turned out negative in both cases.

Tip

You can change the precedence of operations (not operators!) by using parentheses.

The previous expression would evaluate to the different values if parentheses were used:

```
SELECT total_price,
       (total_price + 4) * 0.085 price_increase1,
       total_price + 4 * 0.085 price_increase2
FROM   v_customer_totals;

total_price      value1      value2
-----------    ----------    -------
    7538.20    641.08700     7538.54
    8420.10    716.04850     8420.44
    6630.40    563.92400     6630.74
```

Assignment Operator

The assignment operator is one of the most intuitive to use. It assigns a value to a variable. The only confusion in using this operator could stem from its overloading. All RDBMS overload this operator with an additional function—comparison—in the SQL.

The equals operator (=) is used as an assignment in the following SQL query that updates the price (PROD_PRICE_N) column in the PRODUCT table, raising the existing prices by 2 percent:

```
UPDATE product
SET    prod_price_n = prod_price_n * 1.02

 (10 row(s) affected)
```

And the same operator would be used for comparing values when used, for example, in the WHERE clause of an SQL statement:

```
UPDATE product
SET    prod_price_n = prod_price_n * 1.02
WHERE  prod_id_n = 1880

(1 row(s) affected)
```

This statement assigns a 2 percent increase to a product whose ID is 1880; in the same query, the equals operator (=) is used in its assignment and comparison capacity at the same time.

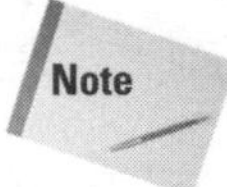

In some SQL procedural languages, there are distinctions between assignment and comparison operators. Oracle PL/SQL uses := for assignment and = for comparison; MS SQL Server's Transact SQL uses only one operator for these purposes, =, as does IBM DB2 UDB.

Comparison Operators

Comparison operators are used to compare two or more values. They are usually found in the WHERE clause of a SELECT statement, though you may use them in any valid SQL expression.

The usage is identical across all three databases except for the nonstandard operators !< and !>—they are recognized by IBM DB2 UDB 8.1 and MS SQL Server 2000, but are excluded from Oracle 9*i*. The nonstandard *not equal to* operator, !=, could be used in all three dialects. Table 11-5 lists all comparison operators.

Table 11-5
Comparison Operators

Operator	*Description*
=	Equals
>	Greater than
<	Less than
>=	Greater than or equal to
<=	Less than or equal to

Operator	Description
<>	Not equal to
!=	Not equal to*
!<	Not less than*
!>	Not greater than*

* Does not follow SQL standards

To illustrate the uses of the operators listed in Table 11-5, we're going to query the ACME database view V_CUSTOMER_TOTALS.

To restrict the number of rows returned by a query SQL uses the WHERE clause, discussed in Chapter 7. Comparison operators logically fit into this strategy, allowing you to limit the number of rows based on some search criteria. Consider the query that returns all rows. (We are showing only five of these here.)

```
SELECT customer_name,
       order_number,
       total_price
FROM   v_customer_totals

customer_name            order_number  total_price
------------------       -----------   -----------
WILE BESS COMPANY        523720           7538.20
WILE BESS COMPANY        523723          11186.00
WILE BESS COMPANY        523724           8745.50
WILE ELECTROMUSICAL INC. 523727           6630.40
WILE ELECTROMUSICAL INC. 523728           6630.40
```

Someone who wanted to see, for instance, only the records for WILE BESS COMPANY would issue the following qucry:

```
SELECT customer_name,
       order_number,
       total_price
FROM   v customer_totals
WHERE  customer_name = 'WILE BESS COMPANY'

customer_name       order_number   total_price
------------------  ------------   -----------
WILE BESS COMPANY   523720             7538.20
WILE BESS COMPANY   523723            11186.00
WILE BESS COMPANy   523724             8745.50
```

This query would go through all customers in the view, and by comparing the value in the column CUSTOMER_NAME with the one supplied in the WHERE clause it would select only those that match WILE BESS COMPANY, excluding all others.

To find out only the records that have TOTAL_PRICE over a certain preset limit (say, $7,500), one would use the greater than operator (>):

```
SELECT customer_name,
       order_number,
       total_price
FROM   v_customer_totals
WHERE  total_price > 7500

customer_name      order_number  total_price
------------------ -----------   -----------
WILE BESS COMPANY  523720            7538.20
WILE BESS COMPANY  523723           11186.00
WILE BESS COMPANy  523724            8745.50
```

As you can see, this effectively excluded all records where the total price was less than $7,500. If you wish to include a cut-off value, operators *greater than or equal to* (>=) and/or *less than or equal to* (<=) might be used:

```
SELECT customer_name,
       order_number,
       total_price
FROM   v_customer_totals
WHERE  total_price <= 7538.20

customer_name                order_number  total_price
---------------------------- -----------   -----------
WILE BESS COMPANY            523720            7538.20
WILE ELECTROMUSICAL INC.     523727            6630.40
WILE ELECTROMUSICAL INC.     523728            6630.40
```

This query returns records from the V_CUSTOMER_TOTALS view that are equal to $7538.20 or less than this value.

To find out the orders that were placed by any of your customers but one, you would use *not equal to* operators — <> or != — the latter being a nonstandard operator, supported nevertheless by all three vendors:

```
SELECT customer_name,
       order_number,
```

```
       total_price
FROM   v_customer_totals
WHERE  customer_name <> 'WILE BESS COMPANY'

customer_name               order_number   total_price
------------------------    ------------   -----------
WILE ELECTROMUSICAL INC.    523727             6630.40
WILE ELECTROMUSICAL INC.    523728             6630.40
```

We have mentioned earlier that the WHERE clause is not the only place where you can use comparison operators. Chapter 10 introduced the CASE expression, which we're going to use here:

```
SELECT order_number,
   total_price
    CASE
        WHEN total_price < 7500 THEN 'medium order'
        WHEN total_price > 7500
         AND total_price < 10000 THEN 'big order'
        WHEN total_price > 10000 THEN 'very big order'
        ELSE 'cannot say'
    END
FROM v_customer_totals

order_number  total_price
-----------   -----------   ---------------
523720            7538.20   big order
523723           11186.00   very big order
523724            8745.50   big order
523727            6630.40   medium order
523728            6630.40   medium order.
```

Bitwise Operators

Bitwise operators perform bit operations on integer data types; all bitwise operators introduced into SQL by RDBMS vendors are listed in Table 11-6. To understand the results of the bitwise operations one must understand the basics of Boolean algebra.

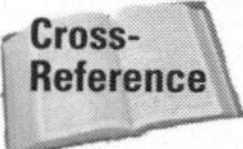

See Appendix L for more information on Boolean algebra.

Table 11-6
Bitwise Operators

Operator	*Description*
&	Bitwise AND
|	Bitwise OR
/\	Bitwise exclusive OR
~	Bitwise NOT

The operands for bitwise operators can be of either the integer data type or the binary string data type (except for IMAGE data type) category. Data type compatibility is given in Table 11-7. Bitwise operations are not typical for a high-level language such as SQL, and one might be hard-pressed to come up with a usage example.

One of the possible uses could be a complex bit mask made for color — after all RDBMS now supports more than just text and numeric data. Consider a combination of zeroes and ones, for example 0101. When a binary AND is applied to this number and to another binary number, for example 1101, it will produce the following result:

```
SELECT  5 & 13 result


result
------
     5
```

The binary representation of 5 is 0101. In this example of logical AND, only 1 and 1 produce 1, any other combinations — namely 1 and 0, or 0 and 0 — produce 0.

```
0101        (decimal 5)
1101        (decimal 13)
----
0101        (decimal 5)
```

To decode or encode a pixel in an image stored in your database you would use bit mask and shifting. Another possible use of the XOR (exclusive OR) operator would be to encrypt data based on some numeric key.

Using Boolean Logic for Data Safety

In the database world, safety of data is of paramount importance; it comes right after getting the software running at all. There are different safety aspects, discussed in Chapter 12, including unauthorized access, malicious data manipulations, and so on. Here we're going to briefly touch the data corruption issue.

Sometimes a technical glitch occurs and data gets corrupted—somewhere in the gazillions of zeroes and ones representing data on your hard drive, a couple of bits get flipped, exchange places, or disappear altogether. You could blame it on a power fluctuation, cosmic rays, earthquakes, and such, but the question remains—how to restore data to a consistent state.

One of the technologies out there is RAID (Redundant Array of Independent Disks). While RAID does not apply directly to SQL, it does have something important to do with RDBMS and Boolean algebra.

The idea behind RAID is to combine several relatively inexpensive disk drives into an array that works as a single unit, thus increasing the reliability and speed of operations. There are different types of RAID architecture (ways these disks can be combined), ranging from RAID0 to RAID5 (the first, RAID0, being just another name for a single disk).

What makes RAID relevant to Boolean logic is that the fundamental technology behind it is *striping.* RAID partitions each of the drives participating in the array into stripes that are interleaved in a sequence.

To visualize that, imagine a stack of wafers where you butter the first, third, and fifth wafers, and spread jam over the second and fourth. In a similar manner, RAID enables you to perform different operations on the data spread across more than one disk (drive) simultaneously, greatly improving input/output operations. In RAID3, RAID4, and RAID5 configurations, an additional benefit of safety comes from *parity*, where one drive is dedicated to storing parity information: In case of one drive failure the whole information can be recovered by using a Boolean exclusive OR (XOR) operation of the bit information on the remaining drives.

Consider the previous example, but performing only an `XOR` operation instead of the logical `AND`. The `XOR` operation follows rules of Boolean logic: `0 XOR 0 = 0`, `0 XOR 1 = 1`, `1 XOR 1 = 0`, and `1 XOR 0 = 1`. Imagine that the first number is written on disk 1, the second is written on disk 2, and their `XOR` result (parity)—on disk 3. Now, disk 2 (containing value `1101`) has failed. By performing an `XOR` operation between data on disk 1 and data on disk 3, you could easily restore the corrupted values:

```
0101    0101
1101    1000
----    ----
1000    1101
```

Continued

Continued

Of course, if more than one drive fails, then this safety system would not work. The bet is on the calculated risk, when failure of more than one drive at the same time is extremely unlikely.

All this is a fairly low level that normally is outside of the SQL programming domain, and chances are that if you find yourself in need of more in-depth coverage of Boolean algebra, you will reach for a topic-specific book, and not the one on general SQL issues.

Table 11-7
Data Type Compatibility for Bitwise Operands

Left Operand	*Right Operand*
BINARY	INT, SMALLINT, TINYINT
BIT	INT, SMALLINT, TINYINT, BIT
INT	INT, SMALLINT, TINYINT, BINARY, VARBINARY
SMALLINT	INT, SMALLINT, TINYINT, BINARY, VARBINARY
TINYINT	INT, SMALLINT, TINYINT, BINARY, VARBINARY
VARBINARY	INT, SMALLINT, TINYINT

Only Microsoft SQL Server provides bitwise operators; the IBM DB2 UDB dialect of SQL does not have bit operations support built into the language itself, and Oracle 9*i* has a BITAND function that works identically to SQL Server's bitwise AND.

User-defined Operators

Oracle 9*i* allows you to create user-defined operators. They are created using the CREATE OPERATOR statement and are identified by names rather than by single characters. Once a user-defined operator is created it can be used just like any of the built-in operators with the notable exception that one has to have EXECUTE privilege to this object.

User-defined operators in Oracle 9*i* behave very similarly to user-defined functions, because Oracle takes sets of operands for input and returns values.

Summary

Though not emphasized in the SQL, operators serve their important role by enabling you to manipulate output and to specify selection criteria and search conditions.

Operators can be unary or binary, depending on whether they are applied to one or two operands.

The argument of what could be considered an operator goes on for at least as long as the existence of RDBMS — some databases insist on keywords such as `LIKE`, `IN`, `EXISTS`, `BETWEEN` and so on to be classified as operators, and some list them as predicates. This is a rather academic discussion, as classification does not affect the way you use either operators or predicates in SQL programming.

Operators are generally uniform across all database vendors with the notable exception of bitwise operators in Microsoft SQL Server and nonstandard comparison operators.

The precedence of operators is an established order in which RDBMS evaluates expressions that contain more than one operator; it is very important to take into consideration the precedence order. Using parentheses, one can specify custom precedence in an expression (as opposed to default precedence order).

✦ ✦ ✦

PART

V

Implementing Security Using System Catalogs

✦ ✦ ✦ ✦

In This Part

✦ ✦ ✦ ✦

CHAPTER 12

SQL and RDBMS Security

In This Chapter

Basic security mechanisms

Defining a database user

Managing security with privileges

Managing security with roles

Using views for security

Using constraints for security

Using stored procedures and triggers for security

Data encryption

Database auditing

Security standards

SQL provides only limited security mechanisms, relying on the software to implement a more robust security framework. Recognizing this, we've decided to give you a comprehensive overview of the RDBMS security, in addition to detailed coverage of SQL specific security statements (both mandated by the SQL99 standard and vendor-specific implementations).

Basic Security Mechanisms

Database security is an enormous topic, and exploring the ways in which leading database vendors implemented its various aspects is even larger. Security was not invented with the relational database; the password authentication, locks, and other security concepts are as ancient as human history, and SQL just added a new twist. Following SQL92/99's lead, all databases essentially comply in establishing the security procedures. There are three levels of security common to all RDBMS:

- **Authentication.** User connects to the RDBMS.
- **Authorization.** User gets access to the database or database schema objects to perform certain actions, based on the set of privileges assigned to the user.
- **Auditing.** For monitoring suspicious (and otherwise) activity, and performing postmortem analysis.

What differs is the way each of these relational database management systems (RDBMS) implement these levels.

Identification and authentication

The first line of defense is authentication. Before you even access RDBMS you must submit sufficient information validated either by RDBMS itself, or by the operating system within which this database is installed. Once the identity is authenticated, you may proceed with the attempt to access the database resources, objects, and data.

Authorization and access control

Once the user is authenticated and granted access to the database, RDBMS employs a complex, finely grained system of privileges (permissions) for the particular database objects. These privileges include permission to access, modify, destroy, or execute relevant database objects, as well as add, modify, and delete data.

Encryption

Encryption provides an additional security layer, protecting the data from unauthorized viewing. Even if access to the database is obtained, it will not be easy to decipher encrypted data into a human readable form.

Integrity and consistency

While security is mostly based on authentication and authorization procedures, data integrity plays a certain role in protecting data from unintentional or malicious manipulation. For example, even if a user gains access to the database (by stealing a password, for example), s/he still has to follow relational rules for data manipulation, which, among others, do not allow orphaned records; s/he wont be able to delete records from a parent table without understanding database relationships (though some vendors had implemented the CASCADE feature that instructs RDBMS to remove child records upon deletion of the parent one), won't be able to insert a duplicate a record into a column protected by the `UNIQUE` constraint, or won't be able to insert invalid data that would violate CHECK constraints.

Auditing

Auditing provides means to monitor database activity, both legitimate and unauthorized. It preserves the trail of database access attempts — either successful or failed, data deletions and inserts (in case one has to find out what had happened), and so on. It is a necessary component in order to be considered for security certification, discussed later in the chapter.

Defining a Database User

The concept of the USER, while being plain and simple in an intuitive layman way, is one of the most confusing across the RDBMS implementations. SQL99 does not specify any special syntax (or even a way) to create a user in the database. Left to their own devices, the database vendors have managed to create some ingenious solutions. For example, Oracle 9*i* makes little distinction between a user and the database schema, IDB DB2 UDB only uses operating system-defined users (or those defined by some external framework), and the Microsoft SQL Server combines both approaches, using Windows accounts and special system procedures for adding users to a database.

By definition, a database user is someone who makes use of the services provided by the RDBMS server. It could be an application, a database administrator, or just anyone who happens to access the database at any given moment. User authentication, as we've mentioned before, is the first line of defense when it comes to security issues.

In **Oracle 9*i*,** the syntax for creating a user is as follows:

```
CREATE USER <user_name>
IDENTIFIED BY [<password> | EXTERNALLY]
[DEFAULT TABLESPACE <def_tablespace_name>]
[TEMPORARY TABLESPACE <tmp_tablespace_name>]
[QUOTA (<integer> (K | M) ON <tablespace_name>],...
[PROFILE <profile_name>]
[PASSWORD EXPIRE]
[ACCOUNT [LOCK | UNLOCK]];
```

In addition to the CREATE USER privilege (explained later in the chapter), to create a user, you need, at the very least, to specify user name and password, since most of the clauses in the statement are optional. To create a user identified by the operating system (OS), use the keyword EXTERNALLY. For more information on OS integration, see the sidebar "OS Security Integration" later in the chapter.

The other options are Oracle-specific, and not found in other RDBMS implementations. For example, by specifying the PASSWORD EXPIRE clause, you are essentially telling Oracle that the password for this user expires immediately, forcing the user to select a different password on the next connection to the database. ACCOUNT LOCK allows you to specify, for example, that access is to be blocked after so many unsuccessful attempts (precluding password guessing), or disable user's account when, say, employee leaves the company. This is a security measure that prevents all "inactive" users from logging onto the database. A detailed discussion of all the Oracle-specific options is well beyond the scope of this book.

Here is a very simple version of the CREATE USER statement:

```
CREATE USER   new_user
IDENTIFIED BY it_is_me;

User created.
```

By omitting all the optional clauses, this statement creates a user that has all the system defaults assigned: it uses system tablespace, his/her password never expires, and so on. Needless to say, this practice has no place in a real, live production environment. In addition to being less secure, it is also very inefficient.

Oracle 9*i* User PROFILE

The PROFILE clause assigns an environmental user profile that governs the user's resource access by setting limits the user cannot exceed. If no profile is specified, then a default profile is used. To create a profile, you must assign the CREATE PROFILE privilege—either directly or through a role (explained later in the chapter).

A profile is created with the CREATE PROFILE statement. The syntax is relatively simple:

```
CREATE PROFILE <profile name>
LIMIT [RESOURCE PARAMETERS | PASSWORD PARAMETERS ];
```

Resource parameters could be set to integer UNLIMITED, or DEFAULT. The first explicitly specifies number of days, retries, and so on; the second removes the limit; and DEFAULT tells Oracle to use its default value, which is set in the system as part of the default profile (assigned to any user for whom no explicit profile was specified).

There are a number of parameters used here, most of which require some Oracle knowledge. Many of these are directly related to security. For example, the resource parameter SESSIONS_PER_USER limits the number of concurrent sessions allowed for this user ID; when the number is exceeded, the logon is denied. Another resource parameter—CONNECT_TIME—sets a limit for the connection time; yet another, IDLE_TIME, tells Oracle exactly how long a particular connection is allowed to remain idle, terminating the connection once the limit is reached. Of course, there are more resource parameters used for allocating system resources to a user, which you will find in the Oracle documentation.

Among password parameters, virtually every one falls into the security domain. Parameters like FAILED_LOGIN_ATTEMPTS, PASSWORD_LIFE_TIME, PASSWORD_REUSE_TIME, PASSWORD_REUSE_MAX, PASSWORD_LOCK_TIME, and PASSWORD_GRACE_TIME all define how passwords are created, used, and expired. The names of the parameters describe their functions. The first, FAILED_LOGIN_ATTEMPTS, guards against guessing the password and locks an account once the allowed number is reached. The PASSWORD_REUSE_MAX parameter specifies number of password changes before the current password is reused, and so on. One of the parameters (PASSWORD_VERIFY_FUNCTION) allows for using custom logic, usually implemented as PL/SQL script, for additional password verification, logging, and so on.

When a user is created, a schema corresponding to that user is also created. The newly created user has no rights or privileges within RDBMS, but must at least be granted the CONNECT privilege to be able to connect to the Oracle database and the set of privileges assigned on "as needed" basis (privileges and the GRANT statement syntax are discussed later in this chapter). After these privileges have been granted, the user ACME might access database ACME using password ACME, and perform actions based on the privileges granted.

In fact, that is the only way to create a "real schema"; the CREATE SCHEMA statement serves a somewhat different purpose. See Chapter 4 for more information on creating database objects.

Of course, as with almost any Oracle database object, a USER could be either dropped or altered later on. Here is the DROP syntax:

```
DROP USER <user name> [CASCADE];
```

CASCADE specifies that all objects in the user's schema should be dropped before dropping the user; Oracle does not allow dropping a user whose schema contains any objects, unless this clause is specified.

The ALTER USER statement specifies a number of changes for a user. It assigns a different profile, changes the resources limit, changes the default tablespace, and much more. It also provides a convenient way to modify a user's properties without the need to drop the user and then recreate it from scratch. For complete syntax of the ALTER USER statement, refer to Oracle documentation.

Information about users in the Oracle database is accessible through the system catalogs, discussed in detail in Chapter 13.

IBM DB2 UDB uses a combination of external security services and internal access controls. The first step in RDBMS security is authentication. IBM DB2 UDB does not provide authentication services, relying instead on external services, which could be implemented within the operating system, or as a third-party software product (especially in the case where the database is installed as part of a distributed environment).

This means that a user cannot be created unless s/he also has an operating system account, be it Windows, Unix, or any other OS. As such, all user authentication is managed outside of the DB2 UDB database. For more information, refer to the OS Security Integration section later in this chapter, or to IBM DB2 UDB documentation.

Microsoft SQL Server 2000 can be configured for user authentication either through the Windows NT/2000 operating system, or through Mixed Mode authentication.

In the first case, the user must belong to some predefined Windows account that allows logon to the SQL Server database with his/her system login, which must be mapped to the internal SQL Server account. Therefore, the OS login must be mapped to an SQL Server login in each and every database within it that this login is allowed to access.

The second case — Mixed Mode — requires the user to (1) have a valid Windows account to establish connection to the SQL Server and (2) supply a user ID/password to be authenticated by the SQL Server.

The Microsoft SQL Server does not have the `CREATE USER` statement. Instead it uses several *system-stored procedures*, which are special precompiled routines stored within the database server, usually written in Transact-SQL. The stored procedures can be executed from ISQL/OSQL command-line utilities, or from the visual interface of the Microsoft SQL Server Query Analyzer (see Appendix E for more information on accessing RDBMS).

Table 12-1 lists stored procedures utilized by user management within the SQL Server. The arguments needed to run these stored procedures are by and large self-describing. If you are new to the MS SQL Server, consult SQL Server Books Online (included with every installation of the RDBMS), as there are some restrictions applicable to the use of these procedures.

Table 12-1
Selected Microsoft SQL Server 2000 User Management System-Stored Procedures

Stored Procedure	***Description***
`sp_grantdbaccess <windows account name>, [<name inside database>]`	Maps security account to one inside SQL server database, adding a user to the users list of the current database. The Windows account must be a valid account (<DOMAIN NAME>\<User Name>). When a second argument is not supplied, the Windows account name is used. If called from within an application, it returns 0 on success or 1 on failure. Only members of the SQL Server fixed role `SYSADMIN` have permission to execute this procedure.
`sp_revokedbaccess <name inside database>`	Removes the account mapping from the current database.
`sp_adduser <windows account name>, [<name inside database>] [<group name>] sp_grantdbaccess`	Adds user (security account) to the current database; Microsoft supplies this procedure for backward compatibility only and recommends using instead. If called from within an application, returns 0 on success or 1 on failure.

Stored Procedure	Description
sp_dropuser <name inside database>	Removes user (security account) from the current database. Microsoft supplies this procedure for backward compatibility only and recommend using sp_revokedbaccess instead.
sp_addlogin <login name>, [<password>], [<default database>], [<default language>], [<security identification number>], [<encryption option>]	Creates a new SQL Server login that allows a user to connect to the SQL Server using SQL Server authentication. Normally used for users connecting to the SQL Server over the network (i.e., they do not have a local account). All arguments, except the login name are optional. If called from within an application, returns 0 on success or 1 on failure.
sp_grantlogin <windows account name>	Grants SQL Server access privileges to a valid Windows account. If called from within an application, returns 0 on success or 1 on failure.
sp_revokelogin <windows account name>	Removes access privileges for a Windows account (either user or group). If called from within an application, returns 0 on success or 1 on failure. Note: This procedure revokes individual privileges; if a user whose login privileges were revoked is a member of a group that has these privileges, the user will still be able to connect.
sp_denylogin <windows account name>	Adds login to 'deny list'; the login for this user will be denied. If called from within an application, returns 0 on success or 1 on failure. Only members of sysadmin and securityadmin fixed SQL Server roles can execute this procedure.
sp_droplogin <windows account name>	Removes a login from the current database. If a login is mapped to a user, the user must first be removed using the sp_dropuser stored procedure; other restrictions also apply. If called from within an application, returns 0 on success or 1 on failure.

Note

The main difference between system-stored procedures and user-created procedures is their scope. The first are global, while the latter are usually local to the database in which they are created. Virtually all system-stored procedures are prefixed with sp_, and they all are located in the Master database.

To execute any of the above stored procedures, either from ISQL/OSQL or the Query Analyzer, type in

```
EXEC <stored procedure name> (arg1,arg2,...,argN)
```

The information about users in the Microsoft SQL Server is accessible in the system catalogs (INFORMATION_SCHEMA), discussed in detail in Chapter 13, as well as in the system-stored procedures.

Managing Security with Privileges

An RDBMS is essentially a collection of objects — schemas, tables, views, procedures, and so on, in addition to the processes that manage these objects. Restricting access to these objects is an essential security mechanism implemented on the SQL level through the *privileges* system.

Privileges represent the rights of a particular user to access, create, manipulate, and destroy various objects inside a database, as well as perform administrative tasks. Privileges can be granted to a user, or ROLE, or both (the concept of ROLE is discussed in the next paragraph).

All the privileges can be divided into two broad categories — *system privileges* and *object privilege* — and they vary widely among different database vendors. For a more detailed look, refer to the section on specific RDBMS implementations later in this chapter.

GRANT statement

The SQL92/99 standard defines privileges as the types of actions a user is authorized to perform on the objects and in the system to which s/he is granted access. All these privileges are valid across the three RDBMS discussed in this book.

A privilege can be granted — either to an individual user or to a role. The GRANT statement can be used for granting either system privileges or object privileges. The syntax for granting the privilege is fairly consistent across all three RDBMS packages, and multiple privileges can be granted in a single statement, such as:

```
GRANT [ALL [PRIVILEGES]] | <privilege,...>
[ON <object_name>]
TO <user> | <group> | <role>
[WITH GRANT OPTION]
```

The privilege can be any of the ones listed in Table 12-6; the options clauses vary among databases, and are listed in Table 12-2.

Table 12-2
GRANT Statement Options

Option	*Description*	*Applies To*
ADMIN OPTION	Allows the grantee to GRANT this system level privilege to other users or roles.	Oracle 9*i*
GRANT OPTION	Allows the grantee to GRANT this object level privilege to other users or roles.	Oracle 9*i*, Microsoft SQL Server 2000, IBM DB2 UDB 8.1 SQL92/99 Standard
HIERARCHY OPTION	The WITH HIERARCHY OPTION (Oracle only) indicates that the object privilege is granted not only for the object itself but also for all derived objects.	Oracle 9*i*

Granting system-level privileges

System privileges in general allow users to perform some administrative tasks within a given RDBMS (creating a database; creating and dropping users; creating, altering, and destroying database objects; and so on). You need a sufficiently high level of authority within the RDBM system to be able to exercise or grant system privileges. The features that distinguish these system privileges from object privileges are their scope and, sometimes, the types of activities they allow the user to perform.

System privileges are strictly database specific: each vendor implements its own set of system privileges and some system privileges may have different meanings for different vendors. Some systems—the Microsoft SQL Server, for instance—do not even define system privileges, using privileges for SQL *statements* instead.

Oracle 9*i* has literally dozens of system privileges (and roles that bundle them together), the most common of which are given in Table 12-3. The SQL statement syntax that grants a system privilege is very much in line with the SQL standard. All granted privileges enable the grantee immediately (if the grantee is a ROLE, it acquires the privileges once enabled). The following code presents a basic syntax for granting system privileges in Oracle 9*i*.

```
GRANT ALL [PRIVILEGES] |
      <system privilege,...> |
      <role>
TO <user> | <role> | <PUBLIC>
[IDENTIFIED BY <password>]
[WITH ADMIN OPTION];
```

System privileges might be any of those listed in Table 12-3 (and some more complex or obscure ones, which were not included here). You can either grant a privilege or a role (that was granted some privileges); the ALL keyword refers to all privileges at once and might be followed by an optional PRIVILEGES keyword, introduced in Oracle for compatibility with the SQL99 standard.

You can view all system privileges associated with a user by querying DBA_SYS_PRIVS in the Oracle dictionary view; the privileges available for the session are shown in the catalog view SESSION_PRIVS. See more on system catalogs in Chapter 13.

The privilege or role can be granted to a user, role (either predefined or created), or PUBLIC (which effectively means all users defined in the RDBMS). The IDENTIFIED BY clause specifies a password for an existing user, or—if a user does not yet exist—tells Oracle to create such a user implicitly. This clause is invalid if the grantee is a role, because it has to be created explicitly.

WITH ADMIN OPTION is an Oracle-specific clause. Essentially it means that the user or members of a role will be allowed to GRANT the assigned *system* privilege to some other users or roles (with the exception of GLOBAL roles), revoke the privilege from another user or role, and so on. In that regard it works very much like the WITH GRANT OPTION clause for the object-level privilege, though there are some subtle differences in usage. Refer to vendor documentation for a full explanation.

Table 12-3
Common Oracle 9*i* System Privileges

System Privilege	***Description***
ALTER DATABASE	Permits grantee to alter Oracle database.
ALTER SYSTEM	Permits grantee to alter Oracle system allowing for execution of system-altering statements.
AUDIT SYSTEM	Permits grantee to issue AUDIT SQL statements.
CREATE [PUBLIC] DATABASE LINK	Permits grantee to create private/public database links in the grantee's schema.
DROP [PUBLIC] DATABASE LINK	Permits grantee to drop public database links.
CREATE ANY INDEX	Permits grantee to create a domain INDEX in any schema, or an index on any table in any schema.
ALTER ANY INDEX	Permits grantee to alter any INDEX in any schema.

System Privilege	*Description*
DROP ANY INDEX	Permits grantee to drop any INDEX in any schema.
CREATE [ANY] MATERIALIZED VIEW	Permits grantee to create a materialized view in his/her own schema (or any schema if the clause is used).
ALTER ANY MATERIALIZED VIEW	Permits grantee to alter a materialized view in any schema.
DROP ANY MATERIALIZED VIEW	Permits grantee to drop a materialized view in any schema.
CREATE [ANY] OPERATOR	Permits grantee to create an operator and its bindings in his/her own schema (or *any* schema if the clause is used).
DROP ANY OPERATOR	Permits grantee to drop an operator in any schema.
EXECUTE ANY OPERATOR	Permits grantee to execute an operator in any schema.
CREATE [ANY] PROCEDURE	Permits grantee to create a procedure (or function), stand-alone or packaged, in his/her own schema (or *any* schema if the clause is used).
DROP ANY PROCEDURE	Permits grantee to drop a procedure (or function), stand-alone or packaged in any schema.
EXECUTE ANY PROCEDURE	Permits grantee to execute a procedure (or function), stand-alone or packaged in any schema.
CREATE PROFILE	Permits grantee to create profiles.
ALTER PROFILE	Permits grantee to alter existing profiles.
DROP PROFILE	Permits grantee to drop existing profiles.
CREATE ROLE	Permits grantee to create a role.
ALTER ANY ROLE	Permits grantee to alter any role in existing the database.
DROP ANY ROLE	Permits grantee to drop any role existing in the database.
GRANT ANY ROLE	Permits grantee to grant any existing role in the database.

Continued

Table 12-3 *(continued)*

System Privilege	***Description***
CREATE [ANY] SEQUENCE	Permits grantee to create a sequence in his/her own schema (or *any* schema if the clause is used).
ALTER ANY SEQUENCE	Permits grantee to alter any sequence in any schema.
DROP ANY SEQUENCE	Permits grantee to drop any sequence in any schema.
SELECT ANY SEQUENCE	Permits grantee to access any sequence in any schema.
CREATE SESSION	Permits grantee to connect to the Oracle Database.
ALTER SESSION	Permits grantee to issue ALTER SESSION statements.
CREATE [ANY | PUBLIC] SYNONYM	Permits grantee to create private or public synonym in his/her own schema (or *any* schema if the clause is used).
DROP [ANY | PUBLIC] SYNONYM	Permits grantee to drop public synonym in his/her own schema (or *any* schema if the clause is used).
CREATE [ANY] TABLE	Permits grantee to create a table in his/her own schema (or *any* schema if the clause is used).
ALTER ANY TABLE	Permits grantee to alter any table in any schema.
DELETE ANY TABLE	Permits grantee to delete data in any table or view in any schema.
DROP ANY TABLE	Permits grantee to drop or truncate any table in any schema.
INSERT ANY TABLE	Permits grantee to insert data into tables and views in any schema.
LOCK ANY TABLE	Permits grantee to lock tables and views in any schema.
SELECT ANY TABLE	Permits grantee to select data from any tables or views in any schema.

System Privilege	*Description*
UPDATE ANY TABLE	Permits grantee to update data or view in any schema
CREATE TABLESPACE	Permits grantee to create a tablespace.
ALTER TABLESPACE	Permits grantee to alter a tablespace.
DROP TABLESPACE	Permits grantee to drop a tablespace.
CREATE [ANY] TRIGGER	Permits grantee to create a database trigger in his/her own schema (or *any* schema if the clause is used).
ALTER ANY TRIGGER	Permits grantee to alter (enable, disable, or compile) any trigger in any schema.
DROP ANY TRIGGER	Permits grantee to drop database trigger in any schema.
CREATE [ANY] TYPE	Permits grantee to create object types and object bodies in his/her own schema (or *any* schema if the clause is used).
ALTER ANY TYPE	Permits grantee to alter object types in *any* schema.
DROP ANY TYPE	Permits grantee to drop any object type and object bodies in any schema.
EXECUTE ANY TYPE	Permits grantee to use any user-defined object type or collection in any schema, and to invoke methods defined within these object types.
UNDER ANY TYPE	Permits grantee to create a subtype of any nonfinal object types.
CREATE USER	Permits grantee to create a user, and, at the same time, assign quotas on any tablespace, set default temporary tablespaces, and assign a PROFILE.
ALTER USER	Permits grantee to alter any user, i.e., change a user's authentication method, assign quotas on any tablespace, set default temporary tablespaces, and assign a PROFILE and default roles.
BECOME USER	Permits grantee to become another user.

Continued

Table 12-3 (continued)	
System Privilege	***Description***
DROP USER	Permits grantee to drop other users.
CREATE [ANY] VIEW	Permits grantee to create a view in his/her own schema (or any schema if the clause is used).
DROP ANY VIEW	Permits grantee to drop views in any schema.
UNDER ANY VIEW	Permits grantee to create subviews for any object views.
COMMENT ANY TABLE	Permits grantee to add comments on any table, view, or column in any schema.
GRANT ANY PRIVILEGE	Permits grantee to grant any system privilege.
SELECT ANY DICTIONARY	Permits grantee to query any data dictionary object in the Oracle SYS schema.

Here are some examples based in the ACME database. To grant a user privilege to create a table in the database and, in turn, pass it onto others, the following statement could be used:

```
GRANT CREATE TABLE
TO new_user
IDENTIFIED BY it_is_me
WITH ADMIN OPTION;

Grant succeeded.
```

If you have sufficient privileges, the user NEW_USER identified by the password IT_IS_ME will be created, but you cannot use this user ID and password to connect to the Oracle database if the user NEW_USER has not been granted the CREATE SESSION system privilege, which it would need to access the database. The error ORA-01045: user NEW_USER lacks CREATE SESSION privilege; logon denied would be generated.

To fix the situation you need to grant the newly created user this privilege:

```
GRANT CREATE SESSION
TO new_user
IDENTIFIED BY it_is_me
WITH ADMIN OPTION;

Grant succeeded.
```

Now you can connect to the database using NEW_USER/IT_IS_ME credentials, and — because of the WITH ADMIN OPTION — grant this privilege to other users.

There are two more system privileges in Oracle deserving separate discussion: SYSDBA and SYSOPER, shown in Table 12-4. These privileges act like roles in that they include a number of other system privileges. When connecting to the Oracle database, you can specify to connect AS SYSDBA or AS SYSOPER, assuming that these privileges had been granted to the user. SYSDBA is one of the highest privileges that can be granted.

Table 12-4
Oracle 9*i* SYSDBA and SYSOPER System Privileges

Privilege	*Description*
SYSDBA	Permits grantee to perform STARTUP and SHUTDOWN operations, CREATE DATABASE, ALTER DATABASE (open, mount, backup and change default character set) ARCHIVELOG and RECOVERY, CREATE SPFILE, and includes the RESTRICTED SESSION privilege.
SYSOPER	Permits grantee to perform STARTUP and SHUTDOWN operations, ALTER DATABASE (only open, mount and backup), ARCHIVELOG and RECOVERY, CREATE SPFILE, and includes the RESTRICTED SESSION privilege.

On some platforms for Oracle 9*i* it is possible to assign privileges to database users through the initialization parameter OS_USERS, which allows you to grant roles using operating system facilities. For such users, you cannot also use the GRANT statement to grant additional roles, though it is possible for all other users and roles.

IBM DB2 UDB is somewhat similar in this aspect to Oracle; it has system privileges, and some of the privileges are associated with authority levels (see more on this later in the chapter). All system-level privileges for DB2 UDB are shown in Table 12-5.

The generic GRANT statement in DB2 UDB follows the syntax:

```
GRANT PRIVILEGES | <system privilege,...>
ON DATABASE
TO USER <user> | GROUP <group> | PUBLIC
```

As you can see, DB2 UDB does not have WITH ADMIN OPTION clause (as in Oracle), and you cannot use ALL PRIVILEGES, though granting DBADM essentially serves the same purpose.

Table 12-5
Common IBM DB2 UDB System Privileges

System Privilege	*Description*
BINDADD	Permits grantee to create packages; the package creator automatically has object level CONTROL privilege.
CONNECT	Permits grantee to access the DB2 UDB database.
CREATETAB	Permits grantee to create tables within the database (with the CONTROL object level privilege granted automatically on all created objects, and retained afterward even if the CREATETAB system privilege is revoked).
CREATE_NOT_FENCED	Grants user the authority to register functions for execution in the database manager main process.
IMPLICIT_SCHEMA	Permits grantee to implicitly create schema.
DBADM	Grants database administrator's authority; the DBA has all the privileges and the ability to grant them to others.
LOAD	Permits grantee to use LOAD utility to transfer data into a database; additional object level permissions are required to successfully perform loading.

Here is the example of granting CREATETAB system privilege to PUBLIC (all users), in the database ACME:

```
GRANT CREATETAB
ON DATABASE
TO PUBLIC

DB0000I The SQL command completed successfully
```

Note that unlike Oracle or the MS SQL Server, the keywords USER and GROUP must be specified in DB2 UDB. Granting the system privilege (database authority in IBM DB2 jargon) to a group called SALES would have the following syntax:

```
GRANT CREATETAB
ON DATABASE
TO GROUP sales

DB0000I The SQL command completed successfully
```

If neither USER nor GROUP keywords are specified, then DB2 UDB employs a set of security authorization rules to resolve potential conflicts: if the name is defined in the OS as GROUP, then GROUP would be assumed; if it is defined in the OS as USER, or is undefined, then USER would be assumed; if the name refers to both GROUP and USER (it is possible to have a GROUP and a USER with the same name) then an error is generated. The same error would also be generated if external DCE authentication were used. There is more on authentication methods later in this chapter, and a detailed discussion can be found in the vendor's documentation.

To GRANT the DBADM authority, a user must have SYSADM authority. Both SYSADM and DBADM can grant the other privileges to users or groups. There is more on IBM DB2 UDB's authorities later in this chapter.

The **Microsoft SQL Server 2000** does not have *system privileges,* or at least not in the sense that Oracle or IBM have it. The privileges are granted to a user (or role) for specific SQL statements. Once the privilege is granted, a user can execute the statement to perform operations that they define. Note that the SQL Server has no WITH ADMIN OPTION clause for these privileges:

```
GRANT ALL | <statement,...>
TO <security_account>
```

The statements that require special permissions (privileges) are those that could do the most harm, if misused: adding new objects to a database, altering existing ones, and performing some administrative tasks. Most of these statements are discussed in detail in Chapter 4. The statement list includes (among others) the following:

- CREATE VIEW
- CREATE TABLE
- CREATE DEFAULT
- CREATE PROCEDURE
- CREATE RULE
- BACKUP DATABASE
- BACKUP LOG

The system permissions are tied to a database (MS SQL Server also uses this concept; the closest Oracle equivalent would be *schema*) and are hierarchical. For example, to GRANT the privilege to execute a CREATE DATABASE statement, you must be in the context of the SQL Server *master* database as this statement produces results affecting the whole instance of the SQL Server 2000.

The security account refers to the SQL Server user, SQL Server role, Windows NT user, or Windows NT group. There is some granularity to the security accounts defined by the SQL Server: privileges granted to a user (either on the SQL Server or Windows NT) affect this user only; privileges granted to a role or Windows NT group affect all members of this role or group. In the case of a privileges conflict between a group/role and their members, the most restrictive privilege — DENY — takes precedence (discussed later in the chapter).

Tip

In order to effectively manage SQL Server security using Windows NT groups and accounts, you must understand underlying Windows OS security.

Granting the CREATE DATABASE statement to a user/role while being in context of the ACME database would produce an error, as follows:

```
USE acme

GRANT CREATE DATABASE
TO PUBLIC

CREATE DATABASE permission can only be granted in the master
database.
```

Note

USE keyword is not a part of the SQL standard; it is valid though in Transact-SQL dialect, which is used by the Microsoft SQL Server and the Sybase Adaptive Server.

Changing the context to the *master* database resolves the issue:

```
USE master

GRANT CREATE DATABASE
TO PUBLIC

The command(s) completed successfully.
```

Granting something more local, pertaining to a database itself, requires a narrower scope. To grant a privilege to create a view in the ACME database, one must be in ACME database context:

```
USE acme

GRANT CREATE VIEW
TO PUBLIC

The command(s) completed successfully.
```

Some Transact-SQL statements cannot be granted through privileges; the grantee must be a member of a predefined *fixed server role* (discussed later in this chapter). This means that in order to be able to execute, for example, the `KILL` statement (that stops a process inside an SQL Server installation) you have to be a member of the `processadmin` fixed role, in order to be able to grant `ALL` statement permissions you have to be a member of the `sysadmin` fixed role, the members of the `db_owner` role can grant and/or revoke any privilege within their database, and so on.

Granting object-level privileges

By their very nature, the object-level privileges are much more fine-grained than system-level ones. This is reflected in the syntax of the `GRANT` statement. These privileges could go all the way down to column level (if the object is a database table or view), or to any other object within the database such as stored procedures, functions, and triggers. The SQL Object-Level privileges are listed in Table 12-6.

Table 12-6
SQL Object-Level Privileges

Object Privilege	*Compliance*	*Description*
`INSERT`	SQL92/99, IBM DB2 UDB, Oracle, Microsoft	Permits the grantee to insert data in a database table (or view). The permission could be further restricted to specific columns.
`SELECT`	SQL92/99, IBM DB2 UDB, Oracle, Microsoft	Permits the grantee to select data from a database table, view, or some other implementation-specific objects (sequences, snapshots, etc.). The permission could be further restricted to specific columns.
`UPDATE`	SQL92/99, IBM DB2 UDB, Oracle, Microsoft	Permits the grantee to update data in a database table or view. The permission could be further restricted to specific columns.
`DELETE`	SQL92/99, IBM DB2 UDB, Oracle, Microsoft	Permits the grantee to delete data in a database table or view.

Continued

Table 12-6 (continued)

Object Privilege	*Compliance*	*Description*
ALTER	IBM DB2 UDB, Oracle, Microsoft	While generally considered a system-level privilege, it permits the grantee to alter certain database objects, e.g., tables and views. Some of the objects might be implementation-specific. Though this privilege is not part of a standard SQL, it is implemented by all three vendors.
INDEX	IBM DB2 UDB, Oracle, Microsoft	Permits the grantee to create an index on the existing table.
UNDER	Oracle	Permits grantee to create a subview under a view.
EXECUTE	IBM DB2 UDB, Oracle, Microsoft	Permits the grantee to execute an existing stored procedure or function.
REFERENCES	SQL92/99, IBM DB2 UDB, Oracle, Microsoft	Permits the grantee to modify an existing table (or create a new one) that incorporates a foreign key constraint referencing some other table.

This is the **Oracle 9*i*** generic syntax for granting privileges to the database objects:

```
GRANT [ALL [PRIVILEGES]] | <object_privilege,...>
[ON [<schema>].<object>]
TO <user> | <role> | <PUBLIC>
[WITH {GRANT OPTION | HIERARCHY OPTION}];
```

As with the GRANT system privileges statement, you need to supply a list of all the privileges you wish to grant (see Table 12-6 for a list of relevant object privileges). Specifying ALL would enable all privileges, but you as a user must have sufficient system privileges to grant this option yourself. Next comes the list of columns to which you may grant access (if applicable, as some database objects do not have columns), then you specify the object itself—table, view, procedure, package, sequence, synonym, and any other valid Oracle database object (the new JAVA and DIRECTORY clauses are not part of SQL and are beyond the scope of this book).

Note that not every object has a given privilege: some privileges are irrelevant to the objects. For example, the REFERENCES privilege does not make much sense if you are trying to assign it to an Oracle sequence, nor does the EXECUTE privilege make sense for a table. Consequently, if you specify ALL privileges, only those allowed for the object type would be granted. The following GRANT statement would generate an error:

```
SQL> GRANT EXECUTE
     ON deduction
     TO PUBLIC;

ORA-02224: EXECUTE privilege not allowed for tables
```

The object privilege could be granted to a user, to a role, or to PUBLIC (which is a specific way to grant privileges to each and every user within that database).

The WITH GRANT OPTION indicates that the grantee will be able in his/her turn to GRANT this privilege to other users or roles.

The WITH HIERARCHY OPTION (Oracle only) indicates that the object privilege is granted not only for the object itself but also for all derived objects. For example, if a view is based upon a table, granting privileges to a table with such an option would automatically grant the same privileges for the view; however, it does not work the other way around — privileges for the view would not give the same access to the base table.

The WITH GRANT OPTION can be specified only when the grantee is a user or PUBLIC; this option is invalid when granting to a role.

Here is a real example that is less confusing; it grants ALL privileges in the ACME database table PRODUCT to the SALES_FORCE role. Whoever belongs to the SALES_FORCE role will be able to exercise these privileges as soon as the following statement is executed:

```
SQL> GRANT SELECT, UPDATE, DELETE
     ON product
     TO sales_force;

Grant succeeded.
```

IBM DB2 UDB has probably the most diverse syntax when it comes to object-level privileges. In addition to the object-level privileges shown in Table 12-6, it has a bunch of its own (Table 12-7).

Table 12-7
IBM DB2 UDB Object-Level Privileges

Object Privilege	*Syntax*	*Description*	*Pertains To*
CONTROL	GRANT CONTROL ON {OBJECT} <object_name> TO USER <user> | GROUP <group> | PUBLIC	Permits grantee to drop the object.	Index package table view nickname
BIND	GRANT BIND ON PACKAGE <package name> TO USER <user> | GROUP <group> | PUBLIC	Permits grantee to bind the package.	Package
ALTERIN	GRANT ALTERIN ON SCHEMA <schema name> TO USER <user> | GROUP <group> | PUBLIC	Permits grantee to alter the existing objects in the schema, or to add comments to them.	Schema
CREATEIN	GRANT ALTERIN ON SCHEMA <schema name> TO USER <user> | GROUP <group> | PUBLIC	Permits grantee to create objects in the schema.	Schema
DROPIN	GRANT ALTERIN ON SCHEMA <schema name> TO USER <user> | GROUP <group> | PUBLIC	Permits grantee to drop objects in the schema.	Schema
USAGE	GRANT USAGE ON SEQUENCE <sequence_name> TO USER <user> | GROUP <group> | PUBLIC	Permits grantee to access the sequence through NEXTVAL or PREVVAL expressions.	Sequence

<table>
<tr><th>Object Privilege</th><th>Syntax</th><th>Description</th><th>Pertains To</th></tr>
<tr><td>USE OF TABLESPACE</td><td>GRANT USE OF TABLESPACE <tablespace_name>
TO USER <user>
| GROUP <group>
| PUBLIC</td><td>Permits grantee to access and use the specified tablespace.</td><td>Tablespace</td></tr>
<tr><td>PASSTHRU</td><td>GRANT PASSTHRU
ON SERVER
<server_name>
TO USER <user>
| GROUP <group>
| PUBLIC</td><td>Permits grantee to access and use a data source in a pass-through mode.</td><td>Server</td></tr>
</table>

Each of these privileges abides by certain rules, and it should not be assumed that these rules are transferable between different objects. Refer to DB2 UDB documentation (or IBM DB2 UDB–specific books) for more information.

The most important thing (and relevant in the sense of being close to the SQL standard) is granting privileges to a table or a view. Here is a more specific syntax for granting such privileges to a table (or view, or nickname):

```
GRANT [ALL [PRIVILEGES]] |
      ALTER |
      CONTROL |
      DELETE |
      INDEX |
      INSERT |
      REFERENCES (<column name>,...) |
      SELECT [(<column name>,...)] |
      UPDATE [(<column name>,...)]
ON [TABLE] <table_name> | <view_name> | <nickname>
TO USER <user> | GROUP <group>| PUBLIC
[WITH GRANT OPTION]
```

In IBM DB2 UDB, the `GRANT ALL` statement grants all privileges except the `CONTROL` privilege.

To grant, for example, a privilege to reference a table (create a foreign key based on the table's column) to `PUBLIC` (all users), the following statement would be issued:

```
GRANT REFERENCES
ON TABLE customer(cust_paytermsid_fn)
TO PUBLIC
WITH GRANT OPTION

DB0000I The SQL command completed successfully
```

This grants privilege to create and drop a foreign key that references the table (as the parent). Of course, the grantor must have sufficient privileges him/herself to execute any of the GRANT statements.

The following generic syntax for granting object-level privileges is valid in **Microsoft SQL Server 2000**:

```
GRANT
    [ALL [PRIVILEGES]]
    | <permission1>,<permission2>,......
        [(<column1>,<column2>...)] ON [<table> | <view>]
    | ON [<stored_procedure> | <extended_procedure>]
    | ON [<user_defined_function>]
TO <security_account>,...
[WITH GRANT OPTION]
[AS <group> | <role>]
```

PRIVILEGES is an optional SQL99 keyword that can be used for standards compliance in any of the three RDBMS discussed.

There are many similarities of the object-level privileges GRANT statement to that used with the system-level one: use of the ALL keyword to grant all the privileges en mass, the security_account refers to exactly the same thing (see previous paragraph), and so on.

Since the statement in the preceding code grants privileges for objects (and object parts — for example, columns within tables), it has many different options. You can grant a privilege (one from the list in the Table 12-6) on a table or a view, on one or more columns within these, and on some other valid *existing* objects within the SQL Server database. The syntax allows you to list several subobjects at the same time (columns, tables, and so on), though you cannot list several objects like tables and views at the same time.

The notable difference between the Microsoft SQL Server and both Oracle and IBM DB2 UDB is an additional AS clause. It is used when privileges (permissions in Microsoft terminology) granted to a group or role are, at the same time, granted to users that are not members of this group/role — and therefore the group does not have sufficient authority. In this case you must use both the WITH GRANT OPTION and AS clauses. This would permit the grantee to GRANT this privilege under the authority of the group/role specified in the AS clause.

The following SQL statement grants SELECT object-level privileges to the Microsoft SQL Server 2000 predefined role PUBLIC for the table PRODUCT (see the paragraph on security models overview later in the chapter):

```
GRANT SELECT
ON product
TO PUBLIC

The command(s) completed successfully.
```

Now any authenticated user belonging to the role PUBLIC would be able to issue a SELECT statement on the table PRODUCT. An example of a more complex statement, which limits columns for user viewing, follows this paragraph. This statement grants PUBLIC role permissions to select and update only two columns from the table PRODUCTS, while hiding the rest:

```
GRANT SELECT,
      UPDATE (prod_id_n,
              prod_price_n)
ON product
TO PUBLIC

The command(s) completed successfully.
```

In the generic MS SQL Server, it makes no difference which of the following syntaxes you choose for the GRANT statement:

```
GRANT <...> (prod_id_n, prod_price_n) ON product
```

or:

```
GRANT <...> ON product (prod_id_n, prod_price_n)
```

The list of columns may either follow or precede the table name.

REVOKE privileges

This command revokes privileges — either system-level or object-level — from a database user, role, or group. Roles, which are just are sets of privileges, are revoked in exactly the same way as users. The syntax that follows revokes *system privileges* using SQL99 standards:

```
REVOKE [GRANT OPTION FOR]
ALL [PRIVILEGES] | <privilege>,...
FROM USER <user> | GROUP <group> | PUBLIC
[CASCADE | RESTRICT]
```

As you can see, you can either revoke a privilege or a GRANT OPTION of that privilege, meaning that the user/role would lose his/her ability to GRANT this privilege in its turn. The privileges themselves remain unaffected.

SQL99 also specifies two optional clauses, RESTRICT and CASCADE. With the first option, the statement succeeds only if there are no abandoned privileges in the database. Such a situation might occur when the user, for example, already granted this privilege to some other user. When you are determined to revoke the privilege no matter what, and propagate this change across all the users that have received this privilege from the user, the CASCADE clause must be specified.

As usual, each of the vendors has its own ideas for implementing this statement.

Revoking system-level privileges

Oracle 9*i* syntax follows that of the SQL99 standard, but does not support the CASCADE and RESTRICT clauses. It also does not allow for revoking GRANT/ADMIN OPTION.

```
REVOKE ALL [PRIVILEGES] | <role> | <system_privilege>,...
FROM   <user> | <role> | PUBLIC;
```

To revoke a system privilege or role requires sufficient privileges, or just the ADMIN OPTION privilege. This preceding statement can only revoke the privileges and roles that have been granted through the GRANT statement; if the privilege was granted with initialization parameter OS_USERS (see GRANT privileges section's Note), you cannot revoke it with the REVOKE statement.

You can revoke the system-level privilege CREATE TABLE from a user NEW_USER with the following statement:

```
SQL> REVOKE CREATE TABLE
     FROM new_user;

Revoke succeeded.
```

The effects of REVOKE are immediate—the user loses the privilege the very moment the statement is executed by Oracle. If the privilege is revoked from PUBLIC, each user loses that privilege *if it was granted through PUBLIC*; privileges granted to the user directly or through a role remain unaffected in this case. The rules for revoking system privileges are complex. For example, if a privilege (or role) is revoked from a role, it is revoked from that role only; if the role had granted the privilege (or role) to another user (or role), the user would continue to exercise the privilege (or role). There is no cascading effect for revoking the system privileges in Oracle. For example, say user1 was granted the system-level privilege WITH ADMIN option, and, in turn, user1 granted this privilege to user2. The latter (user2) retains this privilege even if it is revoked from user1 some time later.

Also, keep in mind that there is no reversal for all the objects that a user had created. When privileges are revoked, all objects created with these privileges up to the moment will remain in the database.

Revoking system-level privileges in **IBM DB2 UDB** is simple—just follow the GRANT statement path in reverse:

```
REVOKE PRIVILEGES | <system privilcgc>,...
ON DATABASE
FROM USER <user> | GROUP <group> | PUBLIC
```

Here is the example from the section discussing the GRANT statement in DB2 UDB, which revokes the CREATETAB system privilege to PUBLIC (all users), in the database ACME:

```
REVOKE CREATETAB
ON DATABASE
FROM PUBLIC

DB0000I The SQL command completed successfully
```

When neither USER nor GROUP is specified, DB2 UDB looks into the system catalog (more on system catalogs in Chapter 13) to determine grantee type. Revoking a privilege does not necessarily revoke the ability to perform the action if the user has some higher authority, or belongs to a group that holds this privilege.

The **Microsoft SQL Server 2000** REVOKE statement for *statement permissions* (which is Microsoft's *system privileges*) is similar to that of Oracle. Like Oracle, it does not support CASCADE and RESTRICT at this level, nor revoking the GRANT OPTION:

```
REVOKE [ALL] | <privilege>,...
FROM <security_account>,...
```

The ALL keyword in the REVOKE statement on the system level can only be used by members of the SYSADMIN fixed role. All restrictions and notes mentioned in the GRANT section of this chapter for the SQL Server 2000 also apply here.

To revoke, for example, the CREATE table privilege from the user NEW_USER, the following statement might be used:

```
REVOKE CREATE TABLE
FROM new_user

The command(s) completed successfully.
```

Revoking object-level privileges

The SQL99 standard does not differentiate between revoking system-level or object-level privileges, providing the same syntax for both. In the vendor RDBMS implementations, the situation is dramatically different; as with the GRANT statement for the object-level privilege, the REVOKE statement is quite complex. The information in this book barely covers the basics of this topic as it is implemented by the vendors; refer to the vendor-specific documentation for more information.

Oracle 9*i* syntax for revoking object privileges is fairly standard, except for the number of the optional clauses like JAVA and DIRECTORY (skipped for simplicity):

```
REVOKE ALL [PRIVILEGES] | <object_privilege,...> [(<column>)]
ON [<schema>].<object>]
FROM <user> | <role> | PUBLIC
CASCADE CONSTRAINTS [FORCE];
```

The object PRIVILEGE can be any of those listed in Table 12-6 (assuming that it is relevant to the object). The COLUMN clause specifies an optional column or a list of columns for which the statement is applicable; the object for which privileges are revoked could be any of the database objects.

The privilege can be revoked from a user, a role, or from PUBLIC. The users cease to exercise the privilege immediately after it is revoked from them.

If the privilege is revoked from a role, all users to whom this role was granted lose this privilege, effective immediately. A privilege revoked from PUBLIC is revoked from every user who had been granted this privilege through the PUBLIC. If, however, a user was granted the privilege directly or through the role, the revoke statement has no effect on him/her.

The following statement revokes INSERT, DELETE , and UPDATE privileges from the PUBLIC for columns CUST_PAYTERMSID_FN and CUST_SALESMANID_FN (assuming that these were granted before) of the table CUSTOMER (database ACME):

```
SQL> REVOKE INSERT,
            DELETE,
            UPDATE (cust_paytermsid_fn, cust_salesmanid_fn)
     ON CUSTOMER
     FROM PUBLIC;
Revoke succeeded.
```

All dependent objects (for example, views created by the user who lost his/her privilege for the underlying table) related to the revoked privilege become invalid.

If there were no privileges granted on the object, Oracle neither takes any action nor returns an error.

The CASCADE CONSTRAINTS clause is relevant only if you revoke the REFERENCES privilege, or ALL. It gets rid of all the referential integrity constraints that were defined by the user using this privilege.

Specifying FORCE when revoking the EXECUTE object privilege causes the privileges to be dropped. Even if it leaves user-defined type objects behind, all dependent objects are invalidated.

Unlike system privileges, revoking object privileges in Oracle has a cascading effect. Say a privilege is granted to user1 via the WITH GRANT option, and user1, in turn, grants the privilege to user2. If the privilege is subsequently revoked from user1, user2 loses this privilege the very moment the user1 loses it.

As with system privileges in **IBM DB2 UDB**, its object-level privileges are revoked with a syntax similar to that of a GRANT statement. DB2 UDB does not support revoking GRANT OPTION nor the CASCADE | RESTRICT clause. For example:

```
REVOKE ALL [PRIVILEGES] | <privilege,...>
ON <object> <object_name>
FROM USER <user> | GROUP <group> | PUBLIC
```

The following example revokes a privilege to reference a table (create a foreign key based on the table's column) to PUBLIC (all users):

```
REVOKE REFERENCES
ON TABLE customer (cust_paytermsid_fn)
FROM PUBLIC

DB0000I The SQL command completed successfully
```

Again, if neither USER nor GROUP is specified, DB2 UDB will look up the information in the system catalog and raise an error if the user from whom the privilege is revoked is authenticated by an external DCE (see OS security integration later in this chapter).

There all rules to follow when revoking a privilege that was used to create a dependent object. For example, the SELECT privilege for a table passed onto a view would be revoked for the user when s/he loses this privilege; the user would be unable to select from the view just as s/he would not be able to select from the table.

Revoking an object-level privilege might not necessarily revoke the ability to perform the action if the user has some higher authority, or belongs to a group that holds the revoked privilege.

The **Microsoft SQL Server 2000** supports revoking GRANT OPTION and the CASCADE clause (but not RESTRICT). The following REVOKE statement is applicable to the context of the current database only:

```
REVOKE [GRANT OPTION FOR]
ALL [PRIVILEGES] | <permission>,...
[(<column,...>)] ON [<table> | <view>] |
ON [<table> | <view>] [(<column>,...)] |
ON [<stored_procedure> | <extended_procedure>] |
ON [<user_defined_function>]
FROM <security_account>,...
[CASCADE]
[AS <group> | <role>]
```

Privileges cannot be revoked from system-fixed roles. When permissions are revoked from a Windows NT group, the security account argument should be in the format BUILTIN\<domain>, where domain represents either a computer name or a domain where this user is defined.

You must have sufficient authority to revoke privileges; members of the SYSADMIN fixed-server role, DB_OWNER, and DB_SECURITYADMIN are granted REVOKE privilege by default, within their corresponding scope.

To revoke, for example, SELECT permission on the table PRODUCT in the ACME database, the following statement would be issued:

```
REVOKE SELECT
ON product
FROM PUBLIC

The command(s) completed successfully.
```

If the privilege was initially granted WITH GRANT OPTION, both GRANT OPTION FOR and CASCADE must be specified. If the CASCADE option is not specified (default), the user who was granted the privilege through the security account, from which this privilege was revoked, does not lose the privilege.

Managing Security with Roles

ROLE is an abstract concept introduced in the relational databases to facilitate user management tasks by grouping users' privileges according to some criteria, usually a job function. If, for example, your accounting staff of 100 people needs privileges for the dozens of objects they access daily—in addition to some system-level privileges—you have two choices: go through each and every user and individually grant him/her all the privileges required; or create a group (role), such as ACCOUNTANTS, grant all the privileges to the role, and thus grant this role to all the users in the group. Revoking the privileges would pose the same choices. It seems fairly obvious which choice is better.

Some RDBMS provide roles-creating capabilities, in addition to having a number of predefined system roles that could be granted to a user. Oracle 9*i* and the Microsoft SQL Server 2000 have this feature, while DB2 UDB employs only fixed, predefined roles (authorities).

The **Oracle 9*i*** roles are collections of privileges that could be granted to (or revoked from) a user or another role, thus providing a hierarchy of privileges. A role must be enabled (with a SET ROLE statement or by the database administrator) before it can pass on all the privileges granted to it.

Oracle 9*i* has a number of predefined roles through which privileges are granted to users. Table 12-8 shows these with short descriptions.

You neither can add new privileges to a predefined role, nor can you revoke any from the role.

Table 12-8
Oracle 9*i* Predefined Roles

Predefined Role	*Description*
CONNECT RESOURCE DBA	Provided for compatibility with the previous versions of Oracle; it is explicitly stated that these roles might not be supported in the future releases. There are a number of privileges associated with each of these roles in Oracle 9*i*. The DBA role, for example, has 124 privileges; RESOURCE and CONNECT have 8 each. Some of these have overlapping privileges—like CREATE TABLE or CREATE VIEW—and some of them are unique. Refer to the DBA_SYS_PRIVS dictionary view for the full list of privileges and their descriptions.
DELETE_CATALOG_ROLE EXECUTE_CATALOG_ROLE SELECT_CATALOG_ROLE	Provided for users who need to access data dictionary views.
EXP_FULL_DATABASE IMP_FULL_DATABASE	Provided for users who need to perform full database export.
AQ_USER_ROLE AQ_ADMINISTRATOR_ROLE	Needed for Oracle's advanced queuing functionality.
SNMPAGENT	Used by Enterprise Manager/Intelligent Agent.
RECOVERY_CATALOG_OWNER	Needed for a user who owns a recovery catalog.
HS_ADMIN_ROLE	Provided to grant access to the DBMS_HS package, which is required for heterogeneous services administration.

The following Oracle syntax, which creates a custom role, is straightforward:

```
CREATE ROLE <role name>
[IDENTIFIED {BY <password> |
             EXTERNALLY |
             GLOBALLY |
             USING [<schema>].[<package>]
            }
];
```

Only the role name is a required argument for this statement, the rest is optional. If the role is to have its own password, then the IDENTIFIED clause must be used. The NOT IDENTIFIED clause indicates that no password is required to enable it.

SQL Server 2000 DENY Statement

The Microsoft-specific DENY statement adds an additional level of granularity to the system of privileges not found in Oracle or DB2 UDB. The SQL92/99 standard does not define such a statement.

If you are using roles to assign a set of privileges to a user, you might find yourself in a situation when this set should be modified for one and only one user, while preserving it for all other users to whom this role was granted. Attempting to revoke a privilege from the user that was granted through a role will result in an error. You could create another role and grant a subset of privileges from the first role and then grant it to a user; or you could grant these privileges to the user directly, bypassing the role. Any of these, while workable, would lead to redundancy and possible confusion. The DENY statement provides an elegant solution to the problem. It allows you to grant a role with a full set of privileges and then deny some of these privileges to a user.

The following DENY statement works both for system-level and object-level privileges, with the syntax very similar to that of GRANT and REVOKE statements:

```
DENY ALL [PRIVILEGES] | <permission>,...
[(<column>)] ON [<table> | <view>] |
ON [<table> | <view>] [(<column>,...)] |
ON [<stored_procedure> | <extended_procedure>] |
ON [<user_defined_function>]
TO <security_account>,...
[CASCADE]
```

The CASCADE clause means that a privilege (permission) denied to the security_account will also be denied to every other user/role/group to that has this security_account permission.

For example, you have a role SALES that has all the privileges in the database, and a user NEW_USER needs all of these, except for CREATE TABLE. The following statements take care of granting the appropriate privileges to the user:

```
GRANT sales TO new_user
GO
DENY CREATE TABLE TO new_user
GO
```

The DENY statement always takes precedence, so while having the inherited privileges of the SALES role, the user NEW_USER will get an error if s/he ever attempts to create a table, though other members granted SALES role will have no problems doing so.

For identified users, the IDENTIFIED BY <password> clause actually creates a local user with this password if none previously existed; a password needs to be specified when enabling the role. The USING [<schema>].[<package>] clause creates an application role (compared to that in the MS SQL Server), which means that the role can be enabled by that specific application using authorized package.

Package in Oracle RDBMS is a collection of pre-compiled routines (usually written in PL/SQL), and residing in RDBMS itself. A user could access database functionality through procedures and functions defined in the package.

Using the EXTERNALLY clause creates an external user (see OS Security integration sidebar later in the chapter), and the GLOBALLY clause creates a global user, authorized by the enterprise directory service.

Here is an example of a role created for the ACME database with a minimal set of default options:

```
CREATE ROLE sales_force;

Role created.
```

Now you can grant privileges to this role (see GRANT statement paragraph earlier in this chapter for more information), and later grant the privileges to everyone who needs them by assigning those people to the sales_force role.

You can enable or disable ROLE for the duration of the current database session using the SET ROLE statement. There might be a limit to the number of concurrent roles that can be set by the database administrator.

A custom role can be altered or dropped by using, respectively, the ALTER ROLE or DROP ROLE statements.

Any user that accesses the **IBM DB2 UDB** database must have a valid OS account. Once authenticated, the user's access to the database's objects is governed by a system of authorities (roles) and privileges inside the RDBMS. DB2 does not support user-defined roles. Instead it relies on the system's predefined authorities (roles), which a user can be a member of, and on GROUP, which behave almost the same as roles that are employed in Oracle or the MS SQL Server 2000.

System authorities (roles) include system administration (SYSADM), system control (SYSCTRL), system maintenance (SYSMAINT), and database administration (DBADM), listed in Table 12-9. Each of these roles implies certain privileges; certain types of privileges are automatically granted to every user authenticated by the OS.

A privilege in DB2 UDB is defined as permission for the authenticated user to access and use database resources such as tables, views, and stored procedures, which will be discussed in greater detail later in the chapter.

Most of IBM DB2 UDB privileges — both on system and object levels — granted to the authorities (Table 12-9) are listed in Table 12-6.

Table 12-9
IBM DB2 UDB System Authorities

System Authority	*Description*
SYSADM	System administration, which includes all the privileges of all other system authorities as well as the ability to grant and revoke DBADM authority.
SYSCTRL	System control, which includes privileges to create, update, or drop a database. It does not allow direct access to the data.
SYSMAINT	System Maintenance, which enables database maintenance tasks in all databases associated with an instance, including the authority to modify configure files, and backup and restore databases.
DBADM	Database administration, which has all the privileges within a single database.

Some privileges for the database objects are not relevant for all discussed RDBMS. For example, the PACKAGE object can be found in the DB2 UDB or Oracle database, but is nonexistent in the MS SQL Server.

The highest authority level belongs to SYSADM, which has full control over all database objects, as well as the DB2 UDB installation that contains this database. It defaults to the Administrators Group on Windows NT/2000/XP; on Unix the initial value is NULL and defaults to the primary group of the database instance owner.

The SYSCTRL and SYSMAINT roles represent a lower level of hierarchy, followed by DBADM. Users that do not belong to any of these roles are granted privileges on an object-by-object basis. A new group can be created by DBADM, and privileges could then be granted to this group and to users in this group. This is a handy way to administer privileges for a number of users with similar responsibilities within the database, and is similar in functionality to the roles in Oracle and the Microsoft SQL Server.

For the syntax of granting system authorities, refer to the GRANT statement section of this chapter.

On the authentication level, the **MS SQL Server 2000** offers two choices: Windows OS authentication and mixed authentication modes. The first is usually rated as the better security provider, because it relies on the more robust security mechanisms of the operating system, and — for accessing the database over the network — it does not require sending login information unprotected. The second offers a more "personal approach" that allows many users to connect to the same SQL Server without needing to be added to the Windows users group. Microsoft defines a special system administrator user — usually *sa,* which is the default — who is responsible for all administrative tasks within the MS SQL Server 2000.

The SQL Server 2000 is tightly integrated with Windows OS: no matter what authentication mode you choose during installation, Windows authentication mode would always allow you to log on.

Authorization is performed by the SQL Server itself. All information about the user's granted permissions is recorded in the server's system tables (partially accessible through INFORMATION_SCHEMA views). Like IBM DB2 UDB and Oracle, the Microsoft SQL Server enforces security through a hierarchical system of users implemented via *fixed roles* and *application roles* (the concept of a role is explained at the beginning of this chapter).

OS Security Integration

It is important to remember that the operating system (OS) was there before the first computer database was invented, and no RDBMS could operate without some kind of OS. Each operating system comes with its own security mechanisms. All the RDBMS discussed in this book — to a certain extent — provide security integration with the OS they are running on. Essentially, it boils down to using operating system accounts and privileges to access the database, instead of relying on the RDBMS itself.

The Microsoft SQL Server 2000, for example, has tight OS-integrated security, which allows users with a valid Windows account to be authenticated based on their Windows NT/2000/XP credentials. Instead of supplying user ID and password, the user is able to access the SQL Server 2000 automatically as soon as s/he logs onto the machine that runs RDBMS.

Both Oracle 9*i* and IBM DB2 UDB extend this functionality to multiple operating systems, and the details of implementation and usage are just as different as the systems they integrate with.

DB2 UDB uses an external facility for user authentication — either the operating system, or a so-called *distributed computing environment* (DCE) facility. A user must have a valid OS account — login and user ID — in order to access the database.

For regular users to be authenticated externally, an Oracle database administrator must create a user account prefixed with a character value from the Oracle initialization parameter OS_AUTHENT_PREFIX and marked as AUTHENTICATED EXTERNALLY. Oracle uses the value of the parameter OS_AUTHENT_PREFIX to check whether any of the users' names created within the database are prefixed with this value if a user name does not have this prefix, it will not be allowed to be authenticated externally. This is only a brief description of the basic mechanism implemented by Oracle, refer to the vendor's documentation for more information on this issue.

For EXTERNALLY authenticated users that intend to administer a database, Oracle 9*i* requires that two predefined OSDBA and OSOPER groups be created on the machine that is running the operating system, and make these users members of one of these groups. In addition, the Oracle start-up parameter REMOTE_LOGIN_PASSWORDFILE has to be set to one of its valid values.

RDBMS running on some operating systems (notably, Windows 9x) do not have OS security integration, as the OS itself does not provide facilities for this.

Fixed server roles provide a server-wide scope hierarchy where each role is allowed to perform certain activities, SYSADMIN being on the top, and having privileges to perform any activity. These roles are listed in Table 12-10.

A fixed role cannot be altered, and new fixed server roles cannot be created. You may add new members to a role, or remove members from the role using SQL Server system-stored procedures, or through graphical user interface (GUI).

Table 12-10
Microsoft SQL Server Fixed Server Roles

Fixed Server Role	*Actions Allowed*
SYSADMIN	Can perform any activity within the SQL Server (this is the highest privileges level).
SERVERADMIN	Able to startup/shutdown server, as well as modify server's configuration.
SETUPADMIN	Able to manage linked servers and modify startup procedures.
SECURITYADMIN	Manages logins, passwords, and permissions; is allowed to read error logs.
PROCESSADMIN	Allowed to manage the SQL Server's processes.
DBCREATOR	Has permissions to create, alter, and drop databases.
DISKADMIN	Allowed to manage SQL Server disk files.
BULKADMIN	Allowed to perform BULK INSERT operations.

The next level in the SQL Server 2000's security hierarchy is *fixed database roles*, shown in Table 12-11. Each database defined within an SQL Server instance has a set of predefined (fixed) database roles to which any of the database users (logins) can be added. The scope of these roles is much more limited — they are confined to the database within which they are declared. As with the fixed server roles, no permissions can be altered for these roles, but new database roles can be created (unlike fixed server roles).

Application roles are unique to the SQL Server 2000 (and Oracle 9*i* with some specifics). They are activated only by the application that accesses RDBMS; there are no predefined application roles. In a way, they just provide another method to manage group permissions — if users always connect to the database server through some accounting program, the SQL Server DBA can create a role for that accounting program and assign all the privileges it needs for normal functioning. When the SQL Server receives a request from the accounting program, it activates the role for this application — no sooner, no later. If the application is phased out and replaced by a new one, all the DBA must do to prevent access from the previous application is to drop an associated application role.

Table 12-11
Microsoft SQL Server Fixed Database Roles

Fixed Database Role	*Actions Allowed*
DB_OWNER	Members of this group have permissions to do anything—within the database scope.
DB_ACCESSADMIN	Members of this role can add or remove users from the database.
DB_SECURITYADMIN	Members of this role manage security: all the privileges, objects, roles, etc.
DB_DDLADMIN	Members of this role may issue any DDL statement, but cannot issue GRANT, REVOKE, or DENY statements.
DB_BACKUPOPERATOR	Members of this role may issue DBCC, CHECKPOINT, and BACKUP statements.
DB_DATAREADER	Members of this role are allowed to select all data from any user table in the database.
DB_DATAWRITER	Members of this role are allowed to modify any data in any user table in the database.
DB_DENYDATAREADER	Members of this role are *not* allowed to select any data from any user table in the database.
DB_DENYDATAWRITER	Members of this role are *not* allowed to modify any data in any user table in the database.

Application roles contain no members, and there are no predefined application roles. There is much more to application roles than described here. If you need to use them, refer to SQL Server (and Oracle) documentation.

The column level privileges are recorded in the system tables and can be viewed through the INFORMATION_SCHEMA view COLUMN_PRIVILEGES. The INFORMATION_SCHEMA views are covered in detail in Chapter 13.

As with other RDBMS, permissions (privileges) can be assigned at the object level, for example, in a table or stored procedure—all the way down to a column. A column is the smallest object for which a user may have privilege. In addition to object granularity, privileges can be differentiated by type—EXECUTE privilege, SELECT privilege, DELETE privilege, and so on, in any combination. The privileges—both on system and object levels—are discussed earlier in this chapter.

The SQL Server does not have the CREATE ROLE statement; it employs system-stored procedures instead. The list of some relevant procedures is given in Table 12-12.

Table 12-12
Selected Microsoft SQL Server 2000 Role Management System-Stored Procedures

`sp_addrole <role name>, [<role owner>]`	Creates a new role in the current database.
`sp_droprole <role name>`	Removes a role from the current database.
`sp_addapprole <role name>, <password>`	Creates a new application role in the current database.
`sp_setapprole <role name>, [<password>], [<encryption>]`	Activates the permissions associated with an application role in the current database.
`sp_dropapprole <role name>`	Removes an application role from the current database.
`sp_addrolemember <role name>, <user name>`	Adds a member to an existing database role.
`sp_droprolemember <role name>, <user name>`	Removes a member from the existing role.
`sp_addsrvrolemember <role name>, <user name>`	Adds a member to an existing fixed server role.
`sp_dropsrvrolemember <role name>, <user name>`	Removes a member from the fixed server role.

Microsoft provides a number of `sp_` help system-stored procedures to obtain information on roles — either fixed or user-defined.

Using Views for Security

One of the mechanisms that can be used to implement security is SQL views, (discussed in Chapter 4). Using views, it is possible to restrict data accessible to a user, the type of operations the user can perform through the views, or both.

Consider the following DDL SQL statement, which is generic enough to be acceptable in all three major RDBMS implementations:

```
CREATE VIEW v_customer_status
(
  name,
  status
)
```

```
AS
SELECT cust_name_s,
       cust_status_s
FROM   customer
```

This view selects only two fields from the table CUSTOMER, which has a total of seven fields. This is called vertical restriction, as it restricts access to the subset of columns (fields). The other fields might contain confidential information that should be accessible only to upper management. If you grant SELECT privilege to the view to some role (for example, ROLE "staff"), then everyone who belongs to that role would be able to see customers' names and statuses, while the rest of the information that the table contains remains inaccessible to them.

If the SELECT statement from the view V_CUSTOMER_STATUS is executed by an authorized person, it will produce the following results (but the same statement issued by a person who was not granted privileges to the view would generate an error):

```
SELECT *
FROM v_customer_status

name                                                 status
---------------------------------------------------- ------
WILE SEAL CORP.                                      Y
MAGNETICS USA INC.                                   Y
MAGNETOMETRIC DEVICES INC.                           Y
. . . . . . . . . . .
CHGO SWITCHBOARD INC.                                N
```

You can also restrict the access horizontally — by specifying a subset of rows. For example, you may want to grant access to the historical data, something that was entered into the table a year ago or earlier, and prevent access to data added after that date; or — using the example from the ACME database — say you have a sales force that is split in two groups according to responsibility and experience level (one group has salespersons that deal with clients whose orders total above 15,000, and the other group handles customers generating less volume). For the latter example, the SQL syntax for all three databases would be as follows:

```
CREATE VIEW v_customer_totals_over_15000
AS
SELECT *
FROM   v_customer_totals
WHERE  total_price > 15000
```

Selecting from the following view will bring up only the records for the customers whose total is over 15000:

```
SELECT *
FROM   v_customer_totals_over_15000

customer_name          order_number    total_price
---------------------- --------------- ------------------
WILE ELECTRONICS INC.  523735          15613.60
WILE BESS COMPANY      523741          15464.10
. . . . . . . . .               . . .
WILE SEAL CORP.        523775          15613.60
WILE SEAL CORP.        523781          15464.10
```

The view V_CUSTOMER_TOTALS_OVER_15000 is built upon another view, V_CUSTOMER_TOTALS, and different privileges can be assigned for each of these objects. Using this method, one can build a sophisticated, fine-grained security hierarchy.

Of course, both horizontal and vertical selection could be combined into a single view.

Views also can limit displayed data to summary information, like in V_CUSTOMER_TOTALS, where information about sales is summed up while being grouped by order number (see Appendix B for the SQL statements that create this view).

Additional restrictions that can be implemented in views include WHERE clauses and JOIN conditions. These are useful when more than one table is involved in a view. For example, you can restrict your view to show only customers that have placed an order and hide all others, as follows (syntax is valid for all three databases):

```
SELECT DISTINCT cust_name_s
FROM   customer cu
  JOIN
       order_header oh
  ON   cu.cust_id_n = oh.ordhdr_custid_fn

CUST_NAME_S
--------------------------------------------------
WILE BESS COMPANY
WILE ELECTROMATIC INC.
WILE ELECTROMUSICAL INC.
. . . .
WILE ELECTRONICS INC.
WILE SEAL CORP.
```

Views are used not only for SELECT but also for UPDATE, INSERT, and DELETE statements. Some of these operations are governed by the inherent properties of a view object, and some can be specified when the view object is created. For example, you cannot update or insert views that were created using aggregate functions — attempting to do so would generate an error. This is an inherent behavior. On the other hand, for an updateable view you could create a constraint, which could accept or reject data modifications based on some criteria. There is more about constraints in the next section.

Using Constraints for Security

Constraints often are used to maintain integrity, be it referential, data integrity (also called *entity* integrity), or domain integrity (discussed in greater detail in Chapter 4). Here we will discuss the use of constraints from a security point of view only.

While all CONSTRAINT examples are given as ALTER TABLE, they also may be created in the CREATE TABLE syntax.

Domain integrity constraints, like the CHECK constraint or the DEFAULT constraint, validate data for correct format and content. For example, in the ACME database the CHK_ADDR_TYPE constraint that follows validates an address as being either a 'SHIPPING' or 'BILLING' type of address:

```
ALTER TABLE address
ADD CONSTRAINT chk_addr_type
CHECK (addr_type_s = 'SHIPPING' OR addr_type_s = 'BILLING')
```

Now any attempt — legitimate or otherwise — to enter invalid data, for example, 'HOME' address type, would generate an error; your data is protected against inconsistency. Validating data before it is committed to the database table is a very efficient security layer.

If the constraint you've trying to add is already in the database, the above example would generate an error. To run the example you might need to drop the constraint.

Another mechanism for enforcing domain integrity is the DEFAULT constraint. When specified, this constraint guarantees that if any data was omitted from the query, a default value will be used instead of blank space or NULL. In the following example (valid for Microsoft SQL Server only, as Oracle 9*i* and IBM DB2 UDB do not consider it a constraint; see Chapter 4 for more information on constraints), the DEFAULT constraint DF_CUSTOMER_CUST_S assigns the default value of 'Y' in every insert statement that does not supply this value:

```
ALTER TABLE customer
ADD CONSTRAINT df_customer_cust_s
DEFAULT ('Y')
FOR cust_status_s
```

It is open for discussion whether DEFAULT represents a security breach or a security enforcement mechanism. On the one hand, it prevents data inconsistency, which is a good thing; on the other, it requires less precision on the data entry end — by preventing omission/sloppiness errors — and less effort for a malicious intruder to insert data.

Entity integrity, which essentially refers to a row of data, is maintained with indices and constraints like the PRIMARY KEY constraint or the UNIQUE constraint. It effectively prevents users from entering duplicate values. Putting these constraints on the Social Security Number (SSN) column would prevent miscreants from applying for a job using stolen SSN cards.

Referential integrity maintains healthy relationships between the tables for which it is declared. It mandates that there cannot be a record in the child table if a corresponding record in the parent table is missing, or that a record in the parent table cannot be deleted as long as it has a corresponding record in the child table. Here is an example using the table ADDRESS from the ACME database. The FOREIGN KEY constraint mandates that there will be no record in the ADDRESS database unless it refers to a valid customer in the CUSTOMER table; the field ADDR_CUSTID_FN from the ADDRESS table is referencing the primary key field CUST_ID_N of the CUSTOMER table:

```
ALTER TABLE address
ADD CONSTRAINT fk_addr_cust
FOREIGN KEY(addr_custid_fn)
REFERENCES customer(cust_id_n)
```

Constraints by themselves cater to a very narrow segment of database security and should be considered supplemental to the more robust mechanisms provided by the overall RDBMS security.

Using Stored Procedures and Triggers for Security

Stored procedures and triggers allow for a very finely grained object-level security. Both are compiled modules implemented in some procedural language and stored inside the RDBMS server.

The idea behind using stored procedures for security is to encapsulate certain business logic inside persistent modules that are stored server-side, and restrict a user's database communication to the use of these procedures only. For example, you can implement a set of stored procedures in such a way that every SELECT, UPDATE, and DELETE would go through the stored procedures. Users could be granted these privileges only through stored procedures and denied direct access to the tables that these stored procedures are based upon. Inside your stored procedures you can implement business security rules that govern the way data is inserted, queried, updated, or deleted. You can even use stored procedures for creating database objects (though there might be some implementation-specific restrictions).

The facilities provided by standard vanilla SQL to implement sophisticated business logic are not adequate. While SQL92 and SQL99 both specify persistent server-side modules, their implementation details developed by the various database vendors are far from being standardized — both in syntax and language. Oracle uses its own PL/SQL procedural extension for the SQL, the Microsoft SQL Server 2000 uses its own Transact-SQL dialect, and IBM uses its own IBM SQL.

Oracle and IBM also allow for using Java for to create stored procedures, and the MS SQL Server 2000 sponsors DTS (Data Transformation Services) that, while not being a stored procedure equivalent, could be used to access and transform data through VBScript and ActiveX objects.

Procedural extensions (as well as Java Programming Language) are beyond the scope of this book, which provides only very basic examples on how they can be used for security purposes.

Here is a simple procedure that handles insert into the CUSTOMER table of the ACME database.

This example assumes existence of the table DELINQUENT_CUSTOMER, which collects information about former customers that were dropped due to nonpayment; the actual ACME database does not contain such a table.

In MS SQL Server syntax, this stored procedure might be implemented as follows:

```
CREATE PROCEDURE sp_cust_insert
    @cust_id    INT,
    @cust_paytermsid  INT,
    @cust_salesmanid  INT,
    @cust_status  VARCHAR(1),
    @cust_name VARCHAR(50),
    @cust_alias  VARCHAR(15),
    @cust_credhold  VARCHAR(1)
AS
   IF NOT EXISTS(
SELECT
```

```
    cust_id_n
FROM delinquent_customer
WHERE cust_name_s = @cust_name)

INSERT INTO customer
(
    cust_id_n,
    cust_paytermsid_fn,
    cust_salesmanid_fn,
    cust_status_s,
    cust_name_s,
    cust_alias_s,
    cust_credhold_s
)
VALUES
(
    @cust_id,
    @cust_paytermsid,
    @cust_salesmanid,
    @cust_status,
    @cust_name,
    @cust_alias,
    @cust_credhold
)
ELSE
  RAISERROR ('Delinquent customer',19,2)
```

What is actually happening here is that the application that calls this stored procedure (`sp_cust_insert`) passes seven parameters to it, one of the parameters being *new customer's name*. Before inserting the data into the table `CUSTOMER`, the procedure checks whether this customer is not already on the delinquent customer list. It allows the record to be added only if no such customer exists there; otherwise, it produces an error and passes it back to the calling application with a description of the error and the severity of it.

This procedure uses Transact-SQL language (which is generally out of scope of this book). The syntax in the sample code was made as simple as possible, and kept to a bare minimum. The syntax for the Oracle RDBMS and IBM DB2 UDB would be quite different, though the idea would be the same.

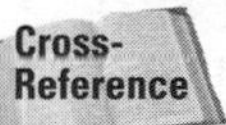

Stored procedures, user functions, and triggers are discussed in Chapter 14.

The same functionality can be implemented as a trigger. A trigger is a special kind of stored procedure that executes automatically, in response to a certain event. In the previous example, the event is the `INSERT` statement executed against the `CUSTOMER` table. You could set up a trigger to fire (execute) whenever an application tries to insert, update, or delete data from the table.

The ACME database has an example of using a trigger for security-related auditing purposes – it fires whenever an update takes place and records data about the user who made the changes.

Data encryption

Encryption is a method to convert information from a human readable format into a format that is unreadable by humans. The encrypted data normally can be decrypted using the same process (algorithm) that was used to encrypt it. Encryption is *not* a part of the SQL standard; therefore each vendor provides different encryption-related services.

The data inside the RDBMS is stored as plain text(ASCII, Unicode), or binary (`BLOBS`, `IMAGE`, and similar data types). To prevent this data from being viewed by unauthorized users (who happen to be granted access to the table that contains it), or to send a data extract over an unsecured network, the data could be encrypted. The data also could be encrypted via some client software before it is entered into the database, or it could be done inside the RDBMS using its own facilities.

This provides an additional level of security, when in order to view data in human readable format — be it text or pictures, audio files, or executable files — a user would need a password and decrypting facilities, either on RDBMS or inside his/her client software.

While maintaining high security for authentication, user access, public key infrastructure, and so on, **Oracle 9*i*** does not provide much of the user-accessible encryption functionality within the database itself, but it compensates with add-on products. The only things you can encrypt using the RDBMS-supplied functionality are the PL/SQL code contained in Oracle's package specifications and package bodies, and stand-alone procedures and functions using the utility *wrap.exe* (found in directory `$ORACLE_HOME/bin` on Unix, and `\Oracle9\bin` on Windows machines). Oracle 9*i* also provides an obfuscation package (`DBMS_OBFUSCATION_TOOLKIT`), which provides a means to hide the source code and data from prying eyes by converting the code into ASCII gibberish. It uses the DES implementation algorithm. Obfuscation differs from encryption by being more secure and not limited to a range of human readable characters.

IBM DB2 UDB 8.1 provides several functions for data encryption (listed in Table 12-13). For example, this query returns product brand from the ACME database table `PRODUCT`:

```
SELECT prod_brand_s
FROM   product

PROD_BRAND_S
----------------
SPRUCE LUMBER
STEEL NAILS
```

To produce encrypted data—for example, a list of brands from the PRODUCT table (to be sent to a branch over an unsecured network)—in IBM DB2 UDB, the following SQL statement could be used:

```
SELECT ENCRYPT(prod_brand_s, 'PASSWORD') encrypted
FROM   product

ENCRYPTED
-----------------------------------------------
x'00E61AFFE404A6D596757C7CC7AC70467884E127B6A50726'
x'00DC24FFE404A0D5F736C8A4156922A6709DD5D609EBE762'
```

To decrypt the above seemingly senseless string of characters, use the DECRYPT_CHAR function (since we are using character data), with exactly the same password, to restore the data into its original form. Numeric data cannot be encrypted with this function directly (you can also encrypt binary or character representation of numbers).

Table 12-13
IBM DB2 UDB Encryption Functions

Function	*Description*
ENCRYPT (<data to encrypt>, <password>, <hint>)	Encrypts CHAR or VARCHAR data (up to 32633 bytes long) using a password—CHAR or VARCHAR string (at least 6 bytes, no more than 127 bytes long). A HINT (CHAR or VARCHAR, up to 32 bytes long) is an optional parameter; if used, it provides capability to recall a password using a hint expression via the GETHINT function.
DECRYPT_BIN (<encrypted data>, <password>)	Decrypts binary data (BLOB,CLOB, etc.) encrypted with ENCRYPT function.
DECRYPT_CHAR (<encrypted data>, <password>)	Decrypts character data encrypted with ENCRYPT function.
GETHINT (<encrypted data>)	This function returns a hint for the encrypted data, if such a hint was found. Hopefully, the user could recall the password using the hint.

The **Microsoft SQL Server 2000** allows you to encrypt (or encrypt by default) the following:

- ✦ Login and application role passwords (stored server-side)
- ✦ Stored procedure body (the actual implementation code)
- ✦ User-defined functions body (the actual implementation code)
- ✦ View definitions (the actual SQL statements)
- ✦ Triggers (the actual implementation code)
- ✦ Rules and defaults definitions
- ✦ Data packets sent between the SQL Server and the client application

Logins and passwords are stored in MS SQL Server 2000 system tables and are always encrypted. The algorithm used for this is proprietary, and passwords cannot be viewed directly (unless NULL is used as a password).

When a stored procedure, function, view, or trigger is compiled and saved in the SQL Server, the creator has an option to encrypt the actual implementation code to prevent it from being viewed by other users or third parties who have access to the database system objects. The encryption option is in the CREATE statement. For example, to encrypt one of the ACME database views inside the MS SQL Server 2000, you would use the following statement:

```
CREATE VIEW v_customer_status
(
  name,
  status
)
WITH ENCRYPTION
AS
SELECT cust_name_s,
       cust_status_s
FROM   customer
```

The WITH ENCRYPTION option saves the actual Transact-SQL code inside the SYSCOMMENTS system table in encrypted form rather than in standard plain text. There is a catch to encrypting SQL Server objects — once encrypted, the object cannot be modified; if you need to do so, you would have to drop the object and recreate it.

Note

There are literally hundreds of data encryption algorithms – both custom and public. To devise and implement an encryption algorithm requires familiarity with programming principles – in addition to advanced math. Here are some popular algorithms in use today: DES (designed by IBM in 1970, adopted by NIST in 1976 for unclassified data), RC5 (from RSA Data Security), CMEA (developed by the Telecommunication Industry Association to encrypt digital cellular phone data), FEAL (developed by Nippon Telephone & Telegraph), TEA, MD5, Tiger, and CAST—to name just a few.

The data sent between the SQL Server 2000 and a client application can be encrypted using Secure Socket Layer (SSL) encryption if TCP/IP is chosen as a communication protocol—which is usually the case for most networks and Internet connections. When multiprotocol is employed, an application must specifically call the Windows RPC encryption API (application programming interface). The actual strength of such an encryption (the length of the encryption key) depends on the version of the Windows OS where the software is installed.

SSL (Secure Socket Layer) is a protocol initially developed by Netscape Communications to secure the transfer of documents over the Internet. It uses so-called *public key* encryption data. By convention, the SSL connection Internet link starts with the prefix https:// as opposed the standard http:// (Hypertext Transfer Protocol).

A very simple password-based data encryption can be implemented in Transact-SQL using the Microsoft SQL Server 2000 bitwise operator `XOR` (logical, exclusive `OR`). This type of encryption is very easy to implement—and break.

How XOR Encryption Works

`XOR` encryption uses a key (password) to encrypt the text. Each letter in the computer world is represented by a specific ASCII/Unicode or ECBCD number. When encrypting data with a key, each character of the data is `XOR`ed with a corresponding character of the key; reversing the operation restores the original data.

The `XOR` operation follows rules of Boolean logic:

```
0 XOR 0 = 0
0 XOR 1 = 1
1 XOR 1 = 0
1 XOR 0 = 1
```

The operation applies to one bit at the time. For more a detailed introduction of Boolean algebra, refer to Appendix L.

Here is an example of encrypting string `ABC` with a password `B`. In the ASCII codes table these letters are assigned codes `65`, `66`, and `67`, respectively. In binary notation they would look like this:

```
A   1000001(ASCII 65)
B   1000010(ASCII 66)
C   1000011(ASCII 67)
```

Continued

Continued

The result of XORing these with B (binary 1000010), bit by bit, would look as follows:

	A	**B**	**C**
Characters to encrypt	1000001	1000010	1000011
Password 'B'	1000010	1000010	1000010
Results of the XOR operation	0000011	0000000	0000001
Result in binary format	ASCII (3)	ASCII (0)	ASCII (1)

The result of the XOR operation gives three nonprintable characters, which could be converted into their previous form using the same operation (XOR) and password (1000010) – shown in bold.

	ASCII (3)	***ASCII (0)***	***ASCII (1)***
Encrypted characters	0000011	0000000	0000001
Password 'B'	1000010	1000010	1000010
Result in binary format	1000001	1000010	1000011

The corresponding SQL statement in the SQL Server 2000 is:

```
SELECT
 65 ^ 66 'a_XOR_b'
,66 ^ 66 'b_XOR_b'
,67 ^ 66 'c_XOR_b'

a_XOR_b     b_XOR_b     c_XOR_b
----------- ----------- -----------
3           0           1

(1 row(s) affected)
```

The result gives a string of ASCII codes, which represent nonprintable characters(since ASCII codes for 3, 0, and 1 are End of Text, NULL, and Start Of Heading, respectively). For passwords longer than one character, you may apply XOR to the consecutive letters in the password with that of the data.

Database Auditing

Auditing provides the ability to trace the information flow inside a database, including connection attempts, data updates, deletes, inserts and selects, execute functionality, and such. It is useful both for postmortem scenarios and for on-going monitoring to prevent unauthorized activity.

Auditing has nothing to do with the SQL standard, and is strictly vendor-dependent — in capabilities, implementation details, and so on. This paragraph gives a brief overview of the RDBMS auditing.

Oracle 9*i* allows you to choose between an operating system auditing trail, a database one, or both. The first option is, of course, operating system dependent, and would contain only such information that the OS is programmed to preserve. An audit trail generated by Windows will be much different from one generated on the Unix box, even if the Oracle database setup is the same.

The database auditing trail will be very much the same, no matter what OS Oracle is installed on; it also has an additional advantage of being able to produce audit reports using Oracle's built-in facilities. The auditing information (database statements, privileges, and so on) is stored in the `SYS.AUD$` catalog table, which is commonly referred to as *audit trail*, in Oracle. Essentially, you select for yourself the events you wish to monitor. A number of events in Oracle are audited by default: instance startup, instance shutdown, and attempts to connect to the database with administrative privileges. You may choose to specify custom auditing options to monitor other events happening within your Oracle installation, with the Oracle-specific `AUDIT` statement. Table 12-14 shows Oracle 9*i* audit levels.

Table 12-14
Oracle 9*i* Audit Levels

Level	*Action*
`STATEMENT`	Initiates auditing of some specific SQL statements. For example, the `AUDIT TABLE` command initiates audits for the `CREATE TABLE`, `TRUNCATE TABLE`, `COMMENT ON TABLE`, and `DELETE [FROM] TABLE` statements.
`PRIVILEGE`	Initiates auditing for the SQL statements created using special system privilege. For example, `AUDIT CREATE USER` will monitor all statements that are issued using this particular system privilege.
`OBJECT`	Initiates audit of the events pertaining to a particular object like `TABLE` or `VIEW`.

When setting the audit level, you also can specify some of the options that narrow the scope of the events you wish to monitor (see Table 12-15).

Table 12-15
Oracle 9*i* AUDIT Level Options

Option	*Description*
BY SESSION / BY ACCESS	The first option accumulates information on all the SQL statements issued for the duration of the session, the second causes Oracle to write one record for each access.
WHENEVER SUCCESSFUL	Records audit information only for statements that succeed.
WHENEVER NOT SUCCESSFUL	Records audit information only for statements that fail or generate in errors.

For example, to audit all failed attempts to perform various database operations, the following statement could be used:

```
AUDIT SELECT TABLE,
      INSERT TABLE,
      DELETE TABLE,
      EXECUTE PROCEDURE
BY ACCESS
WHENEVER NOT SUCCESSFUL;
```

Upon execution of this statement, Oracle begins to collect information on all failed attempts to perform operations listed in the audit clause. Refer to the Oracle 9*i* documentation for more detailed information on auditing capabilities of the RDBMS.

Keep in mind that the amount of accumulated information could easily exceed reasonable limits. Choose wisely what events you wish to monitor and for how long.

IBM DB2 UDB introduces the auditing facility db2audit to monitor database events, and log the collected information. The audit is performed at an instance level, and the user of this facility must have SYSADM authority. The audit trail is generated for a series of predefined events. There are several categories of events for which you may want to generate an audit trail; each of these events can be monitored for failure, success, or both. The categories are listed in Table 12-16.

Table 12-16
IBM DB2 UDB Events Categories Available for Audit

Category	*Description*
AUDIT	Generates a log record whenever auditing settings are changed.
CHECKING	Generates a log record when performing authorization checking.
OBJMAINT	Generates a log record when database objects are created or destroyed.
SECMAINT	Generates a log record when privileges and authorities are granted or revoked; also when security configuration parameters are changed.
SYSADMIN	Generates a log record when an operation requiring high-level authority is performed (e.g., STAERT_DB2, CREATE_DATABASE, etc.).
VALIDATE	Generates a log record when a user is being authenticated, or his/her security information is retrieved.
CONTEXT	Generates a log record of the operation context; it might help when analyzing other events' records. By its very nature, such a record could be very large and should be used with caution (e.g., CONNECT, BACKUP_DB etc.).

The collected information is written into a log file with a predefined structure. Each category of events generates its own file, and has its own structure. The file is a regular ASCII file, optimized for loading into a table; the files are not encrypted but are protected within the operating system's security framework. The loading is also done through the *db2audit* utility, using the *extract* parameter as the argument.

An audit facility runs from the command line and accepts a number of parameters (over 20). Here is a very simple example of the usage:

```
db2audit start checking both
```

This would start auditing all events that fall into the CHECKING category for both failure and succcss.

The audit facility is very complex, and even a brief explanation of its usage would require a chapter of its own; refer to IBM DB2 UDB documentation for more information.

The **Microsoft SQL Server 2000** provides an SQL Profiler tool that can be used for auditing, and, as you would expect in the Windows world, there is a visual interface. It is invoked from the Tools menu of the SQL Server Enterprise manager. However only members of the SYSADMIN security fixed role are allowed to enable it; for all other users, this option is not available.

The SQL Profiler provides a visual interface for auditing events. The events fall into several categories: user activity, database administrative activity, server events, and so on. Each category represents a collection of the events that could be selected separately—or all together. The event categories available for monitoring are shown in Table 12-17.

The information recorded contains date/time stamp, user ID, type of event, outcome (success/failure), the source (machine name, IP address), names of the objects accessed, and full text of the SQL statement. All this information is recorded in the auditing files, placed under operating system security protection.

Table 12-17
Microsoft SQL Server 2000 Event Categories

Event Category	*Description*
CURSOR	Events generated by cursor operations
DATABASE	Events generated by data and log files when an expansion/shrinkage occurs
ERRORS AND WARNINGS	Events generated by an exception that occurred within a process
LOCKS	Events generated by locks occurring during the operation
OBJECTS	Events generated by operations with objects as they are created, destroyed, opened, etc.
PERFORMANCE	Collection of events related to the DML (Data Manipulation Language) execution
SCANS	Events generated by the scan performed on a database object (like table or index)
SECURITY AUDIT	Events generated by security-related operations (like granting privilege, for example)
SESSIONS	Events generated by connecting and disconnecting to and from the SQL Server
STORED PROCEDURES	Events generated by executing stored procedures within SQL Server
TRANSACTIONS	Events produced by the execution of Microsoft Distributed Transaction Coordinator (MS DTC) transactions or by writing to the transaction log.
TSQL	Events generated by execution Transact SQL statements passed to the SQL Server instance from the client
USER CONFIGURABLE	Allows user to specify custom events

The SQL Server provides very fine-grained monitoring capabilities (for example, the amount of CPU time required for the event to occur) for each of the event categories. In addition, you can specify filters, stating, for example, that you would like to monitor the selected events only if they are generated by a specific application, ignoring all others.

The Microsoft SQL Server supports C2 audit requirements (see more information on C2-level security certification later in this chapter). To turn on the C2 auditing option, a member of the SYSADMIN fixed role must run the system-stored procedure sp_configure, and set the *c2 audit mode* option to 1:

```
EXEC sp_configure 'c2 audit mode','1'
```

To access the advanced *audit mode* option, run this script first:

```
EXEC sp_configure 'show advanced options', '0'
RECONFIGURE
```

Enabling this option turns on a security trace template that collects all information needed for the C2-level security audit, as specified by the security standard.

Security Standards

While not related directly to SQL, security standards define the infrastructure within which it is employed, and are therefore of interest to SQL users. Usually, RDBMS software complies with these standards to a certain degree — either voluntarily, or under pressure from the government agencies that mandate requirements for the software's acceptance.

The first nationwide attempt to standardize security procedures for computer systems was undertaken in 1985 by the U.S. National Computer Security Center (NCSC). To be considered for a government contract, the vendors had to achieve a certain level of security for their products through proctored testing. Dozens of vendors went through years (the process has taken three years, on average) of testing procedures just to be able to sell their products to government agencies. The vendors, like Sun, Oracle, and Novell, received their certifications (either C1 or B2) in early 1990s, following a directive that all computer systems storing sensitive information must be C2 certified.

International security standards

BS7799 and its international equivalent ISO 17799 are the most widely recognized security standards in the world. Their closest equivalent in the United States is the level B1 security.

ISO 17799 provides a detailed roadmap in several areas, and every company that seeks this standard's endorsement for its product must address all of these areas:

- **Business Continuity Planning.** Mandates procedures for continuing business activities in spite major failures or disasters.
- **System Access Control.** Focuses on controlling access to information, ensures protection of the networked services, detects and counteracts unauthorized activity, ensures information security for distributed mobile applications.
- **System Development and Maintenance.** Mandates that security be built-in (as opposed to external); deals with data loss prevention and data misuse, as well as with confidentiality, authenticity, and integrity of information
- **Physical and Environmental Security.** Deals with preventing unauthorized access, damage, and interference to top business premises and information, preventing loss, compromise, or theft of information and information processing facilities.
- **Compliance.** Avoids breaches of any criminal or civil law, statutory, regulatory, or contractual obligations; ensures compliance of every system in the organization with established organizational security policies and standards; minimizes interference of the audit process with business practices.
- **Personnel Security.** Reduces risks resulting from human error, theft, fraud, or misuse of facilities, minimizing damage in case such incidents occur; educates users about proper policy procedures.
- **Security Organization.** Manages information security within an organization; maintains security for the organization's facilities accessed by third parties, for example, when the responsibility for information protection has been outsourced to a third party.
- **Computer and Operation Management.** Deals with facility's operational policies, ensures safety of information in the networks and the supporting infrastructure, prevents loss, misuse, or unauthorized modification of data exchanged between organizations.
- **Assets Classification and Control.** Maintains protection of the corporate assets.
- **Policy.** Establishes and manages a viable security policy within an organization.

In spite of the detailed standards, the actual implementations of them might widely differ across the board. One reason for the differences is that there are so many standards; and, since the certification process can be very expensive, it is not a viable option for many businesses. Most banks in the United States, for example, do not use ISO standards, relying instead on SAS 70 auditing standards, while other companies prefer using use ISO 9000/2000 standards.

More information on information systems security can be accessed on one of these sites: `www.infosyssec.com`, `www.firstgov.gov`, `www.sas70.com`, and `http://csrc.nist.gov/`.

There are also emerging standards like the Common Criteria (CC) program. This program was started in 1996, initially by the United Kingdom, Germany, France, and the Netherlands with strong support from the National Information Assurance Partnership (NIAP). Since then 11 more countries have joined the program: Australia, New Zealand, Canada, Finland, Greece, Israel, Italy, Norway, Spain, and Sweden.

What Is C2 Security Level?

Class C2 is a security rating established by the U.S. National Computer Security Center (NCSC). It is granted to the products that pass Trusted Computer System Evaluation Criteria (TCSEC) tests (known as Orange Book) administered by the Department of Defense. This rating is an absolute security minimum required for a product to be considered for employment in government agencies and offices that accumulate and process sensitive secure information.

The TCSEC standards were established in 1985 and updated numerous times since then. According to TCSEC, system security is evaluated at one of four levels, ranging from class A1 to class D.

Class D is defined as *Minimum Security*; meaning essentially — "In God we trust."

Class C1 is defined as *Discretionary Security Protection*; systems evaluated at this level have to meet security requirements by controlling user access to data.

Class C2, defined as *Controlled Access Protection* complements class C1 by adding additional accountability features, such as login procedures, auditing capabilities to verify all users' actions (i.e., attempts to access, read, write, or delete any object), finely grained access privileges, and so on.

Class B1 is defined as *Labeled Security Protection*; systems at this level must have a stated policy model, and specifically labeled data.

Class B2, defined as *Structured Protection*, adds a much more explicit and formal security policy to the B1 requirements.

Class B3, defined as *Security Domains*, adds stringent engineering and monitoring requirements.

Class A1 is defined as *Verified Design*; systems at this level are functionally equivalent to B3 systems, but in addition to all the features of the all previous levels they must undergo formal functional analysis procedures to ensure security.

The National Security Agency (NSA) instituted — beginning July 2002 — that all new national security systems (and that includes RDBMS software) must pass a rigorous test as mandated in CC; there are also indications that this might spread to every government organization.

Usually database vendors are certified on a C2 level. As for the Common Criteria program, only Oracle has certified its products at the EAL4 CC certification level. The Microsoft SQL Server 2000 received the C2 Level of security certification from NSA, and IBM DB2 UDB has yet to be certified.

Summary

SQL by itself provides only limited security mechanisms. It essentially uses `GRANT` and `REVOKE` statements to control access to the database objects through system *privileges*. Relational Database Systems needed more robust security, which have been implemented in a variety of nonstandard ways by the RDBMS vendors.

There are several different macro-layers of security: authentication, authorization, and audit. There are also different techniques used to protect data on the most basic levels.

All RDBMS consider the notion of a user as some entity that connects to a database and performs actions. Further, all three vendors discussed in this book implement, in one way or another, *roles*, which is a method to manage sets of privileges. Roles can be system-defined (fixed) or user-defined.

The user gets authenticated either through RDBMS itself, or through the operating system on which the RDBMS is installed. Once authenticated, the user can perform authorized actions on the database objects. The authorization is handled through a system of *privileges*.

Using `GRANT` or `REVOKE`, authorization (privileges) can be assigned or denied to users or roles, and there are rules that govern the process.

Additional security can be implemented through various mechanisms supplied by the database itself: constraints, views, stored procedures, and triggers. The lowest level of defense is vested in the data itself, via encryption, which renders data unreadable by humans.

There are national and international security standards, which are recommended (but not required); some database vendors choose to get certified, while some do not.

✦ ✦ ✦

CHAPTER 13

The System Catalog and INFORMATION_ SCHEMA

In This Chapter

SQL99 information schema

Oracle data dictionary

IBM DB2 UDB system catalogs

MS SQL Server information schema

MS SQL Server system stored procedures

To keep track of all objects, their relationships, etc., the RDBMS use the same technique they are advocating—a set of relational tables and views. This approach was first defined in the SQL92 standard (ISO/IEC 9075-2:199x) and was implemented across all major RDBMS—to a certain degree.

SQL System Catalogs

In the SQL Standard a CATALOG is a collection of schemas that contains, among other things, INFORMATION_SCHEMA. It comprises the tables and/or views that provide all the information about all the other objects and records defined in the database: schemas, tables, privileges, and so on. The main idea is to provide both users and the RDBMS with a consistent standardized way of accessing metadata (the data about data: table definitions, user-defined types, etc.) as well as some system information. By definition, the INFORMATION_SCHEMA tables and views cannot be updated directly, though some vendors allow this (e.g., IBM DB2 UDB).

Table 13-1 shows INFORMATION_SCHEMA views as specified in SQL99 standards.

Table 13-1
SQL Standard INFORMATION_SCHEMA Views

INFORMATION_SCHEMA view	*Description*	*Implemented in RDBMS*
`ASSERTIONS`	Lists all the assertions created in the database; not implemented by any of the leading vendors.	None
`CHARACTER_SETS`	Describes character set definitions accessible to the user; one row per set.	None
`CHECK_CONSTRAINTS`	Describes check constraints on the tables accessible by the user; one row per constraint.	SQL Server 2000
`COLLATIONS`	Describes collations accessible to the user; one row per collation.	None
`COLUMNS`	Describes columns accessible to the current user for every table in the database; one row per column.	IBM DB2 UDB, SQL Server 2000
`COLUMN_DOMAIN_USAGE`	Contains information about the objects for which the current user has permissions.	SQL Server 2000
`COLUMN_PRIVILEGES`	Describes privileges on the column level granted to the user; one row per privilege per column.	SQL Server 2000
`CONSTRAINT_COLUMN_USAGE`	Describes columns referenced in every constraint; one row per column.	SQL Server 2000
`CONSTRAINT_TABLE_USAGE`	Describes tables referenced in every constraint; one row per table per constraint.	SQL Server 2000

INFORMATION_SCHEMA view	*Description*	*Implemented in RDBMS*
DOMAINS	Describes domains accessible to the user (data type, restrictions, etc.); one row per domain.	SQL Server 2000
INFORMATION_SCHEMA_CATALOG_NAME	Name of the database for the user; one row per name; not implemented by any of the leading vendors.	None
DOMAIN_CONSTRAINTS	Describes domain constraints accessible to the user; one row per domain constraint.	SQL Server 2000
KEY_COLUMN_USAGE	Describes columns used in the key-based constraints (primary key, foreign key, unique, etc); one row per constraint.	SQL Server 2000
REFERENTIAL_CONSTRAINTS	Describes foreign key constrains for the tables accessible to the user; one row per constraint.	SQL Server 2000
SCHEMATA	Describes schemas contained in the database; one row per schema.	IBM DB2 UDB, SQL Server 2000
SQL_LANGUAGES	Contains information about languages supported by the RDBMS (i.e., C, FORTRAN, PL/I etc.).	None
TABLES	Describes every table accessible to the user; one row per table/view.	IBM DB2 UDB, SQL Server 2000
TABLE_CONSTRAINTS	Describes constraints declared for the table (primary key, check constraint etc.); one row per constraint.	SQL Server 2000

Continued

Table 13-1 *(continued)*

INFORMATION_SCHEMA view	*Description*	*Implemented in RDBMS*
TABLE_PRIVILEGES	Describes all the privileges granted to the user; one row per privilege.	SQL Server 2000
TRANSLATIONS	Translation definitions accessible to the user.	None
USAGE_PRIVILEGES	Contains information about privileges granted to a user; one row per privilege.	None
VIEWS	Describes every view accessible to the user; one row per view.	IBM DB2 UDB, SQL Server 2000
VIEW_COLUMN_USAGE	Describes columns referenced by the views accessible to the user; one row per column.	SQL Server 2000
VIEW_TABLE_USAGE	Describes tables referenced by views accessible to the user; one row per table.	SQL Server 2000

Similar functionality has been implemented by the RDBMS vendors in views with different names or in a different way. Please refer to the particular RDBMS section of this chapter for more information. In Table 13-1 the column "Implemented in RDBMS" refers to the actual syntax of the view, that is, its name; some vendors choose to use different names and/or add their own views and tables to the System Catalog.

Oracle 9*i* Data Dictionary

Oracle uses the term "Data Dictionary" for its system catalogs. Each Oracle database has its own set of system tables and views that store information about both the physical and logical database structure. The data dictionary objects are read-only, meaning that no database user ever manually modifies them; however, Oracle RDBMS itself automatically updates data in these objects in response to specific actions. For example, when user ACME creates a new object (table, view, stored procedure, etc.), adds a column or a constraint to a table, and so forth, the appropriate data dictionary tables are updated behind the scenes at once, and the corresponding changes are visible through the system views (discussed later in this chapter).

Oracle's data dictionary consists of hundreds of different views and tables that logically belong to different categories, but most of them are only of interest to the database administrators and are beyond the scope of this book. We list only the main object groups in the information schema and briefly describe the most common objects in each category.

Oracle data dictionary structure

Generally, the data dictionary consists of base tables and user-accessible views.

The base tables contain all database information that is dynamically updated by Oracle RDBMS. Oracle strictly discourages using those tables even for selects; the database users normally have no access to them, and even DBAs do not typically query these tables directly. The information stored in the base tables is cryptic and difficult to understand.

The user-accessible views summarize and display the information stored in the base tables; they display the information from the base tables in readable and/or simplified form using joins, column aliases, and so on. Different Oracle users can have `SELECT` privileges on different database views.

Note

All Oracle data dictionary objects belong to a special user called `SYS`. Oracle creates public synonyms to simplify user access to these objects (see Chapter 4). That means you do not have to, for example, refer to `SYS.DBA_TABLES` with the fully qualified name; simply `DBA_TABLES` will do, assuming you have appropriate privileges to access the view.

The data dictionary views, in turn, consist of static and dynamic views. The name "static" denotes that the information in this group of views only changes when a change is made to the data dictionary (a column is added to a table, a new database user is created, etc.). The dynamic views are constantly updated while a database is in use; their contents relate primarily to performance and are not relevant to this book.

The dynamic data dictionary views can be distinguished by the prefix `V_$`, and the public synonyms for these views start with `V$`.

The static views can be divided into three groups. The views in each group are prefixed `USER_`, `ALL_`, or `DBA_`, as shown in Table 13-2.

Table 13-2
Static View Prefixes

Prefix	*Scope*
USER	User's view (objects in the user's schema).
ALL	Expanded user's view (all objects that the user can access).
DBA	Database administrator's view (all objects in all users' schemas).

The set of columns is almost identical across views, that is, USER_TABLES, ALL_TABLES, and DBA_TABLES have the same columns, except USER_TABLES does not have column OWNER (which is unnecessary because that view only has information about tables that belong to the user who queries the view).

Table 13-3 contains information about the most commonly used static views.

Table 13-3
Selected Oracle Data Dictionary views

Data Dictionary View	*Contains Information About:*
ALL_ALL_TABLES	All object and relational tables accessible to the user.
ALL_CATALOG	All tables, views, synonyms, sequences accessible to the user.
ALL_COL_PRIVS	Grants on columns accessible by the user.
ALL_CONSTRAINTS	Constraint definitions on accessible tables.
ALL_CONS_COLUMNS	Information about columns in constraint definitions accessible by the user.
ALL_DB_LINKS	Database links accessible to the user.
ALL_INDEXES	Indexes on tables accessible to the user.
ALL_OBJECTS	All objects accessible to the user.
ALL_SEQUENCES	Database sequences accessible to the user.
ALL_SYNONYMS	All synonyms accessible to the user.
ALL_TABLES	Relational tables accessible to the user.
ALL_TAB_COLUMNS	Columns of tables, views, and clusters accessible to the user.
ALL_TRIGGERS	Triggers accessible to the current user.

Data Dictionary View	***Contains Information About:***
ALL_USERS	Information about all users of the database visible to the current user.
ALL_VIEWS	Views accessible to the user.
DBA_ALL_TABLES	All object and relational tables in the database.
DBA_CATALOG	All database tables, views, synonyms, and sequences.
DBA_COL_PRIVS	All grants on columns in the database.
DBA_CONSTRAINTS	Constraint definitions on all tables.
DBA_CONS_COLUMNS	Information about all columns in constraint definitions in the database.
DBA_DB_LINKS	All database links in the database.
DBA_INDEXES	All indexes in the database.
DBA_OBJECTS	All database objects.
DBA_SEQUENCES	All sequences in the database.
DBA_SYNONYMS	All synonyms in the database.
DBA_TABLES	All relational tables in the database.
DBA_TAB_COLUMNS	Description of columns of all tables, views, and clusters in the database.
DBA_TRIGGERS	All triggers in the database.
DBA_USERS	Information about all users of the database.
DBA_VIEWS	All views in the database.
USER_ALL_TABLES	All object and relational tables owned by the user.
USER_CATALOG	Tables, views, synonyms, and sequences owned by the user.
USER_COL_PRIVS	Grants on columns for which the user is the owner, grantor, or grantee.
USER_CONSTRAINTS	Constraint definitions on user's own tables.
USER_CONS_COLUMNS	Information about columns in constraint definitions owned by the user.
USER_DB_LINKS	Database links owned by the user.
USER_INDEXES	The user's own indexes.
USER_OBJECTS	Objects owned by the user.

Continued

Table 13-3 (continued)

Data Dictionary View	*Contains Information About:*
USER_SEQUENCES	The user's own database sequences.
USER_SYNONYMS	The user's private synonyms.
USER_TABLES	The user's own relational tables.
USER_TAB_COLUMNS	Columns of user's tables, views, and clusters.
USER_TRIGGERS	Triggers owned by the user.
USER_USERS	Information about the current user.
USER_VIEWS	The user's own views.

The select privilege for USER_ and ALL_ views (as well as for selected V$ views) is granted to PUBLIC by default; DBA_ views are visible to privileged users only.

Oracle data dictionary and SQL99 standards

We already mentioned that Oracle is the least compliant of our three databases with SQL99 INFORMATION_SCHEMA standards. Historically, Oracle has its own naming conventions for the system catalog objects that do not match the standards. However, most of the "SQL99 standardized" information (at least regarding the objects implemented by Oracle) can be retrieved from Oracle's data dictionary. Table 13-4 shows a rough correspondence between SQL99 INFORMATION_SCHEMA views and Oracle data dictionary objects.

Table 13-4
Oracle Data Dictionary Views Correspondence to SQL99 INFORMATION_SCHEMA.

INFORMATION_SCHEMA View	*Oracle Data Dictionary View*
CHECK_CONSTRAINTS	USER_CONSTRAINTS USER_OBJECTS
COLUMNS	USER_TAB_COLUMNS
COLUMN_PRIVILEGES	USER_COL_PRIVS
CONSTRAINT_COLUMN_USAGE	USER_CONS_COLUMNS
CONSTRAINT_TABLE_USAGE	USER_CONSTRAINTS
KEY_COLUMN_USAGE	USER_CONS_COLUMNS

INFORMATION_SCHEMA View	*Oracle Data Dictionary View*
REFERENTIAL_CONSTRAINTS	USER_CONSTRAINTS
TABLES	USER_TABLES USER_OBJECTS
TABLE_CONSTRAINTS	USER_CONSTRAINTS
TABLE_PRIVILEGES	USER_COL_PRIVS
USAGE_PRIVILEGES	USER_COL_PRIVS
VIEWS	USER_VIEWS USER_OBJECTS
VIEW_COLUMN_USAGE	USER_TAB_COLUMNS

The following query (when issued by user ACME in the ACME sample database) retrieves the names and creation dates of all tables that belong to the current user:

```
SELECT object_name,
       created
FROM   user_objects
WHERE  object_type = 'TABLE';

OBJECT_NAME                                          CREATED
---------------------------------------------------- ---------
ADDRESS                                              27-OCT-02
CUSTOMER                                             27-OCT-02
DISCOUNT                                             27-OCT-02
ORDER_HEADER                                         27-OCT-02
ORDER_LINE                                           27-OCT-02
ORDER_SHIPMENT                                       27-OCT-02
PAYMENT_TERMS                                        27-OCT-02
PHONE                                                27-OCT-02
PRODUCT                                              27-OCT-02
RESELLER                                             27-OCT-02
SALESMAN                                             27-OCT-02
SHIPMENT                                             27-OCT-02
STATUS                                               27-OCT-02

13 rows selected.
```

The query results tell us that there are currently 13 tables in the ACME database that belong to user ACME and that all of them were created on October 27, 2002.

The system catalog views can be joined just as any other views or tables in Oracle to produce some combined output. The query below joins USER_TABLES and USER_TAB_COLS data dictionary views to produce the list of all columns in ADDRESS table that belongs to user ACME:

```
SELECT   table_name,
         column_name
FROM     user_tables
  JOIN
         user_tab_cols
  USING  (table_name)
WHERE    table_name = 'ADDRESS';

TABLE_NAME                       COLUMN_NAME
-------------------------------- ------------------------------
ADDRESS                          ADDR_ID_N
ADDRESS                          ADDR_CUSTID_FN
ADDRESS                          ADDR_SALESMANID_FN
ADDRESS                          ADDR_ADDRESS_S
ADDRESS                          ADDR_TYPE_S
ADDRESS                          ADDR_CITY_S
ADDRESS                          ADDR_STATE_S
ADDRESS                          ADDR_ZIP_S
ADDRESS                          ADDR_COUNTRY_S

9 rows selected.
```

One more level deep: Data about metadata

The whole idea of Oracle's data dictionary is to hold data about data that are used both internally by the RDBMS and by Oracle users. However, unlike the SQL99 `INFORMATION_SCHEMA`, which only contains a handful of views, the Oracle 9*i* data dictionary consists of over a thousand objects, with dozens of columns in each. That raises a question — where to look for certain information within the data dictionary. Fortunately, Oracle provides a few objects that contain the information about the system objects. The two main views are `DICTIONARY`, which contains a description of the data dictionary tables and views, and `DICT_COLUMNS`, which describes these objects' columns.

You can use a simple SQL query to look for objects that contain the information you need. For example, if you want to know which columns in which tables you have permission to modify, a query similar to one below can help you to find out:

```
SELECT * FROM dictionary
WHERE  UPPER(comments) LIKE '%UPDAT%';

TABLE_NAME                 COMMENTS
-------------------------- ----------------------------------
ALL_UPDATABLE_COLUMNS      Description of all updatable columns
USER_UPDATABLE_COLUMNS     Description of updatable columns
```

Querying either ALL_UPDATABLE_COLUMNS or USER_UPDATABLE_COLUMNS will provide you with the information you are looking for.

The other view, DICT_COLUMNS, gives you information about the individual columns of the data dictionary objects. The query below displays all the columns in the USER_OBJECTS view along with comments for these columns:

```
SELECT * from dict_columns
WHERE  table_name = 'USER_OBJECTS';

TABLE_NAME        COLUMN_NAME      COMMENTS
----------------  ---------------  ----------------------------
USER_OBJECTS      OBJECT_NAME      Name of the object
USER_OBJECTS      SUBOBJECT_NAME   Name of the sub-object (for
                                   example, partition)
USER_OBJECTS      OBJECT_ID        Object number of the object
USER_OBJECTS      DATA_OBJECT_ID   Object number of the segment
                                   which contains the object
USER_OBJECTS      OBJECT_TYPE      Type of the object
USER_OBJECTS      CREATED          Timestamp for the creation
                                   of the object
USER_OBJECTS      LAST_DDL_TIME    Timestamp for the last DDL
                                   change (including GRANT and
                                   REVOKE) to the object
USER_OBJECTS      TIMESTAMP        Timestamp for the
                                   specification of the object
USER_OBJECTS      STATUS           Status of the object
USER_OBJECTS      TEMPORARY        Can the current session only
                                   see data that it place in
                                   this object itself?
USER_OBJECTS      GENERATED        Was the name of this object
                                   system generated?
USER_OBJECTS      SECONDARY        Is this a secondary object
                                   created as part of icreate
                                   for domain indexes?
12 rows selected.
```

Tip

You can use the DESCRIBE command to obtain some minimal information about the data dictionary views and tables in exactly the same way that you would use it to inquire about any other database objects, for example:

```
DESCRIBE user_sequences

Name              Null?     Type
----------------- --------  -------------
SEQUENCE_NAME     NOT NULL  VARCHAR2(30)
MIN_VALUE                   NUMBER
MAX_VALUE                   NUMBER
```

```
INCREMENT_BY      NOT NULL  NUMBER
CYCLE_FLAG                  VARCHAR2(1)
ORDER_FLAG                  VARCHAR2(1)
CACHE_SIZE        NOT NULL  NUMBER
LAST_NUMBER       NOT NULL  NUMBER
```

IBM DB2 UDB 8.1 System Catalogs

IBM DB2 UDB maintains two sets of the INFORMATION_SCHEMA views — one in SYSCAT schema and a subset in the SYSSTAT schema (used for SQL Optimizer to improve query performance). All views are created whenever the CREATE DATABASE command is run; the views comprising the catalog cannot be explicitly dropped, altered, or updated, except for some columns in the SYSSTAT views.

The INFORMATION_SCHEMA objects in DB2

The Table 13-5 shows some of the views we consider most useful.

INFORMATION_SCHEMA views are introduced for SQL standard compliance and are maintained on top of system base tables.

Table 13-5
Selected IBM DB2 UDB INFORMATION_SCHEMA Views

INFORMATION_SCHEMA View	*Contains Information About*
SYSCAT.ATTRIBUTES	Attributes of the structured data types
SYSCAT.DBAUTH	Database authorities
SYSCAT.CHECKS	Check constraints; corresponds to the SQL99 standard view CHECK_CONSTRAINTS
SYSCAT.COLAUTH	Column level privileges
SYSCAT.COLUMNS	Columns accessible for the current user
SYSCAT.COLCHECKS	Columns referenced by the check constraints
SYSCAT.KEYCOLUSE	Columns used in the keys – either primary or foreign
SYSCAT.CONSTDEP	Constraint dependencies
SYSCAT.DATATYPES	Valid data types
SYSCAT.INDEXAUTH	Privileges for indices
SYSCAT.INDEXCOLUSE	Columns of which indices are comprised

INFORMATION_SCHEMA View	*Contains Information About*
SYSCAT.INDEXDEP	Index dependencies
SYSCAT.INDEXES	Indices
SYSCAT.PACKAGES	Packages
SYSCAT.PACKAGEAUTH	Package privileges
SYSCAT.PACKAGEDEP	Package dependencies
SYSCAT.PROCOPTIONS	Stored procedure options.
SYSCAT.PROCPARMOPTIONS	Stored procedure parameter options
SYSCAT.PROCPARMS	Stored procedures parameters
SYSCAT.REFERENCES	Referential constraints; corresponds to the SQL99 standard REFERENTIAL_CONSTRAINTS
SYSCAT.SCHEMAUTH	Schema privileges
SYSCAT.SCHEMATA	All the schemas defined for the database
SYSCAT.SEQUENCES	Database sequences
SYSCAT.PROCEDURES	Stored procedures
SYSCAT.TABCONST	Constraints defined for the table
SYSCAT.TABAUTH	Table level privileges
SYSCAT.TABLES	Tables created within the database
SYSCAT.TABLESPACES	Database tablespaces
SYSCAT.TABLESPACEAUTH	Tablespace privileges
SYSCAT.TRIGDEP	Trigger dependencies
SYSCAT.TRIGGERS	Triggers created in the database.
SYSCAT.FUNCTIONS	User-defined functions
SYSCAT.VIEWS	Views created in the database

The SELECT privilege to views is granted to PUBLIC by default. IBM explicitly states that columns in the views might be changed from release to release and recommends querying these tables using SELECT * FROM SYSCAT.<view> syntax. Nevertheless, IBM specifies that some columns are "guaranteed" to work with the corresponding views. (See Table 13-6.)

The following query retrieves information about the table CUSTOMER created in the ACME database. To display meaningful results, we've limited the number of columns selected to three, because the table contains over 30 columns.

```
db2 => SELECT tabschema,
              colcount,
              create_time
FROM          syscat.tables
WHERE         tabname = 'CUSTOMER'

TABSCHEMA            COLCOUNT CREATE_TIME
-------------------- -------- --------------------------
ACME                        7 2002-09-23-17.55.50.95300

1 record(s) selected.
```

The information returned shows that the table CUSTOMER belongs to the schema ACME, was created on 9/23/2002, and contains seven columns. It is possible to join tables of the system catalog to produce combined results. The following query joins two tables, SYSCAT.TABLES and SYSCAT.COLUMNS, to give a single set of values extracted from both tables.

```
db2 => SELECT tbl.tabname,
              cl.colname
FROM          syscat.tables tbl, syscat.columns cl
WHERE         syscat.tables.tabname = syscat.columns.tabname
AND           syscat.tables.tabname = 'CUSTOMER'

TABNAME       COLNAME

------------- ------------------------------
CUSTOMER      CUST_ID_N
CUSTOMER      CUST_PAYTERMSID_FN
CUSTOMER      CUST_SALESMANID_FN
CUSTOMER      CUST_STATUS_S
CUSTOMER      CUST_NAME_S
CUSTOMER      CUST_ALIAS_S
CUSTOMER      CUST_CREDHOLD_S
  7 record(s) selected.
```

Table 13-6
INFORMATION_SCHEMA Views Column Names

Object	*Selected Column Names*
TABLE	TABSCHEMA, TABNAME, COLCOUNT, KEYCOLUMNS
INDEX	INDSCHEMA, INDNAME
VIEW	VIEWSCHEMA, VIEWNAME, TABID, COLNO, COLTYPE

Object	Selected Column Names
CONSTRAINT	CONSTSCHEMA, CONSTNAME,
TRIGGER	TRIGSCHEMA, TRIGNAME
PACKAGE	PKGSCHEMA, PCKGNAME
TYPE	TYPESCHEMA, TYPENAME, TYPEID
FUNCTION	FUNCSCHEMA, FUNCNAME, FUNCID
COLUMN	COLNAME, COLNO, DEFAULT, REMARKS
SCHEMA	SCHEMANAME

Some INFORMATION_SCHEMA views contained in the SYSSTAT schema are updateable as shown in Table 13-7.

Table 13-7
Updateable IBM DB2 UDB INFORMATION_SCHEMA Views

INFORMATION_SCHEMA Views	Description
SYSSTAT.COLUMNS	Contains information about columns for each table.
SYSSTAT.INDEXES	Contains information about indices created for the database tables.
SYSSTAT.COLDIST	Contains detailed statistics about column usage.
SYSSTAT.TABLES	Contains information about the database tables.
SYSSTAT.FUNCTIONS	Contains information about user-defined functions.

For the sake of compatibility with the DB2 Universal Database for OS/390, IBM maintains the SYSDUMMY1 catalog table in the SYSCAT schema. This table consists of one row and one column (IBMREQ) of the CHAR(1) data type. See Chapter 8 for more information on the use of this table.

Obtaining information about INFORMATION_SCHEMA objects

The DESCRIBE TABLE <table_name> command can be used to obtain information about the internal structure of the INFORMATION_SCHEMA objects in DB2. For example:

```
db2 =>  describe table syscat.views

Column          Type          Type name  Length  Scale Nulls
name            schema
--------------- ------------- ---------  ------- ----- -----
VIEWSCHEMA      SYSIBM        VARCHAR        128     0 No
VIEWNAME        SYSIBM        VARCHAR        128     0 No
DEFINER         SYSIBM        VARCHAR        128     0 No
SEQNO           SYSIBM        INTEGER          4     0 No
VIEWCHECK       SYSIBM        CHARACTER        1     0 No
READONLY        SYSIBM        CHARACTER        1     0 No
VALID           SYSIBM        CHARACTER        1     0 No
QUALIFIER       SYSIBM        VARCHAR        128     0 No
FUNC_PATH       SYSIBM        VARCHAR        254     0 No
TEXT            SYSIBM        CLOB         65536     0 No

  10 record(s) selected.
```

Microsoft SQL Server 2000 System Catalog

Microsoft SQL Server 2000 provides several ways of obtaining system information — through INFORMATION_SCHEMA views and/or through system stored procedures and functions.

One of the ways to obtain system information about the Microsoft SQL Server 2000 is direct querying of the system tables — that is, tables and views that contain information about the current database (e.g., sysobjects, sysindexes, sysusers, etc. — up to a total of 19 tables). Those stored in Master database contain information about the RDBMS itself. While it is possible — for a user with sufficient privileges — to query these views and tables, Microsoft strongly discourages such practice, stating that the system tables are for the exclusive use of the SQL Server itself, and that the names and structures might change in future releases (and they certainly do — each version of the SQL Server brings new tables, old ones are dropped, and the names get changed). Our advice is to resist the temptation of using this "backdoor" but instead use legitimate interfaces to obtain information.

MS SQL Server 2000 INFORMATION_SCHEMA Views

The INFORMATION_SCHEMA system views were first introduced in Microsoft SQL Server 7.0 for SQL92 standard compliance. These views are defined in each database contained in RDBMS. They are based on system tables, which should not be queried directly (see Tip above).

Table 13-8 contains information about MS SQL Server 2000 INFORMATION_SCHEMA views.

Table 13-8
Microsoft SQL Server 2000 INFORMATION_SCHEMA Views

INFORMATION_SCHEMA View	*Contains Information About*
CHECK_CONSTRAINTS	All check constraints for the current database; based on sysobjects and syscomments system tables. Shows only constraints for which the current user has permission.
COLUMN_DOMAIN_USAGE	All user-defined data types; based on sysobjects, syscolumns, and systypes system tables. Shows only data-types for which the current user has permission.
COLUMN_PRIVILEGES	All privileges either granted to or by the user; based on sysprotects, sysobjects, and syscolumns system tables. Shows only privileges for which the current user has permission.
COLUMNS	Every column in every table in the current database accessible to the user; based on sysobjects, spt_data type_info, systypes, syscolumns, syscomments, sysconfigures, and syscharsets system tables. Shows only columns for which the current user has permission.
CONSTRAINT_COLUMN_USAGE	Every column in the database that has constraint put on it; based on sysobjects, syscolumns, and systypes system tables. Shows only columns for which the current user has permission.
CONSTRAINT_TABLE_USAGE	Each table in the current database that has a constraint defined on it; based on sysobjects system table. Shows only tables for which the current user has permission.
DOMAIN_CONSTRAINTS	Every user-defined data type that has a rule bound to it; based on sysobjects and systypes system tables. Shows only types for which the current user has permission.
DOMAINS	User-Defined Types declared in the current database; based on spt_data type_info, systypes, syscomments, sysconfigures, and syscharsets system tables. Shows only UDT(s) for which the current user has permission.

Continued

Table 13-8 *(continued)*

INFORMATION_SCHEMA View	*Contains Information About*
KEY_COLUMN_USAGE	Each column declared as a key (primary or foreign) for every table in the current database; based on sysobjects, syscolumns, sysreferences, spt_values, and sysindexes system tables. Shows only key columns for which the current user has permission.
PARAMETERS	Each parameter defined for a user-defined stored procedure or function; also shows return parameter for a function; based on sysobjects and syscolumns system tables. Shows only information for the stored procedures and functions for which the current user has permission.
REFERENTIAL_CONSTRAINTS	Each foreign key constraint defined in the current database; based on sysreferences, sysindexes, and sysobjects system tables. Shows only constraints for which the current user has permission.
ROUTINES	Every stored procedure or function defined in the current database; based on sysobjects and sysscolumns system tables. Shows only functions for which the current user has permission.
ROUTINE_COLUMNS	User functions that are table-valued (containing a SELECT statement); based on sysobjects and syscolumns system tables. Shows only functions for which the current user has permission.
SCHEMATA	All databases accessible to a user; based on sysdatabases, sysconfigures, and syscharsets system tables. Shows only databases for which the current user has permission.
TABLE_CONSTRAINTS	Table constraints defined in the current database; based on sysobjects system table. Shows only constraints for which the current user has permission.
TABLE_PRIVILEGES	Each table privilege either granted to or by the user; based on sysobjects and sysprotects system tables. Shows only constraints for which the current user has permission.
TABLES	Every table defined in the current database; based on sysobjects system table. Shows only tables for which the current user has permission.

INFORMATION_SCHEMA View	*Contains Information About*
VIEW COLUMN USAGE	Each column used in a view definition; based on sysobjects and sysdepends system tables. Shows only columns for which the current user has permission.
VIEW_TABLE_USAGE	Tables used as a base table for the views; based on sysobjects and sysdepends system tables. Shows only tables for which the current user has permission.
VIEWS	Views in the current database accessible to a user; based on sysobjects and syscomments system tables.

The INFORMATION_SCHEMA views are queried just like any other view or table in the database with one important distinction: the view name must be preceded with the INFORMATION_SCHEMA qualifier. Each view contains several columns, and search conditions can be specified on the columns these views contain (for the full list of the INFORMATION_SCHEMA views columns, please refer to the vendor documentation).

Here are several examples illustrating the use of the INFORMATION_SCHEMA views in SQL Server 2000.

The following query returns information about every column in the ACME database. (The results displayed were shortened somewhat, because the query returns all rows for each table in the database, including 19 system tables, used by the SQL Server to keep track of the objects; only 4 columns were requested, since the view contains a total of 23 columns.)

```
SELECT table_name,
       column_name,
       column_default,
       data_type
FROM   information_schema.columns

TABLE_NAME         COLUMN_NAME           DATA_TYPE
----------------   ---------------       -------------
ORDER_LINE         ORDLINE_ID_N          int
ORDER_LINE         ORDLINE_ORDHDRID_FN   int
. . .              . . .                 . . .
SHIPMENT           SHIPMENT_ID_N         int
SHIPMENT           SHIPMENT_BOLNUM_S     varchar
SHIPMENT           SHIPMENT_SHIPDATE_D   datetime
SHIPMENT           SHIPMENT_ARRIVDATE_D  datetime
. . .              . . .                  . . .        . . .
STATUS             STATUS_ID_N           int
STATUS             STATUS_CODE_S         char
```

```
STATUS              STATUS_DESC_S          varchar
. . .               . . .                  . . .
v_customer_totals customer_name           varchar
v_customer_totals order_number            varchar
. . .               . . .                  . . .
SALESMAN            SALESMAN_NAME_S        varchar
SALESMAN            SALESMAN_STATUS_S      char

(112 row(s) affected)
```

For example, if you would like to query the table for information only on table SALESMAN, then the query should look like the following:

```
SELECT table_name,
       column_name,
       column_default,
       data_type
FROM   information_schema.columns
WHERE  table_name = 'SALESMAN'

TABLE_NAME          COLUMN_NAME            DATA_TYPE
----------------    ---------------        -------------
SALESMAN            SALESMAN_ID_N          int
SALESMAN            SALESMAN_CODE_S        varchar
SALESMAN            SALESMAN_NAME_S        varchar
SALESMAN            SALESMAN_STATUS_S      char

(4 row(s) affected)
```

It is possible to join INFORMATION_SCHEMA views just as you would the "regular" views or tables, or use any other SQL expressions. For example, to find out what tables do not have constraints declared on their columns, the following query can be used:

```
SELECT tbl.table_name,
       tbl.table_type
FROM   information_schema.tables tbl
WHERE  tbl.table_name NOT IN
  (SELECT table_name
   FROM   information_schema.constraint_column_usage)

TABLE_NAME               TABLE_TYPE
----------------         ---------------
sysconstraints           VIEW
syssegments              VIEW
v_contact_list           VIEW
```

```
v_customer_status     VIEW
v_customer_totals     VIEW
. . .                 . . .
v_fax_number          VIEW
v_phone_number        VIEW
v_wile_bess_orders    VIEW

(10 row(s) affected)
```

As it turns out, every single table in the ACME database has some type of constraint (at least primary or foreign keys) declared for it, but views do not. Note that the final resultset includes two system views.

Microsoft SQL Server system stored procedures

There are many categories of system stored procedures supplied with Microsoft SQL Server 2000, depending on the purpose and tasks performed. Only catalog procedures are discussed at relative length in this chapter.

Table 13-9 contains information about MS SQL Server 2000 `INFORMATION_SCHEMA` system stored procedure categories.

Table 13-9
Microsoft SQL Server 2000 System Stored Procedure Categories

Category	*Description*
Active Directory Procedures	Used to register SQL Server with Microsoft Windows Active Directory.
Catalog Procedures	Returns information about system objects; implements ODBC data dictionary functions.
Cursor Procedures	Implements cursor functionality (see Chapter 14 for more information on cursors).
Database Maintenance Plan Procedures	Used to set up and perform core database maintenance tasks.
Distributed Queries Procedures	Used to execute and manage Distributed Queries.
Full-Text search Procedures	Pertains to the Full-Text search capabilities; requires special setup to use full text indices.
Log Shipping Procedures	Used in configuration and administration of the SQL Server Log shipping.

Continued

Table 13-9 (continued)

Category	*Description*
OLE Automation Procedures	Allows for using ActiveX (OLE) automation objects to be used within standard Transact SQL code.
Replication Procedures	Used to set up and manage replication process.
Security Procedures	Security management procedures.
SQL Mail Procedures	Integrates e-mail operations with SQL Server.
SQL Profiler Procedures	Used by the SQL Profiler add-on to monitor SQL Server performance.
SQL Server Agent Procedures	Used by SQL Server Agent to manage scheduled activities.
System Maintenance Procedures	Used for the entire RDBM system maintenance tasks.
Web Assistant Procedures	Used by SQL Server Web assistant to publish information with Internet Information Server.
XML Procedures	Used to perform operation on XM documents (see Chapter 17 on XML/SQL integration).
General Extended Procedures	Refers to the stored procedures capable of accessing resources of the underlying Windows OS.

The Catalog stored procedures will be the focus of this chapter, and we will look into some of the most useful as examples. The Microsoft SQL Server 2000 lists 12 stored procedures that provide information about the system. You can use these procedures directly from the command-line interface of OSQL, from SQL Query Analyzer, or from a client application accessing the SQL Server through any of the programming interfaces provided. Initially, the purpose of these procedures was to implement ODBC data dictionary functions to isolate ODBC applications from possible changes to the SQL Server system tables structure.

The use of system stored procedures is unique to Microsoft SQL Server and Sybase adaptive Server, since they both have their origins in a joint project initiated by Microsoft, Sybase, and Ashton-Tate in 1988, whereas INFORMATION_SCHEMA views were introduced starting with version 7.0 of the SQL Server.

The information returned by these stored procedures usually pertains to the current database; in the case of the server scope, it pertains to the databases in the current installation. In addition to that, these procedures might return information about objects accessible through a database gateway (i.e., registered as legitimate data sources with the SQL Server). Since the details of implementation differ from data source to data source, some information might be unavailable (for example, Oracle's concept of a "database" is totally different from that of MS SQL Server, so `sp_database` procedure will not be able to return it).

Every procedure listed in the following sections accepts none, one or more arguments; we are going to specify only the most basic of the arguments, often only required arguments in our examples, as a full listing will require many more pages and really belongs in a Microsoft SQL Server book.

sp_tables

This procedure returns a list of tables and views (and some related information about them) in the current database. The format of the returned data set is given in Table 13-10.

Table 13-10
Result Set Returned by sp_tables System Stored Procedures

Column Name	*Description*
TABLE_QUALIFIER	Table qualifier name. In the SQL Server, this column represents the database name. This field can be NULL.
TABLE_OWNER	Contains the table owner name, usually DBO (database owner).
TABLE_NAME	Contains the name of the table.
TABLE_TYPE	Specifies the type of the object: a table, system table, or a view.
REMARKS	Comments can be added to the table, but usually this column returns NULL.

The procedure accepts a number of optional parameters that correspond to the column name in the Table 13-10; if omitted, every single table and view in the current database will be listed. Here is an example:

```
1> exec sp_tables
2> go

TABLE_QUALIFIER  TABLE_OWNER TABLE_NAME  TABLE_TYPE   REMARKS
---------------  ----------- ----------- -----------  ------
acme             dbo         syscolumns  SYSTEM TABLE NULL
. . .             . . .       . . .       . . .        . . .
acme             dbo         ADDRESS     TABLE        NULL
acme             dbo         CUSTOMER    TABLE        NULL
acme             dbo         DISCOUNT    TABLE        NULL
. . .             . . .       . . .       . . .        . . .
acme             dbo         v_fax_number VIEW        NULL
```

Note that this procedure lists all the system tables and views in the context of the current database.

If the server property ACCESSIBLE_TABLES returned by the system stored procedure sp_server_info (see later in the chapter) is Y, then, only tables that the current user has permission to access will be returned.

sp_columns

This procedure returns all the columns (and column-specific information) accessible in the current session. Here is a basic example:

```
exec sp_columns 'CUSTOMER'
```

The procedure is equivalent to the ODBC API SQL columns. See Chapter 16 for more details on ODBC.

sp_server_info

Executing the procedure without any parameters returns 29 rows, while specifying the attribute ID gives you exactly one row of data. The information returned represents a subset of the data provided by an ODBC call SQLGetInfo.

```
1> exec sp_server_info
2> go

attribute_id attribute_name             attribute_value
------------ -------------------------- ---------------------
1            DBMS_NAME                  Microsoft SQL Server
. . .        . . .                      . . .
12           MAX_OWNER_NAME_LENGTH      128
13           TABLE_LENGTH               128
. . .        . . .                      . . .
112          SP_RENAME                  Y
113          REMOTE_SPROC               Y
500          SYS_SPROC_VERSION          8.00.178

(29 row(s) affected)
```

This procedure is capable of returning information about non-SQL Server RDBMS, provided that a database gateway or linked data source is specified.

sp_databases

This procedure returns a list of all SQL Server databases. Here is an example of the returned data, on the MS SQL Server installation performed as described in Appendix D:

```
1> exec sp_databases
2> go

DATABASE_NAME            DATABASE_SIZE REMARKS
------------------------ ------------- --------------
acme                     2176          NULL
master                   14208         NULL
model                    1280          NULL
msdb                     14336         NULL
Northwind                4352          NULL
pubs                     2560          NULL
tempdb                   8704          NULL
```

The data returned are contained in the table SYSDATABASES of the Master database. It has no corresponding ODBC functions.

Getting Help

One of the most useful procedures in obtaining information about any database object is the sp_help<> group of stored procedures.

Stored Procedure	*Description*
sp_help	Returns information about database objects in the current database.
sp_helpuser	Returns information about database users, database roles, etc.
sp_helptrigger (<tabname>)	Returns information about triggers defined on the specified table for the current database.
sp_helprotect	Returns information about user permissions in the current database.
sp_helpindex	Returns information about the indices on a table or view.

SP_HELP is probably the most universal of the lot. If used without any arguments, it will returned information about every single database object (table, view, stored procedure, index, default, etc.) listed in the sysobjects table of the current database.

```
1> exec sp_help
2> go

Name                   Owner         Object_type
---------------------- ------------- -----------------
sysconstraints         dbo           view
. . .
```

Continued

Continued

```
v_fax_number            dbo         view
v_phone_number          dbo         view
. . .                   . . .       . . .
ADDRESS                 dbo         user table
CUSTOMER                dbo         user table
. . .                   . . .       . . .
sysindexes              dbo         system table
. . .                   . . .       . . .
PK_ADDRPRIMARY          dbo         primary key cns
PK_CUSTPRIMARY          dbo         primary key cns
. . .                   . . .       . . .
sp_productadd           dbo         stored procedure
. . .                   . . .       . . .
CHK_ADDR_TYPE           dbo         check cns
CHK_CUST_CREDHOLD       dbo         check cns
```

Queried again, with the object name passed as a parameter, it returns a wealth of information about the object, for example, `CUSTOMER` table of the ACME sample database:

```
exec sp_help 'CUSTOMER'
```

The above example returns multiple resultsets, each describing the table `CUSTOMER`. Because of its sheer size, the output is not shown here.

There is a `sp_help<object>` system stored procedure for virtually every database object. Please refer to the Microsoft SQL Server 2000 documentation for more information. When using these procedures, keep in mind that usually more than one resultset is returned.

Microsoft SQL Server 2000 system functions

Microsoft SQL Server 2000 also provides a number of functions that return information about the RDBMS server and contained objects. The full list of the functions is given in Appendix G. The functions' grouping follows that of Microsoft documentation, and the number of functions might increase in future releases.

Configuration functions

The `@@CONNECTIONS` unary function returns number of connections (or attempted connections) for the period since the RDBMS was started.

```
SELECT @@CONNECTIONS AS 'Connections Total'

Connections Total
-----------------
```

```
49

(1 row(s) affected)
```

The unary function @@VERSION returns the full version information about particular installation of the SQL Server.

```
1> SELECT @@VERSION AS ' SQL Server Info'
2> go
SQL Server Info
----------------------------------------------------------------
Microsoft SQL Server  2000 - 8.00.194 (Intel X86)
Aug  6 2000 00:57:48
Copyright (c) 1988-2000 Microsoft Corporation
Enterprise Evaluation Edition on Windows NT 5.0         (Build
2195: Service Pack 2)


(1 row(s) affected)
```

Microsoft SQL Server 2000 lists 15 functions in the Configuration Functions category.

Metadata functions

The DB_NAME function returns name of the current database if no parameters were specified or a database name corresponding to a numeric database ID. The function DB_ID returns the numeric ID of the current database (if no parameters were specified), or—if a numeric ID was specified—a database name corresponding to that ID.

```
1> USE ACME
2> SELECT DB_NAME() AS 'database',
3>        DB_NAME(7) AS 'db_by_id',
4>        DB_ID() AS 'id'
5> go

db_by_id                 databaseid          id
------------------       -----------         ------
acme                     acme                     7

(1 row(s) affected)
```

The example above uses both the DB_NAME and DB_ID functions; the USE ACME keyword makes sure that the ACME database context is specified. There is a total of 25 metadata functions supplied with MS SQL Server 2000.

System functions

The APP_NAME function returns the name of the application (if set by the application) that initialized connection. For example, the following output was produced using OSQL command-line utility (see Appendix E for more information).

```
1> select app_name() as 'application'
2> go

application
---------------
OSQL-32

(1 row affected)
```

The @@ROWCOUNT returns the number of rows affected by the last SELECT statement for the session's scope. For instance, if issued immediately after the statement from the above example, it will produce the following results:

```
1> select @@ROWCOUNT as 'rows'
2> go

rows
----------
         1

(1 row affected)
```

Note, that the statement itself affects the result: if, for example, the previous statement returned 100 records, the statement SELECT @@ROWCOUNT will return 100, issued immediately after that, it will return 1 (i.e., rows affected by the statement itself).

Here is an example of the SUSER_SNAME and USER_NAME system functions usage. The first function is supposed to return the login identification name, given a user identification number (or the current user, if the number is omitted), and the second function returns the database user name. Start two OSQL sessions or establish two connections in the SQL Query Analyzer; then use Windows authentication for the first session and SQL Server Authentication (UserID 'acme,' password 'acme') for the second session; please see Appendix E for details.

Here are the results returned by the function in the first session (Windows Authentication); the login name is represented by the computer name/user name.

```
1> SELECT suser_sname() AS LOGIN_NAME,
2>        user_name() AS DB_USER
3> go

LOGIN_NAME                    DB_USER
----------------------------- -----------
ALEX-KRIEGEL\alex_kriegel     dbo

(1 row(s) affected)
```

The following example shows the same query executed within a session initiated through SQL Server Authentication:

```
1> SELECT suser_sname() AS LOGIN_NAME,
2>        user_name() AS DB_USER
3> go

LOGIN_NAME                    DB_USER
----------------------------- -----------
acme                          dbo

(1 row(s) affected)
```

There is total of 38 functions in the Microsoft SQL Server 2000.

Summary

`INFORMATION_SCHEMA` was endorsed by the ISO/ANSI body long after the real RDBMS implementations moved into the market. As a result, some of the vendors implemented their own version of the metadata repository in a form of system tables.

The information from these tables can be gathered in a variety of ways, usually through views, provided by the vendor for just this purpose (the idea behind the `INFORMATION_SCHEMA`), through some vendor-supplied stored procedures or functions, or by making your best guess via direct querying of the underlying system tables.

Most vendors explicitly discourage users from accessing the system tables directly because their structure might change without any notice, and the information contained in the table is not guaranteed to mean what you think it should; in short, system tables are for the use of the system, views are for the users.

While introducing the standard is a step in the right direction toward uniform interface to metadata, it probably will not happen overnight (considering that INFORMATION_SCHEMA was first introduced in the SQL92 standard). The system catalog of the structure specified in the SQL92/99 standard is a requirement for achieving higher levels of the standard conformance; most of the RDBMS products are only Level 1 compliant and are likely to remain so in the nearest future.

✦ ✦ ✦

PART

VI

Beyond SQL: Procedural Programming and Database Access Mechanisms

✦ ✦ ✦ ✦

In This Part

✦ ✦ ✦ ✦

Stored Procedures, Triggers, and User-Defined Functions

✦ ✦ ✦ ✦

In This Chapter

SQL procedural extensions

SQL procedural language key elements

Stored procedures

User-defined functions

Triggers

✦ ✦ ✦ ✦

As was mentioned before, SQL is a nonprocedural programming language by definition. That means it lacks procedural constructs, specifically, the ability to perform operations in optionally named hierarchical logical blocks that can accept and return values, perform iterations, execute conditional statements, and so on.

Note

Most programming languages are procedural. A procedural program is a list of step-by-step instructions that tell the computer what to do; for example, repeatedly read user's input, multiply it by some predefined constant, and store the result in a database table. A procedural program can also have error handling – for example, if the value is nonnumeric, do not try to multiply it but rather display an error message; or multiply the input by different values depending on how large the input was. Also, instead of storing the result into a table a procedural program can pass it to a different program (subprogram) that in its order might perform more calculations and pass the results to yet another programming module, and so on.

First RDBMS implementations did not have procedural language capabilities — all procedural database processing was done using embedded programming. All major procedural languages that were popular back then (C, COBOL, Pascal, etc.) had (and still have) special extensions (precompilers) that allow the programmer to embed SQL statements directly into programming language code. The work of precompiles is to translate SQL into appropriate language constructs that can be later compiled into binary code.

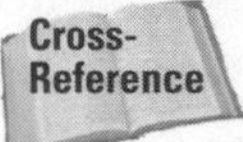

Embedded programming is discussed in Chapter 15.

However, while relational databases became increasingly sophisticated and more internal control was delegated to RDBMS, the idea arose to store procedural programming modules inside RDBMS in compiled (binary) form. The problem was that ANSI/ISO standards specified no (or almost none) guidelines for such elements. As a result, each vendor implemented its own version of internal RDBMS procedural modules.

SQL99 added persistent stored routines (PSR) and triggers to SQL standards when all major RDBMS vendors already had their own procedural languages. Oracle's procedural SQL extension is called PL/SQL; MS SQL Server uses Transact-SQL; and DB2 UDB introduced its own version that does not seem to have an official name, but is sometimes referred to as T-SQL or IBM SQL.

DB2 UDB did not have its own procedural SQL extension until version 7.1. Instead, it provided capabilities to write stored routines using your choice of C or COBOL and, later, Java. Java can also be used as an alternative to PL/SQL in Oracle to be used for writing procedural code.

Even though the basic syntax elements of these three languages are similar, the advanced features differ significantly. It is impossible to cover all three syntaxes in depth in the scope of this book, so we are going to explain the common basic features and encourage you to refer to vendor-specific documentation for more details.

PSR includes stored procedures, user-defined functions, and special constructs called modules that can contain procedures, functions, and shared variable declarations for them. Modules are known in Oracle as *packages;* they are not implemented in MS SQL Server and DB2 UDB and are not covered in this book.

The two main forms of RDBMS procedural routines are stored procedures and triggers that embody two different procedural programming approaches — linear and event-driven, correspondingly. A user-defined function can be envisioned as a special case of a stored procedure, and a module is just a number of stored procedures and functions bundled together.

Procedural Extension Uses and Benefits

Stored procedures, user-defined functions, and triggers can be used in many different ways and for many different reasons. The main categories include performance improvement, network traffic reduction, database security, and code reusability.

Sequential and Event-Driven Programming

In sequential programming, the application controls the order of execution; in other words, the code is executed in a predetermined sequence and requires minimal user interference. Sequential, or linear, programming is typical for batch programs that perform large sequential tasks. The most popular languages for linear programming are COBOL, FORTRAN, and C.

In event-driven programming, the code is executed according to a user action or system event; the user actions and system events control the sequence. Application starts and waits for an event (mouse click, keystroke, or a system event such as time expiring) to occur. Based on the specific event the program performs an action and waits for the next event. Most modern visual applications are event-driven. Order entry, financial, time tracking, banking, and many other applications typically open the main menu screen on startup and then wait for users to perform certain actions. The most typical languages for writing event-driven applications are Visual C++, Visual Basic, and Java. (Of course, you can create an event-driven program using COBOL or a procedural program using C++; we just emphasize the typical or most common scenarios.)

In RDBMS, events are usually more database-related than the ones described here. For example, inserting or deleting table rows, updating certain columns, users logging in and out can trigger other events in a database.

Performance and network traffic

Stored routines can be used to improve application performance. Since they simply appear to be compiled code stored inside the RDBMS, they generally execute faster uncompiled SQL statements (that normally have to be compiled each time a user or program calls them).

Network traffic can also be significantly reduced because there is no need to send SQL statements as they are already compiled and stored on the server. Each individual statement is probably not large enough to improve the overall network performance, but, in a large system with thousands of users and tons of SQL statements, it can make a difference.

Database security

Stored procedures, functions, and triggers can be used for database security purposes.

A stored procedure (or function) is a separate database object with its own database privileges. That means you can design a stored procedure in such way that it would, for example, update only certain columns; or insert rows with `NULL` values for columns that a user who executes the procedure has no permission to update—s/he would only need the privilege to execute that particular stored procedure.

Triggers are even more useful for security implementation. For example, they can be designed in such way that certain actions performed by users on certain objects are written to special database tables or OS files. These records can be reviewed later.

Read more about using stored procedures and triggers to enforce database security in Chapter 12.

Code reusability

Another important thing about stored routines is code reusability—once compiled, a stored procedure or user-defined function can be used over and over again by multiple users (or applications), saving time on retyping large SQL statements and reducing the probability of human errors. Also, when a persistent module needs to be changed, the change won't affect the client programs that access it, as long as all the calling parameters remain the same.

Key Elements of a SQL Procedural Language

In this section we introduce the main elements of a SQL procedural language.

Variables and assignment

Variables can be thought of as storage units for values. They can be of any data type supported by your RDBMS. For example, `NUMBER` and `VARCHAR2` are valid data types for variable declaration in Oracle PL/SQL, but `MONEY` or `SMALLDATETIME` are not.

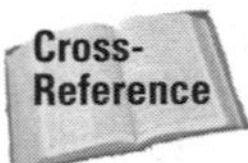

Data types are discussed in Chapter 3.

The declaration syntax is also slightly different for different vendors. The sample declaration for integer type variable `v_prodcount` is shown below.

PL/SQL (Oracle)

Variables are declared in the declaration section of the programming unit (between the header and the word `BEGIN`). All statements in PL/SQL end with semicolon:

```
v_prodcount NUMBER;
```

The assignment can be done on the declaration, but is usually done in the program body; the assignment operator in PL/SQL is a colon followed by an equals sign (`:=`).

```
v_prodcount := 0;
```

DB2 UDB

DB2 procedural language uses the DECLARE keyword for variable declarations. A declaration is done in the stored program body rather than in the declaration section; the statement ends with a semicolon:

```
DECLARE v_prodcount INTEGER;
```

The keyword SET is used for variable assignment:

```
SET v_prodcount = 0;
```

The values stored in variables can be retrieved and/or changed during the execution scope of the programming unit.

Transact-SQL (MS SQL Server)

The keyword DECLARE is also used in Transact-SQL to declare variables. All local variables must be prefixed with the at-sign (@); global variables are prefixed with the double at-sign (@@).

```
declare @v_prodcount INTEGER
```

The variable assignment can be done in two different ways:

```
select @v_prodcount = 0
```

or:

```
set @v_prodcount = 0
```

Modularity, subprograms, and block structure

Modularity is the important feature of the procedural languages that allows developers to improve code reusability and to hide the complexity of the execution of a specific operation behind a name. There are two levels of modularity: the ability to create sequential logical blocks within a single program and the aptitude of a program to call another program, which in its turn can call yet another program, and so on.

The first level of modularity enables you to structure your program and handle errors appropriately (error handling is discussed later in this chapter). This is especially convenient in PL/SQL where each block can have its own EXCEPTION section:

```
BEGIN -- Main program
  ...
  <statement>,...
  BEGIN -- Nested block level 1
    <statement>,...
```

```
      BEGIN -- Nested block level 2
        <statement>,...
      EXCEPTION
        <error_handling_statement>,...
      END; -- Nested block level 2
        <statement>,...
    EXCEPTION
        <error_handling_statement>,...
    END; -- Nested block level 1
    <statement>,...
  EXCEPTION
    <error_handling_statement>,...
  END; -- Main program
```

The other vendors' procedural SQL extensions also have the idea of nested blocks that may be used to implement a similar principle as well as to write large programs with complex functionality. Refer to vendor-specific documentation for more details.

Here is the example of the second level of modularity invoking separate modules. Stored procedure A inserts records into tables BB and CC by calling procedures B and C, each of which inserts records into the corresponding table as shown using PL/SQL-like pseudocode:

```
CREATE PROCEDURE b (field1 INTEGER,
                    field2 INTEGER,
                    field3 INTEGER)
AS
BEGIN
  ...
  INSERT INTO bb
  VALUES (field1, field2, field3);
   ...
END;
```

```
CREATE PROCEDURE c (field1 INTEGER,
                    field2 INTEGER,
                    field3 INTEGER)
AS
BEGIN
  ...
  INSERT INTO cc
  VALUES (field1, field2, field3);
   ...
END;
```

```
CREATE PROCEDURE a (field1 INTEGER,
                    field2 INTEGER,
                    field3 INTEGER)
AS
BEGIN
   b(field1, field2, field3);
   c(field1, field2, field3);
END;
```

Passing parameters

Another procedural programming feature closely tied with modularity is the ability to accept parameters and/or pass them to another programming module. Parameters (sometimes also called arguments) are in a way similar to variables. The main difference is that the variables are local to the program whereas parameters are passed into the program upon the module invocation. For example, a stored procedure or user-defined function could have zero or more parameters that are later used for certain actions determined in the program logic. Parameter names and data types are defined in the header part of the programming unit.

Parameters can be passed to a stored procedure or to a user-defined function, but not to a trigger because of the triggers' event-driven nature.

PL/SQL

The main difference between PL/SQL and other proprietary procedural SQL extensions is that you cannot specify data type precision, scale, or length in the parameter declaration. For example, `v_prodnum VARCHAR2(10)` or `v_prodprice DECIMAL(10,2)` would produce an error. The parameters are enclosed by parentheses.

The declaration section of the `SP_PRODUCTADD` procedure written in PL/SQL is shown here:

```
CREATE PROCEDURE sp_productadd
(
 v_prodid              NUMBER,
 v_prodprice           NUMBER,
 v_prodnum             VARCHAR2,
 v_proddesc            VARCHAR2,
 v_prodstatus          CHAR,
 v_prodbrand           VARCHAR2,
 v_prodpltwid          NUMBER,
 v_prodpltlen          NUMBER,
 v_prodnetwgt          NUMBER,
 v_prodshipwgt         NUMBER
)
...
```

Transact-SQL

The parameters in Transact-SQL are prefixed with at-signs in the same way the variables are; you do not enclose them in parentheses:

```
CREATE PROCEDURE sp_productadd
  @v_prodid                 INTEGER,
  @v_prodprice              MONEY,
  @v_prodnum                VARCHAR (10),
  @v_proddesc               VARCHAR (44),
  @v_prodstatus             CHAR,
  @v_prodbrand              VARCHAR (20),
  @v_prodpltwid             DECIMAL(5, 2),
  @v_prodpltlen             DECIMAL(5, 2),
  @v_prodnetwgt             DECIMAL(10, 3),
  @v_prodshipwgt            DECIMAL(10, 3)
  ...
```

DB2 IBM SQL

The syntax is practically identical to that of PL/SQL except you have to specify the length or precision and scale when required:

```
CREATE PROCEDURE sp_productadd
(
 v_prodid                 INTEGER,
 v_prodprice              INTEGER,
 v_prodnum                VARCHAR(44),
 v_proddesc               VARCHAR(10),
 v_prodstatus             CHAR(1),
 v_prodbrand              VARCHAR(20),
 v_prodpltwid             DECIMAL(5,2),
 v_prodpltlen             DECIMAL(5,2),
 v_prodnetwgt             DECIMAL(10,3),
 v_prodshipwgt            DECIMAL(10,3)
)
...
```

Passing Parameters by Name and by Value

Most procedural languages implement two main types of parameters: `by value` and `by reference`. The main difference is that if you send a variable from the calling module as a `by value` parameter, a copy of this variable is actually sent, so whatever happens to it inside the subroutine does not affect the original variable value. However, if you send the variable `by reference`, the memory address of this variable is passed to the subprogram, so it could actually be changed. The following example (written in pseudocode) illustrates the concept:

```
CREATE PROCEDURE POWER_V (x INTEGER BYVALUE)
-- The parameter x is passed by value
AS
BEGIN
  x := x * x;
END;

CREATE PROCEDURE POWER_R (x INTEGER BYREFERENCE)
-- The parameter x is passed by reference
AS
BEGIN
  x := x * x;
END;

CREATE PROCEDURE SQUARE (x INTEGER)
AS
-- Declare local variable y of type integer
DECLARE y INTEGER;
BEGIN
 -- Assign variable y the value of x
 y := x;
 -- Display the value of variable y
 PRINT (y);
 -- Call procedure POWER_V.
 EXECUTE POWER_V(y);
 -- The value of y does not change
 PRINT (y);
 -- Call procedure POWER_R.
 EXECUTE POWER_R(y);
 -- The variable y was passed by reference
 -- so its value actually changes (squared)
 PRINT (y);
END;

EXECUTE SQUARE(5);
```

Continued

Continued

```
5
5
25
```

All the "big three" databases allow you to pass parameters by value or by reference, with `by value` being a default.

Both Oracle and DB2 have two types of `by reference` arguments, `OUT` and `IN OUT` (`INOUT` in DB2). The first one means you can not pass a value using the argument (you would usually pass `NULL` instead), but the nested program could assign a value to it that is readable by the main module. The second type means you could actually send a value to the subprogram, that it would use in its calculations, optionally change it, and send it back to the calling module. MS SQL Server has only one type of `by reference` variable called `OUTPUT` that roughly corresponds to `IN OUT`.

The syntax varies between implementations:

Oracle 9*i*

```
<variable_name> [IN | OUT IN OUT] <datatype>
```

For example:

```
my_value1 IN OUT NUMBER;
my_value2 OUT VARCHAR2;
my_value3 IN DATE;
```

Note that the last declaration could simply be

```
my_value3 DATE;
```

DB2 UDB 8.1

```
[IN | OUT INOUT]  <variable_name> <datatype>
```

For example:

```
INOUT my_value1 INTEGER;
OUT my_value2 VARCHAR(30);
IN my_value3 DATE;
```

The last statement is an equivalent to the following simple line:

```
my_value3 DATE;
```

MS SQL Server 2000

```
@<variable_name> <datatype> [OUTPUT]
```

For example:

```
@ my_value1 INTEGER OUTPUT
@ my_value3 DATETIME
```

There is no alternative for the last statement; `@my_value3 DATETIME INPUT` is invalid syntax.

Conditional execution

Sometimes you want your program to perform different actions based on different conditions (usually resulting from the previous program code execution). For example, you might want to multiply the amounts retrieved from a table by different factors depending on how large the amounts are.

The main conditional statement in all three proprietary procedural SQL extensions is one or another flavor of the `IF ... ELSE` construct in form:

```
IF <condition1> THEN
  <perform action 1>
[ELSE IF  <condition2>
  <perform action2>
]
...
[ELSE IF <conditionN>
  <perform actionN>]
]
...
[ELSE
  <perform default action>
]
END IF;
```

Here `<condition...>` is a Boolean expression that evaluates to `TRUE` or `FALSE`.

PL/SQL

The syntax is slightly different from the generic one listed previously. The main difference is you use the keyword `ELSIF` instead of `ELSE IF`:

```
IF v_prodcount = 0 THEN
   INSERT INTO product ...
ELSIF v_prodcount = 1 THEN
   ...
   UPDATE product ...
ELSE
   ...
END IF;
```

DB2 UDB

The syntax resembles PL/SQL except the `ELSEIF` keyword is used instead of `ELSIF`:

```
IF (v_prodcount) = 0 THEN
 INSERT INTO product ...
ELSEIF (v_prodcount = 1) THEN
  ...
  UPDATE product ...
ELSE
  ...
END IF;
```

Transact-SQL

The keyword THEN is not used in Transact-SQL; END is only used to end the program or a logical block, not to terminate the conditional statements. The syntax here illustrates the conditional constructs usage in Transact-SQL:

```
IF @v_prodcount = 0
  INSERT INTO product ...
ELSE IF @v_prodcount = 1
  ...
  UPDATE product...
ELSE
  ...
```

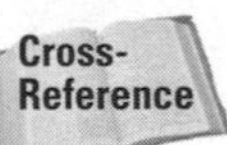

The CASE function, another example of conditional execution, is discussed in Chapter 10.

Repeated execution

Sometimes you want to repeat a certain block of code more than once within the same execution path. For example, you might want your program to read a line from a file, parse it into tokens, assign their values to variables, and insert a row of data into a table, repeating this operation until the end of file is reached. You may also want to read user input some predetermined number of times, or perform some calculations based on your variables until a certain result is obtained, and so on. The programming constructs that allow you to perform the repeated execution are called *loops*.

Most programming languages have three types of loops.

- ✦ WHILE loop repeats a predefined action while some condition remains TRUE.
- ✦ REPEAT UNTIL loop repeats a block of code until some condition becomes TRUE.
- ✦ FOR loop repeats the execution some predefined number of times.

All three types of loops can generally be simulated using just one syntax, for example, you can simulate both REPEAT UNTIL and FOR loops using a WHILE loop. Only Oracle PL/SQL has all three types of loops; however, all our "big three" databases have WHILE loop, so we are going to discuss it in this chapter. For more information on how to simulate other loops using the WHILE loop refer to vendor documentation.

PL/SQL

```
WHILE <condition>
LOOP
  <statement1>;
  [<statement2>;]...
END LOOP;
```

DB2 UDB

```
WHILE <condition>
DO
  <statement1>;
  [<statement2>;]...
END WHILE;
```

Transact-SQL

```
WHILE <condition>
  [BEGIN]
    <statement1>
    [ BREAK ]
    [<statement2>]...
    [ CONTINUE ]
  [END]
```

The two keywords BREAK and CONTINUE are important. BREAK causes an exit from the WHILE loop; any statements after the END keyword are executed. CONTINUE causes the WHILE loop to restart, ignoring any statements after the CONTINUE keyword.

Oracle and DB2 UDB use the EXIT and LEAVE/ITERATE keywords, respectively, for similar purposes. See vendor documentation for more information.

Cursors

Cursor is a special programming construct that allows you to create a named working area and access its stored information. The main advantage of cursors is the ability to work with individual rows one-by-one rather than with the record set as a whole. For example, all DML statements work with record sets, so you could change "all or nothing". If your update statement is changing hundreds of thousands rows, just one single row could cause the whole statement to fail and roll back all the changes if it violates a column constraint, resulting in serious time losses. Fortunately, cursors are able to handle such situations working with each row individually. A logic that combines cursors, loops, and conditional statements could generate a warning, store the unsuccessfull row information in a special table, and continue processing. Also, cursors give you flexibility on commits and rollbacks (you can commit after each row, after ten rows, or after every five hundred rows), which sometimes can be very useful to save system memory space; you can employ conditional logic and perform calculations on certain values before they are used in your DML statements; using cursors, you are able to update multiple tables with the same values, and much more.

Different RDBMS vendors implement cursors in different ways. Both syntax and functionality vary, which makes it difficult to talk about some generic cursor. SQL99 standards require a cursor to be scrollable, that is, you should be able to move back and forth from one record in the record set to another, but until recently only a few RDBMS vendors (notably MS SQL Server) implemented such functionality. The main reason is that a scrollable cursor is a huge resource waste and not every system can afford it. It is a known fact that many MS SQL Server developers are explicitly warned against using cursors unless it is absolutely necessary, whereas for PL/SQL programmers cursor use is an integral part of their everyday work.

In spite of all the differences, all cursor implementations have some common features. In general, the main operations you can perform on a cursor are DECLARE, OPEN, FETCH, and CLOSE.

DECLARE

DECLARE associates a cursor name with a certain SELECT statement and defines a memory structure to hold the appropriate columns (that could be of different data types). The simplified SQL99 syntax is

```
DECLARE <cursor_name> [SENSITIVE | INSENSITIVE] [SCROLL] CURSOR
FOR <select_statement>
[FOR [READ ONLY | UPDATE [OF <column_name>,...]]
```

INSENSITIVE means that a temporary copy of data based on the <select_statement> is made, so the cursor fetches are not sensitive to any DML changes of underlying tables that may happen afterwards; the default is SENSITIVE, which means every subsequent fetch uses the actual data at this particular moment of time.

SCROLL specifies the cursor as scrollable; that is, additional FETCH options (discussed later) are available.

READ ONLY prevents a cursor from changing data while UPDATE specifies updatable columns within the cursor.

The same syntax is valid in Transact-SQL (even though it has many additional advanced cursor features not mentioned in this book); the Oracle PL/SQL cursor declaration is quite different:

```
CURSOR <cursor_name> [<parameter_list>] [RETURN <return_type>]
IS <select_statement>;
```

As you can see, the keyword DECLARE is omitted; and the IS keyword is used instead of FOR; also PL/SQL cursors are not scrollable, but can optionally take parameters and return values.

DB2 cursors also do not allow scrolling; other than that the syntax is similar to the SQL99 one:

```
DECLARE <cursor_name> CURSOR
FOR <select_statement>
```

OPEN

The OPEN statement executes the underlying query and identifies the result set consisting of all rows that meet the conditions specified on the cursor declaration. The basic syntax is consistent between all three RDBMS:

```
OPEN <cursor_name>
```

FETCH

FETCH retrieves the current row (for nonscrollable cursors) or a specific row (for scrollable cursors), parses the row, and puts the column values into predefined set of variables. The Transact-SQL syntax is

```
FETCH [ NEXT | PRIOR | FIRST | LAST  | ABSOLUTE n   | RELATIVE  n ]
FROM <cursor_name>
INTO @<variable_name>,...
```

The PL/SQL and DB2 syntax for nonscrollable cursors is

```
FETCH <cursor_name>
INTO <variable_name>,...
```

The number of columns in the SELECT clause of the <select_statement> specified upon the cursor declaration must exactly match the number of variables specified in the INTO clause of the FETCH statement.

The cursor rows of nonscrollable cursors are usually fetched in a loop until the last row is processed; the scrollable cursors can be used as a part of a more complicated processing logic.

CLOSE

The CLOSE statement deallocates memory, releases locks, and makes the cursor's result set undefined. The syntax is

```
CLOSE <cursor_name>
```

The cursor can be reopened with the OPEN statement.

In addition to the four main cursor operations described in this section, Transact-SQL requires all cursors to be deallocated using the DEALLOCATE statement that releases all data structures comprising the cursor:

```
DEALLOCATE <cursor_name>
```

Cursor examples

As we mentioned before, cursors are used in row-by-row operations and are usually fetched within loop structures. The following examples are very simple; our main goal here is to show how to declare, open, fetch, and close a cursor with emphasis on the implementation differences.

The procedure SP_PRINTCUSTPHONE declares and opens the cursor cur_custphone based on a query retrieving records from the V_CONTACT_LIST view and then fetches them one by one and prints them to the standard output.

The term "standard output" identifies the device to which the program sends its output; usually, by default it's the display of your monitor. The standard output could be redirected into an OS file.

PL/SQL

Each PL/SQL cursor has four attributes associated with it that can be appended to the cursor name to return certain information. The arguments are as follows:

- ✦ **%FOUND.** TRUE if the last FETCH returned a row; FALSE otherwise.
- ✦ **%ISOPEN.** TRUE if the cursor is open; FALSE otherwise.
- ✦ **%NOTFOUND.** The logical opposite of %FOUND.
- ✦ **%ROWCOUNT.** The number of rows fetched so far.

The following example uses %FOUND to determine when to exit the loop (when it yields FALSE there are no more rows to fetch):

```
CREATE OR REPLACE PROCEDURE SP_PRINTCUSTPHONE
-- The procedure displays customer names and phone numbers
IS
 -- Declare local variables to fetch cursor values into
 v_custname VARCHAR(50);
 v_phone VARCHAR(20);
 -- Declare  cursor
 CURSOR cur_custphone IS
 SELECT name,
        phone_number
 FROM   v_contact_list
 WHERE  contact_type = 'customer';
BEGIN
 -- Open cursor
 OPEN cur_custphone;
 -- Fetch cursor for the first time
 FETCH cur_custphone
 INTO  v_custname,
         v_phone;
 -- Fetch records in loop until the last one is reached
 WHILE cur_custphone%FOUND
 LOOP
   FETCH cur_custphone
   INTO  v_custname,
         v_phone;
   -- Enable standard output
   DBMS_OUTPUT.ENABLE;
   -- Put line into the standard output
   DBMS_OUTPUT.PUT_LINE(v_custname || v_phone);
 END LOOP;
 -- Close cursor
 CLOSE cur_custphone;
END SP_PRINTCUSTPHONE;
/
```

Transact-SQL

Transact-SQL uses the so-called cursor global functions to obtain information about the cursor. The two most commonly used are `@@FETCH_STATUS`, which returns `0` (zero) if the last fetch was successful or a negative number otherwise, and `@@CURSOR_ROWS`, which returns the number of qualifying rows currently in the last cursor opened.

As we mentioned before, Transact-SQL cursors can be scrollable. Unlike PL/SQL or DB2 cursors, where you only can go to the next record in the record set while previous rows become unavailable unless you close and reopen the cursor, Transact-SQL gives you the option to navigate the entire record set contained in the cursor—in a way similar to how you would use your compact disk player buttons when jumping between the songs on the CD.

The following example uses `@@FETCH_STATUS` to determine when the loop is to be terminated; the cursor is not declared as scrollable to be consistent with the previous examples:

```
CREATE PROCEDURE SP_PRINTCUSTPHONE
-- The procedure displays customer names and phone numbers
AS
 -- Declare local variables to fetch cursor values into
 DECLARE @v_custname VARCHAR(50)
 DECLARE @v_phone VARCHAR(20)
 -- Declare  cursor
 DECLARE cur_custphone CURSOR FOR
 SELECT name,
        phone_number
 FROM   v_contact_list
 WHERE  contact_type = 'customer'
BEGIN
 -- Open cursor
 OPEN cur_custphone
 -- Fetch cursor for the first time
 FETCH cur_custphone
 INTO  @v_custname,
         @v_phone
 -- Fetch records in loop until the last one is reached
 WHILE @@fetch_status = 0
 BEGIN
   FETCH cur_custphone
   INTO  @v_custname,
         @v_phone
   PRINT @v_custname + @v_phone
 END
 -- Close cursor
 CLOSE cur_custphone
 DEALLOCATE cur_custphone
END
```

More detailed information on how to create stored procedures is given later in this chapter.

Error handling

The error handling varies a lot between the three procedural SQL extensions discussed in this book. Oracle and DB2 use structured error handling to deal with abnormal conditions during the program execution. When an error occurs, RDBMS raises an *exception* (syntax is quite different between Oracle and DB2). Exceptions can be predefined (for example, one of the most common ones in Oracle— `NO_DATA_FOUND` occurs when a `SELECT ... INTO` statement returns no rows) or user-defined. MS SQL Server allows you to raise, trap, and handle errors inside the program body.

The error handling is a quite complicated process. This chapter gives you just the very basics; the vendor-specific documentation is the best source if you need to know more.

PL/SQL

All PL/SQL programming blocks have an optional `EXCEPTION` section where the program control is passed if an error occurs. Oracle has a set of predefined exceptions. We already mentioned `NO_DATA_FOUND`; another common one is `TOO_MANY_ROWS`, which occurs if a single-row subquery returns more than one row; the generic one to be raised for any type of error is `OTHERS`. You could also declare and instantiate your own exceptions in the declaration section of the program and raise them in the program body:

```
CREATE PROCEDURE ...
AS
   ...
   /* To handle error conditions that have no predefined
      name, you must use the pragma EXCEPTION_INIT. A pragma
      is a compiler directive that is processed at compile
      time.
   */

   my_exception EXCEPTION;
   PRAGMA EXCEPTION_INIT(my_exception, -400);
   ...
BEGIN
   ...
   IF <special_condition>
      RAISE my_exception;
   ...
EXCEPTION
  WHEN no_data_found THEN
      <conditions to handle no_data_found>
```

```
    WHEN too_many_rows THEN
        <conditions to handle too_many_rows >
    WHEN my_exception THEN
        <conditions to handle my_exception >
    WHEN others THEN
        <conditions to handle all other exceptions >
  END;
```

The conditions to handle a specific exception can be quite different. For example, you might want to rollback (or commit) a transaction and exit the program; or in some situations you don't want any action at all but simply to continue the execution; you also might want to display (or write into a table or OS file) an error message, and so on.

DB2 UDB

When an error occurs in DB2, the behavior of your SQL program is determined by condition handlers. The three general conditions in DB2 are NOT FOUND, SQLEXCEPTION, and SQLWARNING. If a statement in your SQL program issues an SQLWARNING or NOT FOUND condition and a handler for the appropriate condition has been declared, the control is passed to the corresponding handler; otherwise DB2 passes control to the next statement in the program body. The situation is different when SQLEXCEPTION condition is issued by a statement. The control is still passed to the appropriate handler if the handler is declared; if not, the program execution is terminated and the control is passed to the calling module.

DB2 has three main handler types: CONTINUE, EXIT, and UNDO. CONTINUE means the program execution continues with the next statement after the one that caused the error (after the special error-handling statements are complete); EXIT tells the program to go to the last statement in the program; and UNDO is in a way similar to EXIT, but in addition all DML statements in the program are rolled back:

```
CREATE PROCEDURE ...
...
LANGUAGE SQL
BEGIN ATOMIC
  ...
  DECLARE [CONTINUE | EXIT | UNDO] HANDLER FOR <condition>
    [<error-handling statements>]
  ...
END
@
```

Transact-SQL

In Transact-SQL errors are usually handled using the conditional statements (IF ... ELSE) described above. The way to handle critical problems is to use RAISERROR statement that terminates the program and returns control to the calling module; otherwise if you want to continue the program execution, the GOTO statement can be used to point to the block of statements to execute:

```
CREATE PROCEDURE ...
AS
   ...
BEGIN
   ...
   IF <special_condition>
      RAISERROR(<paramters_for_reiserror>)
   ...
   IF <another_special_condition>
      GOTO <label>
   ...
   <label>
     <error_handling_statements>
   ...
END
```

The special global unary function @@error returns the error number for the last Transact-SQL statement executed. It is set to 0 if the statement executed successfully. If an error occurs, an error message number is returned. (See MS SQL Server documentation for error message numbers and descriptions.)

Stored procedures

As we mentioned before, stored procedures are linear or sequential programs. The syntax varies from implementation to implementation, but some common features can be emphasized. Stored procedures can accept parameters and allow local variable declarations; they are structured and allow the use of submodules; also, they allow repeated and conditional statement execution.

CREATE PROCEDURE syntax

The CREATE PROCEDURE syntax is different among RDBMS implementations. The simplified syntaxes for SQL99 and all our three major RDBMS vendors are provided below:

SQL99

```
CREATE PROCEDURE <procedure_name>
<procedure_definition>
```

PL/SQL

```
CREATE [OR REPLACE] PROCEDURE [qualifier.]<procedure_name>
([<argument_name> IN | OUT | IN OUT <datatype>
                                   [DEFAULT <default>],...])
{IS | AS}
  [<variable_name <datatype> [DEFAULT <default>];],...
BEGIN
  <procedure_body>
[EXCEPTION
  <exception_statements>]
END;
```

DB2 procedural language

```
CREATE PROCEDURE [qualifier.]<procedure_name>
([IN | OUT | INOUT <argument_name> <datatype>,...])
{MODIFIES SQL DATA |
 NO SQL |
 CONTAINS SQL |
 READS SQL DATA}
[[NOT] DETERMINISTIC]
LANGUAGE SQL
BEGIN [ATOMIC]
  <procedure_body>
END
```

Transact-SQL

```
CREATE PROC[EDURE] <procedure_name>
   [@<parameter_name> <datatype> [ = <default>] [OUTPUT] ] ,...
AS
   <procedure_body>
```

Creating a simple stored procedure

Our stored procedure implements the following business logic. New products are often entered into the `PRODUCT` table of the ACME sample database. The problem is the clerks sometimes enter duplicate product names using the different combinations of uppercase and lowercase letters. For example, SPRUCE LUMBER 30X40X50, spruce lumber 30x40x50 and Spruce Lumber 30X40X50 are supposed to be a single entry, but could be entered as three separate entities with different primary keys referred by foreign keys from other tables causing data integrity problems.

The procedure SP_PRODUCTADD adds a row to the PRODUCT table if the product with the given product description does not exist or updates the existing record with new values. It accepts ten parameters, one for each column in the PRODUCT table, then checks if a product with such a description (in uppercase or lowercase letters) already exists, and then performs the appropriate action (INSERT or UPDATE) based on the result.

Oracle 9*i*

A typical Oracle-stored procedure consists of header, declaration part, body, and exception handling component. The header (between keywords CREATE and IS) includes parameter names and data types. The local variables can be declared in the declaration section. The body stores the procedure's logic, and the optional exception section is for handling exceptions — errors that could happen during the execution of the procedure. Here is the syntax to implement this logic:

```
CREATE PROCEDURE sp_productadd
/* This procedure adds new product to PRODUCT table */
(
 v_prodid                NUMBER,
 v_prodprice             NUMBER,
 v_prodnum               VARCHAR2,
 v_proddesc              VARCHAR2,
 v_prodstatus            CHAR,
 v_prodbrand             VARCHAR2,
 v_prodpltwid            NUMBER,
 v_prodpltlen            NUMBER,
 v_prodnetwgt            NUMBER,
 v_prodshipwgt           NUMBER
)

IS
  -- Local variable declaration
  v_prodcount NUMBER := 0;
  v_prodid_existing NUMBER;
BEGIN
  -- Check if product with this name already exists
  SELECT COUNT (*)
  INTO   v_prodcount
  FROM   product
  WHERE  UPPER(prod_description_s) = UPPER(v_proddesc);
  -- Product does not exist
  IF v_prodcount = 0 THEN
   -- Insert row into PRODUCT based on arguments passed
   INSERT INTO product
   VALUES
         (
```

```
                v_prodid,
                v_prodprice,
                v_prodnum,
                v_proddesc,
                v_prodstatus,
                v_prodbrand,
                v_prodpltwid,
                v_prodpltlen,
                v_prodnetwgt,
                v_prodshipwgt
              );
    -- Product with this name already exists
    ELSIF v_prodcount = 1 THEN
      -- Find the product's primary key number
      SELECT prod_id_n
      INTO   v_prodid_existing
      FROM   product
      WHERE  UPPER(prod_description_s) = UPPER(v_proddesc);
      -- Update the existing product with values
      -- passed as arguments
      UPDATE product
      SET    prod_price_n = v_prodprice,
             prod_description_s = v_proddesc,
             prod_status_s = v_prodstatus,
             prod_brand_s = v_prodbrand,
             prod_pltwid_n = v_prodpltwid,
             prod_pltlen_n = v_prodpltlen,
             prod_netwght_n = v_prodnetwgt,
             prod_shipweight_n = v_prodshipwgt
      WHERE  prod_id_n = v_prodid_existing;
    END IF;

    -- No errors; perform COMMIT
    COMMIT;

  -- Exception section -- the execution flow goes here
  -- if an error occurs during the execution
  EXCEPTION
    WHEN OTHERS THEN
      -- Enable standard output
      DBMS_OUTPUT.ENABLE;
      -- Put line into the standard output
      DBMS_OUTPUT.PUT_LINE('Error');
      -- Rollback all changes
      ROLLBACK;
  END sp_productadd;
  /
```

The above stored procedure can be compiled directly from SQL*Plus command line or from a GUI tool like TOAD or Oracle Enterprise Manager and then called using the following syntax:

```
EXEC SP_PRODUCTADD
    (1, 23.67, 1, 'TEST PRODUCT', 'Y', 'TEST', 1, 3, 45, 33);
```

DB2 UDB

The structure of a DB2 stored procedure is similar to one of PL/SQL except it does not have an EXCEPTION section in it. The syntax to create our stored procedure using DB2 SQL procedural language is as follows:

```
CREATE PROCEDURE sp_productadd
/* This procedure adds new product to PRODUCT table */
(
 v_prodid                INTEGER,
 v_prodprice             DECIMAL(10,2),
 v_prodnum               VARCHAR(44),
 v_proddesc              VARCHAR(10),
 v_prodstatus            CHAR(1),
 v_prodbrand             VARCHAR(20),
 v_prodpltwid            DECIMAL(5,2),
 v_prodpltlen            DECIMAL(5,2),
 v_prodnetwgt            DECIMAL(10,3),
 v_prodshipwgt           DECIMAL(10,3)
)

LANGUAGE SQL
-- Transaction has to be atomic if we
-- want to be able to roll back changes
BEGIN ATOMIC
  -- Local variable declaration
  DECLARE v_prodcount INTEGER;
  DECLARE v_prodid_existing INTEGER;
  DECLARE v_result_set_end INTEGER DEFAULT 0;

  DECLARE UNDO HANDLER FOR SQLEXCEPTION
    BEGIN
      SET v_result_set_end = 1;
    END;


  SET v_prodcount = 0;

  SELECT COUNT (*)
  INTO   v_prodcount
  FROM   product
  WHERE  UPPER(prod_description_s) = UPPER(v_proddesc);

  IF (v_prodcount) = 0 THEN
   -- Insert row into PRODUCT based on arguments passed
   INSERT INTO product
   VALUES
         (
```

```
            v_prodid,
            v_prodprice,
            v_prodnum,
            v_proddesc,
            v_prodstatus,
            v_prodbrand,
            v_prodpltwid,
            v_prodpltlen,
            v_prodnetwgt,
            v_prodshipwgt
    );
   ELSEIF (v_prodcount = 1) THEN
     -- Find the product's primary key number
     SELECT prod_id_n
     INTO   v_prodid_existing
     FROM   product
     WHERE  UPPER(prod_description_s) = UPPER(v_proddesc);
     -- Update the existing product with values
     -- passed as arguments
     UPDATE product
     SET    prod_price_n = v_prodprice,
            prod_description_s = v_proddesc,
            prod_status_s = v_prodstatus,
            prod_brand_s = v_prodbrand,
            prod_pltwid_n = v_prodpltwid,
            prod_pltlen_n = v_prodpltlen,
            prod_netwght_n = v_prodnetwgt,
            prod_shipweight_n = v_prodshipwgt
     WHERE  prod_id_n = v_prodid_existing;
   END IF;

   -- perform COMMIT
   COMMIT;
 END
@@
```

To compile the foregoing stored procedure using DB2's Command Line Processor tool (CLP), use this syntax (assuming the above code is saved in file C:\SQLBIB\DB2\SP_PRODUCT.SQL):

```
db2 -td@ -vf "C:\SQLBIB\DB2_ACME\SP_PRODUCT.SQL"
```

MS SQL Server 2000

A MS SQL Server Transact-SQL stored procedure also consists of the header and the body; the variable declarations are done in the procedure body. The syntax to create the stored procedure with the foregoing functionality might be as follows:

```
CREATE PROCEDURE sp_productadd
/* This procedure adds new product to PRODUCT table */
  @v_prodid              INTEGER,
  @v_prodprice           MONEY,
  @v_prodnum             VARCHAR (10),
  @v_proddesc            VARCHAR (44),
  @v_prodstatus          CHAR,
  @v_prodbrand           VARCHAR (20),
  @v_prodpltwid          DECIMAL(5, 2),
  @v_prodpltlen          DECIMAL(5, 2),
  @v_prodnetwgt          DECIMAL(10, 3),
  @v_prodshipwgt         DECIMAL(10, 3)
AS
  -- Local variable declaration and preassignment
  declare @v_prodcount INTEGER
  select @v_prodcount = 0
  declare @v_prodid_existing INTEGER
BEGIN
 -- Begin transaction
 BEGIN TRANSACTION

 -- Check if product with this name already exists
 SELECT @v_prodcount=COUNT(*)
 FROM   product
 WHERE  UPPER(prod_description_s) = UPPER(@v_proddesc)

 -- Check for errors
 IF @@error <> 0 GOTO E_General_Error

 -- Product does not exist
 IF @v_prodcount = 0
  -- Insert row into PRODUCT based on arguments passed
  INSERT INTO product
  VALUES
  (
        @v_prodid,
        @v_prodprice,
        @v_prodnum,
        @v_proddesc,
        @v_prodstatus,
        @v_prodbrand,
        @v_prodpltwid,
        @v_prodpltlen,
        @v_prodnetwgt,
        @v_prodshipwgt
  )

 -- Check for errors
 IF @@error <> 0 GOTO E_General_Error

 -- Product with this name already exists
 ELSE IF @v_prodcount = 1
  -- Find the product's primary key number
```

```
    SELECT @v_prodid_existing = PROD_ID_N
    FROM   product
    WHERE  UPPER(prod_description_s) = UPPER(@v_proddesc)

    -- Check for errors
    IF @@error <> 0 GOTO E_General_Error

    -- Update the existing product with
    -- values passed as arguments
    UPDATE product
    SET    prod_price_n = @v_prodprice,
           prod_description_s = @v_proddesc,
           prod_status_s = @v_prodstatus,
           prod_brand_s = @v_prodbrand,
           prod_pltwid_n = @v_prodpltwid,
           prod_pltlen_n = @v_prodpltlen,
           prod_netwght_n = @v_prodnetwgt,
           prod_shipweight_n = @v_prodshipwgt
    WHERE  prod_id_n = @v_prodid_existing

    -- Check for errors
    IF @@error <> 0 GOTO E_General_Error

   -- No errors; perform COMMIT and exit
   COMMIT TRANSACTION
   RETURN

   -- If an error occurs, rollback and exit
   E_General_Error:
      PRINT 'Error'
      ROLLBACK TRANSACTION
      RETURN
  END
```

You probably notice some differences between Oracle (or DB2 UDB) and MS SQL Server syntax; for example, in MS SQL Server arguments are not enclosed in parentheses, the error handling is done in a different way, the variables are prefixed with at-signs, and so on. The stored procedure can be compiled using OSQL command-line tool, Query Analyzer, or other MS SQL Server-compatible tools; to execute this stored procedure you can use the following syntax:

```
EXEC SP_PRODUCTADD
    1, 23.67, 1, 'TEST PRODUCT', 'Y', 'TEST', 1, 3, 45, 33
```

Removing a stored procedure

The basic syntax to remove a stored procedure is identical for all three databases:

```
DROP PROCEDURE [qualifier.]<procedure_name>
```

Transact-SQL lets you drop multiple procedures within a single DROP PROCEDURE statement. The procedure names have to be separated by commas.

User-Defined Functions

User-defined functions combine the advantages of stored procedures with the capabilities of SQL predefined functions. They can accept parameters, perform specific calculations based on data retrieved by one or more SELECT statement, and return results directly to the calling SQL statement.

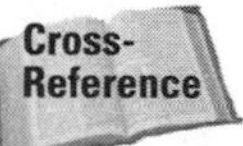

Built-in SQL functions are discussed in Chapter 10.

CREATE FUNCTION syntax

The CREATE FUNCTION syntax is different for different implementations. The simplified SQL99 syntax as well as syntaxes for all "big three" SQL procedural extensions are given here:

SQL99

```
CREATE FUNCTION <function_name>
<function_definition_includes_return_statement>
```

PL/SQL

```
CREATE [OR REPLACE] FUNCTION [qualifier.]<function_name>
([<argument_name> IN | OUT | IN OUT <datatype>
                                      [DEFAULT <default>],...])
RETURN <datatype>
{IS | AS}
  [<variable_name <datatype> [DEFAULT <default>];],...
BEGIN
  <function_body_includes_return_statement>
[EXCEPTION
  <exception_statements>]
END;
```

DB2 procedural language

```
CREATE FUNCTION <function_name>
([<argument_name> <datatype>,...])
RETURNS <datatype>
LANGUAGE SQL
[[NOT] DETERMINISTIC]
{MODIFIES SQL DATA |
 NO SQL |
 CONTAINS SQL |
 READS SQL DATA}
RETURN {<value> | <sql_statement>}
```

Transact-SQL

```
CREATE FUNCTION <function_name>
 ([@<parameter_name> <datatype> [ = <default>]],...)
RETURNS <datatype>
[AS]
BEGIN
   <function_body>
   RETURN <value>
END
```

Creating a simple function

Functions can be very useful in many situations. For example, imagine you need to extract order totals for customers with state sales tax added to the total price. The sales tax rate is different in different states; for example, in California it is 7.25 percent at this writing. In addition, in the ACME database the total price for orders is not stored anywhere (normalization tradeoffs) but has to be calculated dynamically by adding prices for all order items multiplied by item quantities. The latter is done in the ACME view V_CUSTOMER_TOTALS (see Chapter 4); user-defined function UF_ORDERTAX takes two parameters, tax factor and order number, and returns the total order amount multiplied by that factor.

PL/SQL

PL/SQL syntax to create user-defined functions is not much different from that for stored procedures. The main difference is it has to specify the return data type in the header section and return a value somewhere in the function body. Any code after the RETURN statement in the function body will be ignored. The code below creates function UF_ORDERTAX.

The slash (/) at the end is necessary to compile the function code from a SQLPLUS command line. (That is also true for compiling PL/SQL stored procedures and triggers.) It could usually be omitted when using a GUI tool:

```
CREATE OR REPLACE FUNCTION uf_ordertax
(
  v_tax       NUMBER,
  v_ordnum    VARCHAR2
)
RETURN NUMBER
AS
    -- Declare local variables
    v_result NUMBER;
    v_ordamt NUMBER;
BEGIN
    -- This query performs variable v_ordamt assignment
    SELECT  total_price
    INTO    v_ordamt
    FROM    v_customer_totals
    WHERE   order_number = v_ordnum;
    -- Variable v_result is v_ordamt multiplied by tax
    v_result := v_ordamt * v_tax;
    -- Return result
    RETURN v_result;
END;
/
```

PL/SQL user-defined functions have an optional EXCEPTION clause in the same way the stored procedures do. The foregoing example skips the EXCEPTION section.

As we mentioned before, the function could be called from within SQL statements using either literals or actual column names as the parameters:

```
SELECT  ordhdr_nbr_s,
        ordhdr_orderdate_d,
        uf_ordertax(1.0725, ordhdr_nbr_s) AS amt_incl_tax
FROM    order_header
   JOIN
        customer
   ON   (ordhdr_custid_fn  = cust_id_n)
   JOIN
        address
   ON   (cust_id_n = addr_custid_fn)
WHERE   addr_state_s = 'CA'
```

```
ORDHDR_NBR_S                   ORDHDR_ORDERDATE_D      AMT_INCL_TAX
------------------------------ ----------------------- ------------
523774                         2002-08-21 00:00:00.000      7037.52
523775                         2002-08-21 00:00:00.000     16461.49
523776                         2002-08-21 00:00:00.000     13734.45
523777                         2002-08-21 00:00:00.000     10660.65
523778                         2002-08-21 00:00:00.000      7037.52
523779                         2002-08-21 00:00:00.000      7037.52
523780                         2002-08-21 00:00:00.000      7037.52
523781                         2002-08-21 00:00:00.000     16403.34
523782                         2002-08-21 00:00:00.000      8984.34
523783                         2002-08-21 00:00:00.000     12927.60

10 rows selected.
```

Note that the function was executed ten times, once for each row returned by the SELECT statement.

DB2 UDB

DB2 procedural SQL extension has syntax for creating user-defined functions that is quite dissimilar from both PL/SQL and Transact SQL grammar (provided later in this chapter):

```
CREATE FUNCTION uf_ordertax
(
  v_tax       DECIMAL(12,2),
  v_ordnum    VARCHAR(10)
)
RETURNS DECIMAL(12,2)
LANGUAGE SQL NOT DETERMINISTIC
READS SQL DATA
RETURN
    -- This query performs variable v_ordamt assignment
    SELECT  total_price * v_tax
    FROM    v_customer_totals
    WHERE   order_number = v_ordnum
@
```

This function can be compiled in exactly the same way DB2 stored procedures are:

```
db2 -td@ -vf "C:\SQLBIB\DB2_ACME\UF_PRODUCT.SQL"
```

You can then call it from a SQL statement using the syntax given previously in the PL/SQL section.

Transact-SQL

The Transact-SQL syntax for user-defined functions is quite similar to the PL/SQL one — more than it resembles the Transact-SQL syntax for creating stored procedures. The parameters are enclosed by parentheses, and the function body is enclosed by the `BEGIN` and `END` keywords:

```
CREATE FUNCTION uf_ordertax
(
   @v_tax    NUMERIC(12,4),
   @v_ordnum VARCHAR(30)
)
RETURNS NUMERIC(12,4)
AS
BEGIN
     -- Declare local variables
     declare @v_result NUMERIC(12,4)
     declare @v_ordamt NUMERIC(12,4)
     -- Assign variable @v_ordamt using SELECT statement
     SELECT @v_ordamt = total_price
     FROM v_customer_totals
     WHERE ORDER_NUMBER = @v_ordnum;
     -- Variable @v_result is @v_ordamt multiplied by tax
     SET @v_result = @v_ordamt * @v_tax
     -- Return result
     RETURN @v_result
END
```

The call for a user-defined function from a SQL statement must be qualified with the user name, forming the so-called two-part name of the function:

```
SELECT  ordhdr_nbr_s,
        ordhdr_orderdate_d,
        dbo.uf_ordertax(1.065, ordhdr_nbr_s)
FROM    order_header
   JOIN
        customer
   ON   (ordhdr_custid_fn  = cust_id_n)
   JOIN
        address
   ON   (cust_id_n = addr_custid_fn)
WHERE   addr_state_s = 'CA'
```

A function could also be called with literals for both parameters:

```
SELECT dbo.uf_ordertax(1.065, '523774') AS ORDER_TOTAL
GO
```

```
ORDER_TOTAL
-----------------
     7037.5200

(1 row affected)
```

Removing a user-defined function

The basic syntax to remove a user-defined function is identical for all three databases:

```
DROP FUNCTION [qualifier.]<function_name>
```

Again, as in case with the stored procedures, Transact-SQL allows you to drop multiple functions within a single `DROP FUNCTION` statement.

Triggers

A trigger is a special type of stored procedure that fires off automatically whenever a special event in the database occurs. For example, a trigger can be invoked when a row is inserted into a specified table or when certain table columns are being updated.

CREATE TRIGGER syntax

The syntax differs among RDBMS products, none of which complies with the SQL99 standards.

SQL99

SQL99 only mandates triggers that automatically execute on DML events; here is the syntax to create a trigger:

```
CREATE TRIGGER <trigger_name>
[BEFORE | AFTER]
{INSERT | UPDATE | DELETE}
ON <table_name>
[FOR EACH ROW]
<trigger_body>
```

BEFORE and AFTER keywords specify whether the trigger fires off before or after the DML event actually takes place. In other words, if a particular trigger is designed to execute whenever a row is inserted into table A and the BEFORE keyword is specified, the trigger will fire off just before the RDBMS tries to perform the insert; if the trigger produced an error, the insert will never take place. The AFTER triggers execute upon the triggering DML statement completion; if an error occurs, the transaction will be rolled back.

Triggers with a FOR EACH ROW optional clause are sometimes referred as *row triggers*. A row trigger executes once for each row affected by a DML statement; for example if an UPDATE statement modifies column values in ten rows, the trigger will fire off ten times. If the clause is omitted, the trigger will only execute once no matter how many rows are affected (*table trigger*).

PL/SQL

Oracle's PL/SQL has all the options required by the SQL99 standards and many more. The following syntax includes only DML trigger clauses; in addition, PL/SQL allows you to create DDL and database triggers that fire off on specified DDLs (CREATE, ALTER, DROP, etc.) or database events (user logon/logoff, database startup/shutdown, and so on).

```
CREATE [OR REPLACE] TRIGGER [qualifier.]<trigger_name>
{BEFORE | AFTER | INSTEAD OF}
{INSERT | DELETE | UPDATE OF <column_name>,...} [OR],...
ON <table_or_view_name>
[REFERENCING OLD AS <name_for_old> NEW AS <name_for_new>]
[FOR EACH ROW]
[WHEN <condition> <sql_block>],... |
<trigger_body>
```

Like many other Oracle objects (stored procedures, functions, views, synonyms, sequences, etc.). PL/SQL syntax has an optional OR REPLACE clause (discussed in Chapter 4).

In addition to the BEFORE and AFTER keywords, INSTEAD OF could be specified (for views only); in that case Oracle performs actions coded in its body instead of executing the triggering event. That is especially useful when working with nonupdateable views (see Chapter 4) to simulate the updatable view behavior. For example, you cannot use a DML on a view that has a GROUP BY or DISTINCT clause in its definition; however, an INSTEAD OF trigger could include special logic that overrides that rule using procedural language constructs to execute appropriate DML statements.

Another advanced feature is the UPDATE OF clause. Unlike the SQL99 standard that only allows you to execute a trigger if any column of the triggered table is being updated, PL/SQL lets you specify update of which column (or a set of columns) fires off the trigger.

The REFERENCING clause allows you to specify alternative correlation names for OLD and NEW keywords used to prefix column names to access old (not modified) or new (modified) column values, correspondingly.

Some other PL/SQL advanced features include the ability to create triggers for multiple DML events and specify different actions for different events in the trigger body:

```
CREATE TRIGGER multi_action
BEFORE INSERT OR UPDATE ON my_table
...
WHEN INSERTING
   <code_to_execute_on_insert>
WHEN UPDATING
   <code_to_execute_on_update>
...
```

The following example creates trigger TRBU_PRODUCT that inserts a row into special auditing table PRODUCT_AUDIT each time PROD_PRICE_N value changes in PRODUCT table. The information includes the primary key of the modified row, the new and the old price values, the username of the person who modified the record, and the timestamp. The trigger fires off for every modified row in PRODUCT that meets the condition, so if someone issued an UPDATE statement that changes the price for five products, five rows would be inserted into PRODUCT_AUDIT.

```
CREATE OR REPLACE TRIGGER trbu_product
BEFORE  UPDATE OF prod_price_n ON product
FOR EACH ROW
BEGIN
    INSERT INTO  product_audit
    VALUES (:NEW.prod_id_n,
            :OLD.prod_price_n,
            :NEW.prod_price_n,
            USER,
            SYSDATE);
END;
/
```

The name of the trigger in the foregoing example extends the Hungarian notation discussed in other chapters. TRBU stands for Trigger for each Row Before Update.

DB2

DB2's procedural language has the following syntax to create a trigger:

```
CREATE TRIGGER <trigger_name>
[NO CASCADE BEFORE | AFTER]
{INSERT | DELETE | UPDATE [OF COLUMN <column_name>,...]}
ON <table_name>
[FOR EACH ROW MODE DB2SQL | FOR EACH STATEMENT]
[REFERENCING OLD AS <name_for_old> NEW AS <name_for_new>]
<trigger_body>
```

The syntax in general resembles SQL99 specifications with the exception of some minor details. For example, simply BEFORE is not good enough — you have to specify NO CASCADE BEFORE. Also, to create a row trigger, MODE DB2SQL keywords have to be added to the FOR EACH ROW clause.

The MODE clause specifies the mode of triggers; DB2SQL is the only currently supported one in DB2.

The REFERENCING clause is similar to that of PL/SQL except even though the clause itself is optional, you have to specify alternative names for OLD and NEW if you want to use them in the trigger's body.

The trigger TRAU_PRODUCT created using the code in the following example has the same functionality as the trigger TRBU_PRODUCT described in the PL/SQL example earlier in this chapter:

```
CREATE TRIGGER trau_product
AFTER UPDATE OF prod_price_n ON product
REFERENCING NEW AS NNN OLD AS OOO
FOR EACH ROW MODE DB2SQL
BEGIN ATOMIC
        INSERT INTO product_audit
        VALUES (NNN.prod_id_n,
                OOO.prod_price_n,
                NNN.prod_price_n,
                USER,
                CURRENT DATE);
END
@
```

Transact-SQL

Here is the generalized Transact-SQL syntax for creating triggers:

```
CREATE TRIGGER <trigger_name>
ON <table_or_view>
{ FOR | AFTER | INSTEAD OF }
{INSERT | UPDATE | DELETE}
AS
[IF UPDATE ( <column_name> )
          [AND | OR UPDATE ( <column_name> ) ],...]
<trigger_body>
```

FOR is the Transact-SQL equivalent to the SQL99 keyword BEFORE.

Unlike PL/SQL, the INSTEAD OF clause can be specified for both table and view triggers.

The IF UPDATE clause allows you specify the updating of those columns (or combinations of columns) that cause the trigger to fire off.

The following syntax creates a trigger that functions identically to the PL/SQL one discussed in the previous section:

```
CREATE TRIGGER trbu_product ON product
FOR UPDATE
AS
IF UPDATE (prod_price_n)
    INSERT INTO product_audit
    SELECT  i.prod_id_n,
            d.prod_price_n,
            i.prod_price_n,
            USER,
            GETDATE()
     FROM   inserted i
       JOIN
            deleted d
       ON i.prod_id_n = d.prod_id_n
```

Several things in this example require explanation. Unlike PL/SQL or DB2 UDB, Transact-SQL does not have special structures OLD and NEW that hold the original and modified values of table columns. Instead, MS SQL Server provides two special virtual tables, DELETED (stores copies of the affected rows during DELETE and UPDATE operations) and INSERTED (holds copies of the affected rows during INSERT and UPDATE). We can join the two tables as shown above to get the values that have to be inserted into PRODUCT_AUDIT.

Tip

To imitate `FOR EACH ROW` functionality in Transact-SQL, use a cursor. See vendor documentation for details.

Removing a trigger

This syntax removes an existing trigger definition from the system catalog:

```
DROP TRIGGER [qualifier.]<trigger_name>
```

The syntax is identical for all three databases. Transact-SQL allows you to drop multiple triggers just in the same way as when dropping stored procedures, user-defined functions, or any other database objects.

Summary

This chapter introduces the key components of the SQL procedural languages, for which the main purpose is to amend deficiencies of non-procedural nature of SQL proper. The ISO/ANSI standard provides for the existence of the RDBMS-stored modules for data processing without specifying what language should be used for the implementation. Left to their own devices, vendors have implemented it in a variety of ways — from their own proprietary SQL extensions like PL/SQL (Oracle), Transact-SQL (Microsoft SQL Server and Sybase), TSQL or IBM SQL (IBM DB2 UDB), to Java, Cobol, and Visual Basic (Data Transformation Services).

Programming RDBMS using these languages does not differ much from creating programs using any other programming language, with the notable exception that these SQL extensions are database-oriented, and include many specific constructs for specific tasks (like cursors, for row-by-row data manipulation).

The procedural SQL programs can be compiled into a variety of the module types: stored procedures, user-defined functions, and triggers. All these might differ in flavor, with various invocation methods and so on, but the general principles remain the same: the module is compiled and stored server-side using either a proprietary SQL extension language or a general-purpose language (like Java); the module includes constructs of the procedural language and SQL statements, and is executed within RDBMS environment.

The procedural languages are not part of the SQL standard (though persistent modules are mandated), and some popular SQL products did not even have this capability until very recently.

✦ ✦ ✦

Dynamic and Embedded SQL Overview

✦ ✦ ✦ ✦

In This Chapter

SQL statement processing steps

Embedded SQL elements

Dynamic DML and DDL

Dynamic query overview

Static versus dynamic SQL

✦ ✦ ✦ ✦

As you already know, SQL is a nonprocedural language. In the previous chapter, you learned how to create procedural programs using proprietary SQL procedural extensions. These programs (stored procedures, user-defined functions, triggers, etc.) are stored inside RDBMS. This approach, though very popular since the 1990s, was not the first attempt to empower SQL with procedural language capabilities. The idea of the embedded SQL arose long before the SQL procedural extensions were developed. It was introduced by IBM in the beginning of the 1980s and then implemented by many other SQL vendors. The dynamic SQL was the logical continuation of the embedded SQL principles that alleviated some limitations and inconveniences of the latter.

SQL Statement Processing Steps

The internal mechanisms of SQL statement processing are different for each RDBMS, but generally, there are always these five steps involved to process an SQL statement.

1. The RDBMS *parses* the SQL statement by breaking it up into individual words (tokens) and validating the statement syntax. The purpose of this step is to make sure the statement does not have typos and logical errors in it (if it does, the processing stops right there, saving time and system resources). For example, the following statements would be rejected at the first step because the first one has keyword `SELECT` misspelled, and in the second one the order of the `FROM` and `WHERE` clauses is incorrect:

```
SELCT *
FROM CUSTOMER
```

```
SELECT *
WHERE CUST_ID_N = 65
FROM CUSTOMER
```

Generally, any SQL statement consists of three types of tokens: keywords like SELECT, UPDATE, WHERE, etc.; table, view, constraint, or other database object names and column names; and values assigned to the columns or used in WHERE and HAVING clause predicates (or special variables for these values that could be substituted with real values in the runtime). In Step 1 of the process described here, only the first group of tokens is validated.

Parsing is usually the quickest step because it does not require actual database access.

2. The statement is then *validated* by the RDBMS by checking the statement against the information schema. In fact, this step validates the second group of tokens by making sure all the table and column names exist in the database. In addition, it checks the user privileges to execute the statement, ensures the column names are not ambiguous, and so on. For example, the following statement would fail at Step 2 (if you try to execute it against ACME sample database) because column CUST_ID does not exist in the CUSTOMER table:

```
UPDATE CUSTOMER
SET CUST_NAME_S = 'THE BEST CUSTOMER'
WHERE CUST_ID = 65
```

3. The next step is to *optimize* the statement. The query optimization process differs significantly between different RDBMS vendors, but the idea is the same: to find the most efficient way to execute the SQL statement. For example, it determines in which order the tables should be joined, when search conditions are to be applied, whether use the existing indexes on certain columns, and so on. Optimization is usually very CPU-intensive; the RDBMS may need to choose from dozens of different ways to process the same query, especially if it is complex and involves multiple table joins and conditions; however, when done in the right way, optimization could improve the query performance dramatically.

4. The next step is to *generate an execution plan* for the statement based on the optimization process performed during Step 3. The execution plan is simply a binary representation of the optimized sequence of actions.

5. Finally, the set of binary instructions created in Step 4 is executed by the RDBMS. Most database vendors provide mechanisms that allow you to substitute the third group of token variables with the actual values at this point.

In addition to the standard five steps to process any SQL statement, an additional step is necessary when processing a SELECT statement, namely returning the query results in some organized form.

We will be talking about the five steps of SQL statement processing again in this chapter when discussing dynamic SQL.

Embedded (Static) SQL

The idea of embedded SQL is simple — implant the SQL statements into the program written in a traditional procedural language, like C, COBOL, FORTRAN, or Pascal. This approach enables you to combine SQL's capability to work with relational database tables (and more) with all the power of a procedural language (variables, parameters, subprograms, iterations, conditional statements, etc.).

The major elements of a procedural language are introduced in Chapter 14.

Embedded SQL and SQL99 standards

Embedded SQL is a classic example of how de-facto IBM-based standards became SQL99 standards. As we mentioned before, IBM developed and implemented embedded SQL principles in the early 1980s; since then most vendors were simply following these standards with just slight variations. The standards were recognized first by SQL92 and later by SQL99 specifications.

All the "big three" vendors featured in this book support the ANSI/ISO standards to some extent. Oracle provides precompilers for C/C++, COBOL, ADA, PL/I, and FORTRAN; DB2 supports embedded SQL for C, COBOL, PL/I, FORTRAN, and Java; and MS SQL Server allows you to use only C language.

Embedded and Dynamic SQL Terminology

The terminology used in this chapter follows commonly accepted conventions. However, it may look confusing to some. For example, we are talking about embedded and dynamic SQL as if they were two separate topics, whereas dynamic SQL is rather an extension to the embedded SQL; dynamic SQL simply adds some functionality and extends the embedded SQL syntax. It is more appropriate to talk about two variations of the embedded SQL — static and dynamic.

Another commonly misinterpreted issue is the differences between the embedded SQL and the vendor-specific procedural SQL extensions. For example, Oracle allows you to write stored procedures using Java language, or, as an alternative, you could create a C program with embedded SQL. The main difference between a stored procedure and a host program is that the stored procedure is a compiled code stored inside the database, whereas a host program with embedded SQL resides outside the database as a binary file somewhere in the operating system.

Embedded SQL basic elements

Even though the embedded SQL syntax differs slightly for different implementations (mostly because of the proprietary SQL syntax variations), the concept and the elements are the same. You have to declare host variables, establish database connection, execute one or more SQL statements, get the results, and perform some error handling when necessary.

To be able to use embedded SQL in your host program, you must provide it with special instructions on how to find the specific precompiler files for the RDBMS the host program will be using.

Host variables

Host variables are the key to communication between your host program and the server. They are used to pass data to RDBMS and/or to receive the information back from it. In other words, the host variables are necessary to link the SQL statements with the host language (C, COBOL, etc.) statements. For example, your C program could pass parameters accepted from the command line into an SQL statement using previously declared host variables.

Host variables declaration

The declaration of the host variables is done in the `DECLARE` section in the following form:

```
EXEC SQL BEGIN DECLARE SECTION <language-specific delimiter>
      <language-specific variable declaration>,...
EXEC SQL END DECLARE SECTION <language-specific delimiter>
```

The `EXEC SQL` keyword is used to start an embedded SQL block in a host-language program.

The following three examples show how to declare a character-string host variable that can hold fifty characters and another variable of type integer in C, COBOL, and FORTRAN, respectively:

Example 1

```
EXEC SQL BEGIN DECLARE SECTION;
      char custname [51];
      int custid;
      ...
EXEC SQL END DECLARE SECTION;
```

Example 2

```
EXEC SQL BEGIN DECLARE SECTION END-EXEC.
       01 CUSTNAME PIC X(50).
       01 CUSTID   PIC S9(9) COMP.
       ...
EXEC SQL END DECLARE SECTION END-EXEC.
```

Example 3

```
EXEC SQL BEGIN DECLARE SECTION
       CHARACTER*50 CUSTNAME
       INTEGER*4 CUSTID
       ...
EXEC SQL END DECLARE SECTION
```

As you can notice, the delimiter in C is a semicolon (;), COBOL uses the keyword END-EXEC, and no delimiter is necessary in FORTRAN. The host data types are usually declared according to the host-language variable declaration rules using data types valid for this specific language. SQL99 rules require host variable names to be no longer than eighteen characters, but most RDBMS allow longer names.

Input versus output host variables

As we mentioned before, the purpose of using host variables is to provide communication between the host program and the RDBMS. Generally, you can divide host variables into two main categories: input and output host variables. The input host variables transfer information from the host program to RDBMS, and the output host variables receive data from the database. Host variables can be used anywhere an expression can be used; however, in SQL statements, they must be prefixed with a colon (:), to set them apart from database schema names.

Host variables and SQL data types correspondence

The correspondence between host variables and SQL data types is a complex and unintuitive topic. The fact that some host-language data types share their names with incompatible SQL data types adds even more confusion.

Table 15-1 shows the correspondence between SQL99 data types and some host-language data types (C, COBOL, and FORTRAN). You will need to refer to vendor-specific documentation for more information.

Many SQL99 data types do not have exact equivalents in the host languages; for example, all date and time related data types must be converted into host-language-compatible character string data types.

Table 15-1
Data type Correspondence

SQL99	*C*	*COBOL*	*FORTRAN*
`CHAR(n)`	`char[n+1]`	`PIC (n)`	`CHARACTER*n`
`DECIMAL/NUMERIC`	`Double`	`V9(s) COMP-3`	`REAL*8`
`DOUBLE`	`Double`	`COMP-2`	`REAL*8`
`INTEGER`	`Long`	`PIC S9 (9)`	`INTEGER*4`
`REAL`	`Float`	`COMP-1`	`REAL*4`
`SMALLINT`	`Short`	`PIC S9 (4) COMP`	`INTEGER*2`
`VARCHAR(n)`	`char*`	`NO EQUIVALENT`	`NO EQUIVALENT`

Dealing with NULLs and indicator variables

The concept of null is foreign to most programming languages. To deal with that issue, embedded SQL introduces the concept of *indicator variables*. You can associate any host variable with an optional indicator variable. Every time an SQL statement uses the host variable, a result is stored in its associated indicator variable, providing you the capability to monitor host variables and treat them accordingly.

Indicator variables must be declared in the host variable declaration sections, just like any other host variables. The appropriate data type for an indicator variable is `short` in C; `PIC S9(4) COMP` in COBOL; and FORTRAN programs could use `INTEGER*2`.

Indicator variables must be placed immediately after the corresponding host variable specified in the Embedded SQL statement (without separating them with a comma); they can be used with both input and output host variables. The first scenario is typically used to assign `NULL` values in DML statements while the second situation allows you to handle nulls received by `SELECT INTO` (discussed later in this chapter) or as the result of a cursor fetch.

Tables 15-2 and 15-3 show how the value of an indicator variable affects the related host variable.

Table 15-2
Indicator Variable Values (Input)

Value	*Meaning*
`-1`	`NULL` will be assigned to the column; the value of the host variable is ignored.
`>= 0`	The value of the host variable will be assigned to the column.

Table 15-3
Indicator Variable Values (Output)

Value	*Meaning*
-1	The column value is NULL.
0	The column value is not NULL; the original column value is assigned to the associated host variable.
> 0	The column value is not NULL, but the original column value was truncated before it was assigned to the associated host variable.

In the following examples (written in C and COBOL, respectively), we declare host variable price (PRICE) along with indicator variable priceind (PRICEIND), assigned the value of -1 to the latter, and then used the variables in the UPDATE statement to modify the price for product 990 to be NULL.

```
EXEC SQL BEGIN DECLARE SECTION;
       double price;
       short  priceind = -1;
       ...
EXEC SQL END DECLARE SECTION;
...
EXEC SQL UPDATE PRODUCT
SET PROD_PRICE_N = :price:priceind
WHERE PROD_ID_N = 990;
...
```

```
EXEC SQL BEGIN DECLARE SECTION END-EXEC.
       01 PRICE V9(9) COMP-3.
       01 PRICEIND    PIC S9(4) COMP VALUE -1.
       ...
EXEC SQL END DECLARE SECTION END-EXEC.
...
EXEC SQL UPDATE PRODUCT
SET PROD_PRICE_N = :PRICE:PRICEIND
WHERE PROD_ID_N = 990 END-EXEC.
...
```

Database connection

Before your program can start doing anything else, it has to establish connection to the target database. The embedded SQL keyword CONNECT is used for that purpose; the grammar again is vendor-specific with generic syntax specified below:

```
EXEC SQL
   CONNECT <connect_string>
<language-specific delimiter>
```

The `<connect_string>` is different for different RDBMS, and the delimiter is host-language-specific. For example, to connect to Oracle using Pro*C (Oracle's precompiler for C/C++), you can use this embedded SQL statement (assuming the host variables `username` and `password` of appropriate data types are properly declared and some meaningful values are assigned to them):

```
EXEC SQL CONNECT :username IDENTIFIED BY :password;
```

This example is the typical situation when the input host variable is used to pass the information (the user name and the password) from your host program to the RDBMS.

The `<connect_string>` in a C program that connects to DB2 UDB would be slightly different, as shown in the following example:

```
EXEC SQL CONNECT TO :database USER :username USING :password;
```

This example assumes that the additional host variable, `database`, is in place. In the Oracle example, we assumed the default database connection; otherwise the connect string would be slightly different.

The syntax to connect to MS SQL Server is quite similar, except the username and the password must be concatenated with an intervening dot (.):

```
strcat(strcat(username, "."), password);
EXEC SQL CONNECT TO :database USER :username;
```

The first line of code is simply using the C function `strcat()` to represent the username and password in the form `username.password` and store the result in the host variable username; the second line performs the database connection.

All the previous examples are using C as the host language; the syntax for COBOL connecting to Oracle and DB2 UDB, respectfully, follows:

Oracle example

```
EXEC SQL
   CONNECT :USERNAME IDENTIFIED BY :PASSWORD
END-EXEC.
```

DB2 UDB example

```
EXEC SQL
   CONNECT TO :DATABASE USER :USERNAME USING :PASSWORD
END-EXEC.
```

These examples assume three host variables: DATABASE, USERNAME, and PASSWORD.

Data retrieval and SELECT INTO statement

One of the major advantages of embedded SQL over nonprocedural SQL is the ability to retrieve data from a database server into host variables and use that data within the host program. A special variation of the SELECT statement, SELECT INTO, is used to accomplish this task. The syntax is very similar to that of the regular SQL SELECT statement; the main difference is that in the INTO clause of the SELECT INTO statement, you specify the host variables to store the resulting set rather than sending it to the standard output:

```
SELECT     {[<qualifier>.]<column_name> | <expression>},...
INTO       <host_variable>,...
FROM       <from_clause>
[WHERE     <predicate>]
[GROUP BY [<qualifier>.]<column_name>,...
 [HAVING <predicate>]
]
```

SELECT INTO has some limitations, but in general it is capable of doing most things the regular SELECT can do, including grouping, using aggregate functions, and so on. (The SELECT statement was discussed in Chapter 8.) The number of columns listed in the SELECT clause must match the number of host variables in the INTO clause; they also must be of compatible data types. Also, the query must return one and only one row, otherwise either TOO MANY ROWS or NO DATA FOUND RDBMS error is generated.

Assuming host variable declarations earlier in this chapter, the following SELECT INTO statement selects CUST_ID_N and CUST_NAME_S columns from the CUSTOMER table using the ACME sample database for a customer with alias MNGA71396:

C

```
EXEC SQL SELECT CUST_ID_N, CUST_NAME_S
INTO :custid, :custname
FROM CUSTOMER
WHERE CUST_ALIAS_S = 'MNGA71396';
```

COBOL

```
EXEC SQL SELECT CUST_ID_N, CUST_NAME_S
INTO :CUSTID, :CUSTNAME
FROM CUSTOMER
WHERE CUST_ALIAS_S = 'MNGA71396' END-EXEC.
```

The host variables used in these SQL statements are output host variables; you could combine both input and output host variables in a single SELECT INTO statement. For example, assuming another host variable, custalias (CUSTALIAS) was declared and the value MNGA71396 has been assigned to it, the above statements could be written in this form:

C

```
EXEC SQL SELECT CUST_ID_N, CUST_NAME_S
INTO :custid, :custname
FROM CUSTOMER
WHERE CUST_ALIAS_S = :custalias;
```

COBOL

```
EXEC SQL SELECT CUST_ID_N, CUST_NAME_S
INTO :CUSTID, :CUSTNAME
FROM CUSTOMER
WHERE CUST_ALIAS_S = :CUSTALIAS END-EXEC.
```

In this case, CUSTID and CUSTNAME are still used as output host variables, and CUSTALIAS plays the role of an input host variable since it transfers data from the host program to RDBMS.

Using cursors to store multirow query results

SELECT INTO can be useful in many situations, but it has a very serious limitation— it can only return one row at a time. We introduced the concept of the CURSOR in Chapter 14, so not to repeat ourselves let us simply remind you there are four basic operations on a cursor: DECLARE, OPEN, FETCH, and CLOSE. You can use both input and output host variables in DECLARE and FETCH. The following examples show how to use a cursor to retrieve CUST_ID_N and CUST_NAME_S columns from the CUSTOMER table, row by row, and fetch the values into the host variables until the last row is processed:

C

```
...
EXEC SQL DECLARE custcur CURSOR FOR
SELECT CUST_ID_N, CUST_NAME_S
FROM CUSTOMER;
...
EXEC SQL OPEN custcur;
...
do
{
 EXEC SQL FETCH custcur
 INTO :custid, :custname;
 ...
 if (SQLCODE != 0) break;
}
...
EXEC SQL CLOSE custcur;
...
```

COBOL

```
...
EXEC SQL DECLARE CUSTCUR CURSOR FOR
SELECT CUST_ID_N, CUST_NAME_S
FROM CUSTOMER END-EXEC.
...
EXEC SQL OPEN CUSTCUR END-EXEC.
...
FETCH-LOOP.
 EXEC SQL FETCH CUSTCUR INTO :CUSTID, :CUSTNAME END-EXEC.
 ...
GO TO LOOP. EXIT.
...
EXEC SQL CLOSE CUSTCUR END-EXEC.
...
```

Handling errors

Error handling is an important part of any application program. For a program with embedded SQL, error handling means detecting and recovering from SQL statement execution errors (in addition to any other errors in the program). It is critical to check for error conditions after every DML statement to make sure it processed all data it was supposed to; when using a `SELECT INTO` statement, you usually check if a single row query returned no data (`NO DATA` condition) or more than one row (`TOO MANY ROWS` condition).

SQL99 specifies two variables, SQLCODE and SQLSTATE, for error handling needs. SQLCODE is pretty much implementation-specific. A negative value indicates some serious problem; a positive number points to a warning; and zero means successful completion. SQLSTATE is the new SQL99 standard; it consists of error class and error subclass, which are consistent across implementations. Table 15-4 shows several SQLSTATE classes and subclasses and their meanings.

Table 15-4
Selected SQLSTATE Codes

Code	*Code Condition*	*Subcode*	*Subcode condition*
00	Successful completion	00000	Successful completion
01	Warning	01000 01001 01007	Warning Cursor operation conflict Privilege not granted
02	No data	02000	No data
08	Connection exception	08000 08002 08006	Connection exception Connection name is use Connection failure
0A	Feature not supported	0A000 0A001	Feature not supported Multiple server transactions
23	Integrity constraint violation	23000	Integrity constraint violation
27	Triggered data change violation	27000	Triggered data change violation

The error handling is usually done in the host program using programming language-specific conditional statements. For example:

C

```
...
EXEC SQL <embedded_sql_statement>;
if (SQLCODE < 0)
{
  <condition_to_handle_error>,...
}
...
```

```
...
EXEC SQL <single_row_select>;
if (SQLSTATE != "02000")
{
  <do_something>,...
}
...
```

COBOL

```
EXEC SQL <embedded_sql_statement> END-EXEC.
IF SQLCODE LESS THAN 0
  <condition_to_handle_error>,...
...
```

```
...
EXEC SQL <single_row_select> END-EXEC.
IF SQLSTATE NOT = "02000"
  <do_something>,...
...
```

You must declare SQLCODE and/or SQLSTATE before you can use it in your program; refer to vendor-specific documentation for details.

As an alternative to checking SQLCODE and/or SQLSTATE values after each embedded SQL statement, you can use SQL Communications Area (SQLCA) to handle embedded SQL errors. SQLCA is a structure containing components that are filled in at runtime after the SQL statement is processed by RDBMS. Before your program can start using SQLCA, you have to include the structure in your program using the following syntax (usually somewhere before the host variables declaration section):

C

```
EXEC SQL INCLUDE SQLCA;
```

COBOL

```
EXEC SQL INCLUDE SQLCA END-EXEC.
```

The main advantage of using SQLCA is that in addition to explicit checking of its components in a way similar to how you would do it with SQLCODE and SQLSTATE variables, you can perform implicit checking using WHENEVER statement.

Rather than checking errors after every single embedded SQL statement, with the WHENEVER statement you can specify actions to be taken when RDBMS detects errors, warnings, or NOT FOUND conditions. You can tell the program to go to the next (or specifically labeled) statement, call a subprogram, or stop execution.

The general syntax for the WHENEVER statement is:

```
EXEC SQL WHENEVER {SQLERROR | SQLWARNING | NOT FOUND}
{CONTINUE | GOTO <label> | DO | STOP} <language-specific delimiter>
```

The error handling with WHENEVER is less specific, but much simpler than using SCLCODE or SQLSTATE. All you have to do is use the appropriate calls somewhere before the first SQL call in your program:

C

```
...
EXEC SQL WHENEVER SQLERROR GOTO my_error;
EXEC SQL WHENEVER NOT FOUND CONTINUE;
EXEC SQL WHENEVER SQLWARNING CONTINUE;
...
```

COBOL

```
...
EXEC SQL WHENEVER SQLERROR GOTO MYERROR END-EXEC.
EXEC SQL WHENEVER NOT FOUND CONTINUE END-EXEC.
EXEC SQL WHENEVER SQLWARNING CONTINUE END-EXEC.
...
```

Additional useful embedded SQL statements

Some additional useful embedded SQL statements are listed in Table 15-5.

Table 15-5
Useful Embedded SQL Statements

Generic statement syntax	*Explanation*
EXEC SQL COMMIT [WORK] [RELEASE] <language-specific delimiter>	End the current transaction making all database changes permanent. The optional keyword RELEASE also frees resources and disconnects from the database.
EXEC SQL ROLLBACK [WORK] [RELEASE] <language-specific delimiter>	End the current transaction, discarding all database changes. The optional keyword RELEASE also frees resources and disconnects from the database.
EXEC SQL CONNECT RESET <language-specific delimiter> EXEC SQL INSERT INTO <table_name>[<columns_clause>] VALUES <values_clause>	Disconnect for the database.
<language-specific delimiter> EXEC SQL UPDATE <table_name> SET <set_clause> [<where_clause>]	Add rows to a table.
<language-specific delimiter> EXEC SQL DELETE FROM <table_name>	Change existing values in a table.
[<where_clause>] <language-specific delimiter>	Remove rows from a table.

A typical embedded SQL program flow

The following example illustrates the typical flow of a program containing embedded SQL:

```
EXEC SQL BEGIN DECLARE
  <host_variable_declaration>,...
EXEC SQL END DECLARE SECTION <language-specific delimiter>

EXEC SQL INCLUDE SQLCA <language-specific delimiter>

EXEC SQL WHENEVER <condition> <action>
```

```
<language-specific delimiter>,...

EXEC SQL CONNECT <vendor-specific connect string>
<language-specific delimiter>

EXEC SQL SELECT INTO <single_select>
<vendor-specific delimiter>,...

EXEC SQL <embedded_dml_statement>
<language-specific delimiter>,...

EXEC SQL COMMIT <vendor-specific delimiter >

EXEC SQL CONNECT RESET <vendor-specific delimiter >

<error handling section referred from WHENEVER directive>
```

Dynamic SQL Techniques

The embedded static SQL techniques discussed in the previous section can be useful in many situations, but sometimes they are not flexible enough to satisfy all your needs. The classic example is a GUI-based application that allows users to build their own ad hoc queries by using dropdown lists to choose column (or even table) names and conditions for the WHERE clause. The application would build the appropriate query dynamically, send it to the RDBMS, receive the results, and display them in some nice, easily readable form. The static SQL would not allow you to build your queries on the fly because of the way it handles the five steps of a SQL statement execution (discussed in the beginning of this chapter). In fact, the first four steps are carried out during the compile time; that is, the statement parsing, validation, optimization, and the binary execution plan generation are all done when you compile your host-language program. That means your SQL statements are hardcoded in your program, allowing you to substitute values for the third group of tokens only (explained earlier in this chapter).

Dynamic SQL overrides these limitations by postponing all the five steps until the actual runtime. The SQL statements could be built dynamically during the program execution based on user-supplied parameters, such as table names, column names, search conditions, and so on.

Two varieties of dynamic SQL

Generally, all dynamic SQL can be divided into two categories. The first one includes any dynamically built DML and DDL statements, and the other one handles dynamic queries.

The difference between these two categories is rooted in SQL processing specifics. As we mentioned in the beginning of this chapter, there is an additional step in SELECT statement processing that involves returning query results in organized form. Because a DML (or DDL) statement can either be successful or unsuccessful only, all we usually need back from the RDBMS is the return code (SQLCODE or SQLSTATE); an SQL query returns the resulting set that consists of some columns selected from some tables. The exact number of columns may be unknown until the actual program execution, as well as the columns data types. That means the host program has to allocate an appropriate data structure to hold the anticipated resulting set just after the dynamic query has been built and before it is submitted to the RDBMS for execution.

For all these reasons, dynamic DML/DDL processing is much simpler than handling dynamic queries. Fortunately, most modern programming languages, including Visual Basic, Visual C++, PowerBuilder, Delphi, Java, and many others hide the complexity from the programmers by delegating the sophisticated part to the internal mechanisms of the programming language. All a programmer needs to do is to dynamically assemble a character string that represents the dynamic query and assign its value to the appropriate (often predefined within a class) variable. Building and handling dynamic queries manually is generally obsolete, so we are not going to go into great details when discussing dynamic query techniques. You should refer to vendor-specific documentation in case you want to know more.

Dynamic SQL and SQL99 standards

By now, you probably are already used to the fact that ANSI/ISO standards are often quite different from what each vendor has actually implemented. This is also the case for the dynamic SQL that existed long before any ANSI/ISO standards were accepted. IBM implemented its own version of dynamic SQL in the early 1980s; all major RDBMS vendors followed these standards to a certain extent, but with their own twist. This is especially true about dynamic query processing, where each RDBMS has its own mechanism for handling the resulting set returned by a query. For example, all three major databases covered in this book use special dynamic SQL data structure, known as the SQL Data Area (SQLDA), to handle the dynamic query output, but all three implemented their own version of this structure incompatible with the others. SQL99 standards replace SQLDA with a similar construct called Dynamic SQL Descriptor that plays exactly the same role but is structured quite differently.

Dynamic SQL basic elements

Dynamic SQL shares most elements with static embedded SQL. Including SQLCA, connecting to and disconnecting from database, declaring host variables, handling errors, and performing COMMIT and ROLLBACK are exactly the same for both. The embedded statements start with EXEC SQL keywords and end with a language-specific delimiter. However, since the SQL statement processing has to be done in runtime rather than in compile-time, the dynamic SQL introduces some additional elements to enable users to build their statements on the fly. As we mentioned before, DML/DDL statements are easier to handle than dynamic queries, which require additional preparation. In the next sections of this chapter, we introduce the techniques of working with both.

Dynamic DML and DDL

Dynamic SQL provides two methods of executing almost any DML or DDL statement dynamically in your host program. The first method is called `EXECUTE IMMEDIATE` and allows you to submit a programmatically assembled string that represents a DML/DDL statement to the RDBMS in one step. The alternative, also known as two-step dynamic execution, consists of two statements, `PREPARE` and `EXECUTE`.

One-step execution

One-step execution is the simplest way of executing dynamic SQL within your host program. First, the program builds the SQL statement based on user input, command-line arguments, and so on, and stores it in a previously declared character string variable. The variable is then passed to the RDBMS using `EXECUTE IMMEDIATE`; the statement is executed by the database engine. (All five processing steps are performed at this time.) The RDBMS returns the completion status back to the host program using `SCLCA`, `SQLCODE`, `SQLSTATE`, etc. The generalized syntax is

```
EXEC SQL EXECUTE IMMEDIATE <language-specific delimiter>
```

The following examples illustrate how to build and dynamically execute an SQL statement that updates the `PROD_PRICE_N` column of the `PRODUCT` table with a value of 25.50 for row(s) matching user-supplied criteria using C and COBOL syntax, respectively:

C

```
...
EXEC SQL BEGIN DECLARE SECTION;
...
char buffer[101];
...
EXEC SQL END DECLARE SECTION;
...
char searchcond[51];
...
strcpy(buffer, "UPDATE PRODUCT SET PROD_PRICE_N = 25.50 WHERE ");
printf("ENTER SEARCH CONDITION:");
gets(searchcond);
strcat(buffer, searchcond);
EXEC SQL EXECUTE IMMEDIATE :buffer;
...
```

COBOL

```
...
EXEC SQL BEGIN DECLARE SECTION END-EXEC.
...
01  BUFFER    PIC X(100).
...
EXEC SQL END DECLARE SECTION END-EXEC.
...
01  UPDCLAUSE PIC X(50).
01  SEARCHCOND PIC X(50).
...
DISPLAY "ENTER SEARCH CONDITION:".
MOVE "UPDATE PRODUCT SET PROD_PRICE_N = 25.50 WHERE "
 TO UPDCLAUSE.
DISPLAY UPDCLAUSE.
ACCEPT SEARCHCOND.
STRING UPDCLAUSE DELIMITED BY SIZE
 SEARCHCOND DELIMITED BY SIZE INTO BUFFER.
EXEC SQL EXECUTE IMMEDIATE :BUFFER END-EXEC.
...
```

The query billet is in this form:

```
UPDATE PRODUCT
SET PROD_PRICE_N = 25.50
WHERE
```

So, the user can submit any valid search condition to form a legitimate query; for example, PROD_ID_N = 990, PROD_BRAND_S = 'STEEL NAILS', PROD_PRICE_N = 33.28, etc.

The code in this example is just to illustrate the concept of the EXECUTE IMMEDIATE statement; the actual program would probably at least use a host variable for the PROD_PRICE_N rather than a hardcoded constant.

Two-step execution

Two-step execution is more complicated. You build your SQL statement in exactly the same way you would do it for EXECUTE IMMEDIATE; the only difference is, you can use a question mark (?), called the *parameter marker* or *placeholder,* instead of any token from group three (discussed earlier in this chapter) to be later substituted with the actual value. The statement is then submitted as an argument for the PREPARE statement that performs the first four SQL statement processing steps (parse, validate, optimize, and generate execution plan). The last step is to use EXECUTE to replace the parameter markers with the actual values and execute the SQL statement.

Oracle uses the host variable notation (not allowed in DB2 or MS SQL Server) for the parameter markers instead of the question marks.

The generalized syntax for the PREPARE and EXECUTE commands is

PREPARE

```
EXEC SQL
PREPARE <statement_name> FROM  {:<host_string > | <string_literal>}
<language-specific delimiter>
```

EXECUTE

```
EXEC SQL
EXECUTE <statement_name> [USING <host_variable_list>]
<language-specific delimiter>
```

Every parameter marker in the prepared dynamic SQL statement (if any) must correspond to a different host variable in the USING clause. When using Oracle notation, the names of the placeholders need not match the names of the host variables; however, the order of the placeholders in the prepared dynamic SQL statement must match the order of corresponding host variables in the USING clause.

The indicator variables could be used with host variables in the USING clause.

The following examples illustrate how to build and dynamically execute an SQL statement that updates the PROD_DESCRIPTION_S column of the PRODUCT table with a user-supplied value for row(s) matching user-supplied search criteria using C and COBOL syntax, respectively:

C

```
...
EXEC SQL BEGIN DECLARE SECTION;
...
char buffer[150];
char proddesc[45];
...
EXEC SQL END DECLARE SECTION;
...
char searchcond[51];
...
strcpy(buffer, "UPDATE PRODUCT SET PROD_NAME_S = ? WHERE ");
printf("ENTER PRODUCT DESCRIPTION:");
gets(proddesc);
printf("ENTER SEARCH CONDITION:");
gets(searchcond);
```

```
strcat(buffer, searchcond);
...
EXEC SQL PREPARE S FROM :buffer;
...
EXEC SQL EXECUTE S USING :proddesc;
...
```

COBOL

```
...
EXEC SQL BEGIN DECLARE SECTION END-EXEC.
...
01  BUFFER    PIC X(100).
01  PRODDESC  PIC X(44).
...
EXEC SQL END DECLARE SECTION END-EXEC.
...
01  UPDCLAUSE PIC X(50).
01  SEARCHCOND PIC X(50).
...
DISPLAY "ENTER SEARCH CONDITION:".
MOVE "UPDATE PRODUCT SET PROD_PRICE_N = ? WHERE "
 TO UPDCLAUSE.
DISPLAY UPDCLAUSE.
ACCEPT SEARCHCOND.
DISPLAY "ENTER PRODUCT DESCRIPTION:".
ACCEPT PRODDESC.
STRING UPDCLAUSE DELIMITED BY SIZE
 SEARCHCOND DELIMITED BY SIZE INTO BUFFER.
EXEC SQL PREPARE S FROM :BUFFER END-EXEC.
...
EXEC SQL EXECUTE S USING :PRODDESC.
...
```

The `S` in the `PREPARE` statement is not a host variable, but rather, an *SQL identifier*, so it does not appear in the declaration section.

The syntax in these examples works with DB2 and MS SQL Server; you could modify it into Oracle-compliant code by replacing the parameter marker question marks with host variables. Thus, instead of

```
strcpy(buffer, "UPDATE PRODUCT SET PROD_NAME_S = ? WHERE ");
```

and

```
MOVE "UPDATE PRODUCT SET PROD_PRICE_N = ? WHERE "  TO UPDCLAUSE.
```

you use

```
strcpy(buffer, "UPDATE PRODUCT SET PROD_NAME_S = :n WHERE ");
```

and

```
MOVE "UPDATE PRODUCT SET PROD_PRICE_N = :N WHERE " TO UPDCLAUSE.
```

Two-step execution benefits

The two-step execution yields better performance than `EXECUTE IMMEDIATELY`, especially when the prepared statement is executed multiple times with different parameter markers. This is so because the `PREPARE` statement could be executed only once for numerous `EXECUTE` statements with different values substituted for the placeholders, so RDBMS does not have to execute SQL statement processing Steps 1 through 4 over and over again. A simple loop in the host program will do. However, if the SQL statement is used only once during the program execution, `EXECUTE IMMEDIATE` is the appropriate choice.

Dynamic queries

As we mentioned earlier in this chapter, dynamic queries are more complicated than dynamic DML and DDL and are characterized by serious discrepancies between vendor implementations. In this section, we introduce dynamic query using ANSI/ISO syntax.

To make the examples more usable, we created them using Oracle's version of SQL99 compliant syntax. In fact, this is just one of many possible ways to work with dynamic queries in Oracle; for example, you could use `SQLDA` as an alternative to the dynamic SQL descriptor.

Dynamic query syntax

Before you can start working with dynamic queries, you have to learn some more dynamic SQL statements.

The `ALLOCATE DESCRIPTOR` command allocates descriptor areas for "in" and "out" parameters:

```
EXEC SQL ALLOCATE DESCRIPTOR <'descriptor_name'>
<language-specific delimiter>
```

The `DESCRIBE` statement obtains information on a prepared SQL statement. `DESCRIBE INPUT` describes input host variables for the dynamic statement that has been prepared. `DESCRIBE OUTPUT` gives the number, type, and length of the output columns:

```
EXEC SQL DESCRIBE [INPUT | OUTPUT] <sql_statement>
USING [SQL] DESCRIPTOR <'descriptor_name'>
<language-specific delimiter>
```

The SET DESCRIPTOR statement lets you specify input values for the WHERE clause of your SELECT statement. A separate SET DESCRIPTOR statement must be used for each host variable. You can specify type, length, and data value; also, you have to specify VALUE, which is the host variable relative position in the dynamic SQL statement:

```
EXEC SQL SET DESCRIPTOR <'descriptor_name'>
[VALUE <item_sequence_number>,]
[TYPE = <:host_variable1>,]
[LENGTH = <:host_variable2>,]
DATA = <:host_variable3>
<language-specific delimiter>
```

For example, if your statement is: SELECT :v1, :v2, :v3, ... then the VALUE for :v1 is 1; the value for :v2 is 2, and so on.

TYPE is the ANSI Type Code selected from the values in Table 15-6.

Table 15-6
ANSI/ISO SQL Data type Codes

Data type	*Type Code*
CHARACTER	1
CHARACTER VARYING	12
DATE	9
DECIMAL	3
DOUBLE PRECISION	8
FLOAT	6
INTEGER	4
NUMERIC	2
REAL	7
SMALLINT	5

DEALLOCATE DESCRIPTOR spares memory allocated for the descriptor when it is no longer needed:

```
EXEC SQL DEALLOCATE DESCRIPTOR <'descriptor_name'>
<language-specific delimiter>
```

In addition to these statements, you need to know how to use dynamic cursors. A dynamic cursor is not much different from a static cursor; it allows you to perform the same four basic operations: DECLARE, OPEN, FETCH, and CLOSE. The main difference is, when you declare a dynamic cursor, the query is not specified using a hard-coded SELECT statement but rather referred indirectly using the statement name prepared by the PREPARE statement. The syntax for dynamic cursor statements is

```
EXEC SQL DECLARE <cursor_name> CURSOR FOR <statement_id>
<language-specific delimiter>
```

```
EXEC SQL OPEN <cursor_name> CURSOR
USING DESCRIPTOR <'descriptor_name'>
<language-specific delimiter>
```

```
EXEC SQL FETCH <cursor_name>
INTO DESCRIPTOR <'descriptor_name'>
<language-specific delimiter>
```

```
EXEC SQL CLOSE <cursor_name> <language-specific delimiter>
```

Steps to execute a dynamic query

Perform the following steps to execute a dynamic query:

1. Declare variables, including a string buffer to hold the statement to be executed.
2. Allocate descriptors for input and output variables.
3. Prepare the statement with a PREPARE ... USING DESCRIPTOR statement.
4. Describe input for the input descriptor.

5. Set the input descriptor.
6. Declare and open a dynamic cursor.
7. Set the output descriptors for each output host variable.
8. Fetch the cursor in a loop; use GET DESCRIPTOR to retrieve the data for each row.
9. Use the retrieved data in your program.
10. Close the dynamic cursor.
11. Deallocate the input and output descriptors.

Dynamic query example

The following examples (in C and COBOL, respectively) show how to use a dynamic query in your host program using the steps described in the previous section:

C

```
...
EXEC SQL BEGIN DECLARE SECTION;
 ...
 char* buffer= "SELECT CUST_ID_N, CUST_NAME_S FROM CUSTOMER
               WHERE CUST_PAYTERMSID_N = :payterm_data";
 int payterm_type = 4, payterm_len = 2, payterm_data = 28;
 int custid_type = 4, custid_len = 4;
 int custid_data;
 int name_type = 12, name_len = 50;
 char name_data[51] ;
 ...
EXEC SQL END DECLARE SECTION;
...
long SQLCODE = 0 ;
...
main ()
{
 ...
 EXEC SQL ALLOCATE DESCRIPTOR 'in' ;

 EXEC SQL ALLOCATE DESCRIPTOR 'out' ;

 EXEC SQL PREPARE S FROM :buffer;

 EXEC SQL DESCRIBE INPUT S USING DESCRIPTOR 'in' ;

 EXEC SQL SET DESCRIPTOR 'in' VALUE 1 TYPE = :payterm_type,
             LENGTH = :payterm_len, DATA = :payterm_data ;

 EXEC SQL DECLARE cur CURSOR FOR S;
```

```
  EXEC SQL OPEN cur USING DESCRIPTOR 'in' ;

  EXEC SQL DESCRIBE OUTPUT S USING DESCRIPTOR 'out' ;

  EXEC SQL SET DESCRIPTOR 'out' VALUE 1 TYPE = :custid_type,
    LENGTH = :custid_len, DATA = :custid_data ;

  EXEC SQL SET DESCRIPTOR 'out' VALUE 2 TYPE = :name_type,
    LENGTH = :name_len, DATA = :name_data ;

  EXEC SQL WHENEVER NOT FOUND DO BREAK ;

  while (SQLCODE == 0)
  {
    EXEC SQL FETCH cur INTO DESCRIPTOR 'out' ;
    EXEC SQL GET DESCRIPTOR 'out' VALUE 1 :custid_data = DATA;
    EXEC SQL GET DESCRIPTOR 'out' VALUE 2 :name_data = DATA ;
    printf("\nCustomer ID = %s Customer Name = %s",
           custid_data, name_data) ;
  }

  EXEC SQL CLOSE cur;

  EXEC SQL DEALLOCATE DESCRIPTOR 'in';

  EXEC SQL DEALLOCATE DESCRIPTOR 'out' ;
  ...
}
```

COBOL

```
EXEC SQL BEGIN DECLARE SECTION END-EXEC.
...
01  BUFFER PIC X(100)
    VALUE "SELECT CUST_ID_N, CUST_NAME_S FROM CUSTOMER WHERE
           CUST_PAYTERMSID_N = :payterm_data".
01  PAYTERM-DAT  PIC S9(9)  COMP  VALUE 28.
01  PAYTERM-TYP  PIC S9(9)  COMP  VALUE 4.
01  PAYTERM-LEN  PIC S9(9)  COMP  VALUE 2.
01  CUSTID-TYP   PIC S9(9)  COMP  VALUE 4.
01  CUSTID-LEN   PIC S9(9)  COMP  VALUE 4.
01  CUSTID-DAT   PIC S9(9)  COMP.
01  NAME-TYP     PIC S9(9)  COMP  VALUE 12.
01  NAME-LEN     PIC S9(9)  COMP  VALUE 50.
01  NAME-DAT     PIC X(50).
EXEC SQL END DECLARE SECTION END-EXEC.
...
01  SQLCODE      PIC S9(9)  COMP  VALUE 0.
...
     EXEC SQL ALLOCATE DESCRIPTOR 'in' END-EXEC.
     EXEC SQL ALLOCATE DESCRIPTOR 'out' END-EXEC.
```

```
      EXEC SQL PREPARE S FROM :BUFFER END-EXEC.
      EXEC SQL DESCRIBE INPUT S USING DESCRIPTOR 'in'
         END-EXEC.

      EXEC SQL SET DESCRIPTOR 'in' VALUE 1 TYPE=:PAYTERM-TYP,
         LENGTH=:PAYTERM-LEN, DATA=:PAYTERM-DAT END-EXEC.
      EXEC SQL DECLARE cur CURSOR FOR S END-EXEC.
      EXEC SQL OPEN cur USING DESCRIPTOR 'in' END-EXEC.
      EXEC SQL DESCRIBE OUTPUT S USING DESCRIPTOR 'out'
         END-EXEC.
      EXEC SQL SET DESCRIPTOR 'out' VALUE 1 TYPE=:CUSTID-TYP,
         LENGTH=:CUSTID-LEN, DATA=:CUSTID-DAT END-EXEC.
      EXEC SQL SET DESCRIPTOR 'out' VALUE 2 TYPE=:NAME-TYP,
         LENGTH=:NAME-LEN, DATA=:NAME-DAT END-EXEC.

LOOP.
      IF SQLCODE NOT = 0
         GOTO BREAK.
      EXEC SQL FETCH cur INTO DESCRIPTOR 'out' END-EXEC.
      EXEC SQL GET DESCRIPTOR 'OUT' VALUE 1 :CUSTID-DAT = DATA
         END-EXEC.
      EXEC SQL GET DESCRIPTOR 'OUT' VALUE 2 :NAME-DAT = DATA
         END-EXEC.
      DISPLAY "CUSTOMER ID = " WITH NO ADVANCING
      DISPLAY CUSTID-DAT  WITH NO ADVANCING
      DISPLAY "CUSTOMER NAME = " WITH NO ADVANCING
      DISPLAY NAME-DAT.
      GOTO LOOP.
 BREAK:
      EXEC SQL CLOSE cur END-EXEC.
      EXEC SQL DEALLOCATE DESCRIPTOR 'in' END-EXEC.
      EXEC SQL DEALLOCATE DESCRIPTOR 'out' END-EXEC.
...
```

The Future of Embedded SQL

The Embedded SQL was born of the first attempts to extend SQL with procedural language capabilities. Its main function was to carry on the internal RDBMS control and administration. The other goal was to provide the ability to write programs that could connect to the database, retrieve, process, modify data, and so on. The first task is being gradually delegated to stored procedures, functions, and triggers that have better mechanisms of doing that. The second is still mostly done using various programming languages; however, the mechanics of databases constantly evolve. Most modern programming languages provide different (sometimes more efficient and/or easier to use) means of accessing RDBMS. These include ODBC, JDBC, CLI, along with the object-oriented interfaces (like Microsoft ADO) — to name just a few.

Embedded (Static) Versus Dynamic SQL: Advantages and Disadvantages

One may ask, what is more efficient, embedded or dynamic SQL? Most sources (SQL books, Web sites, etc.) unambiguously answer this question in favor of the embedded SQL. The reason is simple—in the embedded SQL, the first four steps of SQL statement processing are done in compile-time and do not need to be repeated again in runtime. In theory, these speculations are difficult to argue, but in real life, not everything is that simple.

The key to the understanding of the issue lies in Step 3, which is the optimization step of SQL processing. Most modern RDBMS have special built-in components called *optimizers* that create an execution plan for each single SQL statement, usually based on dynamic system catalog information. That means the execution plan for a SQL statement that was optimal one day may be far from optimal in a month, and even less so in a year. This is especially true for large DML-intensive databases where the optimal execution plan may change within days or even hours. The problem is that the plan is hardcoded into your program and you will have to recompile it to change it. The price for bad execution plans for SQL statements in your program can thus be very high; in fact, it could be much higher than repeating all five SQL processing steps multiple times.

Using the two-step dynamic SQL could help to improve performance even more—you might need to `PREPARE` your SQL statement just once and then `EXECUTE` it as many times as you need during the run of the program.

However, none of previously mentioned advantages apply to databases that are static—the optimal execution plan for such databases is probably not going to change for many years.

The final answer is—it all depends; there is no silver bullet, and developers have to make decisions for each particular case.

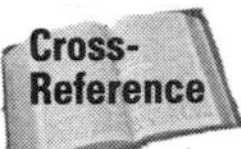

ODBC, JDBC, CLI, and other alternative methods of accessing RDBMS are discussed in Chapter 16.

In spite of all this, embedded/dynamic SQL still has its niche in the contemporary programming world—the embedded database market. Embedded databases are widely used in mobile and wireless devices, consumer electronics, medical equipment, and more. Using embedded/dynamic SQL requires less memory and processor power and provides fast and reliable access to relatively static embedded databases, and with embedded databases making their way into a vast array of the new devices—cell-phones, microwaves, personal digital assistants (PDA), and the like—embedded SQL is experiencing a revival.

Summary

Embedded SQL was the first commercial solution to extend SQL with the capabilities of a procedural language. It allows a host-language-written computer program to connect to RDBMS and perform virtually any SQL operation (retrieve and modify data, create, change, and drop database objects, grant and revoke privileges, etc.).

Dynamic SQL is a logical extension to the embedded (static) SQL that enables you to build and execute SQL statements in runtime.

Dynamic DML and DDL statements are relatively simple to implement because they do not have to return data back to the host program. Dynamic query standards are more complex and difficult to implement. Most modern programming languages delegate their implementation complexities to the internal mechanisms of the programming language — thus sparing the programmers.

Even though most sources say that dynamic SQL is generally less efficient than embedded SQL, that may or may not be true in different real-life situations. Understanding the general five steps of a SQL statement processing is the key to the appropriate use of embedded/dynamic SQL in each particular case.

Embedded/dynamic SQL is gradually becoming obsolete in the face of arising new database technologies, but it is far from being dead because of large amounts of legacy programming code. Embedded SQL has also found its place inside some modern technologies where it is the only choice — i.e., embedded databases.

✦ ✦ ✦

CHAPTER 16

SQL API

✦ ✦ ✦ ✦

In This Chapter

SQL/CLI standard

Microsoft ODBC standard

Java database connectivity

IBM BD2 call-level interface

Oracle call-level interface

Oracle objects for OLE

Microsoft data access interfaces

✦ ✦ ✦ ✦

Before a single SQL statement can execute, a client application that submits this statement must somehow establish connection with RDBMS. The connection can be established through a variety of mechanisms — ranging from proprietary call-level interface to the buzz-of-the-day like Java Database Connectivity and .NET Providers.

While not being in the domain of SQL proper, application programming interface concepts should be understood by anyone serious enough to go to the trouble of learning RDBMS and their native SQL.

SQL/CLI Standard

The call-level interface (CLI) standard was created by the subcommittee of the SQL Access Group (SAG). SAG was formed in 1989 with its declared purpose "to define and promote standards for database interoperability." The group included Oracle, Informix, and Hewlett-Packard, among others. The list keeps growing and now includes virtually every sizable company exploring the database field.

At about the same time, Microsoft, Lotus, Sybase, and DEC joined the effort in creating the SQL Connectivity specification, which later made its way into SAG base specification.

The CLI standard was published as a work in progress in 1992, and that same year Microsoft shipped the first commercial implementation of the standard CLI specification — Open DataBase Connectivity for Windows version 1.0. In this release, the original specification was extended and divided into three compatibility layers, the core of which corresponded directly to the SAG CLI standard.

In 1994, after several transformations, the original SAG CLI specification (amended and expanded) was dubbed X/Open Preliminary Specification. Microsoft released ODBC for

Windows version 2.0 the same year. That year also marks the release of the ODBC Software Development Kit (SDK) for non-Windows platforms by Visigenic Software, under an exclusive source-code license.

In 1993 ODBC was accepted as a base document for the SQL/CLI by the ISO/ANSI SQL committees. In 1995 it was completed as ISO/IEC document 9075-3:1995 Information Technology–Database Languages–SQL–Part 3: Call-Level Interface (SQL/CLI). Later it was expanded to include SQL99 standard extensions. The standard was commercialized as Microsoft ODBC 3.0 in 1996.

In the SQL/CLI standard terminology we are speaking about *binding styles* — e.g., embedded SQL, module language, and direct invocation — which represent traditional binding mechanisms.

Embedded SQL, discussed in more detail in Chapter 15, received its name because SQL statements were directly embedded into the host language program. Before an application that contained Embedded SQL can be compiled and executed, it had to go through a precompiling process, using a vendor-supplied precompiler.

Module Language refers to the compiled modules stored on the server, utilizing C, PL/1, Cobol, or Java, as well as vendor-proprietary languages like Oracle's PL/SQL or Microsoft/Sybase Transact-SQL.

Direct Invocation defined a set SQL statements that can be executed directly in RDBMS, using some specific vendor-defined mechanism.

The absence of the common standard hindered development of portable applications and reuse of the code, when almost the entire application had to be rewritten to accommodate peculiarities of the RDBMS access and handling of returned data.

The CLI/SQL standard allows for relative independence from a proprietary database interface, through encapsulation of all vendor-specific details into a number of uniform functions. Table 16-1 provides a list of SQL/CLI functions (over 50), as defined by the standard.

Table 16-1
SQL/CLI and ODBC Functions

SQL/CLI Function	*Conforms to the Standard*	*Description*
Allocating and De-allocating Resources		
`SQLAllocHandle()`	SQL/CLI	Allocates environment, connection, statement, or descriptor handle.
`SQLAllocEnv()`	SQL/CLI	Allocates environment resources, returns handle.

SQL/CLI Function	*Conforms to the Standard*	*Description*
`SQLAllocConnect()`	SQL/CLI	Allocates connection resources, returns handle.
`SQLAllocStmt()`	SQL/CLI	Allocates statement resources, returns handle.
`SQLFreeHandle()`	SQL/CLI	Releases allocated environment, connection, etc., by handle.
`SQLFreeEnv()`	SQL/CLI	Releases allocated environment resources.
`SQLFreeConnect()`	SQL/CLI	Releases allocated connection resources.
`SQLFreeStmt()`	SQL/CLI	Stops statement processing and frees all the resources associated with its handle.
Opening and Closing Database Connections		
`SQLConnect()`	SQL/CLI	Connects to a specific driver.
`SQLDisconnect()`	SQL/CLI	Terminates database connection established with SQLConnect.
`SQLDriverConnect()`	ODBC	Connects to a specific driver; if connection parameters are omitted, displays Driver Manager dialog box.
`SQLBrowseConnect()`	ODBC	Returns hierarchy of connection attributes.
SQL Statement Execution		
`SQLExecDirect()`	SQL/CLI	Executes an SQL statement (without preparation).
`SQLPrepare()`	SQL/CLI	Prepares an SQL statement for execution.
`SQLExecute()`	SQL/CLI	Executes a prepared SQL statement.
`SQLCancel()`	SQL/CLI	Cancels SQL statement execution.
`SQLBindParameter()`	ODBC	Allocates storage for parameters in SQL statements.
`SQLParamData()`	SQL/CLI	Supplies parameters value at runtime.
`SQLDescribeParam()`	ODBC	Describes a specific parameter in the statement.
`SQLNumParams()`	SQL/CLI	Returns a number of parameters for a statement.
`SQLNativeSql()`	ODBC	Returns text of an SQL statement, as it is translated by the ODBC driver.
`SQLCloseCursor()`	SQL/CLI	Closes opened cursor (by handle).

Continued

Table 16-1 (continued)

SQL/CLI Function	Conforms to the Standard	Description
SQLSetCursorName()	SQL/CLI	Defines cursor name.
SQLGetCursorName()	SQL/CLI	Retrieves cursor name.
SQLSetScrollOptions()	ODBC	Sets scroll options for a cursor.
SQLPutData()	SQL/CLI	Sends part or all of the data for a parameter.
Attributes Management		
SQLSetConnectAttr()	SQL/CLI	Sets connection attribute.
SQLGetConnectAttr()	SQL/CLI	Retrieves value of the connection attribute.
SQLSetEnvAttr()	SQL/CLI	Sets environment attribute.
SQLGetEnvAttr()	SQL/CLI	Retrieves value of the environment attribute.
SQLSetStmtAttr()	SQL/CLI	Sets statement attribute.
SQLGetStmtAttr()	SQL/CLI	Retrieves value of the statement attribute.
Setting and Retrieving Descriptor Fields		
SQLGetDescField()	SQL/CLI	Returns the value of a single descriptor field.
SQLGetDescRec()	SQL/CLI	Returns the value of multiple descriptor fields.
SQLSetDescField()	SQL/CLI	Sets the value of a single descriptor field.
SQLSetDescRec()	SQL/CLI	Sets the value of multiple descriptor fields.
Query Results Retrieval		
SQLRowCount()	SQL/CLI	Returns the number of rows affected by SQL statement.
SQLDescribeCol()	SQL/CLI	Describes a column in a resultset.
SQLColAttribute()	SQL/CLI	Describes the attributes of a column in a resultset.
SQLBindCol()	SQL/CLI	Assigns storage of a specific data type for a return value.
SQLFetch()	SQL/CLI	Returns a resultset.
SQLFetchScroll()	SQL/CLI	Returns scrollable resultset.
SQLGetData()	SQL/CLI	Returns part or whole of a column's value for single row in the resultset.
SQLSetPos()	ODBC	Positions cursor at specific location within a fetched resultset.
SQLBulkOperations()	ODBC	Performs bulk operations.

SQL/CLI Function	Conforms to the Standard	Description
`SQLMoreResults()`	ODBC	Returns additional resultsets, if they exist.
`SQLGetDiagField()`	SQL/CLI	Returns additional diagnostic information (single record).
`SQLGetDiagRec()`	SQL/CLI	Returns additional diagnostic information (multiple records).
Accessing Systems Catalogs		
`SQLColumnPrivileges()`	ODBC	Returns list of columns and associated privileges.
`SQLColumns()`	X/Open	Returns list of columns for the specified table.
`SQLForeignKeys`	ODBC	Returns list of all columns that comprise the foreign keys for the table, if any.
`SQLPrimaryKeys()`	ODBC	Returns list of all columns that comprise the primary key for the table, if any.
`SQLProcedureColumns()`	ODBC	Returns list of input/output parameters and columns included into returned resultset.
`SQLProcedures()`	ODBC	Returns list of all stored procedures and functions from a data source.
`SQLSpecialColumns()`	X/Open	Returns information about optimal set of columns that uniquely identifies a row in the table, or a list of the columns updated automatically when any value in a row is updated.
`SQLStatistics()`	SQL/CLI	Returns statistic information for specific table, as well as the list of all indices for the table.
`SQLTablePrivileges()`	ODBC	Returns list of tables and all the privileges for the specific table.
`SQLTables()`	X/Open	Returns list of table names from the data source.
Transaction Management		
`SQLEndTran()`	SQL/CLI	Commits or rolls back a transaction.
Drivers and Data Source Information		
`SQLDataSources()`	SQL/CLI	Returns list of all available data sources.

Continued

Table 16-1 *(continued)*

SQL/CLI Function	***Conforms to the Standard***	***Description***
`SQLDrivers()`	ODBC	Returns list of all installed drivers on the system.
`SQLGetInfo()`	SQL/CLI	Returns information about a specific driver and the data source.
`SQLGetFunctions()`	SQL/CLI	Returns list of all functions supported by the driver.
`SQLGetTypeInfo()`	SQL/CLI	Returns information about all supported data types.

ODBC standard does not address security concerns; in fact, unless encryption is used, all information sent through API calls is up for grabs. Using an ODBC driver with built-in encryption alleviates this potential problem.

Microsoft Open Database Connectivity (ODBC)

ODBC stands for Open Database Connectivity. It started as a Microsoft-only standard and was adopted as a vendor-independent SQL/CLI standard. There were several iterations of the ODBC interfaces, with the latest being in version 3.0, and it remains a Microsoft product.

ODBC 3.0 aligns itself with the existing X/Open CAE specification, Data Management: SQL Call-Level Interface (CLI), and ISO/IEC 9075-3:1995 (E) Call-Level Interface (SQL/CLI).

The functions in the ODBC API are implemented in a variety of the ODBC drivers, which can be called by applications through the ODBC Driver Manager, which handles communications between the functions and the drivers.

Both the drivers and the Driver Manager were ported on platforms different from Windows (e.g., Unix, Macintosh). When the driver manager receives a call from an application, it loads the corresponding ODBC driver that in turn forwards the call to the RDBMS interface. When a response is received from the database, the driver forwards it to the Driver Manager, which returns the results of the call to the application. Only the Driver Manager is loaded and unloaded by an application that requests ODBC connection to the database; the rest is the task of the Manager itself. The Driver Manager also performs ODBC functions basic checking (correct parameters, data types, and the like).

The drivers represent the libraries implementing the ODBC functions. Each RDBMS requires its own ODBC driver. You may think of the driver as an interpreter: understanding a common language (ODBC API calls) of the application and translating it into the RDBM-specific terms. Drivers are not supposed to understand, execute, or even translate SQL; those tasks are solely the responsibility of the RDBMS.

The tasks performed by ODBC drivers are the following:

- Establishing and closing connections to data source
- Checking ODBC function calls for errors
- Initiating transactions in a manner apparent to the application
- Passing SQL to DBMS for execution
- Sending data to and retrieving data from the DBMS
- Mapping DBMS vendor-specific errors to ODBC `SQLSTATES` collection of predefined errors

Configuring an ODBC Data Source Name on Windows

On Microsoft Windows OS, the Driver Manager resides in the Settings⇨Control Panel⇨Administrative Tools⇨Data Sources (ODBC) (assuming that you are using Windows 2000; the path might be different if the data source is configured on Windows 9*x* or Windows XP). It maintains information about all ODBC drivers installed on the system and assists in creating and configuring ODBC Data Source Names (DSN).

The only exception to the "speak no SQL" rule are drivers for the DBMS that do not have a stand-alone database engine (Xbase, for instance). In this case, the driver is supposed to process the SQL as well.

The DSN can be used by an application to connect to the RDBMS for which it was configured. The use of ODBC DSN is illustrated later in this chapter, in the paragraph discussing ADO interface.

We will guide you through the process of creating an ODBC Data Source Name (DSN) on a Windows 2000 Professional machine. The DSN will be used later in this chapter in the example in which the Microsoft Visual Basic application connects to IBM DB2 UDB database.

From the Control Panel (Start⇨Settings⇨Control Panel; again, we assume Windows 2000 configuration, the path might different for other flavors of Windows) menu, select the Administrative Tools option and double-click it. From the Administrative Tools, select the Data Sources (ODBC) option and double-click it. This brings up the ODBC Data Source Administrator. Figure 16-1 shows several tabs for the three different types of ODBC DSN that can be created on a Windows machine; they differ primarily in scope — the System DSN has global scope, the User DSN is visible for the user account only, and the File DSN is represented by a standard OS file. Select the User DSN tab.

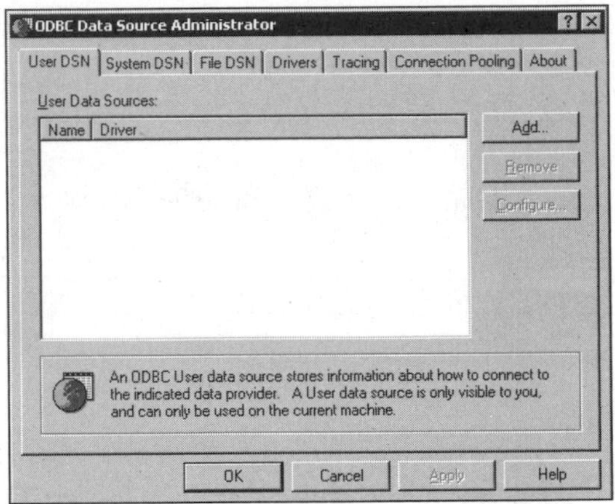

Figure 16-1: Microsoft ODBC Driver Manager console

The screen will list all the DSN entries created on the machine; from here you can add new DSN or remove and configure existing ones. Click the Add button to add a new DSN entry. The next screen (Figure 16-2), Create New Data Source, presents you with the list of all ODBC drivers installed on the machine. Select the IBM DB2 ODBC driver from the list and click the Finish button.

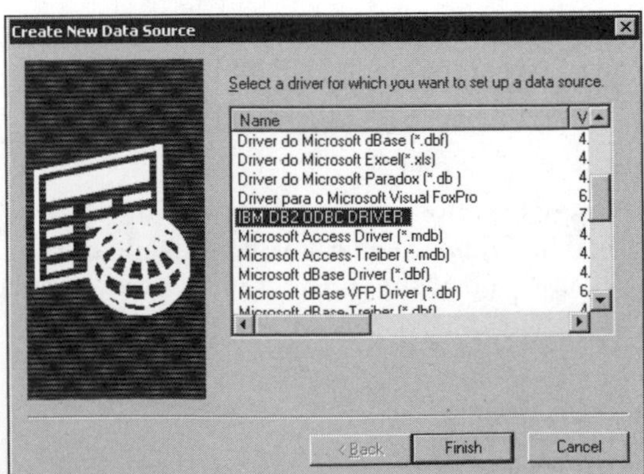

Figure 16-2: ODBC drivers selection

From this point on, you will be guided by the IBM-specific driver interface, shown in Figure 16-3. This interface is not uniform, as it reflects RDBMS specifics. The Oracle driver will display a different screen and set of options; and the SQL Server driver, yet another.

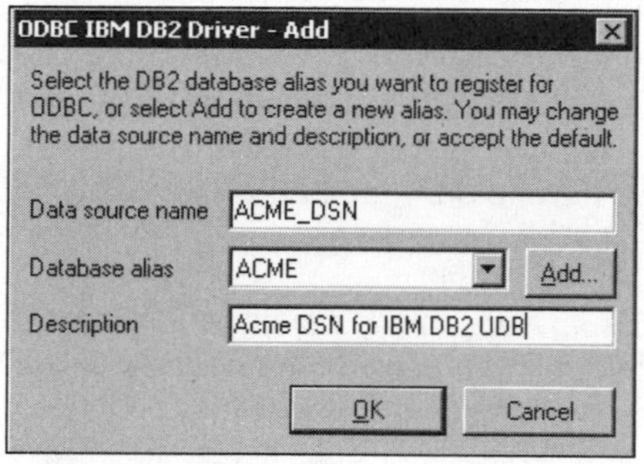

Figure 16-3: IBM DB2 UDB ODBC driver configuration

A DSN needs a unique name, so choose one and type it in to the Data Source Name field, as shown in Figure 16-3. Since we are creating a Data Source on the same machine where IBM DB2 UDB is installed, the Database Alias field defaults to ACME (you should have the same, if you've followed the instructions for the sample database installation given in Appendix F). Click the OK button.

The final screen (Figure 16-4) shows the User DSN for the IBM DB2 UDB. This DSN can be used by any ODBC-compliant application to establish connection to the DB2 UDB database ACME.

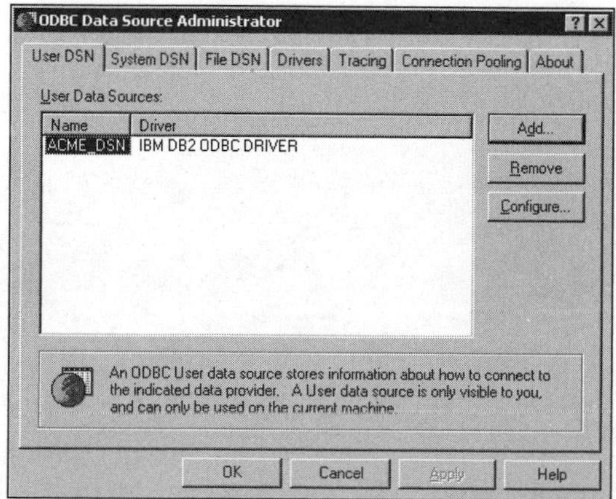

Figure 16-4: New user DSN entry IBM DB2 UDB

Java Database Connectivity (JDBC)

Java Database Connectivity was proposed (and implemented) by the Sun Corporation to provide its popular Java programming language (some would say "programming platform," but we will not fight holy wars here) with a uniform set of database access methods. Using JDBC you can connect to a data source (which might not necessarily be an RDBMS data source), execute SQL statements (i.e., forward them to the SQL processing software — like RDBMS — for execution), and process the output of these SQL statements. The most current JDBC standard is JDBC v.3.0 standard, which is included with J2SE (Java 2 Standard Edition) and J2EE (Java 2 Enterprise Edition), version 1.4.

The difference between J2SE and J2EE is in scope and capabilities. Both are standards for developing applications, applets in Java programming language; but J2EE adds a component-based model (EJB – Enterprise Java Beans) for building enterprise level multi-tier applications.

JDBC provides two sets of interfaces: one for the database application programmers, and one for the database driver programmers, and its core set is included with Java2 Platform.

Many industry heavyweights support the JDBC standard for their products; among the others the following RDBMS vendors are IBM, Oracle, Gupta Technologies, Borland, Compaq, Pervasive Software, and POET software. Microsoft supports JDBC/ODBC bridging with its recently released SQL Server 2000 driver for JDBC.

Figure 16-5 illustrates generic RDBMS access using JDBS drivers.

The JDBC functionality — basic and extended — is contained in the java.sql package (shipped with Java2 Core) and javax.sql package, listed in Table 16-2.

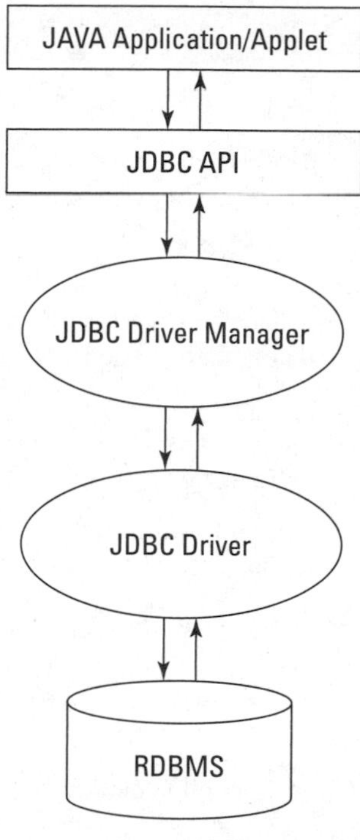

Figure 16-5: Accessing RDBMS through JDBC interface

Table 16-2
JDBC 3.0 Features

Feature	*Package*	*Description*
Enhanced resultset manipulations: scrollable set and updateable resultset	java.sql	Facilitates programmatic manipulation of the resultsets fetched with SQL statements or returned by stored procedures.
New Data Types Support	java.sql	Ability to manipulate with structured data types like `CLOB` and `BLOB` server-side, without transferring them over to the client application.
Batch Updates	java.sql	Ability to combine SQL statements into a single batch, to reduce network traffic and control overhead.

Continued

Table 16-2 *(continued)*

Feature	*Package*	*Description*
Transactional Support	java.sql	Declares, rolls back, and commits transactions on the client-side, including `SAVEPOINT` support.
JNDI (Java Naming and Directory Interface) Support	javax.sql	Facilitates deployment of Java applications by abstracting JDBC driver into independently managed components.
Connection Pooling	javax.sql	Maintains a cache of the database connections for future reuse.
Distributed Transactions Support	javax.sql	Provides support for distributed transactions processing (see Chapter 7).
Java Beans	javax.sql	Encapsulates data and functionality (rowset objects).
Reference to JDBC Rowset	javax.sql	Encapsulates a driver as a Java Bean component.
Statement Pooling	javax.sql	Pools parameterized statements for reuse.

There are four types of the JDBC drivers available today:

- ✦ **JDBC-ODBC drivers (Type 1).** These provide JDBC API access on top of the standard ODBC drivers. Essentially, they add an additional level of communications slowing the whole process down. The advantage of using this approach is that the current infrastructure can be used for the Java-based applications.
- ✦ **Native API Partly Java technology-enabled drivers (Type 2).** These drivers translate JDBC calls into direct calls to the RDBMS native interface (CLI).
- ✦ **Net-Protocol Fully Java technology-enabled drivers (Type 3).** These drivers translate JDBC calls into a DBMS independent network protocol, which is subsequently translated into a DBMS-specific protocol by some middleware server.
- ✦ **Native-Protocol Fully Java technology-enabled drivers (Type 4).** These drivers translate JDBC calls into a DATABASE-specific network protocol directly.

Drivers usually implement a subset of the functions and features available in RDBMS; check for the compliance level, and do not assume that every feature will be supported. Vendor's drivers are usually most complete.

Table 16-3 lists several JDBC drivers of different types for the big three RDBMS vendors: Oracle, IBM DB2 UDB, and Microsoft SQL Server 2000.

Table 16-3
Selected JDBC Drivers Vendors

Vendor	*Oracle 9i*	*IBM DB2 UDB*	*Microsoft SQL Server 2000*	*Remarks*
Atinav Inc.	n/a	n/a	✓	Types 3, 4
Attunity	✓	✓	n/a	Types 2, 2
Bea Weblogic	✓	n/a	✓	Types 2, 3
Computer Associates	✓	✓	✓	Type 3
CONNX Solutions	✓	✓	✓	Type 3
DataDirect Technologies	✓	✓	✓	Types 3, 4
Recital Corp.	✓	✓	n/a	Type 3
OpenLink Inc.	✓	✓	✓	Types 1, 3
Oracle	✓	n/a	n/a	Types 2, 3, 4
Object Industries	✓	✓	✓	Types 1, 2, 3, 4
Microsoft	n/a	n/a	✓	Type 4
IBM	✓	n/a	n/a	Types 3, 4
IDS Software	✓	✓	✓	Types 3, 4

JDBC Connector and Java Data Objects (JDO)

Sun Corporation has introduced the JDBC Connector to facilitate integration of the databases with Java 2 Enterprise Edition (J2EE) application servers. It forms an intermediate layer between the JDBC driver and an applications server.

Another development from Sun is the Java Data Object. It is a complementary technology that provides object-relational mappings between Java classes and object databases. From the Java programmer's standpoint, it provides a standard, familiar, SQL-free approach to the RDBMS.

JDO integrates well into Enterprise Java Beans technology and is part of the Java Community Process, which comes close to giving it the status of being an open standard.

In addition to the JDBC standard, Oracle provides enhanced support for Java technology through JServer, which is Oracle's own Java Virtual Machine (JVM). It runs within RDBMS address space and provides for Java to be used for stored procedures (instead of PL/SQL). For the outside world, Oracle complies with "regular" JDBC access and adds a couple of its own: JDBC OCI drivers accessing RDBMS directly from Java code through Oracle Call Interface (discussed later in this chapter), and JDBC KPRB drivers for executing Java-stored procedures and database JSP (Java Server Pages).

The following code snippet illustrates the use of the JDBC thin driver to establish a connection to Oracle:

```
import java.sql
class JDBC_access
{
    public static void main (Strings args[ ] )
    throws SQL Exception
{
    DriverManager.registerDriver (new
oracle.jdbc.driver.Oracledriver());
//
//connecting string includes
//machine name (@alexhome)
//port (1522)
//SID (Oracle's ID) ORA_TEST
//User ID (acme), Password (acme)
//
    Connection objConn = DriverManager.getConnection
    ("jdbc:oracle:thin:@alexhome:1522:ORA_TEST",
                                   "acme",
                                    "acme");
//
// Create a statement object
// using the connection object
//
    Statement objStatement = objConn.CreateStatement();
//
// assemble SQl statement
//
    String s_SQL = "SELECT * FROM customer";
//
// retrieve the result set
//
    ResultSet objRecordset = s_SQL.ExecuteQuery(s_SQL);
//
// scroll the recordset object
//
    while (objRecordset.next())
//
// print the fourth column value
// onto the standard output
//
        System.out.println(objRecordset.getString(4);
```

```
//
// clean up
// close the connection
// all other objects will be dereferenced
// automatically
//
    objConnection.Close();
}
}
```

The syntax for any other RDBMS accessible through JDBC is essentially the same, though some differences may appear in the connection string and, of course, you need an RDBMS-specific JDBC driver installed on your machine.

IBM DB2 UDB Call-Level Interface (CLI)

The DB2 Call-Level Interface (DB2 CLI) is an IBM standard for the DB2 family of database servers. It is tuned up for C/C++ API programming, and it is used for establishing connections, passing dynamic SQL statements, or calling persistent modules (like stored procedures).

DB2 CLI is based on the ODBC specification and the international standard for SQL/CLI, discussed earlier in this chapter. The DB2 CLI driver acts like a comparable ODBC driver, and it conforms to level 2 of ODBC 2.0 and level 1 of the ODBC 3.0. Some features of ODBC 3.0 level-2 conformance are also supported.

Figure 16-6 illustrates the way an application accesses DB2 RDBMS server using the CLI driver, the main difference being that the ODBC driver scenario does not have the additional access layer of the ODBC Driver Manager.

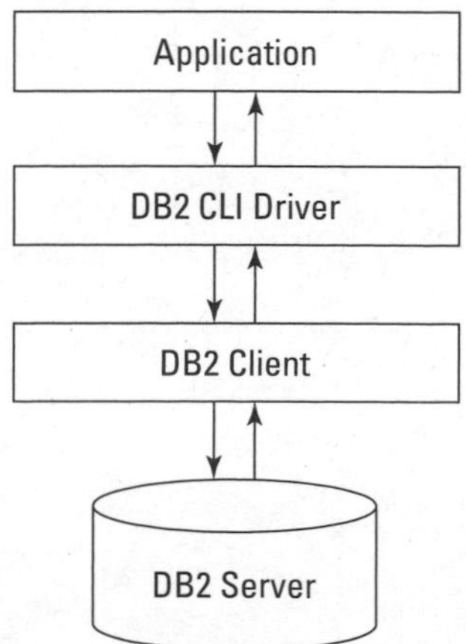

Figure 16-6: Accessing IBM DB2 UDB through CLI

Table 16-4 lists DB2 CLI driver features and ODBC driver for DB2 side by side with the ODBC Standard Specification.

Table 16-4
DB2 CLI vs. DB2 ODBC Driver Comparison

ODBC Features	*DB2 CLI*	*DB2 ODBC driver*
Core level functions	Implemented.	Implemented.
Level 1 functions	Implemented.	Implemented.
Level 2 functions	Implemented (except for `SQLDrivers()`, as nonapplicable).	Implemented.
Additional DB2 CLI functions	`SQLSetConnection()`, `SQLGetEnvAttr()`, `SQLSetEnvAttr()`, `SQLSetColAttributes()`, `SQLGetSQLCA()`, `SQLBindFileToCol()`, `SQLBindFileToParam()`, `SQLExtendedPrepare()`, `SQLGetLength()`, `SQLGetPosition()`, `SQLSetSubstring()`	Implemented all functions; can be accessed by dynamically loading DB2 CLI Library.
SQL data types	`SQL_BIGINT`, `SQL_BINARY`,`SQL_BLOB`, `SQL_BLOB_LOCATOR`, `SQL_CHAR`, `SQL_CLOB`,`SQL_CLOB_LOCATOR`, `SQL_DCLOB`, `SQL_DCLOB_LOCATOR`, `SQL_DECIMAL`, `SQL_DOUBLE`, `SQL_FLOAT`, `SQL_GRAPHIC`, `SQL_INTEGER`, `SQL_LONGVARBINARY`, `SQL_LONGVARCHAR`, `SQLLONGVARGRAPHIC`, `SQL_NUMERIC`, `SQL_REAL`, `SQL_SMALLINT`, `SQL_TYPE_DATE`, `SQL_TYPE_TIME`, `SQL_TYPE_TIMESTAMP`, `SQL_VARBINARY`, `SQL_VARCHAR`, `SQL_VARGRAPHIC`.	Supports all types listed for DB2 CLI, in addition to the ODBC standard.
C data types	`SQL_C_BINARY`, `SQL_C_BIT`, `SQLC_BLOB_LOCATOR`, `SQL_C_CHAR`, `SQL_C_CLOB_LOCATOR`, `SQL_C_DATE`, `SQL_C_DBCHAR`, `SQL_C_DBCLOB_LOCATOR`, `SQL_C_DOUBLE`, `SQL_C_FLOAT`, `SQL_C_LONG`, `SQL_C_SHORT`, `SQL_C_TIME`, `SQL_C_TIMESTAMP`, `SQL_C_TINYINT`, `SQL_SBIGINT`, `SQL_C_UBIGINT`. `SQL_C_NUMERIC` (supported for Win32 environment only).	

ODBC Features	DB2 CLI	DB2 ODBC driver
Return codes	SQL_SUCCESS, SQL_SUCCESS_WITH_INFO, SQL_STILL_EXECUTING, SQL_NEED_DATA, SQL_NO_DATA_FOUND, SQL_ERROR, SQL_INVALID_HANDLE.	Supports all types listed for DB2 CLI, in addition to the ODBC standard.
SQLSTATES (SQL standard compliance)	Some codes are not present (e.g., ODBC Type 08S01); otherwise the same as ODBC driver.	Mapped to X/Open SQLSTATES standard (in addition to the IBM-specific SQLSTATES codes).
Multiple connections for the client application	Supported.	Supported.
Dynamic loading of driver	N/A	Supported.

The main advantage of using DB2 CLI over embedded SQL is flexibility and convenience. Embedded SQL requires a precompiler to convert SQL Statements into executable code, which must be then bound to the DB2 database. DB2 CLI implementation is not tied to a particular product or environment, resulting in portable code; it is SQL standards (X/Open) compliant, can connect to a multiple databases (so much for the binding concept!), can use dynamic parameters, and, in general, is more suited for GUI (graphical user interface) applications. There is a performance penalty to pay for all this; embedded SQL is inherently faster because it does not go through all the layers of communication and translation.

Compared to DB2 ODBC driver, there's not much difference. True, elimination some of the middleware (ODBC Driver Manager) offers increased speed of execution and fewer environment setup problems (no ODBC Driver Manager). But it comes at the price of more limited set of features, and it relies squarely on IBM implementation (as opposed third-party ODBC drivers for DB2).

Oracle Call Interface (OCI)

The Oracle Call Interface (OCI) is a set of APIs (application programming interfaces) that allow a developer to programmatically access Oracle RDBMS and submit and control all the phases of the SQL statement execution.

The OCI provides a standard dynamic runtime library, OCILIB, that an application can link to. Essentially, this means that the embedded SQL is a thing of the past.

The OCI interface can be used by a number of third-generation programming languages like C/C++, COBOL, and Fortran. To use fourth-generation languages (4GLs) like Java, Visual Basic, C#, and so forth, a programmer must use some other interface like ODBC, JDBC, or OLEDB. Even in that case, while the application is using its respective interface driver, Oracle is using OCI.

Oracle supplies JDBC OCI drivers that provide access to the Oracle database using Java on the application side and Oracle's OCI on the other; it allows you to call OCI interface directly, without incurring the overhead of JDBC.

Oracle tests client and server compatibility with every new version released. There is always an issue of compatibility between the version of the client software with that of the server. Table 16-5 shows compatibility between various versions of the Oracle software. The EMS acronym refers to an extended maintenance contract, a special arrangement for the existing customers — there is usually cut-off date after which the system is no longer supported.

Table 16-5
OCI Compatibility Between Different Versions of Server and Client Software

Client Version/ Server Version	7.3.4	8.0.6	8.1.7	9.0.1	9.2
7.3.4	EMS	EMS	EMS	EMS	EMS
8.0.6	EMS	EMS	EMS	EMS	EMS
8.1.7	EMS	EMS	Supported	Supported	Supported
9.0.1	EMS	EMS	Supported	Supported	Supported
9.2	Not Supported	EMS	Supported	Supported	Supported

The typical OCI development process — that is, the stages involved in building embedded SQL applications — is bypassed, and an application can link into the OCI library directly.

It is possible to mix OCI calls and Embedded SQL in a program. Please refer to the vendor documentation for more information.

Oracle OCI functions can be grouped by functionality; Table 16-6 shows main groups of functions as well as some examples from each group.

Table 16-6
Selected Oracle OCI Functions

Functional Group	*Examples*	*Uses*
Relational Functions	`OCIAttrGet(), OCIAttrSet(), OCIBreak(), OCILogoff(), OCILogon(), OCISessionBegin(), OCISessionEnd(), OCIStmtExecute(), OCIStmtFetch(),OCIStmtPrepare(), OCIStmtSetPieceInfo(), OCITransCommit(),OCITransPrepare(), OCITransRollback(),OCITransStart()`	Manage database access and processing SQL statements.
Navigational Functions	`OCICacheFlush(),OCICacheFree(), OCICacheRefresh(),OCICacheUnmark(), OCICacheUnpin(),OCIObjectArrayPin(), OCIObjectCopy(),OCIObjectExists(), OCIObjectFlush(),OCIObjectFree(), OCIObjectGetAttr(),OCIObjectRefresh(), OCIObjectSetAttr(),OCIObjectUnmark(), OCIObjectUnmarkByRef(), OCIObjectUnpin(),OCITypeArrayByName(), OCITypeArrayByRef(),OCITypeByName(), OCITypeByRef()`	Manipulate the records and objects retrieved from the Oracle RDBMS.
Data-type Mapping and Manipulation Functions	`OCICollAppend(),OCICollAssign(), OCICollAssignElem(),OCIDateGetDate(), OCIDateGetTime(),OCIDateLastDay(), OCIDateNextDay(),OCIDateSetDate(), OCINumberIntPower(),OCINumberIsZero(), OCIStringSize(),OCITableDelete(), OCITableExists(),OCITableFirst(), OCITableLast(),OCITableNext(), OCITablePrev(),OCITableSize()`	Manipulate the data attributes and ensure proper data casting.
External Procedure Functions	`OCIExtProcAllocCallMemory(), OCIExtProcRaiseExcp(), OCIExtProcRaiseExcpWithMsg(), OCIExtProcGetEnv()`	Implement C-type callbacks from PL/SQ programs.

To use OCI, a C/C++ program, at the very minimum, should include an OCI.H header file and link with OCI.LIB. Here is example of a very basic C program using OCI:

```
#include <stdio.h>
#include <stdlib.h>
```

```
#include <string.h>
#include <oci.h>

static OCIEnv           *p_OCI_env;
static OCIError         *p_OCI_error;
static OCISvcCtx        *p_OCI_svc;
static OCIStmt          *p_OCI_sql;
static OCIDefine        *p_OCI_def    = (OCIDefine *) 0;

void main()
{
   char             p_data [30];
   int              ret;

/* Initialize OCI */
   ret = OCIInitialize((ub4) OCI_DEFAULT, (dvoid *)0,
          (dvoid * (*)(dvoid *, size_t)) 0,
          (dvoid * (*)(dvoid *, dvoid *, size_t))0,
          (void (*)(dvoid *, dvoid *)) 0 );

   /* Initialize the environment */
   ret = OCIEnvInit( (OCIEnv **) &p_OCI_env, OCI_DEFAULT,
(size_t) 0, (dvoid **) 0 );

   /* Initialize handles */
   ret = OCIHandleAlloc((dvoid *) p_OCI_env,
         (dvoid **)&p_OCI_err,
         OCI_HTYPE_ERROR,(size_t) 0,
         (dvoid **) 0);

   ret = OCIHandleAlloc((dvoid *)p_OCI_env,
        (dvoid **)&p_OCI_svc, OCI_HTYPE_SVCCTX,
        (size_t) 0, (dvoid **) 0);

   /* Connect to the RDBMS */
   ret = OCILogon(p_OCI_env,
            p_OCI_err,
            &p_OCI_svc,
            "acme",
            4,
            "acme",
            4,
            "acme",
            4);
   if (ret!= 0)
 {
 /* handle the possible errors */
  }

   /*Prepare the SQL statement */
   ret = OCIHandleAlloc( (dvoid *) p_OCI_env,
```

```
            (dvoid **) &p_OCI_sql,
            OCI_HTYPE_STMT,
            (size_t) 0,(dvoid **) 0);
            ret = OCIStmtPrepare(p_OCI_sql,p_OCI_err,
           "SELECT
                  cust_name_s
           FROM customer
           WHERE cust_id_n = 1",
             (ub4) 37,
             (ub4) OCI_NTV_SYNTAX,
             (ub4) OCI_DEFAULT);

   /* Define the select list items */
   ret = OCIDefineByPos(p_OCI_sql, &p_OCI_def, p_OCI_err, 1,
(dvoid *)&p_data,(sword) 20, SQLT_STR,(dvoid *) 0, (ub2
*)0,(ub2 *)0,OCI_DEFAULT);

   /* Execute the SQL statement */
   ret = OCIStmtExecute(p_OCI_svc, p_OCI_sql, p_OCI_err,
(ub4) 1,(ub4) 0, (CONST OCISnapshot *) NULL,
          (OCISnapshot *) NULL,

OCI_DEFAULT);

  /* Fetch the data */
   while (ret != OCI_NO_DATA) {
      printf("%s\n",p_data);
      ret = OCIStmtFetch(p_OCI_sql, p_OCI_err, 1, 0, 0);
   }

/* Disconnect */
   ret = OCILogoff(p_OCI_svc, p_OCI_err);
   ret = OCIHandleFree((dvoid *) p_OCI_sql, OCI_HTYPE_STMT);
/* Free handles */
   ret = OCIHandleFree((dvoid *) p_OCI_svc, OCI_HTYPE_SVCCTX);
   ret = OCIHandleFree((dvoid *) p_OCI_err, OCI_HTYPE_ERROR);
   return;
}
```

The sequence of the program above follows:

- **OCIInitialize.** Initializes the OCI process environment.
- **OCIEnvInit.** Allocates and initializes an OCI environment handle.
- **OCIHandleAlloc.** Returns a pointer to an allocated and initialized handle.
- **OCILogon.** Creates a simple logon session.
- **OCIStmtPrepare.** Prepares an SQL or a PL/SQL statement for execution.

✦ **OCIDefineByPos.** Associates an item in a select-list with the type and output data buffer.

✦ **OCIStmtExecute.** Associates an application request with a server.

✦ **OCIStmtFetch.** Fetches rows from a query.

✦ **OCILogoff.** Terminates a connection and session created with `OCILogon()`.

✦ **OCIHandleFree.** Explicitly deallocates a handle and frees up resources.

The use of OCI programming interface results in faster programs, though most often than not this advantage is minuscule compared to the hurdles to create it. Most database applications today use a 4GL like Java, Visual Basic, or PowerBuilder. If you need to squeeze out the last drop of performance for your application, use OCI. Refer to the Oracle documentation for more information.

Oracle Objects for OLE (OO4O)

The Oracle Objects for OLE (OO4O) were introduced to capitalize on the huge success of the Microsoft COM (Component Object Model) standard. Implementing OO4O allowed COM-compliant applications to connect to the Oracle RDBMS directly, bypassing ODBC, and thus increasing efficiency and raw speed of the applications.

The OO4Os consist of an in-process OLE automation server (DLL), which provides an OLE/ActiveX interface to COM-compliant applications, specifically Visual Basic and Visual Basic for Application (VBA); OCX custom Data Control, to facilitate data manipulations; and two C++ class libraries — one for Microsoft Foundation Classes (MFC) specification and one for Borland (OWL).

Note

In Microsoft ActiveX world there is a notion of "early bound" and "late bound" objects. The former refers to the object's data type resolved at compilation thus requiring explicit reference to the library containing the class (from which object is to be created) to be added to the project. The latter allows for use of generic variables of Object type or Variant to be used in code, and their data type is resolved and assigned at run-time. Each of the methods has its advantages and disadvantages. Early bound objects are usually faster to load and execute since all dependencies were resolved at compile time, while being prone to "DLL Hell"–a scourge created by introducing Dynamic Link Libraries (DLL). Application compiled with one version of the library does not work with a different version of the same library. Late Bound objects are more immune to the DLL Hell (not completely, though), but are slower to load as all dependencies must be resolved in run-time.

The OO4Os are installed with Oracle Client. Once you've configured SQL*Net on the machine (see Oracle documentation for more information), you may use the interface to connect to the Oracle RDBMS. The following short example demonstrates the use of OO4O from within Microsoft Visual Basic 6.0:

```
' The following example assumes that Service Name 'ACME'
' was configured using the Oracle Net Configuration Assistant
' Please refer to the Oracle documentation for additional
' information on Oracle configuration
'
' declare object variables as VARIANT (VB default)
' alternatively, you may add reference to the Oracles
' ActiveX DLL and use strongly typed variables
'(if you do, the code below cannot be used
' within "classic" Active Server Pages(ASP))
'
Dim objSession
Dim objDB
Dim objDynaset
Dim objFields

Dim strSQL
'
' create late bound Oracle session object
'
    Set objSession =
CreateObject("OracleInProcServer.XOraSession")
'
' connect to the database
'
    Set objDB = objSession.DbOpenDatabase("ACME", _
            "ACME/ACME", 0&)
'
' assemble SQL query
'
     strSQL = "SELECT * FROM customer"
'
' create OraDynaset object using the SQL statement
'
     Set objDynaset = objDB.CreateDynaset(strSQL, 0&)
'
' get handle to the fields collection of the
' dynaset object
'
     Set objFields = objDynaset.Fields
'
'position the dynaset to the very first record
'
     objDynaset.MoveFirst
'
' scroll the dynaset object
'
    Do While Not objDynaset.EOF
'
' display the value of the first field in the result set
' in a message box
```

```
'
        MsgBox objFields(1).Value
'
'move to the next record
'
        objDynaset.MoveNext
    Loop
```

OO4O do offer an advantage over ODBC but are very similar to the OLEDB provider for Oracle; the latter offers the advantage of a more standard interface and naming conventions.

Oracle Gateways

The Oracle Open Gateway interface is used to access data from non-Oracle databases like IBM DB2 UDB, Microsoft SQL Server, Sybase, and so on; it even provides limited capabilities to access nonrelational data sources.

There are four types of Oracle Open Gateways, presented in the table below:

Oracle Gateway	***Uses***
Transparent Gateways	The most commonly used type to link non-Oracle RDBMS; when used, they handle complexities of intercommunication, details of syntax, and so on. They also manage distributed queries and transactions (i.e., heterogeneous queries).
Procedural Gateways	Used to communicate with nonrelational data sources via mapping of the foreign database functions into custom Oracle PL/SQL procedures.
Access Managers	Used exclusively for IBM AS/400 and MVS platforms.
Oracle Replication Servers	Used for heterogeneous data replication.

The Oracle Open Gateways are available for every major database product, including Microsoft SQL Server and IBM DB2.

Microsoft Data Access Interfaces

Microsoft went through many stages of data access mechanisms in its products. Call Level Interface, while fast, was not easy to use and had a steep learning curve. Realizing that, Microsoft introduced classes that encapsulated the same functionality but provided a much more programmer-friendly interface. With the advent of Rapid Development Tools (Visual Basic, Delphi, PowerBuilder, etc.), a programmer-friendly interface that allows the user to concentrate on the implementation of the business logic, without being bogged down with low-level manipulations, became a strategic point for Microsoft. The data access objects (classes) followed in the rapid succession: Data Access Objects (DAO), Remote Access Objects (RDO), Active Data Objects (ADO), and finally Active Data Objects.NET. (Some may even recall ODBCDirect — a data access library introduced specifically for Visual Basic programmers to access MS SQL Server 6.0/6.5.) Make no mistake: While serving the same purpose, these interfaces are all different. DAO, for instance, uses the JET Engine — Microsoft Access library — even when connecting to SQL Server, while RDO does not have to use it; the syntax is quite different and not always straightforward.

The component-based architecture became a mainstream in the late 1990s. While who introduced the technology (and when) can be disputed, there is no doubt that it was Microsoft who brought it to the widest audience with its OLE/ActiveX technology (its equivalent in non-Microsoft camp is CORBA). ADO was a hierarchy of the ActiveX objects, assembled in a collection of the ADO data library. It was working with OLEDB data providers — assuming there was one available; for the standard ODBC connection you would have to use the OLEDB provider for ODBC. This meant more and more layers of data access abstraction, which slowed down the process of data retrieval and manipulation. To make things worse, initially ADO was limited to working in connected environment; that is, a permanent connection had to be maintained to the data source); the disconnected data access model was introduced later, and it had problems of its own (e.g., being limited to using Microsoft Internet Explorer version 4 or above). Even now, while the .NET initiative is taking firm hold on the developer community, ADO is still very much alive and will continue for a few more years at least. (Microsoft announced that support for "classic" Visual Basic would cease in 2008.)

The following Visual Basic example illustrates the process of connecting to the IBM DB2 UDB RDBMS and executing an SQL query.

```
' this example uses late bound objects
' (see note later in the chapter), which
' makes it possible to use in ASP projects
' and makes it less DLL-versions-error prone
' there is a price to pay in terms of speed and
' typing errors (no IntelliSense help for the
' late-bound ActiveX objects
```

```
Dim objConnection
Dim objCommand
Dim objADORecordset
Dim strConnectString
Dim strSQL
'
' assemble the connection string
' uses Microsoft ODBC bridge for OLEDB
' the user DSN ACME_DSN was created earlier in the chapter
'
     strConnectString = "Provider=MSDASQL;DSN=ACME_DSN;"
     strConnectString = strConnectString &
"User ID=ACME;Password=ACME;"
'
' create late-bound ADODB Connection object
'
    Set objConnection = CreateObject("ADODB.Connection")
'
' open connection to the IBM DB2 UDB database
'
    objConnection.Open strConnectString
'
' create late-bound ADODB Command object
'
    Set objCommand = CreateObject("ADODB.Command")
'
' assign objConnection to its ActiveConnection property
'
    objCommand.ActiveConnection = objConnection
'
' assign SQL statement to the CommandText property
'
    objCommand.CommandText = strSQL
'
' set type of the command to adCmdText
' meaning that raw SQL statement would be executed
' as opposed to stored procedure, for instance
'
    objCommand.CommandType = 1
'
' the execute command returns an ADO Recordset (if succeeded)
'
    Set objADORecordset = objCommand.Execute
'
' scroll the recordset
'
    With objADORecordset
'
' position the cursor on the very first row
' in the recordset
'
```

```
        .MoveFirst
        Do While Not objADORecordset.EOF
      '
      ' display the value of the first field
      ' of the result set in a message box
      '
            MsgBox .Fields(1).Value
      '
      'move to the next record
      '
            .MoveNext
        Loop
    End With
  '
  ' clean up: close all the connections
  ' and destroy objects; usually done
  ' automatically by Visual Basic once the object
  ' goes out of scope
    objADORecordset.Close
    Set objADORecordset = Nothing
    Set objCommand = Nothing
    objConnection.Close
    Set objConnection = Nothing
```

ADO.NET is the latest incarnation of the Microsoft data access mechanisms, and it was specifically designed to work with the new .NET framework, which is supposed to be a programming paradigm shift. While retaining part of the old name, ADO.NET is a completely different data access mechanism. First, it is not an external library that you link one way or another into your application and distribute afterward. ADO.NET is a part of the .NET framework (and—eventually—a part of the Windows operating system itself); second, it is not OLE/ActiveX based; that is, it has nothing to do with COM (Microsoft Component Object Model).

ADO.NET was designed to support a connected environment as well as disconnected one, and to support XML natively. To maintain compatibility with the previous interfaces, there are .NET Data Providers for OLEDB.

The following example, of a console application written in VB.NET, uses OLEDB provider for Microsoft SQL Server and ADO.NET classes to connect to a local server and retrieve some information:

```
Sub Main()
    Dim objDataReader As SqlClient.SqlDataReader
    Dim strConn As String
    Dim strSQL As String
    Dim lCount As Integer = 0
    '
```

```
        ' assemble connection string using SQLOLEDB provider
        '
        strConn = "Provider=SqlOleDb;Data Source=localhost;"
        strConn = "Initial Catalog=Acme;"
        strConn = "User ID=acme;Password=acme;"
        '
        ' assemble SQL query
        '
        strSQL = "SELECT * FROM customer"
        strSQL = strSQL & " WHERE CUST_NAME_S LIKE 'WI%'"
'
        ' write comments onto console
        '
        Console.WriteLine("An example of using SQLOLEDB")
        Console.WriteLine("Provider with VB.NET")
        Console.WriteLine("-------------------")
        '
        ' connect to the SQL Server and fetch the data
        '
        Try
            '
            ' create new Connection object
            ' using the connection string
            Dim objConnection As New
SqlClient.SqlConnection(strConn)            '
            ' open connection to the SQL server
            '
            objConnection.Open()
            '
            ' create a command object, with the SQL statement
            ' and connection object as initialization params
            '
            Dim objCommand As New
SqlClient.SqlCommand(strSQL, objConnection)
            '
            ' retrieve results into DataReader object
            '
            objDataReader = objCommand.ExecuteReader()
            '
            ' scroll the data reader, and reteieve
            ' value from the 4th field in the recordset
            ' CUST_NAME_S, and increment counter
            '
            Do While objDataReader.Read
                Console.WriteLine
                    (objDataReader.GetSqlString(4).ToString)
                    lCount = lCount + 1
            Loop
```

```
            '
            ' output the final message
            '
            Console.WriteLine("------------------")
            Console.WriteLine("Total records:" & lCount)
            '
            ' wait for the input
            '
            Console.ReadLine()
            '
            ' close the connection within
            ' an appropriate scope
            '
            objConnection.Close()
        Catch e As SqlClient.SqlException
            Console.WriteLine(e.Message)
        Finally
            '
            ' close DataReader
            '
            objDataReader.Close()
        End Try
End Sub
```

The results of the execution of the code above are shown in Figure 16-7.

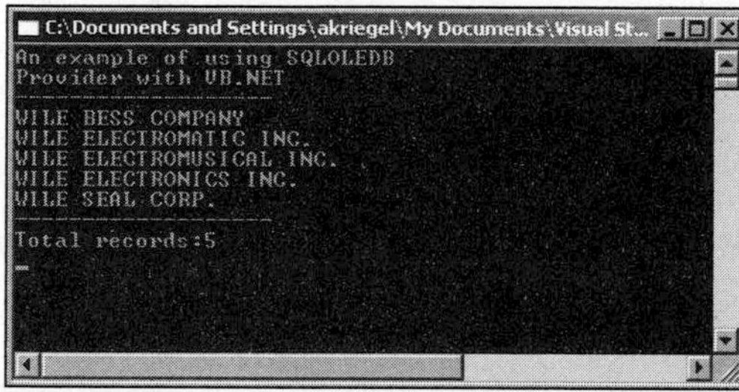

Figure 16-7: Connecting to Microsoft SQL Server 2000 through OLEDB

The functionality of ADO.NET is contained in the following Namespaces (a .NET concept but fairly intuitive—similar to the library, header file, or Java class), listed in Table 16-7. Both are used with VB.NET and C# (pronounced C sharp).

Table 16-7
ADO.NET Top Level Namespaces

Namespace	*Description*
`System.Data`	The top level class in the ADO.NET hierarchy
`System.Data.Common`	Shared "groundwork" classes for .NET providers
`System.Data.OleDb`	.NET for OLEDB classes
`System.Data.SqlClient`	SQL Server specific classes; optimized for SQL server 7.0 and later
`System.Data.SqlTypes`	Mapping RDBMS data types to handle return values

We illustrate ADO.NET usage with one of the .NET family languages, C#; the syntax for the other languages ported to .NET (VB.NET, COBOL, Eiffel, C++ with managed extensions, to name a few) might differ, but the underlying mechanisms remain exactly the same, since ADO.NET is incorporated into the .NET framework.

Microsoft DBLIB Legacy

DBLIB (stands for DataBase Library) is a Microsoft proprietary Call Level Interface consisting of C functions and macros (compare to Oracle OCI) that can be used to access Microsoft SQL server 2000 from the applications programmed in third-generation languages (mostly C). It was the original interface, and it became a legacy interface with introduction of Microsoft SQL Server version 7.0.

The DB-Library API has not been enhanced beyond the level of SQL Server version 6.5, which means that even if you are able to use it for communication with Microsoft SQL Server 2000, you would be limited to only the feature set of its 6.5 version (which was all the rave back in 1997).

The principles of DBLIB do not differ much from Oracle's OCI interface: you include the header files to get all the definitions into your C program, then you compile and link it. Samples of the DBLIB applications are installed with the Microsoft SQL Server 2000 in default directory \Microsoft SQL Server\80\Tools\Devtools\Samples\DBLib.

DBLIB is the fastest interface to the MS SQL Server. You can find more help about programming DBLIB in the Microsoft documentation, but keep in mind that this interface quickly becomes obsolete (though you might not have much choice if your server is version 6.5, or 6, or—just don't tell anyone—version 4.2, capable of running in MS-DOS and OS/2 environments).

The following code snippet in C# demonstrates using ADO.NET SQLData to connect to Microsoft SQL Server 2000. To try the example, start the Visual Studio.Net IDE (Integrated Development environment), select Console Application, name it `SQL_Connect`, then type in the code shown below, then compile it and run. Keep in mind that C# is a case-sensitive language, and `SqlConnection` is not the same as `SQLConnection`. You may or may not use the namespace that automatically appears in your code pane.

```
using System;
using System.Data;
using System.Data.SqlClient;

class SQL_Connect
{
static void Main(string[] args)
{
//
//prepare connection string
//use integrated security (Windows Authentication)
//as opposed to UserID/Password pair
 //
    string s_conn = @"server=(local);" +
        "Integrated Security=true;" +
        "database=ACME";
//
//Create SqlConnection object instance
//
    SqlConnection connSQL = new SqlConnection(s_conn);
try
{
//
//open connection to the local instance
//of your SQL Server
//
    connSQL.Open();
string s_SQL = "SELECT * FROM customer
           WHERE CUST_NAME_S LIKE 'MA%'";
//
//create command object and pass to it
//connection object and SQL query string
//
    SqlCommand commSQL = new SqlCommand(s_SQL,connSQL);
//
//retrieve all the records returned by the
//query into SqlDatReader object
//
    SqlDataReader sqlRead=commSQL.ExecuteReader();
    Console.WriteLine("Example demonstrating .NET Data
Provider");
```

```
    Console.WriteLine("connection to Microsoft SQL Server
2000");
//
//scroll the result set and print the output
//onto standard  output console
//
while (sqlRead.Read())
 {
     Console.WriteLine("{0}|{1}",
          sqlRead["CUST_NAME_S"].ToString().PadRight(30),
          sqlRead["CUST_ID_N"].ToString());
     Console.WriteLine("--------------");
 }
}
catch(Exception e)
{
//
// in the case an error occurred
// display a message, including error source
//
     Console.WriteLine("Error occurred:" + e.Message);
     Console.WriteLine("Error Source:" + e.Source);
}
finally
{
//
//Close connection to SQL Server
//
     connSQL.Close();
     Console.WriteLine("Connection closed.");
//
//wait for user input
//to keep MS-DOS Window
//
     Console.ReadLine();
          }
     }
}
```

If you are using VisualStudio.NET IDE, run the program either from the taskbar or by pressing F5 button on your keyboard, or from the command line by going into the directory where the executable was compiled. Figure 16-8 shows the output results produced by the above program.

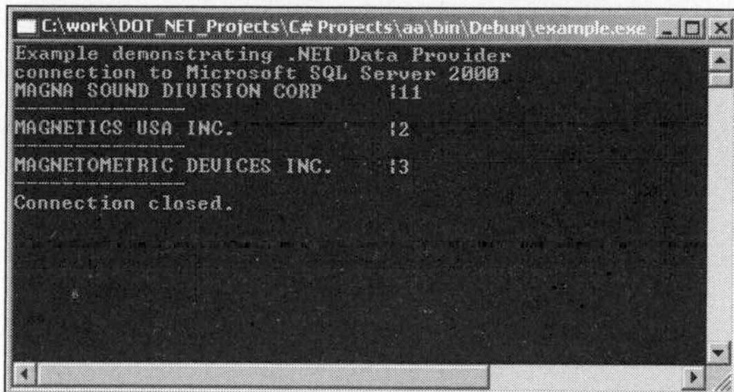

Figure 16-8: Results of the database C# program

Oracle's native .NET Data Provider is not included with the Visual Studio.NET and must be downloaded separately from Microsoft site. Once downloaded and installed, you need to add a reference to System.Data.OracleClient.dll assembly to your project.

Summary

The database connectivity standard is an established fact, with its most successful commercial implementation being Microsoft ODBC 3.0 interface. There are dozens of ODBC drivers for all types of data sources ranging from RDBMS to flat text files, available on virtually every platform — Microsoft Windows, various Unix flavors, and Mac OS, to name just a few.

The CLI/SQL standard establishes a set of functions that are used by applications in a uniform fashion to access data sources and perform data-related tasks.

All communication between the application and the data source is conducted through ODBC drivers, which are loaded and unloaded on demand by the Driver Manager. The ODBC (CLI/SQL) drivers work in a way similar to a live interpreter — it speaks a common language (ODBC functions set) to the application (through the Driver Manager) and also speaks native RDBMS dialect.

There are a number of emerging technologies for defining the application-RDBMS interaction. The most popular are Java Database Connectivity (JDBC), Microsoft Active Data Objects (ADO), and ADO.NET (an object-oriented interface to the OLEDB API or ODBC API), in addition to the new "native" .NET providers.

Every RDBMS vendor has its own version of Call Level Interface: Oracle's Oracle Call Interface (OCI), IBM DB2 UDB Call Level Interface (CLI), and Microsoft DBLIB. Some of these are becoming increasingly obsolete, although they provide the maximum performance in terms of the raw speed.

✦ ✦ ✦

CHAPTER 17

New Developments: XML, OLAP, and Objects

In This Chapter

XML

OLAP and business intelligence

Objects in relational databases

SQL has been around for more than 20 years, and its age has begun to show — especially in the face of other developments. First, the object-oriented programming paradigm, introduced at about the same time as SQL, became mainstream at the beginning of the 1990s. And the Internet has now created a seemingly insatiable demand for structured data and opened new ways of using and creating information. As computers become more powerful, new uses have emerged — for example, analyzing vast amounts of data for uncovering hidden trends, replication over the Internet, storing data in new data formats like video, MP3 and more.

These developments have all placed pressure on SQL to transform and adapt. SQL3 standards have introduced new data types, bridging gaps between text-oriented SQL and object-oriented software. RDBMS vendors have added capabilities to utilize objects within standard relational framework (e.g., Java-stored procedures, ActiveX (OLE) Automation, XML etc.). New object-oriented database systems (OODBS) and object-oriented relational database systems (OORDBMS) have sprouted.

This chapter discusses some major new technologies that relate to SQL. Some of the emerging technologies — for instance EJB (Enterprise Java Beans) or Web services (exposing functionality over the Internet) — would be only briefly touched. Readers interested in using these technologies in conjunction with SQL, are encouraged to read books dedicated to the topic.

We recommend in particular *Mastering Enterprise JavaBeans, Second Edition*, by Ed Roman, Scott W. Ambler, and Tyler Jewell (Wiley, 2001).

XML

One can hardly open a trade magazine without seeing yet another article describing how *eXtensible Markup Language* (XML) will make our life easier, and touting it as the solution for all our problems. While the jury is still out, there is no question that XML has made its way into virtually every area of data exchange. Every major RDBMS vendor has made a pledge to XML, and some have already incorporated it into their products.

XML was initially designed as a more rigorous approach to presenting information on the Web, as inadequacies of traditional *HyperText Markup Language* (HTML) became apparent. Essentially, XML is a way to describe data — in addition to data itself. Unlike HTML, it does not say how the data is to be presented (i.e., color, font, font size etc). To be viewed in, say, a Web browser, the XML document must be first translated into some other form (e.g., HTML), using style sheets to specify how the document should be rendered with the help of *Extensible Style Language* (XSL). Because of the separation between the data and the presentation level, it is possible to transform the same set of data into different representations.

The *document type definitions* (DTD) define the XML elements that make up the document; because of the DTD — to which an XML document contains a link — the XML documents are considered self-describing.

Well-formed XML refers to an XML document that strictly adheres to the standards; being well formed is crucial for seamless integration between applications; there are numerous programs available on the Internet to check whether an XML document is well-formed.

The core specification of XML has achieved universal acceptance, and is ubiquitous over the Internet and is used in many custom-designed applications that previously were the domain of the *Electronic Data Interchange* (EDI) standard. The term itself sometimes refer to related specifications of XSL, XML Linking Language (XLink), Simple API for XML (SAX), XML Pointer Language (XPointer), and document object model (DOM).

The *document object model* (DOM) is an application programming interface (API) representing an XML document in a hierarchical treelike structure. Once parsed into the DOM, an XML document is referred to as *infoset.* An infoset can is manipulated through the DOM objects, and using XPath API — a set of functions for querying/manipulating XML document's values — one could extract and/or modify information contained in the document, which could be later written into a file, rendered into HTML for posting on the Web, and so on.

Extensible Style Language for Transformation (XSLT, XSL) steps in to compensate for XML's inability to communicate just how the contained information is to be presented. It defines a process of transforming one XML document into another, even reformatting it into non-XML format.

Oracle 9*i*

Oracle supports XML through its built-in *XML Developer Kits* (XDK) (which allow developing for XML in Java or C/C++, as well as in PL/SQL), which in the last version — Oracle 9*i* Release 2 — was replaced by XML DB Repository. Both names refer to a collection of the XML related features and technologies built into RDBMS itself.

Procedures written in PL/SQL access the XDK from inside the RDBMS, whereas Java and/or C/C++ procedures have the ability to access its functionality from outside.

These kits allow you to create and manipulate XML documents via a number of objects including XML/XSLT parsers, XML class generators, XSQL servlets, and so on. To use these packages you must know these languages and the underlying XML/XSLT principles.

XDK is written in Java, and is integrated with Oracle 9*i*. Owners of earlier versions of Oracle (prior to Oracle 8*i* Release 8.1.7) may download it from the Oracle Web site. The kit contains an XSLT processor, an XSQL page processor and servlet engine, as well as an XML/SQL utility (a separate, Oracle-specific tool for parsing XML documents into relational tables structure).

Using XSQL, you can set up publishing information in XML format. XSQL includes a page processor, XSQL Java servlet, and a command line interface. The page processor could be called through the servlet (running on Apache Web Server, for instance) or through the command line interface. Essentially, it enables querying relational data and getting results back formatted as XML documents

The XDK will not work with Oracle 8.0 or earlier; to add XML capabilities (somewhat limited) to legacy versions, Oracle introduced the PLSXML package, written in PL/SQL. This package can be called within an SQL or PL/SQL query and will produce XML document output. It requires Oracle Application Server or Oracle 9*i*AS, to operate.

Within its XML DB Repository, Oracle 9*i* Release 2 also introduced a new native XML type to store XML documents instead of parsing them into relational rows. It also enables non-XML data to be treated as XML by creating the document from the data extracted from the tables. There are numerous packages provided by Oracle that you could use to build solutions based on XML — DBMS_XDB, DBMS_XMLSCHEMA, to name a few — in addition to XML-related functions and data types. Please refer to Oracle documentation for more information on these features.

XML and Web Services

Distributed computing has been with us for quite a while. The idea behind *distributed computing* is that programs spread across a network may collaborate on a single task or related tasks. The *Web services* paradigm takes distributed architecture to the next level. Instead of binary formats (like Microsoft Distributed COM [COM/DCOM] and Enterprise Java Beans [CORBA]), it uses XML and Simple Object Access Protocol (SOAP) to send and process requests among library components spread over the Internet or intranet. It works like a giant Lego, only each piece can be used by more than one application and the binding between the pieces comes over HTTP as a standard XML document.

Web services run on their respective Web servers across the globe; a Universal Description, Discovery and Integration (UDDI) directory—very similar to that of URL server—maintains a registry of all available Web services. When an application requires the functionality provided by a Web service, it requests it over HTTP, using an XML document composed according to SOAP rules, describing the function requested, arguments, etc.; the application on the other end receives the document, parses it, processes the request, and sends a response to the calling app in very much the same way.

With the convergence of database and Internet technologies, every major vendor provides support for Web services with their flagship products—either built-in, or through add-on components.

IBM DB2 UDB 8.1

DB2 UDB supports XML through XML Extender component. It serves as an XML document repository, as well as a repository for the DTD. DB2 UDB provides two options for the storage—XML column and XML collection. The first option—XML column—enters the entire document into a column of XML data type, while the second option—XML collection—maps the document onto the set of relational tables. IBM provides a number of stored procedures for storing, retrieving, searching, and modifying data in the XML collection.

The DB2 XML Extender includes a visual tool that facilitates mapping of the XML document elements to the columns in the database table. The mapping, once performed, is stored in the database as a *document access definition* (DAD).

DB2 also provides XML-native data type (`XMLVARCHAR` and `XMLCLOB`). Using it you could store the whole XML document in a single column (as opposed to disassembling the document into row-level data for insertion into the "standard" relational tables).

To generate an XML document through SQL queries against DB2 UDB (or any ODBC-compliant source), one has to use an IBM Net.Data component that defines a collection of macros for XML.

Microsoft SQL Server 2000

SQL Server 2000 provides native support for XML using additional XML-related keywords (built into the Transact-SQL dialect). The XML data is disassembled into text-based tables, and could be assembled back on request. There is no XML data type in the SQL Server 2000.

The requests could be made through usual SQL Server data access channel (ADO, ADO.NET, ODBC,DBLIB — see Chapter 16 for more information about accessing RDBMS), or sent to the SQL Server directly using HTTP (HyperText Transfer Protocol — the Internet standard for transferring text-based data). While exciting, the full description of these features belongs to a Microsoft SQL Server 2000– or XML-specific book. Here we are going to cover just the basics of the XML/SQL convergence.

The new Microsoft extensions for SQL enable you to query SQL Server 2000 tables and receive the data in XML format, as well as to submit an XML document for saving the data into the database. The new `FOR XML` clause with a standard `SELECT` query instructs SQL Server 2000 to produce XML output of the data. The clause should be used with additional XML-related keywords to specify the mode: `RAW`, `AUTO`, or `EXPLICIT`; the mode refers to the XML output formatting, and is explained in Microsoft documentation or numerous books on the subject.

Here is an output produced by querying the two tables `ORDER_HEADER` and `ORDER_LINE` from the ACME database. The query returns records for two orders (`30607` and `30608`) and all the order items for them:

```
SELECT    ORDER_HEADER.ORDHDR_ID_N,
          ORDER_LINE.ORDLINE_ID_N,
          ORDER_LINE.ORDLINE_CREATEDATE_D
FROM      ORDER_HEADER,ORDER_LINE
WHERE     ORDER_HEADER.ORDHDR_ID_N =
          ORDER_LINE.ORDLINE_ORDHDRID_FN
AND       ORDER_HEADER.ORDHDR_ID_N IN (30608, 30607)
ORDER BY  ORDER_HEADER.ORDHDR_ID_N
FOR XML AUTO

XML_F52E2B61-18A1-11d1-B105-00805F49916B
---------------------------------------------------
<ORDER_HEADER ORDHDR_ID_N="30607">
<ORDER_LINE ORDLINE_ID_N="87234"/>
<ORDER_LINE ORDLINE_ID_N="87235"/>
</ORDER_HEADER>
<ORDER_HEADER ORDHDR_ID_N="30608">
<ORDER_LINE ORDLINE_ID_N="87236"/>
<ORDER_LINE ORDLINE_ID_N="87237"/>
</ORDER_HEADER>

(4 row(s) affected)
```

Future of XML

While XML is an established standard, there are several new developments that might undermine it: Electronic Business eXtensible Markup Language (ebXML), Universal Business Language (UBL), and Open Financial Exchange standard (OFEX) are only three of these. XML itself might undergo some transformation as it is being adapted to Web services and mobile computing using telephony. Several database products are built for XML exclusively (including SoftwareAG, eXelon, Ipedo, and others), with integrated support for SOAP, ODBC, JDBC, Xpath, and so on. Microsoft built its .NET technology around XML, and IBM and Oracle incorporate it into many of their products (WebSphere and Application Server respectively); SUN pushes integration of XML and J2EE.

Touted as the most important development since the invention of the Internet, XML may or may not live up to the hype that surrounds it nowadays. We believe that it is not a "silver bullet" solution for everything but a very useful format for storing and retrieving text data, and that it eventually will take its place as one of the useful niche technologies.

Using `AUTO` mode makes SQL Server 2000 format document according to the best guess it can make, based on the relationships between the tables; note the hierarchical structure of the XML document. Combined with DTD, this document can be sent over the Internet to be displayed or used as input for some application.

To enter the data into an RDBMS from an XML document, Microsoft SQL Server provides the `OPENXML` keyword. Its use is much more complicated than simply querying for XML. First, you must call a stored procedure `sp_xml_preparedocument`, which parses the XML document and returns a handle (a memory pointer) to the prepared document in computer memory. This handle is passed to the `OPENXML` statement, which converts it into RDBMS standard rows, ready to be inserted. A number of parameters have to be specified for the data to be correctly formatted and interpreted.

OLAP and Business Intelligence

Every deployed database system could be arbitrarily divided into two broad categories — OLTP databases and OLAP databases; some deployed systems could represent a mix of both.

An *online transaction processing* (OLTP) system is optimized to support transactions: order processing, inventory tracking, recording employee data, and so on. Such systems are designed to process large volumes of concurrent transactions as quickly as possible. In short, the main purpose of such a system is to accumulate structured information.

OLAP Rules

The term *OLAP* was introduced in 1993 by Dr. E.F. Codd, who also was the first to propose the relational data model about 20 years earlier. With its various flavors — ROLAP (relational OLAP), MOLAP (multidimensional OLAP), and HOLAP (hybrid OLAP) — it is taking data analysis from a manual, tedious combination of art and science into a computer-aided, exact science. (OLAP does not remove need to program for data analysis; yet it is a major improvement over just about any other way of analyzing large amount of data.) Dr. Codd established 12 OLAP rules to follow, and most OLAP products conform to these in one way or another.

- **Multidimensional conceptual view.** OLAP operates with CUBEs of data that represent multidimensional construct of data. Event though the name implies three dimensional data, the number of possible dimensions is practically unlimited.
- **Transparency.** OLAP systems should be part of an open system that supports heterogeneous data sources.
- **Accessibility.** The OLAP should present the user with a single logical schema of the data.
- **Consistent reporting performance.** Performance should not degrade as the number of dimensions in the model increases.
- **Client/server architecture.** Should be based on open, modular systems.
- **Generic dimensionality.** Not limited to 3-D and not biased toward any particular dimension. A function applied to one dimension should also be able to be applied to another.
- **Dynamic sparse-matrix handling.** Related both to the idea of nulls in relational databases and to the notion of compressing large files, a sparse matrix is one in which not every cell contains data. OLAP systems should accommodate varying storage and data-handling options.
- **Multiuser support.** OLAP systems should support more than one user at the time.
- **Unrestricted cross-dimensional operations.** Similar to rule of generic dimensionality; all dimensions are created equal, and operations across data dimensions should not restrict relationships between cells.
- **Intuitive data manipulation.** Ideally, users shouldn't have to use menus or perform complex multiple-step operations when an intuitive drag-and-drop action will do.
- **Flexible reporting.** Save a tree. Users should be able to print just what they need, and any changes to the underlying financial model should be automatically reflected in reports.
- **Unlimited dimensional and aggregation levels.** The OLAP cube can be built with unlimited dimensions, and aggregation of the contained data also does not have practical limits.

Most OLAP tools — either integrated or stand-alone — generally conform to these rules. There are many more rules defined by theorists, as well as de-facto ones, established by the heavyweight database market players; please refer to OLAP-specific literature and vendor's documentation for more information.

An *online analytical processing* (OLAP) system is designed to make sense out of the accumulated data. These systems are used to discover trends and analyze critical factors, perform statistical analysis, and so on. While important, speed is not the main feature of such systems, as OLAP queries typically process large amounts of data. Normally, OLAP databases extract information from several OLTP databases called *data warehouses*.

What is OLAP used for? Decision support, sales analysis, marketing, data consolidation — the list goes on. Once data is accumulated, OLAP steps in to make actual sense out of it. OLAP provides multidimensional representation of data contained in OLTP data warehouses through the `CUBE` structure, which allows for creating views of data according to different sets of criteria, and manipulate those using sophisticated analytic functions.

Oracle, IBM, Microsoft, Hyperion, Cognos are among the leading OLAP vendors. While an RDBMS can be a base for OLAP services, the tools are usually not integrated or tied to a particular database. Oracle's Data Mining utility and Oracle Express, for example, can utilize a "native" Oracle database or Hyperion Essbase or IBM DB2 UDB.

ROLAP, MOLAP, and HOLAP...

All these acronyms refer to the way data for the `CUBE` — the primary operational unit for the OLAP queries — is stored. The functionality, methods, and principles of OLAP remain identical across all three.

- ✦ *Multidimensional OLAP* (MOLAP) refers to the situation when relational data for a CUBE, along with aggregation data, are stored in the CUBE itself. It provides for the fastest response, and is most appropriate for frequent use (like on-demand OLAP, without the need for real-time data).
- ✦ *Relational OLAP* (ROLAP) refers to the situation when relational data for a CUBE, along with aggregation data, are stored in the relational database. This provides for real-time querying, though response might be slower than MOLAP as all the data need to be assembled from scratch.
- ✦ *Hybrid OLAP* (HOLAP) refers to the situation when relational data for a CUBE is stored in a relational database, while the aggregation data are stored in the CUBE itself. It was designed to get best of both worlds: it is somewhat faster than ROLAP, and CUBE structure is much smaller than in MOLAP case.

Oracle 9*i*

Of course, Oracle also has incorporated business intelligence capability directly into Oracle 9*i* Database. It allows OLAP queries to be executed directly against an OLTP database without transferring it into a specialized OLAP database. This approach has its pluses and minuses; one plus would be that there is no need for a time-consuming and expensive data transfer (and transformation) process; on the minus side is the fact that running an ad-hoc OLAP query against your production database may slow down your operation with a resource intensive process.

Oracle 9*i* Database provides the foundation for the Oracle OLAP, providing data storage and management capabilities, analytic functions, security, and so on, whereas the OLAP services themselves support multidimensional calculations, forecast functions, models, and the like. A number of wizards are provided to guide users through the maze of choices.

Oracle provides a set of Java OLAP APIs to program additional functionality, which enables building cross-platform solutions using Java applications, applets, Java Server Pages, and so on. It could be installed separately, on middle tier hardware, or integrated with a RDBMS.

Oracle OLAP CUBE does not relate to the `GROUP BY CUBE` clause that groups the selected rows, based on the values of all possible combinations, and produces a single aggregate row for each group (cross-tabulation).

IBM DB2 UDB 8.1

IBM DB2 UDB provides OLAP capabilities through DB2 OLAP Server and OLAP Server Analyzer. Both are add-ons developed in collaboration with Hyperion (and its Essbase product).

The product is Java-based and uses JAPI from Essbase. IBM supports only ROLAP and MOLAP functionality IBM DB2 UDB also features OLAP Miner — branded by IBM as an "opportunity-discovery" component of the IBM OLAP Server. It applies data mining algorithms to the OLAP CUBEs to pinpoint the "surprise" areas and present them to an analyst for further investigation.

Microsoft SQL Server 2000

Microsoft provides OLAP capabilities through Microsoft Analysis Services, which are bundled with SQL Server 2000 (OLAP Services Components in SQL Server 7.0).

The Multidimensional Expressions (MDX) language is used to manipulate the base unit of any OLAP analysis — CUBE. The language is similar to SQL in many respects, and enables the manipulation of data stored in OLAP CUBEs Microsoft also provides external access interfaces like OLEDB,Active Data Objects and SQL-DMO (Data Management Objects) to access OLAP functionality within SQL Server 2000.

See Chapter 16 for more information on programming interfaces.

In addition to its predefined functions, MDX permits the creation of custom functions. While having somewhat similar syntax to SQL, MDX is not an SQL extension; it is a different language, designed specifically for OLAP.

Objects

The object-oriented approach — an interesting academic topic in the 1980s — became mainstream in the early 1990s and the de-facto standard for every new development thereafter (the object-oriented term is explained later in the chapter).

Nearly any modern programming language is (or claims to be) object-oriented. However, even though the object-oriented approach proved to be successful in computer programming (in terms of increased development speed, increased robustness etc.), it is not a very popular concept in the database market so far. Although there are some purely object-oriented databases (which we discuss later in this chapter), their market share is rather insignificant. The implementations of the different concept — supplying objects and tools for working with RDBMS — seems to be more practical. Many major RDBMS vendors — including Oracle and DB2 UDB — provide some kind of using objects with traditional RDBMS (the Object Oriented RDBMS — OORDBMS — approach). Therefore, even though the object-oriented paradigm is not directly related to the contents of this book, we will briefly introduce it in the database context in this chapter.

In the RDBMS world, OO refers to the ability of the database to store and retrieve instances (explained in the following paragraph) of the objects — very much the same way as XML documents: either by being parsed into text and reconstituted on demand, or by saving the entire object AS-IS — be it Java, ActiveX or .NET object. In addition, some databases sponsor *object data types*, which introduce OOP principles into their procedural SQL programming (see Chapter 14 for more information on SQL procedural extensions). You may think of these as User Defined Data types (see Chapter 3 for more information on data types) that also contain some methods or functions.

OOP Paradigm

Object-oriented approach treats everything as objects — i.e. programming structures that are capable of containing data and have some relevant methods. Usually, objects are representations of real-life entities, reduced in their complexity to a few well defined features and tasks they should be able to perform. A person, a tree, a car, an organization — all can be represented as objects; the same goes for some abstract objects like 'bank account', or 'data access object'. Consider an object that models, say, a bank account: it might to have an attribute 'balance' and 'account ID', methods 'withdraw' and 'deposit' — all representing some functionality that is expected of an object of this type. The main principles of Object Orientation are encapsulation, inheritance, polymorphism, and identity, all of which will be discussed in the next paragraphs.

Objects and classes

Each *object* has its own attributes and methods. For example, for object CAR you can have such attributes as engine size, engine type, wheel size, interior color, exterior color, shift type, and so on. The methods may include 'drive', 'turn(left | right)' and so on. The objects are defined through programming concept of *classes*. An object is an instance of a class. The common analogy here is the blueprint of a house and the actual house built based on that blueprint. You can instantiate many objects of the same class in the very same way as many houses could be built from the same blueprint, being different only in their attributes — color, location etc.

Encapsulation

The main idea of encapsulation is to hide details of implementation, and make it accessible only by explicitly defined methods that reduce the impact of changes made to the internals of the objects, and enforce security. The non-programmer's world analogy would be any programmable electronic device you may have at home like a VCR or a microwave oven: you normally can manipulate those only through buttons devised for this purpose, though it might be possible to open the cover and use one's best judgment to control its operations through manipulating electronic components.

Security is usually enforced by using public, private, and protected methods. Public methods are available for all users; private methods limit the internal code access, and protected methods forbid access to all objects instantiated from classes inherited from the parent class.

Inheritance

Inheritance is a mechanism that allows the programmer to create a new class based on (or inherited from) the old (existing) class. The new class, called (unsurprisingly) child class, has all the attributes (properties) and methods of the old class (parent), but some of them could be ignored or modified, while some new characteristics could be added. For example, subclasses Chevrolet, Ford, Honda, Toyota, and Nissan could be derived from class CAR. This allows for reuse of the code this class contains, and makes development process more rigorous.

Polymorphism

Polymorphism means that a given method could be applied to different objects. For example, the same method could perform logically consistent actions when it gets a different number of arguments or arguments of different data types. For example, a hypothetical function `ADD` could add numbers, concatenate strings, and increment a date by the given number of days, depending on the internal implementation. For the programmer that means that as long as s/he calls the method with correct arguments, s/he does not have to worry about details of implementation, and expect correct results.

Identity

Since two objects can be inherited from the same class and all their characteristics can be exactly the same, their identities must be different in order to tell them apart. Each object has its own unique identifier, or *handle*. Usually handles are assigned to the objects implicitly by the system.

The term "object" might cause some confusion when used within common relational database terminology. From the very beginning, in RDBMS language, *database object* means a table, a view, an index, and so on. An object within your program is not a database object.

Oracle 9*i* support

Oracle allows you to create *object types*—special structures with object attributes and methods. The syntax consists of two parts. First, you declare the object type itself:

```
CREATE [OR REPLACE] TYPE <object_name> AS OBJECT
(
 <attribute_name> <attribute_datatype>,...
 [MEMBER FUNCTION <function_name>
  [<function_parameter> <parameter_datatype>,...
   RETURN <datatype>]...
 [MEMBER PROCEDURE <procedure_name>
 [<procedure_parameter> <parameter_datatype>,...]...);
```

Then you define the object type body, where all the functionality implementation code would be contained. This part is optional unless you had any member functions/procedures in the object type declaration. The syntax is as follows (assuming one member function and one member procedure were declared in the CREATE OBJECT TYPE section):

```
CREATE OR REPLACE OBJECT TYPE BODY <object_name>
AS
  MEMBER FUNCTION <function_name>
 [<function_parameter> <parameter_datatype>,...
   RETURN <datatype>]...
 IS
 [<declaration_section>]
 BEGIN
  <function_body>
 [EXCEPTION
  <exception_body>]
 END;
MEMBER PROCEDURE <procedure_name>
[<procedure_parameter> <parameter_datatype>,...]...
IS
 [<declaration_section>]
 BEGIN
  <procedure_body>
 [EXCEPTION
  <exception_body>]
 END;
END;
```

The instances of this object could be stored in the Oracle tables, and invoked in Oracle's PL/SQL stored procedures.

IBM DB2 UDB 8.1 support

DB2 allows you to create objects in a similar way to that of Oracle, but the syntax is quite different and more complex. Here is the simplified version adopted from IBM DB2 UDB:

```
CREATE TYPE <type_name> [UNDER <supertype_name>]
AS ( <attribute_name> <attribute_datatype>,...)
INSTANTIABLE | NOT INSTANTIABLE
[WITHOUT COMPARISSONS] [NOT FINAL]
MODE DB2SQL
METHOD <method_name>
(<attribute_name> <attribute_datatype>,...)
RETURNS <datatype>
<method_specification>
```

In addition to optional user-defined types, the execution of the CREATE TYPE statement generates methods for retrieving and updating the values of attributes, as well as for constructing instances of a structured type and for supporting the comparison operators (=, <>, <, <=, >, and >=).

For each method declared with the CREATE TYPE statement, you can use the CREATE METHOD statement to associate a method body with a method specification. Here is the syntax:

```
CREATE METHOD <method_name>
RETURNS <datatype>
FOR TYPE <type_name>
RETURN {<value> | <sql_statement>}
```

Microsoft SQL Server 2000

Microsoft SQL Server 2000 does not provide object-oriented features with its RDBMS product; the next closest thing would be the TABLE system data type that allows you to arrange data returned by the SQL query as a set of rows. It cannot be used as a column data type, and therefore cannot be used as permanent storage. An instance of an object created by some external application could be saved in the binary format in the database, but it is no different from any other binary data stored in the RDBMS.

The user-defined data type in MS SQL Server does not allow for creation of a structure data type (like a record field), and cannot contain methods.

Compensating the lack of OOP features, SQL Server 2000 provides the ability to invoke and use ActiveX/OLE objects from within Transact-SQL code through system stored procedures.

SQL Server 2000 also provides Meta Data Services that allow for storage and management of meta data about information systems and applications. It serves as a central repository for data and component definitions, development and deployment models, reusable software components, and data warehousing descriptions; it facilitates development and modeling processes through establishing a common framework for developers and analysts, borrowing heavily from UML (Universal Modeling Language).

Abstract data types

SQL99 introduced the abstract data type (ADT) that is in fact undistinguishable from the definition of class. ADT specification consists of two parts: attribute specification and method specification. ADT behavior is completely encapsulated within the type definition. The ADT enables database programmers to construct application-specific data types in the database with built-in methods to manipulate these data types. As usual, implementation of the standard lags behind — none of the three major vendors have implemented this feature.

Collections and Arrays

Long-time standard tools of every programming language, *collections* and *arrays* have made inroads into the domain of RDBMS. They mostly facilitate programming process, eliminating need for additional tables. Both arrays and collections contain data elements, the main difference between these data types being that, as a rule, an array contains elements of the same data type, whereas collections can accommodate different data types.

Imagine that you have decided, in spite of all the talk about good database design (see Appendix C for more information on RDBMS design), to store an employee's educational credentials inside the same table where you store other employee information. If your employees generally have three diplomas, you might consider declaring an `EDUCATION_CREDENTIALS` column as a `VARRAY(5) OF VARCHAR(25)`—using Oracle 9*i* features. Now for each employee there will be five potential records to store information.

Employee ID	*Educational Institution*
1	Stanford University
	Massachusetts Institute of Technology
	Kalamazoo Community College

To accommodate the case, when more than five educational credentials are acquired, you may want to use a nested table (i.e., a column is of table type, and could therefore contain unrestricted amount of data—Oracle's feature). Both Oracle and IBM DB2 UDB support arrays and collections, while Microsoft does not.

Object-oriented databases

The topic of object-oriented databases is clearly out of scope for this book; we are going to give you only a high-level overview of the current state of affairs.

With the advent of the object-oriented programming came the idea of *object storage*. Relational databases, in spite of all modernization, new data types, and functionality, remain by and large text-based—that is, they parse, store, and search textual data. While various new media formats—video, sound, PowerPoint presentations, Microsoft Word structured storage—were accommodated by inclusion of the new data types, essentially it remains the same text-based approach, somewhat expanded.

As OO languages (C++, Java, C#, Visual Basic.NET, Delphi, Smalltalk, Eiffel, etc.) become increasingly popular, it begins to make sense to store information in objects as they are defined by the classes implemented in these languages. Imagine a Java class `EMPLOYEE`, which has its properties (attributes) and methods defined; when an application creates an instance of this class to add a new employee, it populates its properties and then saves the whole object into a database. For an

RDBMS that would mean populating a number of tables with textual information; for an object-oriented database, it would mean saving the object as it is — either as a binary, byte-code, or text description version, and still being able to track this object by, say, employee ID. This is what OODBMS and OORDBMS are all about.

While pure object-oriented databases try to implement their own "pure OO" method of storing information, OORDBMS rely on proven relational technology to establish a hierarchy of the objects. There are new standards emerging (Table 17-1), and new ideas taking hold.

Table 17-1
The RDBMS/OODBMS Standards Comparison

	SQL-92	*SQL-99*	*JDBC and SQLJ*	*JDO*	*ODMG 3.0*
Model	Relational	Relational/ Object	Relational/ Object	Enhanced Java object model	Java, C++, Smalltalk, etc. object model; OMG common object model
DDL	SQL	SQL, PL/SQL, Transact-SQL	SQL	Java and XML	Object definition (ODL), language partly based on SQL92
DML	Embedded/ dynamic SQL, CLI	CLI for SQL, Java, PL/SQL, Transact-SQL	Embedded SQL, CLI	Java	Java, C++, C#, Smalltalk, etc.
DQL	Embedded/ dynamic SQL, CLI	CLI, OCI, ODBC	CLI, Embedded SQL, Java	JDO query language (JQL)	Object query language (OQL), partly based on SQL92

Because of a tight coupling of the OO database with the programming language, the application written for one database might be impossible to use with some other products. There are several initiatives to establish a standard for OODBMS, which so far have resulted in the ODMG 3.0 standard, in addition to a number of proprietary ways to do things.

While still a novelty, OODBMS are making it into the mainstream of the academic and corporate worlds, fueled mainly by adoption of object-oriented technologies like Java (and EJB — Enterprise Java Beans) and Smalltalk.

Some object-oriented databases available on the market today are shown in Table 17-2.

Table 17-2
Database Products Supporting Pure OO Technology

Company	*Product*	*Release*
db4o	db4o - database for objects	*1.0*
eXcelon Corporation, Object Design Division	ObjectStore Enterprise Edition	*6.05*
	PSE Pro for C++	*4.0*
	PSE Pro for Java	*6.05*
	Javlin	*1.1*
	JavlinOne	*1.0*
Fresher Information Corporation	MATISSE	*5.0*
JYD Software Engineering Pty Ltd.	JYD Object Database	*2.0*
Micro Data Base Systems, Inc.	TITANIUM	*8.1*
Objectivity, Inc.	Objectivity/DB	*6.1*
Orient Technologies	Orient Enterprise Edition	*2.0*
	Orient Just Edition	*2.0*
The Ozone Database Project	ozone	*1.0*
Poet Software Corporation, FastObjects Division	FastObjects j2	*2.0*
	FastObjects e7	*7.0*
	FastObjects t7	*7.0*
InterSystems Corp	Cache	*5.0*
Sysra	EyeDB	*2.6*
Versant Corporation	Versant Developer Suite	6.0.1
Computer Associates	Jasmine ii Object Database	2.02

The main advantage of the OODBMS over OORDBMS comes from eliminating the mapping of the objects from the application (client) to RDBMS structure. In the current environment, in which data is still coming as text or numbers, RDBMS are much faster than comparable OODBMS/OORDBMS; at the same time there are situations when the object approach might prove to be superior to the "old" relational model. The jury is still out.

Summary

New developments like XML, OLAP, and object-oriented technologies continue to change the ways we are collecting, storing, and consuming information; the very nature of the information keeps changing and often involves new media and new formats.

XML emerged as the de-facto information exchange standard and not surprisingly, relational databases responded by incorporating XML into their cores. The approaches taken by each of the RDBMS vendors might be different (XML documents might be mapped and parsed in familiar text-based records, or be stored as complete documents), but the details of these implementations have become increasingly irrelevant to the vast majority of developers and users.

OLAP became a standard for BI — business intelligence. With the enormous amount of data — structured or otherwise — accumulated since the dawn of civilization, it was only a matter of time before someone would take data comprehension to the next level, which is to discover statistical trends. While not part of the RDBMS technology, BI does not make much sense without some kind of a database — relational, in our case. The main processing unit of this information is a multidimensional CUBE, which can be manipulated using either some general-purpose language (like Java) or some proprietary language (like Microsoft MDX). Some vendors bundle business intelligence tools with their RDBMS, some BI tools are stand-alone tools built by third-party companies.

The object-oriented approach became the de-facto application programming standard, and as such made a compelling case for object-oriented databases. As we model the surrounding world in terms of objects, we need a place to store these objects. An RDBMS maps the objects to words; an OODBMS will accept them as they are. You may compare it to a book, where images are created by your brain from mere words; the movie stores and communicates visual objects directly to your senses, bypassing the verbalization step.

OODBMS may well be the wave of the future, which is notoriously unpredictable. As of today, many companies have implemented object-oriented databases, designed to store and retrieve objects created within some particular language (Java, C++, Smalltalk). Eventually, new standards will emerge and performance gaps — if any — will be eliminated, making RDBMS outdated. For now, RDBMS remain the pillars of the business community, though they do pay lip service to the objects, incorporating them as data types but warning against the inefficiency of using them.

✦ ✦ ✦

What's on the CD-ROM

This appendix provides you with information on the contents of the CD that accompanies this book. For the latest and greatest information, please refer to the ReadMe file located at the root of the CD. Here is what you will find:

- ✦ System Requirements
- ✦ Using the CD with Windows
- ✦ What's on the CD
- ✦ Troubleshooting

System Requirements

Make sure that your computer meets the minimum system requirements listed in Appendix D. If your computer doesn't match up to most of these requirements, you may have a problem using the contents of the CD.

Using the CD with Windows

To install the items from the CD to your hard drive, follow these steps:

1. Insert the CD into your computer's CD-ROM drive.
2. A window will appear with the following options: Install, Browse, eBook, Links, and Exit.

   Install: Gives you the option to install the supplied software and/or the author-created samples on the CD-ROM.

   Explore: Allows you to view the contents of the CD-ROM in its directory structure.

eBook: Allows you to view an electronic version of the book.

Exit: Closes the autorun window.

If you do not have autorun enabled or if the autorun window does not appear, follow the steps below to access the CD.

1. Click Start⇨Run.
2. In the dialog box that appears, type ***d*:\setup.exe**, where *d* is the letter of your CD-ROM drive. This will bring up the autorun window described above.
3. Choose the Install, Browse, eBook, Links, or Exit option from the menu. (See Step 2 in the preceding list for descriptions of these options.)

When installing RDBMS software, please refer to Appendix D for more-detailed installation instructions.

What's on the CD

The following sections provide a summary of the software and other materials you'll find on the CD.

Author-created materials

All author-created material from the book, including code listings and samples, are on the CD in the folder named "sqlbib." The CD also contains complete authors' SQL scripts and examples used in the book, with different versions for Oracle 9*i*, IBM DB2 UDB 8.1, and Microsoft SQL Server 2000.

Please run the specific version for the RDBMS of your choice as from the respective directories: `/sqlbib/acme_oracle/`, `/sqlbib/acme_db2/`, and `/sqlbib/acme_mssql/`.

The following files are supplied for you to create and populate the sample ACME database:

- *create_acme_ora.sql*: creates database and all database objects for Oracle 9*i*
- *load_data_oradat*: populates the ACME database with the appropriate data for Oracle 9*i*
- *load.sql:* runs *create_acme_oracle.sql* and then *load_data_oracle.sql*
- *create_acme_db2.sql*: creates database and all database objects for IBM DB2 UDB 8.1

- *load_data_db2.dat*: populates the ACME database with the appropriate data for IBM DB2 UDB 8.1
- *create_acme_mssql.sql*: creates database and all database objects for Microsoft SQL Server 2000
- *load_data_mssql.dat*: populates the ACME database with the appropriate data for Microsoft SQL Server 2000
- *triggers_ora.sql*, *triggers_db2.sql*, and *triggers_mssql.sql* demonstrate topics discussed in Chapter 16
- *empty_acme.sql* (found in the vendor-specific directories): creates empty schema for Oracle 9i and an empty database for MS SQL Server 2000 (required for examples in Chapters 3, 4, 5, and 6)

The use of these files is described in Appendixes D, E, and F, as well as in chapters where they are mentioned. Examples in Chapters 3 through 6 assume an empty ACME database created with *empty_acme.sql*. The rest of the chapters rely on the database structures installed as described in Appendix F.

Applications

The following applications are on your CD:

- IBM DB2 Universal Database Personal Edition Version 8.1 for Microsoft Windows Operating Environments Evaluation Copy (Windows NT/2000/XP). It provides a single-user database engine for deployment to PC-based users. The PE includes the ability to be remotely managed, which makes it the perfect choice for deployment in occasionally connected or remote office implementations that don't require multi-user capability. Detailed installation instructions are provided in Appendix D.

  Note: This is a time-limited version of DB2 and will expire and become unoperational on or about November 30, 2004.
- Adobe Acrobat Reader free software for viewing and printing Adobe Portable Document Format (PDF) files on all major hardware and operating system platforms.

Shareware programs are fully functional, trial versions of copyrighted programs. If you like particular programs, register with their authors for a nominal fee and receive licenses, enhanced versions, and technical support. *Freeware programs* are copyrighted games, applications, and utilities that are free for personal use. Unlike shareware, these programs do not require a fee or provide technical support. *GNU software* is governed by its own license, which is included inside the folder of the GNU product. See the GNU license for more details.

Trial, demo, or evaluation versions are usually limited either by time or functionality (such as being unable to save projects). Some trial versions are very sensitive to system date changes. If you alter your computer's date, the programs will "time out" and will no longer be functional.

eBook version of *SQL Bible*

The complete text of this book is provided in Adobe's Portable Document Format (PDF). It does not include the scripts required to create sample database. You can read and search through the file with the Adobe Acrobat Reader (also provided).

Troubleshooting

If you have difficulty installing or using any of the materials on the companion CD, try the following solutions:

- **Close all running programs.** The more programs you're running, the less memory is available to other programs. Installers also typically update files and programs; if you keep other programs running, installation may not work properly.
- **Reference the ReadMe.** Please refer to the ReadMe file located at the root of the CD-ROM for the latest product information at the time of publication.

If you still have trouble with the CD, please call the Customer Care phone number: (800) 762-2974. Outside the United States, call 1 (317) 572-3994. You can also contact Customer Service by e-mail at `techsupdum@wiley.com`. Wiley Publishing, Inc., will provide technical support only for installation and other general quality control items; for technical support on the applications themselves, consult the program's vendor or author.

✦ ✦ ✦

The ACME Sample Database

ACME is the database for a company of the same name that sells some kind of building materials. It has 13 tables described in detail in this chapter.

The database creation scripts on your CD have an additional table, PRODUCT_AUDIT, that is not a part of the ACME business schema but rather is used for auditing. We refer to it in Chapter 14 when discussing triggers.

General Information and Business Rules

ACME has customers who buy different products. Each customer has one or more addresses — for example, billing and shipping — and one or more phone and/or fax numbers. Customers also have default payment terms that specify how many days they have to make a payment to get a specified discount; for example, a customer who pays within 31 days might qualify for a 2 percent discount. Customers who do not pay in time may be put on credit hold, which means they cannot order any more until their debts have been paid. Also, customers who did not buy from ACME for over two years are marked inactive. Customers are referred to by aliases given to them (for internal company use only).

Every customer is assigned to a default salesperson who is a liaison between the customer and the company. Each salesperson has address, phone, and fax numbers, a code he or she is referred by, and some other properties. If all customers for a salesperson become inactive, the salesperson is inactivated within the system.

ACME implements a kind of multi-level marketing. It sells products to resellers, who in turn either sell the products to a lower-level reseller or directly to a customer. That means any of ACME's customers could either be a reseller (the one who buys and resells products) or a supplier (the one from whom products are bought), or both.

ACME sells multiple products. Each product has a price, description, brand, weight, and some other characteristics.

Customers can order products. When a customer orders more than one product at a time, all order items are logically grouped within one order. Order stores general information, such as order number, default salesperson and customer information, quantities ordered, dates, invoice number, and so on. The actual shipped quantity can differ from the ordered one (for example, because of a lack of sufficient inventory).

Some fields (payment terms, salesman) are populated by default when customer is selected, but can later be changed. Some other fields have to be populated manually. Order and invoice numbers are populated automatically and cannot be modified. Some orders are eligible for volume discount based on total order price. For example, all orders with total amount between $15,000 and $20,000 are eligible for a 3 percent discount.

When a new order is created, the `COMPLETE` status is assigned to it. It is now ready to be shipped to the customer after which the status is to be changed to `SHIPPED`. A sales department clerk creates an invoice for this order and changes its status to `INVOICED`. The order can be canceled by the customer; the status is then changes to `CANCELED`.

The database also contains specific shipping information—for example, bill of lading number, total number of cases shipped, trailer number, freight terms, dates, and so on. Usually one shipment contains one order, but special situations when one order is distributed between more than one shipment, or one shipment can contain more than one order, can also be handled.

Naming Conventions

The ACME database is using a simplified concept of the *Hungarian notation* in its naming conventions. The idea is to encode the information about the objects in their names. Many database developers find this concept very helpful, especially when working with huge databases which contain hundreds tables and thousands of columns.

Hungarian notation is a naming convention that allows the developer to determine the type and use of an identifier. It was invented by Dr. Charles Simonyi who has worked for Microsoft since 1981. The notation is very popular with C++ and Java developers. Dr. Simonyi says it was called "Hungarian" as a joke. The notation is supposed to make code more readable, but in fact it looks so unreadable it might as well be written in Hungarian.

The main ACME naming rules are as follows:

1. Each table has an abbreviation used as a part of every column, index, or constraint name for the table. For example, ADDRESS table is abbreviated with ADDR. Index names are prefixed with IDX, check constraints start with CHK, and so on:

   ```
   ADDR_ID_N (column name)
   CHK_ADDR_TYPE (check constraint name)
   IDX_ADDR_CUST (index name)
   FK_ADDR_CUST (referential integrity constraint)
   ```

   The foreign key name on the last line also indicates the referential integrity direction (from ADDRESS to CUSTOMER).

2. All columns have a postfix that symbolizes the general data type of the column (N for numeric datatypes; S for character strings, D for dates, etc.). For example:

   ```
   ADDR_ID_N
   ```

3. The primary key columns include a suffix ID:

   ```
   ADDR_ID_N
   ```

4. The foreign key columns include the name of the primary key of their parent table as well as suffix F. For example,

   ```
   ADDR_CUSTID_FN
   ```

   is a foreign key to CUSTOMER_ID_N in CUSTOMER table.

ACME naming conventions are simplified and for demonstration purposes only. For example, S stands for any character string datatype and does not distinguish between CHARACTER and VARCHAR; N stands for any numeric data type (INTEGER, DECIMAL, FLOAT), etc.

Relationships Between Tables

Tables in ACME are connected by primary/foreign key relationships (as in any relational database). The database is normalized to a certain degree (see Appendix C for relational database design basics and Normalization rules). Figure B-1 shows ACME tables and relationships between them.

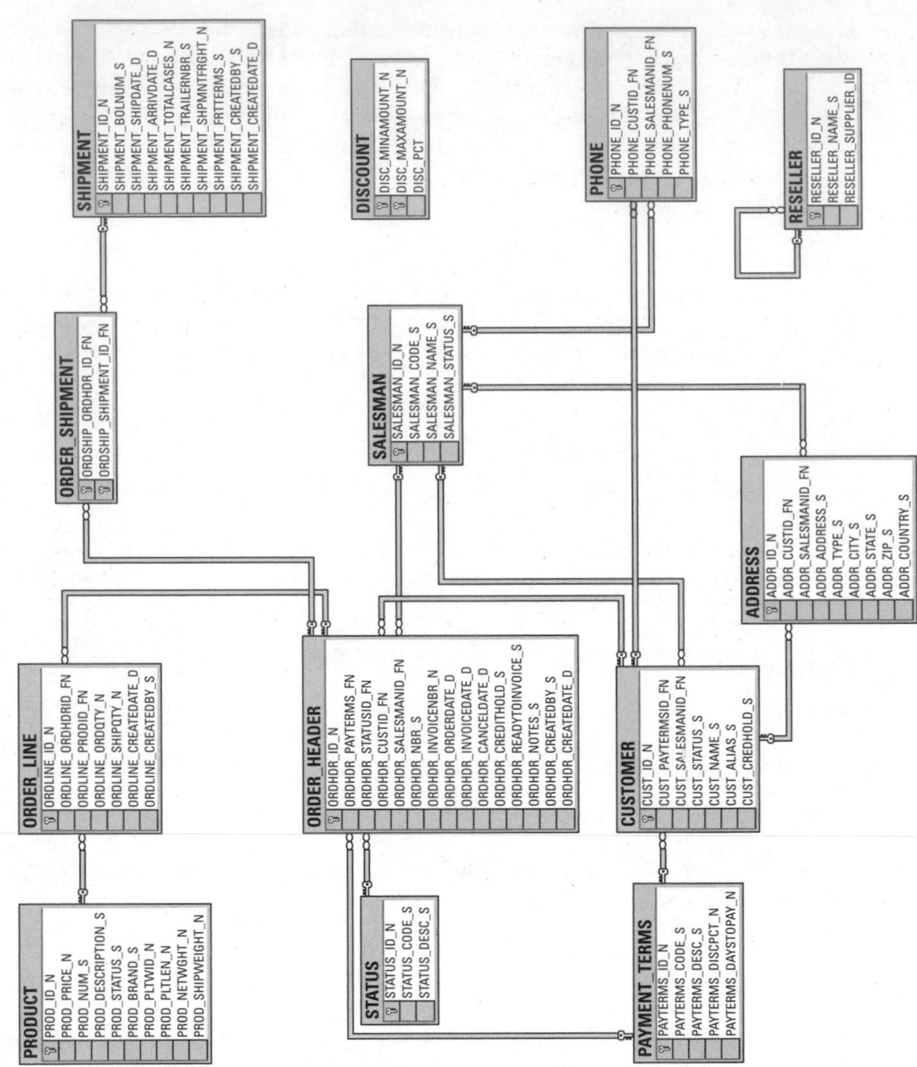

Figure B-1: ACME database schema

Column Constraints and Defaults

Column constraints in ACME are based on the business rules and design principles discussed earlier in this appendix. For example, invoice number and invoice date are undefined until the order is invoiced; canceled date makes sense for canceled orders only, so fields ORDHDR_INVOICENBR_N, ORDHDR_INVOICEDATE_D, and ORDHDR_CANCELDATE_D in ORDER_HEADER table allow null values. ACME defines only two valid values for freight terms, prepaid (PPD) and collect (COL), so there is a check constraint on the SHIPMENT_FRTTERMS_S column of the SHIPMENT table. Most tables have referential integrity constraints to enforce parent/child relationships. Every table has a meaningless primary key, that is, each record in every table has a unique number hidden from nontechnical users that is used only by database programmers for table joins and other purposes.

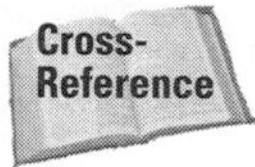

The procedure to populate meaningless primary keys differs from implementation to implementation. Oracle uses sequences, MS SQL Server employs identity columns, and DB2 allows both. See Chapter 4 for more details.

Some columns have default values. For example, the value Y in the ORDER_HEADER.ORDHDR_READYTOINVOICE_S column that indicates that the order has been finalized, shipped, and signed off by the sales department, so it is ready to be invoiced. The default value for this column is N, so when a new order is created, it is populated automatically.

Indexes

All primary and foreign key columns in ACME are indexed. All indexes are prefixed with IDX.

Indexes on the foreign keys are unnecessary and even ineffective for a database of this size, but we created them anyway, as if we are working with a huge database with thousands of customers and millions of orders.

SQL Scripts to Create ACME Database Objects

These statements create ACME database in DB2:

```
--
-- TABLE: ADDRESS
--

CREATE TABLE ADDRESS(
```

```
    ADDR_ID_N           INTEGER          NOT NULL,
    ADDR_CUSTID_FN      INTEGER,
    ADDR_SALESMANID_FN  INTEGER,
    ADDR_ADDRESS_S      VARCHAR(60),
    ADDR_TYPE_S         VARCHAR(8),
    ADDR_CITY_S         VARCHAR(18)      NOT NULL,
    ADDR_STATE_S        CHAR(2),
    ADDR_ZIP_S          VARCHAR(10)      NOT NULL,
    ADDR_COUNTRY_S      CHAR(3),
    CONSTRAINT CHK_ADDR_TYPE
        CHECK (ADDR_TYPE_S IN ('BILLING', 'SHIPPING')),
        CONSTRAINT PK_ADDRPRIMARY PRIMARY KEY (ADDR_ID_N)
)
;

--
-- TABLE: CUSTOMER
--

CREATE TABLE CUSTOMER(
    CUST_ID_N            INTEGER          NOT NULL,
    CUST_PAYTERMSID_FN   INTEGER,
    CUST_SALESMANID_FN   INTEGER,
    CUST_STATUS_S        VARCHAR(1)       DEFAULT 'Y' NOT NULL,
    CUST_NAME_S          VARCHAR(50)      NOT NULL,
    CUST_ALIAS_S         VARCHAR(15),
    CUST_CREDHOLD_S      VARCHAR(1)       DEFAULT 'Y' NOT NULL,
    CONSTRAINT CHK_CUST_STATUS CHECK (CUST_STATUS_S IN ('N', 'Y')),
    CONSTRAINT CHK_CUST_CREDHOLD CHECK (CUST_CREDHOLD_S IN ('N', 'Y')),
    CONSTRAINT PK_CUSTPRIMARY PRIMARY KEY (CUST_ID_N)
)
;

--
-- TABLE: ORDER_HEADER
--

CREATE TABLE ORDER_HEADER(
    ORDHDR_ID_N                 INTEGER          NOT NULL,
    ORDHDR_PAYTERMS_FN          INTEGER,
    ORDHDR_STATUSID_FN          INTEGER,
    ORDHDR_CUSTID_FN            INTEGER,
    ORDHDR_SALESMANID_FN        INTEGER,
    ORDHDR_NBR_S                VARCHAR(30)      NOT NULL,
    ORDHDR_INVOICENBR_N         INTEGER,
    ORDHDR_ORDERDATE_D          DATE,
    ORDHDR_INVOICEDATE_D        DATE,
    ORDHDR_CANCELDATE_D         DATE,
    ORDHDR_CREDITHOLD_S         CHAR(1),
    ORDHDR_READYTOINVOICE_S     CHAR(1)          DEFAULT 'N',
    ORDHDR_NOTES_S              VARCHAR(60),
```

```
    ORDHDR_CREATEDBY_S          VARCHAR(10),
    ORDHDR_CREATEDATE_D         DATE,
    CONSTRAINT CHK_ORDHDR_READY CHECK
            (ORDHDR_READYTOINVOICE_S IN ('N', 'Y')),
    CONSTRAINT CHK_ORDHDR_CREDH CHECK (ORDHDR_CREDITHOLD_S IN ('N', 'Y')),
    CONSTRAINT PK_ORDHDRPRIM PRIMARY KEY (ORDHDR_ID_N),
    CONSTRAINT IDX_ORDHDR_ORDNBR  UNIQUE (ORDHDR_NBR_S)
)
;

--
-- TABLE: ORDER_LINE
--

CREATE TABLE ORDER_LINE(
    ORDLINE_ID_N            INTEGER          NOT NULL,
    ORDLINE_ORDHDRID_FN     INTEGER          NOT NULL,
    ORDLINE_PRODID_FN       INTEGER,
    ORDLINE_ORDQTY_N        INTEGER,
    ORDLINE_SHIPQTY_N       INTEGER,
    ORDLINE_CREATEDATE_D    DATE,
    ORDLINE_CREATEDBY_S     VARCHAR(10),
    CONSTRAINT PK_ORDLINEPRIM PRIMARY KEY (ORDLINE_ID_N)
)
;

--
-- TABLE: ORDER_SHIPMENT
--

CREATE TABLE ORDER_SHIPMENT(
    ORDSHIP_ORDHDR_ID_FN      INTEGER    NOT NULL,
    ORDSHIP_SHIPMENT_ID_FN    INTEGER    NOT NULL,
    CONSTRAINT PK_ORDHDRSHIP
         PRIMARY KEY (ORDSHIP_ORDHDR_ID_FN,ORDSHIP_SHIPMENT_ID_FN)
)
;

--
-- TABLE: PAYMENT_TERMS
--

CREATE TABLE PAYMENT_TERMS(
    PAYTERMS_ID_N           INTEGER          NOT NULL,
    PAYTERMS_CODE_S         VARCHAR(6),
    PAYTERMS_DESC_S         VARCHAR(60),
    PAYTERMS_DISCPCT_N      DECIMAL(5,2),
    PAYTERMS_DAYSTOPAY_N    INTEGER,
    CONSTRAINT PK_PAYTERMS PRIMARY KEY (PAYTERMS_ID_N)
)
;
```

```
--
-- TABLE: PHONE
--

CREATE TABLE PHONE(
    PHONE_ID_N          INTEGER         NOT NULL,
    PHONE_CUSTID_FN     INTEGER,
    PHONE_SALESMANID_FN INTEGER,
    PHONE_PHONENUM_S    VARCHAR(20),
    PHONE_TYPE_S        VARCHAR(20),
    CONSTRAINT CHK_PHONE_TYPE CHECK (PHONE_TYPE_S IN ('PHONE', 'FAX')),
    CONSTRAINT PK_PHONERIMARY PRIMARY KEY (PHONE_ID_N)
)
;

--
-- TABLE: PRODUCT
--

CREATE TABLE PRODUCT(
    PROD_ID_N             INTEGER          NOT NULL,
    PROD_PRICE_N          DECIMAL(10,2),
    PROD_NUM_S            VARCHAR(10),
    PROD_DESCRIPTION_S    VARCHAR(44)      NOT NULL,
    PROD_STATUS_S         CHAR(1)          DEFAULT 'Y',
    PROD_BRAND_S          VARCHAR(20)      NOT NULL,
    PROD_PLTWID_N         DECIMAL(5,2)     NOT NULL,
    PROD_PLTLEN_N         DECIMAL(5,2)     NOT NULL,
    PROD_NETWGHT_N        DECIMAL(10,3),
    PROD_SHIPWEIGHT_N     DECIMAL(10,3),
    CONSTRAINT CHK_PRODSTATUS CHECK (PROD_STATUS_S in ('N', 'Y')),
    CONSTRAINT PK_PRODUCTPRIM PRIMARY KEY (PROD_ID_N)
)
;

--
-- TABLE: SALESMAN
--

CREATE TABLE SALESMAN(
    SALESMAN_ID_N         INTEGER          NOT NULL,
    SALESMAN_CODE_S       VARCHAR(2)       NOT NULL,
    SALESMAN_NAME_S       VARCHAR(50)      NOT NULL,
    SALESMAN_STATUS_S     CHAR(1)          DEFAULT 'Y',
    CONSTRAINT CHK_SALESSTATUS CHECK (SALESMAN_STATUS_S in ('N', 'Y')),
    CONSTRAINT PK_SALESMANPRIM PRIMARY KEY (SALESMAN_ID_N)
)
;

--
```

```
-- TABLE: SHIPMENT
--

CREATE TABLE SHIPMENT(
    SHIPMENT_ID_N              INTEGER          NOT NULL,
    SHIPMENT_BOLNUM_S          VARCHAR(6),
    SHIPMENT_SHIPDATE_D        DATE,
    SHIPMENT_ARRIVDATE_D       DATE,
    SHIPMENT_TOTALCASES_N      INTEGER,
    SHIPMENT_TRAILERNBR_S      VARCHAR(12),
    SHIPMENT_SHPMNTFRGHT_N     DECIMAL(12,2),
    SHIPMENT_FRTTERMS_S        VARCHAR(3),
    SHIPMENT_CREATEDBY_S       VARCHAR(10),
    SHIPMENT_CREATEDATE_D      TIMESTAMP,
    CONSTRAINT CHK_SHIPFRTTERMS
           CHECK (SHIPMENT_FRTTERMS_S IN ('COL', 'PPD')),
    CONSTRAINT PK_SHIPMENTRPRIM PRIMARY KEY (SHIPMENT_ID_N)
)
;

--
-- TABLE: STATUS
--

CREATE TABLE STATUS(
    STATUS_ID_N      INTEGER          NOT NULL,
    STATUS_CODE_S    CHAR(2),
    STATUS_DESC_S    VARCHAR(30),
    CONSTRAINT PK_STATUSPRIM PRIMARY KEY (STATUS_ID_N)
)
;

--
-- TABLE: DISCOUNT
--

CREATE TABLE DISCOUNT(
    DISC_MINAMOUNT_N DECIMAL(14,4)      NOT NULL,
    DISC_MAXAMOUNT_N DECIMAL(14,4)      NOT NULL,
    DISC_PCT         DECIMAL(5,3),
    CONSTRAINT PK_DISCOUNT
               PRIMARY KEY(DISC_MINAMOUNT_N, DISC_MAXAMOUNT_N)
)
;

--
-- TABLE: RESELLER
--

CREATE TABLE RESELLER (
  RESELLER_ID_N         INT     NOT NULL,
```

```
  RESELLER_NAME_S        VARCHAR(30),
  RESELLER_SUPPLIER_ID  INT,
  CONSTRAINT PK_RESELLER
  PRIMARY KEY (RESELLER_ID_N)
)
;

--
-- INDEXES
--

CREATE INDEX IDX_ADDR_CUST ON ADDRESS(ADDR_CUSTID_FN)
;

CREATE INDEX IDX_CUST_PAYTERMS ON CUSTOMER(CUST_PAYTERMSID_FN)
;

CREATE INDEX IDX_CUST_SALESMAN ON CUSTOMER(CUST_SALESMANID_FN)
;

CREATE INDEX IDX_ORDHDR_CUST ON ORDER_HEADER(ORDHDR_CUSTID_FN)
;

CREATE INDEX IDX_ORDHDR_STATUS ON ORDER_HEADER(ORDHDR_STATUSID_FN)
;

CREATE INDEX IDX_ORDHDR_PAYTERM ON ORDER_HEADER(ORDHDR_PAYTERMS_FN)
;

CREATE INDEX IDX_ORDHDR_SALES ON ORDER_HEADER(ORDHDR_SALESMANID_FN)
;

CREATE INDEX IDX_ORDLINE_ORDHDR ON ORDER_LINE(ORDLINE_ORDHDRID_FN)
;

CREATE INDEX IDX_ORDLINE_PROD ON ORDER_LINE(ORDLINE_PRODID_FN)
;

CREATE INDEX IDX_ORDSHIP_ORD ON ORDER_SHIPMENT(ORDSHIP_ORDHDR_ID_FN)
;

CREATE INDEX IDX_ORDSHIP_SHIP ON ORDER_SHIPMENT(ORDSHIP_SHIPMENT_ID_FN)
;

CREATE INDEX IDX_PHONE_CUST ON PHONE(PHONE_CUSTID_FN)
;

CREATE INDEX IDX_RESELLER_RESSUPID ON RESELLER(RESELLER_SUPPLIER_ID)
;

--
```

```
--  FOREIGN KEYS
--

ALTER TABLE ADDRESS ADD CONSTRAINT FK_ADDR_CUST
    FOREIGN KEY (ADDR_CUSTID_FN)
    REFERENCES CUSTOMER(CUST_ID_N)
;

ALTER TABLE ADDRESS ADD  CONSTRAINT FK_ADDR_SALESMAN
    FOREIGN KEY (ADDR_SALESMANID_FN)
    REFERENCES SALESMAN (SALESMAN_ID_N) ;

ALTER TABLE CUSTOMER ADD CONSTRAINT FK_CUST_PAYTERMS
    FOREIGN KEY (CUST_PAYTERMSID_FN)
    REFERENCES PAYMENT_TERMS(PAYTERMS_ID_N)
;

ALTER TABLE CUSTOMER ADD CONSTRAINT FK_CUST_SALESMAN
    FOREIGN KEY (CUST_SALESMANID_FN)
    REFERENCES SALESMAN(SALESMAN_ID_N)
;

ALTER TABLE ORDER_HEADER ADD CONSTRAINT FK_ORDHDR_PAYTERMS
    FOREIGN KEY (ORDHDR_PAYTERMS_FN)
    REFERENCES PAYMENT_TERMS(PAYTERMS_ID_N)
;

ALTER TABLE ORDER_HEADER ADD CONSTRAINT FK_ORDHDR_CUSTOMER
    FOREIGN KEY (ORDHDR_CUSTID_FN)
    REFERENCES CUSTOMER(CUST_ID_N)
;

ALTER TABLE ORDER_HEADER ADD CONSTRAINT FK_ORDHDR_STAT
    FOREIGN KEY (ORDHDR_STATUSID_FN)
    REFERENCES STATUS(STATUS_ID_N)
;

ALTER TABLE ORDER_HEADER ADD CONSTRAINT FK_ORDHDR_SALES
    FOREIGN KEY (ORDHDR_SALESMANID_FN)
    REFERENCES SALESMAN(SALESMAN_ID_N)
;

ALTER TABLE ORDER_LINE ADD CONSTRAINT FK_ORDLINE_ORDHDR
    FOREIGN KEY (ORDLINE_ORDHDRID_FN)
    REFERENCES ORDER_HEADER(ORDHDR_ID_N)
;

ALTER TABLE ORDER_LINE ADD CONSTRAINT FK_ORDLINE_PRODUCT
    FOREIGN KEY (ORDLINE_PRODID_FN)
    REFERENCES PRODUCT(PROD_ID_N)
;
```

```
ALTER TABLE ORDER_SHIPMENT ADD CONSTRAINT FK_ORDSH_ORD
    FOREIGN KEY (ORDSHIP_ORDHDR_ID_FN)
    REFERENCES ORDER_HEADER(ORDHDR_ID_N)
;

ALTER TABLE ORDER_SHIPMENT ADD CONSTRAINT FK_ORDSH_SHIP
    FOREIGN KEY (ORDSHIP_SHIPMENT_ID_FN)
    REFERENCES SHIPMENT(SHIPMENT_ID_N)
;

ALTER TABLE PHONE ADD CONSTRAINT FK_PHONE_CUST
    FOREIGN KEY (PHONE_CUSTID_FN)
    REFERENCES CUSTOMER(CUST_ID_N)
;

ALTER TABLE PHONE ADD CONSTRAINT FK_SALESMAN_CUST
    FOREIGN KEY (PHONE_SALESMANID_FN)
    REFERENCES SALESMAN (SALESMAN_ID_N)
;

ALTER TABLE RESELLER ADD CONSTRAINT FK_RESELLER_SUPPLIER
    FOREIGN KEY (RESELLER_SUPPLIER_ID)
    REFERENCES RESELLER (RESELLER_ID_N)
;

--
-- VIEW V_CUSTOMER_TOTALS
--

CREATE VIEW   v_customer_totals
(
              customer_name,
              order_number,
              total_price
)
 AS
(
 SELECT       customer.cust_name_s,
              order_header.ordhdr_nbr_s,
              sum(product.prod_price_n * order_line.ordline_ordqty_n)
 FROM         customer,
              order_header,
              order_line,
              product
 WHERE        customer.cust_id_n = order_header.ordhdr_custid_fn
 AND          order_header.ordhdr_id_n = order_line.ordline_ordhdrid_fn
 AND          product.prod_id_n = order_line.ordline_prodid_fn
 AND          order_line.ordline_ordqty_n IS NOT NULL
 GROUP BY     customer.cust_name_s,
              order_header.ordhdr_nbr_s
```

```
)
;
--
-- CREATE VIEW V_CUSTOMER_STATUS
--

CREATE VIEW    v_customer_status
(
               name,
               status
)
AS
SELECT         cust_name_s,
               cust_status_s
FROM           customer
;

--
--CREATE VIEW V_PHONE_NUMBER
--

CREATE VIEW    v_phone_number
(
               phone_id,
               phone_number
)
AS
SELECT         phone_id_n,
               phone_phonenum_s
FROM           phone
WHERE          phone_type_s = 'PHONE';


--
--CREATE VIEW V_FAX NUMBER
--

CREATE VIEW    v_fax_number
(
               fax_id,
               fax_number
)
AS
SELECT         phone_id_n,
               phone_phonenum_s
FROM           phone
WHERE          phone_type_s = 'FAX'
WITH CHECK OPTION
;
```

```
--
-- CREATE VIEW V_CUSTOMER_TOTALS_OVER_15000
--

CREATE VIEW   v_customer_totals_over_15000
AS
SELECT        *
FROM          v_customer_totals
WHERE         total_price > 15000;



--
-- CREATE VIEW V_CONTACT_LIST
--

CREATE VIEW   v_contact_list
(
              name,
              phone_number,
              contact_type
)
AS
SELECT        cust_name_s,
              phone_phonenum_s,
              'customer'
FROM          customer,
              phone
WHERE         cust_id_n = phone_custid_fn
AND           phone_type_s = 'PHONE'
UNION
SELECT        salesman_name_s,
              phone_phonenum_s,
              'salesperson'
FROM          salesman,
              phone
WHERE         salesman_id_n = phone_salesmanid_fn
AND           phone_type_s = 'PHONE';


--
--CREATE VIEW V_WILE_BESS_ORDERS
--

CREATE VIEW   v_wile_bess_orders
(
              order_number,
              order_date
)
AS
SELECT        ordhdr_nbr_s,
```

```
                ordhdr_orderdate_d
FROM            order_header
WHERE           ordhdr_custid_fn IN
           (
            SELECT   cust_id_n
            FROM     customer
            WHERE    cust_name_s = 'WILE BESS COMPANY'
           )
;

CREATE VIEW    v_customer_totals_wilebess
AS
SELECT         customer_name,
               total_price
FROM           v_customer_totals
WHERE          customer_name = 'WILE BESS COMPANY'
;
```

The same set of scripts with just a slight modification will create the ACME database with Oracle. All you would need to do is to replace the SHIPMENT_CREATEDATE_D column data type from TIMESTAMP to DATE in table SHIPMENT.

To create an MS SQL ACME database, the SHIPMENT_CREATEDATE_D column data type has to be changed to DATETIME (or SMALLDATETIME); in addition, all DATE columns need to be altered to the appropriate MS SQL datatypes.

Note The script above is as generic as possible; the actual SQL statements on your CD-ROM are more implementation-specific.

✦ ✦ ✦

Basics of Relational Database Design

✦ ✦ ✦ ✦

Database design still remains more of an art than exact science. A database does not exist in a vacuum; it serves some specific business purpose. General database types could be divided into two broad categories: operational databases and analytical databases. The operational database handles day-to-day operations: recording data, printing payroll checks, and so on. The data in such a database changes rather frequently. Examples of this kind of database include the ACME database supplied in this book.

Analytical databases are used to store historical data, which is analyzed for reporting purposes, used to generate statistics, and so on. The information in such a database is static; new data can be added, but the historic data cannot be modified.

We've listed several database types in Chapter 1, and the examples throughout the book use the ACME database, which is a fictitious database of a fictitious hardware company.

Database design is a two-phase process. In the first phase you need to determine and define tables and fields, establish relationships, and so on. You start with collecting user requirements and formalizing them, then you analyze these requirements and identify entities in the specific business model; each entity is a prime candidate for being a table in your database.

Once you've identified the tables, you must define their *attributes*. An attribute is like an adjective; it describes an entity, as "sweet" describes sugar. For the Customer entity you might think of something that identifies a customer, such as name, address, phone number, and so on. These attributes will become columns in your table. Logical relationships are signified via a primary-foreign key pair.

The second phase deals with the actual creation of the conceived database inside some RDBMS package. The process is by no means linear: you'll find yourself traveling back and forth between these two phases as you fine-tune your database requirements. *SQL Bible* teaches the SQL syntax for creating database objects (Chapter 4), which is virtually independent of vendor implementations.

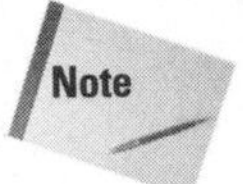

The design of the database objects could be done completely independently of the particular RDBMS software, or it could be tied up to it. While one might argue that designing specifically for Oracle or Microsoft would increase performance, sticking with a plain generic approach (when possible) makes your design more portable and spares you some of the maintenance and upgrading headaches.

Identifying Entities and Attributes

Think of the purpose of your database. For a brief example, to create a database that records orders placed by your customers, you might start with a `CUSTOMER` table. What are the attributes of a customer? Name, physical address, products s/he orders, order information, credit rating, and so on.

An important part of this stage is the selection of proper data types to represent desired attributes. There are a number of trade-offs to be considered while choosing data types, usually concerning performance versus clarity of a logical design. For example, sales amounts or prices might perfectly fit into a numeric data type in Oracle (and Oracle advocates using the `NUMBER` data type as opposed to specific numeric types like `DECIMAL`, `INTEGER`, and so on). Making this data an `INTEGER` in the Microsoft SQL Server would be a mistake, because the value will be rounded to the nearest dollar; selecting the `MONEY` or `SMALLMONEY` data type would be the correct choice. In addition to this, searches are usually performed faster on numeric fields than on character-containing columns. When you need to store more complex information like images or binary files, use data types appropriate for the data the column is supposed to hold.

See Chapter 3 for more information on data types.

Table C-1 is an example of the flat file design described in Chapter 1 — everything is dumped into one single table. Such a design would hardly be adequate for anything but a kitchen table enterprise. To create a relational database, this raw table must undergo the normalization process.

Table C-1
"One Table" Design

CUST_ NAME	ADDRESS	SALES_ REGION	SALES_ REGION_ID	ORDER_ID	DESCRIP- TION	CREDIT_ RATING
Lone Dove Ent.	1234 Elm Street, Salem, OR 95679	North Pacific	3	NA1234-89	Paper Pulp	Excellent
ACME, Inc.	567 Pine Street, Chicago, IL 07891	Midwest	4	GA4358-92	Sawdust	Average

Normalization

Once the relationships between the database entities have been established, it is time for your database to undergo the *normalization* process.

Normalizing means disassembling your large database tables into a number of smaller ones to reduce redundancy. This, of course, means revising some relationships between the tables, even discovering new entities. The normalization steps are called *forms*, and database theoreticians have so far defined five Normal Forms; this is as far as you can possibly take your database on the way to normalization.

As you may see, designing a database is an iterational process — the same steps get repeated over and over again to the highest level until you're quite satisfied with the results. The same goes for the normalization phase. There is no such thing as a completely normalized database: for one thing, any database that goes beyond third Normal Form incurs a significant performance hit (as it struggles with all the additional joins needed to accommodate additional tables); for another, it could be difficult to detect any clues for further separation of data into the fourth and fifth Normal Forms. Use your best judgment as to where to stop while normalizing your database. Third Normal Form is adequate for most uses.

Note

A *Normal Form* is a set of rules applied to a table to ensure that there is no redundant information (not only duplicate information but also information that could be derived on demand). For example, if you store an employee's age in addition to the employee's date of birth, you would be stuck with updating the employee age column every year.

First Normal Form

The first Normal Form deals with repeating groups. Let's normalize the table CUSTOMER shown in Table C-1.We start by recording all the information we feel would be relevant: customer name, address, orders they've placed, and so on.

Now, while orders definitely belong to the customer, putting them into the CUSTOMER table would be an enormous waste of storage space, and it breaks relational database principles. Customer information would have to be replicated for each new order, and the order's information (such as description, suppliers) would be repeated for each customer that placed a similar order. The logical (as well as relational) solution would be to remove orders from the CUSTOMER table and create an ORDER table. Each customer would get a unique ID, which would be the primary key for the table CUSTOMER, and all information about orders would be moved into the ORDER table. To tie customers with their orders, the ORDER table would have to have a column with CUSTOMER_ID as a foreign key, as shown in Table C-2 and Table C-3.

Table C-2
Table CUSTOMER after First Normal Form

CUST_ID	*CUST_NAME*	*SALES_ REGION*	*SALES_ REGION_ID*	*ADDRESS*	*CREDIT_ RATING*
1	Lone Dove Ent.	North Pacific	3	1234 Elm Street, Salem, OR 95679	Excellent
2	ACME Corp	Midwest	4	567 Pine Street, Chicago, IL 07891	Average

Table C-3
New ORDER Table

CUST_ID	*ORDER_ID*	*PRODUCT_ID*	*DESCRIPTION*
1	NA1234-89	P01245	Paper Pulp
2	GA4358-92	SD3457	Sawdust
1	HA5432-02	WC7863	Wood Chips

While removing redundancy for *customer* information, this solution does nothing to alleviate the problem of redundancy for *order* information. The order is unique, and the tables CUSTOMER and ORDER are in a one-to-many relationship, where for each customer there may be one or more orders, but for each order there can be one and only one customer. Here, the order is for some products, and keeping product alongside with orders results in repeating product information, as new orders for the same product are entered.

The same process would be repeated for every other irrelevant group: customer's address, bank accounts, credit rating, and so on.

Second Normal Form

The second Normal Form eliminates redundant data; it establishes that there can be no nonkey attributes (fields) that depend on a portion (or the whole) of the primary key. The ORDER table needs to be normalized further: a composite primary key made up of ORDER_ID and PRODUCT_ID is a possible answer. But the product description depends on PRODUCT_ID only, not on the ORDER_ID. This works fine if each order consists of only one product; what if a customer places an order for multiple products to save on shipping? Or the product description changes — and now you have to update each and every order that contains this product? This calls for introducing the PRODUCT table. The PRODUCT_ID remains in the ORDER table but becomes a foreign key.

Table CUSTOMER for again normalized to the first Form with the column CREDIT_RATING removed to CREDIT table (not shown). See Tables C-4, C-5, and C-6.

Table C-4
Table CUSTOMER after Second Normal Form

CUST_ID	***CUST_NAME***	***SALES_REGION***	***SALES_REGION_ID***	***ADDRESS***
1	Lone Dove Ent.	North Pacific	3	1234 Elm Street, Salem, OR 95679
2	ACME Corp.	Midwest	4	567 Pine Street, Chicago, IL 07891

Table C-5
New ORDER Table

CUST_ID	***ORDER_ID***	***PRODUCT_ID***
1	NA1234-89	P01245
2	GA4358-92	SD3457
1	HA5432-02	WC7863

Table C-6
New PRODUCT Table

PRODUCT_ID	*QUANTITY*	*DESCRIPTION*
P01245	20000	Paper Pulp
SD3457	400000	Sawdust
WC7863	70000	Wood Chips

Third Normal Form

The third Normal Form declares that there should not be attributes (fields) that depend on other nonkey attributes. That means that only relevant information describing an entity's primary key has a place in your table. The table `CUSTOMER` contains `SALES_REGION_ID` and `SALES_REGION_NAME`, which do not describe a customer. This data must be moved into a separate table called, say, `REGIONS` to achieve the third Normal Form as shown in Table C-7 and Table C-8.

Table C-7
Table CUSTOMER After First Normal Form

CUST_ID	*CUST_NAME*	*SALES_REGION_ NAME*	*SALES_ REGION_ID*	*ADDRESS*
1	Lone Dove Ent.	North Pacific	3	1234 Elm Street, Salem, OR 95679
2	ACME Corp.	Midwest	4	567 Pine street, Chicago, IL 07891

Table C-8
New REGION Table

SALES_REGION_ID	*SALES_REGION_NAME*
3	North Pacific
4	Midwest
5	North Atlantic

The fourth Normal Form states that independent multiple relationships should be isolated. It applies only to designs that include one-to-many and many-to-many relationships. The theory states that no table may contain two or more one-to-many and many-to-many relationships that are not directly related.

The fifth Normal Form requires isolation of semantically related multiple relationships. There might be reasons for separating even logically related attributes into separate tables, but you would pay dearly in performance if you decide to go there.

Things are moving along quite nicely, but now you have a problem: your customers opened more than one location and now one order could be related to more than one customer and shipped to more than one destination; at the same time one customer still could place more than one order. To resolve many-to-many relationships, an intermediary table is introduced. As an example, you may look at the `ORDER_SHIPMENT` table in the ACME database (see Appendix B). It links table `ORDER` and table `SHIPMENT`, since for one shipment there could be more than one order, and each order could be sent out in more than one shipment. It consists of two columns, which represent foreign keys — one (`ORDSHIP_ORDHDR_ID_FN`) from the table `ORDER_HEADER`, and another (`ORDSHIP_SHIPMENT_ID_FN`) from the table `SHIPMENT`.

Specifying Constraints

You should consider a number of constraints to enforce the integrity of the database. Primary keys and foreign keys enforce *Referential Integrity*, which means that each record in the child table is linked to a record in the parent table (*no orphaned records*). The database model is evolving during the database design process, and is inseparable from RDBMS principle.

Primary key and `UNIQUE` constraints also enforce *Entity Integrity* — this concept refers to making sure that a row in the table is unique within the table (that is, its combination of column values is unique throughout the table). Entity Integrity is also enforced with `NOT NULL` constraints (`NULL` values are not allowed within this particular column). You should select a primary key for each table you create and apply the `NOT NULL` constraint for each column of every table that should never be `NULL` (for example, if you have a record for a customer, it must have a `CUST_ID` field populated with some unique value — no two customers should share the same ID).

Domain Integrity refers to the data itself and is enforced by using the appropriate data type, for example, `CHECK` constraints and DEFAULTs. `CHECK` constraints ensure that only specific data — in a range of values or formats — is entered into the column; while `DEFAULT` constraints specify default values for the column in case you do not have a value for it when inserting new records.

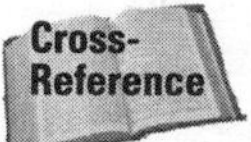

Constraints are discussed in Chapters 4 and 5.

Data types for the column guard against entering invalid data into it. There can be no VARCHAR data in a NUMBER column, and SQL Server's IMAGE data cannot possibly be inserted into the column of an INTEGER data type.

In addition to these integrity constraints, it is possible to enforce custom constraints through use of triggers, stored procedures, and other RDBMS-specific features (see Chapter 14 for more information).

Pitfalls of Relational Database Design

As the saying has it, if the only tool you have is a hammer, every problem starts to look like a nail. Nothing could be truer with regard to the mistakes that people often make while trying their hands at database design.

Programmers with previous experience in nonrelational databases may tend to design databases that resemble hierarchical or network databases, or even flat files and spreadsheet designs, described in Chapter 1.

If you have the luxury of designing your database from scratch — consider yourself lucky and use every technique you can find in the database literature. More often you face the task of redesigning a database to fit new business requirements, improve performance, and so on. Whatever you do, never try reusing existing database structures as a basis for a new database. It is wrong for your particular task if it cannot accommodate the new features you are trying to implement. Take a fresh look without limits imposed by a previous design, already in place. If you seem to be able to re-use some parts and pieces, maybe there is no need for redesign. Maybe you need only to improve upon an existing database? Redesigning databases to preserve legacy data is not a small task and should be approached with caution.

Another common problem arises from the tendency to utilize every single feature offered by a particular RDBMS vendor. While improving performance — most of the time — this approach could lock you into that vendor's product; and it costs you dearly both in terms of time and money to move your database onto a different vendor. Believe it or not, there were times when dBASE, Btrieve, FoxPro, and Sybase were all the rage. Sticking to a few sound principles might not give you the very last drop of performance you could squeeze out of a database, but it would serve you well should you decide to go with a different RDBMS vendor down the road, or even to simply facilitate database maintenance tasks.

This short introduction to database design is clearly inadequate to turn you into a database design guru, but rather its purpose is to offer you help with your very first step on the road. We encourage you to look for more comprehensive books on the subject.

✦ ✦ ✦

Installing RDBMS Software

✦ ✦ ✦ ✦

Please keep in mind that no matter which RDBMS you have chosen to install, it is for educational/evaluation purposes only. Oracle, IBM DB2 UDB, and the MS SQL Server can be installed in many different ways, but for the scope of this book we recommend that you follow the proposed instructions and naming conventions. That will simplify the creation and population of the ACME database (regardless of the RDBMS you have chosen) used in the examples and exercises given throughout this book.

Installing Oracle 9*i*

Undoubtedly, Oracle 9*i* is the most resource-demanding (and one of the most powerful) RDBMS engine out of the three discussed in this book. From our personal experience we know that installing just for the "minimal hardware requirements" combined with the installation defaults does not result in acceptable performance. Oracle is a really great system, but to work well it needs to be tuned, and database tuning is a very serious undertaking usually performed by experienced DBAs; as such, it is definitely beyond the scope of this book.

To install Oracle in a production environment, you need the help of an experienced professional.

Our general recommendation is that if you want to install Oracle 9*i* on your machine, don't rely on the minimum hardware requirements, but rather try to exceed what is recommended. If you don't have enough resources for Oracle, try DB2 or MS SQL Server.

If you've decided to try out Oracle 9i RDBMS, you may download it from the vendor's site (`otn.oracle.com`).We recommend that you install the Personal Edition of Oracle 9*i*, which is only available for Windows. You would need one set of three disks (per platform) to install Personal, Standard, or Enterprise, so it's actually up to you which version to choose; but in order to try out our SQL examples, the Personal Edition is more than sufficient.

We also include instructions on how to install Oracle 9*i* on Sun/Solaris and Linux, but be advised that you have to be familiar with those operating systems to be able to proceed with the installation. For more detailed installation instructions (for any platform) visit `technet.oracle.com`.

Oracle 9*i* installation disks are not included with your book; you can download the disk images from Oracle Technology Network site (`otn.oracle.com`) after completing a registration form.

Installing Oracle 9*i* software on Windows NT/2000/XP

Oracle 9*i* requires quite a bit of resources. Table D-1 contains Oracle's own principal guidelines; from our own experience, we recommend at least a Pentium 400-MHz machine with 192 MB of RAM.

System requirements

Table D-1 lists the minimal and recommended requirements to install Oracle 9*i* on Windows.

Table D-1
Installation of Oracle on Windows: Platforms Requirements

Processor (CPU)	Minimal: Pentium 200 Recommended: Pentium 266
Operating system	Windows NT Workstation 4.0 Windows NT Server 4.0 Windows NT Server Enterprise Edition 4.0 Windows NT 4.0 Server Terminal Server Edition Windows 2000 Professional Windows 2000 Server Windows 2000 Advanced Server Windows 2000 Datacenter Terminal Services

	Windows XP Professional
	Windows XP Home Edition
	Windows 98 (special installation disk required; Oracle 9.1 only)
Service packs	Windows NT: Service pack 5 or higher
	Windows 2000:Service pack 1 or higher
Memory	RAM:
	Minimal: 128M
	Recommended: 256 MB
	Virtual Memory:
	Initial size 200 MB
	Maximum size 400 MB
Hard disk FAT	System drive: 140MB
	Oracle home drive: 4.75 GB
Hard disk NTFS (recommended)	System drive: 140MB
	Oracle home drive: 2.75 GB
Web browser	Netscape Navigator 4.76 or higher
	Microsoft Internet Explorer 5.0 or higher
	Microsoft Internet Explorer 6.0 (with Windows XP)
Other	Video Adapter: 256 color
	CD-ROM Drive

Though Oracle 9*i* is not certified for the Windows XP Home Edition, it is possible to install and run it on this operating system version.

You need a special Oracle 9*i* installation disk for Windows 98; the set of three disks mentioned previously is good for any other approved version of Windows.

Installation instructions

Follow these instructions to install Oracle 9*i* on your computer:

1. Insert the first Oracle 9*i* component CD into your CD-ROM drive. The installation will start automatically (see Figure D-1.) If the *Autorun* window does not appear, find your CD-ROM from Windows Explorer, open the `autorun` directory, and double-click on `autorun.exe`.

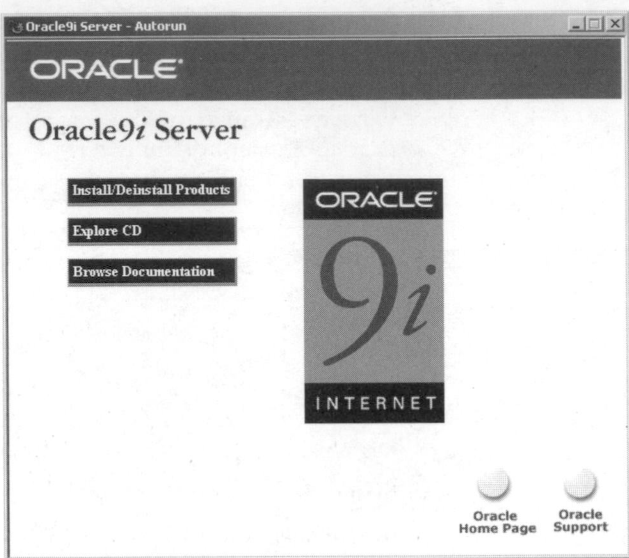

Figure D-1: Oracle 9*i* Autorun window

2. Choose Install/Deinstall Products from the *Autorun* window. The *Welcome* window appears. See Figure D-2.

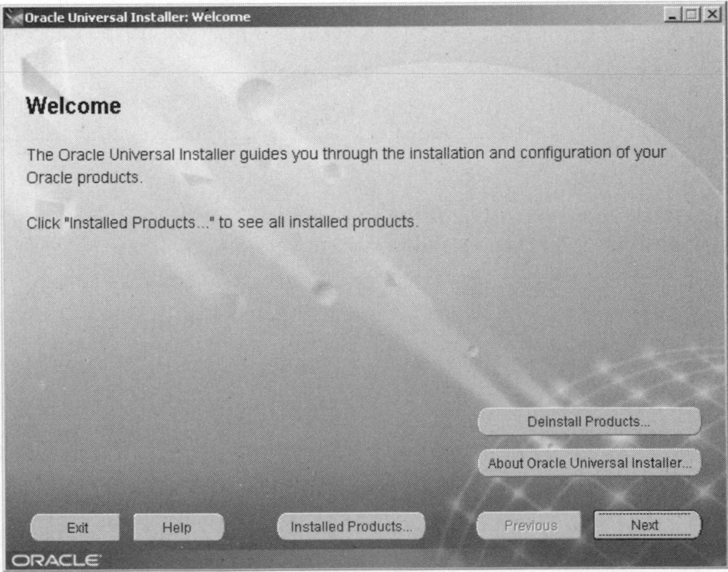

Figure D-2: Oracle Welcome window

3. Choose Next. The *Inventory Location* window appears (assuming that this is your first Oracle installation on this computer). Accept default location and click OK.
4. The *File Locations* window appears. Do not change the directory path in the Source field. We also recommend that you accept defaults for the Oracle Home and Directory path in the Destination fields as shown in Figure D-3.

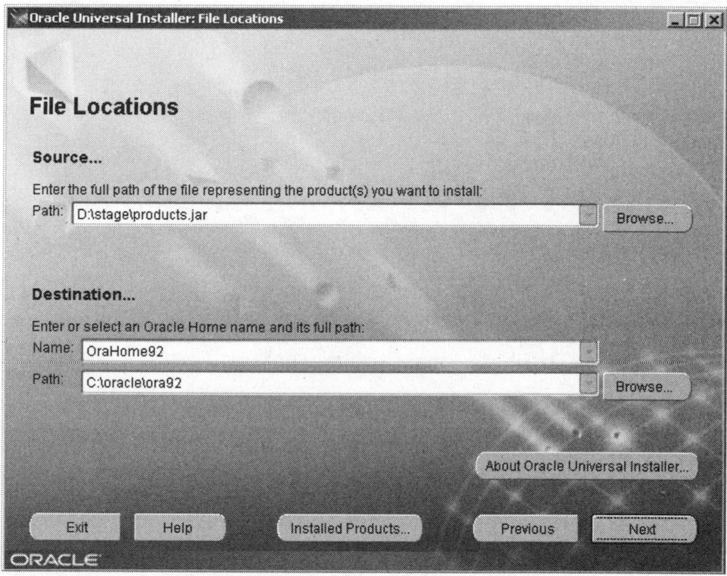

Figure D-3: Oracle File Locations window

5. Choose Next. You will see the *Available Products* window. Select Oracle 9*i* Database.
6. Choose Next. Select Personal Edition on the *Installation Types* window.
7. From the *Database Configuration* window, select General Purpose.
8. If the Microsoft Transaction Server is detected, then the *Oracle Services for Microsoft Transaction Server* window will appear. Accept the default port number for this service (2030).
9. Choose Next. Enter ACME in both the Global Database Name and SID fields on the *Database Identification* window. This information is used by the Database Configuration Assistant to create your database during the installation process. See Figure D-4.
10. Choose Next. The *Database File Location* window appears. Enter the directory location where you wish to place the database files. We recommend that you accept the defaults.

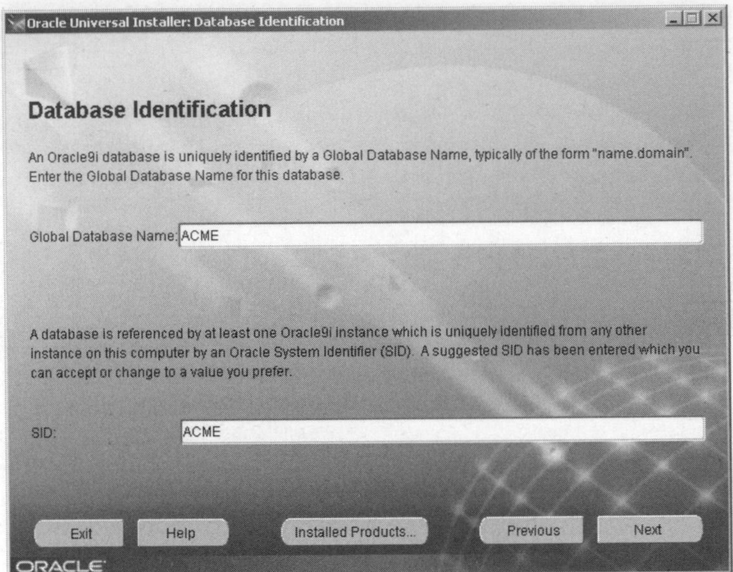

Figure D-4: Oracle Database Identification window

11. Choose Next. Select the database character set. We recommend that you accept the defaults (which are based on your operating system's local settings) as shown in Figure D-5.

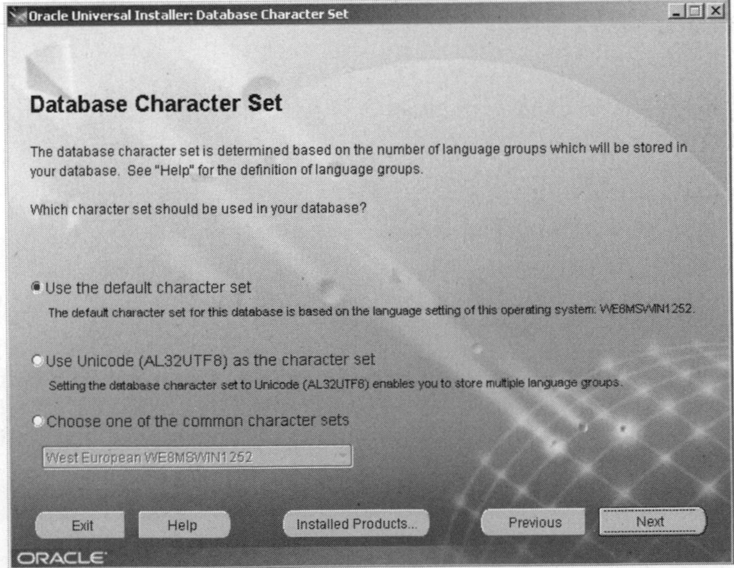

Figure D-5: Oracle Database Character Set window

12. Choose Next. You will see the *Summary* window (Figure D-6.) Review the space requirements to ensure you have enough space on your hard disk. Click the Install button.

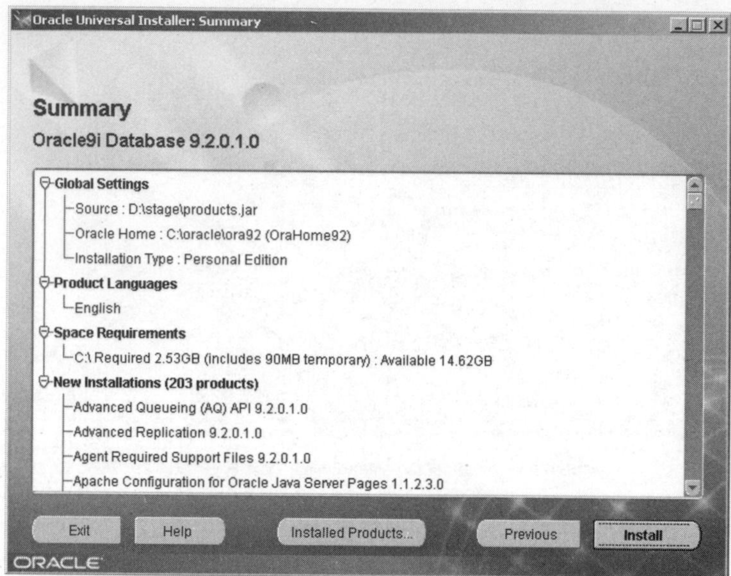

Figure D-6: Oracle Summary window

13. Wait for the installation process to complete. During the installation you will be prompted to insert the second and the third CDs (Figure D-7.)
14. When the software installation process is complete, the *Configuration Tools* window appears (Figure D-8). The default installation configures Oracle Net Services and Agent, creates the sample database, and starts the Oracle HTTP server. The End of Installation window appears when all tasks are complete.

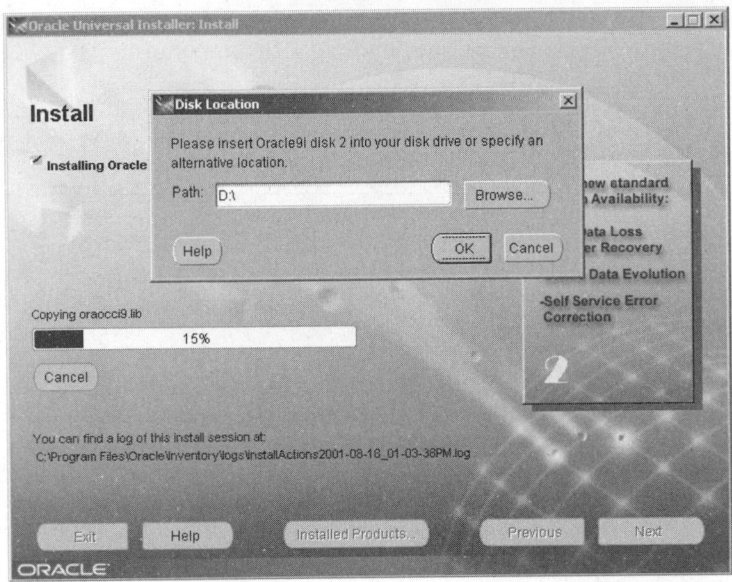

Figure D-7: Oracle Install window / Disk Location pop-up screen

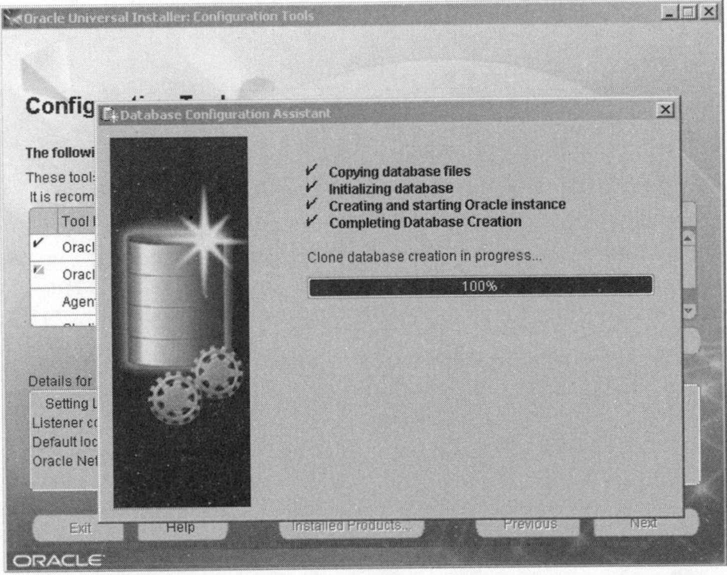

Figure D-8: Oracle Configuration Tools and Database Configuration assistant windows

Note

For the purposes of this book you don't really need to configure the aforementioned services except for the sample database. Regrettably, there is no way to create the default database alone unless you do it manually after the install. For simplicity's sake, we suggest that you let the installation program configure all the default options, and then disable them as described later in this chapter.

15. The *Database Configuration Assistant* window prompts you for new super user (`SYS` and `SYSTEM`) passwords as shown in Figure D-9. Type in your passwords, write them down, and click OK.

Database Configuration Assistant
Database creation complete. Check the logfiles at C:\oracle\admin\ACME\create for details.
Database Information:
Global Database Name: ACME
System Identifier(SID): ACME
Server Parameters Filename: C:\oracle\ora92\database\spfileACME.ora
Change Passwords
For security reasons, you must specify a password for the SYS and SYSTEM accounts in the new database.
SYS Password: ****
Confirm SYS Password: ****
SYSTEM Password: ****
Confirm SYSTEM Password: ****
Note: All database accounts except SYS, SYSTEM, DBSNMP, and SCOTT are locked. Select the Password Management button to view a complete list of locked accounts or to manage the database accounts. From the Password Management window, unlock only the accounts you will use. Oracle Corporation strongly recommends changing the default passwords immediately after unlocking the account.
Password Management...
OK

Figure D-9: Oracle Change passwords for system users on the Database Configuration assistant window

16. The *End of Installation* window appears. Choose Exit and click Yes on the Exit confirmation pop-up window. The Oracle Enterprise Manager Console window may open. Unless you intend to administer the Oracle database, you should simply close this window.

Tip

You can review your installation session logs in the `<SYSTEM_DRIVE>:\Program Files\Oracle\Inventory\logs` directory.

Note

These installation instructions assume you don't have a previous version of Oracle software installed on your computer. Go to `technet.oracle.com` for upgrade instructions.

Postinstallation tasks

Usually there are no special tasks to be performed after Oracle 9*i* installation on the Windows platform. See the *Starting and stopping Oracle 9i* section later in this chapter for basic recommendations.

Uninstalling Oracle 9*i*

At some point you might want to uninstall Oracle. To do so, follow the instructions below. If after the uninstall process is complete some elements were left behind, go to `technet.oracle.com` for instructions on how to completely remove Oracle from your system.

1. Go to the Windows Services control panel (Figure D-10) and stop all Oracle Services (anything that starts with Oracle or Ora).

To go to the Services panel, on Windows NT, select Start⇨Settings⇨Control Panel⇨Services; on Windows 2000, choose Start⇨Settings⇨Control Panel⇨Administrative Tools⇨Services; on Windows XP, go to Start⇨Control Panel⇨Administrative Tools⇨Services. To stop a service, right-click on it and select Stop.

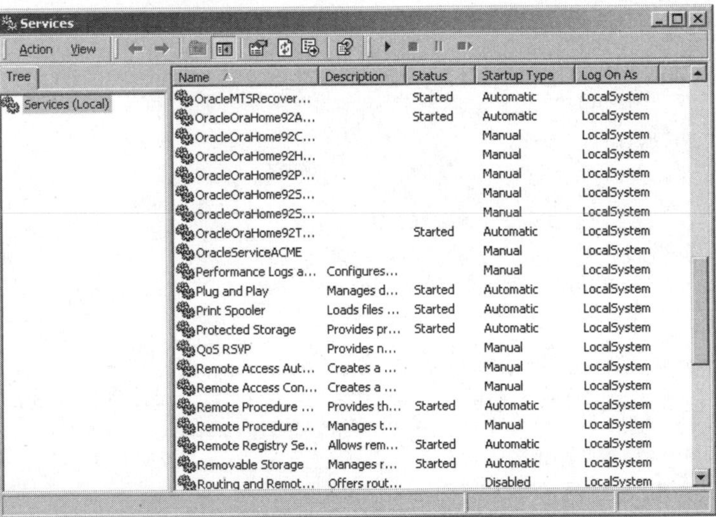

Figure D-10: Oracle Windows Services window

2. Start the Oracle Universal Installer from Start⇨Programs⇨Oracle Installation Products.
3. Choose Deinstall Products from the *Welcome* window. The *Inventory* window appears.

4. Expand the tree of installed components and check the Oracle 9i Database 9.x.x.x box.

5. Choose Remove. Click the Yes button on the *Confirmation* window. See Figure D-11 for details.

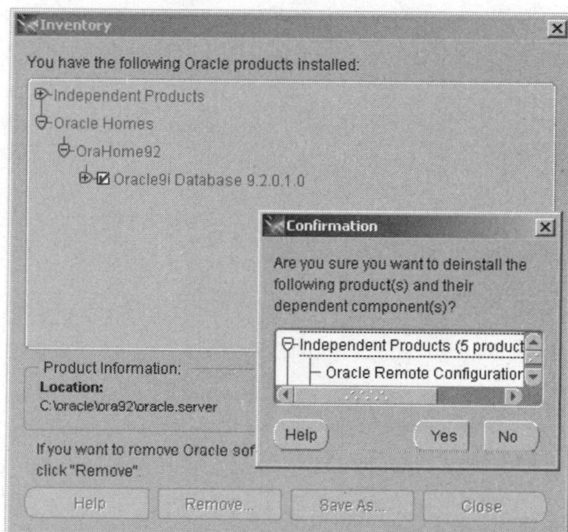

Figure D-11: Removing Oracle software with the Inventory window

6. Close the *Inventory* window and exit the Universal Installer.

Starting and stopping Oracle 9*i*

Oracle 9*i* takes a lot of your computer's resources, so it's good to know how to start and stop it, especially since it is configured to start automatically after default installation. That might not be bad for a production server, but if you installed if for educational purposes only, you probably don't want it to start automatically every time you boot your PC because of resources drain. The following procedure disables the automatic startup:

1. Go to Start➪Programs➪Oracle — OracleHome92➪Configuration and Migration Tools and choose Administration Assistant for Windows NT.

2. Expand the tree all the way to your ACME database, right-click on ACME database, and choose Startup/Shutdown Options.

3. Go to the Oracle NT Service tab, select Manual under Oracle NT Service Startup Type, and click OK (Figure D-12.) Next time you boot your computer, Oracle will not start automatically.

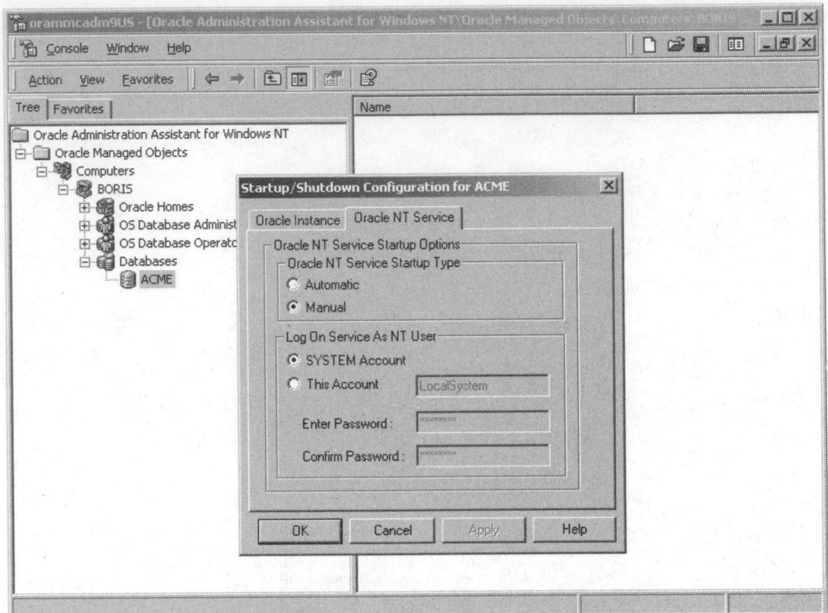

Figure D-12: Oracle Administration Assistant for Windows NT

4. To start Oracle manually, repeat the procedure described in Step 1, expand the tree, right-click on the ACME icon, and select the Start Service option. To stop Oracle, select the Stop Service icon from the same right-click menu.

When you choose to start database service, the message window pops up almost immediately saying, "Service started successfully." In fact, the startup procedures are still in progress, so give it a little time before you try to log in.

Another service that takes your computer's resources is the Oracle HTTP Server. This is powered by the Apache Web Server and also starts automatically by default. To change its default behavior, go to the Windows Services panel, find OracleOraHome92HTTPServer, double-click on it, and change Startup type to manual on the *General* tab.

You will need the Oracle HTTP Server running if you are planning to configure iSQL*Plus (more about iSQL*Plus in Appendix E).

Installing Oracle software on SUN Solaris

Oracle installation on Unix platforms requires solid knowledge of the operating system and `root` privileges. Also, the Oracle 9*i* Personal Edition is not available for Unix, so minimal DBA skills are also desirable. We assume you don't have any previous version of Oracle installed on your server.

System requirements

Table D-2 lists the minimal and recommended requirements to install Oracle 9*i* on Sun Solaris.

Table D-2
Installation of Oracle on Sun Solaris: Platforms Requirements

Operating System	Solaris 32-bit: 2.6(5.6), 7 (5.7), 8 (5.8)
	Solaris 64-bit: 8 (5.8) with update 5 (07/01)
Memory	RAM: 512 MB
	Swap space: 1 GB or 2 × RAM (whichever is greater)
Hard Disk	4.5 GB for database software and seed database
	400 MB in /tmp directory
Web Browser	Netscape Navigator 4.76 or higher
Other	CD-ROM Drive capable of reading ISO 9660 format CDs with RockRidge extensions
	JRE 1.1.8_12 is required for Solaris 32-bit.
	JRE 1.1.8_15 is required for Solaris 64-bit.
	Windows manager (any Sun-supported)
	`make`, `ar`, `ld`, `nm` executables

Preinstallation tasks to perform as root

You must perform the following tasks as `root` before you can start the Oracle installation.

1. Configure Kernel parameters. Edit the `/etc/system` file, and make sure the Kernel parameters are at least at the levels defined below:

   ```
   semsys:seminfo_semmni=100
   semsys:seminfo_semmns=1024
   semsys:seminfo_semmsl=256
   shmsys:shminfo_shmmax=4294967295
   shmsys:shminfo_shmmin=1
   shmsys:shminfo_shmmni=100
   shmsys:shminfo_shmseg=10
   ```

   If any of the above values is not large enough, change it appropriately; save the file, and restart the server.

2. Create mount points. Oracle requires a minimum of two mount points: one for the software, and one for the database files. The conventions are `/u01` and `/u02`.

Oracle recommends that you create at least four mount points to follow the rules of the Oracle Flexible Architecture (OFA).

3. Create a Unix group called `dba`. Everybody who belongs to this group will have all database privileges, so use it carefully.

4. Create user `oracle` as a member of the `dba` group with a home directory consistent with other user home directories (not the same as Oracle Home directory). The default shell can be Bourne, Korn, or C.

You can create Solaris groups and users with the `admintool` utility.

5. Set file creation permissions for user `oracle` by adding this line to `.profile` or `.login` file:

```
umask 022
```

Preinstallation tasks to perform as user oracle

You must perform the following tasks as user `oracle` (created in the previous set of steps) before you can start the Oracle installation.

1. Set environment variables in `.profile` or `.login` file of the `oracle` account as described in Table D-3. We assume you used the `/u02` mount point for the Oracle software installation.

Table D-3
Unix Environment Variables Necessary for Oracle 9*i* Installation on Sun Solaris Platform

Variable	*Explanation*	*Recommended value*
ORACLE_BASE	Top of the Oracle software structure	/u01/app/oracle.
ORACLE_HOME	Directory that contains software for a particular release	/u01/app/oracle/product/9.?.?.?.?, where ?.?.?.? corresponds to the current release.
ORACLE_SID	System identifier to be used by Oracle server instance during the installation	ACME (for purposes of this book).

Variable	Explanation	Recommended value
PATH	Shell's search path for executables (The order *is* important.)	$ORACLE_HOME/bin:/usr/ccs/bin:/usr/bin:/etc:/usr/openwin/bin:/usr/local/bin (if exists).
LD_LIBRARY_PATH		Add $ORACLE_HOME/lib at the beginning of your LD_LIBRARY_PATH variable.

We assume that you installed the Oracle 9*i* software from the server X Window console. Otherwise, the DISPLAY environment variable must be set appropriately.

2. Update the environment for current oracle session (the one that will perform the installation).

Installation instructions

You have several options on how to install Oracle 9*i*. We assume you've chosen the installation that uses the CD-ROMs.

Oracle uses a platform-independent, Java-based graphical user interface (GUI) called Universal Installer for software installations. That means the screenshots from the Windows installation section are identical (or very similar) to what you will see during installation on Sun Solaris, Linux, or any other OS.

1. Insert the first Oracle 9*i* CD (Disk1) into your CD-ROM drive. Mount your CD-ROM. The CD-ROM is mounted automatically if you have Volume Management software installed (Solaris default).
2. Log in as user oracle. Start the Oracle Universal Installer by running the runInstaller command from the CD-ROM root directory. The *Welcome* window appears.
3. Click Next. The *Unix Group Name* window appears. Specify the dba group created during preinstallation steps in the appropriate field.
4. Click Next. The *Installer* window will pop up asking you to run /tmp/OraInstall/orainstRoot.sh as root, which creates the /var/opt/oracle directory on your machine and gives user oracle the appropriate permissions on it. When done, click Retry. The installation will continue.
5. The *File Location* window will appear. Do not change the Source field; we also recommend that you do not change the Destination field that defaults to the directory path specified in your $ORACLE_HOME environment variables.

If you did not complete all preinstallation requirements, another Installer window might appear asking you to run the `orainstRoot.sh` script as root. Run it and click Retry.

6. Click Next. The *Available Products* window will appear. Choose Oracle 9*i* Database.
7. Click Next. The *Installation Types* window appears. Select Standard Edition.
8. Click Next. The *Database Configuration Types* window appears. Select General Purpose.
9. Click Next. Enter `ACME` for both Global Database Name and SID.
10. Click Next. The *Database File Location* window appears. Enter the directory for the database files in the appropriate field, for instance, `/u02` if you've created it during the preinstallation steps.
11. Click Next. The *Database Character Set* window appears. We recommend that you accept defaults.
12. Click Next. The *Summary* window appears. Review the information and click Install. The Install window appears showing a progress bar.
13. You will be prompted to insert Disk2 and Disk3 during the installation. You will also be prompted to run the `root.sh` script as root. The script sets appropriate permissions and configures Oracle software. When done, click OK in the *Alert* pop-up window.
14. The *Configuration Tools* window appears. This window helps you to configure your network, database, HTTP Server, and Oracle Intelligent Agent. We recommend that you accept all defaults.
15. The *End of Installation* window appears. Click Exit.

You can review your installation session logs. The location of the logs is defined in file `/var/opt/oracle/oraInst.loc`.

Noninteractive installation of Oracle 9*i* on Unix platforms is also available.

Postinstallation tasks

Postinstallation tasks can vary. You might want to create additional Unix accounts, check file permissions, change group membership of the Apache user (for security reasons), and automate database startup and shutdown procedures. If you've installed Oracle only to run examples in this book, there is no need for any of these tasks.

Uninstalling Oracle 9*i*

Please follow instructions below to uninstall Oracle.

1. Start the Oracle Universal Installer.
2. Choose Deinstall Products from the *Welcome* window. The Inventory window appears.
3. Expand the tree of installed components and check the boxes of components to uninstall.
4. Choose Remove. Choose Yes on the *Confirmation* window.
5. Close the *Inventory* window and exit the Universal Installer.

Starting and stopping Oracle 9*i*

Oracle 9*i* does not automatically start on Unix. To start and stop Oracle you have to be logged in as user `oracle` or as another member of the `dba` group. Also, make sure your session's environment variables are properly set as shown in Table D-3.

1. At the Unix prompt, type `sqlplus /nolog`.
2. At SQL prompt type `connect / as sysdba`.
3. Either type `startup` (to the start Oracle 9*i* instance) or `shutdown immediate` (to stop it).
4. Type `quit` to exit to the Unix prompt.

Tip

You can also use Oracle's GUI to perform database startup and shutdown.

Installing Oracle software on Linux

For all the practical purposes, Linux is a Unix dialect, just as Sun Solaris is, so the installation procedures are similar for these two operating systems. These installation instructions assume familiarity with the Linux operating system.

System requirements

Even though Oracle 9*i* is only currently certified for the SuSE Linux Enterprise Server 7 (SLES-7), we know from experience that it is also installable on Red Hat 7.0 and Mandrake 8.0. If you are a Linux expert, you are more than welcome to try to install Oracle 9*i* on other Linux flavors. Please refer to Oracle documentation for detailed instructions.

Table D-4 lists the recommended requirements for Oracle 9*i* installation on Linux.

Table D-4
Installation of Oracle on Linux: Requirements Overview

Operating system	SuSE 7 with kernel 2.4.7 and glibc 2.2.2 Red Hat 7.0 (7.1) with kernel 2.4.x Mandrake 8.0 with kernel 2.4.3
Memory	RAM: 512 MB Swap space: 1 GB or 2 x RAM (whichever is greater)
Hard disk	4.5 GB for database software and seed database 400 MB in /tmp directory
Web browser	Netscape Navigator 4.76 or higher
Other	CD-ROM Drive capable of reading ISO 9660 format CDs with RockRidge extensions Blackdown JRE 1.1.8 v3 X Windows (Gnome, KDE, or anything you like) `make`, `ar`, `ld`, `nm` executables

Binutils for Red Hat 7.2 seems to be incompatible with Oracle 9*i*. You can use binutils-2.10.0.18 (Red Hat 7.0) or binutils-2.10.1.0.2 (Mandrake 8.0)

Preinstallation tasks to perform as root

You must perform the following tasks as `root` before you can start the Oracle RDBMS installation.

1. Configure kernel parameters. The minimum recommended values are listed below:

```
semmsl      100
semmns      256
semomp      100
semmni      100
shmmax      2147483648
shmmni      100
shmall      2097152
shmmin      1
shmseg      4096
shmvmx      32767
```

The 2.4.x default kernel parameters are usually sufficient for an Oracle 9*i* installation. If not, modify these values; write a script to initialize them, and include the script in your system initialization files, for example:

```
# cd /proc/sys/kernel
# echo 100 256 100 100 > sem
# echo 2147483648 > shmmax
# echo 100 > shmmni
# echo 2097152 > shmall
# echo 1 > shmmin
# echo 4096 > shmseg
# echo 32767 > shmvmx
# echo 65536 > /proc/sys/fs/file-max
# ulimit -n 65536
# echo 1024 65000 > /proc/sys/net/ipv4/ip_local_port_change
# ulimit -u 16384
```

2. Create mount points. Oracle requires a minimum of two mount points; one for the software, and one for the database files. The conventions are /u01 and /u02.
3. Create a Linux group called dba. Everyone who belongs to this group has all database privileges, so use it carefully.
4. Create user oracle as a member of the dba group with the home directory consistent with other user home directories (but not the same as the Oracle Home directory). The default shell can be Bourne, Korn, or C.
5. Set file creation permissions for user oracle by adding this line to .bash_profile or /etc/profile:

```
umask 022
```

Preinstallation tasks to perform as user oracle

You must perform the following tasks as user oracle (created in the previous set of steps) before you can start the Oracle RDBMS installation.

1. Set environment variables in .bash_profile of the oracle account as described in Table D-5. We assume you used the /u02 mount point for Oracle software installation.

Table D-5
Environment Variables Necessary for Oracle 9*i* Installation on Linux

Variable	*Explanation*	*Recommended value*
ORACLE_BASE	Top of the Oracle software structure	/u01/app/oracle.
ORACLE_HOME	Directory that contains software for a particular release	/u01/app/oracle/product/9.?.?.?.?, where ?.?.?.? corresponds to the current release.
ORACLE_SID	System identifier to be used by Oracle server instance during the installation	ACME (for purposes of this book)
PATH	Shell's search path for executables (The order IS important.)	$ORACLE_HOME/bin:/usr/bin:/bin:/usr/bin/X11:/usr/local/bin (if exists).
LD_LIBRARY_PATH		Add $ORACLE_HOME/lib at the beginning of your LD_LIBRARY_PATH variable.

2. Update the environment for the current oracle session (the one that will perform the installation).

Installation instructions

You have several options on how to install Oracle 9*i*. We assume you've chosen the installation that uses the CD ROMs.

1. Insert the first Oracle 9*i* CD (Disk1) into your CD-ROM drive. Mount your CD-ROM. The CD-ROM is mounted automatically to the directory specified in your auto mount configuration if you are using mounting software.
2. Log in as user oracle. Start the Oracle Universal Installer by running the runInstaller command from the CD-ROM root directory. The *Welcome* window appears.
3. Click Next. The *Unix Group Name* window appears. Specify the dba group created during preinstallation steps in the appropriate field.

Tip If the /etc directory does not exist on your system or user oracle does not have appropriate permissions on it, the Installer window will pop up asking you to run /tmp/OraInstall/orainstRoot.sh as root. When done, click Retry. The installation will continue.

4. Click Next. The *File Location* window will appear. Do not change the Source field; we also recommend that you do not change the Destination field that defaults to directory path specified in your $ORACLE_HOME environment variables.

Tip If you did not complete all the preinstallation requirements, another Installer window might appear asking you to run the `orainstRoot.sh` script as root. Run it and click Retry.

5. Click Next. The *Available Products* window will appear. Choose Oracle 9i Database.
6. Click Next. The *Installation Types* window appears. Select Standard Edition.
7. Click Next. The *Database Configuration* Types window appears. Select General Purpose.
8. Click Next. Enter `ACME` for both Global Database Name and SID.
9. Click Next. The *Database File Location* window appears. Enter the directory for the database files in the appropriate field, for example, `/u02` if you've created it during the preinstallation steps.
10. Click Next. The *Database Character Set* window appears. We recommend that you accept the defaults.
11. Click Next. The *Summary* window appears. Review the information and click the Install button. The Install window appears showing a progress bar.
12. You will be prompted to insert Disk2 and Disk3 during the installation. You will also be prompted to run the `root.sh` script as root. The script sets appropriate permissions and configures Oracle software. When done, click OK in the *Alert* pop-up window.
13. The *Configuration Tools* window appears. This window helps you to configure your network, database, HTTP Server, and Oracle Intelligent Agent. We recommend that you accept all the defaults.
14. The *End of Installation* window appears. Click Exit.

Tip You can review your installation session logs. The location of the logs is defined in the file `/var/opt/oracle/oraInst.loc`.

Postinstallation tasks

Postinstallation tasks may vary. You might want to create additional Linux accounts, check file permissions, change group membership of the Apache user (for security reasons), and automate database startup and shutdown procedures. If you've installed Oracle only to run examples in this book, there is no need for any of these tasks.

Tip If you create any additional OS users to work with Oracle, then you have to make sure all environment variables discussed above are added to their `.bash_profile` (unless `/etc/profile` is used for everybody).

Uninstalling Oracle 9*i*

The following are used to uninstall Oracle:

1. Start the Oracle Universal Installer.
2. Choose Deinstall Products from the *Welcome* window. The Inventory window appears.
3. Expand the tree of installed components and check the boxes of components to uninstall.
4. Choose Remove. Choose Yes on the *Confirmation* window.
5. Close the *Inventory* window and exit the Universal Installer.

Starting and stopping Oracle 9*i*

Oracle 9*i* does not automatically start on Linux. To start and stop Oracle you have to be logged in as user `oracle` or as another member of the `dba` group and start it manually. Also, make sure your session's environment variables are properly set as shown in Table D-5.

1. At the Linux prompt, type `sqlplus /nolog`.
2. At SQL prompt type `connect / as sysdba`.
3. Either type `startup` (to start the Oracle 9*i* instance) or `shutdown immediate` (to stop it), and hit the Return key.
4. Type `quit` to exit to the Linux prompt.

Installing IBM DB2 UDB 8.1 Personal Edition

Unlike Oracle, DB2 requires fewer system resources. It also has a reputation for being fast and reliable, but its user friendliness still lags behind its rivals' (even though it became much better in version 8.1). In this book, however, we use command-line interface.

Installing DB2 UDB 8.1 software on Windows NT/2000/Me/XP

DB2 installation on Windows is fast and simple and does not require much user interaction and is very straightforward.

System requirements

Table D-6 lists the requirements for DB2 UDB 8.1 installation on Windows.

Table D-6
Installation of DB2 UDB on Windows: Platforms Requirements

Processor (CPU)	Minimal: Pentium 200 Recommended: Pentium 266
Operating System	Windows NT 4.0 Windows 2000 Windows XPWindows 98 Windows 95 v. 4.00.950 or later
Service Packs	Windows NT: Service pack 6a or higher
Memory	RAM:128 MB (Personal Edition)
Hard Disk	350 M
Web Browser	Netscape Navigator 4.76 or higher Microsoft Internet Explorer 4.01 with service pack 2 or higher
Other	Java Runtime Environment (JRE) v. 1.3.1 CD-ROM Drive

Preinstallation tasks

You have to have a locally defined user account that is a member of the local Administration group. By default, any user who is a member of the local OS Administration group also belongs to the DB2 System Administrative (SYSADM) group. The user needs the following rights:

✦ Act as part of the operating system

✦ Create a token object

✦ Increase quotas

✦ Replace a process level token

If the user is missing any of these rights, you will see the Information window during the installation (after Step 6) saying that user does not have the necessary rights. You can ignore this message and click OK. While it is important for a properly configured production installation, it is irrelevant for the purposes of this book.

Tip

It is recommended to shut down any other programs before you start installation.

Installation instructions

Follow these steps:

1. Insert DB2 UDB installation CD-ROM into the CD-ROM drive. The installation will start automatically. If the installation window does not appear, find your CD-ROM from Windows Explorer, and double-click on `setup.exe`.
2. The DB2 *Setup* screen opens as shown in Figure D-13. Click Install Products.

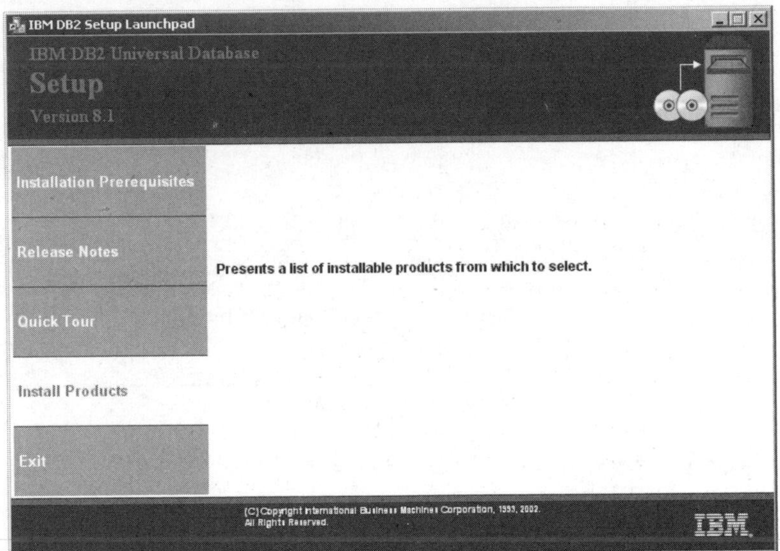

Figure D-13: DB2 UDB 8.1 Installation window

3. The *Select the product you would like to install* screen appears (Figure D-14.) Select DB2 UDB Universal Database Personal Edition and click Next.

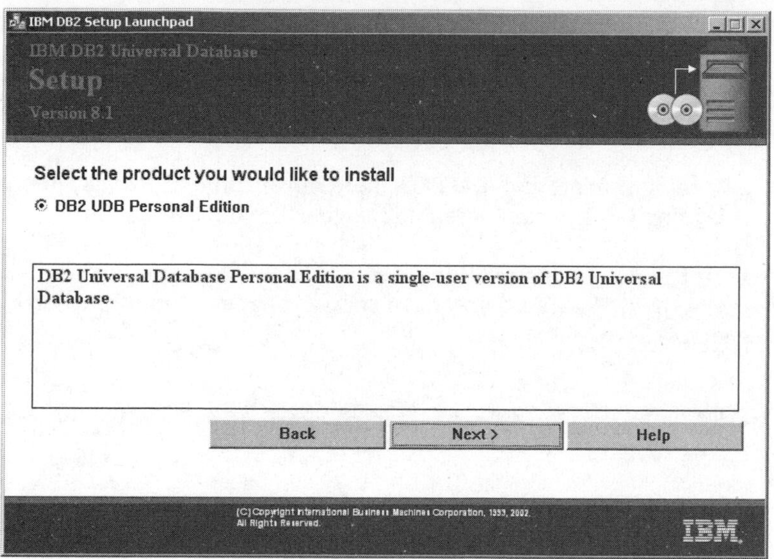

Figure D-14: DB2 UDB 8.1 Products selection screen

4. The *Preparing to Install* window appears; *DB2 Setup wizard* starts automatically then (Figure D-15.) Click Next.

The Next button on the *DB2 Setup wizard* screen will be grayed out for a short period of time. Wait until it becomes enabled.

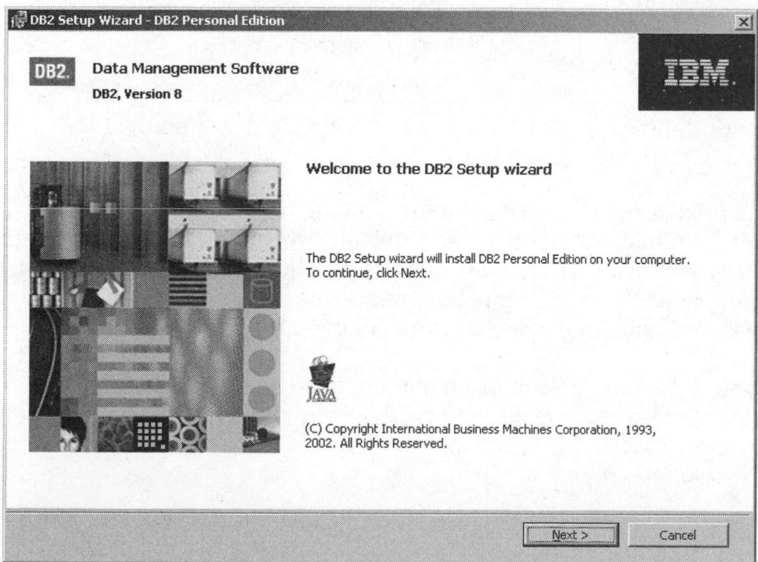

Figure D-15: DB2 UDB 8.1 Setup wizard screen

5. The *License Agreement* screen appears. You may read the agreement (or skip it); you have to select "I accept the terms in the license agreement" option, and click Next.

6. The *Select the installation type* screen appears. Select Typical and click Next.

Note

The Warning window about APPC remote server connections may pop up; ignore it by clicking OK. It is not relevant to the goals of your installation.

7. Accept the default installation drive and directory from the *Select installation folder* screen. Make sure you have enough space on your hard disk (partition). See Figure D-16.

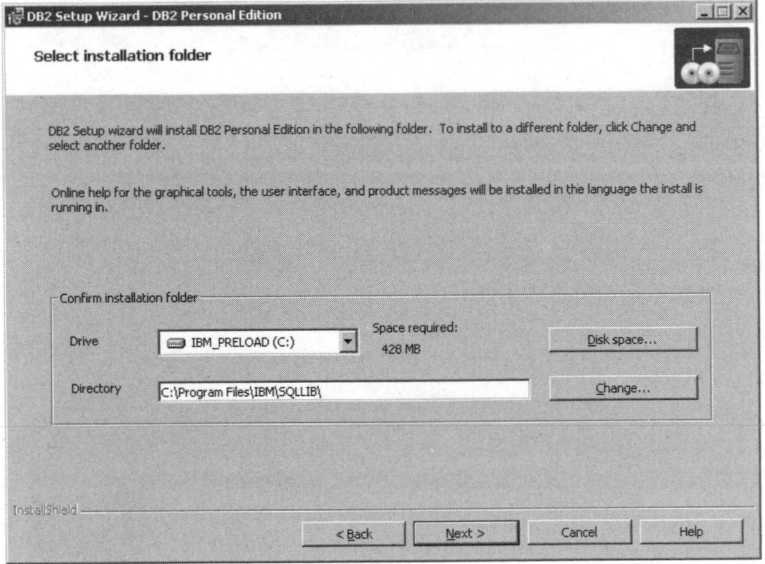
DB2 Setup Wizard - DB2 Personal Edition
Select installation folder
DB2 Setup wizard will install DB2 Personal Edition in the following folder. To install to a different folder, click Change and select another folder.
Online help for the graphical tools, the user interface, and product messages will be installed in the language the install is running in.
Confirm installation folder
Drive
IBM_PRELOAD (C:)
Space required:
428 MB
Disk space...
Directory
C:\Program Files\IBM\SQLLIB\
Change...
InstallShield
< Back
Next >
Cancel
Help

Figure D-16: DB2 UDB 8.1 Select installation folder screen

8. The next screen prompts you for domain, username, and password for the DB2 Administration Server. The default username is `db2admin`. Overtype it with your own OS username and supply the password. Leave the Domain field blank, leave "Use the same user name and password for the remaining DB2 services" checkbox checked, and click Next.

Tip

If you accept the default username `db2admin`, the installation program will ask you if you want to create the user. You can answer Yes and use the `db2admin` account to access your DB2 database later on.

9. The *Set up the administration contact list* screen appears. Leave all the defaults intact and click Next. You may see a warning about SMTP server not being specified. Ignore it by clicking OK, it is irrelevant for the purposes of the current installation.

10. Click Next on the *Configure DB2 instances* screen.

Tip

We recommend that you accept the default options of the *Configure DB2 instances* screen. Otherwise, if you don't want to start DB2 automatically, click Startup button on the abovementioned screen, select "Do not autostart the instance..." option, click OK, and continue. You will have to start the DB2 instance manually every time you reboot your machine. The instructions are given later in this appendix.

11. Accept default settings on the *Prepare the DB2 tools catalog* screen by clicking Next.

12. The *Specify a contact for health monitor notification* screen appears. Select "Defer the task until after installation is complete" option and click Next.

13. Click Install on the *Start copying files* screen (Figure D-17). Installation will start.

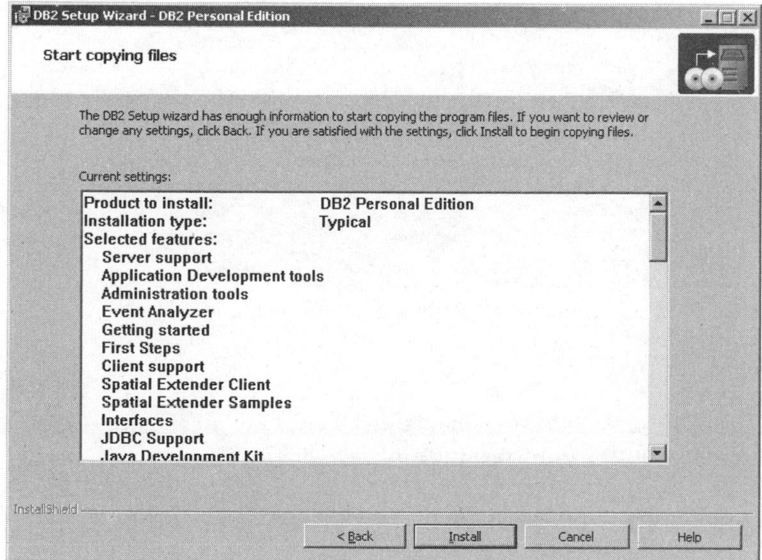

Figure D-17: DB2 UDB 8.1 Start copying files screen

14. When installation and setup of DB2 are complete, the *Setup is complete* screen appears, asking you to shut down all programs running on your computer now. Do so and click Finish.

15. The *First Steps* window appears, displaying the Congratulations message. Click Exit First Steps unless you feel like browsing tutorials or taking the DB2 UDB Quick Tour.

Postinstallation tasks

To create an empty ACME database now:

1. Open the DB2 Control Center (Start⇨Programs⇨IBM DB2⇨General Administration Tools⇨Control Center).

2. Expand the tree view all the way to the databases.

3. Right-click on the Databases folder and select Create⇨Database Using Wizard (Figure D-18.) The *Create Database Wizard* window appears.

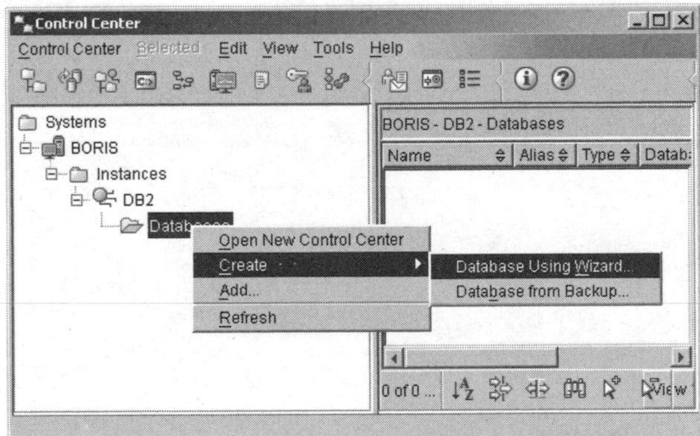

Figure D-18: DB2 UDB 8.1 Creating database using Control Center window

4. Type ACME in Database name field and click Finish (Figure D-19.) The Progress window pops up, showing elapsed time.

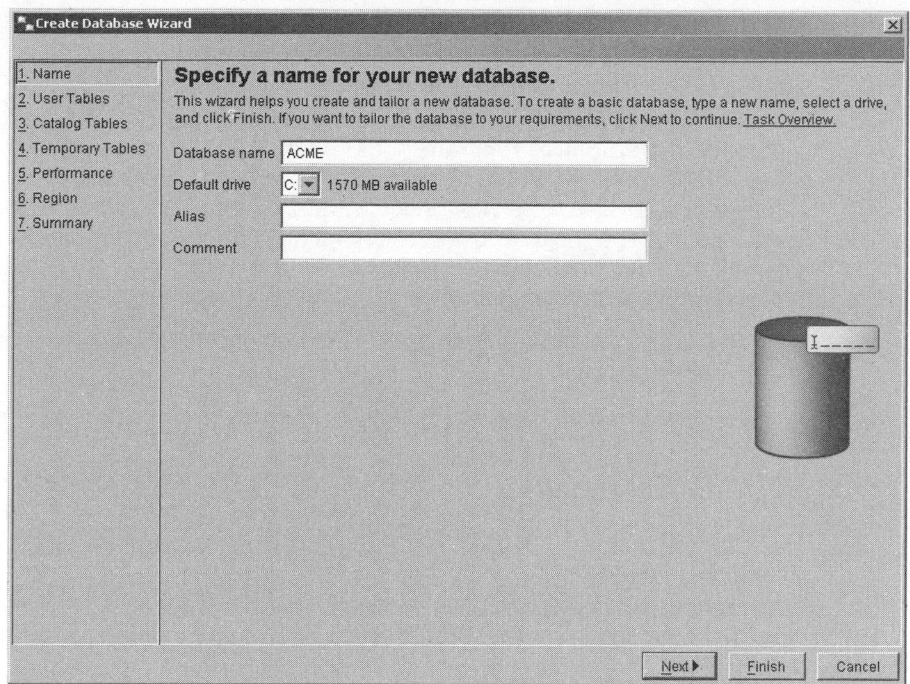

Figure D-19: DB2 UDB 8.1 Creating ACME database in using Database Wizard

If your screen resolution is 800 × 600, the Database Wizard window may appear too large and out of the screen bounds. Resize it manually and continue.

5. When done, the *DB2 Message* window pops up saying the database was created successfully and asking if you want to run the Configuration Advisor to tune your database. Click No to decline.

6. You will see the ACME icon under the Databases folder. The postinstallation tasks are now complete.

You don't have an option to create a database user who is not also an operating system user. All OS users who have Administrator privileges are also DB2 users with administrative privileges by default.

Uninstalling DB2 UDB

The following instructions are used to uninstall DB2 UDB:

1. Drop database ACME (and any additional databases you've created). Open the Control Center (Start⇨Programs⇨IBM DB2⇨General Administration Tools⇨Control Center), expand the tree view all the way to the Databases folder (Instances⇨DB2⇨Databases), select ACME, and choose Remove from the right-click menu (or from the Selected menu). The Confirmation window appears. Leave the Remove checkbox checked and click OK. Repeat for any other databases you might have.
2. Close the Control Center window and any other DB2-related programs you might have opened.
3. Go to My Computer⇨Control Panel⇨Add/Remove Programs.
4. Find DB2 Personal Edition and click the Remove button. Click Yes on the Confirmation window.
5. The INFORMATION window might appear asking if you want to terminate running the DB2 processes. Answer Yes to continue.
6. You might still need to remove some directories manually (`C:\Program Files\IBM\SQLLIB; C:\DB2; C:\DB2LOG`, assuming default locations).

Starting and stopping DB2 UDB

DB2 will automatically start on startup if you accepted the *Configure DB2 instances* screen defaults during the installation process. Otherwise, open the Control Center (Start⇨Programs⇨IBM DB2⇨General Administration Tools⇨Control Center); expand the tree view all the way to the DB2 folder, right-click on the DB2, and select Start. To stop the instance, repeat the same procedure but select Stop option instead.

You can also stop the database manager instance using the `db2start` and `db2stop` commands from the command line.

For DB2 UDB 8.1 installation instructions on different platforms (Linux, Solaris, etc.) go to `www-3.ibm.com/software/data/db2/udb`. The trial DB2 downloads are also available from that Web site.

Installing Microsoft SQL Server 2000

The installation instructions for MS SQL Server 2000 follow.

Prerequisites for the MS SQL Server 2000 Evaluation Edition

SQL Server is native to Windows and, as such, it is highly optimized to work with it. Before you embark on installing MS SQL Server 2000 check your system for software and hardware requirements.

Minimum system requirements

Table D-7 lists the minimum system requirements for the MS SQL Server 2000 Evaluation Edition.

Table D-7
Requirements for MS SQL Server Installation on Windows 2000

Processor (CPU)	Intel Pentium 166MHz or higher
Operating system	Windows XP Professional Windows XP Home Edition Windows 2000 Professional Windows NT 4.0 (SP5 or later) For MS SQL Server 2000 Personal Edition: Windows 98 Windows Millennium Edition (Me)
Memory (RAM)	64 MB (128 MB recommended)
Hard disk	250 MB for typical installation
Web browser	Internet Explorer 5.0 or higher (usually included with any Windows edition)

If you are using Windows 95, you only can install client connectivity software (that is, a client to connect to a server installed somewhere on the network).

Installing on Windows NT/2000/Me/XP

The installation instructions for these flavors of Windows are essentially the same, assuming your choice is Evaluation Edition of Microsoft SQL Server 2000.

Installation instructions

Perform the following steps to install MS SQL Server 2000 on your machine:

1. Insert the Microsoft SQL Server 2000 Evaluation Edition CD into your CD-ROM drive. (These instructions assume that you obtained an evaluation CD from Microsoft.) The installation will start automatically if your computer supports the autorun feature; if it does not, find your CD-ROM from Windows Explorer and double-click on `autorun.exe`. Alternatively, use the Add/Remove Program utility from your Control Panel. Select *SQL Server 2000 Components* menu option

2. The next screen gives you three options:

   - Install Database Server
   - Install Analysis Services
   - Install English Query

   Select the Install Database Server option.

3. The Installation Wizard will guide you through the process. You can go back and forth to amend your choices — until you click the Finish button. SQL Server 2000 can be installed either locally or on a remote machine, as shown in Figure D-20. For the purposes of this book we recommend that you use the Local Computer installation.

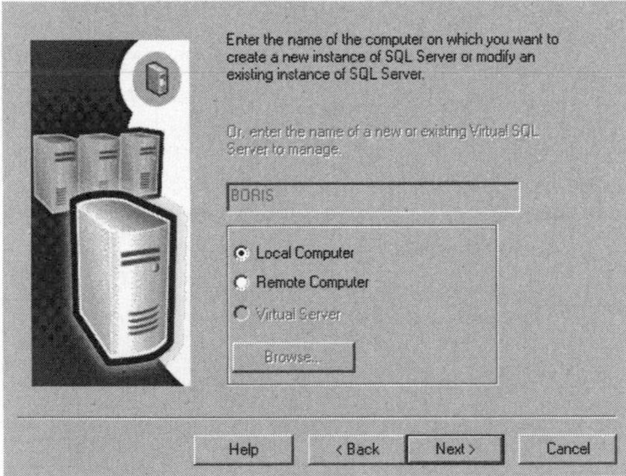

Figure D-20: This MS SQL 2000 installation window allows you to choose the destination computer name.

The installation program detects any previous instances of SQL Server running on your machine and gives you appropriate install and/or upgrade options.

We assume that you're creating a new instance of SQL Server; if so, select the default option shown in Figure D-21. Click Next to continue.

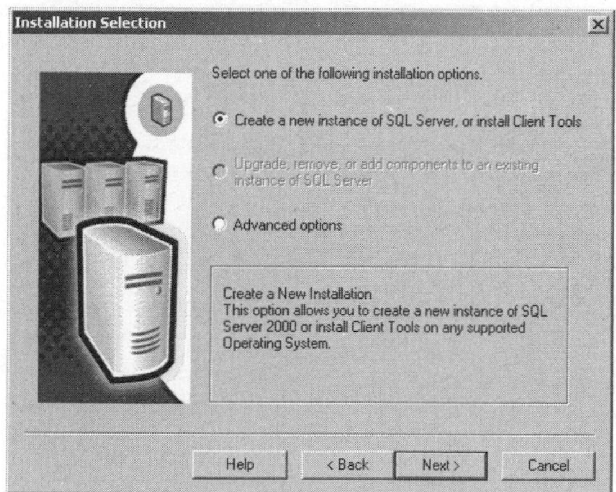

Figure D-21: MS SQL 2000 Installation Selection window

4. The next screen prompts you for your name and the name of your company; fill in the appropriate information (or leave it blank). Click Next to continue to the *License Agreement* screen.
5. Before you can proceed, you need to agree to the terms of the license agreement that comes with your copy of SQL Server 2000.
6. Select installation options as shown in Figure D-22. Click Next.

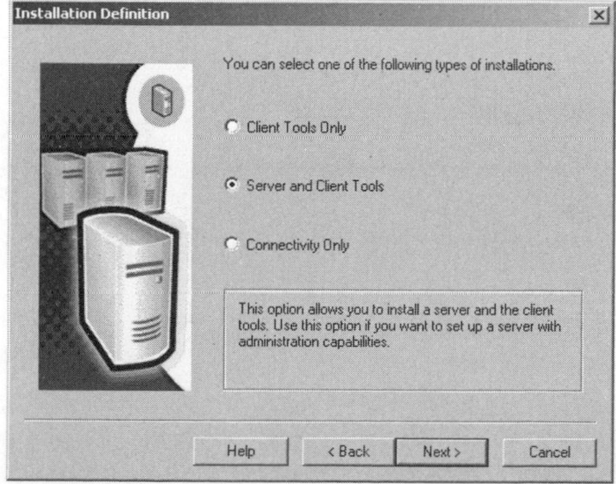

Figure D-22: MS SQL 2000 Installation Definition screen

7. Leave Default checked as you are performing a default installation. We recommend that you do not install *Named* installation as it could complicate configuration and startup tasks. Click Next to proceed.

8. For the purposes of this book we recommend sticking with the Typical setup type. You also may wish to change the physical location of the program and database files by clicking the Browse button. Click Next. See Figure D-23.

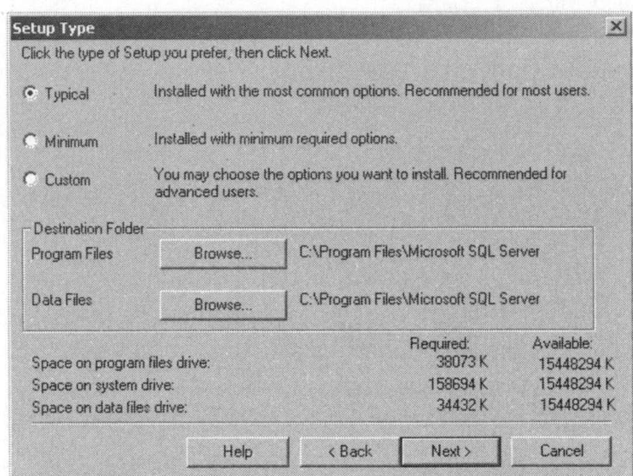

Figure D-23: MS SQL 2000 Setup Type screen

9. You need to specify Services Accounts (see Figure D-24). You can start each service on a different account (for fine-tuning access privileges). We recommend selecting the same account for each service as well as auto-start for the SQL Server. By doing so, you will have SQL Server and SQL Server Agent started each time you start up your computer. Uncheck it if you wish to start SQL Server manually. Choose the Use a Domain User account radio button and use your OS login name and password (Windows 98 would not have this requirement). Click Next.

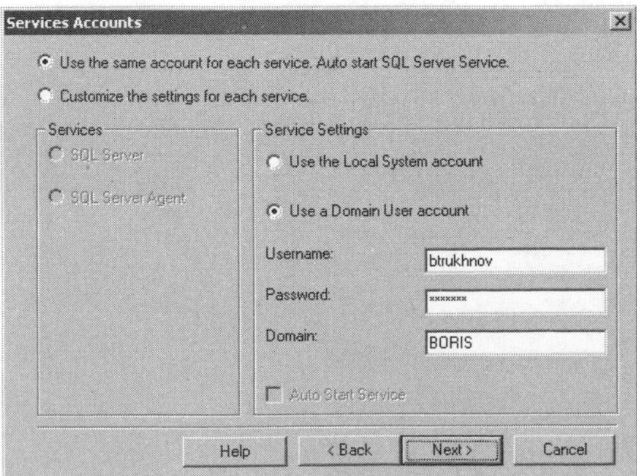

Figure D-24: MS SQL 2000 Services Accounts screen

10. Specify the authentication mode for SQL Server as shown in Figure D-25. Choosing Windows Authentication Mode makes your on-line SQL Server databases accessible as soon as you log on to your account with your Windows NT/XP/2000 login; Mixed Mode requires you to supply a user ID and password to connect to SQL Server after you log on. Select Mixed Mode (for the purposes of this book as we intend on using userID/Password), specify a password, and click Next.

The password you specify on this screen is for user `sa`; you will need it when installing the ACME database (see Appendix F).

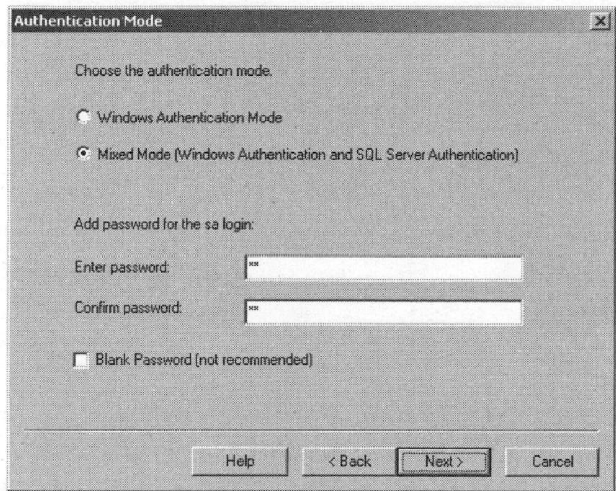

Figure D-25: MS SQL 2000 Authentication Mode screen

11. The setup process has collected enough information to start the installation. Click Next to finish the installation.

You might see additional screens prompting you to choose licensing mode, collation order, network protocols, and so on. We recommend accepting defaults unless you have valid reasons for doing otherwise.

Assuming that all the steps of the installation routine have completed successfully, after reboot and logging on you should see a small icon (a computer tower and a small encircled green triangle) in your system tray (usually found in the lower right-hand corner of the Windows desktop). This means that MS SQL Server has been installed and started successfully. Now you can connect to it and run the SQL scripts provided with this book to install the ACME database and populate it with data; please refer to Appendix E.

Postinstallation tasks

Usually you do not need to do anything additional to run MS SQL Server on your machine after the install. However, if you selected the option not to start SQL Server services at system startup, you need to know how to do it manually. Microsoft provides an SQL Server Service Manager utility through which you can start, stop, or pause any SQL Server-related service (see Figure D-26).

Figure D-26: MS SQL 2000 Server Service Manager

You could access the Service Manager from Start⇨Programs⇨Microsoft SQL Server menu, or from the system tray icon (usually found at the lower right corner of the Windows taskbar). Make sure that the SQL Server Service Manager is running before attempting to execute any of the SQL examples from the book — either through the command line or through the Query Analyzer interface; otherwise you will get the "SQL Server does not exist or access denied" error.

MS SQL Server Administration is beyond the scope of this book, but for the most common scenarios, you do not need to know much about the RDBMS administration.

Uninstalling MS SQL Server 2000

You have two options for uninstalling MS SQL Server:

- ✦ Re-run the initial setup program and choose the Uninstall option.
- ✦ Add/Remove Programs utility from your computer's Control Panel.

To uninstall MS SQL Server 2000 using the setup program perform the following steps:

1. Start SQL Server Installation.
2. On the first screen, select the option SQL Server Components.
3. On the second screen, select the option Install Database Server.

4. Click Next on the *Welcome* screen.
5. The Computer Name screen prompts you to select installation on Local or Remote computer; if you followed our installation instructions, then your choice will be Local.
6. Select the option "Upgrade, remove, or add components to an existing instance of SQL Server."
7. Select the option "Uninstall your existing installation."
8. Click the Finish button on the final dialog box to complete the process.

The second option does not differ from any other program removal. If you installed several named instances of MS SQL Server, you must remove each instance separately.

Note

Some directories and files created during operation of the SQL Server on your computer may remain, and will require manual removal; these are found under the folder you've installed your SQL Server into: \Microsoft SQL Server\80 or \Microsoft SQL Server\MSSQL.

In January 2003, the "Slammer" worm attacked a vulnerability in MS SQL Server 2000. If you have a copy of MS SQL Server 2000 Evaluation Edition, you should verify that it is a recent version that is not vulnerable to "Slammer." Additionally, Microsoft recommends that you should not run the trial version in a production environment and it should be kept separate from your production network. The SQL Server 2000 Evaluation Edition installation coverage in this appendix was written based on a version prior to the "Slammer" worm and it is possible that future evaluation edition versions will have installation procedures that vary from the steps described here. For non-evaluation MS SQL Server 2000 installations, you should verify that you have updated your servers with SQL Server 2000 Service Pack 2 and update MS02-061 or with SQL Server 2000 Service Pack 3.

✦ ✦ ✦

APPENDIX E

Accessing RDBMS

Believe it or not, the graphical user interface (GUI) so prevalent on today's computers did not always exist; it evolved along with the use of the cathode-ray tube (CRT) monitors and really took off with the advent of the pointing device, popularly known as the mouse. Consequently, every database capable of interactive access has, as a legacy of the non-GUI days, some sort of command-line interface that allows users to submit a request (usually an SQL query), and eventually receive some response — be it requested data or an error message from the RDBMS.

Using ORACLE 9*i* Utilities to Access RDBMS

Oracle provides three utilities for communicating with its RDBMS: SQL*Plus, SQL*Plus Worksheet, and iSQL*Plus. Many third-party products can work with Oracle 9*i* Database, the most popular being TOAD by Quest Software Ltd. (`www.quest.com`).

SQL*Plus

SQL*Plus is an interactive query tool that provides a mechanism to submit SQL commands to Oracle RDBMS for execution, retrieving results, performing database administration, and more. All Oracle examples in this book are produced using the Oracle SQL*Plus interface, and this appendix provides the basic knowledge you need to access an Oracle database and run either interactive commands or script files against it. SQL*Plus also has the advantage of being platform-independent — exactly the same commands can be used on Windows, Sun Solaris, Linux, or VAX VMS.

You have two choices starting SQL*Plus application: from MS-DOS (or Unix, etc.) command prompt or from Windows Start menu; Oracle 9*i* also gives you iSQL*Plus — a Web browser–based interface to SQL*Plus that allows you to query database and receive results over the Internet. This section explains how to use SQL*Plus on a local computer, assuming that you followed the Oracle 9*i* installation instructions in Appendix D. At the command-line prompt, type `sqlplus /nolog;` and press Enter; the screen should look similar to what you see in Figure E-1.

```
Command Prompt - sqlplus /nolog
Microsoft Windows 2000 [Version 5.00.2195]
(C) Copyright 1985-2000 Microsoft Corp.

C:\>sqlplus /nolog

SQL*Plus: Release 9.2.0.1.0 - Production on Tue Aug 28 21:43:16 2001

Copyright (c) 1982, 2002, Oracle Corporation.  All rights reserved.

SQL> _
```

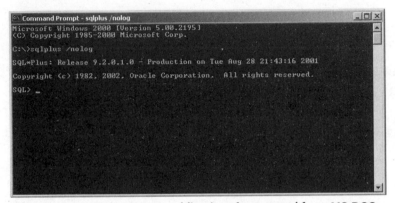

Figure E-1: SQL*Plus command-line interface started from MS-DOS

Now you need to connect to your database. The syntax for the `connect` command is `connect` <*username*>/<*password*>[@<database_sid>]. For example, assuming you already ran scripts from the book's CD-ROM that create user `ACME`, type `connect acme/acme`. If everything went as it was supposed to, you will get the SQL prompt and can start typing and executing SQL statements. To actually send an SQL statement to Oracle you need to add a semicolon at the end of the query and press Enter. If you press the Enter key without including the semicolon, SQL*Plus will continue on the new line; each line will be prefixed with a sequence number. See Figure E-2.

```
Command Prompt - sqlplus /nolog
SQL> select cust_id_n, cust_name_s
  2  from customer
  3  where cust_id_n = 152;

 CUST_ID_N CUST_NAME_S
---------- --------------------------------------------------
       152 WILE BESS COMPANY

SQL> _
```

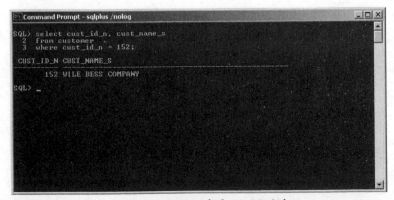

Figure E-2: Executing SQL commands from SQL*Plus

Tip

You can use a slash (/) instead of a semicolon, but this is mainly used in PL/SQL and for batch processing.

The results will be displayed in the same window. You can set a number of parameters to customize the look and feel of the SQL*Plus interface. Please refer to the SQL*Plus manual for more details.

To load a script file use the syntax `@["][<path>]<file_name>["]`, for example

```
SQL> @"C:\sqlbib\oracle_acme\load.sql"
```

or

```
SQL> @load.sql
```

The first example assumes the file `load.sql` is not in the current directory, so you must specify a fully qualified path to the file. Double quotes are optional and needed only when directory names in your path contain blank spaces. The second example loads the file from the current directory.

Oracle does not make an assumption that the script from a file has to be run immediately; because of that, if your script does not end with a semicolon it would not run until you add it and press Enter.

Tip

To access help from within SQL*Plus, type `help <topic>` (providing Help is installed).

You can edit your SQL statements using either SQL*Plus commands or the operating system default editor (usually Notepad for Windows OS and `vi` on Unix). To edit a query from SQL*Plus, type `edit` or `ed` at the SQL*Plus prompt. This brings up the default editor with your last SQL statement. Edit, save, and exit; you would see your modified statement in the SQL*Plus window. Type semicolon or slash to execute.

Note

The modified text will be stored in the buffer file afiedt.buf located in the same directory where you've started your SQL*Plus session.

There are about 50 SQL*Plus commands you can use; refer to Oracle documentation should you require more information on this interface. In Table E-1 we've included only the most commonly used commands you'll need in order to feel comfortable with SQL*Plus.

Note

The commands in Table E-1 are not to be considered as a part of SQL; Oracle calls them SQL*Plus commands.

Table E-1
Most Commonly Used SQL*Plus Commands

SQL*PLUS COMMAND	DESCRIPTION	EXAMPLE
@ (at sign)	Runs the SQL statements in the specified script. The script can be called from the local file system or from a Web server.	`SQL> @load_data_ora.dat`
@@ (double at sign)	Similar to @; often used to call a script from another script (nested scripts).	`@@load_data_ora.dat`
/ (slash)	Executes the contents of the SQL buffer.	`SQL> /` `<query results>`
`CLEAR SCREEN`	Clears your monitor screen.	`SQL> clear screen`
`CONN[ECT]`	Connects a specified Oracle user.	`SQL> connect acme/acme`
`DEF[INE]`	Specifies a user variable.	`SQL> define cust_id = 152`
`DESC[RIBE]`	Lists the column definition for the specified object (table, view, etc.).	`SQL> desc address`
`DISC[ONNECT]`	Disconnects current user after committing pending changes.	`SQL> disc`
`ED[IT]`	Invokes the default OS editor.	`SQL> ed create_acme.sql`
`EXIT`	Exits SQL*Plus. All changes will be committed.	`SQL> exit`
`GET`	Loads an OS file into the SQL buffer (but does not execute).	`SQL> get create_acme.sql`
`HELP`	Accesses SQL*Plus help.	`SQL> help get`
`HOST`	Executes a host OS command without leaving SQL*Plus.	`SQL> host dir`
`PASSW[ORD]`	Allows to change user's password.	`SQL> passw acme`
`QUIT`	Same as `EXIT`.	`SQL> exit`
`R[UN]`	Lists and executes the contents of the SQL buffer.	`SQL> run create_acme.sql`
`SAV[E]`	Saves the contents of the SQL buffer in a host OS file.	`SQL> save tmp.out`

SQL*PLUS COMMAND	DESCRIPTION	EXAMPLE
SPOOL	Stores query result in an OS file.	SQL> spool tmp.out SQL> select * from status; SQL> spool off
SET	Sets system variables for current session (automatic commit, the line and page size, etc.).	SQL> set autocommit on SQL> set linesize 1000 SQL> set pagesize 300 SQL> set pause on
START	Same as @.	SQL> start create_acme.sql
UNDEFINE	Deletes a user variable (previously created with the DEFINE command).	SQL> undefine cust_id
WHENEVER SQLERROR	Stops execution of a script and exits SQL*Plus if an SQL statement returns an error.	SQL> whenever sqlerror continue
WHENEVER OSERROR	Stops execution of a script and exits SQL*Plus if an operating system error occurs (i.e., connection to the databases lost).	SQL> whenever oserror exit

SQL*Plus commands are case insensitive.

SQL*Plus Worksheet utility

Oracle provides this simple graphical user interface to execute SQL and SQL*Plus commands, Windows style. To start SQL*Plus Worksheet type `oemapp worksheet` at your command-line prompt (OS-independent). The Oracle Enterprise Manager Login screen appears asking for Username, Password, and, optionally, Service Name. Supply the information and click OK. The SQL*Plus Worksheet window opens. It gives you a somewhat easier way to communicate with the RDBMS. Figure E-3 shows the SQL*Plus Worksheet window.

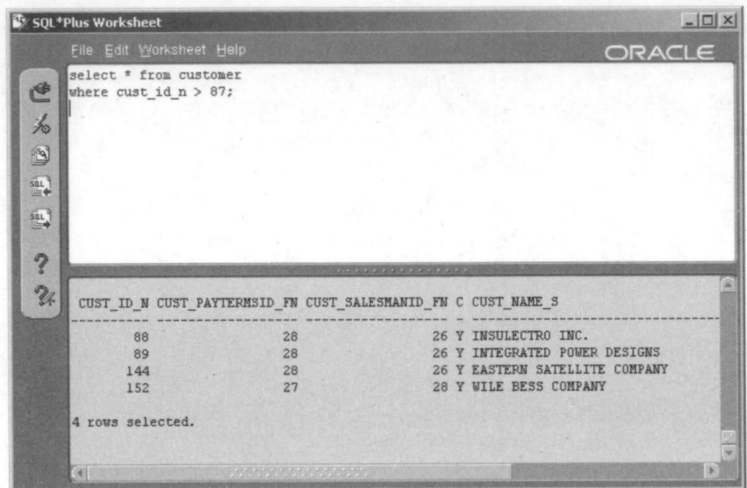

Figure E-3: SQL*Plus Worksheet window

You can use all SQL*Plus commands from Table E-1 (and more) when using SQL*Plus Worksheet.

iSQL*Plus utility

iSQL*Plus is a Web browser–based interface to Oracle 9*i* that can be considered a component of SQL*Plus. It enables you to perform the same tasks as you would through the command-line version of SQL*Plus, but using a Web browser instead of a command line.

You will have to configure Oracle HTTP Server to use iSQL*Plus. The configuration of the server is beyond the scope of this book.

Using IBM DB2 UDB 8.1 Command-Line Processor (CLP)

CLP is IBM DB2 command-line utility that allows you to execute SQL statements and invoke online help. This appendix provides the basic commands and options you can use with CLP to run either interactive commands or scripts against your DB2 database. Akin to Oracle's SQL*Plus, CLP is platform-independent. You can use it in interactive input mode, command mode, or batch mode.

Interactive mode

To enter the interactive mode, open the Command Line Processor window (Start⇨Programs⇨IBM DB2⇨Command Line Tools⇨Command Line Processor):

```
(c) Copyright IBM Corporation 1993,2002
Command Line Processor for DB2 SDK 8.1.0

...
For general help, type: ?.
...
db2 =>
```

For the most commonly used options, see Table E-2.

Command mode

Open the Command Line Processor window (Start⇨Programs⇨IBM DB2⇨Command Line Tools⇨Command Window). That initializes environment variables for you, so you can type the CLP commands prefixed with db2, for example:

```
C:\Program Files\IBM\SQLLIB\BIN> db2 connect to acme

 Database Connection Information

 Database server        = DB2/NT 8.1.0
 SQL authorization ID   = BORIS
 Local database alias   = ACME

C:\Program Files\IBM\SQLLIB\BIN> db2 select * from status

STATUS_ID_N STATUS_CODE_S STATUS_DESC_S
----------- ------------- ------------------------------
          2 20            COMPLETE
          6 60            SHIPPED
          8 70            INVOICED
          9 80            CANCELLED
  4 record(s) selected.
```

Batch mode

Batch mode allows you to execute SQL statements stored in the operating system's files. It is invoked with -f option (see Table E-2). For example,

```
C:\Program Files\IBM\SQLLIB\BIN> db2 -f C:\myfiles\query.sql
```

executes the contents of file query.sql in the myfiles directory of the C:\ drive (presuming it does exist).

Table E-2
Common CLP Options

Option	*Explanation*
`-c`	Automatically commits SQL statements. This option is turned on by default; i.e., all your statements will be automatically committed unless you start your session with `+c` option (`db2 +c`).
`-f <filename>`	Reads command input from file *<filename>*. You have to specify the full path to your file unless it is in the current directory: `db2 -f /home/btrukhnov/db2/queries/my_query.sql`
`-l <filename>`	Creates a log of commands. For example: `db2 -f my_query.sql -l logfiles/my_query.log`
`-r <filename>`	Logs the command output to file *<filename>*.
`-s`	Stops execution on error; usually used with `-t` option, when script execution termination is desirable if a statement fails.
`-t`	Uses semicolon as the statement termination character.
`-v`	Echoes command text to standard output.
`-w`	Displays SQL statement warning messages.
`-z <filename>`	Redirects all output to file *<filename>*.

Command Line Processor has many commands; most of them are for database administration and not relevant to this book. Table E-3 lists some CLP commands that you may find useful.

Table E-3
Common CLP commands

CLP command	*Description*	*Example*
`!`	Invokes an operating system command.	db2=> !dir
`?`	Invokes online help.	db2=> ? db2=> ? echo
`DESCRIBE`	Describes table columns or indexes for a table.	db2 describe table address db2 describe indexes for table customer
`ECHO`	Writes to standard output.	db2 echo "Enter your query"

CLP command	Description	Example
GET CONNECTION STATE	Displays the state of the current connection.	db2 get connection state
HELP	Invokes the Information Center.	db2 help
LIST ACTIVE DATABASES	Displays the list of databases ready for connection.	db2 list active databases
QUIT	Exits CLP interactive input mode.	db2=> quit C:\
TERMINATE	Similar to QUIT, but terminates all background processes and frees memory.	db2=> terminate

Using Microsoft SQL Server Utilities to Access Database

Microsoft SQL Server 2000 provides two command-line utilities — ISQL and OSQL — to access databases. In addition, Microsoft SQL Server 2000 includes Microsoft Query Analyzer — a graphical user interface to execute ad hoc queries and scripts and analyze output.

Using Microsoft SQL Server command line interface

ISQL is a legacy application maintained for backward compatibility. It uses DBLIB (a native call level interface [CLI] for MS SQL Server) and does not support all new features of MS SQL Server 2000. When using it, a user is limited to MS SQL Server 6.5 capabilities only — for example, it has no support for Unicode scripts. The only advantage of using it is that it might offer a slightly faster performance in comparison to ODBC-based OSQL.

OSQL was introduced for the first time with MS SQL Server 7.0. It uses an Open Database Connectivity (ODBC) API to connect to the RDBMS (see Chapter 16 for more information on SQL API), and it uses default ODBC settings as defined in the SQL2 standard. It has full support for all the new features of MS SQL Server 2000 and is recommended for use whenever there is no need to be bound by the restrictions of earlier versions of SQL Server. Here we are giving only the basics to help you feel comfortable while trying on examples from this book; for the full list of available options, refer to MS SQL Server 2000 documentation. (Books Online are included with its installation.)

To start OSQL from an MS-DOS prompt, type the following command:

```
C:\> osql /U sa /P <pasword>
```

This command opens connection to the default database (usually Master) for user (/U) sa identified by password (/P). If you installed MS SQL Server 2000 with all defaults as described in Appendix D, then your user ID will be sa, and your password will be whatever you've specified during the installation, and they would not be case sensitive.

To connect to a specific database, you would need to supply an additional parameter — the database name. For example

```
C:\> osql /d acme /U acme /P acme
```

This example assumes existence of database acme in your MS SQL Server installation, as well as that of user acme with password acme.

If you missed one of the required parameters (like /P), you will be prompted for it. If none of the parameters are specified, OSQL checks environmental variables on your computer OSQLUSER=(user) and OSQLSERVER=(server); if these are undefined, then the workstation name is used; it also will attempt to use Windows Authentication Mode to log onto SQL Server; thus, it will use your Windows account under which the OSQL utility is running.

Once a connection is established, your screen would look like that on Figure E-4. Now you can type in your SQL statements as they are given in this book, or you could load a script file — that is, a file that contains prepared SQL statements.

To run the SQL statement — or multiple statements — (i.e., to submit them to MS SQL Server for execution) you'd need to type GO at the end of the last statement, and press Enter; if you enter the scripts via file then the GO is assumed and the statements in the file are executed immediately.

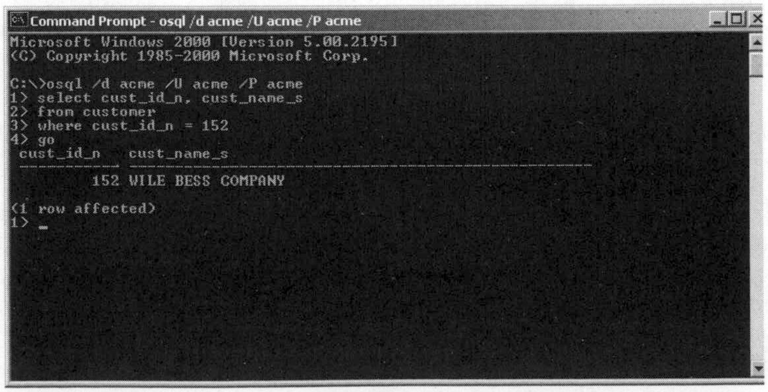

```
Command Prompt - osql /d acme /U acme /P acme
Microsoft Windows 2000 [Version 5.00.2195]
(C) Copyright 1985-2000 Microsoft Corp.

C:\>osql /d acme /U acme /P acme
1> select cust_id_n, cust_name_s
2> from customer
3> where cust_id_n = 152
4> go
 cust_id_n   cust_name_s
 ----------- --------------------------------------------------
         152 WILE BESS COMPANY

(1 row affected)
1> _
```

Figure E-4: OSQL session window

To run scripts stored in a file, you must specify the file name as well as a fully qualified path to that file if it is located in the directory other than the current one. Assuming that the file is in the current directory, the syntax might look like this:

```
C:\>osql /d acme /U acme /P acme /i create_tables.sql
```

The GO statement to actually run the query is a default requirement for MS SQL Server; it is possible to specify a different command terminator. For example, if you wish to have a semicolon in place of the GO (syntax a la Oracle), then add one more parameter when starting OSQL:

```
C:\>osql /d ACME /U acme /P acme /c ;
```

GO, however, serves more than one purpose. For example, if you need to run the same SQL statement 10 times, then you can type GO 10 as the last statement of your script or query.

The results of the executed query are printed at the end of execution (or an error message is displayed). There is a limit of 1,000 characters per line, and results that exceed this limit would be split across multiple lines.

The output could be redirected to a file instead of standard screen. You need to specify that along with the name of the file (which will be created in the current directory unless some other directory is specified):

```
C:\>osql /d acme /U acme /P acme /i create_tables.sql /o output.log
```

In addition to SQL statements (rather Transact-SQL statements) you could use the OSQL commands in Table E-4 to control the utility behavior.

Table E-4
Basic OSQL Commands

Command	*Description*
!! (double exclamation mark)	Executes MS-DOS command.
Ctrl-C (key combination)	Ends query without exiting to MS-DOS.
ED	Invokes default built-in editor.
EXIT	Exits the OSQL utility into MS-DOS.
GO	Executes cached SQL statements.
QUIT	Same as EXIT.
RESET	Clears all statements that are currently displayed in the window.

The default editor is `EDIT` — a rather old cumbersome MS-DOS editor program. If you intend using it make sure you know how to control it with your keyboard; press Alt to access the menu bar and then use the arrow keys to navigate it. To change the default editor to, say, Notepad, you would need to execute `SET EDITOR = notepad` command from the MS-DOS command prompt. To edit an SQL query type `ED` (or `EDIT`) while connected to the server; your editor would be brought up, and you may type in your query or edit the one you've just entered at the SQL prompt. Once you've closed the editor (do not forget to save your query first!) the edited text will appear at the SQL prompt; type `GO` and press Enter to execute it.

To get full list of OSQL commands, just type `osql /?` at the MS-DOS prompt.

Using Microsoft Query Analyzer to execute queries

Windows is a graphical environment and MS SQL Server comes with a full-featured GUI utility — MS Query Analyzer. You can invoke this utility from MS SQL Server Enterprise Manager Console, from the Start⇨Programs⇨Microsoft SQL Server⇨Query Analyzer menu option, or from the command line by its name ISQLW. It is the most commonly used query interface to Microsoft SQL Server.

While it is possible to run ISQLW without the user interface by specifying connect information and output/input files, there is no reason for doing this if you use it interactively.

From the MS-DOS command line type `isqlw`. For example:

```
C:\>isqlw
```

This will bring up the dialog box shown in Figure E-5.

If you set up your SQL Server to use Windows Authentication, press the OK button — you will be logged in with your Windows login/password credentials; otherwise select SQL Server Authentication and supply User ID and Password to connect.

Once connected, you can type in and execute any query, load script file, and so on. Of course, Query Analyzer provides a much richer set of tools than a humble command-line interface, but the use of these tools would be a topic for a Microsoft SQL Server book. All we need to know for the purpose of running and executing our sample queries is how to load and execute them, and — hopefully — to see the results.

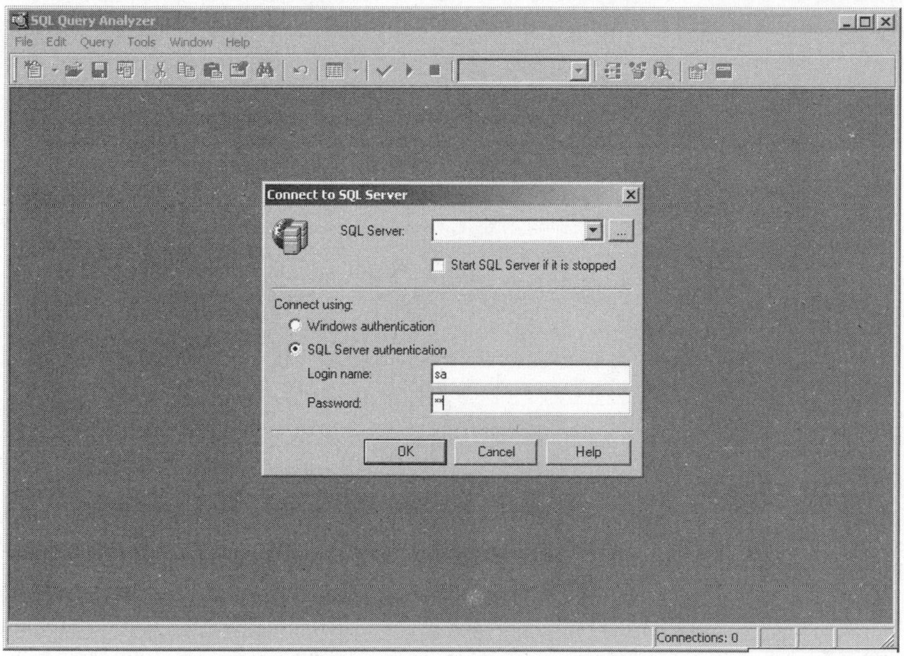

Figure E-5: MS SQL Server Query Analyzer dialog box

An SQL query is always executed in the context of some database. If your query brings back an error, complaining about Invalid Object, chances are that you executed the query against wrong database. Make sure that you have selected ACME as the database context in the drop-down list (it has Master by default). To run interactive queries you may just type SQL statement in the query pane; there is no need to add the GO statement at the end — press F5 (or click on the green triangle on the toolbar). The results of the query (or an error message — in case the query was unsuccessful) will be displayed at the lower part of the split pane (see Figure E-6).

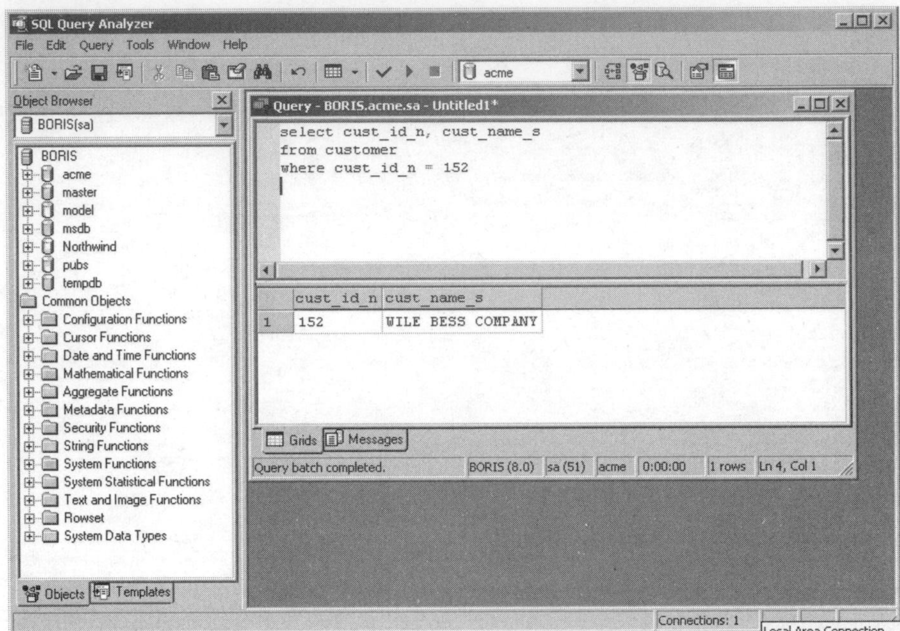

Figure E-6: Executing SQL commands using Query Analyzer

Loading and running SQL script file is very intuitive. Click the Load Script button on the toolbar of the Query Analyzer (or press Ctrl-Shift-P); the standard dialog box appears to allow you to select a file very much in the same way as you would open any other file in Windows OS. Once the SQL statements from the file are loaded into the query pane, you may run them just as any other query—by pressing F5 key on the keyboard or Run button (the triangle to the right of the checkmark) on the toolbar.

✦ ✦ ✦

Installing the ACME Database

This appendix explains how to install the sample ACME database on the RDBMS of your choice. Refer to the section that corresponds to the database platform you've created.

Installing the ACME Sample Database on Oracle 9*i* (Windows) Using SQL*Plus

Following are instructions on how to install ACME sample database on Oracle 9*i* (Windows) using the SQL*Plus utility (explained in Appendix E).

1. If the Oracle services are not started, start them as described in Appendix D.
2. Copy the `D:\sqlbib\oracle_acme` (where *D* is the letter of your CD-ROM drive) directory from the CD-ROM that comes with your book to the `C:\` directory of your computer.
3. Start SQL*Plus from the command line by typing:

   ```
   C:\> sqlplus /nolog
   ```

4. If you want to create a log file, use the `spool` command (described in Appendix E). For example, if you want the resulting log file `load.log` to be created in the same directory, the other files you need are:

   ```
   SQL> spool C:\sqlbib\oracle_acme\load.log
   ```

5. Run script `C:\sqlbib\oracle_acme\load.sql`:

   ```
   SQL> @C:\sqlbib\oracle_acme\load.sql
   ```

6. This script creates the Oracle ACME database. Stop spooling (if started) by issuing:

```
SQL> spool off
```

7. Type `quit` to exit SQL*Plus.

Script `load.sql` runs two other scripts, `create_acme_ora.sql` and `load_data_ora.dat`. The first one creates RDBMS objects (tables, indexes, constraints, views, and so on) and the second script populates ACME tables with data. You may want to run the first script by itself before trying the examples from Chapter 6. You can run `load.sql` and `create_acme_ora.sql` as many times as you want to create a loaded or empty ACME database, correspondingly.

When you run your script for the first time, you may see ORA-00942 errors (table or view does not exist). That is not a problem; the script is trying to drop tables that do not yet exist.

The most common errors you may see in your log file are in Table F-1.

Table F-1
Common Errors from Running Oracle Scripts

Error	*Explanation*	*Solution*
`ORA-12560: TNS: protocol adapter error`	Oracle is not started.	Start Oracle and try running your scripts again.
`ORA-12154: TNS: could not resolve service name`	You supplied an incorrect service name.	You don't need to supply a service name, just user ID and password.
`ORA-01031: insufficient privileges`	You are not a member of `ORA_DBA` OS group.	Either log in as a user who is a member of the `ORA_DBA` group or add current user to the `ORA_DBA` group.
`ORA-01033: Oracle initialization or shutdown in progress`	Oracle is being started.	Wait and try again.

Installing the ACME Database on Oracle 9*i* (Unix/Linux) Using SQL*Plus

Following are instructions on how to install ACME sample database on Oracle 9*i* (Unix/Linux) using the SQL*Plus utility (explained in Appendix E).

1. Start your Oracle instance. Make sure that your session's ORACLE_HOME environment variable points to the correct instance:

```
# echo $ORACLE_SID
ACME
#
```

The Unix/Linux Environment Variables required to run sqlplus utility are listed in Table D-3 and Table D-5 of Appendix D.

2. Insert the book's CD-ROM into your CD-ROM drive. Mount the CD-ROM and copy the /sqlbib/oracle_acme directory from the CD to your home directory.
3. Start SQL*Plus from your home directory by typing:

```
# sqlplus /nolog
```

4. If you want to create the log file, use the spool command (described in Appendix E). For example, if you want the resulting log file load.log to be created in the same directory as your other files, type:

```
SQL> spool sqlbib/oracle_acme/load.log
```

5. Run the script sqlbib/oracle_acme/load.sql:

```
SQL> @sqlbib/oracle_acme/load.sql
```

6. This script creates your Oracle ACME database. Stop spooling (if started) by issuing

```
SQL> spool off
```

7. Type quit to exit SQL*Plus.

Script load.sql runs two other scripts, create_acme_ora.sql and load_data_ora.dat. The first one creates RDBMS objects (tables, indexes, constraints, views, and so on) and the second script populates ACME tables with data. You may want to run the first script by itself before trying the examples from Chapter 6. You can run load.sql and create_acme_ora.sql as many times as you want to create a loaded or empty ACME database, correspondingly.

Installing the ACME Database on DB2 UDB 8.1 (Windows) Using CLP

Following are instructions on how to install ACME sample database on DB2 UDB 8.1 (Windows) using the CLP utility (explained in Appendix E).

1. Copy the D:\sqlbib\db2_acme (where *D* is the letter of your CD-ROM drive) directory from the CD-ROM that comes with your book to the C:\ directory of your computer.
2. Make sure you created the ACME database as described in the *Postinstallation tasks* section of Appendix D, and that your database has been started.

3. Open the DB2 UDB Command window (Start➪Programs➪IBM DB2➪Command Line Tools➪Command Window).

4. Issue the two following commands at the prompt (if you want your log files in `C:\sqlbib\db2_acme\`):

```
C:\Program Files\IBM\SQLLIB\BIN> db2 -tvf
C:\sqlbib\db2_acme\create_acme_db2.sql -z
C:\sqlbib\db2_acme\create_acme_db2.log

C:\Program Files\IBM\SQLLIB\BIN> db2 -tvf
C:\sqlbib\db2_acme\load_data_db2.dat -z
C:\sqlbib\db2_acme\load_data_db2.log
```

Each of these is actually one command, although the physical dimensions of the printed book dictate that they be presented in this way.

Script `create_acme_ora.sql` creates RDBMS objects (tables, indexes, constraints, views, and so on) and script `load_data_ora.dat` populates ACME tables with data. You may want to run the first script by itself before trying the examples from Chapter 6. You can run `create_acme_ora.sql` as many times as you want to create empty ACME database.

When you run your scripts for the first time, you may see some messages at the beginning of your log file saying something like: `<TABLE_NAME> IS UNDEFINED NAME`. The message is not an error but rather a warning; your tables have not been created yet, so ignore it.

Some common errors from running DB2 scripts are shown in Table F-2.

Table F-2
Common Errors from Running DB2 Scripts

Error	*Explanation*	*Solution*
`DB21061E Command line environment not initialized.`	You are trying to execute db2 commands from a command line prompt rather than from the DB2 Command Window.	Start the DB2 Command Window and try again.

Error	*Explanation*	*Solution*
`SQL0900N The application state is in error. A database connection does not exist. SQLSTATE=08003`	You supplied an incorrect service name.	Specify the correct service name.
`SQL1032N No start database manager command was issued. SQLSTATE=57019`	Database services are not started.	Start database services as described in Appendix D.

Installing ACME Database on Microsoft SQL Server 2000 Using OSQL Utility

Following are instructions on how to install ACME sample database on MS SQL Server 2000 using OSQL utility (explained in Appendix E).

1. If your MS SQL Server services are not running, start them as described in Appendix D.
2. Copy the D:`\sqlbib\mssql_acme` (where *D* is the letter of your CD-ROM drive) directory from the CD-ROM that comes with your book to the `C:\` directory of your computer.
3. Issue the following commands:

```
osql /U sa /P sa /I
C:\sqlbib\mssql_acme\create_acme_mssql.sql /o
C:\sqlbib\mssql_acme\create_acme_mssql.log

osql /U sa /P sa /I
C:\sqlbib\mssql_acme\load_data_mssql.dat /o
C:\sqlbib\mssql_acme\load_data_mssql.log
```

Each of these is actually one command, although the physical dimensions of the printed book dictate that they be presented in this way.

This example assumes that during the MS SQL Server installation you specified password '`sa`' for user `sa` (see Appendix D). If a different password and user ID were specified, replace values accordingly. After execution, a log file is created in the specified directory (in this case `C:\sqlbib\mssql_acme`).

Some common errors from running MS SQL Server scripts are shown in Table F-3.

Table F-3
Common Errors from Running MS SQL Server Scripts

Error	*Explanation*	*Solution*
`Login failed for user 'sa'.`	You specified an incorrect password for user `sa`.	Specify the correct password or change it using the MS SQL Server Enterprise Manager.
`[Shared Memory]SQL Server does not exist or access denied.`	MS SQL Server is not running.	Start MS SQL Server (see Appendix D).
`Procedure sp_grantdbaccess, Line 126 User or role 'acme' already exists in the current database.`	Script is trying to create user `acme` that already exists.	No action required, FYI only.

✦ ✦ ✦

SQL Functions

Every RDBMS maintains an ever-expanding list of the SQL functions specific to its own version. Some of the most useful functions were covered in Chapter 10 of this book. This appendix provides a comprehensive list of the functions available for each RDBMS in its current version: Oracle 9*i*, IBM DB2 UDB 8.1, and Microsoft SQL Server 2000.

All the functions are grouped in Tables G-1 through G-24 similarly to the way they are organized in each corresponding vendor's documentation. Oracle 9*i* allows overloading of the functions, meaning that some functions can be used in more than one way depending on the data type and number of arguments; because of that such functions are listed in several categories. IBM rarely provides overloaded functions, and Microsoft stands somewhere between Oracle and IBM in this regard.

Certain functions require appropriate privileges to be run, as well as specific output result holders. We've omitted the arguments of the functions from the tables, because the purpose of the appendix is to show what is available, without going into too much detail. Refer to each vendor's documentation for more detailed syntax and explanations.

Table G-1
Oracle 9*i* SQL Number Functions

Function Name	***Brief Description***
`ABS`	Returns the absolute value of *n*.
`ACOS`	Returns the arc cosine of *n*.
`ASIN`	Returns the arc sine of *n*.
`ATAN`	Returns the arc tangent of *n*.
`ATAN2`	Returns the arc tangent of *n* and *m*.
`BITAND`	Returns an integer.
`CEIL`	Returns the smallest integer greater than or equal to *n*.
`COS`	Returns the cosine of *n*.
`COSH`	Returns the hyperbolic cosine of *n*.
`EXP`	Returns *e* raised to the *n*th power, where `e=2.71828183`.
`FLOOR`	Returns the largest integer equal to or less than *n*.
`LN`	Returns the natural logarithm of *n*, where *n* is greater than 0.
`LOG`	Returns the logarithm, base *m*, of *n*.
`MOD`	Returns the remainder of *m* divided by *n*. Returns *m* if *n* is 0.
`POWER`	Returns *m* raised to the *n*th power.
`SIGN`	If `n<0`, `SIGN` returns –1. If `n=0`, the function returns 0. If `n>0`, `SIGN` returns 1.
`SINH`	Returns the hyperbolic sine of *n*.
`SQRT`	Returns the square root of *n*.
`TAN`	Returns the tangent of *n*.
`TANH`	Returns the hyperbolic tangent of *n*.
`TRUNC`	Returns a value truncated to *m* decimal places. If *m* is omitted, *n* is truncated to 0 places. *m* can be negative to truncate (make zero) *m* digits left of the decimal point.
`WIDTH_BUCKET`	Lets you construct equiwidth histograms, in which the histogram range is divided into intervals that have identical size.

Table G-2
Oracle 9*i* SQL Character Functions

Function Name	*Brief Description*
`CHR`	Returns the character having the binary equivalent to *n*.
`CONCAT`	Returns `char1` concatenated with `char2`.
`INITCAP`	Returns `char`, the first letter in uppercase, all other letters in lowercase.
`LOWER`	Returns `char`, all letters in lowercase.
`LPAD`	Returns `char1`, left-padded to length *n* with the sequence of characters in `char2`; if `char1` is longer than *n*, this function returns the portion of `char1` that fits in *n*.
`LTRIM`	Removes characters from the left of `char`, with all the leftmost characters that appear in `set` removed; `set` defaults to a single blank.
`NLS_INITCAP`	Returns `char`, with the first letter of each word in uppercase, all other letters in lowercase.
`NLS_LOWER`	Returns `char`, with all letters lowercase.
`NLSSORT`	Returns the string of bytes used to sort `char`.
`NLS_UPPER`	Returns `char`, with all letters uppercase.
`REPLACE`	Returns `char` with every occurrence of `search_string` replaced with `replacement_string`.
`RPAD`	Returns `char1`, right-padded to length *n* with `char2` replicated as many times as necessary.
`RTRIM`	Returns `char`, with all rightmost characters that appear in `set` removed.
`SOUNDEX`	Returns a character string containing the phonetic representation of `char`.
`SUBSTR`	Returns a portion of `string`, beginning at a specified character position that is `substring_length` characters long. `SUBSTR` calculates lengths using characters defined by the input character set.
`SUBSTRB`	Same as `STRING`, except `SUBSTRB` uses bytes instead of characters.
`SUBSTRC`	Same as `STRING`, except `SUBSTRC` uses Unicode-complete characters.

Continued

Table G-2 (continued)

Function Name	*Brief Description*
SUBSTR2	Same as STRING, except SUBSTR2 uses UCS2 codepoints.
SUBSTR4	Same as STRING, except SUBSTR4 uses UCS4 codepoints.
TRANSLATE	Returns char with all occurrences of each character in from_string, replaced by its corresponding character in to_string.
TREAT	Returns a declared type of expression.
UPPER	Returns char, with all letters uppercase. char can be any of the data types CHAR, VARCHAR2, NCHAR, NVARCHAR2, CLOB, or NCLOB. The return value is the same data type as char.

Table G-3
Oracle 9*i* SQL Datetime Functions

Function Name	*Brief Description*
ADD_MONTHS	Returns the date *d* plus *n* months.
CURRENT_DATE	Returns the current date and time in the session's time zone, with a value in Gregorian calendar format with the data type DATE.
CURRENT_TIMESTAMP	Returns the current date and time in the session's time zone, with the value of data type TIMESTAMP WITH TIME ZONE.
DBTIMEZONE	Returns the value of the database time zone.
EXTRACT	Returns the value of a specified datetime field from a datetime or interval value expression.
FROM_TZ	Converts a timestamp value in a time zone to a TIMESTAMP WITH TIME ZONE value. time_zone_value is a character string in the format 'TZH:TZM' or a character expression that returns a string in TZR with optional TZD format.
LAST_DAY	Returns the date of the last day of the month that contains this date.
LOCALTIMESTAMP	Returns the current date and time in the session's time zone in a value of the data type TIMESTAMP.
MONTH_BETWEEN	Returns the number of months between dates date1 and date2.

Function Name	*Brief Description*
NEW_TIME	Returns the date and time in time zone zone2 when the date and time in time zone zone1 are the date argument.
NEXT_DAY	Returns the date of the first weekday named by char that is later than the date argument.
NUMTODSINTERVAL	Converts *n* to an INTERVAL DAY TO SECOND literal. *n* can be a number or an expression resolving to a number.
NUMTOYMINTERVAL	Converts *n* to an INTERNAL YEAR TO MONTH literal. *n* can be a number or an expression resolving to a number.
ROUND	Truncates time portion of the date.
SESSIONTIMEZONE	Returns the value of the current session's time zone.
SYS_EXTRACT_UTC	Extracts the UTC (Coordinated Universal Time) from a datetime with time zone displacement.
SYSTEMSTAMP	Returns the system date, including fractional seconds and the time zone of the database.
SYSDATE	Returns the current date and time.
TO_DSINTERVAL	Converts a character string of the CHAR, VARCHAR2, NCHAR, or NVARCHAR2 data type to an INTERVAL DAY TO SECOND TYPE.
TO_TIMESTAMP	Converts char of the CHAR, VARCHAR2, NCHAR, or NVARCHAR2 data type to a value of the TIMESTAMP data type.
TO_TIMSTAMP_TZ	Converts char of the CHAR, VARCHAR2, NCHAR, or NVARCHAR2 data type to a value of TIMESTAMP WITH TIME ZONE.
TO_YMINTERVAL	Converts a character string of the CHAR, VARCHAR2, NVARCHAR, or NVARCHAR2 data type to an INTERVALYEAR TO MONTH type.
TRUNC	Returns the date with the time portion of the day truncated to the unit specified by the format model format. If you omit format, date is truncated to the nearest day.
TZ_OFFSET	Returns the time zone offset corresponding to the value entered based on the date the statement is executed. You can enter a valid time zone name, a time zone offset from UTC (which simply returns itself), or the keyword SESSIONTIMEZONE or DBTIMEZONE. For a listing of valid values, query the TZNAME column of the V$TIMEZONE_NAMES dynamic performance view.

Table G-4
Oracle 9*i* SQL Conversion Functions

Function Name	***Brief Description***
ASCIISTR	Returns an ASCII string in the database character set. The value returned contains only characters that appear in SQL, plus the forward slash (/).
BIN_TO_NUM	Converts a bit vector to its equivalent number. Each argument in this function represents a bit in the bit vector. Each expression must evaluate to 0 or 1. This function returns NUMBER.
CAST	Converts one built-in data type or collection-type value into another built-in data type or collection-type value.
CHARTOROWID	Converts a value from the CHAR, VARCHAR2, NCHAR, or NVARCHAR2 data type to the ROWID data type.
COMPOSE	Returns a Unicode string in its fully normalized form in the same character set as the input.
CONVERT	Converts a character string from one character set to another. The data type of the returned value is VARCHAR2.
DECOMPOSE	Returns a Unicode string after canonical decomposition in the same character set as the input.
HEXTORAW	Converts char containing hexadecimal digits in the CHAR, VARCHAR2, NVARCHAR, or NVARCHAR2 character set to a raw value.
NUMTODSINTERVAL	Converts *n* to an INTERVAL DAY TO SECOND LITERAL. *n* can be a number or an expression resolving to a number.
NUMTOYMINTERVAL	Converts number *n* to an INTERVAL YEAR TO MONTH literal. *n* can be a number or an expression resolving to a number.
RAWTOHEX	Converts raw data type to a character value containing its hexadecimal equivalent.
RAWTONHEX	Converts raw data type to an NVARCHAR2 character value containing its hexadecimal equivalent.
ROWIDTOCHAR	Converts a rowid value to a VARCHAR2 data type. The result of this conversion is always 18 characters long.
ROWIDTONCHAR	Converts a rowid value to a NVARCHAR2 data type. The result of this conversion is always 18 characters long.
TO_CHAR	Converts the NCHAR, NVARCHAR2, CLOB, or NCLOB data type to the database character set.

Function Name	Brief Description
TO_CHAR	Converts date of the DATE, TIMESTAMP, TIMESTAMP WITH TIME ZONE, or TIMESTAMP WITH A LOCAL TIME ZONE data type to a value of the VARCHAR2 data type in the format specified by the date format.
TO_CHAR	Converts *n* of the NUMBER data type to a value of the VARCHAR2 data type.
TO_CLOB	Converts NCLOB values in an LOB column or other character string to CLOB values.
TO_DATE	Converts char of the CHAR, VARCHAR2, NCHAR, or NVARCHAR2, data type to a value of the DATE data type.
TO_DSINTERVAL	Converts a character string of the CHAR, VARCHAR2, NCHAR, or NVARCHAR2 data type to an INTERVAL DAY TO SECOND TYPE.
TO_LOB	Converts LONG or LONG RAW values in the column long_column to LOB values.
TO_MULTI_BYTE	Returns char with all of its single-byte characters converted to their corresponding multibyte characters. The value returned is in the same data type as char.
TO_NCHAR	Converts a character string, CLOB, NCLOB, from the database character set to the national character set.
TO_NCHAR	Converts a character string of the DATE,TIMESTAMP, TIMESTAMP WITH TIME ZONE ......etc. data type from the database character set to the national character set.
TO_NCHAR	Converts a number to a string in the NVARCHAR2 character set.
TO_NCLOB	Converts CLOB values in a LOB column or other character string to NCLOB values.
TO_NUMBER	Converts char to a value of the NUMBER data type.
TO_SINGLE_BYTE	Returns char with all of its multibyte characters converted to their corresponding single-byte characters.
TO_YMINTERVAL	Converts a character string of the CHAR, VARCHAR2, NCHAR, or NVARCHAR2 data type to an INTERVAL YEAR TO MONTH data type, where char is the character string to be converted.
TRANSLATE ... USING	Converts text into the character set specified for conversions between the database character set and the national character set.
UNISTR	Takes as its argument a string in any character set and returns it in Unicode in the database Unicode character set.

Table G-5 **Oracle 9*i* SQL Miscellaneous Single-Row Functions**	
Function Name	***Brief Description***
BFILENAME	Returns a BFILE locator that is associated with a physical LOB binary file on the server's file system.
COALESCE	Returns the first non-NULL expression in the expression list.
DECODE	Compares an expression to each search value one by one. If expression is equal to a search, Oracle returns the corresponding result. If no match is found, returns default, or, if default is omitted, returns NULL.
DUMP	Returns a VARCHAR2 value containing the data type codelength in bytes, and internal representation of expression.
EMPTY_BLOB	Returns an empty LOB locator that can be used to initialize an LOB variable or, an INSERT or UPDATE statement.
EMPTY_CLOB	Returns an empty LOB locator that can be used to initialize an LOB variable or, an INSERT or UPDATE statement.
EXISTSNODE	Determines whether traversal of the document using the path results in any nodes. It takes as arguments the XMLType instance containing an XML document and a VARCHAR2 string designating a path.
EXTRACT	Returns the value of specified datetime field from a datetime or interval value expression.
GREATEST	Returns the greatest value on the list of expressions.
LEAST	Returns the least value on the list of expressions.
NLS_CHARSET_DECL_LEN	Returns the declaration width (in number of characters) of an NCHAR column.
NLS_CHARSET_ID	Returns the character set ID number corresponding to the character set name text.
NLS_CHARSET_NAME	Returns the name of the character set corresponding to the ID number.
NULLIF	Returns NULL, if expression1 and expression2 are equal. If they are not equal, the function returns expression1.
NVL	If expression1 is NULL, NVL returns expression2. If not NULL, NVL returns expression1.

Function Name	Brief Description
NVL2	If expression1 is not NULL, NVL2 returns expression2, If expression2 is NULL, NVL2 returns expression3.
SYS_CONNECT_BY_PATH	Returns the path of a column value from root to node, with column values separated by char for each row returned by the CONNECT BY condition.
SYS_CONTEXT	Returns the value of the parameter associated with the context namespace.
SYS_DBURIGEN	Takes as its argument one or more columns or attributes, and optionally a rowid, and generates a URL of data type DBUriType to a particular column or row object. You can then use the URL to retrieve an XML document from the database.
SYS_EXTRACT_UTC	Extracts the UTC (Coordinated Universal Time—formerly Greenwich Mean Time) from a datetime with time zone displacement. Returns datetime with time zone displacement.
SYS_GUID	Returns a globally unique identifier (RAW value) made up of 16 bytes.
SYS_TYPEID	Returns the typeid of the most specific type of the operand.
SYS_XMLAGG	Aggregates all of the XML documents or fragments represented by an expression and produces a single XML document.
SYS_XMLGEN	Takes an expression that evaluates to a particular row and column of the database, and returns an instance of type SYS.XMLType containing an XML document.
UID	Returns an integer that uniquely identifies the session user (the user who logged on).
USER	Returns the name of the session user (the user who logged on) with the data type VARCHAR2.
USERENV	Returns information from the VARCHAR2 data type about the current session. USERENV is a legacy function that is retained for backward compatibility; use the SYS_CONTEXT function instead.
VSIZE	VSIZE returns the number of bytes in the internal representation of expression. If expression is NULL, this function returns NULL.

Table G-6
Oracle 9*i* SQL Aggregate Functions

Function Name	***Brief Description***
AVG	Returns the average value of an expression, could be used with GROUP BY.
CORR	Returns the coefficient of correlation of a set of number pairs.
COUNT	Returns the number of rows in the query.
COVAR_POP	Returns the population covariance of a set of number pairs.
COVAR_SAMP	Returns the sample covariance of a set of number pairs.
CUME_DIST	As an aggregate function, calculates, for a hypothetical row R identified by the arguments of the function and a corresponding sort specification, the relative position of row R among the rows in the aggregation group.
DENSE_RANK	As an aggregate function, calculates the dense rank of a hypothetical row identified by the arguments of the function with respect to a given sort specification.
FIRST	Returns the value from the first row of a sorted group.
GROUP_ID	Distinguishes duplicate groups resulting from a GROUP BY specification. It is therefore useful in filtering out duplicate groupings from the query result. It returns a NUMBER to uniquely identify duplicate groups.
GROUPING	Distinguishes superaggregate rows from regular grouped rows. GROUP BY extensions such as ROLLUP and CUBE produce superaggregate rows where the set of all values is represented by NULL. Using the GROUPING function, you can distinguish a NULL representing the set of all values in a superaggregate row from a NULL in a regular row.
GROUPING_ID	Returns a number corresponding to the GROUPING bit vector associated with a row. GROUPING_ID is applicable only in a SELECT statement that contains a GROUP BY extension, such as ROLLUP or CUBE, and a GROUPING function.
LAST	Returns the value from the last row of a sorted group.
MAX	Returns the maximum value of an expression.
MIN	Returns the minimum value of an expression.

Function Name	*Brief Description*
PERCENTILE_CONT	Is an inverse distribution function that assumes a continuous distribution model. It takes a percentile value and a sort specification, and returns an interpolated value that would fall into that percentile value with respect to the sort specification. Nulls are ignored in the calculation.
PERCENTILE_DISC	Is an inverse distribution function that assumes a discrete distribution model. It takes a percentile value and a sort specification and returns an element from the set. Nulls are ignored in the calculation.
PERCENT_RANK	Is similar to the CUME_DIST (cumulative distribution) function. The range of values returned by PERCENT_RANK is 0 to 1, inclusive. The first row in any set has a PERCENT_RANK of 0.
RANK	As an aggregate function, calculates the rank of a hypothetical row identified by the arguments of the function with respect to a given sort specification. The arguments of the function must all evaluate to constant expressions within each aggregate group, because they identify a single row within each group.
STDDEV	Returns the sample standard deviation of an expression, a set of numbers; differs from STDDEV_SAMP in that STDDEV returns zero when it has only 1 row of input data, whereas STDDEV_SAMP returns a NULL.
STDDEV_POP	Computes the population standard deviation and returns the square root of the population variance.
STDDEV_SAMP	Computes the cumulative sample standard deviation and returns the square root of the sample variance.
SUM	Returns the sum of the values of an expression.
VAR_POP	Returns the population variance of a set of numbers after discarding the NULLs in this set.
VAR_SAMP	Returns the sample variance of a set of numbers after discarding the NULLs in this set.
VARIANCE	Returns the variance of an expression. Can be used as an aggregate or analytic function.

Table G-7
Oracle 9*i* SQL Analytic Functions

Function Name	***Brief Description***
AVG	Returns the average the value of an expression, could return multiple rows within group
CORR	Returns the coefficient of correlation of a set of number pairs.
COVAR_POP	Returns the population covariance of a set of number pairs.
COVAR_SAMP	Returns the sample covariance of a set of number pairs. You can use it as an aggregate or analytic function.
COUNT	Returns the number of rows in the query.
CUME_DIST	Calculates the cumulative distribution of a value in a group of values. The range of values returned by CUME_DIST is >0 to <=1.
DENSE_RANK	Computes the rank of a row in an ordered group of rows. The ranks are consecutive integers beginning with 1. The largest rank value is the number of unique values returned by the query. Rank values are not skipped in the event of ties. Rows with equal values for the ranking criteria receive the same rank.
FIRST_VALUE	Returns the first value in an ordered set of values.
LAG	Provides access to more than one row of a table at the same time without a self-join. Given a series of rows returned from a query and a position of the cursor, LAG provides access to a row at a given physical offset prior to that position.
LAST	Returns the value from the last row of a sorted group.
LAST_VALUE	Returns the last value in an ordered set of values.
LEAD	Provides access to more than one row of a table at the same time without a self-join. Given a series of rows returned from a query and a position of the cursor, LEAD provides access to a row at a given physical offset beyond that position.
MAX	Returns the maximum value of an expression.
MIN	Returns the minimum value of an expression.
NTILE	Divides an ordered dataset into a number of buckets indicated by an expression and assigns the appropriate bucket number to each row. The buckets are numbered 1 through expression, and expression must resolve to a positive constant for each partition.

Function Name	*Brief Description*
PERCENT_RANK	Is similar to the CUME_DIST (cumulative distribution) function. The range of values returned by PERCENT_RANK is 0 to 1, inclusive. The first row in any set has a PERCENT_RANK of 0.
PERCENTILE_COUNT	Is an inverse distribution function that assumes a continuous distribution model. It takes a percentile value and a sort specification, and returns an interpolated value that would fall into that percentile value with respect to the sort specification. Nulls are ignored in the calculation.
PERCENTILE_DISC	Is an inverse distribution function that assumes a discrete distribution model. It takes a percentile value and a sort specification and returns an element from the set. Nulls are ignored in the calculation.
RANK	Calculates the rank of a value in a group of values. Rows with equal values for the ranking criteria receive the same rank; the ranks may not be consecutive numbers.
RATIO_TO_REPORT	Computes the ratio of a value to the sum of a set of values. If expression evaluates to NULL, the ratio-to-report value also evaluates to NULL.
ROW_NUMBER	Assigns a unique number to each row to which it is applied (either each row in the partition or each row returned), in the ordered sequence of rows specified in the order_by_clause, beginning with 1.
REGR_SLOPE REGR_INTERCEPT REGR_COUNT REGR_R2 REGR_AVGX REGR_AVGY REGR_SXX REGR_SYY REGR_SXY	The linear regression functions that follow fit an ordinary-least-squares regression line to a set of number pairs: REGR_SLOPE returns the slope of the line. The return value is a number and can be NULL. REGR_INTERCEPT returns the *y*-intercept of the regression line. REGR_COUNT returns an integer that is the number of non-NULL number pairs used to fit the regression line. REGR_R2 returns the coefficient of determination (also called "R-squared" or "goodness of fit") for the regression. REGR_AVGX evaluates the average of the independent variable (expr2) of the regression line. REGR_AVGY evaluates the average of the dependent variable (expr1) of the regression line. REGR_SXY, REGR_SXX, and REGR_SYY are auxiliary functions that are used to compute various diagnostic statistics.

Continued

Table G-7 *(continued)*

Function Name	*Brief Description*
STDDEV	Returns the sample standard deviation of an expression, a set of numbers; differs from STDDEV_SAMP in that STDDEV returns zero when it has only 1 row of input data, whereas STDDEV_SAMP returns a NULL.
STDDEV_POP	Computes the population standard deviation and returns the square root of the population variance.
STDDEV_SAMP	Computes the cumulative sample standard deviation and returns the square root of the sample variance.
SUM	Returns the sum of the values of an expression.
VAR_POP	Returns the population variance of a set of numbers after discarding the NULLs in this set.
VAR_SAMP	Returns the sample variance of a set of numbers after discarding the NULLs in this set.
VARIANCE	Returns the variance of an expression. Can be used as an aggregate or analytic function.

Table G-8
Oracle 9*i* SQL Object Reference Functions

Function Name	*Brief Description*
DEREF	Returns the object reference of an argument expression, where expression must return a REF to an object.
MAKE_REF	Creates a REF to a row of an object view or a row in an object table whose object identifier is primary-key based.
REF	Returns a REF value for the object instance that is bound to the variable or row.
REFTOHEX	Converts an argument expression to a character value containing its hexadecimal equivalent. The expression must return a REF.
VALUE	Takes as its argument a correlation variable (table alias) associated with a row of an object table and returns object instances stored in the object table. The type of the object instance is the same type as the object table.

Table G-9
IBM DB2 UDB Built-in Scalar Functions

Function Name	*Brief Description*
`ABS[VAL]`	Returns the absolute value of a number *n*.
`ACOS`	Returns the arccosine of the argument as an angle expressed in radians.
`ASCII`	Returns the ASCII code of the first character of a string.
`ASIN`	Returns the arcsine of the argument as an angle expressed in radians.
`ATAN`	Returns the arctangent of the argument as an angle expressed in radians.
`ATAN2`	Returns the arctangent of *x* and *y* coordinates as an angle expressed in radians. The *x* and *y* coordinates are specified by the first and second arguments, respectively.
`BIGINT`	Returns a 64-bit integer representation of a number or character string in the form of an integer constant.
`BLOB`	Returns a `BLOB` representation of a string of any type.
`CEIL[ING]`	Returns the smallest integer that is greater than or equal to *n*.
`CHAR`	Converts argument expression into a character string.
`CHR`	Returns a character for the ASCII code.
`CLOB`	Returns a `CLOB` representation of a character string type.
`COALESCE`	Returns the first argument on the list that is not `NULL`.
`CONCAT`	Returns result of concatenation of two strings.
`COS`	Returns the cosine of the argument, where the argument is an angle expressed in radians.
`COT`	Returns the cotangent of the argument, where the argument is an angle expressed in radians.
`DATE`	Returns a date from a value.
`DAY`	Returns the day part of a value.
`DAYNAME`	Returns a mixed-case character string containing the name of the day for the day portion of the argument based on the locale where the database was started.
`DAYOFWEEK`	Returns the day of the week in the argument as an integer value in the range of 1–7, where 1 represents Sunday.

Continued

Table G-9 *(continued)*	
Function Name	***Brief Description***
DAYOFWEEK_ISO	Returns the day of the week in the argument as an integer value in the range of 1–7, where 1 represents Monday.
DAYOFYEAR	Returns the day of the year in the argument as an integer value in the range of 1–366.
DAYS	Returns an integer representation of a date.
DBCLOB	Returns a DBCLOB representation of a graphic string type.
DEC[IMAL]	Returns a decimal representation of a number, a character string representation of a decimal number, or a character string representation of an integer number.
DECRYPT_BIN	Returns a value that is the result of decrypting encrypted data.
DECRYPT_CHAR	Returns a value that is the result of decrypting encrypted data.
DEGREES	Returns the number of degrees converted from the argument expressed in radians.
DEREF	Returns an instance of the target type of the argument.
DIFFERENCE	Returns a value from 0 to 4 representing the difference between the sounds of two strings based on applying the SOUNDEX function to the strings. A value of 4 is the best possible sound match.
DIGITS	Returns a character-string representation of a number.
DLCOMMENT	Returns the comment value, if it exists, from a DATALINK value.
DLLINKTYPE	Returns the linktype value from a DATALINK value.
DLURLCOMPLETE	Returns the data location attribute from a DATALINK value with a linktype of URL.
DLURLPATH	Returns the path and file name necessary to access a file within a given server from a DATALINK value with a linktype of URL.
DLURLPATHONLY	Returns the path necessary to access a file within a given server from a DATALINK value with a linktype of URL.
DLURLSCHEME	Returns the scheme from a DATALINK value with a linktype of URL.
DLURLSERVER	Returns the file server from a DATALINK value with a linktype of URL.
DLVALUE	Returns a DATALINK value.

Function Name	*Brief Description*
DOUBLE	Returns a floating-point number corresponding to a number if the argument is a numeric expression character string, or a representation of a number if the argument is a string expression.
ENCRYPT	Returns a value that is the result of encrypting a data-string expression.
EVENT_MON_STATE	Returns the current state of an event monitor.
EXP	Returns the exponential value of *n*.
FLOAT	Returns a floating-point representation of a number.
FLOOR	Returns the largest integer less than or equal to *n*.
GETHINT	Returns will return the password hint if one is found in the encrypted data.
GENERATE_UNIQUE	Returns a bit-data character string 13 bytes long (CHAR(13) FOR BIT DATA) that is unique when compared to any other execution of the same function.
GRAPHIC	Returns a GRAPHIC representation of a graphic string type.
HEX	Returns a hexadecimal representation of a value as a character string.
HOUR	Returns the hour part of a value.
IDENTITY_VAL_LOCAL	Returns the most recently assigned value for an identity column, where the assignment occurred as a result of a single row INSERT statement using a VALUES clause.
INSERT	Returns a string where expression3 bytes have been deleted from expression1 beginning at expression2, and where expression4 has been inserted into expression1 beginning at expression2.
INTEGER	Returns an integer representation of a number or character string in the form of an integer constant.
JULIAN_DAY	Returns an integer value representing the number of days from January 1, 4712 B.C. (the start of the Julian date calendar) to the date value specified in the argument.
LOWER	Converts all characters in a string to lowercase.
LCASE	Converts all characters in a string to lowercase.
LEFT	Returns *n* number of characters starting from the left.
LENGTH	Returns the number of characters in a string.

Continued

Table G-9 *(continued)*

Function Name	***Brief Description***
LN	Returns the natural logarithm of the argument.
LOCATE	Returns the position of an occurrence of a substring within the string.
LOG	Returns the natural logarithm of the argument (same as LN).
LOG10	Returns the base 10 logarithm of the argument.
LONG_VARCHAR	Returns a LONG VARCHAR representation of a character string data type.
LONG_VARGRAPHIC	Returns a LONG VARGRAPHIC representation of a double-byte character string.
LTRIM	Trims leading spaces off the string.
MICROSECOND	Returns the microsecond part of a value.
MIDNIGHT_SECONDS	Returns an integer value, which represents the number of seconds between midnight and the time value specified in the argument.
MINUTE	Returns the minute part of a value.
MOD	Returns the remainder of *n* divided by *m*.
MONTH	Returns the month part of a value.
MONTHNAME	Returns a mixed-case character string containing the name of month for the month portion of the argument, based on the locale where the database was started.
MQPUBLISH	Returns published data to MQSeries.
MQREAD	Returns a message from the MQSeries location specified by receive-service. The read is non-destructive—i.e. the message itself remains in the queue.
MQRECEIVE	Same as above, but the message in the queue is destroyed.
MQSEND	Sends the data contained in message data to the MQSeries location specified by send-service, using the quality of service policy defined by service-policy.
MQSUBSCRIBE	Used to register interest in MQSeries messages published on a specified topic.
MQUNSUBSCRIBE	Used to unregister an existing message subscription.
MULTIPLY_ALT	Returns the product of the two arguments as a decimal value.
NODENUMBER	Returns the partition number of the row.

Function Name	*Brief Description*
NULLIF	Returns a NULL value if the arguments are equal, otherwise it returns the value of the first argument.
PARTITION	Returns the partitioning map index of the row obtained by applying the partitioning function on the partitioning key value of the row.
POSSTR	Returns the position of an occurrence of a substring within the string. The POSSTR test is case-sensitive
POWER	Returns value of *m* raised to the *n*th power.
QUARTER	Returns an integer value in the range of 1 to 4, which represents the quarter of the year for the date specified in the argument.
RADIANS	Returns the number of radians converted from an argument, which is expressed in degrees.
RAISE_ERROR	Causes the statement that includes the function to return an error with the specified SQLSTATE, SQLCODE, and diagnostic-string.
RAND	Returns a random floating-point value between 0 and 1 using the argument as the optional seed value.
REAL	Returns a single-precision, floating-point representation of a number.
REC2XML	Returns a string formatted with XML tags and containing column names and column data.
REPEAT	Returns string1 repeated *n* times.
REPLACE	Replaces all occurrences of expression2 in expression1 with expression3.
RIGHT	Returns a string consisting of the rightmost expression2 bytes in expression1.
ROUND	Returns number *n* rounded to *m* decimal places.
RTRIM	Returns the characters of the argument with trailing blanks removed.
SECOND	Returns the seconds part of a time value/expression.
SIGN	Returns an indicator of the sign of the argument. If the argument is less than zero, -1 is returned. If argument equals zero, 0 is returned. If argument is greater than zero, 1 is returned.

Continued

Table G-9 (continued)

Function Name	*Brief Description*
SIN	Returns the sine of the argument, where the argument is an angle expressed in radians.
SMALLINT	Returns a small integer representation of a number or character string in the form of a small integer constant.
SOUNDEX	Returns a four-character code representing the sound of the words in the argument.
SPACE	Returns a string of *n* blanks.
SQRT	Returns the square root of the argument.
SUBSTR	Returns a part of a string starting from *n*th characters for the length of *m* characters.
TABLE_NAME	Returns the unqualified name of the object found after any alias chains have been resolved.
TABLE_SCHEMA	Returns the schema name of the object found after any alias chains have been resolved.
TAN	Returns the tangent of the argument, where the argument is an angle expressed in radians.
TIME	Returns a time from a value.
TAMESTAMP	Returns a timestamp from a value or a pair of values.
TIMESTAMP_ISO	Returns a timestamp value based on date, time, or timestamp argument.
TIMESTAMPDIFF	Returns an estimated number of intervals of the type defined by the first argument, based on the difference between two timestamps.
TRANSLATE	Replaces all occurrences of `string1` within `string2` translated into `string3`.
TRUN[CATE]	Returns *n* truncated to *m* decimal places.
TYPE_ID	Returns the internal type identifier of the dynamic data type of the expression.
TYPE_NAME	Returns the unqualified name of the dynamic data type of the expression.
TYPE_SCHEMA	Returns the schema name of the dynamic data type of the expression.
UCASE	Returns a string converted into `UPPER` case.
UPPER	Returns a string converted into `UPPER` case.
VALUE	Returns the first argument that is not `NULL`.

Function Name	Brief Description
VARCHAR	Returns a varying-length character string representation of a character string, datetime value, or graphic string.
VARGRAPHIC	Returns a graphic string representation of a character string value, converting single-byte characters to double-byte characters; or a graphic string value, if the first argument is any type of graphic string.
WEEK	Returns the week of the year of the argument as an integer value in the range of 1–54. The week starts with Sunday.
WEEK_ISO	Returns the week of the year of the argument as an integer value in the range 1–53.
YEAR	Returns the year part of a value.

Table G-10
IBM DB2 UDB Built-in Column Functions

Function Name	Brief Description
AVG	Returns the average of a set of numbers.
CORR[ELATION]	Returns the coefficient of correlation of a set of number pairs.
COUNT	Returns the number of rows or values in a set of rows or values.
COUNT_BIG	Returns the number of rows or values in a set of rows or values. It is similar to COUNT except that the result can be greater than the maximum value of integer.
COVARIANCE	Returns the (population) covariance of a set of number pairs.
GROUPING	In conjunction with the GROUP BY clause, returns a value that indicates whether a row returned in a GROUP BY set is a row generated by a grouping set that excludes the column represented by an expression.
MAX	Returns the maximum value in a set of values.
MIN	Returns the minimum value in a set of values.
STDDEV	Returns the standard deviation of a set of numbers.
SUM	Returns the sum of a set of numbers.
VAR[IANCE]	Returns the variance of a set of numbers.

Table G-11
IBM DB2 UDB Built-in Table Functions

Function Name	Brief Description
MQREADALL	Returns a table containing the messages and message metadata from the MQSeries location specified by receive service, using the quality of service policy.
MQRECEIVEALL	Returns a table containing the messages and message metadata from the MQSeries location specified by receive service.. The read is non-desctructive – i.e. the message itself remains in the queue.
SQLCACHE_SNAPSHOT	Returns the results of a snapshot of the DB2 dynamic SQL statement cache.

Table G-12
IBM DB2 UDB Built-in Procedures

Function Name	Brief Description
GET_ROUTINE_SAR	Retrieves the necessary information to install the same routine in another database server, running at the same level on the same operating system.
PUT_ROUTINE_SAR	Passes the necessary file to create an SQL routine at the server and then defines the routine.

Table G-13
Microsoft SQL Server 2000 Built-in String Functions

Function Name	Brief Description
ASCII	Returns the ASCII code of the first character in the expression.
CHAR	Returns the character for the ASCII code.
CHARINDEX	Returns the first position of the first occurrence of the expression within another expression.
DIFFERENCE	Returns the integer difference between two SOUNDEX expressions.
LEFT	Returns part of the expression starting from a specific character to the left.

Function Name	*Brief Description*
LEN	Returns number of characters in the expression, excluding trailing blank spaces.
LOWER	Returns an expression with all characters converted to lowercase.
LTRIM	Returns an expression without left trailing blanks.
NCHAR	Returns a Unicode character from the code number.
PATINDEX	Returns starting position of the first occurrence of a pattern within a specified expression.
REPLACE	Returns string where all occurrences of the second expression within the first expression are replaced with the third expression.
QUOTENAME	Returns a Unicode expression with delimiters added for validation.
REPLICATE	Returns an expression consisting of first argument repeated *n* times.
REVERSE	Returns a reversed-character expression.
RIGHT	Returns part of the expression starting from a specific character to the right.
RTRIM	Returns the expression with trailing blanks removed.
SOUNDEX	Returns four characters code to evaluate similarity between the sounds of two expressions.
SPACE	Returns string comprised of the blank spaces, repeated *n* times.
STR	Returns character data of numeric data type.
STUFF	Deletes a specified number of characters, and inserts another set of characters at the specified point.
SUBSTRING	Returns part of a string, starting from a specified point and spanning a specified number of characters.
UNICODE	Returns a Unicode integer code for the first character in the expression.
UPPER	Returns a character string converted to uppercase letters.

Table G-14
Microsoft SQL Server 2000 Built-in Mathematical Functions

Function Name	*Brief Description*
ABS	Returns the absolute value of the expression.
ACOS	Returns the angle in radians for the given cosine.
ASIN	Returns the angle in radians for the given sine.
ATAN	Returns the angle in radians for the given tangent.
ATN2	Returns the angle in radians whose tangent is in between two given floats.
CEILING	Returns the smallest integer greater than or equal to a given expression.
COS	Returns the cosine from a given angle (in radians).
COT	Returns the cotangent from a given angle (in radians).
DEGREES	Returns a degrees value from a given expression (in radians).
EXP	Returns the exponential value of the expression.
FLOOR	Returns the largest integer that is less than or equal to the given expression.
LOG	Returns the natural logarithm of a given expression.
LOG10	Returns the base 10 logarithm of the given expression.
PI	Returns number PI (3.1415926535897931...).
POWER	Returns the result of an expression in power *n*.
RADIANS	Returns radians from degrees.
RAND	Returns the random float number in the range of 0 to 1.
ROUND	Returns a numeric expression rounded to a specified length or precision.
SIGN	Returns +1 for positive expressions, 0 for zero, and –1 for negative expressions.
SIN	Returns the sine from a given angle (in radians).
SQUARE	Returns the expression squared.
SQRT	Returns the square root of the given expression.
TAN	Returns the tangent of the given expression.

Table G-15
Microsoft SQL Server 2000 Built-in Date and Time Functions

Function Name	*Brief Description*
DATEADD	Returns a new datetime value based on the passed value plus a specified interval.
DATEDIFF	Returns number of time units (seconds, days, years, etc.) passed between two dates.
DATENAME	Returns character string representing a specified date part of the date.
DATEPART	Returns an integer representing the specified date part.
DAY	Returns an integer representing the day part of a date.
GETDATE	Returns the current system's date and time.
GETUTCDATE	Returns date/time value for the current UTC time.
MONTH	Returns an integer representing the month part of a date.
YEAR	Returns an integer representing the year part of a date.

Table G-16
Microsoft SQL Server 2000 Built-in Aggregate Functions

Function Name	*Brief Description*
AVG	Returns the average of all the group values; NULLs are ignored.
BINARY_CHECKSUM	Returns the binary checksum value computed over a row of a table or a list of expressions.
CHECKSUM	Returns the checksum value computed over a row of a table or a list of expressions.
CHECKSUM_AGG	Returns the checksum of values in a group.
COUNT	Returns the number of selected rows or input values.
COUNT_BIG	Returns the number of selected rows or input values.
GROUPING	Causes an additional column to be output with a value 1 or 0.
MIN	Returns the lowest input value.
MAX	Returns the greatest input value.
STDEV	Returns the statistical standard deviation for values in the expression.

Continued

Table G-16 *(continued)*

Function Name	*Brief Description*
`STDEVP`	Returns the statistical standard deviation for the population of the values in the expression.
`SUM`	Returns the sum of the input values.
`VAR`	Returns the statistical variance for the values in a given expression.
`VARP`	Returns the statistical variance for a population of *s* in the values in a given expression.

Table G-17
Microsoft SQL Server 2000 Built-in Text and Image Functions

Function Name	*Brief Description*
`PATINDEX`	Returns the starting position of a first occurrence of the specified pattern within an expression.
`TEXTPTR`	Returns the text pointer value that corresponds to a text, ntext, or image in varbinary format.
`TEXTVALID`	Returns the results from checking whether text, ntext, or image text-pointer is valid.

Table G-18
Microsoft SQL Server 2000 Built-in Cursor Functions

Function Name	*Brief Description*
`@@CURSOR_ROWS`	Returns the number of rows in the last opened cursor.
`@@FETCH_STATUS`	Returns the status of the last `FETCH` statement from any cursor within the current session.
`CURSOR_STATUS`	Is a scalar function that shows whether the procedure has returned a cursor and a result set for a given parameter.

Table G-19
Microsoft SQL Server 2000 Built-in Metadata Functions

Function Name	*Brief Description*
COL_LENGTH	Returns the defined length of a column.
COL_NAME	Returns the column name from the column ID.
COLUMNPROPERTY	Returns information about a column or a parameter in a procedure.
DATABASEPROPERTY	Returns the property value of a given database.
DATABASEPROPERTYEX	Returns the current setting for the specified property.
DB_ID	Returns database identification number.
DB_NAME	Returns the current database name.
FILE_ID	Returns the file identification number for a given logical file.
FILE_NAME	Returns the file name from a given identification number.
FILEGROUP_ID	Returns the file identification number for a given filegroup.
FILEGROUP_NAME	Returns the filegroup name from a given identification number.
FILEGROUPPROPERTY	Returns a specified filegroup property value for a given filegroup.
FILEPROPERTY	Returns a specified file property value for a given file.
FULLTEXTCATALOGPROPERTY	Returns information about full-text catalog.
FULLTEXTSERVICEPROPERTY	Returns information about full-text service level properties.
INDEX_COL	Returns indexed column name.
INDEXKEY_PROPERTY	Returns information about the index key.
INDEXPROPERTY	Returns the property value from a given index name and table ID.
OBJECT_ID	Returns database object's ID given name.
OBJECT_NAME	Returns database object's name by ID.
OBJECTPROPERTY	Returns information about objects in the current database.
@@PROCID	Returns stored procedure identifier for the current procedure.
TYPEPROPERTY	Returns information about data types.
SQL_VARIANT_PROPERTY	Returns information about the base data type in addition to other property information.
FN_LISTEXTENDEDPROPERTY	Returns extended property values of the database objects.

Table G-20
Microsoft SQL Server 2000 Built-in Configuration Functions

Function Name	*Brief Description*
@@CONNECTION	Returns the number of opened or attempted connections.
@@DATEFIRST	Returns the value of the SET DATEFIRST parameter.
@@DBTS	Returns the current value of the datestamp data type.
@@LANGUAGE	Returns the name of the language for the current session/database.
@@LANGID	Returns ID of the language for the current session/database.
@@LOCK_TIMEOUT	Returns lock timeout in seconds.
@@MAX_CONNECTION	Returns the maximum number of simultaneous user connections.
@@MAX_PRECISION	Returns the precision level used by numeric data types.
@@NESTLEVEL	Returns the nesting level of the current stored procedure.
@@OPTIONS	Returns bitmask information about current SET options.
@@REMSERVER	Returns name of the remote server.
@@SPID	Returns the number (ID) of the current process/session.
@@SERVERNAME	Returns the name of the local server.
@@SERVICENAME	Returns the name of the registry key under which the SQL Server instance is running.
@@TEXTSIZE	Returns the current value of the TEXTSIZE option.
@@VERSION	Returns the date, version, and processor type for the current version of SQL Server.

Table G-21
Microsoft SQL Server 2000 Built-in Security Functions

Function Name	*Brief Description*
IS_MEMBER	Indicates whether the user is a member of a Windows NT group or an SQL Server role.
IS_SRVROLEMEMBER	Indicates whether current login is a member of the specified role.
SUSER_ID	Returns login ID for the current user.

Function Name	Brief Description
SUSER_NAME	Returns login name for the current user.
SUSER_SID	Returns user's security identification number (SID) from login name.
SUSER_SNAME	Returns user's login name from security identification number (SID).
USER_ID	Returns user's database identification number from user name.
USER_NAME	Returns database user's name from identification number.
USER	Returns the current user's database name.
HAS_DBACCESS	Indicates whether current user has access to the specified database.
fn_trace_geteventinfo	Returns information about events being traced.
fn_trace_getfilterinfo	Returns information about filters applied to a specified trace.
fn_trace_getinfo	Returns information about traces.
fn_trace_gettable	Returns trace information in a table format.

Table G-22
Microsoft SQL Server 2000 Built-in System Functions

Function Name	Brief Description
APP_NAME	Returns the application name of the current session (if set).
CASE	Evaluates a list of conditions and returns one value.
CAST	Explicitly converts one data type into another data type.
COALESCE	Returns the first non-Null expression on the list.
CONVERT	Explicitly converts one data type into another data type, behaves similar to the CAST function.
CURRENT_TIMESTAMP	Returns the current date/time; equivalent of GETDATE().
CURRENT_USER	Returns the current user; equivalent of USER_NAME.
DATALENGTH	Returns the number of bytes in an expression.
@@ERROR	Returns the error number of the last Transact-SQL statement.

Continued

Table G-22 *(continued)*

Function Name	***Brief Description***
FORMATMESSAGE	Formats a message from the existing one in the sysmessages table.
GETANSINULL	Returns the default NULL ability for the database for the session.
HOST_ID	Returns the ID of the computer.
HOST_NAME	Returns the name of the host computer.
IDENT_INCR	Returns the increment value of any identity column in a table or a view.
IDENT_SEED	Returns the identity seed value of any identity column in a table or a view.
@@IDENTITY	Returns the last inserted identity value.
IDENTITY	Used to insert into an identity column.
ISDATE	Determines whether an expression is a valid date type (or could be converted into one).
ISNULL	Determines whether the expression is NULL.
ISNUMERIC	Determines whether the expression is numeric.
NEWID	Returns a unique value for the UNIQUEIDENTIFIER data type.
NULLIF	Returns NULL if two expressions are equivalent.
PARSENAME	Returns the specified path of the object name.
PERMISSIONS	Returns a value for the bitmap specifying permissions for the object for the current user.
@@ROWCOUNT	Returns the number of rows affected by the last statement.
ROWCOUNT_BIG	Returns the rows affected by the last statement (bigint).
SESSION_USER	Returns the user's name that is to be inserted into a table when no default is specified.
STATS_DATE	Returns the date when the index statistics were updated.
SYSTEM_USER	Returns the name of the current user with admin privileges (Windows authenticated).
@@TRANCOUNT	Returns the number of pending transactions for the current session.
USER_NAME	Returns the database user name from a given identification number.
COLLATIONPROPERTY	Returns the property of a given collation.

Function Name	Brief Description
SCOPE_IDENTITY	Returns the last identity value inserted in the identity column for the current scope.
SERVERPROPERTY	Returns the value for the specified server property.
SESSIONPROPERTY	Returns the value for the specified session property.
fn_helpcollation	Returns a list of all collation supported.
fn_servershareddrives	Returns the names of the shared drives that could be used by the clustered server.
fn_virtualservernodes	Returns a list of nodes on which a virtual server can run.

Table G-23
Microsoft SQL Server 2000 Built-in System Statistical Functions

Function Name	Brief Description
@@CPU_BUSY	Returns the time (in milliseconds) since the start of the SQL Server.
@@IDLE	Returns idle time (in milliseconds) since the start of the SQL Server.
@@IO_BUSY	Returns the time (in milliseconds) since the start of the SQL Server, when it was busy with I/O operations.
@@PACK_RECEIVED	Returns the number of input packets received since the start of the SQL Server.
@@PACK_SENT	Returns the number of output packets received since the start of the SQL Server.
@@PACKET_ERRORS	Returns the number of error packets on the network that have occurred since the start of the SQL Server.
@@TIMETICKS	Returns the number of milliseconds per CPU tick.
@@TOTAL_ERRORS	Returns the number of disk write/read errors since the start of the SQL Server.
@@TOTAL_READ	Returns the number of physical disk reads since the start of the SQL Server.
@@TOTAL_WRITE	Returns the number of physical disk writes since the start of the SQL Server.
fn_virtualfilestats	Returns I/O statistics for the database files.

Table G-24
Microsoft SQL Server 2000 Built-in Rowset Functions

Function Name	*Brief Description*
CONTAINSTABLE	Returns a table for those columns containing character-based data types for precise or fuzzy matches of a single word or phrase.
FREETEXTTABLE	Returns a table for those columns containing character-based data types for values that match the meaning but not the exact word.
OPENQUERY	Executes a specified pass-through query on a linked OLEDB data source.
OPENROWSET	Provides an ad-hoc method of connecting and accessing remote data through OLEDB.
OPENDATASOURCE	Provides ad-hoc connection information, as a part of a four-part object name, without using a linked server.
OPENXML	Provides a rowset view of the XML document.

✦ ✦ ✦

SQL Syntax Reference

SQL99 syntax uses BNF (Backus-Naur Form) notation to specify the standard syntax for SQL.

Note The notation is named after John Backus and Peter Naur, who first introduced a formal notation to describe the syntax of a given language.

The notation is quite complicated, so in this book we simplified it by using the most important elements only. In addition, because the syntaxes for our "big three" differ significantly among themselves (and also are different from the SQL99 standards), our purpose was to provide as generic notation as possible that would be applicable to them all. For additional features not mentioned in this appendix, refer to vendor-specific documentation.

The symbols used in our notation are listed in Table H-1 along with their meanings.

Table H-1
Simplified BNF Notation

Symbol	*Meaning*
< >	Encloses term names.
|	Separates alternatives (exclusive OR).
[ ]	Designates optional term.
{ }	Indicates at least one of the required terms is required.
,...	Indicates term can be optionally repeated more than once.

In addition, all SQL keywords are in uppercase letters; everything else is in lowercase.

DDL Statements

This section provides BNF notation for DDL statements.

Tables

The notations below are to create, modify, and drop database tables, respectively:

```
CREATE TABLE <table_name>
(
 column_name <datatype> [<column_constraint>,...]
                        [DEFAULT <default_value>],...
 [<table_constraint>,...]
 [physical_options]
)
```

```
ALTER TABLE <table_name>
{ <vendor_specific_add_column_clause> |
  <vendor_specific_alter_column_clause> |
  <vendor_specific_add_constraint_clause> |
  <vendor_specific_drop_constraint_clause>
}
```

ALTER TABLE statement clauses vary for different implementations and can hardly be generalized. See Chapter 5 for more information.

```
DROP TABLE <table_name>
```

Indexes

The following two notations are to create and drop database indexes:

```
CREATE [UNIQUE] INDEX <index_name>
ON <table_name> (<column_name> [ASC|DESC],...)
```

```
DROP INDEX <index_name>
```

Views

The notations below are to create, modify, and drop database views, respectively:

```
CREATE VIEW <view_name> [(column_name,...)]
AS <select_statement>
[WITH CHECK OPTION]
```

```
ALTER VIEW <view_name>
<vendor_specific_alter_view_clause>
```

```
DROP VIEW <view_name>
```

Schemas

The following two notations are to create and to drop database schemas:

```
CREATE SCHEMA <schema_name>
AUTHORIZATION <authorization_id>
<create_object_statement>,...
<grant_privilege_statement>,...
```

In Oracle, the `schema_name` token is invalid. You can create schemas in Oracle in your own schema only, and only with your own `authorization_id`.

```
DROP SCHEMA <schema_name> RESTRICT
```

The foregoing syntax is for DB2 only; Oracle and MS SQL Server don't have `DROP SCHEMA` statements in their syntaxes.

Stored procedures

The BNF notation to create a stored procedure follows:

```
CREATE PROCEDURE <procedure_name> [<parameter_section>]
<procedure_definition>
```

The preceding specification is generic; the actual syntax is implementation-specific. Refer to vendor-specific documentation for details.

The following notation is to drop a stored procedure:

```
DROP PROCEDURE <procedure_name>
```

User-defined functions

The BNF notation to create a user-defined function follows:

```
CREATE FUNCTION <function_name>
<function_definition_includes_return_statement>
```

The preceding specification is generic; the actual syntax is implementation-specific. Refer to vendor-specific documentation for details.

The following notation is to drop a user-defined function:

```
DROP FUNCTION <function_name>
```

Triggers

The BNF notation to create a trigger follows:

```
CREATE TRIGGER <trigger_name>
[BEFORE | AFTER]
{INSERT | UPDATE | DELETE}
ON <table_name>
[FOR EACH ROW]
<trigger_body>
```

The preceding syntax describes only basic trigger functionality; the actual implementations have more options.

The following notation is to drop a trigger:

```
DROP TRIGGER [qualifier.]<trigger_name>
```

DCL Statements

The BNF notations for the main two DCL statements are:

```
GRANT {[ALL [PRIVILEGES]] | <privilege,...>}
[ON <object_name>]
TO <user_group_or_role>
[WITH GRANT OPTION]
```

```
REVOKE {[ALL [PRIVILEGES]] | <privilege,...>
ON <object_name>
FROM <user_group_or_role>
```

DML Statements

The BNF notations for DML statements follow:

```
INSERT INTO <table_or_view_name>
[(<column_name>,...)]
{{VALUES (<literal> |
```

```
            <expression> |
            NULL |
            DEFAULT,...)} |
   {(<select_statement>} }
```

```
UPDATE <table_or_view_name>
SET {<column_name> = <literal> |
                     <expression> |
                     <single_row_select_statement> |
                     NULL |
                     DEFAULT,...}
[WHERE <predicate>]
```

```
DELETE FROM <table_or_view_name>
WHERE <predicate>
```

DQL Statements

Data query language (DQL) is comprised of SELECT statements only. A SELECT statement can be single-table (selecting records from one table only) or multitable (selecting rows from more than one table, usually using some kind of join).

Single table select

The BNF notation for single table select follows:

```
SELECT [ALL | DISTINCT]
{[<qualifier>.]<column_name> | * | <expression>}
    [AS <column_alias>],...
FROM <table_or_view_name> | <inline_view> [<table_alias>]
[WHERE <predicate>]
[GROUP BY [<qualifier>.]<column_name>,...
    [HAVING <predicate>]]
[ORDER_BY [<qualifier>.]<column_name> | <column_number>
    [ASC | DESC],...];
```

Multitable SELECT

A multitable SELECT can be done using either "new" or "old" syntax; also, there are slightly different syntaxes for inner and outer joins.

"New" syntax (inner join)

```
SELECT [ALL | DISTINCT]
{[<qualifier>.]<column_name> | * | <expression>}
    [AS <column_alias>],...
FROM <table_or_view_name> | <inline_view> [<table_alias>]
   [INNER | NATURAL | CROSS] JOIN
     <table_or_view_name> | <inline_view> [<table_alias>]
   [ON [<qualifier>.]<column_name>
          <join_condition>
       [<qualifier>.]<column_name>]
   [[INNER | NATURAL | CROSS] JOIN
     <table_or_view_name> | <inline_view> [<table_alias>]
   [ON [<qualifier>.]<column_name>
          <join_condition>
       [<qualifier>.]<column_name>],...]
[WHERE <predicate>]
[GROUP BY [<qualifier>.]<column_name>,...
    [HAVING <predicate>]]
[ORDER_BY [<qualifier>.]<column_name> | <column_number>
    [ASC | DESC],...];
```

"New" syntax (outer join)

```
SELECT [ALL | DISTINCT]
{[<qualifier>.]<column_name> | * | <expression>}
  [AS <column_alias>],...
FROM <table_or_view_name> | <inline_view> [<table_alias>]
  {[LEFT | RIGHT | FULL [OUTER]} JOIN
     <table_or_view_name> | <inline_view> [<table_alias>]
  {ON [<qualifier>.]<column_name>
          <join_condition>
       [<qualifier>.]<column_name>}
  [{[LEFT | RIGHT | FULL [OUTER]} JOIN
     <table_or_view_name> | <inline_view> [<table_alias>]
  {ON [<qualifier>.]<column_name>
          <join_condition>
       [<qualifier>.]<column_name>},...]
[WHERE <predicate>]
[GROUP BY [<qualifier>.]<column_name>,...
    [HAVING <predicate>]]
[ORDER_BY [<qualifier>.]<column_name> | <column_number>
    [ASC | DESC],...];
```

The "new" syntax for inner and outer joins can be combined in a single query; that is, you might want to join to tables using an inner join and then join the resulting set with another table using an outer join, and so on.

"Old" syntax (inner join)

```
SELECT [ALL | DISTINCT]
{[<qualifier>.]<column_name> | * | <expression>}
    [AS <column_alias>],...
FROM <table_or_view_name> | <inline_view> [<table_alias>]
[WHERE [<qualifier>.]<column_name>
           join_condition
       [<qualifier>.]<column_name>
[AND [<qualifier>.]<column_name>
           join_condition
     [<qualifier>.]<column_name>],...
[AND <predicate>],...]
[GROUP BY [<qualifier>.]<column_name>,...
    [HAVING <predicate>]]
[ORDER_BY [<qualifier>.]<column_name> | <column_number>
    [ASC | DESC],...];
```

The "old" syntax for outer join is implementation-specific; please see Chapter 9 or refer to vendor documentation.

Transactional Control Statements

The BNF syntax for the transactional control statements is given below:

```
COMMIT [WORK]
```

```
ROLLBACK [WORK]
```

Predicates

In our simplified BNF, predicate can be defined as a statement that can be evaluated to either TRUE or FALSE. Table H-2 "decodes" SQL syntax for predicates.

<table>
<tr><th colspan="2">Table H-2
Predicates</th></tr>
<tr><th>Element</th><th>Syntax</th></tr>
<tr><td><predicate></td><td><boolean_term> [{AND | OR} <boolean_term>,...]</td></tr>
<tr><td><boolean_term></td><td>[NOT] <search_test></td></tr>
<tr><td><search_test></td><td><comparison_test> |
<between_test> |
<in_test> |
<like_test> |
<null_test> |
<exists_test> |
<quantified_comparisson_test></td></tr>
<tr><td><comparison_test></td><td><column_value>
{= | <> | != | < | > | <= | >=}
{<expression> | <single_row_subquery>}</td></tr>
<tr><td><between_test></td><td><column_value>
[NOT] BETWEEN
<expression> AND <expression></td></tr>
<tr><td><in_test></td><td><column_value> [NOT] IN <expression_list> |
<table_subquery></td></tr>
<tr><td><like_test></td><td><column_value> [NOT] LIKE <pattern>
[ESCAPE <value>]</td></tr>
<tr><td><null_test></td><td><column_value> IS [NOT] NULL</td></tr>
<tr><td><exists_test></td><td>EXISTS <table_subquery></td></tr>
<tr><td><quantified_
comparisson_test></td><td><column_value>
{= | <> | != | < | > | <= | >=}
{ALL | SOME | ANY}
<table_subquery></td></tr>
<tr><td><expression_list></td><td>(<expression>,...)</td></tr>
<tr><td><expression></td><td><sub-expression>
{+ | - | * | /}
<sub-expression></td></tr>
</table>

Continued

Table H-2 *(continued)*

Element	*Syntax*
<sub-expression>	[- | +] {<value> | <function>}
<value>	<literal> | <variable>
<column_value>	[qualifier.]<column_name>

✦ ✦ ✦

SQL-Reserved Keywords

With a limited vocabulary, SQL is a relatively efficient language (compared with many other programming languages); the SQL99 standard defines about 300 keywords out of which vendors have thus far implemented only a small subset.

Oracle 9i lists over 100 keywords, IBM DB2 UDB has over 290 keywords, and Microsoft SQL Server 2000 reserves over 170 keywords. Most of the vendor-reserved keywords are found in the SQL99 standard, but many more exist. None of these reserved words should be used as a variable identifier as such use would affect portability of your SQL code. On some systems, doing so will generate an error (`SQLSTATE 42939`).

Asterisks appear after the vendor-supported keywords whenever they also are part of SQL standard.

In addition to keywords listed here, each vendor also has a list of keywords reserved for future use. These lists are constantly updated. Refer to the particular RDBMS documentation.

SQL99 standard reserved keywords:

ABSOLUTE
ACTION
ADD
ADMIN
AFTER
AGGREGATE
ALIAS
ALL
ALLOCATE
ALTER
AND
ANY
ARE
ARRAY
AS
ASC
ASSERTION
AT
AUTHORIZATION
BEFORE
BEGIN
BINARY
BIT
BLOB
BOOLEAN
BOTH
BREADTH
BY
CALL
CASCADE
CASCADED
CASE
CAST
CATALOG
CHAR
CHARACTER
CHECK
CLASS
CLOB
CLOSE
COLLATE
COLLATION
COLUMN
COMMIT
COMPLETION
CONDITION
CONNECT
CONNECTION
CONSTRAINT
CONSTRAINTS
CONSTRUCTOR
CONTAINS
CONTINUE
CORRESPONDING
CREATE
CROSS
CUBE
CURRENT
CURRENT_DATE
CURRENT_PATH
CURRENT_ROLE
CURRENT_TIME
CURRENT_TIMESTAMP
CURRENT_USER
CURSOR
CYCLE
DATA
DATALINK
DATE
DAY
DEALLOCATE
DEC
DECIMAL
DECLARE
DEFAULT
DEFERRABLE
DELETE
DEPTH
DEREF
DESC
DESCRIPTOR
DIAGNOSTICS
DICTIONARY
DISCONNECT
DO
DOMAIN
DOUBLE
DROP
END-EXEC
EQUALS
ESCAPE
EXCEPT
EXCEPTION

EXECUTE
EXIT
EXPAND
EXPANDING
FALSE
FIRST
FLOAT
FOR
FOREIGN
FREE
FROM
FUNCTION
GENERAL
GET
GLOBAL
GOTO
GROUP
GROUPING
HANDLER
HASH
HOUR
IDENTITY
IF
IGNORE
IMMEDIATE
IN
INDICATOR
INITIALIZE
INITIALLY
INNER
INOUT
INPUT
INSERT
INT
INTEGER
INTERSECT
INTERVAL
INTO
IS
ISOLATION
ITERATE
JOIN
KEY
LANGUAGE
LARGE
LAST
LATERAL
LEADING
LEAVE
LEFT
LESS
LEVEL
LIKE
LIMIT
LOCAL
LOCALTIME
LOCALTIME-STAMP
LOCATOR
LOOP
MATCH
MEETS
MINUTE
MODIFIES
MODIFY
MODULE
MONTH
NAMES
NATIONAL
NATURAL
NCHAR
NCLOB
NEW
NEXT
NO
NONE
NORMALIZE
NOT
NULL
NUMERIC
OBJECT
OF
OFF
OLD
ON
ONLY
OPEN
OPERATION
OPTION
OR
ORDER
ORDINALITY
OUT
OUTER

OUTPUT
PAD
PARAMETER
PARAMETERS
PARTIAL
PATH
PERIOD
POSTFIX
PRECEDES
PRECISION
PREFIX
PREORDER
PREPARE
PRESERVE
PRIMARY
PRIOR
PRIVILEGES
PROCEDURE
PUBLIC
READ
READS
REAL
RECURSIVE
REDO
REF
REFERENCES
REFERENCING
RELATIVE
REPEAT
RESIGNAL
RESTRICT
RESULT
RETURN
RETURNS
REVOKE
RIGHT
ROLE
ROLLBACK
ROLLUP
ROUTINE
ROW
ROWS
SAVEPOINT
SCHEMA
SCROLL
SEARCH
SECOND
SECTION
SELECT
SEQUENCE
SESSION
SESSION_USER
SET
SETS
SIGNAL
SIZE
SMALLINT
SPECIFIC
SPECIFICTYPE
SQL
SQLEXCEPTION
SQLSTATE
SQLWARNING
START
STATE
STATIC
STRUCTURE
SUCCEEDS
SUM
SYSTEM_USER
TABLE
TEMPORARY
TERMINATE
THAN
THEN
TIME
TIMESTAMP
TIMEZONE_HOUR
TIMEZONE_MINUTE
TO
TRAILING
TRANSACTION
TRANSLATION
TREAT
TRIGGER
TRUE
UNDER
UNDO
UNION
UNIQUE
UNKNOWN
UNTIL
UPDATE

USAGE
USER
USING
VALUE
VALUES
VARIABLE
VARYING
VIEW
WHEN
WHENEVER
WHERE
WHILE
WITH
WRITE
YEAR
ZONE

Oracle 9i SQL reserved keywords:

ACCESS
ADD *
ALL *
ALTER *
AND *
ANY *
AS *
ASC *
AUDIT
BETWEEN *
BY *
CHAR *
CHECK *
CLUSTER
COLUMN *
COMMENT
COMPRESS
CONNECT *
CREATE *
CURRENT *
DATE *
DECIMAL *
DEFAULT *
DELETE *
DESC *
DISTINCT *
DROP *
ELSE *
EXCLUSIVE
EXISTS
FILE
FLOAT *
FOR *
FROM *
GRANT *
GROUP *
HAVING *
IDENTIFIED
IMMEDIATE *
IN *
INCREMENT
INDEX
INITIAL
INSERT *
INTEGER *
INTERSECT *
INTO *
IS *
LEVEL *
LIKE *
LOCK
LONG
MAXEXTENTS
MINUS
MLSLABEL
MODE
MODIFY *
NOAUDIT
NOCOMPRESS
NOT *
NOWAIT
NULL *
NUMBER
OF *
OFFLINE
ON *
ONLINE
OPTION *
OR*

ORDER *
PCTFREE
PRIOR *
PRIVILEGES *
PUBLIC *
RAW *
RENAME
RESOURCE
REVOKE *
ROW *
ROWID
ROWNUM
ROWS *
SELECT *
SESSION *
SET *
SHARE
SIZE *
SMALLINT *
START *
SUCCESSFUL
SYNONYM
SYSDATE
TABLE *
THEN *
TO *
TRIGGER *
UID
UNION *
UNIQUE *
UPDATE *
USER *
VALIDATE
VALUES *
VARCHAR *
VARCHAR2
VIEW *
WHENEVER *
WHERE *
WITH *

IBM DB2 UDB 8.1 reserved keywords:

ACQUIRE
ADD *
AFTER *
ALIAS *
ALL *
ALLOCATE *
ALLOW
ALTER *
AND *
ANY *
AS *
ASC *
ASUTIME
AUDIT
AUTHORISATION *
AUX
AUXILIARY
AVG
BD2GENERAL
BEFORE *
BEGIN *
BETWEEN
BINARY *
BUFFERPOOL
BY *
CALL *
CALLED
CAPTURE
CASCADED *
CASE *
CAST *
CCSID
CHAR *
CHARACTER *
CHECK *
CLOSE *
CLUSTER
COLLECTION
COLLID
COLUMN *
COMMENT
COMMIT *
CONCAT
CONDITION *
CONNECT *

CONNECTION *
CONSTRAINT *
CONTAINS *
CONTINUE *
COUNT
COUNT_BIG
CREATE *
CROSS *
CURRENT *
CURRENT_DATE *
CURRENT_LC_PATH
CURRENT_PATH
CURRENT_SERVER
CURRENT_TIME *
CURRENT_TIMESTAMP *
CURRENT_TIMEZONE
CURRENT_USER *
CURSOR *
DATA *
DATABASE
DATE *
DAY *
DAYS
DB2SQL
DBA
DBINFO
DBSPACE
DECLARE
DEFAULT *
DELETE *
DESC *
DESCRIPTOR *
DETERMINISTIC
DISALLOW
DISCONNECT *
DISTINCT
DO *
DOUBLE *
DROP *
DSSIZE
DYNAMIC
EDITPROC
ELSE
ELSEIF
END
END-EXEC
ERASE
ESCAPE *
EXCEPT *
EXCEPTION *
EXCLUSIVE
EXECUTE *
EXISTS
EXIT *
EXPLAIN
EXTERNAL
FENCED
FETCH
FIELDPROC
FILE
FINAL
FOR *
FOREIGN *
FREE *
FROM *
FULL
FUNCTION *
GENERAL *
GENERATED
GO
GOTO *
GRANT
GRAPHIC
GROUP *
HANDLER *
HAVING
HOUR *
HOURS
IDENTIFIED
IF *
IMMEDIATE *
IN *
INDEX
INDICATOR *
INNER *
INOUT *
INSENSITIVE
INSERT *
INTEGRITY
INTERSECT *
INTO *
IS *
ISOBID

ISOLATION *
JAVA
JOIN *
KEY *
LABEL
LANGUAGE *
LC_TYPE
LEAVE *
LEFT *
LIKE *
LINKTYPE
LOCAL *
LOCALE
LOCATOR *
LOCATORS
LOCK
LOCKSIZE
LONG
LOOP *
MAX
MICROSECOND
MICROSECONDS
MIN
MINUTE *
MINUTES
MODE
MODIFIES *
MONTH *
MONTHS
NAME
NAMED
NHEADER
NO *
NODENAME
NODENUMBER
NOT *
NULL *
NULLS
NUMPARTS
OBID
OF *
ON *
ONLY
OPEN *
OPTIMIZATION
OPTIMIZE
OPTION *
OR *
ORDER *
OUT *
OUTER *
PACKAGE
PAGE
PAGES
PARAMETER
PART
PARTITION
PATH
PCTINDEX
PCTREE
PIECESIZE
PLAN
POSITION
PRECISION
PREPARE *
PRIMARY *
PRIQTY
PRIVATE
PRIVILEGES *
PROCEDURE *
PROGRAM
PSID
PUBLIC *
QUERYNO
READ *
READS *
RECOVERY
REFERENCES *
RELEASE
RENAME
REPEAT *
RESET
RESOURCE
RESTRICT *
RESULT *
RETURN *
RETURNS *
REVOKE *
RIGHT *
ROLLBACK *
ROW *
ROWS *
RRN

RUN
SCHEDULE
SCHEMA *
SCRATCHPAD
SECOND *
SECONDS
SECQTY
SECURITY
SELECT *
SET *
SHARE
SIMPLE
SOME
SOURCE
SPECIFIC *
SQL *
STANDARD
STATIC
STATISTICS
STAY
STOGROUP
STORES
STORPOOL
STYLE
SUBPAGES
SUBSTRING
SUM *
SYNONYM
TABLE *
TABLESPACE
THEN *
TO *
TRANSACTION *
TRIGGER *
TRIM
TYPE
UNDO *
UNION *
UNIQUE *
UNTIL *
UPDATE *
USAGE *
USER *
USING *
VALIDPROC
VALUES *
VARIABLE *
VARIANT
VCAT
VIEW *
VOLUMES
WHEN *
WHERE *
WHILE *
WITH *
WLM
WORK
WRITE *
YEAR *
YEARS

Microsoft SQL Server 2000 reserved keywords:

ADD *
ALL *
ALTER *
AND *
ANY *
AS *
ASC *
AUTHORIZATION *
BACKUP
BEGIN *
BETWEEN *
BREAK
BROWSE
BULK
BY *
CASCADE *
CASE *
CHECK *
CHECKPOINT
CLOSE *
CLUSTERED
COALESCE
COLLATE *
COLUMN *
COMMIT *
COMPUTE
CONSTRAINT *

CONTAINS *
CONTAINSTABLE
CONTINUE *
CONVERT
CREATE *
CROSS *
CRRENT_TIME *
CURREN *T
CURRENT_DATE *
CURRENT_TIMESTAMP *
CURRENT_USER *
CURSOR *
DATABASE
DBCC
DEALLOCATE *
DECLARE *
DEFAULT *
DELETE *
DENY
DESC *
DISK
DISTINCT *
DISTRIBUTED
DOUBLE *
DROP *
DUMMY
DUMP
ELSE *
END *
ERRLVL
ESCAPE
EXCEPT *
EXEC
EXECUTE *
EXISTS
EXIT *
FETCH
FILE
FILLFACTOR
FOR *
FOREIGN *
FREETEXT
FREETEXTTABLE
FROM *
FULL
FUNCTION *
GOTO *
GRANT *
GROUP *
HAVING
HOLDLOCK
IDENTITY *
IDENTITY_COL
IDENTITY_INSERT
IF *
IN *
INDEX
INNER *
INSERT *
INTERSECT *
INTO *
IS *
JOIN *
KEY *
KILL
LEFT *
LIKE
LINENO
LOAD
NATIONAL *
NOCHECK
NONCLUSTERED
NOT *
NULL *
NULLIF
OF *
OFF *
OFFSETS
ON *
OPEN *
OPENDATASOURCE
OPENQUERY
OPENROWSET
OPENXML

OPTION *
OR *
ORDER *
OUTER *
OVER
PERCENT
PLAN
PRECISION *
PRIMARY *
PRINT *
PROC
PROCEDURE *
PUBLIC *
RAISERROR
READ *
READTEXT
RECONFIGURE
REFERENCES *
REPLICATION
RESTORE
RESTRICT *
RETURN *
REVOKE *
RIGHT *
ROLLBACK *
ROWCOUNT
ROWGUIDCOL
RULE
SAVE
SCHEMA *
SELECTSESSION_USER *
SET *
SETUSER
SHUTDOWN
SOME
STATISTICS
SYSTEM_USER *
TABLE *
TEXTSIZE
THEN *
TO *
TOP
TRAN
TRANSACTION *
TRIGGER *
TRUNCATE
TSEQUAL
UNION *
UNIQUE *
UPDATE *
UPDATETEXT
USE
USER *
VALUES *
VARYING *
VIEW *
WAITFOR
WHEN *
WHERE *
WHILE *
WITH *
WRITETEXT

Future Keywords

Microsoft has also reserved a number of keywords for future use. These are not implemented in MS SQL Server 2000 and hence do not represent valid SQL commands. Nevertheless, it will be a good idea to avoid these altogether in your code (as identifiers, for instance) as they might render your code invalid in future versions. You may notice that some of the keywords listed here are, in fact, mandated by the SQL99 standard.

Microsoft SQL Server reserved future keywords:

ABSOLUTE	CONNECTION	EQUALS
ACTION	CONSTRAINTS	EVERY
ADMIN	CONSTRUCTOR	EXCEPTION
AFTER	CORRESPONDING	EXTERNAL
AGGREGATE	CUBE	FALSE
ALIAS	CURRENT_PATH	FIRST
ALLOCATE	CURRENT_ROLE	FLOAT
ARE	CYCLE	FOUND
ARRAY	DATA	FREE
ASSERTION	DATE	GENERAL
AT	DAY	GET
BEFORE	DEC	GLOBAL
BINARY	DECIMAL	GO
BIT	DEFERRABLE	GROUPING
BLOB	DEFERRED	HOST
BOOLEAN	DEPTH	HOUR
BOTH	DEREF	IGNORE
BREADTH	DESCRIBE	IMMEDIATE
CALL	DESCRIPTOR	INDICATOR
CASCADED	DESTROY	INITIALIZE
CAST	DESTRUCTOR	INITIALLY
CATALOG	DETERMINISTIC	INOUT
CHAR	DIAGNOSTICS	INPUT
CHARACTER	DICTIONARY	INT
CLASS	DISCONNECT	INTEGER
CLOB	DOMAIN	INTERVAL
COLLATION	DYNAMIC	ISOLATION
COMPLETION	EACH	ITERATE
CONNECT	END-EXEC	LANGUAGE

LARGE
LAST
LATERAL
LEADING
LESS
LEVEL
LIMIT
LOCAL
LOCALTIME
LOCALTIMESTAMP
LOCATOR
MAP
MATCH
MINUTE
MODIFIES
MODIFY
MODULE
MONTH
NAMES
NATURAL
NCHAR
NCLOB
NEW
NEXT
NO
NONE
NUMERIC
OBJECT
OLD
ONLY
OPERATION
ORDINALITY
OUT
OUTPUT
PAD
PARAMETER
PARAMETERS
PARTIAL
PATH
POSTFIX
PREFIX
PREORDER
PREPARE
PRESERVE
PRIOR
PRIVILEGES
READS
REAL
RECURSIVE
REF
REFERENCING
RELATIVE
RESULT
RETURNS
ROLE
ROLLUP
ROUTINE
ROW
ROWS
SAVEPOINT
SCOPE
SCROLL
SEARCH
SECOND
SECTION
SEQUENCE
SESSION
SETS
SIZE
SMALLINT
SPACE
SPECIFIC
SPECIFICTYPE
SQL
SQLEXCEPTION
SQLSTATE
SQLWARNING
START
STATE
STATEMENT
STATIC
STRUCTURE
TEMPORARY
TERMINATE
THAN
TIME
TIMESTAMP
TIMEZONE_HOUR
TIMEZONE_MINUTE
TRAILING
TRANSLATION
TREAT
TRUE

UNDER	VALUE	WORK
UNKNOWN	VARCHAR	WRITE
UNNEST	VARIABLE	YEAR
USAGE	WHENEVER	ZONE
USING	WITHOUT	

ODBC Reserved Keywords

While not being within the mandated SQL core, these keywords should be avoided in applications to preserve compatibility with SQL99-compliant drivers.

ODBC 3.0 reserved keywords:

ABSOLUTE	BOTH	CONSTRAINT
ACTION	BY	CONSTRAINTS
ADA	CASCADE	CONTINUE
ADD	CASCADED	CONVERT
ALL	CASE	CORRESPONDING
ALLOCATE	CAST	COUNT
ALTER	CATALOG	CREATE
AND	CHAR	CROSS
ANY	CHAR_LENGTH	CURRENT
ARE	CHARACTER	CURRENT_DATE
AS	CHARACTER_LENGTH	CURRENT_TIME
ASC	CHECK	CURRENT_TIMESTAMP
ASSERTION	CLOSE	CURRENT_USER
AT	COALESCE	CURSOR
AUTHORIZATION	COLLATE	DATE
AVG	COLLATION	DAY
BEGIN	COLUMN	DEALLOCATE
BETWEEN	COMMIT	DEC
BIT	CONNECT	DECIMAL
BIT_LENGTH	CONNECTION	DECLARE

DEFAULT
DEFERRABLE
DEFERRED
DELETE
DESC
DESCRIBE
DESCRIPTOR
DIAGNOSTICS
DISCONNECT
DISTINCT
DOMAIN
DOUBLE
DROP
ELSE
END
END-EXEC
ESCAPE
EXCEPT
EXCEPTION
EXEC
EXECUTE
EXISTS
EXTERNAL
EXTRACT
FALSE
FETCH
FIRST
FLOAT
FOR
FOREIGN
FORTRAN
FOUND
FROM
FULL
GET
GLOBAL
GO
GOTO
GRANT
GROUP
HAVING
HOUR
IDENTITY
IMMEDIATE
IN
INCLUDE
INDEX
INDICATOR
INITIALLY
INNER
INPUT
INSENSITIVE
INSERT
INT
INTEGER
INTERSECT
INTERVAL
INTO
IS
ISOLATION
JOIN
KEY
LANGUAGE
LAST
LEADING
LEFT
LEVEL
LIKE
LOCAL
LOWER
MATCH
MAX
MIN
MINUTE
MODULE
MONTH
NAMES
NATIONAL
NATURAL
NCHAR
NEXT
NO
NONE
NOT
NULL
NULLIF
NUMERIC
OCTET_LENGTH
OF
ON
ONLY
OPEN
OPTION

OR
ORDER
OUTER
OUTPUT
OVERLAPS
PAD
PARTIAL
PASCAL
POSITION
PRECISION
PREPARE
PRESERVE
PRIMARY
PRIOR
PRIVILEGES
PROCEDURE
PUBLIC
READ
REAL
REFERENCES
RELATIVE
RESTRICT
REVOKE
RIGHT
ROLLBACK
ROWS
SCHEMA
SCROLL
SECOND
SECTION
SELECT
SESSION
SESSION_USER
SET
SIZE
SMALLINT
SOME
SPACE
SQL
SQLCA
SQLCODE
SQLERROR
SQLSTATE
SQLWARNING
SUBSTRING
SUM
SYSTEM_USER
TABLE
TEMPORARY
THEN
TIME
TIMESTAMP
TIMEZONE_HOUR
TIMEZONE_MINUTE
TO
TRAILING
TRANSACTION
TRANSLATE
TRANSLATION
TRIM
TRUE
UNION
UNIQUE
UNKNOWN
UPDATE
UPPER
USAGE
USER
USING
VALUE
VALUES
VARCHAR
VARYING
VIEW
WHEN
WHENEVER
WHERE
WITH
WORK
WRITE
YEAR
ZONE

✦ ✦ ✦

SQL99 Major Features Compliance Across Different RDBMS

Table J-1 shows which of 350 major features defining SQL99 standard compliance have been implemented in IBM UDB2 (version 7.2), Oracle 9*i,* and Microsoft SQL Server 2000. Whenever an alternative implementation is available the vendor's feature is marked as compliant. For example, the ANSI/ISO standard mandates a `CHARACTER_LENGTH` function, which Oracle and UDB2 implement with their function `LENGTH` and Microsoft with its function `LEN`—for our purposes they are considered to be compliant, though strictly speaking they are not. For practicality's sake, we follow the spirit, not the letter, of the standard.

Table J-1
SQL99-Defined Features across RDBMS

Identifier	*Description*	*IBM*	*Oracle*	*Microsoft*
E011	Numeric data types	✓	✓	✓
E011-01	`INTEGER` and `SMALLINT` data types	✓	✓	✓
E011-02	`REAL`, `DOUBLE PRECISON`, and `FLOAT` data types	✓	✓	✓
E011-03	`DECIMAL` and `NUMERIC` data types	✓	✓	✓
E011-04	Arithmetic operators	✓	✓	✓
E011-05	Numeric comparison	✓	✓	✓
E011-06	Implicit casting among the numeric data types	✓	✓	✓
E021	Character data types	✓	✓	✓
E021-01	`CHARACTER` data type	✓	✓	✓
E021-02	`CHARACTER VARYING` data type	✓	Partial	Partial
E021-03	Character literals	✓	Partial	✓
E021-04	`CHARACTER_LENGTH` function	✓	✓	✓
E021-05	`OCTET_LENGTH` function	✓	✓	✓
E021-06	`SUBSTRING` function	✓	✓	✓
E021-07	Character concatenation	✓	✓	✓
E021-08	`UPPER` and `LOWER` functions	✓	✓	✓
E021-09	`TRIM` function	✓	✓	✓
E021-10	Implicit casting among the character data types	✓	✓	✓
E021-11	`POSITION` function	✓	✓	✓
E011-12	Character comparison	✓	✓	✓
E031	Identifiers	✓	✓	✓
E031-01	Delimited identifiers	✓	✓	✓
E031-02	Lower case identifiers	✓	✓	✓
E031-03	Trailing underscore			
E051	Basic query specification	✓	✓	✓
E051-01	`SELECT DISTINCT`	✓	✓	✓
E051-02	`GROUP BY` clause	✓	✓	✓
E051-04	`GROUP BY` can contain columns not in select list	✓	✓	✓

Identifier	*Description*	*IBM*	*Oracle*	*Microsoft*
E051-05	Select list items can be renamed	✓	✓	✓
E051-06	`HAVING` clause	✓	✓	✓
E051-07	Qualified * in select list	✓	✓	✓
E051-08	Correlation names in the `FROM` clause	✓	✓	✓
E061	Basic predicates and search conditions	✓	✓	✓
E061-01	Comparison predicate	✓	✓	
E061-02	`BETWEEN` predicate	✓	✓	✓
E061-03	`IN` predicate with list of values	✓	✓	✓
E061-04	`LIKE` predicate	✓	✓	✓
E061-05	`LIKE` predicate `ESCAPE` clause	✓	✓	✓
E061-06	`NULL` predicate	✓	✓	✓
E061-07	Quantified comparison predicate	✓	✓	✓
E061-08	`EXISTS` predicate	✓	Partial	✓
E061-09	Subqueries in comparison predicate	✓	✓	✓
E061-11	Subqueries in `IN` predicate	✓	✓	✓
E061-12	Subqueries in quantified comparison predicate	✓	✓	✓
E061-13	Correlated subqueries	✓	✓	✓
E061-14	Search condition	✓	✓	✓
E071	Basic query expressions	✓		✓
E071-01	`UNION DISTINCT` table operator	✓	✓	
E071-02	`UNION ALL` table operator	✓	✓	✓
E071-03	`EXCEPT DISTINCT` table operator	✓	Partial	
E071-05	Columns combined via table operators need not have exactly the same data type	✓	✓	✓
E071-06	Table operators in subqueries	✓	✓	✓
E081	Basic Privileges	✓	✓	✓
E081-01	`SELECT` privilege	✓	✓	✓
E081-02	`DELETE` privilege	✓	✓	✓
E081-03	`INSERT` privilege at the table level	✓	✓	✓
E081-04	`UPDATE` privilege at the table level	✓	✓	✓
E081-06	`REFERENCES` privilege at the table level	✓	✓	✓

Continued

Table J-1 (continued)

Identifier	*Description*	*IBM*	*Oracle*	*Microsoft*
E081-08	WITH GRANT OPTION	✓	✓	✓
E081-05	UPDATE privilege at the column level	✓	✓	✓
E081-07	REFERENCES privilege at the column level	✓	✓	✓
E091	Set functions	✓	✓	✓
E091-01	AVG	✓	✓	✓
E091-02	COUNT	✓	✓	✓
E091-03	MAX	✓	✓	✓
E091-04	MIN	✓	✓	✓
E091-05	SUM	✓	✓	✓
E091-06	ALL quantifier	✓	✓	✓
E091-07	DISTINCT quantifier	✓	✓	✓
E101	Basic data manipulation	✓	✓	✓
E101-01	INSERT statement	✓	✓	✓
E101-03	Searched UPDATE statement	✓	✓	✓
E101-04	Searched DELETE statement	✓	✓	✓
E111	Single row SELECT statement	✓	✓	✓
E121	Basic cursor support	✓	✓	✓
E121-01	DECLARE CURSOR	✓	✓	✓
E121-02	ORDER BY columns need not be in select list	✓	✓	✓
E121-03	Value expressions in ORDER BY clause	✓	✓	✓
E121-04	OPEN statement	✓	✓	✓
E121-06	Positioned UPDATE statement	✓	✓	✓
E121-07	Positioned DELETE statement	✓	✓	✓
E121-08	CLOSE statement	✓	✓	✓
E121-10	FETCH statement implicit NEXT		✓	
E121-17	WITH HOLD cursors	✓		✓
E131	Null value support (nulls in lieu of values)	✓	✓	✓
E141	Basic integrity constraints	✓	✓	✓
E141-01	NOT NULL constraints	✓	✓	✓
E141-02	UNIQUE constraints of NOT NULL columns	✓	✓	✓
E141-03	PRIMARY KEY constraints	✓	✓	✓

Identifier	Description	IBM	Oracle	Microsoft
E141-04	Basic FOREIGN KEY constraint with the NO ACTION default for both referential delete action and referential update action	✓	✓	✓
E141-06	CHECK constraints	✓	✓	✓
E141-07	Column defaults	✓	✓	✓
E141-08	NOT NULL inferred on PRIMARY KEY	✓	✓	✓
E141-10	Names in a foreign key can be specified in any order			
E151	Transaction support	✓	✓	✓
E151-01	COMMIT statement	✓	✓	✓
E151-02	ROLLBACK statement	✓	✓	✓
E152	Basic SET TRANSACTION statement	✓	✓	✓
E152-01	SET TRANSACTION statement: ISOLATION LEVEL SERIALIZABLE clause	✓	✓	✓
E152-02	SET TRANSACTION statement: READ ONLY and READ WRITE clauses	✓	✓	✓
E153	Updateable queries with subqueries	✓	✓	✓
E161	SQL comments using leading double minus	✓	✓	✓
E171	SQLSTATE support	✓	✓	✓
E182	Module language	✓	Partial	
F021	Basic information schema	✓	✓	✓
F021-01	COLUMNS view	✓	✓	✓
F021-02	TABLES view	✓	✓	✓
F021-03	VIEWS view	✓	✓	✓
F021-04	TABLE_CONSTRAINTS view	✓	✓	✓
F021-05	REFERENTIAL_CONSTRAINTS view	✓	✓	✓
F021-06	CHECK_CONSTRAINTS view	✓	✓	✓
F031	Basic schema manipulation	✓	✓	✓
F031-01	CREATE TABLE statement to create persistent base tables	✓	✓	✓
F031-02	CREATE VIEW statement	✓	✓	✓
F031-03	GRANT statement	✓	✓	✓
F031-04	ALTER TABLE statement COLUMN clause	✓	✓	✓

Continued

Table J-1 (continued)				
Identifier	***Description***	***IBM***	***Oracle***	***Microsoft***
F031-13	DROP TABLE statement clause	✓		✓
F031-16	DROP VIEW statement RESTRICT clause	✓		
F031-19	REVOKE statement RESTRICT clause	✓		
F033	ALTER TABLE statement: DROP COLUMN clause	✓	✓	✓
F041	Basic joined table	✓	✓	✓
F041-01	Inner join (but not necessarily the INNER keyword)	✓	✓	✓
F041-02	INNER keyword	✓	✓	✓
F041-03	LEFT OUTER JOIN	✓	✓	✓
F041-04	RIGHT OUTER JOIN	✓	✓	✓
F041-05	Outer joins can be nested	✓	✓	✓
F041-07	The inner table in a left or right outer join can also be used in an inner join	✓	✓	✓
F041-08	All comparison operators are supported (rather than just =)	✓	✓	✓
F051	Basic date and time	✓	✓	✓
F051-01	DATE data type (including support of DATE literal)	✓	✓	✓
F051-02	TIME data type (including support of TIME literal) with fractional seconds precision of at least 0	✓	✓	✓
F051-03	TIMESTAMP data type (including support of TIMESTAMP literal) with fractional seconds precision of at least 0 and 6	✓	✓	✓
F051-04	Comparison predicate on DATE TIMESTAMP data types	✓	✓	✓
F051-05	Explicit CAST between datetime types and character types	✓	✓	
F051-06	CURRENT_DATE	✓	✓	✓
F051-07	LOCALTIME	✓	✓	✓
F051-08	LOCALTIMESTAMP	✓	✓	✓
F081	UNION and EXCEPT in views	✓	✓	Partial
F111	Isolation levels other than SERIALIZABLE	✓	✓	✓

Identifier	*Description*	*IBM*	*Oracle*	*Microsoft*
F111-01	`READ UNCOMMITTED` isolation level	✓	✓	✓
F111-02	`READ COMMITTED` isolation level	✓	✓	✓
F111-03	`REPEATABLE READ` isolation level	✓	✓	✓
F121	Basic diagnostics management	✓	✓	✓
F121-01	`GET DIAGNOSTICS` statement			
F121-02	`SET TRANSACTION` statement: `DIAGNOSTICS SIZE` clause			
F131	Grouped operations	✓	✓	✓
F131-01	`WHERE`, `GROUP BY` and `HAVING` clauses supported in queries with grouped views	✓	✓	
F131-02	Multiple tables supported in queries with grouped views	✓	✓	✓
F131-03	Set functions supported in queries with grouped views	✓	✓	✓
F131-04	Subqueries with `GROUP BY` and `HAVING` clauses and grouped views	✓	✓	✓
F131-05	Single row `SELECT` with `GROUP BY` and `HAVING` clauses and grouped views	✓	✓	✓
F201	`CAST` function	✓	✓	✓
F221	Explicit defaults	✓	✓	✓
F231	Privilege Tables	✓	✓	✓
F231-01	`TABLE_PRIVILEGES` view	✓	✓	✓
F231-02	`COLUMN_PRIVILEGES` view	✓	✓	✓
F231-03	`USAGE_PRIVILEGES` view	✓	✓	✓
F261	`CASE` expression	✓	✓	✓
F261-01	Simple `CASE`	✓	✓	✓
F261-02	Searched `CASE`	✓		
F261-03	`NULLIF`	✓	✓	✓
F261-04	`COALESCE`	✓		✓
F311	Schema definition statement	✓	✓	✓
F311-01	`CREATE SCHEMA`	✓	✓	✓
F311-02	`CREATE TABLE` for persistent base tables	✓	✓	✓
F311-03	`CREATE VIEW`	✓	✓	✓

Continued

Table J-1 *(continued)*

Identifier	*Description*	*IBM*	*Oracle*	*Microsoft*
F311-04	CREATE VIEW: WITH CHECK OPTION	✓	✓	✓
F311-05	GRANT statement	✓	✓	✓
F471	Scalar subquery values	✓	✓	✓
F481	Expanded NULL predicate	✓	✓	✓
F032	CASCADE drop behavior	✓	✓	✓
F034	Extended REVOKE statement	✓	✓	✓
F034-01	REVOKE statement performed by other than the owner of a schema object	✓	✓	✓
F052	Intervals and datetime arithmetic	✓	✓	✓
F171	Multiple schemas per user	✓	✓	✓
F191	Referential delete actions	✓	✓	✓
F222	INSERT statement: DEFAULT VALUES clause	✓	✓	✓
F251	Domain support			
F281	LIKE enhancements	✓	✓	✓
F291	UNIQUE predicate	✓	✓	✓
F301	CORRESPONDING in query expressions	✓		
F302	INTERSECT table operator	✓	✓	
F302-01	INTERSECT DISTINCT table operator	✓	✓	
F302-02	INTERSECT ALL table operator	✓	✓	
F304	EXCEPT ALL table operator	✓	✓	
F321	User authorization	✓	✓	✓
F341	Usage tables	✓	✓	✓
F361	Subprogram support	✓	✓	✓
F381-01	ALTER TABLE statement: ALTER COLUMN clause	✓	✓	✓
F381-02	ALTER TABLE statement: ADD CONSTRAINT clause	✓	✓	✓
F381-03	ALTER TABLE statement: DROP CONSTRAINT clause	✓	✓	✓
F391	Long identifiers	✓	✓	✓
F401	Extended joined table	✓	✓	✓

Identifier	*Description*	*IBM*	*Oracle*	*Microsoft*
F401-01	NATURAL JOIN	✓	✓	✓
F401-02	FULL OUTER JOIN	✓	✓	✓
F401-03	UNION JOIN	✓	✓	✓
F401-04	CROSS JOIN	✓	✓	✓
F411	Time zone specification	✓	✓	✓
F421	National character	✓	✓	✓
F431	Read-only scrollable cursors	✓	✓	✓
F431-01	FETCH with explicit NEXT	✓	✓	
F431-02	FETCH FIRST	✓		✓
F431-03	FETCH LAST	✓		✓
F431-04	FETCH PRIOR	✓		✓
F431-05	FETCH ABSOLUTE	✓		✓
F431-06	FETCH RELATIVE	✓		✓
F451	Character set definition	✓	✓	✓
F461	Named character sets	✓	✓	✓
F491	Constraint management	✓	✓	✓
F501-01	SQL_FEATURES view			
F501-02	SQL_SIZING view			
F501-03	SQL_LANGUAGES view			
F502	Enhanced documentation tables	✓	✓	✓
F502-01	SQL_SIZING_PROFILES view			
F502-02	SQL_IMPLEMENTATION_INFO view			
F502-03	SQL_PACKAGES view	✓	✓	
F511	BIT data type	✓	✓	✓
F521	Assertions	✓	✓	✓
F531	Temporary tables	✓	✓	✓
F555	Enhanced seconds precision	✓	✓	✓
F561	Full value expressions	✓	✓	✓
F571	Truth value tests	✓	✓	✓
F591	Derived tables	✓	✓	
F641	Row and table constructors	✓	✓	

Continued

Table J-1 *(continued)*

Identifier	*Description*	*IBM*	*Oracle*	*Microsoft*
F661	Simple tables	✓	✓	✓
F671	Subqueries in CHECK	✓	✓	✓
F691	Collation and translation	✓	✓	✓
F701	Referential update actions	✓	✓	✓
F711	ALTER domain			
F721	Deferrable constraints	✓	✓	✓
F731	INSERT column privileges	✓	✓	✓
F751	View CHECK enhancements	✓	✓	✓
F761	Session management	✓	✓	✓
F771	Connection management	✓	✓	✓
F781	Self-referencing operations	✓	✓	✓
F791	Insensitive cursors	✓	✓	✓
F801	Full set function	✓	✓	✓
F811	Extended flagging			
F812	Basic flagging	✓	✓	✓
F813	Extended flagging for "Core SQL Flagging" and "Catalog Lookup" only	✓	✓	
F821	Local table references	✓	✓	✓
F831	Full cursor update			✓
F831-01	Updateable scrollable cursors	✓		✓
S011	Distinct data types	✓		✓
S011-01	USER_DEFINED_TYPES view	✓	✓	✓
S023	Basic structured types	✓	✓	✓
S024	Enhanced structured types	✓	✓	
S041	Basic reference types	✓	✓	✓
S051	Create table of type	✓	✓	✓
S071	SQL paths in function and type name resolution	✓	✓	✓
S081	Subtables	✓	✓	
S091	Basic array support	✓	✓	Partial
S091-01	Arrays of built-in data types	✓	✓	

Identifier	*Description*	*IBM*	*Oracle*	*Microsoft*
S091-02	Arrays of distinct types	✓		
S091-03	Array expressions			
S092	Arrays of user-defined types	✓	✓	
S094	Arrays of reference types	✓		
S111	`ONLY` in query expressions	✓	✓	✓
S161	Subtype treatment	✓	✓	
S201	SQL routines on arrays	✓	✓	
S201-01	Array parameters	✓		
S201-02	Array as result type of functions	✓	✓	
S211	User-defined cast functions	✓	✓	✓
S232	Array locators	✓	✓	
S241	Transform functions	✓	✓	✓
S251	User-defined orderings			
S261	Specific type method	✓	✓	
T011	Timestamp in INFORMATION_SCHEMA	✓	✓	
T031	`BOOLEAN` data type			
T041-01	`BLOB` data type	✓	✓	
T041-02	`CLOB` data type	✓	✓	
T051	Row types	✓	✓	
T111	Updateable joins, unions, and columns	✓	✓	✓
T121	`WITH` (excluding `RECURSIVE`) in query expression	✓	✓	✓
T131	Recursive query	✓	✓	✓
T171	`LIKE` clause in table definition			
T271	Savepoints	✓	✓	✓
T281	`SELECT` privilege with column granularity	✓	✓	✓
T301	Functional Dependencies	✓	✓	✓
T141	`SIMILAR` predicate			
T151	`DISTINCT` predicate	✓	✓	✓
T191	Referential action `RESTRICT`	✓		
T201	Comparable data types for referential constraints	✓	✓	✓

Continued

Table J-1 (continued)

Identifier	*Description*	*IBM*	*Oracle*	*Microsoft*
T211	Basic trigger capability	✓	✓	✓
T211-01	Triggers activated on `UPDATE`, `INSERT`, or `DELETE` of one base table	✓	✓	✓
T211-02	`BEFORE` triggers	✓	✓	✓
T211-03	`AFTER` triggers	✓	✓	✓
T211-04	`FOR EACH ROW` triggers	✓	✓	✓
T211-05	Ability to specify a search condition that must be true before the trigger is invoked	✓	✓	
T211-06	Support for run-time rules for the interaction of triggers and constraints			✓
T211-07	`TRIGGER` privilege			
T211-08	Multiple triggers for the same the event are executed in the order in which they were created	✓	✓	✓
T212	Enhanced trigger capability			✓
T231	`SENSITIVE` cursors	✓	✓	✓
T241	`START TRANSACTION` statement			✓
T251	`SET TRANSACTION` statement: `LOCAL` option	✓	✓	✓
T312	`OVERLAY` function			
T321	Basic SQL-invoked routines	✓	✓	✓
T321-01	User-defined functions with no overloading	✓	✓	✓
T321-02	User-Defined procedures with no overloading	✓	✓	✓
T321-03	Function invocation	✓	✓	✓
T321-04	`CALL` statement	✓	✓	
T321-06	`ROUTINES` view	✓	✓	✓
T321-07	`PARAMETERS` view	✓	✓	✓
T321-05	`RETURN` statement	✓	Partial	✓
T322	Overloading of SQL-invoked functions and procedures	✓	Partial	
T323	Explicit security for external routines	✓	✓	✓
T331	Basic roles	✓	✓	✓

Identifier	*Description*	*IBM*	*Oracle*	*Microsoft*
T332	Extended roles	✓	✓	✓
T351	Bracketed SQL comments (`/*...*/` comments)	✓	✓	✓
T401	`INSERT` into a cursor			✓
T411	`UPDATE` statement: `SET ROW` option	✓	✓	✓
T431	`CUBE` and `ROLLUP` operations	✓	✓	✓
T471	Result sets return value	✓	✓	✓
T441	`ABS` and `MOD` functions	✓	✓	Partial
T461	Symmetric `BETWEEN` predicate	✓	✓	✓
T501	Enhanced `EXISTS` predicate	✓		✓
T511	Transaction counts	✓	✓	✓
T541	Updateable table references	✓	✓	✓
T551	`OPTIONAL` keyword for default syntax			
T561	Holdable locators	✓		✓
T571	Array-returning external SQL-invoked functions	✓	✓	✓
T581	Regular expression substring function	✓	✓	
T591	`UNIQUE` constraints of possibly null columns		✓	✓
T601	Local cursor references	✓	✓	✓

✦ ✦ ✦

The Other RDBMS

This book concentrates on three big vendors — Oracle, IBM, and Microsoft — but of course, they are not the only providers of relational database software. We intentionally tried to steer away from the "holy wars" of the RDBMS vendors, and we hope we've succeeded.

There are virtually dozens of lesser-known RDBMS packages out there, and their merits are not always reflected by their market share. Most of them compare very favorably with the "big three" in terms of costs (some of these are distributed free of charge), and even performance. Some of the most popular are listed in Table K-1; the list is by no means complete.

Table K-1
RDBMS Software Vendors

RDBMS	*SQL*	*Operating System*	*Vendor Info*
ADABAS	92	Unix, Linux, mainframe	Software AG `www.softwareagusa.com`
Cloudscape DBMS	92/99	Any platform for which JVM is implemented	IBM `www.cloudscape.com`
Daffodil DB Java	99	Any platform for which JVM is implemented	Daffodil Software `www.daffodilwoods.com`

Continued

Table K-1 (continued)

RDBMS	SQL	Operating System	Vendor Info
Empress	92	Sun Solaris, HP_UX, IBM AIX, True64 UNIX, IRIX, LINUX, FreeBSD, UNICOS, MS Windows NT/ 2000/XP LynxOS, QNX, RTU, Bluecat, RTLinux	Empress Software Inc. `www.empress.com`
FirstBase v9.3.2	92	Unix, Linux	FirstBase Software `www.firstbase.com` Open Source Database, GNU General Public License
FoxPro/FoxBase	92	Microsoft Windows 9x/ NT/2000/XP	Microsoft Corporation `www.microsoft.com`
INGRES II	92	Windows NT/2000, Unix, Open VMS, Linux	Computer Associates `www.cai.com`
Informix	92	IBM AIX, SGI IRIX; Linux; Reliant UNIX; Sun Solaris; Compaq Tru64; Windows NT/ 2000/ XP; UNIXWare, HP-UX	IBM `www.informix.com`
InterBase	92	Windows NT/2000/XP, UNIX, Linux	Borland Software Corporation `www.borland.com`
LEAP RDBMS v1.2.6	92	Unix, Linux	`http://leap .sourceforge.net` Open Source Database, GNU General Public License
Linter RDBMS SQL/RelX Enterprise	92/99	Linux (Red Hat, Caldera, SuSe, Mandrake) FreeBSD, NetBSD, OpenBSD, BSDi Sun Solaris (ix86, Sparc) SGI IRIX, IBM AIX (Power PC) Digital UNIX, OpenVMS HP-UX, Novell Netware SINIX, USIX WindRiver Tornado/ VxWorks, QNX OS9, OS9000, SCO UNIX UnixWare, Windows 95/ 98/ME/NT/2000/XP	RelX Corporation `www.relxnet.com`

RDBMS	*SQL*	*Operating System*	*Vendor Info*
MS Access 2000	92	Windows 9x/NT/2000/XP	Microsoft Corporation www.microsoft.com
mSQL		Unix, Linux	Hughes Technologies Pty. Ltd. www.hughes.com Open Source
MySQL	92/99	Linux, FreeBSD, Windows 9x/NT/2000/XP, Sun Solaris, HP-UX, Mac OS X, AIX, SGI Irix, SCO Unix, DEC OSF, BSDi	MySQL AB, www.mysql.com GNU General Public License
Non-Stop SQL	92	Unix, Windows NT/2000	Hewlett-Packard Company http://thenew.hp.com
Ocelot SQLDBMS	99	Windows NT/2000/XP/9x	Open Source; available for download on the Internet, but the company is no longer in business. www.ocelot.ca GNU General Public License
PostgreSQL v7.2.1	92/99	AIX, BeOS, FreeBSD, BSD, Tru64 Unix, DG/UX, Linux, Mac OS X, SCO OpenServer, SCO UnixWare, SGI Irix, Sun Solaris, MS Windows NT/2000	Open Source Software www.postgresql.org GNU General Public License
Progress v9.0	92	Sun Solaris, SCO Open Server, IBM AIX, True64 UNIX, HP-UX, Linux, DG/UX Intel, Citrix MetaFrame, MS Windows 9x/NT/2000/XP	Progress Software Corp. www.progress.com
Pervasive SQL 2000i	92/99	NetWare, Windows 9x/NT/2000, MS-DOS, Linux	Pervasive Software www.pervasive.com
Quadbase SQL Server v4.x	92	Novell Netware, Windows 9x/NT/2000	Quadbase Systems Inc. www.quadbase.com
RedBase Pure Java RDBMS	92	Any platform for which JVM is implemented	Bungisoft, Inc www.bungisoft.com
SQLBase v8.0	92	Windows 98/NT/2000/XP NetWare 5.1 & 6	Gupta Technologies, LLC www.centurasoft.com

Continued

Table K-1 *(continued)*			
RDBMS	***SQL***	***Operating System***	***Vendor Info***
StorHouse/RM	92	HP-UX, Sun Solaris	FileTek, Inc. `www.filetek.com`
Sybase Adaptive Server	92/99	Sun Solaris, HP-UX, SGI Irix, IBM AIX, Windows NT/2000/ XP, Linux, Mac OS X	Sybase, Inc. `www.sybase.com`
TimesTen RDBMS		Sun Solaris, HP-UX, AIX, Windows NT/2000/XP, LynxOS, Linux	TimesTen, Inc. `www.timesten.com`
UniVerse	92	Windows NT, Linux, Unix	IBM `www.3.ibm.com/software/data/u2/universe/`
Versant/SQL v6.0	92/99	Solaris, Microsoft Windows NT, IBM AIX and HP/UX	Versant Corporation `www.versant.com`

✦ ✦ ✦

A Brief Introduction to the Number Systems, Boolean Algebra, and Set Theory

We believe strongly that daily users of RDBMS and SQL will greatly benefit by understanding the basics of discrete math and set theory that serve as the foundation for SQL.

You don't need a math degree to write and read SQL code, but the knowledge of how binary and hexadecimal numbers are different from decimals and how they can be converted to each other can help you to better understand issues directly related to it. Such issues include security issues, data encryption, data storage principles, and the Oracle `ROWID` data type — to mention just a few.

Understanding set theory is even more important. Basically, the result of any database query is a set of values, so it would benefit you immediately to know the rules of working with sets to create efficient queries.

The Number Systems

The decimal number system we casually use in our everyday lives is not the only number system in the world. Most of us are used to the decimal system, take it for granted, and maybe even consider it the only possible collection of numbers. But that assumption is valid only if we are talking about modern humans. Machines don't use the decimal system. Moreover, humans themselves, now and in the past, have used other systems. For example, the ancient civilization of Sumerians used a base-sixty number system six thousand years ago; that is, they had 60 different characters to represent digits. In our own time, the English word "dozen" points to the existence of a numbering system different from decimal.

The RDBMS connection

The bases relevant to computer science in general and to SQL in particular are represented in Table L-1.

Table L-1
Number Systems

System	*Elements*
Decimal	{0,1,2,3,4,5,6,7,8,9}
Binary	{0,1}
Hexadecimal	{0,1,2,3,4,5,6,7,8,9,A,B,C,D,E,F}

The hexadecimal system is useful to represent large binary numbers. For example, a 16-bit binary sequence, called a *word* in programming jargon, can be divided into four groups with four bits in each group, and then each group can be easily represented as a hexadecimal number (Table L-2) that is more convenient to use.

Table L-2
Binary Number Represented in Hexadecimal Groups

Binary number	0010111011111100			
Binary groups	0010	1110	1111	1100
Hexadecimal groups	2	E	F	C

Since the largest possible four-bit number (1111) is a decimal 15, you cannot represent it (as well as numbers 10,11, 12, 13, and 14) using just one character in the decimal number system. The hexadecimal system is very convenient in this case because 1111 can be represented as hexadecimal F (the equivalent to decimal 15).

Converting numbers

Numbers can be converted from one number system to another using a mathematical algorithm — a sequence of operations.

Binary to decimal conversion

A binary number could be converted into decimal using the following algorithm: Count the elements comprising the number (zeroes and ones) from right to left using 0 for the first element, 1 for the second, and so on until the last element *n*. Then, starting from the *n*th (leftmost) element, calculate the sum of each element times 2 powered by *n*:

$$(A_n * 2)^{n} + (A_{n-1} * 2)^{n-1} + \ldots + (A_0 * 2)^{0}$$

Table L-3 illustrates the conversion of binary number 10011 to its decimal equivalent.

Table L-3
Binary to Decimal Conversion

Binary Number	1	0	0	1	1
n	4	3	2	1	0
Calculation	$(2 * 1)^{4}$	$(2 * 0)^{3}$	$(2 * 0)^{2}$	$(2 * 1)^{1}$	$(2 * 1)^{0}$
Result	16	0	0	2	1
Subtotal	16+0+0+2+1=19				

Decimal to binary conversion

A decimal number can be converted into binary using this logic: Divide a decimal number by 2 using integer division. Write down the remainder (from right to left). Repeat the operation using the resulting number. Repeat until the resulting number becomes zero:

```
SET j to 0
SET n_j to N
WHILE n_j <> 0
{
```

```
    a_j := remainder of n_j / 2
    n_j + 1 := floor (n_j / 2)
    j := j + 1
  }
```

Table L-4 illustrates the conversion of decimal number 123 to its binary equivalent. The resulting binary number is 1111011.

Table L-4
Decimal to Binary Conversion

N = 123	123						
J	0	1	2	3	4	5	6
n_j	123	61	30	15	7	3	1
a_j	61	30	15	7	3	1	0
Remainder	1	1	0	1	1	1	1

Logic Elements of Boolean Algebra

Boolean algebra is a system named after George Boole, a mid-nineteenth-century English mathematician. It is based on the binary number system described earlier in this chapter. In addition to the binary elements (0 and 1) it also includes a number of operators. The four fundamental Boolean operators are:

- NOT
- AND
- OR
- XOR

There are two other operators derived from the three basic ones:

- NAND
- NOR

As you know from Chapter 11, operators can be unary and binary (in this case the word "binary" is by no means related to binary numbers; it only means that the operator requires two operands). NOT is a unary operator; all other operators covered in this appendix are binary.

NOT (complement or inverter)

The NOT operator accepts the value of one Boolean variable as input and outputs the opposite of this value. See Table L-5.

Table L-5
NOT Truth Table

VALUE	0	1
NOT (VALUE)	1	0

AND (Boolean product)

The AND operator accepts two Boolean variables as input and outputs their Boolean product. See Table L-6.

Table L-6
AND Truth table

VALUE1	0	0	1	1
VALUE2	0	1	0	1
VALUE1 *AND* VALUE2	0	0	0	1

OR (Boolean sum)

The OR operator accepts two Boolean variables as input and outputs their Boolean sum. See Table L-7.

Table L-7 **OR Truth table**				
VALUE1	0	0	1	1
VALUE2	0	1	0	1
VALUE1 *OR* VALUE2	0	1	1	1

XOR (exclusive OR)

The XOR operator accepts two Boolean variables as input and outputs their exclusive Boolean sum (*exactly one* of the variables must be 1 for XOR output to be 1). See Table L-8.

Table L-8 **XOR Truth table**				
VALUE1	0	0	1	1
VALUE2	0	1	0	1
VALUE1 *XOR* VALUE2	0	1	1	0

NAND (inversed AND)

The NAND operator accepts two Boolean variables as input and outputs the opposite of their Boolean product. See Table L-9.

Table L-9 **NAND Truth table**				
VALUE1	0	0	1	1
VALUE2	0	1	0	1
VALUE1 *NAND* VALUE2	1	1	1	0

NOT(A AND B) **is not the same as** NOT(A) AND NOT(B).

NOR (inversed OR)

The NOR operator accepts two or more Boolean variables as input and outputs the complement of their Boolean sum. See Table L-10.

Table L-10
NOR Truth table

VALUE1	0	0	1	1
VALUE2	0	1	0	1
VALUE1 *NOR* VALUE2	1	0	0	0

NOT(A OR B) **is not the same as** NOT(A) + NOT(B).

Rules of precedence

Table L-11 shows the precedence rules of the Boolean algebra operators.

Table L-11
Boolean Algebra Operator Precedence

Precedence level	***Operator***
1	brackets ( )
2	Boolean complement NOT
3	Boolean product AND
4	Boolean sum OR

Brackets have the highest precedence, i.e., everything inside brackets is evaluated first.

Table L-12 illustrates how the precedence rules are used when evaluating the expression: NOT (TRUE OR FALSE) OR TRUE AND FALSE.

Remember, 1 in Boolean algebra means TRUE and 0 means FALSE.

Table L-12
Precedence Rules Illustration

Step	*Expression*	*Explanation*
1	NOT(1 OR 0) OR 1 AND 0	1 OR 0 is inside the brackets, so evaluate it first. The result is 1, so replace (1 OR 0) with 1.
2	= NOT(1) OR 1 AND 0	Evaluate the complement next. NOT(1) = 0. Replace NOT(1) with 0.
3	= 0 OR 1 AND 0	Evaluate the product next. 1 AND 0 = 0. Replace 1 AND 0 with 0.
4	= 0 OR 0	Now, evaluate the sum. 0 OR 0 = 0, so the result of the expression is 0.
5	= 0	We are done.

Table L-13 contains the main identities of Boolean algebra.

Table L-13
Identities of Boolean Algebra

Name	*Corresponding Notation*
Complement laws	X OR NOT(X) = TRUE X AND NOT(X) = FALSE
Law of the double complement	NOT(NOT(X)) = X
Idempotent laws	X OR X = X X AND X = X
Identity laws	X OR FALSE = X X AND TRUE = X
Dominance laws	X OR TRUE = TRUE X AND FALSE = FALSE
Commutative laws	X OR Y = Y OR X X AND Y = Y AND X
Associative laws	X OR (Y OR Z) = (X OR Y) OR Z X AND (Y AND Z) = (X AND Y) AND Z

Continued

Name	*Corresponding Notation*
Distributive laws	X OR (Y AND Z) = (X OR Y) AND (X OR Z) X AND (Y OR Z) = (X AND Y) OR (X AND Z)
DeMorgan's laws	NOT(X AND Y) = NOT(X) OR NOT(Y) NOT(X OR Y) = NOT(X) AND NOT(Y)
Absorption law	X AND (X OR Y) = X

Set Theory

Set is a fundamental concept in all branches of mathematics and is also a very important concept for SQL because SQL queries operate with record sets. The idea of set is very intuitive: a collection of objects. The objects may be of the same type or of different types. In math terminology, *set* is a collection of well-defined objects; these objects are called the *elements* of the set. The elements (or members) of the set are said to *belong* to the set.

The listing of sets

Sets are usually denoted by capital letters and their elements by lowercase letters (or numbers). A set can contain anything and the elements of a set need not be the same kind of objects. In math notation a set can be defined by listing its elements between braces or by using set builder notation:

$A = \{1,2,5,8\}$

$B = \{x \mid x \text{ in } N, 10 <= x <= 200\}$

The order of the elements does not matter:

$\{1,5,2,6\} = \{1,2,5,6\} = \{6,1,2,5\}$

Sets can contain other sets as elements

$A = \{1,3,\{1,2\},4,7\}$

assuming $B = \{1,2\}$ and $C = \{7\}$, $A = \{1,3,B,4,C\}$.

The *empty set* is a set with no elements, denoted by {} or {∅}.

In conventional set theory, repeated elements are ignored, or more specifically, repeated elements are treated as if they were a single element:

$\{a,a,c,b,c\} = \{a,b,c\}$

Sets need not be finite, and a typical example of an infinite set is the set of all integers:

$Z = \{...,-2,-1,0,1,2,...\}$

Another typical example is the set of natural numbers, which consists of all nonnegative integers:

$N = \{1,2,3,...\}$

Yet another example is the set of whole numbers:

$W = \{0,1,2,...\}$.

Sometimes a set is difficult or impossible to list; for example, the set of all natural numbers from 10 to 200. In such cases we can define the set by stating the properties of its elements:

$A = \{x \mid x \text{ in } N, 10 <= x <= 200\}$

This notation is read as *A* is the set of all *x* such that *x* is a natural number (*N*) and *x* lies between 10 and 200 inclusive.

Subsets

We say that a set P is a *subset* of set *Q* if every element of *P* is also an element of *Q*. This does not exclude the possibility that *P* = *Q*.

For example, if:

$A = \{1,2,3,4,5,6\}$

$B = \{1,3,7\}$

$C = \{2,4,6\}$

then *C* is a subset of *A*, but *B* is not a subset of *A* because it contains element 7 that is not a member of set *A*.

Related to the concept of subsets is that of the superset. *A* is a superset of *C*, which means that *A* contains *C*.

Set equality

Two sets, *A* and *B*, are equal if *A* is a subset of *B* and *B* is a subset of *A*. In other words, *A* = *B* if every element of *A* is also in *B* and every element of *B* is also in *A*.

Operations on sets

Operations on sets include union, intersection, complement, difference, and Cartesian product.

UNION

The union of two sets *A* and *B* is the set containing all elements in *A* or *B* or both. It is written as *A* U *B*. The union of *n* sets, A_1, A_2, ..., A_n is the set of all objects which belong to at least one of the sets:

A = {2,5}

B = {1,9}

A U *B* = {1,2,5,9}.

Figure L-1 illustrates the concept.

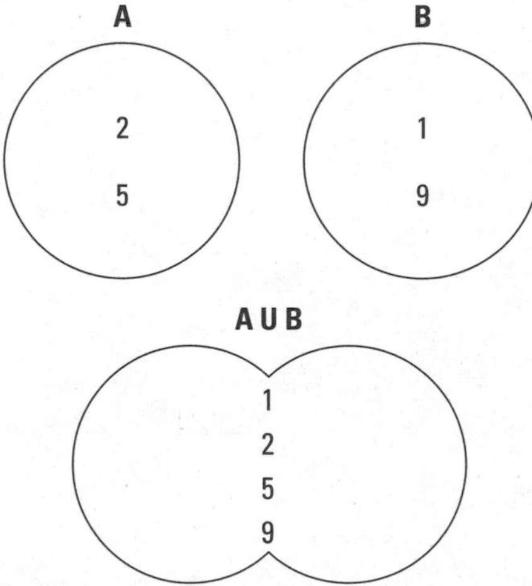

Figure L-1: Set union

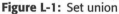

In SQL, the `UNION` operator works exactly as described here. If the resulting set contains duplicates, they are excluded. For example, {1,2,5} U {1,5,9} = {1,2,5,9}. To preserve duplicates SQL uses another operator, `UNION ALL` that is not a part of the classical set theory. If you denote `UNION ALL` with UA, then {1,2,5} UA {1,5,9} = {1,1,2,5,5,9}.

INTERSECTION

The intersection of two sets *A* and *B* is the set of all common elements that are found in both *A* and *B*. It is written as *A* ^ *B*. The intersection of *n* sets, A_1, A_2, ..., A_n is the set of all objects that belong to every one of the sets:

A = {a,b,d}

B = {d,e,f}

A ^ B = {d}

Intersection is shown on Figure L-2.

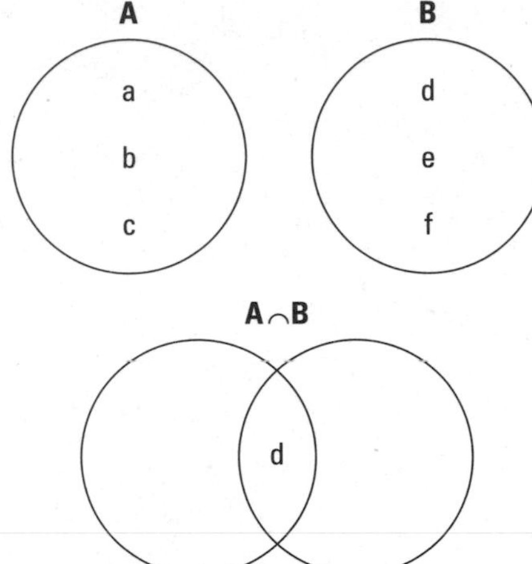

Figure L-2: Set intersection

COMPLEMENT

The complement (or absolute complement) of a set *A* is the set NOT(*A*) or *A'* consisting of all elements not in *A*. This definition requires the existence of a Universal set *U*:

A = {a,b,c}

U = {$a,b,c,...,z$}

A' = {$d,e,f,...,z$}

In the SQL99 standards (and all the "big three" databases) the complement is denoted by the `NOT` operator.

DIFFERENCE

The difference of sets *A* and *B* is defined as the set $A - B$ consisting of all elements of *A* that are not also in *B*. The difference of *A* and *B* is not the same as the difference of *B* and *A*. The definition of set difference does not imply that *A* and *B* have anything in common, nor does it say anything about their relative sizes:

$$A = \{1,3,5,7,8\}$$

$$B = \{3,4,6,8,10\}$$

$$A - B = \{1,5,7\}$$

$$B - A = \{4,6,10\}.$$

Set difference is illustrated in Figure L-3.

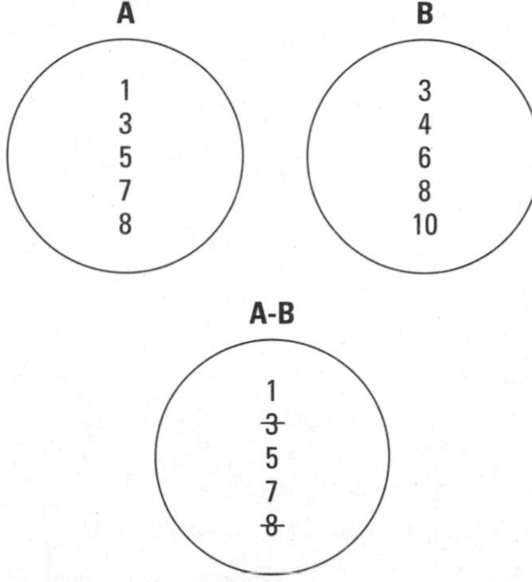

Figure L-3: Set difference

The `DIFFERENCE` set operator is represented by `EXCEPT` in SQL99 and DB2 (`MINUS` in Oracle). MS SQL Server does not have any operator for set difference; the result can be simulated using `NOT EXISTS`. See Chapter 8 for more information.

CARTESIAN PRODUCT

The Cartesian product of two sets *A* and *B* denoted by $A \times B$ (also called the product set or the product of *A* and *B*) is a set of ordered pairs where the first component is a member of the first set and the second component is a member of the second set:

A = {1,2,3}

B = {7,8}

A × B = {(1,7), (1,8), (2,7), (2,8), (3,7), (3,8)}

Figure L-4 represents the Cartesian product.

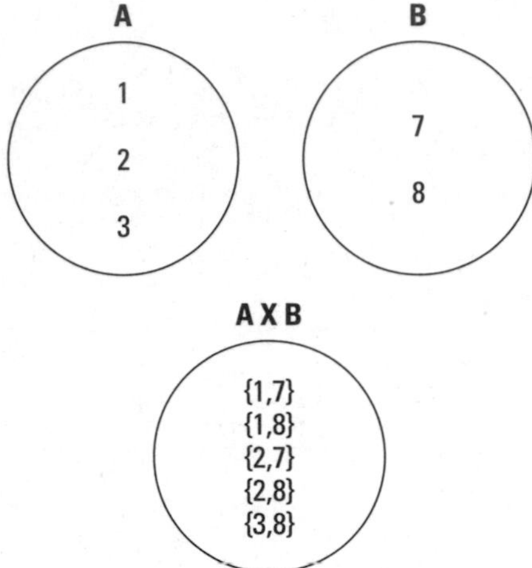

Figure L-4: Cartesian product

Cartesian product is also known as a `CROSS JOIN` in SQL99 and MS SQL Server.

Multiple operations

For multiple unions and intersections, brackets can be used to clarify the order of operations, e.g., (*A* ^ *B*) U *C*.

Set cardinality

Cardinality is the term describing the number of elements in a set. It is denoted by $|A|$:

A = {1,3,5}

$|A|$ = 3

B = {a,b,f,r,t,y}

$|B|$ = 6

Set Operations on Multielement Operands

Set theory is fully applicable to the resultsets returned in SQL queries. In most cases, a query returns more than one column, which implies two main rules.

First, you can only perform set operations on two sets if they have exactly the same number of subelements. (Don't confuse this rule with set cardinality!) That means you can have a union of sets *A* = {(1,2), (5,6), (10,12)} and *B* = {(1,3), (16,18)} (*A* U *B* = {(1,2), (5,6), (10,12), (1,3), (16,18)}), but the union becomes impossible (in SQL) if *A* = {(1,2), (5,6), (10,12)} and *B* = {(1,3,5), (16,18,7)}.

Second, the subelements within the element are treated as a single entity; that's why the resulting set *A* U *B* from the previous example includes both (1,2) and (1,3).

For the empty set, |{}| = 0.

Identities of Set algebra

Set algebra identities are listed in Table L-14.

Table L-14
Identities of Set Algebra

Name	Identity
Idempotent laws	*A* U *A* = *A* *A* ^ *A* = *A*
Associative laws	*A* U (*B* U *C*) = (*A* U *B*) U *C* *A* ^ (*B* ^ *C*) = (*A* ^ *B*) ^ *C*
Commutative laws	*A* U *B* = *B* U *A* *A* ^ *B* = *B* ^ *A*
Distributive laws	*A* U (*B* ^ *C*) = (*A* U *B*) ^ (*A* U *C*) *A* ^ (*B* U *C*) = (*A* ^ *B*) U (*A* ^ *C*)
Identity laws	*A* U {} = *A* *A* U U = U *A* ^ {} = {} *A* ^ U = *A*

Continued

Table L-14 *(continued)*

Name	***Identity***
Complement laws	$A \cup A' = U$ $A \wedge A' = \{\}$ $(A')' = A$ $U' = \{\}$ $\{\}' = U$
DeMorgan's laws	$(A \wedge B)' = A' \cup B'$ $(A \cup B)' = A' \wedge B'$

✦ ✦ ✦

Index

SYMBOLS

A

B

C

Continued

Continued

E

G

H

I

J

K

L

M

Continued

Continued

Continued

P

Continued

Continued

S

Continued

Continued

U

Continued